Water and American Government

Water and American Government

The Reclamation Bureau, National Water Policy, and the West, 1902–1935

Donald J. Pisani

UNIVERSITY OF CALIFORNIA PRESS

Berkeley   Los Angeles   London

University of California Press
Berkeley and Los Angeles, California

University of California Press, Ltd.
London, England

© 2002 by
The Regents of the University of California

Library of Congress Cataloging-in-Publication Data

Pisani, Donald J.

   Water and American government : the Reclamation Bureau,
national water policy, and the West, 1902–1935 / Donald J. Pisani.
      p.   cm.
   Includes bibliographical references and index.
   ISBN 0-520-23030-2 (cloth : alk. paper)
   1. United States. Bureau of Reclamation.   2. Reclamation
of land—West (U.S.)—History—20th century.   3. West (U.S.)—
Economic conditions—20th century.   4. Water-supply—
Government policy—West (U.S.)—History—20th century.
I. Title.
TC823.6.P57 2002
333.91'15'0978—dc21   2002008939

Manufactured in the United States of America

10 09 08 07 06 05 04 03 02

10 9 8 7 6 5 4 3 2 1

The paper used in this publication is both acid-free and totally
chlorine-free (TCF). It meets the minimum requirements of
ANSI/NISO Z39.48–1992 (R 1997) (*Permanence of Paper*).♾

To the memory of Robert Kelley

CONTENTS

Illustrations follow page 180.

MAPS

PREFACE AND ACKNOWLEDGMENTS

This is the second in a multivolume history of water in the American West. The first installment, *To Reclaim a Divided West: Water, Law, and Public Policy, 1848–1902*, appeared in 1992.[1] *Water and American Government: The Reclamation Bureau, National Water Policy, and the West, 1902–1935* surveys water policy from the adoption of the federal irrigation program in 1902 to the completion of Boulder Dam in 1935. Should fate permit, a third volume will carry the story forward from the beginning of the New Deal into the 1980s. The thesis of this book is simple. Historians have portrayed federal reclamation as a sharp break with the past—as a symbol of modernization, or at the least a symptom of the expansion and centralization of national power over natural resources.[2] But it makes more sense to see the Reclamation Act of 1902 and the events that followed as evidence of the persistence of "frontier America" and traditional nineteenth-century values, rather than as the emergence of "modern America." The Reclamation Act of 1902 had a far closer relationship to the laissez-faire natural resource policies of the nineteenth century than to the ethic of a rationalized, planned economy. It was consistent with the nineteenth-century vision of an America built on the striving of autonomous individuals—the agricultural model of 1800 or 1850.

Most historians have studied irrigation apart from other elements in federal water policy. Although this book is not a comprehensive history of federal water policies, I attempt to show how irrigation, flood control, and hydroelectric power intersected; Congress preferred to treat different uses of water discretely, but they were closely related. A second goal is to demonstrate that water policy often obliterated boundaries between East and West, federal and state, or even "public" and "private." The American system of government encouraged balance and accommodation, not just competition; the efforts of federal, state, and local governments complemented as well as competed with one another. There was no monolithic "central government." Finally, I examine the many constraints that affected federal water policy, including water law, the competition among western states, land speculation, interagency rivalries, and the conflict between Congress and the executive agencies. This book is as much about politics and government as about water policy, but it is not a social history of how irrigation farmers settled the land, or an assessment of the impact of irrigation on rural society.

In the nineteenth century, easy access to "public land" became the cornerstone of individual autonomy and national economic prosperity. Between 1870 and 1900, the opening of the Great Plains to agriculture more than doubled the nation's cultivated land. That increase, along with millions of acres abandoned in New England and the South, suggested that the United States could absorb an unlimited amount of new cultivated land. There could never be too much. Once the best land on the Great Plains had been taken, the United States resorted to a form of continental imperialism—reclaiming the arid and semiarid West. Reclamation, it was hoped, would save wasted lives along with wasted land; it would drain the crowded tenements of eastern cities as it salvaged the remaining arable land within the public domain. It would resuscitate the ideal of the family farm, revive civic virtue, and serve as an antidote to a variety of social diseases associated with industrialization and urbanization.[3]

The water story reflected the "back to the land" movement of the late nineteenth and early twentieth centuries. In his famous 1896 "Cross of Gold" speech, William Jennings Bryan of Nebraska—later a strong advocate of the Reclamation Act of 1902—warned that "the great cities rest upon our broad and fertile prairies. Burn down your cities and leave our farms, and your cities will spring up again as if by magic; but destroy our farms and the grass will grow in the streets of every city in the country." Bryan spoke not just for the virtuous rural life; he articulated a widely held and deeply felt faith that lacking a proper agricultural foundation, the American West would forever remain the nation's backwater. To Bryan and many of his contemporaries, including the young historian Frederick Jackson Turner, the family farm had to spread across the West before the region could be anything more than a colony or province of the East. The West's nineteenth-century economy, based on mining and cattle, did not offer a sound foundation for future economic and population growth.[4]

Nostalgia for rural America helped make irrigation a popular panacea. So did irrigation's importance as the cornerstone of Progressive Era conservation policy. In 1900, 90 percent of the population of the United States lived in the eastern half of the nation, while less than 10 percent resided in the western half. Progressive Era politicians sought to move people to resources as well as resources to people. Conservation represented not just "the greatest good for the greatest number for the longest time," but also "planned economic development" in lieu of the haphazard, boom-and-bust regime of the nineteenth-century West. It also symbolized conquest and subordination— the forceful amalgamation of the West into the nation and the complete management of nature. "The destiny of man is to possess the whole earth," agricultural specialist John Widtsoe proclaimed in 1928, "and the destiny of the earth is to be subject to man. There can be no full conquest of the earth, and no real satisfaction to humanity, if large portions of the earth remain beyond his highest control." Water not used by human beings was wasted, and federal reclamation nominally began with the goal of *systematically and completely* developing the arid lands. In 1902, there was little doubt that land-hungry Americans would flock to the government's irrigated farms and that the nation's population growth would forever sustain the demand for desert homesteads.[5]

Although in some ways the Reclamation Act of 1902 reflected the ideals of the conservation movement, conservation does not explain why Congress enacted the legislation when it did. The Reclamation Act of 1902 was a product of the 1890s, one of the darkest decades in the history of the United States. The depression of 1893–98, a flood of European immigrants that exceeded 4 million for the decade, the spectacular growth of American cities, the expansion of tenant farming, and the proliferation of large institutions, including the manufacturing corporation, deepened the fears of the nation's social critics and political reformers. The corporate consolidation movement that began in the mid-1890s reinforced fears of monopoly and the subversion of democracy by "new immigrants" and urban political bosses, as well as industrial tycoons. From 1893 to 1898, an average of 20 percent of the industrial workforce lacked jobs, reaching a peak of 30 percent in 1894. The 1892 strike at the Carnegie Homestead plant near Pittsburgh and the Pullman strike in Chicago in 1894 suggested that the country was coming apart. Fears of class warfare became epidemic. In 1894 alone, fourteen hundred strikes involved more than five hundred thousand workers. To make matters worse, a severe drought visited many parts of the West in 1893–95, with a complete crop failure in 1894. Drought reinforced demands for federal aid, as it did in 1899–1900.[6]

The depression of the 1890s suggested that the nation could not survive without defusing urban tensions, without a return to the land and to the family farm. Yet the West faced more immediate economic problems. Money for reclamation projects dried up during the 1890s, and the value of rural land fell precipitously. The future of the region, which looked so bright in the 1880s, now appeared ominous and forbidding. Could the West sustain its mines and ranches, let alone develop farms and factories?

In the nineteenth century, the federal government promoted the economic development of the West in many ways, including mapping the land, constructing military forts, and subsidizing railroads. But during the 1890s, westerners began to argue that they were *entitled* to federal aid not just because of their region's economic backwardness, but because they had been shortchanged by Congress in the decades after the Civil War: the two major sources of pork in the federal budget, Civil War veterans' pensions and river and harbor appropriations, both benefited the eastern half of the nation almost exclusively.

The crusade for federal reclamation, like the campaign for free silver, erupted in large part because of the West's increasing power in Congress. In 1889 and 1890, the western states doubled in number as North and South Dakota, Montana, Washington, Idaho, and Wyoming entered the union, joining California, Nevada, Colorado, Kansas, Nebraska, and Texas. The region west of the Mississippi contained less than 10 percent of the nation's population, and only a handful of seats in the House of Representatives, but it now had substantial power in the Senate. Nevertheless, profound differences divided the Great Plains, Rocky Mountain, Great Basin, and Pacific Coast states. These subregions vied for settlers and for federal aid. The West was not unified economically or politically—nor would it become unified in the years immediately following 1902.

The grazing states had been hard hit by the blizzard and drought of the late 1880s. As the open range dried up, livestock prices tumbled and politicians in the Rocky Mountain West searched for ways to promote agriculture and attract new settlers. Counties in western Kansas and Nebraska lost up to half of their residents during the drought, and Wyoming politicians hoped to attract some of those dispossessed to their water-rich state. Elwood Mead, who plays a prominent part in this book, became Wyoming's first state engineer, and in that capacity he prepared many congressional bills designed to water the West during the 1890s. Senator Francis E. Warren, Mead's benefactor and confidant, introduced most of those bills in Congress. At the beginning of the nineties, Warren favored the unconditional cession of all or at least the arable part of the public domain to the states. Convinced that the federal government would not build dams and canals, Warren hoped to grant the land to private companies, which, in turn, would reclaim the deserts of the West under terms set by the states. This campaign culminated in the Carey Act of 1894, which awarded each western state up to a million acres.[7]

The Carey Act had limited success in the 1890s. In 1896, therefore, Warren called for a federal survey of potential reservoir sites in Colorado and Wyoming, insisting, "It is no more than fair and just that these arid-land States shall participate hereafter in the deliberations, emoluments, and perquisites of river and harbor bills. If money is to be distributed with some little regard for local benefits, then give us our share." Two years later, the depression had lifted sufficiently so that Warren changed strategies. He now asked that the federal government build reservoirs at the headwaters of the West's most important streams and pay for them using proceeds from river and harbor

appropriations or from leases on public grazing lands. Upon their completion, Warren wanted the dams turned over to the states, which would then
build distribution canals under state laws or assign that job to private enterprise. The federal government would build dams, but they would be administered entirely by the water users or states.[8]

Westerners did not agree with one another on the shape federal reclamation should take, even in 1902. As early as 1900, there was widespread
support for federal construction of dams, but it was not clear whether those
structures would be built from river and harbor appropriations or from the
sale of public lands. How many dams should be built, where the first dams
should be built, whether the Great Plains states should be included in the
national irrigation program or only the region from the Rocky Mountains
to the Pacific, whether the federal government or states should dole out the
stored water, and whether the program should benefit private as well as public land were all open questions. Still, the first task was to find a way to pay
for reclamation that did not rely on appropriations from the general treasury. Many westerners in the Rocky Mountain states resisted paying anything
for grazing cattle and sheep on the public domain, but by that year sales of
public land, which had slumped during the 1890s, were picking up. This offered a new source of potential funding, a source more acceptable to eastern
politicians than river and harbor appropriations.

At 11:40 P.M. on the night of March 3, 1901, Senator Thomas Carter of
Montana took the floor of the Senate and, with brief breaks, talked for twelve
straight hours, ending within a half hour of the inauguration of President
William McKinley. Carter filibustered the Rivers and Harbors Bill to death,
and Senator Warren predicted that "before another River and Harbor bill
passes and becomes a law, there will be reservoirs built and provided for
by this nation, either in the River and Harbor bill or by some other appropriation bill, or in an independent measure." In 1902, eastern fears and
western hopes forged a political coalition capable of overcoming the ignorance, disdain, and suspicion most members of Congress felt toward the West.
Nevertheless, reclamation was still a western measure. The West had the
power to block important legislation in the Senate. That, not the appeal of
reclamation as an instrument of social reform, explains the passage of the
Reclamation Act of 1902.[9]

By the turn of the twentieth century, Congress had plenty of experience
administering natural resources. It had parceled out the minerals and timber of the public domain, as well as its farmland. It had appropriated money
to improve the nation's rivers and harbors. It had ordered the United States
Geological Survey, an agency within the Interior Department, to study dam
and canal sites on the public domain (1888–90), and in the middle of the
1890s asked the USGS to measure the volume of the nation's rivers. Always
careful to balance the power of new executive agencies against old, in 1898

Congress created the Office of Irrigation Investigations within the Office of Experiment Stations in the U.S. Department of Agriculture to explore practical problems of desert agriculture, including the amount of water needed to grow various crops and how to reduce litigation over water rights. Nevertheless, when the Reclamation Act passed Congress, federal officials knew surprisingly little about how much unclaimed or "surplus" water the region's lakes and rivers contained, and almost nothing about its underground water sources, or the nature of desert soils, or how much experience was needed to become a successful irrigation farmer, or how much it would cost to clear and level desert land or construct irrigation and drainage works. Federal reclamation was a program begun with great confidence, with the assumption that all problems could be reduced to matters of engineering and, once the correct facts were gathered, easily solved. Government could turn nature into a productive machine just as the assembly line had rationalized the manufacture of factory goods.

The Reclamation Act of 1902 promised water management on a scale far beyond the nineteenth-century efforts of the states or private companies, and the nation's engineering organizations well understood that more was at stake than making the desert bloom. "If it can be shown that the task undertaken by the Reclamation Service has been carried out with a high degree of success," the nation's leading engineering journal editorialized in 1913, "it argues well for the extension of the work of engineers to larger fields in connection with our Federal public works. On the other hand, if the Reclamation Service can be shown to have been extravagant and inefficient in its work, then a strong weapon is placed in the hands of those who declare that the federal government should keep its hands off from all public works and leave their execution to the States or to private enterprise."[10] Not surprisingly, many professional engineering societies made the Reclamation Service a poster child and strenuously tried to protect the agency from criticism.

Federal reclamation was the boldest public-works scheme ever undertaken in the United States, and leaders in the Reclamation Service tried repeatedly to extend reclamation to the swamps and cutover lands in the South and upper Midwest. By doing so, they hoped to give the service a national mission and constituency. At the beginning of the twentieth century, the main responsibility of national water policy was to maintain and improve navigable rivers and harbors. Irrigation, flood control, and the drainage of wetlands were state, local, and private concerns. Hydroelectric power played no part in government water planning, and flood control was a relatively minor consideration. Much changed during the years from 1902 to 1935. During the second and third decades of the twentieth century, cities and farms invaded the vulnerable floodplains of the Mississippi River and its tributaries, and the technology developed to transmit hydroelectricity great distances from its point of origin. Meanwhile, reclamation as homemaking lost much of its appeal during the 1920s. By then a good farm was beyond the reach of most families. By the mid-1930s federal reclamation watered only a few million acres, and it was limited entirely to the American West. The grandeur of Boulder Dam masked a failed dream.

Scholarship is collaborative work, so acknowledgments are hardly a stale formality. No book is completely original, and this one is no exception. My narrative challenges existing scholarship, particularly the work of Samuel P. Hays. Nevertheless, like all environmental historians, I am deeply indebted to Hays, as well as to Norris Hundley, Robert Kelley, Lawrence B. Lee, Donald Worster, and countless others whose publications appear in the notes. To credit all the scholars who have provided aid, advice, insight, and encouragement over the past fifteen years would be impossible. Some, inevitably, will be left out. That said, my list of thanks includes Brett Adams, Daniel Carpenter, William Cronon, Robert Dunbar, Gail Evans, Robert Fayles, Paul Wallace Gates, Gene Gressley, Robert Griswold, Norris Hundley, Albert Hurtado, Donald C. Jackson, W. Turrentine Jackson, Robert Kelley, Howard Lamar, Lawrence B. Lee, Douglas Littlefield, Toni Linenberger, Laura Lovett, Richard Lowitt, H. Wayne Morgan, Gerald Nash, Karen O'Neill, Richard Orsi, Rodman Paul, Earl Pomeroy, Brad Raley, Martin Reuss, Martin Ridge, Hal Rothman, William Rowley, Harry N. Scheiber, Jeffrey Stine, Brit Storey, Garrit Voggesser, David Weber, Richard White, and Donald Worster.

Historians depend on the publications, advice, and friendship of specialists in their field. They also benefit from the time for research and writing and the financial support provided by the colleges and universities that employ them, from grants awarded by charitable academic foundations, and from the indispensable assistance of publishers, editors, archivists, manuscript curators, librarians, and other civil servants. Research for this book was conducted at archives and libraries throughout the United States. Many thanks to the staffs of the National Archives, the Library of Congress, and the Smithsonian Institution Archives in Washington, D.C.; the Federal Records Centers in Denver, Colorado, and Suitland, Maryland; the Army Corps of Engineers Library, Alexandria, Virginia; the Sterling Library, Yale University; the Wyoming State Archives (Cheyenne); the American Heritage Center, University of Wyoming (Laramie); the Louisiana State Museum (New Orleans); Special Collections at the University of Southwestern Louisiana (Lafayette), Idaho State University (Pocatello), Idaho Historical Society (Boise), University of California (Los Angeles), University of Nevada (Reno), and University of Washington (Seattle); the James J. Hill Library (St. Paul), and the Minnesota Historical Society (Minneapolis); the Huntington Library (San Marino, California); and the Water Resources Archives at the University of California, Berkeley. The Bancroft Library at U.C. Berkeley provided a particularly ex-

xviii PREFACE AND ACKNOWLEDGMENTS

citing place to work. Thanks also to Brit Storey, Toni Linenberger, and the staff of the Bureau of Reclamation in Denver for their invaluable assistance in providing photographs. Finally, the University of California Press deserves recognition for the efficiency, imagination, patience, and care with which its editorial employees perform their jobs. I particularly want to thank Stanley Holwitz, Suzanne Knott, Marian Olivas, and Jacqueline Volin. They worked hard to make this a better book. So did Joyce Appleby as well as Norris Hundley jr. and an anonymous reader, all of whom evaluated the manuscript for the press and offered many useful suggestions. None of these generous people, of course, bears any responsibility for any errors of fact or interpretation that may remain.

Financial assistance came from the American Council of Learned Societies, the National Endowment for the Humanities, the American Bar Foundation, the American Philosophical Society, and the Texas A&M University Summer Grant and Mini-Grant programs. Since much of the research for this book was done at the Bancroft Library, I also want to thank my parents-in-law, Engel and Shirley Sluiter, who provided a home away from home in Berkeley. Mary Alice knows her contribution. Most of all, I am indebted to Elizabeth Merrick Coe and her family, who endowed the chair in western United States history I hold at the University of Oklahoma. I have benefited enormously from their benevolence.

Ultimately, we measure the quality of our lives by the people we have known. This book is dedicated to Robert Kelley, whose death several years ago took from the historical profession one of its ablest students of politics, public policy, and water, depriving me and many others of a dear friend. I cherish memories of his passion for history, as well as his generosity, humor, grace, courage, and wise counsel. Bob was a real gentleman, and he is missed.

Map 1. Major U.S. rivers discussed in the text.

○ ACTIVE ◎ ABANDONED

1. BELLE FOURCHE
2. BOISE-PAYETTE
3. BUFORD-TRENTON
4. CARLSBAD
5. GARDEN CITY
6. GRAND VALLEY
7. HONDO
8. HUNTLEY
9. KLAMATH
10. YELLOWSTONE
11. MILK RIVER
12. MINIDOKA
13. NORTH PLATTE
14. OKANOGAN

15. ORLAND
16. RIVERTON
17. RIO GRANDE
18. SALT RIVER
19. SHOSHONE
20. STRAWBERRY VALLEY
21. SUN RIVER
22. TRUCKEE-CARSON
23. UMATILLA
24. UNCOMPAHGRE
25. OWYHEE-VALE
26. WEBER RIVER
27. YAKIMA
28. YUMA

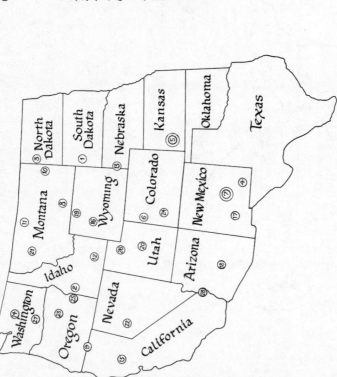

Map 2. Federal reclamation projects as of 1928.

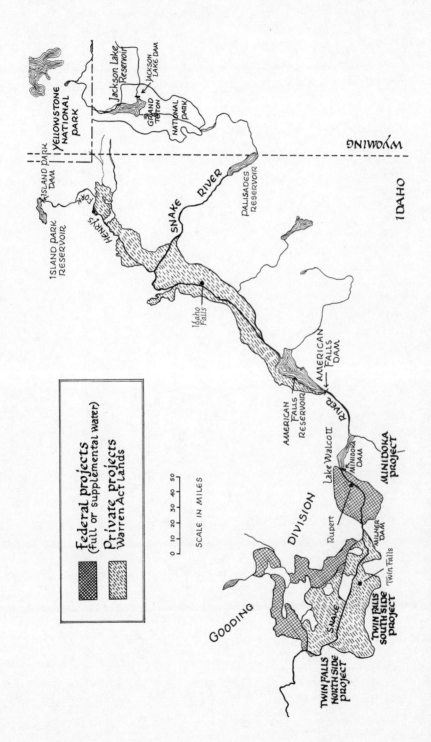

Map 3. Snake River irrigation, central Idaho.

Saving Lost Lives

Irrigation and the Ideology of Homemaking

*If there is one lesson taught by history it is that the permanent greatness of any State
must ultimately depend more upon the character of its country population than upon
anything else. No growth of cities, no growth of wealth can make up for a loss in either the number or the character of the farming population. . . . We cannot afford to
lose that pre-eminently typical American, the farmer who owns his own farm.*
THEODORE ROOSEVELT, *"The Man Who Works with His Hands,"*
address at Michigan State University, May 31, 1907

On June 1, 1902, President Theodore Roosevelt signed the Reclamation Act
into law—often called the Newlands Act in honor of the legislation's sponsor in the House of Representatives, Francis G. Newlands of Nevada.[1] The
legislation directed the national government to construct irrigation projects
in sixteen western states and territories. It entrusted the job to the Reclamation Service, which was created within the Interior Department's United
States Geological Survey. Money from sales of public land paid for the first
projects. To prevent some parts of the West from securing federal aid at the
expense of others, at least 51 percent of the proceeds had to be spent within
the state or territory in which the land had been sold. The secretary of the
interior could limit the size of project farms to as little as 40 acres (after 1906
to as little as 10 acres), but no settler could claim more than 160 acres of
public land. The public land *within* project boundaries cost settlers nothing,
save for a filing fee, but entrants were required to repay their share of the
cost of constructing dams and canals over ten years. That debt carried no
interest. Federal reclamation promised to be self-supporting. As settlers repaid their obligation to the government, money would become available to
build new projects. Proceeds from land sales outside the projects would cease
when the public domain was gone, but by that time the revolving fund would
be perpetual.

Never had the federal government undertaken such a bold program of
public works or regional economic development. In 1902, no one understood how far the federal government would go beyond building dams and
canals; many expected it to engage in large-scale social planning as well. "The
passage of the National Irrigation Law was one of the greatest steps, not only

in the forward progress of the states, but to that of all mankind," President Theodore Roosevelt boasted in 1903. "The settlement of the great arid West by the makers of homes is the central object, both of the irrigation and the forest policy of the United States."[2] Frederick Haynes Newell, the first director of the Reclamation Service, predicted that ultimately the reclaimed lands of the arid and semiarid West would support a population twice as large as that of the entire United States in 1900: "The dead and profitless deserts need only the magic touch of water to make arable lands that will afford farms and homes for the surplus people of our overcrowded Eastern cities, and for that endless procession of home-seekers filing through [Ellis Island]."[3] "The object of the reclamation law," Newell emphasized, "is primarily to put the public domain into the hands of small land owners." In 1910, Senator William E. Borah of Idaho remembered what many champions of federal reclamation had already forgotten: "The law as it was passed was intended to be, as was said in the public prints and as was generally understood, a poor man's law; that is to say, it was designed that men of most moderate means might go upon the public lands and, under these projects, initiated and carried on by the Government, obtain homes."[4]

Nevertheless, federal reclamation could not be restricted to the public domain. The West contained plenty of vacant government land, but few extensive tracts suited to irrigation. Moreover, restricting the national program to public land would penalize farmers who had already proven their agricultural ability by breaking, grading, plowing, and fencing, as well as by building houses, barns, and roads. Neither urban workers nor eastern farmers had any experience with desert agriculture. Established irrigation farmers were more likely to repay their debt to the government than were poor settlers new to the West.

In 1880, three hundred thousand acres were irrigated in the entire United States. That amount increased to more than 4.1 million acres in 1890 and 7.3 million acres in 1900.[5] In 1902, Frederick Newell estimated that between 60 million and a hundred million acres could be reclaimed in the West, a body of land roughly the size of California, and he crowed that "there seems to be ground for the most optimistic view." Every state and territory could benefit from irrigation. In 1900, most of the region's irrigated land was in California, Colorado, and Utah, but in the 1880s and early 1890s, prior to the devastating depression of 1893–98, the *percentage growth* of irrigated land was greatest in states such as Idaho, Montana, and Wyoming. This suggested that the West's poorer states might use irrigation to compete with their more favored neighbors for settlers, in effect providing a more equitable division of the region's wealth.[6]

In 1901, the sale of public land produced more revenue than in any previous year in American history and more than three times the return in 1897.

Soon after the Reclamation Act passed Congress, the *New York Times* predicted that the reclamation fund would be five times greater than the friends of federal reclamation had expected. In 1904, when construction began on the first national water projects, the fund contained more than $16 million.[7]

But where should the new water projects be situated? When Congress met in December 1901, it considered two alternatives: a comprehensive bill that covered the entire West and a bill to construct experimental projects adjacent to the Great Northern, Southern Pacific, and Santa Fe railroads.[8] At that time, Theodore Roosevelt warned against launching too many government irrigation projects at once: "It would be unwise to begin by doing too much, for a great deal will doubtless be learned, both as to what can and what can not be safely attempted, by the early efforts, which must of necessity be partly experimental in character. At the very beginning the Government should make clear, beyond shadow of doubt, its intention to pursue this policy on lines of the broadest public interest. No reservoir or canal should ever be built to satisfy selfish personal or local interests."[9]

Nevertheless, when the Reclamation Act passed Congress in June 1902, the fall elections loomed, and Roosevelt, always a canny politician, recognized that limiting federal reclamation to a few model projects would reduce its value to the Republican Party. Francis Newlands, the leading sponsor of the Reclamation Act in Congress, was nominally a Democrat, as were many others who had voted for the legislation. They took full credit for the measure. The winning of the West was vital to the Republican Party's future, and Arizona, New Mexico, and Oklahoma were soon expected to join the union. On July 2, 1902, T. R. advised Secretary of the Interior Ethan A. Hitchcock that "instead of starting on a few large [model] enterprises, I should think it would be best to divide up the work among the different States as fairly [widely] as possible; and be sure we can carry out whatever we undertake." The bigger the project, the longer it would take to complete. If the law did not provide immediate benefits, and if those benefits were not spread relatively evenly throughout the arid West, the Republican Party would pay the price.[10]

A week later, Secretary Hitchcock informed Roosevelt that he had met with Newell and Charles Walcott—head of the U.S. Geological Survey—to underscore the importance of paying close attention to the politics of reclamation: "I dwelt upon this financial feature of the situation with Messrs. Walcott and Newell, and impressed upon them the necessity of avoiding any large expenditures upon any particular scheme or locality, and the necessity of such distribution of our available funds as would protect the Department from the charge of partiality, your desire being for such wide distribution of both work and capital as will secure the earliest demonstration of the value of the Irrigation program to the arid and semiarid States and Territories."

Hitchcock assured the president that irrigation surveys were planned for *all* the western states and territories.[11]

In March 1903, Hitchcock approved the first five government irrigation projects: the Sweetwater in Wyoming, the Milk River in Montana, the Truckee-Carson in Nevada, the Gunnison in Colorado, and the Salt River in Arizona. By August, construction had begun on the Nevada project. Publicly, Hitchcock insisted that in the selection of projects "[n]o consideration of expediency or sentiment can be tolerated. Great care is being exercised in selecting [irrigation] projects which will be of the greatest benefit to the country; which will settle upon the land the greatest number of people, and which will return to the Treasury the cost of the undertaking."[12] In 1904, five more projects were authorized; in 1905, nine; and in 1906, four. By the end of 1906, twenty-three reclamation schemes had been approved, one or more in every western state and territory. Between 1907 and the 1920s, only four new projects were approved—all of them small—but more than fifty "secondary projects" were identified and surveyed.[13]

From the beginning of the federal reclamation program, efficiency took a backseat to politics. And once Roosevelt and Newell decided to begin construction as rapidly as possible and distribute federal aid as widely as possible, the Reclamation Service came under siege. "I have personally talked with about every man in this audience, about some pet project in his country [region] or State," Newell drolly told the National Irrigation Congress, which met in Colorado in the fall of 1902, "so I am fully convinced that every State, county and locality has the best scheme, and the best crops and water supply, and that we ought to build a reservoir there at once. I am fully convinced that we ought to do everything right now." Western politicians had worked hard to push the Reclamation Act through Congress; now they expected a payoff. They hounded the president, Newell, and other officials in the Interior Department. In 1904, for example, Wyoming senator Francis E. Warren informed a constituent that he had "kept strenuously busy in preventing the Government from passing us by on the Shoshone proposition." And in the following year, he appealed to Newell: "I beg to transmit herewith copy of resolutions adopted at a meeting of citizens of Wyoming, held at Meeteetse, Wyoming, on April 12th, relative to the desired reclamation of lands along the Grey Bull River and streams tributary thereto, under the national irrigation act. I add my *earnest* request to the prayer of the petitioners and ask that the proposed enterprise be undertaken by the Reclamation Service." So it was throughout the West.[14]

RECLAMATION AS A NATIONAL ISSUE

Reclamation was not just a western issue—a fact historians have failed to appreciate.[15] Aside from 600,000 acres planted to rice in Louisiana and Texas, at the dawn of the twentieth century a scant 6,000 acres were irrigated in the humid half of the nation, including 134 acres in Massachusetts, 73 in New Jersey, 123 in New York, and 758 in Pennsylvania.[16] The proponents of federal reclamation hoped, therefore, that building dams and canals in the West would make this method of agriculture attractive to eastern and southern farmers, permitting federal reclamation to become a national program. Eventually, it was hoped, the Reclamation Service would salvage abandoned, cutover, and swamp land in the humid states. In the words of Frederick H. Newell, the "will of man" would be substituted for "unregulated natural forces"—and the Reclamation Service would become an immense bureau with vast new responsibilities. The conservationist Charles Van Hise claimed that 750 million acres "should be irrigated" in the United States—virtually *all* the arable land within the nation. This was a domain worthy of the bold new program.[17]

In the last decades of the nineteenth century, eastern newspapers worried about how the nation's farms could provide sufficient food to a burgeoning population at a reasonable price. As early as 1871, the *New York Times* speculated that "in the regions supplying our great cities, a system of irrigation might . . . be adopted that would put the inhabitants beyond the reach of meteorological caprices." Drought afflicted eastern as well as western farmers, and many high-value crops—such as celery and rice—could not be cultivated without irrigation. Connecticut received an average fifty inches of precipitation per year, but the state's Board of Agriculture estimated that at least three inches of rain were needed during the summer growing season to raise good crops. From 1888 to 1895, however, only one June and four Julys saw that much moisture. Similarly, Professor E. B. Voorhees of the New Jersey Experiment Station noted that in nine out of ten years from 1825 to 1895, Philadelphia's rainfall had been inadequate in at least one month during the growing season, and more than half those years showed a rainfall deficit for two months. Given the East's abundance of water, and the cost of crop damages in dry years, irrigation canals promised to pay for themselves even if they were not used every year.[18]

In the 1870s and 1880s, the use of irrigation by market gardeners around Boston and New York increased. The water provided insurance against drought, and, applied at the right time, dramatically increased crop yields. Water carried by unlined ditches was assumed to absorb natural fertilizers from the soil, nutrients more potent than those contained in solid fertilizers. "In all the civilized countries of the world, even in humid regions, farmers are gradually resorting more and more to irrigation for the purpose of permanently improving the soil and fertilizing the growing crops," John Wesley Powell noted in a letter to a North Dakota congressman in 1890. "Water artificially supplied to the land is the great source of fertilization, compared with which all others sink into insignificance."[19] Liberty Hyde Bailey, professor of horticulture at Cornell University, observed that "the more water the soil has, the more plants will grow." Irrigation boosters guaranteed that crop yields would increase as much as four or five times, and experiments confirmed that irrigation paid off. A Wisconsin study showed that irrigation cost an average $6.68 per acre per year, but irrigated hay returned $20 an acre and irrigated potatoes $73 per acre. A New Jersey study demonstrated that irrigation increased the yield of lima beans by 24 percent and sweet potatoes by 73 percent.[20]

During the 1890s, Frederick H. Newell, then head of the Hydrographic Division of the United States Geological Survey, and George H. Maxwell, federal reclamation's chief publicist in the years from 1896 to 1902, sought to broaden the membership of the annual National Irrigation Congress, whose conferences traditionally were held in the West, to include representatives from all parts of the nation, particularly the South. The drought that blanketed much of the South and East in 1899 and 1900 aided their efforts, as did the rapid expansion of rice cultivation in Louisiana, where more miles of irrigation canals were constructed during those two years than in any arid or semiarid state. In 1904, the annual Irrigation Congress devoted part of its program to irrigation in the humid region, and Herbert Myrick, editor of the *American Agriculturist*, declared that irrigation was a "practical necessity" in the East as well as West.[21]

In the West, irrigation attracted social reformers who wanted to promote the family farm and break up large landholdings.[22] But the South also offered vast opportunities to social engineers. Once drained, 50 million acres of submerged land could become small farms. Florida contained nearly 19 million acres of swampland, Louisiana about 10 million, and Mississippi more than 6 million. The same dams and canals used to dry out the land might later be used to water it. To be sure, irrigation in the South would be very different from irrigation in the West. Unlike western rivers, most southern streams were sluggish and flat. Gravity could not be relied upon to feed water from these streams into diversion ditches. Therefore, irrigation canals would be little more than long ponds from which water would be pumped onto adjoining lands. Moreover, the flatness of the South's alluvial land dictated the use of flood rather than furrow irrigation.[23]

Two kinds of reclamation bills appeared before Congress in 1906: those authorizing specific drainage projects and those providing for wetland reclamation throughout the nation. Senator Henry C. Hansbrough of North Dakota wanted to divert $1 million from the reclamation fund created in 1902 to pay for drainage in his state, under supervision of the Office of Irrigation Investigations in the Department of Agriculture. Congressman John H. Small of North Carolina asked for $1 million from the same fund to dry up the Dismal Swamp in Virginia and his state.[24] Congressman Halvor Steenerson of Minnesota wanted to create a new reclamation fund to be replenished by the sale of reclaimed flood land. He entrusted all work to the Reclamation Service, bypassing the Army Corps of Engineers and the Office of Irrigation Investigations. *Forestry and Irrigation,* part of the Forest Service and Reclamation Service's substantial publicity mill, jubilantly supported the legislation. "It is but natural," the journal editorialized, "that the advocates of national drainage works for the vast swamp land areas . . . should look to the Reclamation Service to take charge of the work. Irrigation and drainage go hand in hand. . . . Detailed surveys of vast areas of submerged lands have been made and maps and other data are on file in the office of the U.S. Geological Survey. . . . The National Drainage Congress will find in the well organized body of men in the Geological Survey and the Reclamation Service willing assistants to any general plans that may be proposed."[25]

In 1907 and 1908, Senator Frank Flint of California—a loyal friend of the Reclamation Service—introduced bills in the Senate Public Lands Committee similar to the Steenerson legislation that would have created a drainage fund from the sale of government lands *outside* the arid states. He promised that 80 million acres of swampland could be drained for an average cost of five dollars an acre, providing homes for 5 million people. The Irrigation Congress supported the legislation, and Frederick Newell urged various business organizations, including the Trans-Mississippi Commercial Congress, to discuss and publicize it. The Senate Public Lands Committee favorably reported Flint's 1907 bill, but it never reached the floor. Such a program would be unconstitutional, critics argued, and it would result in massive raids on the treasury. Why should the federal government aid some private landowners and not others, and what assurance did Congress have that the cost of drainage and irrigation would be repaid? The attempt to expand reclamation also encountered strenuous resistance from federal agencies threatened by the Reclamation Service's ambitions—particularly the Army Corps of Engineers and the Office of Irrigation Investigations in the Agriculture Department.[26]

Nevertheless, federal arid land reclamation set a precedent. If the central government could assist the economic development of the West, how could other sections of the country be denied? In his December 1907 address to Congress, Theodore Roosevelt called for the expansion of irrigation into "large portions of the South Atlantic and Gulf States."[27] In the same month, Francis G. Newlands introduced legislation to create a permanent Inland Waterways Commission that would treat the nation's major streams as units and coordinate irrigation, drainage, flood control, navigation, and the generation of electrical power throughout the nation. The National Drainage Association stimulated interest in both drainage and irrigation, and high crop prices and the increasing demand for farmland during World War I kept interest high. But Congress did not authorize a survey of swamplands until

1918, and not until the end of World War I were national schemes to reclaim swamp and cutover lands seriously entertained.

GOVERNMENT FARMERS

In its early years, federal reclamation was sold to the public as a series of technological triumphs and individual success stories—often in the nineteenth-century rags-to-riches style. The Reclamation Service boasted about the cosmopolitan population of its projects, where opportunity was open to all. Danes settled on the Yellowstone Project, in Montana and North Dakota; Belgians, Germans, and Russians on the Huntley Project, in Montana; Italians and Russians on the Uncompahgre, in Colorado; and Bohemians on the Klamath, in California and Oregon. Mexican American farmers preferred the Rio Grande and Carlsbad Projects in New Mexico, the Salt River Project in Arizona, and the Yuma Project in California. European American settlers ran the gamut from former tenant farmers who had saved enough from sharecropping to buy their own land on the Rio Grande Project to at least one Harvard graduate on the Shoshone Project, in Wyoming. Few settlers came from the crowded cities of the East, nor did more than a handful flee worn-out farms in New England or the South. A 1912 survey of homesteaders on Idaho's Minidoka Project revealed that 29 percent had resided in Idaho before entering the project, and taken collectively, about the same percentage came from Utah, Montana, Colorado, Oregon, Washington, and Nebraska. Less than 2 percent hailed from Indiana and Ohio, and less than 1 percent from Pennsylvania and New York. From the beginning of the federal reclamation program, government farmers came from *within* the West; most moved no more than five hundred miles to reach their new homes.[28]

New settlers on government projects were mainly refugees from rural America, but the Reclamation Service eagerly publicized former city dwellers on the projects. The message of the Service's propaganda was clear: character and hard work could overcome a lack of capital and agricultural experience. One young man—employed in Washington, D.C., as a stenographer in the Post Office Department—saw little future in his job and headed west in search of a new life. He inspected the government's proposed Huntley Project, near Billings, Montana, and returned to Washington deeply impressed. He remained in Washington until the project opened, then resigned his clerical position, purchased a forty-seven-acre farm, cleared thirty-five acres of sagebrush, leveled and plowed the ground, and put in twenty-four acres of oats and four of wheat. He also set out 250 apple trees and planted strawberries, potatoes, currants, grapes, and other berries between the rows. His wife supplemented the family's income by tending a garden and raising chickens. In November 1908, he reported an oat crop of sixty-two bushels to the acre and a wheat crop of thirty bushels. He also expected to net fifty to eighty dollars an acre from apples and sugar beets.[29]

Then there was a young "wood polisher" from Buffalo, New York, who filed for 160 acres on the Yellowstone Project. He arrived with fifty dollars in his pocket, but his hard work paid off. C. J. Blanchard, the Reclamation Service's chief statistician (and chief publicist), recounted that the man found work as a teamster, saved his money, bought a team and wagon of his own, and then secured a contract for hauling supplies: "He now has nine good horses and two wagons. On his farm he has erected a good house, has fenced his land, and will henceforth devote his time to harvesting bountiful crops. He has done all this within three years." Nor was that unusual. Edgar Silvers moved from Nebraska to a government farm in Washington state and grossed $2,727.60 from 7.5 acres of apple trees, with vegetables and clover grown between the rows of trees. On the same project, another farmer netted $3,755 from nine acres of apple trees, and a third reaped an average of $407.14 per acre from six acres of apple and pear trees.[30]

The wealth of the West was not reserved to men. *Reclamation Record,* the Reclamation Service's monthly publication, told the story of a "Miss Ward" and a "Miss Peebles," two ambitious bookkeepers from El Paso. They started with a few hundred dollars, "a whole lot of determination, and some good practical ideas." While employed in El Paso, the women took up two acres on the Rio Grande Project nearby and tended their farm on mornings, evenings, and holidays. First one, then the other, resigned to devote full time to ranching. Poultry provided their main income, but they also raised corn and beets and cultivated a small orchard of pear, plum, peach, apple, and apricot trees. They planted a half acre to alfalfa, baled it for winter feed, and on three-quarters of an acre put in Tokay, mission, muscat, and Cornishon grapes. The land cost $1,000 an acre, and the women spent an additional $1,500 on improvements, including three lighted poultry houses. Within two years they had paid for the land and improvements. "Except for irrigating," the *Record* noted, "all the work is done by the two women, and so far they have been exchanging such practical Christmas and birthday gifts as an ax, a saw, a steam-pressure cooker, or a wheelbarrow. Miss Ward is maid of all work. She has built a quite presentable kitchen sink and drain board, poultry fence, and all gates on the farm. Both women are members of the El Paso Egg Producers Association."[31]

At age twenty-two, Joe Bianchi came to the United States from Italy. For twenty years he worked in the coal mines at Cle Elum, Washington. When the Yakima Project opened, he risked his entire savings, $2,500, as a down payment on nineteen acres near Prosser priced at $7,000. He then borrowed $300 from friends to get started. Initially, the farm had no improvements save for a three-room shack worth less than $150. With utterly no agricultural experience, Bianchi watched his neighbors and did as they did, setting out one acre of strawberries and a half acre of eggplant during the first year, as well as corn and wheat. He later added asparagus, cherries, tomatoes, onions, rhubarb, and potatoes. A $3,000 annual gross return permitted him to build a five-room bungalow for his wife and four children, and within a few years he owned the land and home free and clear, along with an automobile. Four other Italian coal miners bought farms on the Yakima Project during the mid-1920s, and apparently, all prospered.[32]

For all the Reclamation Service's successes, there were far more failures—though few of them made the pages of the *Reclamation Record* (later *New Reclamation Era*). The rags-to-riches stories seldom mentioned family and community life on the government projects, nor did they consider such important matters as the quality of schools, roads, or local government. Success was an individual matter, measured purely in economic terms. When Henry Wallace, who was destined to become secretary of agriculture during the 1930s and vice president from 1941 to 1945, toured the West in 1909, he foresaw a bright future for irrigation agriculture and for federal reclamation. Nevertheless, he recounted some heartbreaking stories. Many residents of government projects abandoned their farms in despair after concluding that irrigation agriculture took too much work and capital for the potential rewards. Others complained about problems ranging from isolation to alkali in the soil, which proved inhospitable to crops. Women were more prone to disappointment than men. On the Garden City Project, in Kansas, Wallace ate dinner with a couple who found life on the Great Plains unbearable. "She spoke of the continual blowing of the wind which made things all the lonelier," Wallace recounted. "She and her husband both lamented the lack of people in the country." Project homes were scattered on isolated quarter sections, and irrigation was so demanding that the couple had little time to socialize. In the Salt River Valley, in Arizona, Wallace asked a woman who had recently arrived from Detroit how she liked the desert. "Oh, I just hate it," she replied. "If I could get away I wouldn't stay here if you would give me the whole town of Glendale. My husband brought me out here for my health, but I would rather go back to Detroit and die."[33]

The isolated pioneer phase of settlement would quickly pass—or so the Reclamation Service promised. Such complaints were limited to inexperienced and incompetent farmers, its leaders insisted, malcontents who lacked character and spunk. In 1913 or 1914, the *Reclamation Record* launched a strident campaign against "knockers." Its basic theme was that one critic could undo the good work of a hundred boosters. "The tone of this paper is going to remain cheerful," the *Record*'s editor observed at the end of 1914. "Other irrigation papers may sing their doleful tunes for the delectation of the knockers, but such warbling never yet helped a project or a real man."[34]

The *Record* told the cautionary tale of a rich man who wanted to settle on the Elephant Butte Project, near Las Cruces. He liked the climate and hoped to see his children educated at the nearby New Mexico Agricultural College. After touring the project, however, he changed his mind. The settlers disappointed him:

> They are pessimistic and have no hopeful outlook. They tell me of a drouth last summer and of a frost last spring, of rains on their last crop of alfalfa, and they seem to set so little store by this magnificent work that the government is doing in building the great dam at Elephant Butte, that it makes me sick, and I don't want to live among such a pessimistic people. It's too depressing. I am tired with years of steady application to business, and I want to live among cheerful people who look forward to good times and stable conditions and who are satisfied in some measure at least, with their surroundings. I do not want to fight the windmill of pessimism and neighborhood contention.

The man was confident that the knockers would eventually leave, but meanwhile, he decided to go elsewhere. The *Record* suggested that each new settler on the Elephant Butte Project be provided with a list of the disgruntled.[35]

On occasion, *Reclamation Record* published poems to inspire confidence. "Be a Booster," appeared in 1923:

> Boost and the world boosts with you;
> Knock and you're on the shelf;
> For the booster gets sick of the man who kicks,
> And wishes he'd kick himself.
>
> Boost when the sun is shining;
> Boost when it starts to rain;
> If you happen to fall, don't lie there and bawl,
> But get up and boost again.[36]

Seldom did the *Record* publish letters from farmers who complained about Reclamation Service policies or disagreed with the magazine's rosy editorials.[37]

The crusade against knockers reflected the inability and unwillingness of the Reclamation Service to design model farms or agricultural communities. For example, the new agency paid little attention to project towns until passage of the Townsite Act of 1906. That law raised the possibility of town building on the government projects, and the "father" of national reclamation, Francis G. Newlands, predicted that

> in the near future the Reclamation Service, in laying out the public lands under the various projects, will provide for well-planned towns, in which the owners of the adjoining farms will gather for social, educational, and religious purposes. . . . Reservations will be made for schools, libraries, churches, and public squares. Water, sewerage, and electric-light systems will be planned and provided, and thus farm life will lose much of its unattractiveness and isolation. Our frontier towns will not be, as heretofore, accidental growths, devoid of comfort and attractiveness. Collectivism will be employed with great economic advantage in comprehensive plans covering town development, sani-

tation, and architecture, and ending in the individualized home near the out-lying farm, associated with all the advantages of religious, education, and so-cial life.

Well-designed communities would encourage farmers to live in town and par-ticipate in civic and social affairs.[38]

In 1906, the Reclamation Service drafted plans for a model town a half mile square, built around a school and business district. Eight boulevards ra-diated out from the center of town like spokes on a wheel. This design es-caped the monotony of typical midwestern farm towns and permitted lots ranging from 36 by 140 feet in the business district to garden farms of 325 by 610 feet on the edge of the town. The line between urban and rural was imperceptible; residential district gave way gradually to countryside. Farms varied in size, as did town lots.[39] The Reclamation Service created the plan largely as propaganda, not to take the initiative in social planning. It sought to compete for settlers with railroads and townsite development companies, which often promised model towns to would-be settlers.[40]

The Reclamation Service's model was never put into practice, and a hand-ful of urban planners, led by J. Horace McFarland and the American Civic Association (ACA), badgered the service to hire a specialist to lay out its towns, or at least to employ designs provided by the ACA. "Modern types of town plans . . . are . . . incomparably superior to the old T-square plans," an official in the association informed Frederick Newell at the end of 1912. "It seems fair to expect that these new communities established under government plans should be models of their sort; and it is depressing to learn that they are merely repeating the thoroughly bad types of planning which heretofore prevailed in the prairie states." McFarland proclaimed that he was "painfully familiar with the outrages done by [the service's] engineers," and with their lack of attention to the "sociological and economical sides" of communities. He insisted that "town planning is as much a science as is the expert handling of reclamation projects" and offered the services of the ACA.[41]

At the beginning of 1913, the ACA sent the Reclamation Service a set of recommendations on the design of project towns. Above all, the report emphasized, rural communities should not be "mechanically standardized." Traditional rectilinear land surveys produced uniform and monotonous blocks and lots, as well as long, flat, straight, dull roads and streets that fol-lowed section lines and ignored the contour and character of the land. In the judgment of ACA planners, moreover, the typical pattern of plotting com-mercial buildings around a park or town square made no sense, because the business district should be compact, with stores and shops as close together as possible. The ACA recommended that the main park be at the center of the town's civic and administrative buildings, with smaller parks scattered throughout the town so that playgrounds could be situated within a quarter-mile of each home. No park should interrupt the major thoroughfares.[42]

In the years before World War I, the Reclamation Service showed little interest in social planning, and its project towns exhibited the same forlorn, ramshackle look as frontier towns everywhere in the West. As chapter 3 notes, Congress opposed any form of "paternalism," whether it took the form of planting trees, building urban water supply and sanitation systems, or providing inexpensive power to schools.[43] Nor were project farmers enthusiastic about planning. For example, they showed little interest when the Reclamation Service attempted to provide them with free house plans. Some project communities *were* more modern and up-to-date than nineteenth-century towns, but only because they were newer, not because the Reclamation Service guided or influenced their development.[44]

THE IDEOLOGY OF RECLAMATION: THE "BIG THREE" AFTER 1902

From 1898 to 1902, such champions of federal reclamation as George H. Maxwell, William Ellsworth Smythe, and Frederick H. Newell sold irrigation mainly as a scheme to build *new* homes and communities. Reclaiming desert land became a crusade to transform American society.[45] But within a few years of passage of the Reclamation Act, reclamation's leading ideologues parted company. Reclamation as homemaking gave way to reclamation as dam building, and social reform gave way to a massive federal program for the construction of dams and canals.

Reclamation and the Railroads

No one did more to make federal reclamation a national issue than railroad lobbyist George H. Maxwell.[46] From 1899 to 1902, he forged a coalition of politicians, manufacturers, chambers of commerce, labor unions, and railroads—all of whom stood to benefit directly from the government reclamation projects. The Reclamation Act would never have passed Congress without political and financial support from the nation's largest railroads. Maxwell first appeared on the railroad payroll in the late 1890s, and he remained there until 1905.[47]

James J. Hill, one of the most ambitious American railroad barons, who by 1902 controlled both the Great Northern and Northern Pacific lines, was the glue that held the coalition of railroads together. "Where irrigation prevails," he observed, "agriculture knows three admirable conditions: certainty, abundance, and variety." The population of the United States had increased by an average of 1.6 million each year since the end of the Civil War. At that rate of growth, by 1920 there would be twice as many people to feed as in

1865, and the population would double again by 1950. To make matters worse, the public domain was fast disappearing, and in many humid parts of the nation the soil had been abused and exhausted. Displaced farmers had nowhere to go. Farming had to be made more profitable, and its financial risks reduced, or newly arrived immigrants would continue to cluster in American cities, contributing to the danger of social revolution. In 1905, Hill proclaimed, "Of all the actual or suggested activities of our time, of all the wide aims that workers and lovers of their land have in view, none will take precedence of the reclamation of those vast spaces of our country now closed to productive activity."[48]

Hill's interest in irrigation was self-serving. The two railroads he was most interested in—the Great Northern and Northern Pacific—were closely allied, although the Great Northern's primary concern was the Milk River Valley, in Montana, and the Northern Pacific focused on the Yakima Valley, in Washington. Congress had granted the Northern Pacific Railroad 17.5 million acres in Montana and another 11 million acres in Washington.[49] In 1900, the Northern Pacific still held 13,450,816 acres in Montana, and millions more in North Dakota and Washington. "The largest area for cheap irrigation in the United States is south of the Sweet Grass Hills and in the Milk River Valley on our line, in Northern Montana," Hill wrote one month before Congress adopted the Reclamation Act. "At an expense of five or six dollars an acre, covering a period of say, eight or ten years, four or five million acres can be put under a full supply of water. . . . That district, with a good supply of water, would produce nearly as much grain as is produced on our entire System at the present time." The Northern Pacific would profit from federal reclamation in two ways. It could expect to receive fifteen to twenty-five dollars an acre for the land it owned—land previously leased to stockmen—and irrigation agriculture would expand freight traffic, increasing the line's profits.[50]

The Milk River Valley was several hundred miles long, with the potential to produce more sugar beets than any other agricultural region in the United States, Hill predicted. Land not planted to beets would grow alfalfa to carry the state's cattle herds through the harsh Montana winters. Hill favored a scheme to dam the outlet of St. Mary Lake and divert its water into the north fork of the Milk River via a twenty-seven-mile canal. The augmented stream would carry the water 150 to 200 miles east—including more than a hundred miles within Canada—until it reached 250,000 acres of potential farmland near Chinook and Malta. The U.S. Geological Survey began preliminary surveys for a Milk River Project in 1900.[51]

Two months before passage of the Reclamation Act, the USGS withdrew from settlement a million acres in the Milk River and Marias valleys, and the Milk River Project was one of the first authorized by the secretary of the interior.[52] To limit speculation, Newell forbade government surveyors from talking to Montana newspaper editors and booster groups, and in March 1904, he warned Maxwell that an "apparent indifference" to the project—to use his words—was necessary to prevent a speculative mania that would inflate private land prices far beyond what potential government farmers could afford to pay. The railroad used the mere promise of government aid to sell its land, but that land had not ended up in the hands of small farmers. "If we could be freed from the pest of petty speculators and amateur lobbyists who are taking up the time of the responsible [Reclamation Service] men," Newell complained, "we could make far more rapid progress. I trust you will use every effort in your power to keep this thing out of the public press and to avoid discussion of it during the present critical situation."[53]

Land speculation was only one of the Reclamation Service's problems. Canada and the United States shared the Milk River, and Newell hesitated to begin construction in the Milk River Valley until an international treaty had defined each nation's rights to the river. Meanwhile, he hoped to find a project that included more government land. But the more projects that were proposed, the more intractable the differences between the railroads and the Reclamation Service became. Each side accused the other of duplicity.[54]

By the spring of 1904, railroad executives and politicians in the northwest had lost faith in Newell and the Reclamation Service. Senator Henry C. Hansbrough charged Newell with incompetence and favoritism. The northern plains had contributed far more to the reclamation fund than Arizona, but Hansbrough claimed that Newell and Maxwell had favored the Salt River Project in Arizona from the beginning. "I think his [Newell's] interests are all in the southwest," Louis Hill, vice president of the Great Northern Railroad, wrote. "The more I hear from Maxwell and Newell, the more satisfied I am that we are getting the worst of it. . . . I cannot help but feel that the question of irrigation is being sidetracked along our line in Montana and through the State of North Dakota."[55]

James J. Hill's enthusiasm faded even more when he discovered the reluctance of Montana farmers to irrigate, or to practice scientific agriculture. They preferred to risk relying on nature for moisture. If the canals were built, would they be used? And if farmers refused to help themselves, what could the railroads do? "I have long ago concluded that local selfishness would prove the bane of the whole question of irrigation," he wrote in March 1905, "and I am so well satisfied of that that I am prepared to see the work fail. I think . . . that it would have been much better if what we had done towards National Irrigation [the money spent by the railroads to push the 1902 law through Congress] had been done [spent] in the Milk River Valley. We then would have had something to show for it; at present, there is nothing." By 1913, Hill was one of federal reclamation's harshest critics, arguing that the government works were far more expensive, and no better built, than those constructed by private enterprise.[56]

Eventually, the Reclamation Service constructed several projects along or near the Great Northern line, including the Buford-Trenton pump project in North Dakota, the Sun River Project in Montana, and the Yakima Project in Washington State. All but the Washington project were spectacular failures. "Some of the projects would have never been considered if it had not been for the influence of those who helped secure the law," Elwood Mead, the former director of the Office of Irrigation Investigations, advised Senator John D. Works of California in 1912, "and of these the Sun River project in Montana and the one on the lower Colorado [the Yuma Project] will never return 10 cents on the dollar." In the end, only the Yellowstone Project in Montana and the Minidoka Project in Idaho served substantial tracts of railroad land.[57]

George H. Maxwell and the Homecroft Movement

Officials of the northern railroads became convinced that Maxwell was speculating in land along the Southern Pacific line.[58] In the late 1890s, Maxwell had served as Arizona's territorial delegate in Congress. He moved to the Salt River Valley in December 1902 and spent the next seven or eight months organizing the Salt River Valley water users' association as an inducement for the federal government to build a reservoir to aid landowners around Phoenix. Prior to reaching Arizona, he informed the secretary of the Salt River Valley Water Storage Committee: "In the strictest *personal confidence* I have no hesitancy in expressing to you my belief that the Tonto will be the first reservoir built by the national government."[59] Maxwell knew that Arizona would soon become a state, and Theodore Roosevelt was eager to ensure that its first two U.S. senators would be Republican.[60]

On June 7, 1904, the railroads decided to end payments to Maxwell at the end of the year.[61] By the time the northern railroads fired Maxwell as their lobbyist, he had already decided that the Reclamation Act was a failure. The irrigation movement, Maxwell insisted, should go "far beyond the mere building of dams and reservoirs and canals." It should include large-scale colonization as well as the management of water. Yet not only did Congress refuse to appropriate money to train and relocate those trapped in American cities, it even refused to protect the best public land from speculators. Little wonder that few urban poor wanted to move West.[62]

Maxwell never questioned the power of irrigation to transform American society, but by 1905 he considered the land surrounding America's largest cities as a more practical safety valve than the West. America's most important social problems, according to Maxwell, had their roots in rapid industrialization, the concentration of workers in cities, and the decline of the family. Mechanization had methodically reduced the demand for labor on the farm and in the factory. The average American worker paid 43 percent of his or her wages for food and another 18 percent for rent, and, Maxwell argued, wages were unlikely to increase. Yet despite the large amount of arable land within a few miles of most cities, workers crowded into tenement houses. Hunger and malnutrition, crippling diseases such as tuberculosis, the decline of civic virtue and public responsibility, the increasing concentration of wealth, and the corrosive effects of socialism and anarchism on American values all worried Maxwell. Without a revival of the independence and individualism that once characterized rural America, the next depression would touch off a massive war between the haves and the have nots.

The lesson Maxwell learned between 1902 and 1905 was simple: The United States did not have to become *either* a nation of small farms *or* a nation of sprawling cities. It was possible, he insisted, to combine the efficiency, organization, and productivity of industrial America with the time-honored values and open space of rural America. A one-acre irrigated plot on the edge of a city could feed a family and produce enough eggs and vegetables to make the difference between a precarious subsistence and a life of comfort and security.[63] A home in the country would also improve the health and productivity of workers. "You are developing race-horses and fat cattle and fine hogs and all kinds of domestic animals, and how much attention are you giving to improving the human machine in your factories in health, strength and physique?" Maxwell asked.[64]

The historian Laura Lovett has observed that Maxwell drew his ideas from many sources, including the Back to the Land movement, the Parks and Playground campaign (which "used open space and trees as curative antidotes for urban life"), and the City Beautiful crusade, which sought to eliminate tenement houses and slums. All of these campaigns sought to bring the countryside to the city. The most important influence on Maxwell's thinking was the homecroft idea, pioneered in the late 1870s by the Cadbury brothers, who moved their chocolate factory four miles outside Birmingham, England, erected houses for their workers, and encouraged employees to grow their own vegetables and raise their own poultry. They sought to provide workers and their families with healthier surroundings and an improved diet, not just to make wages go further. The homecroft, in Maxwell's mind, was the only solution to the perils of industrialization, and he publicized the "homecroft idea" in frequent speeches and in the pages of several magazines he edited, including *Maxwell's Talisman*. Previous back-to-the-land movements had failed because they transplanted factory workers to the country, where they were expected to make their living solely from the land. Maxwell sought to break down the artificial barrier between rural and urban life.

Each issue of the *Talisman* carried an eloquent statement of principle:

We believe that the Patriotic Slogan of the whole People of this Nation should be "Every Child in a Garden—Every Mother in a Homecroft—and Individual Industrial Independence for Every Worker in a Home of his Own on the Land,"

and that until he owns such a Home, the concentrated purpose and chief inspiration to labor in the life of every wage worker should be his determination to "Get an Acre and Live on it."

We believe that the Slums and Tenements and Congested Centers of population in the Cities are a savagely deteriorating social, moral and political influence, and that a great public movement should be organized, and the whole power of the nation and the states exerted for the betterment of all the conditions of Rural Life, and to create and upbuild Centers of Social and Civic Life in Country and Suburban Towns and Villages, where Trade and Industry can be so firmly anchored that they cannot be drawn into the Commercial Maelstrom that is now steadily sucking Industry and Humanity into the Vortex of the Great Cities. . . .

We believe that, as a Nation, we should be less absorbed with Making Money, and should pay more heed to raising up and training Men who will be Law-Abiding Citizens; that the welfare of our Workers is of more consequence than the mere accumulation of Wealth; and that Stability of National Character and of Social and Business Conditions is of greater importance to the people of this country as a whole than any other one question that is now before them; and we believe that the only way to Preserve such Stability, and to Permanently Maintain our National Prosperity, is to carry into immediate effect and operation the Platform of the Talisman.[65]

Maxwell called for a "great national campaign" to teach gardening in the public schools. Gardening would imbue children with a love of the land, and the food from those gardens, as well as handicrafts produced by the children not employed in factories, would eliminate "wage slavery." Maxwell also proposed the creation of homecroft schools for the unemployed; heavy federal taxes to discourage large estates; government purchase and subdivision of land and low-interest loans to settlers to help them get started; and homecroft tax exemptions. Nominally, Maxwell remained loyal to federal reclamation, and his platform favored many reforms supported by the Reclamation Service, such as welding water rights to the land (to limit speculation in water) and the abolition of riparian rights in the arid West. But the homecroft scheme also underscored the failure of federal reclamation to address the ills of industrial America.[66]

Maxwell established homecrofts in Arizona, Massachusetts, Minnesota, and Indiana. Early in 1905, he selected a block of land served by the Salt River Valley Canal, one mile from the terminus of Phoenix's street railway system, as the site of one of his first homecroft experiments. After leveling the tract, he planted palm and olive trees, subdivided the land into five-acre plots, and sold them exclusively to farmers skilled in truck gardening, berry and small fruit culture, and poultry raising. "This movement for the building of Homecrofts," Maxwell explained, "is a logical enlargement of the central idea around which the National Irrigation Movement was organized. . . . The success of the Homecroft Village near Phoenix will lead to its duplication in the neighborhood of many other cities and towns throughout the country." Unfortunately, Phoenix contained few factories, and the price of land ($150 an acre) was well beyond the means of most workers. At about the same time he launched the experiment in Arizona, Maxwell renamed his home in Newton, Massachusetts, "Homecroft-on-the-Charles" and turned the grounds into a garden school that enrolled more than a hundred children. He also bought fifty acres forty-five minutes from Boston by trolley as a second homecroft.[67]

Maxwell tried, but failed, to persuade railroads, labor unions, and philanthropic organizations to fund the homecroft scheme. Finally, he turned to the federal government. In most European countries, postal savings banks raised money for public works. If such banks were created in the United States, and the ratio of depositors to the total population corresponded to the ratio in England—about one in four—the United States could count on 20 million savings accounts and $700 million for the central government to invest. In 1906, Maxwell drafted a bill to create a postal savings plan, the proceeds from which would be devoted to establishing homecrofts on the outskirts of major cities, ranging in size from a quarter of an acre to ten acres. The legislation would have created a Homecroft Service in the Interior Department, with the secretary of the interior empowered to spend up to $100 million a year—$1 billion in all—to purchase private land and clear, fence, and level it. The money could also be used to drain swamps. The Homecroft Service would plant trees, construct streets and sewers, and provide parks and electric power before the land went on the market, and homecrofters would have twenty years to repay their debt to the government at 4 percent interest. The Maxwell bill posed an obvious threat to the Reclamation Service and to many of the assumptions upon which the national reclamation program had been built.[68]

Maxwell carried the homecroft message to Duluth, Detroit, Michigan City, Indianapolis, Pittsburgh, and many other industrial cities, but with little success.[69] As the years wore on, disappointment took its toll, and anger and bitterness crept into his letters. "I think the American people are mentally dead and refuse to think or be informed on any subject which does not relate to the way they make their living or the fun they can get out of spending what little surplus money they have," Maxwell wrote to a close associate in 1915. "I used to have a lot of patriotic admiration for the American people but I am sorry to say that I think a great majority of them, in these days, have been so degenerated mentally and physically by our wrong educational system, and [by] the city life that they are as superficial and rapidly growing to be as helpless and thoughtless in the matters relating to their own welfare and the eventual welfare of the nation as were the rabble of Rome."[70]

The wages and working conditions of factory workers improved markedly during the first three decades of the twentieth century, but Maxwell's thinking changed little. If American factories went to two six-hour shifts, he suggested in 1920, working men could spend two hours a day in the garden, producing "practically all the food the family needs, and much better food than they get now, and of a value to him of at least one-half of the wage he now receives." And at the beginning of the Great Depression he observed: "The invention of labor-saving machinery the world over, is driving human labor out of the game in both agriculture and industry, and the only way to avoid revolution is by evolution into the Homecroft system, where every family will be anchored to its own food factory." It was "almost a miracle" that the depression had "fallen on the United States of America. No matter what anybody else may think about it, there is no human possibility of ever avoiding such evils periodically in the future, unless they are safeguarded against by the adoption of the entire homecroft system of education, industry and life."[71]

Frequently strapped for money, particularly after the 1917 death of his patron and benefactor, Francis G. Newlands, Maxwell also suffered occasional bouts of crippling depression.[72] During World War I, and into the 1920s and 1930s, he opposed the Colorado River Compact and Boulder Dam Project. Construction of the dam, he predicted, would prevent Arizona from watering its unused irrigable land and would create a Japanese colony in Mexico—a colony that would become the launching pad for an Asian invasion of the United States. Such ideas branded him as a crackpot, and by the time Boulder Dam was completed he was all but forgotten. He spent the last years of his life as a penniless invalid in Phoenix. To the end, he sought a balance or accommodation between rural and urban life, farm and factory. He died in 1946 at the age of eighty-six.[73]

William E. Smythe and the Little Landers

In the early years of the twentieth century, William Ellsworth Smythe's *Conquest of Arid America,* first published in 1900 and revised in 1905, became the bible of arid-land reclamation.[74] Smythe turned irrigation into a crusade, almost a religious movement. He regarded the subjugation of the "Great American Desert" as the last chapter in the westward course of Anglo-Saxon empire. He welcomed the age of industrial organization, but he also celebrated a democratic, egalitarian rural past, particularly the compact agricultural villages of New England and Utah. Smythe's ideas were attractive to those who favored centralized government control over water and land— the planned settlement of the West—as well as to those who promoted the autonomous family farm. Watering the West, they believed, would fulfill the nation's destiny and symbolize the triumph of planning, organization, and order. Without scientific agriculture—and in the West scientific agriculture demanded irrigation—society could not evolve beyond a primitive form.

Irrigation was also part of the modernization of American institutions.

The United States, Smythe thought, was caught in an inevitable historical process: the transition from an economy characterized by individualism, competition, waste, and selfishness, into one defined by efficiency, cooperation, planning, order, and equity. Images of the depression of the 1890s haunted him, including the strikes, class conflict, and vast numbers of jobless and homeless vagabonds. "The starving strikers at Fall River, the pale little children driven from bed and herded into the cotton mills of North Carolina, the ten million American citizens walking hand in hand with hopeless poverty—these are like the slaves of ante-bellum days," Smythe observed.[75]

Antebellum slavery had torn the nation apart, and so might the "slavery" of the late nineteenth century. Yet Smythe did not want to return to the agricultural America of 1800 or 1850. Unlike Maxwell, he did not fear large institutions. Industrial concentration, he believed, was both inevitable and good; he feared an economy of small units built on individualism far more than he feared the new industrial order. Monopoly offered many advantages: it reduced the cost of manufacturing, prevented overproduction, promoted foreign trade, raised the standard of living, and limited the fluctuation of prices. Nor could the process of centralization be resisted. "Consolidation, combination, cooperation—these tend toward unity, and they are true. The Nation and the States sought to restrain them with their puny hands—sought to restore the false doctrine of competitive diversity—but the truth was stronger than legislatures, courts, and executives, and truth would have its way. So the centralizing tendency in corporate ownership and management went on, with its palpable tendency toward harmony and away from discord." The problem was not industrial consolidation or monopoly, but the "surplus" men and women mechanization produced. Once these people had turned to agriculture. It was foolish and dangerous, Smythe thought, that the United States had not done more to develop the West as a refuge for the human beings machines put out of work.[76]

In the years after 1902, Smythe, like Maxwell, recognized that federal reclamation would never provide enough new homes in the West to eliminate poverty in America. "What are we doing for that class of homeseekers—always a large element in every American movement of population—who are without sufficient means to come here, get a foothold in the reclaimed desert, and await the slow return? Nothing—worse than nothing." The national government, Smythe argued, should pay as much attention to colonizing the land as to providing it with water. Just as Maxwell borrowed the homecroft idea from England, Smythe was one of the first to publicize New Zealand's settlement plan. That country's central government purchased private land, improved and subdivided it, then leased it for long periods to prevent the speculation and monopolies that often prevented poor families in the United States from securing a farm.[77]

Smythe did not seek to integrate city and country, or industry and agriculture, as Maxwell did. In his mind, intensive farming and the compact rural village provided *alternatives* to the congestion of large American cities and to the numbing routine of factory life. Properly used, one acre of land could sustain a higher standard of living than a factory job—and provide an ideal retirement home and income as well. Smythe had seen the value of one-acre farms at Orland, California, in the Sacramento Valley, where an old man named Samuel Cleek managed to live comfortably on one acre and to save an average of four hundred dollars a year—the equivalent of one year's wages for a factory worker. Smythe was also influenced by the Garden City movement of Englishman Ebenezer Howard; the proposal of Liberty Hyde Bailey, professor of agriculture at Cornell University and chair of Theodore Roosevelt's Country Life Commission, to build rural homes on the outskirts of American cities; and Wall Street lawyer Bolton Hall's 1908 book *A Little Land and a Living*.[78] In the years from 1895 to 1901, Smythe established irrigation colonies in the Payette Valley of Idaho and in California's Tehama and Lassen Counties. But Smythe's biggest agricultural experiment came at "Little Landers," near San Ysidro, California, a suburb of San Diego just north of the Mexican border.[79]

Smythe established the community of Little Landers in January 1909. He had four goals: to create small irrigated farms; to concentrate the colonists in a village adjoining their farms; to provide new settlers with expert advice from experienced farmers; and to eliminate marketing middlemen by selling crops directly to consumers in San Diego. The colony's motto was "A Little Land and a Living Surely Is Better than Desperate Struggle and Wealth Possibly." A family could buy only as much land within Little Landers as it could cultivate without hiring outside labor. The community covered 550 acres, divided into farms ranging in size from a quarter to seven acres, with an average size of two and a quarter acres. Smythe hoped to sell the farms over many months, so that the community would profit from the "unearned increment." All money beyond the original purchase price went into an Improvement Fund to build streets, sidewalks, sewers, and public buildings, and to provide loans to needy farmers. This endowment was also expected to eliminate the need for taxation. The village included a clubhouse, its own utilities, and a library of several hundred volumes.

At the end of 1911, the community contained sixty-nine families. A year later that number climbed to 116 families—about three hundred people—but all was not well. Smythe could not keep land speculators out of the project, and many residents refused to live in the village. The settlement suffered from other problems as well. As transplanted urbanites, few Little Landers knew anything about farming, and the marketing cooperative created resentment: the best vegetables grew on river-bottom lands, but farmers who raised lower-quality produce demanded the same price. Many withdrew from the cooperative and sought their own buyers. Meanwhile, the community's cooperative store fell into debt and was turned over to a private enterprise in 1915. Subsequently, the irrigation works proved inadequate, and a massive flood at the beginning of 1916 crippled the water system. (It also destroyed twenty-five homes and caused a hundred families to flee.) World War I, the Mexican Revolution, and violence and disorder across the international border discouraged other settlers from coming to San Ysidro. After the death of Smythe's wife in 1918, he left California for Washington, D.C., to help Secretary of the Interior Franklin K. Lane plan soldier-settlement schemes for the postwar reconstruction. After the war, he tried to sell the Little Landers plan in the East through his American Homesteaders Society, but he was unsuccessful. He died in October 1922.[80]

Frederick H. Newell and the "New Engineers"

Frederick H. Newell had little sympathy for the attempts of Maxwell and Smythe to improve the quality of life in rural America. Born in Bradford, Pennsylvania, in 1862 and educated in Massachusetts public schools, Newell enrolled at the Massachusetts Institute of Technology in 1883. After taking a degree in mining engineering in 1885, he entered the graduate engineering program. In his quest for a thesis topic, he first studied coal and oil deposits for the State Geological Survey of Ohio and the Mining and Geological Survey of Virginia and did consulting work in Virginia and Pennsylvania. In the summer of 1888 he met John Wesley Powell, then head of the U.S. Geological Survey, and when Congress appropriated one hundred thousand dollars to investigate possible irrigation projects in the West, Newell, in his words, "entered on duty expecting to remain a year or two until I had accumulated material for a thesis but actually continuing for nearly 30 years."[81]

Newell's appointment as assistant hydraulic engineer in the USGS marked a turning point in his career. Following a brief stint as a topographer in Nevada's Humboldt River basin, he took charge of sixteen men at a camp near Embudo, New Mexico, on the Rio Grande. There he tested surveying instruments and devised methods of stream measurement for the Irrigation Survey. Subsequently, Newell examined streams in Utah, Colorado, Wyoming, and California. After Congress cancelled the Irrigation Survey in 1890, he remained an employee of the Geological Survey, mapping rivers in the East and the West. His big break came in 1894. Plagued with crop surpluses in a time of falling prices, Congress refused to revive the Irrigation Survey, let alone build dams and canals. Instead, it placated those who demanded federal action by appropriating a small amount of money to gauge streams—which could be interpreted as the prelude to a comprehensive federal water program or a stalling tactic. In the following year, Congress abolished the Office of Irrigation Inquiry in the Department of Agriculture (predecessor of the Office of Irrigation Investigations, which was established in 1898). The money saved was reallocated to a new Hydrographic Division in the USGS. By strengthening the USGS, Congress ensured that if a federal reclamation program were ever initiated, it was likely to end up in Interior rather than Agriculture. Newell directed the stream-gauging work and appointed Arthur P. Davis, John Wesley Powell's nephew, as his assistant.[82]

During the late 1890s, Newell made the political connections that permitted him to take control of the federal reclamation program in 1902. Active in the American Forestry Association, the National Geographic Society, and many other scientific organizations, he maintained close ties to influential scientists, including John Wesley Powell and G. K. Gilbert. He demonstrated intellectual breadth by preparing the federal census on irrigation in 1890 and 1900, by drafting maps of the vacant public lands of the United States in 1893 and the dry-farmed regions of the nation in 1894, and by advising New York governor Theodore Roosevelt concerning the Adirondack forests in 1900. Along with Gifford Pinchot, he became one of T. R.'s principal advisers following William McKinley's assassination in September 1901. For example, he and Pinchot drafted the section on natural resources in Roosevelt's first message to Congress.[83]

Newell was a new breed of engineer. Most nineteenth-century engineers, particularly those who worked in the West, were self-taught entrepreneurs, technocrats, scientists, boosters, and master-builders rolled into one. From 1850 to 1880, the number of medical doctors and clergymen in the United States more than doubled and the number of architects increased sixfold, but civil engineers multiplied by sixteen times. Then, from 1880 to 1920, the engineering profession increased by almost 2,000 percent, from 7,000 to 136,000. In 1870 there were 21 engineering colleges in the nation; by 1896 there were 110.[84]

Engineering societies encouraged their members to take a broad view of their profession. Deeply held articles of faith united the "new engineers." The world was governed by knowable natural laws, laws that engineers were best equipped to understand and to harness. Human progress was defined in materialistic terms. The engineer was the master of technology—and the logical arbiter of economic progress. The scientific method made him a rationalist free of bias, suited both to lead and to mediate between economic interests and conflicting classes. Human beings could remake the world and build a harmonious society. "We are the priests of material development, of the work which enables other men to enjoy the fruits of the great sources of power in Nature, and of the power of mind over matter," one engineer commented. "We are the priests of the new epoch, without superstitions." The notion that immutable natural law governed society was best seen in Frederick Taylor's scientific management, which prompted many engineers to suggest structural reforms in government, higher education, and even religion.[85]

By nature, the new engineers were above politics and beyond business; they distrusted politics and politicians. Their professional ethics emphasized organization, rationality, efficiency and expertise, not democratic ideals.[86] Representative government rested on common sense, the consent of the governed, majority rule, and leadership by the "generalist." These principles clashed with bureaucratization and professionalization. The new engineers worried little about the size of big business or the problems of labor, though they might demand more planning and better management and administration. (Capitalism needed reform not because it was morally wrong, but because it was wasteful.) Yet being suited to lead, or deserving to lead, were different from the *will* to lead. In 1907, President Arthur T. Hadley of Yale University, an economist by training, credited engineers with "having in one brief century established science as the arbiter of the material affairs of mankind, and of having enforced her worship upon a world once reluctant, but now gloriously admiring." Nevertheless, he did not think engineers had shown the same leadership as financiers, journalists, and politicians. "If the engineer and the lawyer accept positions as servants, simply putting their technical knowledge at the disposal of merchants, journalists or politicians who will pay the highest price for it," he warned, "it is not simply a confession of inferiority, it is a dereliction of public duty."[87]

Newell embraced Hadley's message wholeheartedly. In May 1912, he delivered the commencement address to the graduating class of Case Engineering School in Cleveland. He called the twentieth century the "age of the engineer," and he characterized the engineer as the "pioneer of a better and higher degree of civilization." Engineering was "the study and application of the so-called laws of nature." Too many engineers confined their work to the construction of roads, bridges, buildings, and other public works, ignoring their responsibility to lead and to shape society. But the age of the generalist was over. The behavior of human beings could be predicted and controlled much like the behavior of nature. "The most important of the machines with which the engineer has to do is the human machine. . . . the engineer is concerned not simply with a single man, as such, but particularly with men in organizations."[88] Time and again, Newell attacked the conservatism of engineering societies and announced the need for engineers to plan and to lead. He also exhibited impatience with "public opinion." For example, in 1915 he wrote: "In this work [in Newell's words, the 'careful, impartial measurement and weighing of facts'] the engineer is far ahead of the public. The latter in many ways has not yet caught up with the growth of knowledge and does not appreciate the possibilities that are awaiting realization under the magic touch of the skilled engineer."[89]

Yet Newell was not as modern as he appeared, and the memory of the hard times and social disorder of the 1890s never left him.[90] In a 1911 speech before the Congress of Technology, he observed

> The reclamation of the arid west is simply one of a number of items of national importance upon whose correct solution by true scientific methods rests largely not merely the material prosperity of the nation, but, more than this, the perpetuation of free government, and of high standards of individual liberty. The stability of a republic or democracy . . . rests not upon its wealth, but upon the character of the individual citizen and voter. . . . The strength of the unit, the family or the voter, is not derived from material wealth, but from the ability to act and think independently and to exercise that intelligent self-interest which binds him to the great mass of his fellow men.

Put a man onto a forty-acre farm and his view of the world changed. He was no longer a nomad moving from flat to flat or town to town, a man indifferent to the welfare of the community in which he lived. The small farm reinforced the family, which, in turn, strengthened the local community and the republic. As a landowner and a voter, the yeoman became interested in improving roads, schools, city government, and the other institutions of a free people.[91]

Newell was not the only leader in the Reclamation Service to play on the homemaking theme. He also spoke through C. J. Blanchard, the Reclamation Service's publicist. "America has furnished a safety-valve against the overcrowding of the great centers of population in the Old World for 50 years," Blanchard wrote in 1907. "Is it not about time to look to our problem and prepare against the day when there shall be a glut of population in our cities? Thoughtful men are predicting a population of 200,000,000 in 1950 and 300,000,000 at the close of the century. How shall we take care of this vast increase?" In the following year Blanchard warned that "the menace of a great population underfed and poorly housed looms more darkly each year. . . . What is the use of preaching love of home and country when we offer nothing but crowded tenements to the toiler who seeks to earn a roof over his family. There is no national stability in a citizenship born and reared in tenements. Patriotism, loyalty, and civic pride are not bred and fostered in the crowded centers of population." As late as 1909, Blanchard insisted that "the work of reclamation is of national interest . . . because it will tend in some measure to relieve the overcrowding and congestion of older settled portions of the country." As Smythe had done in the 1890s, Blanchard reminded his listeners that federal reclamation offered the opportunity to build a new civilization in the West. The job was not just to arrest the flow of Americans from country to city, but to urbanize farm life. "The narrow provincialism which has marked life where farms are large is not found here," he observed in 1909. "Rural delivery of mails, with daily papers, the county telephone, traveling libraries, centralized schools, and trolley lines to the towns are all serving to bring the desert farmer within the stimulating currents of the world's thought." In the West, near perfect conditions of rural life would make possible near perfect rural institutions. As late as 1918, Blanchard noted that reclaiming the desert would fulfill the West's "manifest destiny," which was "the upbuilding of Man."[92]

The key to understanding Frederick H. Newell is the tension between his admiration for the technology and organization of the new bureaucratic age and his respect for the virile, "character-building" frontier society. In 1902, it was unclear whether the farmers who settled government projects would be treated like the pioneer farmers of the nineteenth century, as agricultural entrepreneurs, as wards of the state, or as participants in a social experiment. But unlike Maxwell and Smythe, Newell could not bring himself to manage the lives of those who settled on government farms.

Newell quickly came to believe that the typical government farmer lacked the will, determination, and moral fiber of those who had "opened" the West in the decades after the Civil War. The fact that only a small minority of the first generation of project farmers succeeded reinforced this assumption. If one farmer in three prospered, Newell reasoned, then the failure of the other two could not be blamed on the Reclamation Service. Those most likely to default on payments to the government, he insisted, were either speculators or incompetents. When the parasites and the unfit fled, the projects would be cleansed of those who lacked the discipline and patience to make a go of it. The success of any project, therefore, rested on the broken dreams of those who had first settled the land. Time and again, Newell complained that farmers on the national irrigation projects refused to help themselves, and, he claimed, the large number of drifters or loafers would have failed no matter what policies the Reclamation Service had followed. "The characteristics of present settlers are in many respects entirely different from those of the older pioneer communities," he lamented in 1912. "[T]here is not the spirit of cooperation which ruled the early pioneers." A decade later Newell observed, "The reasons for success or failure lie not so much in climate, soil, or markets, but rather in the character of the landowner, his experience, strength, health, and especially the 'will to win,' or possession of qualities which distinguish the pioneer."[93]

In his 1916 textbook on irrigation, written after he left the Reclamation Service and could express his opinions freely, Newell noted that more than 75 percent of the original inhabitants of federal irrigation projects fled their homesteads within a few years of entry. He concluded:

> The irrigators as a body are not only inexperienced, but many of them are disappointed in that they have expected easier things. Thus they do not always appreciate the efforts made in their behalf. There has been attracted to the locality [the arid West] a considerable number of men who have never made

a success elsewhere; these attribute their failure to make good under the new conditions not to their own inability, but largely to the faults of the country or system. . . . He [the would-be twentieth century farmer] is attracted usually by glowing accounts of the relative ease of acquiring wealth in the West, and with erroneous ideas concerning the conditions to be met. . . . There has thus arisen a class which has been called the "professional pioneer," always seeking for something a little better or for conditions where life will be easier; staying in any locality only a few months and then again seeking El Dorado.[94]

The Reclamation Service, in Newell's judgment, did its best. For example, it encouraged farmers to plant high-value crops, but found that they preferred crops that required less effort rather than those that yielded the largest profits. "It is difficult to interest many of them in the experiments being carried on for their benefit," Newell concluded, "and the tendency has been to rely upon advice or suggestions of some near neighbor, who may be misinformed." Many farmers, he believed, were simply too lazy to seek professional advice.[95]

In 1912, Newell asked C. J. Blanchard to investigate a thousand settler complaints. Blanchard found that "over 95 percent . . . were made by men who were not actually cultivating the ground themselves, but were of the type of farmer who drives into town and tells how local affairs should be run rather than getting in and doing the work. It is obvious that many of the irrigation projects must be resettled by a selected lot of men who have a fair amount of capital, who appreciate that irrigation means hard work." A year later, Newell observed in a letter to Gifford Pinchot, "On the whole, we have done too much in taking the initiative and in trying to expedite development. [W]hat we now need is to bring about by indirect methods the building up of cooperative societies." If the farmers could not do for themselves, no amount of government aid would help.[96]

Newell knew that project farmers were not entirely at fault. At the beginning of the federal reclamation program, no one could have anticipated how the percentage of rural Americans would shrink between 1900 and 1920, as the income of industrial workers increased and farms were abandoned in New England, New York, Ohio, Indiana, Illinois, Iowa, Nebraska, Virginia, North Carolina, and Kentucky. As early as 1915, Newell confided to a friend that he now doubted whether irrigation could be made profitable under the best of circumstances. The average irrigation farmer "under present conditions is obtaining little more than 5% interest on his investment and the day wages of an ordinary laborer." Newell referred mainly to *private* irrigation projects, where interest was tacked on to the cost of reclamation, but by 1927 he insisted that "all large reclamation enterprises, with a few notable exceptions, must be subsidized directly or indirectly. This is because the land when ultimately reclaimed and settled does not have an economic value equalling the cost of reclamation and other work put on it."[97]

Two years before his death in 1932, an embittered Newell looked back on the early years of federal reclamation and admitted that "there was not a real need for more farm land [in 1902]. The demand which seemed to exist for irrigated land was largely artificial, stimulated by the speculative spirit; it did not come from true economic needs of the country." The stubborn and irrational persistence of the homestead ethic had convinced Congress to adopt the Reclamation Act. Congress, Newell now argued, had paid too much attention to the arid West; the farms of the humid United States were more than adequate to feed the entire nation. The crops produced on government projects represented less than 1 percent of the value of all farm products raised in the United States and only 6 percent of the value of the arid region's output. There was no demand for new homes and— given farm mechanization, the labor-saving value of electricity, and the continuing migration to cities—the family farm had no future in the West. There was no need for national reclamation and no need to continue farming marginal land in the West. Above all, the interest-free provision of the 1902 law had proved to be a disaster. The Department of Agriculture had estimated that farmers on the Salt River Project in Arizona paid only one-fourth of the full cost of reclamation. Not only had these farmers gotten something for nothing, federal reclamation had eroded "the higher ideals of citizenship." In Newell's words, "insidious forms of [government] paternalism" had undermined self-reliance. Federal reclamation had created a debtor class, and the promise of repudiating that debt held out by local politicians robbed project farmers of discipline, energy, and independence.[98]

Newell's bitter condemnation of federal reclamation was the postscript to a long and distinguished career. In the same year that he issued the preceding indictment, workers began building the gigantic dam on the Colorado River that would dwarf all the structures erected by the federal government during the Progressive Era. It was fitting that Newell did not live to see the national reclamation program rise from the ashes in the 1930s and after. In the end, he was a man of the nineteenth century who clung to the belief that a generation of farmers had let him down. He carried that disappointment to the grave.[99]

CONCLUSION

In 1902, Theodore Roosevelt made a fatal mistake. He was one of the first presidents to have lived in the West, and he saw that region's political support as vital to the future success of his Republican Party. Nineteenth-century river and harbor appropriations had been allocated on the basis of politics more than need. Some parts of the country, such as the Great Lakes and Atlantic Seaboard, had received more benefits than others, but Congress had scattered the benefits as widely as possible. Six months before passage of the

Reclamation Act, Roosevelt promised that federal reclamation would be different. He proposed the construction of a few model reclamation projects so that government engineers could concentrate their energies and learn from experience. The insistence of some western states that 51 percent of the proceeds from public land sales be spent within the state or territory where that land was located did not mean that all parts of the West should benefit equally from the start of the program. But after passage of the Reclamation Act, Roosevelt had second thoughts. He decided to push through as many reclamation projects as possible as rapidly as possible. Many Democrats, including Francis G. Newlands, had taken credit for passage of the legislation, and many Republicans had opposed it. If the projects were spread out over time, they might not be completed until after a Democrat assumed the presidency, and he might then take credit for T. R.'s pet program. And with Arizona, New Mexico, and Oklahoma waiting to enter the union, identifying federal reclamation with the Republican Party became imperative.

Roosevelt's decision influenced the course of federal reclamation in countless ways. Not all western states and territories had sufficient blocks of public land to create projects that would provide new homes, so most projects had to include large tracts of private land and many already-established farmers. T. R.'s decision to push construction on as many projects as possible also left relatively little money to move settlers onto the land, provide economic support during the difficult years when they prepared the land for water and crops, and find markets for their products. Historians have argued that the Reclamation Service became a construction agency rather than a social welfare agency primarily because it was staffed and administered by engineers. To be sure, Congress refused to permit any federal agency to engage in large-scale "social planning." Yet the political decisions made by Theodore Roosevelt in 1902 had just as profound an effect on the agency's subsequent history.

Another result of emphasizing rapid construction was that federal reclamation quickly became a public works program and rapidly lost the idealism of 1902. Like Frederick H. Newell, Theodore Roosevelt looked to the past. He advocated what he called "the strenuous life," and he deeply admired the strength, independence, and versatility of frontier Americans. Traditional Jeffersonian ideals, particularly the autonomous family farm, motivated him far more than such twentieth-century values as planning, efficiency, and interdependence. His Darwinian view of life also suggested that most farmers who failed lacked the "pluck" and "grit" of earlier generations of frontier Americans. Frederick H. Newell shared these convictions. William Ellsworth Smythe and George H. Maxwell envisioned federal reclamation as a much larger and bolder program that would integrate the city and countryside. Once they saw that federal reclamation would do little to change the

SAVING LOST LIVES   *31*

lives of government farmers, or to transform rural society, they turned to new crusades. By 1905, Smythe and Maxwell's interest in federal reclamation had cooled, and neither Newell, nor A. P. Davis, nor any other leader of the Reclamation Service had their ability to sell federal reclamation to the nation. The Reclamation Bureau spent plenty of money publicizing and justifying its actions, but very little defining the long-range goals of the program. Seldom did it pause to reconsider the promises and ideals of 1902.

Federal reclamation could not live up to original expectations purely as a regional development program. The only hope of recapturing the idealism of 1902 was to nationalize reclamation to eliminate the strong hostility toward it within Congress, and the Reclamation Bureau attempted to do so. Meanwhile, it had to face not just the loss of its original ideals but weaknesses in the Reclamation Act itself.

2

The Perils of Public Works

Federal Reclamation, 1902–1909

"There is probably no law on the statute books," *Forestry and Irrigation* editorialized in 1906, "which puts in the hands of a single official of government such unlimited powers of expenditure as the [Reclamation Act]."[1] In theory, the secretary of the interior selected new projects, determined the size of farms, withdrew from entry public lands needed for projects or towns, purchased or condemned private property, determined construction costs and the amount each farmer owed the government, approved construction contracts, set operation and maintenance charges, decided how rapidly new farmers should open their land to irrigation and how much land they had to irrigate to perfect their claims, fixed the terms under which water was used, and specified when and under what conditions project ownership and operation passed from the federal government to the water users. In reality, of course, the secretary did none of these things. During the administration of Theodore Roosevelt, most important decisions were made by the president or in the offices of the Reclamation Service, then rubber-stamped by the secretary and the director of the U.S. Geological Survey, of which the service was a part until 1907.

As the idealism and zeal for reform that animated the irrigation crusade in the years from 1898 to 1902 faded, federal reclamation encountered a series of crippling political, economic, and legal obstacles. Some were the product of divided authority: the federal government regulated the disposal of the public lands, while the states administered water law. In addition, Congress resented the power Theodore Roosevelt had vested in new executive agencies, and the Department of Agriculture and Department of the Interior competed for control of the new program. Other problems resulted from the ambiguous nature of the Reclamation Act itself, the conflict between federal reclamation and private enterprise, the loss of the major railroads' political support for the program, and extensive land speculation on the government water projects. Noble dreams foundered on the rocks of federalism, localism, and a welter of interest groups that made centralized or coordinated planning impossible.

WATER LAW

In 1891, President Benjamin Harrison lamented that the dramatic growth of irrigation in the West during the 1870s and 1880s had occurred without a comprehensive study of the region's water supply. In the absence of federal control over surplus water, Harrison feared that "the patentees of the arid lands will be tenants at will of the water companies." The nation could and should, he believed, take a more active role in allocating water. "In the Territories this whole subject is under the full control of Congress," Harrison noted, "and in the States it is practically so as long as the Government holds the title to the reservoir sites and water sources and can grant them upon such conditions as it chooses to impose."[2] When the Reclamation Act passed Congress, many friends of federal reclamation assumed that the Supreme Court would soon grant or acknowledge national control over all interstate streams—and perhaps all the West's surplus water.

During the 1890s, the president, Congress, the U.S. Supreme Court, and the federal courts suggested or implied the existence of federal water rights independent of state law. Congress required the War Department to approve the construction of all dams in navigable streams.[3] It also authorized the president to declare quarantine zones when cholera, yellow fever, or other communicable diseases threatened to spread from one state to another. Since many of these diseases were transmitted through sewage dumped into interstate rivers, some legal scholars expected that Congress or the courts would use the Constitution's General Welfare Clause to assert a federal police power over those streams.[4] Moreover, during the 1890s Congress specified that all water flowing through the nation's forest reserves could be used for "domestic, mining, milling, or irrigation purposes, under the laws of the state wherein such forest reservations are situated or *under the laws of the United States and the rules and regulations established thereunder.*"[5] This language, little noticed by westerners at the time, *intimated* that Congress might soon take charge of water within the public domain, laying the foundation for future national public works.

Federal and state courts also suggested that the central government had some claim to the West's unused water.[6] In an 1898 contest over a small stream that originated in Montana but flowed into Wyoming, the Montana circuit court proclaimed that the water within any stream on the public domain was "part thereof, and the national government can sell or grant the same, or the use thereof, separate from the estate [the land itself], under such conditions as may seem to it proper." After the federal government had disposed of the water, the court conceded, the rights to it "must always be a question pertaining to private persons." Once private rights had vested, they could not be rescinded, and the federal government had merely a right of disposal, not a right of use.[7]

In 1899, the U.S. Supreme Court provided the champions of national control with additional ammunition. In a suit pertaining to the navigability of the Rio Grande, Justice David Josiah Brewer acknowledged that each state had the right to "permit the appropriation of flowing waters for such purposes as it deems wise." But Brewer also ruled that if any part of a river was used for transportation, then the entire stream—including its nonnavigable tributaries—fell under national control. Where navigability was at issue, the congressional failure to define or assert federal water rights could not be taken as the acknowledgment or recognition of superior state authority. This suggested that the federal government retained paramount authority over such rivers as the Columbia, Colorado, and Rio Grande—all of which were navigable for at least part of their course.

The Rio Grande case went beyond navigability. In a cryptic passage that lawyers have pondered for a century, Brewer warned that "in the absence of specific authority from Congress a State cannot by its legislation destroy the right of the United States, as the owner of lands bordering on a stream, to the continued flow of its waters; so far at least as may be necessary for the beneficial uses of government property."[8] This was a tantalizing but ambiguous statement. The phrase "lands bordering on a stream" implied the existence of some kind of federal riparian right. But what land was Brewer referring to: the national forests, potential government irrigation projects, Indian reservations, or all the public domain? Furthermore, what constituted "beneficial uses," and who would determine the government's rights? The Rio Grande case was the last major U.S. Supreme Court decision relating to western waters prior to passage of the Reclamation Act in 1902, and it seemed to suggest that the high court, as well as Congress, was ready to expand federal control.

Not only did Congress and the Supreme Court appear to favor federal control over water, but federal officials and water lawyers devised elaborate theories to justify paramount federal rights. In the American West, sovereignty over water hinged on two competing explanations of the origins of water rights. The first interpretation appeared in California during the 1880s, the second in Colorado during the late nineteenth and early twentieth centuries. They came to be called the "California Doctrine" and the "Colorado Doctrine."[9]

The California Doctrine—the theory that the federal government owned not just the public lands but all the resources they contained—served as the foundation for national water rights. The chief legal officer of the Reclamation Service, Morris Bien, distinguished between sovereignty, ownership, and management.[10] The central government's status as "original proprietor" of the public domain, Bien claimed, gave it special water rights. The Constitution granted Congress power to make all laws necessary to administer "property belonging to the United States." In their zeal to encourage the mining industry, the western states had granted the right to *sell*, not just *use* water. But when the public lands passed into private ownership, the federal government retained control over all *unused* water. Titles to land and water passed from the federal government to individual patentees, not from the federal government to the states to individuals. The significance of Bien's theory was obvious: if Congress had granted the states merely a right to dole out water, rather than sovereignty over the water itself, then the central government retained authority over *surplus* water and could reassert it at any time.[11]

Bien's biggest challenge was to explain the intent of legislation enacted by Congress in 1866, 1870, and 1877. Congress's first official statement concerning water rights came in 1866, when it deferred to the prevailing rules of the mining camps: "Whenever, by priority of possession, rights to the use of water for mining, agricultural, manufacturing, or other purposes, have vested and accrued, and the same are recognized and acknowledged by the local customs, laws, and the decisions of [local] courts, the possessors and owners of such vested rights shall be maintained and protected in the same."[12] State courts merely defined and interpreted "local customs." In 1870 Congress subjected all public land titles "to any vested and accrued water-rights" recognized by the 1866 law,[13] but not until 1877 did it require that "all surplus water over and above such actual and use, together with the water of all lakes, rivers and other sources of water supply on the public lands and not navigable shall remain and be held free for the appropriation and use of the public for irrigation, mining and manufacturing purposes subject to existing rights."[14] After 1877, then, water rights on the public domain could be acquired *only* through prior appropriation, but, according to Bien, this restriction did not limit federal authority.

The 1877 law, according to Bien, granted the states authority to *distribute* water, nothing more. No federal right had been relinquished, nor could it be. Therefore, he reasoned, in the years after 1877, federal bureaus could dispose of land and water either separately or together. The Reclamation Act of 1902 changed nothing. Section 8 of that law required the federal government to honor state water laws, but only so that—in Bien's words— "the State records of water appropriations shall not be rendered useless by the failure to make record of the appropriation of the relatively large proportion of the water supply which would be used by the United States in any drainage area in which it may construct works."[15]

The Reclamation Service and Justice Department eagerly embraced what

would come to be called federal "reserved rights."[16] It also won the approval
of such leading scholars and interpreters of western water law as C. S. Kinney and S. C. Wiel.[17] Nevertheless, Bien's interpretation of the origins of
western water law had little value during the first few decades of federal
reclamation. Most remaining government land adjoined the headwaters of
streams far removed from arable land, so little could be gained by claiming
riparian rights. Even more important, the Reclamation Service depended
on western votes in Congress. "In practice we only use the theory of Federal
ownership as an anchor to the leeward," a Justice Department lawyer remarked in 1918. "We strive strenuously to show that we have complied with
every State law and that therefore our rights are good upon that theory; but
we say that even if we have failed in some particular, they would be good anyway because the Government does not have to comply with State statutes."[18]

Bien's theory of federal ownership encountered intense opposition in
Colorado, whose political leaders insisted that long before passage of the
Reclamation Act the federal government had irrevocably relinquished
control over water to the states. Colorado had no stronger champions of state
sovereignty than U.S. senator Henry M. Teller and the region's best-known
water lawyer, Denver's Delph E. Carpenter. Both regarded the Constitution
as a document that sharply limited the authority of the central government,
and both regarded the U.S. Supreme Court as an impartial referee or medi-
ator between sovereignties of equal power and standing. The theory of states'
rights that emerged in the West during the early decades of the twentieth
century closely corresponded to what legal historian E. S. Corwin later called
"dual federalism." In this view, the Constitution was simply a compact among
the states, whose relationship with the central government had never
changed. The Tenth Amendment reserved to the states a field of action
within which the central government could not operate. State and federal
functions complemented each other, and the central government was restricted to the "external relations" of the individual states.[19]

Senator Teller denied that the federal government had *any* right to manage the nation's rivers, even in the name of navigability. Since the states
owned the land under navigable streams, Congress could claim nothing more
than the power to regulate commerce. The English rule of navigability, he
maintained, still prevailed in the United States: "rivers are navigable as far
as the tide ebbs and flows and not farther." From this principle he inferred
that the federal government "has not the slightest interest in the water, not
even in the navigable waters. . . . The court has said that all the Government
has in navigable water is an easement, the right to run a ship, or a boat over
it, the right to see that it is not obstructed." This position had far-reaching
implications. If Congress had no authority over the nation's water, then it
had no right to charge for the use of that water. In that case, the states had
exclusive jurisdiction over the construction of all dams designed to store

water for irrigation and, eventually, over the construction of hydroelectric power plants as well.[20]

Delph Carpenter developed a much more elaborate, sophisticated theory than Teller. It rested on two assumptions: first, that the federal government relinquished sovereignty over water when the territories became states, and second, that the administration of water could be performed successfully only at the state level. All states that entered the union after 1790 acquired the same rights as the original parties to the Constitution, and all states "retain every shred of inherent sovereignty, power, and dominion not granted to the United States by the Constitution, and it is incumbent upon those asserting a power in the United States to point out the grant of any such power. If there is no [specific] grant, the power remains in the States." Admission to the Union was not a grant *from* the United States "but a turning over to the State of the powers and sovereignty which always existed and which had been held in trust for her." Either the nation or the states controlled the water; power could not be shared. "The Federal theory . . . necessitates abandonment of long-established principles," Carpenter warned, "and proposes to set up a new scheme. It either must fail or finally occupy the entire field. It is more a plan of what its authors conceive should have been our plan of government in the first instance than it is an effort to conform to what has been and is." Like Teller, Carpenter claimed that the states enjoyed sovereignty over *all* the waters of the West, navigable or not.[21]

For the proponents of states' rights, the clinching argument was that Colorado had been admitted to the union in 1876 with a constitution that proclaimed state sovereignty over water. Article 16, paragraph 5 of that document declared, "The water of every natural stream not heretofore appropriated within the state of Colorado, is hereby declared to be the property of the public, and the same is dedicated to the use of the people of the state subject to appropriation as hereinafter provided." Congress did not protest this declaration in 1876, or at any time thereafter. According to the champions of the Colorado Doctrine, therefore, the central government tacitly accepted that state's interpretation of the origin of western water rights, thereby forfeiting its original, inchoate rights.

When the Reclamation Service began its work, Morris Bien foresaw little conflict between the central government and the states over water, "for the reason that the aim in all cases will be to make the best possible use of the waters from both an engineering and an economic standpoint."[22] Nevertheless, he recognized the dangers faced by the federal projects. "[A national] project might be completed and fail because of interference with water rights," he warned the director of the Reclamation Service in 1904. "In nearly every project the Reclamation Service will develop the whole water resources of the stream. . . . The government cannot compete with private parties as to time of completion as it will build better and must do more preliminary work on that account. . . . It [the act of claiming all the water that would ultimately be needed at the outset] is our only safety against speculative water filings."[23] The Reclamation Service was forced to launch many grandiose, impractical projects simply to set aside sufficient water for the day it might be needed.[24]

The use of blanket water claims coincided with the Reclamation Service's attempt to standardize western water laws, which varied from state to state. The differences grew out of how state courts and legislatures answered some fundamental questions. What created a water right: the filing of a claim, the submission of construction plans to state officials, or the actual diversion of water? What limited the right: the claim itself, the quantity of water actually used, the size of a ditch, the acreage subject to irrigation, the crops grown, or each farmer's fair share determined by state officials? In theory, all water rights were restricted to "beneficial use." But since the courts had little way to collect unbiased information about the amounts of water diverted, "beneficial use" was often interpreted as "reasonable use." No water user could claim more than a fair share of the available supply, and that water had to be put to use within a stated period of time, often five years. Within the same state, however, different courts granted different amounts of water to irrigate the same amount of land planted to the same crop. What was "reasonable" in one locale was considered wasteful and extravagant in another.[25]

In 1903, water law reform received close attention in the California, Nevada, Arizona, and Montana legislatures, but the Reclamation Service— working behind the scenes—did everything possible to defeat it. Officials in the service favored new laws, but only if those laws suited their purposes. By late 1904 or early 1905, the campaign at the state level prompted Morris Bien to draft a model water code.[26]

The Pacific Northwest served as a battleground for that code. Oregon and Washington were particularly well suited to federal reclamation, owing to their numerous broad, deep streams, their many lakes, and their mild climates and long growing seasons. Equally important, they had contributed substantial revenue from public land sales to the reclamation fund—at a time when the Reclamation Act required 51 percent of those proceeds be spent within the state where the sales occurred. Oregon provided more revenue to the reclamation fund than any other state, and Washington was third on the list of largest contributors. Both recognized riparian as well as appropriative rights, and the existence of those rights made predicting the volume of surplus water available for federal use nearly impossible.

The summer of 1904 was the driest on record in the Pacific Northwest, resulting in a sharp increase in litigation over water. Portland's *Oregonian* of December 2, 1904, warned that Reclamation Service director Frederick H. Newell was "very desirous" of launching a major project in Oregon, but "wherever he has turned he has been barred by lack of water supply, or by high cost, or by unwillingness of private owners to yield the ground." The service desperately needed assurances that it could reserve sufficient water in the Pacific Northwest to meet future needs. It wanted the western states to abandon the riparian doctrine, and Oregon and Washington—in their eagerness to attract a national project—seemed the most likely states to comply.[27]

At the turn of the twentieth century, most arid states had no record of existing diversions, no standardized procedure for filing new claims, no method of supervising the distribution of water, and no inexpensive procedure by which established water rights could be adjudicated and protected. Bien's model code addressed each of these needs. It required each state to create an office of state engineer, whose first duty would be to compile stream-by-stream lists of water claims for submission to the state attorney general. To quiet titles, the attorney general would, in turn, file suit against all claimants within a watershed. Only rights secured through prior appropriation would be recognized, and no future rights could be acquired without approval from the state engineer, who would reduce speculative claims by requiring the completion of water works within a reasonable period. Each state would be divided into four hydrographic districts under the supervision of water commissioners appointed by the state supreme court. The commissioners were, in effect, officers of the court charged with enforcing court decrees and selecting watermasters to distribute the water. Rights would be limited to water put to beneficial use, but in no case could they exceed one cubic foot per second for each seventy acres irrigated. Most important, the Bien Code required state officials to reserve *all* water requested by Reclamation Service officials for an unlimited period.[28]

In August 1904, Bien met with a joint Oregon-Washington irrigation code commission to ready his model law for consideration by the two legislatures that winter.[29] In his farewell address, outgoing Washington governor Henry McBride underscored the urgency of the task before the Washington legislature. Reclamation Service officials had warned him that "under our laws, as they now are, it would not be feasible to undertake any irrigation project in this state."[30]

Nevertheless, at the end of 1904 and the beginning of 1905, harsh criticism of the proposed legislation surfaced in both states. Holders of riparian rights, including power and mining companies, regarded Bien's proposed code as an illegal confiscation of their property. Irrigation companies feared that the carte blanche promised to the Reclamation Service would lock up the state's surplus water and prevent the construction of private water projects. Those who held rights under prior appropriation feared a flood of expensive litigation as individual water users hired lawyers to defend long-established rights. (On some Washington streams, as many as five thousand diverters would be required to participate in adjudication suits—sawmills, municipal water companies, and hydroelectric companies as well as farmers.) The proposed law was also criticized for granting the state engineer quasi-judicial powers—he could scale down wasteful claims and weed out fraudulent or bogus filings—and for creating an expensive new state bureaucracy.[31] Both the Washington and Oregon legislatures rejected the Bien Code, and in no part of the West did it meet with enthusiasm.[32]

The Reclamation Service suffered an even greater blow when the U.S. Supreme Court delivered its 1907 opinion in *Kansas* v. *Colorado,* a contest over the Arkansas River.[33] The stream originated in Colorado but flowed through Kansas, Oklahoma, and Arkansas before emptying into the Mississippi River. Kansas argued that diversions upstream in Colorado threatened the future of irrigation in western Kansas. The Reclamation Service entered the case hoping that the decision would set a precedent for other interstate streams, and it also hoped to persuade the high court to rule that riparian rights did not prevail on such streams. The Justice Department had several plausible arguments to choose from. Kansas maintained that Colorado's diversions had destroyed the navigability of the Arkansas River from Fort Gibson, in Indian Territory, to the mouth of the river, so the government attorneys might have claimed that the 1899 Supreme Court opinion in the Rio Grande case justified national control over the Arkansas River.[34] This course, however, posed great dangers. In building irrigation projects, the federal government planned to alter the flow of many streams that were useful or potentially useful for transportation. In addition, staking a claim on navigability might expand the responsibilities of the Army Corps of Engineers—the Reclamation Service's potential rival in western regional development.[35]

Other alternatives included claiming exclusive federal control over interstate streams on grounds that only the national government had the ability to develop and maintain them, or claiming that Congress had tacitly reserved sufficient water to improve the West's public lands when it approved the Reclamation Act. In the end, the Justice Department argued that the federal government had an implied federal power to *regulate* interstate streams. It proposed the creation of a national administrative tribunal to take charge of these waterways to protect the interests and needs of federal agencies.[36]

The Reclamation Service deeply feared riparian rights. As one of its legal advisers noted later: "One of the chief reasons for the intervention of the United States in behalf of the Reclamation Service in the case of Kansas vs. Colorado was to attempt to secure the abrogation of the riparian doctrine in all of the western states."[37] The Reclamation Service opposed riparian rights not just because their indeterminate nature threatened its western irrigation projects, but because its leaders hoped that eventually the central government would take charge of drainage and reclamation in the eastern United States. Defeating the doctrine in the West, where it was weakest, might serve as a springboard to modernizing water laws nationwide, laying the foundation for the Reclamation Service to assume the main responsibility for water planning from coast to coast.

David Josiah Brewer delivered the opinion in *Kansas* v. *Colorado,* as he had in the Rio Grande case. Strict construction, not a particular conception of western water rights or a transcendent vision of western economic development, dictated Brewer's reasoning. "The primary question is, of course, of national control," Brewer noted as he began his discussion of the government's arguments. "For if the nation has the right to regulate the flow of waters, we must inquire what it has done in the way of regulation. If it has done nothing the further question will then arise, What are the respective rights of the two states, in the absence of national regulation?" Brewer distinguished between his strong support for federal rights in the Rio Grande case and the case at issue: the protection of commerce and navigation was an enumerated power in the United States Constitution, and "the constant declaration of this court from the beginning is that this government is one of enumerated powers." Thus the dispute between Kansas and Colorado could not be compared to the earlier contest over the Rio Grande.[38]

Brewer might simply have denied any national power to regulate water use on interstate streams. But because the government had staked its case on the need to reclaim arid public lands, he went further. Whatever the government's *theoretical* powers, its failure to act in the past limited its authority once the states took administrative control over the nonnavigable waters within their borders. Moreover, the Constitution did not justify the irrigation of public lands even by implication. "It would be a strange rule of construction," Brewer observed, "that language granting powers is to be liberally construed, and that language of restriction is to be narrowly and technically construed." The clear intent of the Tenth Amendment to limit federal responsibilities took precedence over the general welfare and property clauses. Without formally or explicitly declaring the Reclamation Act of 1902 unconstitutional, Brewer dismissed the petition of the United States, leaving the door open for the nation "to take such action as it shall deem necessary to preserve or improve the navigability of the Arkansas River."[39]

Kansas v. *Colorado* smashed the grand dream of the Reclamation Service to develop entire river basins, ensuring that both its dams and water projects would be small. It denied that the federal government had any right to control interstate streams, and it cast a long shadow over the future of the bureau. Even before the Supreme Court handed down its decision, the National Irrigation Congress—western reclamation's leading booster organization—appointed a committee headed by Elwood Mead and Morris Bien to propose a method to manage interstate streams.[40] The committee distributed a questionnaire to lawyers, engineers, and other water experts in the arid West. Questions included who should exercise control over interstate streams;

whether streams ought to be administered by commissions, special tribunals, or the existing courts; what principles should govern the division of water between upstream and downstream states; and how appropriative and riparian rights could be reconciled across state borders.

Twenty-eight of the forty-seven experts who responded to the Mead-Bien questionnaire supported absolute state control over *all* streams; thirteen favored federal control—over intrastate as well as interstate waters. Twelve preferred a special commission to arbitrate interstate disputes; twenty-six subscribed to the status quo—allowing the courts to deal with interstate conflicts as they arose. On only one point did the respondents agree unanimously: where riparian rights were recognized in one state but only prior appropriation in another, the riparian doctrine should give way.

The Mead-Bien Committee did not favor leaving interstate conflicts in the hands of the federal courts. "A decision of a Court, once rendered, remains fixed and only settles the particular questions involved in that case," the committee warned, "while the conditions surrounding irrigation on the other side of the State line are constantly changing and the use of water for irrigation rapidly growing. If there is to be any protection of priorities across State lines it should be by a Federal administrative system corresponding in character to that needed for the establishing and protection of rights within a state." When it failed to reach consensus on how to manage interstate streams, the committee recommended the formation of yet another committee to continue the study. It was appointed, but never met. The annual Irrigation Congresses were dominated by westerners who considered home rule far more important than justice or efficiency in the use of interstate waters.[41]

In May 1913, a member of the defunct Mead-Bien Committee, Oregon state engineer John H. Lewis, proposed that the American Society of Civil Engineers draft a comprehensive interstate water code for the entire country, not just the West.[42] *Kansas* v. *Colorado* (1907) promised an "equitable apportionment" of the benefits from interstate streams without spelling out who would monitor the allocation. That, according to Lewis, presented Congress with an opportunity and responsibility.[43] Following Lewis's suggestion, in 1913 the ASCE appointed a committee to study interstate water problems, with the director of the Reclamation Service, Frederick Haynes Newell, as chair. Long a proponent of federal control over interstate streams, Newell maintained that court cases settled only the rights of litigants and could not regulate the use of waterways.[44] In the summer of 1914, he sent a questionnaire to engineers engaged in interstate water projects asking them to describe the water conflicts they had encountered. The survey uncovered more than a hundred interstate conflicts in the West alone.[45]

Soon after completion of the survey, Newell drafted a set of principles to guide the committee. He put "public welfare" and "unity" at the top of his list. Each interstate stream, he reasoned, should be administered as a unit from beginning to end, regardless of state lines. No permanent water rights should be granted on these streams. "Priority of use of water and appurtenance [attachment of rights] to land should at all times be subject to modification or reconsideration in the matter of economic use," Newell observed. "No right to the use of water should be recognized as being of such permanence that it may not be modified by the requirement of the public welfare calling for economic as well as beneficial use." Efficiency should count for more than chronological priority: it was not enough for water users to demonstrate that they put water to a "beneficial use"; sometimes the *best* use should take precedence over the *oldest* use. The states could not solve the jurisdictional problem on their own. They would reject any constitutional amendment that gave the federal government exclusive control over interstate streams. And even if all the states could be convinced to adopt uniform water laws, their legislatures and courts would interpret the statutes differently. Time would compound the different interpretations, necessitating the need for yet another model law. The quest for uniformity would never end.[46]

Newell proposed that an administrative commission or tribunal regulate all water rights on interstate streams. The commission should have the power "to determine as between the various claimants and the needs of the public the extent and limit of existing rights and consider the relative value of these and of any unutilized or unappropriated water." It should be able to block the construction of any hydraulic works not deemed to serve the public interest, whether hydroelectric plants or irrigation reservoirs. It should be national, "composed of a few men representing engineering and financial wisdom as well as legal knowledge[,] with a view to deciding water questions with greater equity and certainty." It should be guided by "priority" regardless of state lines, but only in evaluating "claims of approximately equal right or necessity." The commission, not the courts, should determine the "equitable apportionment of benefits" called for in *Kansas* v. *Colorado*. A national water law should provide for the appeal of administrative decisions to the courts, but "only to one of the highest courts, and then [only] upon questions of law."[47]

From its inception in 1913, the Newell Committee encountered serious obstacles. Some members of the ASCE wanted to open the committee to members of the Reclamation Service's chief rival, the Army Corps of Engineers—which Newell understandably opposed. Moreover, Newell, who was then under heavy fire for his administration of the reclamation projects, received no support from superiors in Interior. In a July 14, 1914, letter, Secretary of the Interior Franklin K. Lane doubted "the wisdom of our leading in this matter now," presumably because of rising hostility toward the Reclamation Service in the West. In many parts of the region, the Reclamation Service had gained a reputation as dictatorial and arbitrary; the last thing it needed, in Lane's view, was another confrontation over states' rights.[48]

When Newell's interstate water committee filed its first report with the ASCE at the end of 1915, it acknowledged that a massive campaign of public education would be needed to convince Congress to adopt a comprehensive national water law. Some members of the committee refused to accept Newell's recommendations. They wanted the administration of water laws and water rights to remain in the hands of state authorities. They accepted Newell's statement of principles, but refused to draft a model national water code until the ASCE as a whole had had a chance to discuss the proposals.[49]

The ASCE soon became preoccupied with World War I, and at about the same time, Newell left the Reclamation Service. By 1916, Newell was losing patience with his committee and with the American Society of Civil Engineers. His committee was so strapped for money that in March, he had to ask each member for a five-hundred-dollar contribution to carry on its work for that year. He also polled the committee as to what course it should follow in the future. Three members sent no reply; the remainder urged cooperation with other engineering societies and bar associations. Subsequently, Newell invited thirty-one bar associations and thirty-two engineering societies to participate in drafting a national water code, but the response was lukewarm. Conflict had erupted among the engineering societies over which, if any, should speak for the entire profession, and engineers and lawyers took a fundamentally different view of reform: the engineers favored executive commissions staffed by experts in engineering and the law, while the lawyers wanted to expand the court system. In January 1917, the American Society of Civil Engineers' Committee on Committees concluded: "It is no function of an engineering society to prepare water laws, either State or Federal, and . . . the whole question of legislation and preparation of laws can better be dealt with by other professional organizations."[50] The Newell Committee limped along for three more years, its work hampered by a pending suit involving Wyoming and Colorado over the Laramie River and by a large number of bills related to the construction and operation of hydroelectric facilities.[51] The ASCE formally dissolved the committee in May 1920.[52]

TURF WARS

The professionalization and bureaucratization of the federal government is a major theme in the evolution of the "modern American state" during the Progressive Era. Ironically, this process did more to fragment than to unify federal authority. In many ways, the nineteenth-century political system was more accountable, if not more efficient, than the administrative system of the early twentieth century. In the 1870s and 1880s, most bureaucrats were generalists who placed their loyalty with those who appointed them, and with their political party, ahead of the ethics and standards of their profession—if they had a profession other than politics. No realm of public policy illustrated this phenomenon better than natural resources. A host of jurisdictional conflicts arose between the Interior, Agriculture, and War Departments, and the proliferation of bureaus made it all the more difficult to plan and to co-ordinate national water policy.[53]

In 1888, Congress gave John Wesley Powell and the USGS the responsi-bility for locating potential reservoir sites and canal lines in the arid West. It represented the only major survey of its kind ever conducted, but two years later Congress abruptly cut off the Irrigation Survey's funding.[54] The survey had done little to promote the construction of irrigation works, and it placed many of the best reservoir sites off-limits to private enterprise. Meanwhile, the Agriculture Department appointed journalist Richard J. Hinton to com-pile information on irrigation, and some western politicians, led by Nevada's U.S. senator William Morris Stewart, wanted to assign *all* government irri-gation work to the Agriculture Department. Hinton's first report appeared in 1887, his last in 1892. In that year, the secretary of agriculture appointed him as the first director of the Office of Irrigation Inquiry. The new agency suffered from meager appropriations, from being part of a department whose major constituency was eastern farmers deeply afraid of competition from the West, and from USGS antagonism. The secretaries of agriculture, espe-cially J. Sterling Morton (1893–97), prohibited employees of the irrigation office from attending meetings of the National Irrigation Congress, and from lobbying for bills pertaining to land and water.[55]

Even after Powell resigned as director of the Geological Survey in 1894, the USGS had plenty of friends in Congress. In 1895, Congress abolished the Office of Irrigation Inquiry and created a new Hydrographic Division within the Geological Survey. Three years later, however, when the depres-sion began to lift, Wyoming U.S. senator Francis E. Warren persuaded Con-gress to create a new Office of Irrigation Investigations in Agriculture, within the Division of Experiment Stations, which he hoped Elwood Mead, then the Wyoming state engineer, would fill. "Now, my dear Mead, the water melon is about ready to cut," Warren wrote to his friend on March 4, 1898. "I do not know whether the amount is going to be enough; whether the certainty of continuance of appropriation is sufficiently assured, or whether the way in which the Secretary is to appoint or employ is satisfactory so that you will have the interest in this that you once thought you might have." Mead jumped at the chance but prudently retained his Wyoming job for a year following his July 1898 appointment to the federal post.[56]

As had long been the case, rival bureaus reinforced localism by providing competing interest groups with access to power. That these federal agencies performed essentially the same job was less important than that they served constituencies with different objectives. Politicians in the Rocky Mountain West worried that if the USGS took up the work of irrigation, it would un-settle water rights and reward politically powerful states at the expense of those with smaller populations. Warren claimed that the Department of Agriculture's new irrigation office complemented rather than competed with the USGS. The major hydrographic work of the USGS had been measuring the volume of streams—essentially an engineering job. Plenty of important work remained open to the Agriculture Department. There had never been a thorough study of soils in the arid region, including their ability to hold and to transmit moisture, or of the crops best suited to those soils and the amount of water they required. Westerners deserved a bureau, Warren thought, that would provide *practical information* on how to farm in that part of the nation— a bureau that would build up the West, particularly Wyoming, not just collect scientific data.[57]

Mead's mandate was consistent with the traditional fact-gathering mission of the Department of Agriculture. The department had long studied how to improve crop production, and irrigation was widely considered the best "fertilizer" available in the arid region. Mead's office investigated such subjects as evaporation rates, pump systems, and the design of irrigation and drainage works. The Office of Irrigation Investigations also assumed responsibility for surveying water laws and water rights in the western states. Much of the work undertaken by Mead's office between 1898 and 1902 took the form of cooperative studies, and Mead worked closely with the agricultural colleges and experiment stations. Over time, he forged strong alliances with state officials, particularly in California and the Rocky Mountain region.[58]

Nevertheless, Mead was not entirely happy with his new job. He wanted to direct an independent bureau rather than an office within the Division of Experiment Stations, and he wanted to build dams and canals using proceeds from the leasing of federal grazing lands. He faced criticism from within the Department of Agriculture because officials in the Forestry, Plant Industry, and Soils Offices thought that his work overlapped with theirs. In 1901, Mead attempted to transform his office into a "Bureau of Rural Engineering," with a wide range of responsibilities, including the reclamation of swampland in the East.[59] Neither Secretary of Agriculture James Wilson nor Director of Experiment Stations A. C. True favored enlarging the responsibilities of his office, however. "I was given to understand," Mead noted in a December 21, 1898, letter, "that the [irrigation] program for the indefinite future would be restricted to an investigation of irrigation laws and to such physical investigations as the Experiment Stations could undertake." The secretary of agriculture nominally favored Mead's plan to levy rental fees for the use of public grazing lands and use them to build hydraulic works, but he thought that the work belonged "to the engineering officials of the Government"—the Corps of Engineers.[60]

Relations cooled between Mead and other officials in the Department of Agriculture at the same time that he began a feud with Frederick Newell and George Maxwell. In the years after 1898, relations between Mead and Newell went from bad to worse.[61] The leading publicist for federal reclamation, George H. Maxwell, had close ties to the USGS, and he claimed that Mead was a stooge of the cattle industry, which wanted to limit the expansion of agriculture in the West. In the months leading up to passage of the Reclamation Act in June 1902, Mead warned that no more than 11 million acres of the public domain could be irrigated—not the 60 million to 100 million widely predicted by the leading proponents of national reclamation. Since virtually every western stream suffered from unsettled water rights and extensive litigation, and since the study of western soils was in its infancy, Mead considered such a construction program premature at best. And since the federal government administered the disposal of the public lands and the states administered the allocation of water, he feared that a national program would be unworkable—particularly interstate projects that attempted to store water in one state for use in another. He also feared that the Reclamation Service would grow so rapidly that Congress would eliminate his agency.[62]

In Mead's judgment, state control over water was vital to the independence and autonomy of the West. Once the USGS began to build dams, and once it had secured firm control over western water rights, a massive and tyrannical new bureau would be required to maintain centralized control. The arid states would cease to exist as independent entities. Take away the water, or even threaten to take it, and land values would plummet—with devastating effects on the western economy.[63] Officials in the USGS charged that Mead wanted the western states to copy the water laws he had written for Wyoming because those laws would sharply limit the Reclamation Service's freedom of action. As Maxwell put it: "The state ownership and control of water through a central state board of control as advocated by Elwood Mead and his supporters, would be the greatest misfortune that could happen to retard irrigation development in the West, and the operations under the National Irrigation Act."[64]

The Mead-Newell feud crested at the October 1902 National Irrigation Congress, held in Colorado Springs four months after passage of the Reclamation Act. Maxwell orchestrated the meeting and served as a spokesperson for Newell, just as he had directed many previous irrigation conventions. He waited until the last possible moment to send invitations to members of the Department of Agriculture, then attempted to prevent Mead and other critics of the USGS from addressing the delegates. He hoped to persuade the Irrigation Congress—which included many partisans of Mead and states' rights—to fuse with the Trans-Mississippi Commercial Congress in order to dilute western opposition to federal reclamation. That plan failed, but Maxwell engaged in a hot verbal exchange with Mead. There was, he concluded, no need to consult the state legislatures at all, "no necessity of State legislation of any kind to carry into effect the beneficial purposes of the National Irrigation Act." A few weeks later, Maxwell modified his position, but only slightly. The only state action needed, he wrote, was a constitutional amendment to guarantee that water used for irrigation would be attached to the plot of land irrigated and that "beneficial use" would be the "basis, the measure, and the limit of all rights to water."[65]

In response to Maxwell's charges, Mead distributed a six-page broadside to convention delegates and to prominent western politicians.[66] Nevertheless, the Reclamation Service held the upper hand—at least outside the Rocky Mountain West. One of Maxwell's aides urged Thomas R. Bard, U.S. senator from California, to launch a full-scale investigation of Mead's office, charging that "a large portion of the work done under Mr. Mead's direction is simply a duplication . . . of work which properly belongs to other departments."[67] The battle between Mead, Maxwell, the Office of Irrigation Investigations, and the Reclamation Service continued for years in the pages of prominent conservation journals. *Irrigation Age* and *Country Gentleman* supported Mead; *Forestry and Irrigation* came to the defense of Newell and Maxwell.[68]

In 1903 Theodore Roosevelt appointed a Committee on the Organization of Government Scientific Work, headed by Newell's close friend, Gifford Pinchot, to study the structure and administration of the federal government's "scientific" bureaus. Newell used the occasion to launch a fresh attack on the Agriculture Department. He complained that "a considerable portion of the appropriation for irrigation investigations is being used more or less directly to defeat the object of the reclamation law." In his judgment, the large number of engineers on the staff of Irrigation Investigations signaled Mead's clear intent to take over the work of the Reclamation Service. At the least, Mead's office served as a lightning rod for western champions of state's rights and for critics of the Reclamation Service who were disappointed that their region had not secured one of the first projects. Newell recommended that the Office of Irrigation Investigations be abolished or merged with the Reclamation Service, or that its functions be transferred to the soil and plant bureaus within the Agriculture Department.[69]

Mead claimed that the two agencies complemented each other and denied any substantial duplication of effort. The U.S. Geological Survey—of which the Reclamation Service was still a part—gauged streams, selected public lands suited to irrigation, and constructed dams and canals. Mead's office studied the *methods* of applying water to the land. According to Mead, the paramount need was better coordination, not reorganization.[70]

Mead's boss, A. C. True, went further. Congress, he explained in a letter to Pinchot, had given the Department of Agriculture the mission of gathering and disseminating "useful information on subjects connected with agriculture in the most general and comprehensive sense of that term." Creation of the Office of Irrigation Investigations in 1898, True reasoned, tacitly circumscribed or preempted much of the Geological Survey's work. Therefore, the Reclamation Service was the interloper, not Mead's agency. The fact that

Irrigation Investigations employed a large number of hydraulic engineers proved nothing. The study of drainage, according to True, was as natural a function of Irrigation Investigations as the most economical use of water. "There are large areas of marsh land along the Atlantic and northern seaboards and in the valleys of our great rivers," True observed, "which will be needed for agricultural purposes, and already there is much demand that the Department shall aid in the reclamation of such areas." National irrigation works would water only a small portion of the arid West, so "a great majority of the present and prospective owners of water for irrigation in this country will be outside the operations of this reclamation service." One day the Office of Irrigation Investigations might build dams, canals, and drainage works in the humid half of the nation. In any case, True concluded, the job of constructing irrigation works properly belonged to a department or bureau of public works, not to the Geological Survey.[71]

True need not have worried. The recommendations to President Roosevelt of Pinchot's Committee on the Organization of Government Scientific Work were wildly impractical. They constituted a raid on the Department of the Interior by Gifford Pinchot. Pinchot wanted to transfer the Geological Survey (including the Reclamation Service) to Agriculture, along with the General Land Office, Indian Office, Coast Geodetic Survey, and even the National Zoological Park, then part of the Smithsonian Institution. (The justification for the latter move was that specialists in agriculture knew more than pure scientists about the treatment of animals.) He also wanted Agriculture to assume control over the national forests and parks. The Interior Department had enough friends to block such wholesale and not entirely rational transfers. Nevertheless, Pinchot accomplished his paramount goal in 1905, when Congress transferred control over the national forests from Interior to Agriculture.[72]

The Committee on the Organization of Government Scientific Work reflected Gifford Pinchot's desire to build up the Agriculture Department more than it did a quest for efficiency. Newell had as much to fear from Pinchot as from Mead and True. There had long been tension among foresters and irrigators because farmers assumed that the *primary* reason for the creation of national forests was to protect watersheds and stream flow, not timber. The Reclamation Act dedicated proceeds from the sale of public lands solely to reclamation. The more public land that was sold, the greater the revenue. But the Roosevelt administration's efforts to reserve large parts of the public domain as national parks, national forests, game preserves, and mineral reserves clashed with this policy. As president, T.R. withdrew from entry nearly 148 million acres of public land, which reduced the revenue available for irrigation. Although Newell originally favored the transfer of control over national forests to Agriculture, he also recognized that if control over the forests were returned to Interior, proceeds from timber sales and grazing leases could be diverted into the reclamation fund. Pinchot's grazing policy also clashed with reclamation policy. The Forest Service adopted a permit system that rewarded the oldest and largest grazing interests in an area, restricting the opportunities for new settlers who farmed on government irrigation projects near national forests but also raised livestock.[73]

During and after Theodore Roosevelt's presidency, employees of the Agriculture Department continued to snipe at the Reclamation Service. In 1902, Newell boasted that in the arid West, "practically every quarter-section of the flat or gently rolling country is as good as the next." Differences in crop productivity depended largely on the proximity to water, he insisted, not on the inherent quality of its soil. This view was remarkably persistent. As late as 1919, the myth of the uniform fertility of desert soil lived on in a history of the first years of federal reclamation published in that year: "Thus, climate and soil are given consideration [in the selection of projects], but they are so generally found to be good or fair that few, if any, projects are rejected or seriously modified on account of them." Mead's office and the USDA challenged this assumption from the beginning of the federal reclamation program, and the chronic tension between Interior and Agriculture help explain the Reclamation Service's reluctance to conduct soil tests. To do so would have required the service to enlist the aid of the Bureau of Soils, Office of Irrigation Investigations, and perhaps other agencies in the USDA. And to do so would raise doubts about the competence of the Reclamation Service and give rival bureaus a claim to managing federal reclamation.[74]

In 1905, Mead observed in a popular engineering journal, "This tendency to magnify the construction side of irrigation is still manifest. While we may not give too much attention to problems connected with dam and canal building, we fail to give enough to those connected with the agricultural and economic sides. It is the work of the farmer which, after all, determines the value of irrigation properties."[75] On South Dakota's Belle Fourche Project—one of the government's least successful ventures—the Department of Agriculture was not invited to inspect the soil until two years *after* construction began.[76] The survey proved what farmers had already discovered: no amount of water could make the heavy clay soils productive. The myth of the fertility of all desert soil, and the fertilizing qualities of water, died hard.[77]

NATIONAL VS. PRIVATE ENTERPRISE

The Reclamation Act left many questions unanswered. Should the federal government build only storage dams, leaving the excavation of canals and distribution ditches to the states, private enterprise, or the farmers themselves, or should it design and construct entire systems? Should it give preference to small projects that delivered immediate results or to larger, more efficient units that took longer to construct? Should it concentrate on hydraulic works beyond the financial capacity or legal reach of private water companies—such as those that tapped interstate streams—or should it compete directly with those companies, using the interest-free repayment provision to provide cheaper farms to more Americans than private enterprise could?

Private water companies expected direct benefits from federal reclamation. By selling out to the government, companies and irrigation districts impoverished by the depression of the 1890s hoped to recapture their investment, if not turn a profit. And, indeed, many government projects consolidated private ditch systems, the construction of which had been delayed by the hard times and the owners of which had gone bankrupt. In addition, the Interior Department promised to gather information about crops, soils, climate, and other details of western agriculture useful to private companies, and federal efforts were expected to touch off a land rush that would stimulate all reclamation work, especially in the vicinity of government projects.[78] In 1909, Frederick Newell claimed that since 1902, private irrigation companies had spent ten dollars for every dollar expended by the Reclamation Service. That could have happened, he reasoned, only because the national government had restored the faith of investors in arid land reclamation.[79]

Conflict between federal, state, and private reclamation was not inevitable. The Reclamation Act's sponsor in the Senate, Henry C. Hansbrough, predicted that while the federal government might reclaim as little as 20 million acres, "this would serve as a nucleus about which private effort would reclaim an equal amount." Although the federal reclamation program had been instituted in large part because private irrigation companies had all but disappeared during the depression of the 1890s, initially, the Reclamation Service sought—in the words of its second-in-command, A. P. Davis— to "lend every legal encouragement to such [private] construction." The central government would tackle the large projects, particularly those involving interstate streams; the states would build the medium-size projects, or contract with Carey Act companies to construct them; and private companies would undertake the smaller ones. Or, the federal government would build reservoirs, leaving the construction of canals and the distribution of water to the states and to individual companies.[80]

Nevertheless, Reclamation Service officials scorned and distrusted private enterprise. Even before the depression of 1893, few irrigation companies made money, and after 1895 virtually none did. In 1904, Newell reported that he knew of *no* large corporate irrigation schemes that were legitimate: "They are exploited probably more for selling stocks and bonds than for watering land." In Newell's words, irrigation was "too big for individual or corporate enterprise." The discharge of western streams varied dramatically from year to year, and few streams had been measured over a long enough time to make reliable estimates of their flow; this could be done only by the national government. The "normal flow" had been exhausted, so the expansion of irrigation depended on the construction of storage reservoirs to capture the spring and summer runoff from melting snow. Since larger projects took more time to build, and more time to "settle up," only the federal government could afford the long delay between construction and repayment. Moreover, since many reservoirs would be built at the headwaters of streams in one state to serve agricultural land in another, neither the states nor private companies had the legal authority to erect such structures.[81]

The officers of the Reclamation Service feared that private reclamation would encourage land speculation and the engrossment of reservoir sites necessary for the construction of comprehensive government projects. The construction of small dams, moreover, would prevent the later construction of more substantial, and thus more efficient, structures. Therefore, private companies had to satisfy the Reclamation Service that, in the words of A. P. Davis, "the project to be constructed would be a real public benefit, and not operate as an obstruction to a development of the irrigation resources, in a comprehensive and economical manner [by the federal government]."[82]

In 1902, the champions of federal reclamation claimed that the government had distinct advantages over private enterprise. It charged nothing for government land, it did not have to make a profit, it charged no interest on construction charges, and it could achieve economies of scale. "As the government charges no interest and seeks no profit," *National Geographic* crowed, "government irrigation works cost the people considerably less than works built by private corporations." Interest alone made a big difference. The cost of a federal irrigation project repaid in ten years without interest ran 25 percent lower than the cost of a private project that charged 6 percent interest on the same amount over the same period. Moreover, since the federal government would settle water rights before building its projects, it could avoid expensive litigation, which often increased the cost of watering desert land by 50 percent or more. Little wonder that many private companies feared they would be priced out of the market.[83]

Nevertheless, the national government also labored under distinct disadvantages. Private companies often built lower-quality, and hence less expensive, dams and canals, and the Reclamation Act drove up costs by limiting construction workers to an eight-hour workday and by prohibiting the use of Chinese laborers. Newell and other officials within the Interior Department pointed out that inflation, the settlers' demand that the government build distribution and drainage ditches as well as main canals, and the fact that operation and maintenance charges were initially added to construction costs, also drove up project costs.[84]

Reclamation Service officials based their initial calculations of construction costs on the experience of the West and British India.[85] In 1902, some proponents of federal reclamation predicted an average expense of as little as five dollars an acre. Francis G. Newlands, Newell, and USGS director Charles D. Walcott knew better; they estimated the cost at ten to fifteen dollars per acre. When the secretary of the interior approved the first five reclamation projects in March 1903, the cost was still pegged at twelve or thirteen dollars an acre. Yet by the end of 1903, *Forestry and Irrigation* reported that the Reclamation Service was "gravely concerned" that the cost of the works might reach twenty dollars an acre—more than potential farmers were willing to pay—and by May 1904, the service predicted that the first million acres would cost twenty-seven dollars an acre to reclaim.[86] Private reclamation also increased in cost during the first decade of the twentieth century, but at a slower rate. Ray P. Teele, an employee of the Agriculture Department and a sharp critic of federal reclamation, claimed that while the cost of private projects tripled between 1900 and 1910, the price of government works increased by six times during the same period, reaching fifty-five dollars an acre in 1910.[87]

Cost was never the paramount concern of federal reclamation. "The question of immediate profits and of tempting interest returns is not considered in the case of reclamation by the Government," Newell observed in 1901. "The matter of time also is not one always pressing, and if it is necessary to wait ten or even twenty years before all the reclaimed land is disposed of there is not the ever-threatening bankruptcy such as is involved in speculative enterprises where the land and conserved waters are not disposed of at once." Two years later he repeated that while smaller water projects might turn a profit, "the great works can never be commercially successful, and vast tracts of fertile land will be condemned to sterility unless the Government intervenes."[88]

Despite public statements to the contrary, from the beginning Reclamation Service officials feared that sales of public land would be inadequate to pay for federal reclamation and that the projects would not pay for themselves. In a 1914 letter to Secretary of the Interior Franklin K. Lane, George Maxwell admitted, "We accepted the plan of repayment from the land because it enabled us to get our bill through. Those who understood political conditions never believed the money would be paid back." Small wonder that the dream of a partnership between public and private reclamation was never realized.[89]

The strongest criticism of federal reclamation was not that it "undersold" private companies, but that it locked up land that private companies wanted to develop. Acting through the secretary of the interior, the Reclamation Service frequently refused to grant private companies the right to build reservoirs within, or ditches across, public land. Soon after passage of the Reclamation Act, the government withdrew 40 million acres from entry, including the best reservoir sites and the best public land adjoining streams. This included 2.7 million acres in California, 1.5 million acres in Colorado, 3.7 million acres in Idaho, 8.5 million acres in Montana, and 4.4 million acres in Nevada. There was no opportunity to appeal the withdrawal policy. As late as 1910, 2.5 million acres remained reserved in California—as much land as was contained in all the federal projects—even though there was no immediate plan to water it. The reservation policy protected the West's surplus water as well as land. If the public domain could not be developed by private water companies or crossed by private ditches, the water would remain available for government use ten, twenty, or fifty years in the future.[90]

The Rio Grande provided a prime example of how the Reclamation Service blocked private projects on interstate streams. In that basin, the conflict between private enterprise and the federal government stretched back to a protracted drought at the end of the 1880s, when upstream diversions in the Mesilla Valley of New Mexico and the San Luis Valley of Colorado had sharply reduced the water available to American farmers near El Paso. Diversions by Mexican farmers near Juárez, west of El Paso, also limited the water available in Texas. In April 1888, the city council of El Paso asked Colonel Anson Mills, a longtime resident of El Paso who owned land along the river and was on leave from his job with the Army Corps of Engineers, to select a reservoir site where spring floodwater could be stored to relieve future shortages.[91]

Mills recommended federal construction of a dam three miles above El Paso, a plan approved by John Wesley Powell and the U.S. Geological Survey. Congress, however, rejected it. If the federal government built the structure, other western states would demand their own dams, and many members of Congress wanted the State Department to negotiate an international treaty dividing the Rio Grande between the United States and Mexico prior to construction. Prospects for a government dam evaporated once the depression of 1893 hit the West, but in that year the irrigation promoter Nathan Boyd formed the Rio Grande Dam and Irrigation Company to plug the river at Elephant Butte, 120 miles north of El Paso. That dam was capable of watering 230,000 to 500,000 acres in the Mesilla Valley, eighty miles south of the proposed construction site, land adjoining present-day Las Cruces, New Mexico. In 1895 Secretary of the Interior Hoke Smith approved the company's application to dam the river. Boyd demanded that farmers in the valley convey half their land to the company in exchange for a guaranteed water right covering the other half. Like most irrigation companies, it expected to make more money from land speculation rather than from the sale of water. The company had other financial incentives as well, including the New Mexico legislature's promise that its hydraulic works would be exempt from all taxes for six years.[92]

El Paso farmers favored a dam closer to their land, and logic was on their side. Their water rights were much older than those upstream in the Mesilla Valley, and Mexico's minister to the United States raised doubts that the river could fill two reservoirs. Therefore, the secretary of state asked the secretary of the interior to revoke the 1895 permit authorizing private construction of the dam. The Army Corps of Engineers also entered the picture. Since the Rio Grande floated logs and flatboats, the army now deemed the stream "navigable." A dam at Elephant Butte would interfere with commerce, and since the corps had clear authority over navigable streams, construction could not begin without prior approval from the secretary of war. The McKinley administration won a temporary injunction against construction, touching off a twelve-year legal battle. The government's suit was based entirely on navigability. It did not challenge the grant of a virtual monopoly over the Rio Grande's surplus water to a private company, nor did it question whether that company's attempt to secure half the land within the Mesilla Valley violated 1887 legislation that limited land ownership in territories of the United States to American citizens. Given the company's large number of English investors, that was an attractive legal option.[93]

In 1899, the U.S. Supreme Court upheld the navigability of the Rio Grande.[94] Nevertheless, support for the Rio Grande Dam and Irrigation Company remained high until 1902, when the Reclamation Service began enlisting support for a federal dam among farmers in the Mesilla Valley who had promised to buy water from the company. The federal dam at Elephant Butte was even more likely to interfere with navigation than the Rio Grande Dam and Irrigation Company's proposed structure. Therefore, the Interior Department did everything possible to portray the company's officials as wildcat operators. The 1895 permit required construction to begin within five years on pain of forfeiture. Holding the company to this requirement was grossly unfair, however, because private investors could not be expected to sink money into a dam when the project could have been stopped at any time by court injunction. In 1906, Mexico agreed to relinquish all claims to the Rio Grande in exchange for a guaranteed supply of sixty thousand acre-feet annually in the Juárez area. District and territorial courts then turned against the company, and in 1909 the U.S. Supreme Court revoked its permit. The Reclamation Service christened its dam at Elephant Butte in 1916.[95]

In an effort to monopolize dam construction, the Reclamation Bureau blocked private water projects on the Rio Grande, as it did on other rivers, including the North Platte, in Colorado and Wyoming. The secretary of the interior did not authorize the Rio Grande's first private dam until 1925. The Bureau's heavy-handed tactics persuaded the National Association of Manufacturers, the national Chamber of Commerce, and other business groups that supported the Reclamation Act in 1901 and 1902 to turn against federal reclamation. The loss of these allies, along with the loss of support from the railroads, ensured that federal reclamation would remain a regional program.[96]

LAND SPECULATION

One glaring weakness in the Reclamation Act of 1902 was its failure to regulate the price of *private* land within federal reclamation projects. Private land
was generally more productive than public land, but the purchase of that
land also increased the debt-burden of project farmers. Private landowners
exercised a disproportionate influence over reclamation policies. They consistently blocked the Reclamation Service's feeble efforts to limit land prices
and provide for the orderly settlement of projects.

Western historians have often portrayed land speculators as parasites who
feasted on profits they did little or nothing to create. But nearly everyone
bought, sold, and traded land on the frontier, settlers no less than land companies, small farmers as well as large, residents as well as nonresidents, and
town dwellers as well as rural folk. The motives of speculators varied. Small
farmers hoped to use the "unearned increment" to pay for livestock, fences,
seed, lumber, and other necessities, and also to tide themselves over until
their first crops came in (a process that could take years). This form of speculation became increasingly common as the cost of breaking "virgin land"
and operating a farm rapidly advanced during the early decades of the twentieth century. Small farmers also held land for children whom they hoped
would remain in the same neighborhood after reaching adulthood. Within
their own communities these speculators had a different image from nonresident landowners, whose profits did nothing to build up the local economy. Nevertheless, speculative profits more than offset the interest-free subsidy provided by the Reclamation Act, and—because large tracts of private
land remained vacant for years after projects opened—speculation drove up
the operation and maintenance charges of actual farmers. The per-acre cost
of land often exceeded the government's per-acre cost of constructing irrigation works by several times. Therefore, speculation contributed to farmers'
defaulting on their debt to the government.

Nominally, Progressive Era conservation policies discouraged monopoly.
In 1901 and 1902, Frederick Newell hoped that the Reclamation Act would
force large landowners within government projects to divide up their holdings. Since the legislation required settlers to live on the land for five years
and cultivate it, there was, in Newell's hopeful words, "little, if any, possibility of speculation by individuals. Our efforts are centered on getting the land
into the hands of men who will live there and cultivate it; and we are studying every possible scheme a speculator can put up, so as to forestall it." The
Reclamation Act , in Newell's words, was "carefully guarded in every respect,
putting the lands into the hands of small owners."[97]

Officials in the Reclamation Service assumed that market forces would
encourage the sale of holdings over 160 acres. Farmers could reap a princely
income if they properly managed an estate of 160 acres. Irrigation would in-

crease the value of the land, and it was not humanly possible for the average farmer to water even 160 acres without a large family or hired help. Unfortunately, large landowners proved to be as powerful as they were stubborn. As *Forestry and Irrigation* editorialized in 1905:

> The government cannot carry out the terms of the Reclamation Act without the consent and active cooperation of these monopolists [i.e., owners of large tracts of private land within government projects]. They appreciate this position, and believing that the government must spend its funds on these particular tracts, they are holding out for the very best terms [prices] obtainable [from prospective settlers]. The values of these reclaimable lands have increased enormously; but not content with this, the owners are trying to force the government to most liberal concessions. On the one hand public clamor is being stimulated to immediately spend the reclamation fund without waiting for necessary safe-guards; and on the other hand the men who own the land . . . do not display anything like this eagerness [to see the land reclaimed]. Many of them state frankly that they will not irrigate; that they do not want the water; that for the last year or two they have had good crops, and do not wish to be bothered with the necessary change in form of agriculture. More than this they prefer to cultivate on a large scale—several hundred acres—rather than confine themselves by intensive farming to 40 or 80 acres. . . . The owners of these lands are perfectly willing that the government should put in irrigating plants, build the ditches, and be in a position to supply them with water if they should ever want it; but they absolutely refuse to bind themselves to use this water or pay for it. . . . In other words, they would like to see the money spent in their vicinity; would like to be in a position to enjoy the benefits of such expenditure, provided they are not put to any inconvenience, or called upon to pay for the improvements unless they so desire.[98]

In 1905, the secretary of the interior noted: "It is obviously not the intent of the reclamation act to irrigate at public expense large private holdings and increase the wealth of a small number of men unless the public receives an equivalent gain. The strongest argument for the law is, not that it adds to the wealth of the State, but that it builds the greatest number of homes and creates a community of owners of the soil who live on the land and derive their sustenance from it."[99]

In 1899, slightly more than 9 million acres were filed on under the Homestead Act, Desert Land Act, and Timber and Stone Act. That amount increased to 13.5 million acres in 1900, 15.6 million acres in 1901, 19.5 million acres in 1902, and 23 million acres in 1903.[100] In Montana, eleven great ranches, with an average acreage of fifty-five thousand, were pieced together by stretching or bending the land laws. In 1901, the Desert Land Act and Homestead Act were used to claim more than 2.5 million acres in that state, even though its agricultural population showed practically no increase. "All this land has been taken up by speculators," the *New York Tribune* warned, "much of it in anticipation of national irrigation enterprises, which would make desert lands extremely valuable." Paris Gibson, one of the state's U.S. senators, commented, "At this rate of land grabbing . . . all the desirable lands of Montana will be taken up in a very short time, and the national work of reclaiming and settling the farm lands will be at an end, so far as this State is concerned."[101]

The Reclamation Act permitted the secretary of the interior to limit farms to as little as 40 acres, but the General Land Office routinely accepted 160-acre claims before the secretary announced the formal opening of a project. Settlers claimed land under the Homestead Act months and sometimes years before government canals were ready to deliver water. And since a married couple could file on 320 acres, those first on the scene could acquire legally up to eight times the minimum farm size subsequently set by the secretary. Not until 1908 did Congress give the General Land Office and Reclamation Service power to withdraw from entry land within *proposed* federal reclamation projects, and not until 1910 did it amend the land laws so that no claims could be filed until the secretary had announced the size of farms and construction costs. Secretary of the Interior Richard Ballinger concluded that "the major portion of all the difficulties have arisen from this condition of the settlers rushing in the moment the surveys are undertaken, and being compelled to reside thereon several years before water can be available, trying to eke out an existence in the interim, thereby exhausting themselves financially as well as physically."[102]

When Henry Wallace visited the proposed Boise-Payette project in Idaho, he reported that "there are little unpainted shacks scattered over the plain. The people in these shacks are hanging on until water comes."[103] The engineer in charge of Nevada's Truckee-Carson Project warned that water for most of the land would not be available until 1906 or 1907. Nevertheless, as soon as the contract was let to construct the Truckee Canal in the summer of 1903, settlers and speculators filed on twenty thousand acres under the Homestead Act before they knew exactly what land would be irrigated. Much of the land selected proved to be far beyond the reach of the government water system. Of the original 544 homesteaders who filed on the Truckee-Carson Project, only 143 remained on their land in 1911. Most failures resulted from the requirement that entrants move onto the land within six months of filing—whether water was available or not. A residence requirement designed to protect against speculation encouraged it: unless settlers were willing to buy the land from speculators at an inflated price, they had little choice but to file their claim as early as possible.[104]

Between 1902 and 1913, the price of improved land within the twenty-five government irrigation projects increased 759 percent, as opposed to a 111 percent increase for all of the West's farmland. The largest increases occurred where high-value crops such as apples and citrus were cultivated. Land within Arizona's Salt River Project advanced in value from $17.50 an acre in 1903 to $67.50 an acre in 1913 to as high as $175 an acre during World War I. On Washington's Yakima Project the per-acre price soared from $2.75 in 1907 to $150 in 1913.[105] On California's Orland Project, in the Sacramento Valley, Charles F. Lambert candidly recounted his experience:

> I bought land at $10 an acre and put it into the Orland Project at the time the project was organized [1906?]. I had a 440 acre tract along the highway; I sold it for $40 an acre. That was a very good profit. Then, one day at a time of weakness, I bought it back for $75 an acre, speculating upon being able to turn it during the ten year period [allowed private landowners to divest themselves of surplus acreage]. I sold it off in forty-acre lots [the size of farms within the project] at $125 an acre, where by water alone it built up that valuation from $10 an acre. Everyone was happy along the line. Everybody made money.

The Sacramento Valley was well suited to the cultivation of high-value fruits and nuts, hence speculation was much more lucrative there than in Nevada, Wyoming, or Montana. Many speculators, according to Lambert, appreciated the forty-acre project limitation because smaller holdings gave them more opportunity to buy and sell.[106]

In theory, the Reclamation Service required large landowners to sell excess lands or convey them to the local water users' association for resale *prior* to the completion of each project. The association was supposed to sell surplus land at prices set by the secretary of the interior, then turn the proceeds over to the original owner once the irrigation works had been completed. Only a few projects complied, however, and the service was slow to enforce the 160-acre restriction. It feared losing the political support of established large farmers more than it feared violating the spirit of the Reclamation Act. At a public meeting held in Klamath Falls, California, for example, Frederick Newell solicited support for the Klamath Project by minimizing the importance of the Reclamation Act's excess-lands provision. Private landowners could deed surplus land to their children or relatives, he advised, and in ten years, when their water right was paid for, resume ownership. An attendee of the meeting reported to Secretary of the Interior Richard Ballinger: "The owner of a large tract of land arose and asked Mr. Newell, 'How old must a child be before he can hold one hundred and sixty acres and get water from the Government?' Mr. Newell smiled and replied, 'I suppose about five days,' at which the deluded people cheered wildly."[107]

Newell was in a quandary. As early as 1906, he recognized that the tendency of project residents to hold too much land threatened the federal reclamation program as much as the high cost of irrigation works. "It is probable that an attempt will be made to initiate the doctrine of repudiation of the obligations to return the reclamation fund," he wrote California governor George Pardee. "The first step is to try to get the farm units so large that the farmers can not possibly pay back the cost of the water; then, with a few cases of actual hardship will be mingled a large number of cases of speculation, and the attempt will be made to induce Congress to grant relief, extension of payments, and finally rescinding of payments." Government farmers who bought private land were more likely to renege on their obligation to the government than to their other creditors. The question was what to do about it. Newell's answer was to ignore the 160-acre provision of the Reclamation Act—which was difficult, if not impossible, to enforce—and instead expand the supply of irrigated land so rapidly that the market would be saturated and the incentive for speculation destroyed. To keep down the price of land, the Reclamation Service had to provide more irrigated farms than could be used. Ultimately—in part because of the demand for land during World War I—Newell lost his gamble. Attempting to open farms in advance of need did not curb speculation, at least not before the 1920s.[108]

OTHER WEAKNESSES IN THE RECLAMATION ACT

The Reclamation Act's requirement that at least 51 percent of revenue from public land sales be spent within the state or territory that contained those lands seriously compromised the ability of government engineers to select projects objectively. At the end of fiscal year 1904, the reclamation fund contained slightly more than $23 million. The largest amount, more than $4 million, came from land sales in Oregon. North Dakota generated $3.4 million; Washington, $2.7 million; Oklahoma, $2.5 million. At the bottom of the list were South Dakota, with $300,000; Arizona, with $170,000; Kansas, with $100,000; and Nevada, with a paltry $50,000. Only 4 percent of Kansas remained part of the public domain in 1902, and only 17 percent of Nebraska. And although 96 percent of Nevada and 93 percent of Arizona still belonged to the nation, most of that land was too mountainous or too far removed from water to be arable. In that state and territory, proceeds from land sales were expected to pay only 2 percent of the total cost of federal reclamation, but opportunities for reclamation were far greater there than in the Midwest. The Reclamation Act created the appearance, therefore, that money which "belonged" to the Great Plains was being shifted to the Far West, and money that belonged to the Northwest was being shifted to the Southwest.[109]

The Reclamation Service faced a dilemma: the states that produced the largest amount of revenue had the least need for irrigation—and vice-versa. In his report for 1904–05, Frederick Newell noted that "it has been found that the greatest obstacles [to federal reclamation], both from the engineering and human standpoint, are encountered in States from which the largest funds have been derived. This is because these states are not truly arid, for dry farming is now successfully carried on in them, and most of the

farmers do not desire to change their methods and take up the more labo-
rious work of intensive cultivation under irrigation." In addition, states such
as North Dakota and Oklahoma contained few large streams or potential
reservoir sites. In 1904, President Daniel E. Willard of the North Dakota Agricultural College predicted that irrigation "on any large scale in North Dakota
is impracticable if not impossible." The same was true of the other states on
the Great Plains—at least in 1902.[110] Looking back on the beginnings of federal reclamation from the vantage point of 1927, Newell argued that using
proceeds from public land sales to pay for reclamation had given "a number of the States a feeling that they were contributing inordinately to developments in other States. There should have been no reclamation law until
the country was ready to make a budget allotment for a well-considered reclamation program." Congress repealed the 51 percent requirement in 1910,
but by that time many marginal projects had already been constructed or
were under construction.[111]

For example, after discovering that only twenty thousand acres could be
irrigated from gravity-fed canals in the entire state of North Dakota, the Reclamation Service concocted the disastrous Buford-Trenton Project to pump
water from the Missouri River onto eighteen thousand acres of benchlands
adjacent to that stream in North Dakota and Montana. The surrounding land
contained plenty of lignite to drive the pumps, but the cost of raising the
water 140 to 400 feet was high. The Southwest—where agriculture was impossible without irrigation and where high-value citrus fruit compensated
for the cost of applying water to the land—offered many practical pump projects. But they were infeasible on the northern plains. In most years, sufficient
rain fell in western North Dakota to raise wheat without irrigation. Farmers
there preferred to gamble with nature rather than to invest in expensive
pumps. The lack of interest in federal reclamation exhibited by local farmers, and the high cost of constructing the Buford-Trenton Project, made it
a white elephant from the beginning. So was the pump project in Lawton,
Oklahoma.[112]

Of all the Reclamation Act's omissions, the most glaring was its failure to
force government farmers to organize and to accept the terms of the Reclamation Act. The Reclamation Service had many reasons for urging farmers
to cooperate. It needed to create uniform water rights within each project,
it needed to ensure that landowners reimbursed the government for the cost
of construction, and it needed to force landowners to divest themselves of
holdings of more than 160 acres. As early as 1903, Newell anticipated that
the service would have a difficult time getting farmers to pull together, given
the multitude of conflicts over water rights that divided existing communities between "old" and "new" settlers.[113] There was as much need to coordinate or consolidate existing water systems as to build new ones. In an effort
to place all water rights on an equal footing, the Reclamation Service at-

tempted to persuade water users who had farmed their land before a federal project had been created to relinquish their water title to the central government. Many farmers saw that as dictatorial. They refused to give up their seniority, which forced the Reclamation Service to buy up private ditches to establish control over the water supply (and this expense drove up construction costs). To farmers and state officials alike, the process of creating uniform claims with the same chronological priority looked like the prelude to the destruction of *all* state water rights.[114]

The first project water users' association was formed in the Salt River Valley of Arizona on February 9, 1903. Membership was a function of stock ownership. The association sold shares for fifteen dollars apiece, but no member could acquire more than one share per acre or more than 160 in all. Each share entitled the bearer to one vote in the association and one measure of the water supply created by the federal government's promised storage project. Virtually all farmland around Phoenix consisted of privately owned tracts larger than 160 acres, and many of the owners were nonresidents. To prevent speculation in water rights, title to the stock passed with title to the land. The landowners pledged two hundred thousand acres as a mortgage to ensure that they would repay the cost of construction. Only after this was done did the secretary of the interior approve the Salt River Project.[115]

The constitution of the Salt River Water Association became a model for other projects. By 1910, farmers had formed similar organizations on all federal projects except the Minidoka, Shoshone, and Truckee-Carson. The Reclamation Service welcomed such institutions in the hope that they would guarantee the repayment of construction charges. They did not. Nor did they promote "home rule" or democracy, curb speculation, or force the sale of "excess lands." The largest landowners—many of whom did not reside on their land—dictated the policies followed by the association, and often they evaded promises made to the Department of the Interior. Because the water users' association controlled only the allocation of "new water" stored by the government dam, the Salt River's existing stream flow continued to be distributed according to older appropriative rights. Most projects ultimately formed themselves into irrigation districts to escape the weaknesses and limitations of water users' associations.[116]

CONCLUSION

Chapter 1 demonstrated how the idealism of the reclamation crusade faded in the years after 1902. But the structure of American government also hampered federal reclamation. Turf wars within the federal bureaucracy, particularly between the Interior and Agriculture Departments, limited the Reclamation Service's authority and autonomy. A handful of officials in the

Agriculture Department—led by Elwood Mead—thought that the Reclamation Service focused far too narrowly on engineering. The Agriculture Department, with bureaus devoted to extension work, rural engineering, soils, plant pathology, and other related fields, was far more capable of planning and administering a successful irrigation program. That view was not shared by the secretaries of agriculture, however. They considered the low crop prices in the last three decades of the nineteenth century a direct result of opening too much land to cultivation. By 1902, crop prices had begun to rise, but the secretary remained reluctant to encourage the expansion of cultivated land in the West for fear of returning to the depression of the 1890s and alienating Midwest farmers, the Agriculture Department's major constituency. Mead and his lieutenants became strident and effective critics of the Reclamation Service, and they exercised great power in Congress. Their criticism, for example, helped prevent the expansion of federal reclamation into the wetlands of the South and upper Midwest. But, given the secretary of agriculture's opposition to taking over federal reclamation, Mead and his lieutenants could criticize but not lead. And despite his friendship with Frederick Newell, Gifford Pinchot's successful efforts to transfer control over the national forests from Interior to Agriculture, completed in 1905, and his desire to consolidate the management of all the public lands within a Department of Conservation in Agriculture, contributed to criticism of the Reclamation Service.

Equally important, in many matters the Reclamation Service was forced to defer to the states. In 1902, the Reclamation Act seemed to confer vast new powers on the secretary of the interior, and by implication the president. These powers were more apparent than real. The Reclamation Service tried to "stockpile" water for its projects by rewriting state water laws and by asserting "inchoate" rights to part or all of the West's surplus water. But the U.S. Supreme Court exhibited little sympathy for the service's legal arguments, and the agency had no choice but to defer to state control. One justification for the Reclamation Act was that only the central government could afford to undertake vast water projects on the Colorado, Rio Grande, and Sacramento Rivers. But those ambitious plans faded as the Supreme Court's persistent refusal to grant the national government special rights to water ensured that the states would have great influence over the government projects. The federal government resorted to subterfuge to "protect" as much of the West's surplus water as possible. It could not remodel water law, but it could reserve public land from entry. Yet in doing so, it limited the appropriation of water by private companies.

The Reclamation Act fueled the hopes of large landowners and private irrigation companies alike. In 1902, proponents of the Reclamation Act hoped that the nation and private enterprise would operate in different, but complementary, realms. Each would benefit from the other. By the end of

Theodore Roosevelt's presidency in 1909, however, the federal government and most private companies were at odds. The Snake River Valley of Idaho offers an excellent example of the competition between the federal government and private enterprise, and also of the conditions faced on a typical government water project. A private project at Twin Falls clashed with the government's Minidoka Project. The story of the two illustrates not just the triumphs and pitfalls of reclamation, but also the impact irrigation had on the creation of western towns and communities.

3

Case Studies in Irrigation and Community

Twin Falls and Rupert

This book mainly concerns national water policies, but those policies cannot be understood solely from the perspective of Washington, D.C. Water policy exemplifies the dictum that all politics in the United States is local. Therefore, this chapter looks at two agricultural communities in the Snake River Valley of Idaho in the opening years of the twentieth century, one at Twin Falls and the other at Rupert. It analyzes irrigation as a matter private and public, local and national, and rural and urban. It shows the constraints that limited the nature and implementation of natural resource laws at all levels of government. It also suggests how irrigation shaped communities in the arid West.

The Snake River Valley served as a laboratory for new towns, and Twin Falls and Rupert were two of the most notable experiments. Contrary to the promises of promoters and ideologues, irrigation was a deeply divisive force during the early life of new communities. Sometimes it generated great wealth, but individual ambitions took precedence over cooperation, planning, and efficiency. Irrigation did more to divide people than to draw them together. Twin Falls was the creature of capitalists who gambled in land. Fifty miles to the east, in the government town of Rupert, on the Minidoka Irrigation Project, speculation was restrained. Each town experienced economic problems common to new communities, but in population and wealth, Twin Falls surged ahead while Rupert languished. Henry Wallace visited the Snake River Valley in September and October 1909, a few years after the towns were created. He observed that "the Twin Falls project is years in advance of the Minidoka project merely because it has had more advertising, more booming, and has attracted a more progressive class of people." The primary difference between the two towns, Wallace thought, was that land values at Twin Falls had increased much more rapidly.[1]

THE CAREY ACT AND EARLY IRRIGATION IN IDAHO

Land developers and would-be farmers found two great gifts in Idaho's Snake River Valley: plenty of water and remarkably fertile volcanic soil. "The only nutrient seriously lacking in this arid soil is nitrogen," historian William Gertsch has written, "but farmers have compensated for this deficiency by systematic crop rotation and by the growing of alfalfa, clover, or other leguminous crops which return humus and nitrogen to the soil, in turn providing greater yields of potatoes, beans, beets, and grains. This particular composition of soil with its lava structure has rendered negligible the problem of drainage which has particularly bedeviled irrigation in many parts of the West. The broken and porous lava facilitates irrigation water drainage from farm lands and prevents water-logging of the soil which dissolves its minerals and results in the formation of alkali on the surface." As early as 1885, an employee of the Oregon Short Line wrote to the company's president, Charles Francis Adams, extolling the valley's agricultural potential: "I have never seen a more perfect farming country in any of my travels. I consider it far superior to anything I have ever seen in Nebraska, Colorado, Utah, or even Oregon." The land adjoining the Snake River was relatively easy to clear, and its gradual slope made it cheap to irrigate. In 1890, John Wesley Powell's Irrigation Survey estimated the cost of irrigation at five dollars an acre.[2]

No state relied more heavily on the 1894 Carey Act than Idaho.[3] That law donated up to a million acres of federal land to those states willing to irrigate it either directly or by contracting with private companies. The land itself sold for fifty cents an acre, and the fee went entirely to the states to pay for administering the act. The private companies profited solely from the sale of water rights and land they owned in the vicinity of the public land. The Carey Act contributed to a doubling of Idaho's population during the 1890s—when most western states experienced little or no increase—and the population doubled again in the first decade of the twentieth century, rising from 88,600 in 1890 to 326,000 in 1910. Between 1895 and 1930, private land and water companies launched sixty-five Carey Act projects in Idaho, covering more than half the land patented under the legislation in the entire West. Idaho's largest Carey Act project contained more acres than *all* the Carey Act projects patented in Wyoming, the second most active state. Promoters proposed the first Carey Act project to Idaho officials in December 1895, but the boom did not come until after the Twin Falls South Side Project opened in 1905.[4] In 1908, the success of the early projects prompted Congress to grant Idaho an additional 2 million acres and Wyoming an additional 1 million—even though much of that land might have been included in federal reclamation projects.[5]

The boom was short-lived. In the first decade of the twentieth century, so many Carey Act projects were opened that in 1910 the bottom fell out of the irrigation bond market, and in the following year two Chicago bond houses that had sold the majority of Idaho irrigation securities—Trowbridge and Niver and Farwell Trust—collapsed. In July 1913, the financial and industrial empire of two of the heaviest investors in Carey Act projects, James S. and W. S. Kuhn, toppled. Land prices plummeted, and angry investors within and without the state were left holding the bag. The Carey Act became a leading issue in the Fall 1910 election. Democrats charged that Republican state officials had admitted Carey Act promoters to "secret" meetings of the state land board that passed judgment on which water projects would be built; that those meetings were orchestrated by the companies; and that at least one member of the board had been bribed to approve questionable projects.[6] High crop prices and the great demand for land produced by World War I temporarily revived interest in the Carey Act, but the wild enthusiasm of 1906 or 1908 did not recur.

TWIN FALLS: ORIGINS

Twin Falls is thirty-eight hundred feet above sea level and enjoys an average of only 129 frost-free days each year. Nevertheless, its surface is remarkably uniform, and a silt loam well-endowed with lime, potash, and phosphorus covers the tract to a depth of three feet and more. From the beginning of white settlement, the land's gentle slope encouraged furrow rather than flood irrigation and ensured good drainage. Few farms became waterlogged or suffered from the alkali buildup that afflicted so much irrigated land in the West.[7]

Of all the Carey Act ventures, the Twin Falls South Side Project—the dream of irrigation promoter Ira B. Perrine—was the most successful. Born in Indiana and schooled in Iowa, Perrine moved to Idaho in 1883 and joined his uncle and aunt in the mining town of Bullion, sixty miles north of present-day Twin Falls. In the following year, after failing as a miner, Perrine purchased twenty cows, located good pasture near Shoshone Falls, and opened a dairy. Later, at Blue Lakes in the Snake River Canyon, twelve miles downriver from Twin Falls, Perrine engaged in placer mining and staging, built a hotel, and planted several hundred acres to grain and fruit. In 1895, the Oregon Short Line hired him to find the best location for a bridge across the river. While employed in that work, he discovered that even though it was twenty-eight miles from the nearest railroad and devoted entirely to grazing cattle, the fertile plain destined to become the Twin Falls South Side Project could be watered with a relatively simple diversion dam and gravity canal.[8]

Investment capital was scarce during the 1890s. Not until 1900 did Perrine convince Salt Lake City banker S. B. Milner to put up thirty-two thousand dollars for a canal survey. In the same year, the two men incorporated the

Twin Falls Land and Water Company, and soon thereafter Idaho state engineer D. W. Ross joined the enterprise. Ross completed the canal survey in 1901, and that interested Boise investors in the project. But Perrine's big break came late in 1902, when he convinced Frank Buhl, an iron and steel magnate from Sharon, Pennsylvania, to bankroll construction. The company reorganized in January 1903, with Buhl as principal stockholder. Buhl then persuaded business associates in Pittsburgh to invest in the project, beginning with Peter L. Kimberley.[9]

Idaho's constitutional debt limit prevented the state from building its own irrigation works. Therefore, it turned to private enterprise. "The State must be prepared," State Engineer Ross advised the land board that reviewed Carey Act applications, "to offer very liberal inducements to capital seeking investment or these lands will remain in their desert condition for generations to come." The South Side Project involved the construction of a diversion dam two thousand feet wide and eighty feet high to raise water from the river fifty feet to the headgate of an eighty-mile canal. The company promised to water 270,000 acres of land south of the river, and construction began in March 1903; the cost was initially estimated at $1.5 million. Ross claimed that the South Side Project would increase the state's irrigable land by more than 40 percent. Eventually, the company hoped to reclaim an additional thirty thousand acres northeast of the Snake River.[10]

In March 1903, the *New York Times* took note of the project, whose anticipated cost had tripled to $5 million (in part because the *Times* included the cost of reclaiming the relatively inaccessible land north of the river). "When completed the system will be the most perfect in existence in the irrigated world," the newspaper gushed. The promoters also hoped to build a power plant at Shoshone Falls and electrify the project. "It is planned to have electric car lines reaching every farm and orchard, and, when the country is settled, to secure the rural mail system. Public telephones and all modern conveniences are to be added to the comforts of making homes." The Twin Falls Project offered wonderful opportunities to raise fruit, the *Times* promised. Many of the farms would be "the twenty-acre Utah class," not the much larger grain farms of the Midwest.[11]

In August 1903, the company selected a townsite on school land purchased from the state—land that could be sold without Carey Act restrictions. In April 1904, surveyors laid out Twin Falls and divided it into lots, and the town began to take shape in the summer and fall of the same year. The promoters hired E. L. Masqueray, the architect responsible for the 1904 St. Louis World's Fair, to design it. He platted the business district around a large park and civic center. The irrigation company donated four blocks for the park and two blocks adjoining the park for a courthouse and high school, stipulating that no temporary buildings could be erected on this land. Masqueray wanted to give Twin Falls an image of stability, permanence, wealth, and modernity.[12]

Not surprisingly, the first frame building, built in 1905, housed the Twin Falls Investment Company. Perrine created this company, and later the Twin Falls Townsite Company, solely to sell land. Like most Carey Act projects, the Twin Falls Land and Water Company did not profit exclusively from the sale of water rights. Once construction began on the canal, eastern investors hoped that a land rush would permit the company to sell town lots as well as agricultural land within and adjoining the project. But the first sale of project land, held on July 1, 1903, inspired only twenty-eight buyers among the fifty-five who registered for the drawing. As the *Twin Falls News* recounted in 1911, "It required more nerve to buy this land at $25.50 an acre [50 cents an acre for the land and $25 for the water right] than it does today at $125[,] for the soil was untried, the canal uncompleted, and no water was available for man or beast." Some land sold in 1904, but sales did not become brisk until 1905.[13]

Twin Falls incorporated in April 1905, and by the end of the year it contained general stores, livery stables, restaurants, saloons, rooming houses, a lumber yard, blacksmith shop, bank, newspaper, six-room school that served almost five hundred students, and the usual complement of physicians, lawyers, dentists, and barbers. Baptists organized the first Protestant church in January 1905, and Methodists formed their first congregation a month later. By the end of the year, there were many other churches, including Presbyterian and Mormon; the first Catholic church appeared in 1907.[14]

At the beginning of March 1905, the company completed its diversion dam, and soon thereafter it turned water into the partially completed main canal. When the House Committee on Irrigation and Reclamation visited Twin Falls in June, the committee's chair, Congressman Frank Mondell of Wyoming, proclaimed that "the Twin Falls project is decidedly the best of its age I have ever seen."[15] In August, the Minidoka and Southwestern Railroad—a spur of the Oregon Short Line—reached Twin Falls, ending the town's reliance on a thirty-mile freight wagon line from Shoshone across the Snake River canyon. The crowning achievement came shortly before Christmas 1905, with the opening of the thoroughly modern Hotel Perrine. On any given day, two hundred to five hundred strangers visited the town in search of farms and investment property. The Twin Falls Investment Company considered the hotel a business necessity as well as a symbol of prosperity, gentility, and permanence. The Perrine sported crystal chandeliers, massive oak furniture, private baths, electric lights (generated by a threshing-machine engine), steam heat, individual telephones, and its own water and sewage system. Its illuminated sign could be seen for miles and, in the words of the *Twin Falls News*, "shone like a beacon of progress far across the desert." Perrine also built the first general store—the Pioneer Store—just across the street from the hotel.[16]

By the end of 1905, Twin Falls counted a population of two thousand to three thousand. (In 1890, when Idaho entered the union, its largest town, Boise, contained only twenty-three hundred people.) More than a hundred thousand acres of farmland had been sold (half the total), and hundreds of farms dotted the countryside, though only about fifteen thousand acres were under irrigation. By the standards of the time and place, Twin Falls qualified as an instant city. By the end of 1906, all the best agricultural land adjoining Twin Falls had been sold. By 1909, the town's population had reached nearly six thousand.[17]

Just as Ira Perrine provided the town with a first-class hotel, the Twin Falls Land and Water Company granted substantial subsidies to the new community. Idaho's new state engineer, James Stephenson, noted that "it may be said that the company takes the desert, builds irrigation works, and completely furnishes the country with all the modern comforts required by civilization. . . . This method condenses within three or four years the progress which, under ordinary circumstances, requires twenty years."[18] The company donated town lots for schools, churches, an opera house, a fire station, and public buildings. It constructed the first schools. It erected bridges, planted trees, provided cheap oil to spray the streets, and hosted public celebrations on the Fourth of July.[19] The Twin Falls Land and Water Company was allied with the Twin Falls Waterworks Company, which delivered water to homes and businesses in town, and with the Shoshone Falls Power Company, which provided the city with electricity. In 1908, the power company installed arc lamps in the town and, in an effort to attract industry, sold power at the lowest rates in the Pacific Northwest, save for Spokane.[20]

The Twin Falls Land and Water Company also provided valuable advice to farmers, many of whom came to Idaho from the Midwest with little knowledge of desert agriculture. In 1905, the company opened a forty-acre experimental farm under the direction of Alex McPherson. He studied the best crops to raise and the optimum amount of water needed to produce the largest harvests. Potatoes, sugar beets, and dairying were admirably suited to the soils of the Snake River Valley, he discovered, but alfalfa required much more water per harvested ton than beets or carrots. By watering land in the fall, after the summer harvest, the irrigation season could be extended beyond the traditional four-month period from May through August. This prepared the soil for winter wheat, which could then be grown without further irrigation. McPherson found that local farmers used twice as much water as their crops needed. To reduce the number of irrigation days, however, farmers would have to alternate watering their fields, which most refused to do. Twin Falls' farmers demonstrated little trust for or cooperation with one another.[21]

SPECULATION IN A COMPANY TOWN

Ira Perrine, Frank Buhl, and the other investors in the Twin Falls Land and Water Company were not visionaries driven to create a new society in the American West. Their main goal was to sell real estate, and despite their concern with creating an impression of permanence, Twin Falls was a society of gamblers. For better *and* worse, it was a company town, and it remained so for years after its creation. The Twin Falls Land and Water Company's chief engineer simultaneously served as the town's first mayor, and another company employee served as city clerk.[22]

Irrigation was the handmaiden of speculation. Rural and urban residents both speculated, and many migrants to the Twin Falls area purchased 160 acres of farmland and two town lots simultaneously. In some cases, they poured so much money into land that they had little capital left to improve it, to invest in local industries, or even to pay taxes. The Twin Falls Land and Water Company, as well as the local newspaper, fanned the flames. "We have a deep and fertile soil, a delightful climate, and one of the best water rights in the United States," the company's secretary crowed to a Chicago resident in 1906. "All crops can be raised here which can be raised in the Mississippi Valley and the climate and soil especially adapt this tract to the raising of sugar beets and fruit, more particularly apples, two of the most profitable products to be raised in the West."[23] Clearing, plowing, leveling, ditching, and seeding the land cost about $15 an acre, and fencing eighty acres ran about $112. But within a couple of years, the company promised, farmers could expect alfalfa to return more than a hundred dollars an acre a year. In other words, the profits from one year's crop could easily pay for the land and all improvements.[24]

The first issue of the *Twin Falls News* assured readers that the editor had no ties to the Twin Falls Land and Water Company or to the Twin Falls Investment Company. It proclaimed that the paper was "in no sense a professional boomer. It will aim at all times to be conservative in its statements, with the end in view that no one who may depend upon it for reliable information may be misled."[25] Nevertheless, the *News* circulated among investors far beyond the borders of Idaho, and the editor did everything possible to keep the market for land at white heat. In September 1907, he observed, "Hundreds of farmers have sold part or all of their lands for three times the original cost. Every entryman on the tract has made money, or can make money today by turning over his land." In 1909, the paper reported: "Purchasers of Twin Falls real estate and of Twin Falls County irrigated land, at this time, need only pay the nominal taxes and sleep the balance of the time, to make money out of these investments, during the next ten years. If they want to make more money they can have the lands in crops and improvements on their city lots. Either course is a winner." As early as the summer of 1905, the *News* reported that "choice agricultural lands" in lots of from 20 to 160 acres were available to lease on favorable terms. They were owned by nonresident investors in northern Idaho "who wish to have them cleared and cultivated at once. Intending tenants will find the terms very advantageous."[26]

The price of land within the Twin Falls South Side Project more than doubled from 1905 to 1910, when it reached an average of $100 an acre. It doubled again by 1915 and soared to $373 in 1919.[27] Urban land prices kept pace. Two lots at the center of the business district that sold for $1,750 in August 1904 fetched $23,600 four years later. By August 1905, the Twin Falls Investment Company and Twin Falls Townsite Company had sold one-third of the land they owned within the city limits. Another one-third was on the market, and the remainder was reserved for future sale. The company had pocketed more than $500,000 from town lot sales even before the project opened, and sales of company land within the town limits more than paid for the irrigation system.[28]

The state board that administered the Carey Act did not require landowners to improve their land before they could sell it. Nominally, the board required residence within six months of the date water became available, but that could be evaded by paying others to clear, plow, and fence, or by leasing the land to actual farmers. Frequently, the company chose parcels for nonresidents knowing that the land would be resold within a few months of purchase. Privately, the company secretary called the residence requirement "a farce"—"the lighter you make it the better from the standpoint of the state and the canal company."[29]

For all its power to generate interest in a new community, land speculation based on irrigation had a dark side. Gamblers in land had little desire to make permanent improvements unless they benefited directly. In any new agricultural district, moreover, farmers faced the high cost of readying land for cultivation and waiting until the first crops came in. Taxes had to be kept low at a time when the community faced its greatest need for revenue. But if taxes were too low, how could Twin Falls provide the public services that would attract future residents? The Twin Falls Land and Water Company, Investment Company, and Townsite Company attempted to transfer the tax burden to patented land.[30] In 1906, it succeeded in reducing the book value of its property in Cassia County from $645,000 to $200,000, and its assessment in Lincoln County from $200,000 to $10,000. The Twin Falls townsite paid a higher assessment than the dam, canal, and unsold agricultural land.[31]

Irrigation works were subject to taxation until the water users assumed control over the project. But assessing taxes and collecting them were two different things. As one of the two largest taxpayers in the county (along with the railroad), the Twin Falls Land and Water Company was able to "negotiate" its tax debt. By threatening to take the county to court each year—adding an enormous legal expense to the cost of local government—it transferred much of the cost of government and public services to those who cultivated the soil.[32]

To attract investors, the company also fought to keep taxes low on patented, unimproved land. Much to its regret, initially the county assessed unimproved and improved land at the same rate. "The position I took on this question," the county assessor explained, "was that the speculator owned as good land and had the same water right as his industrious neighbor who was cultivating his property and thereby making the property of the speculator more valuable. For that reason, the speculator should pay the same rate of tax on his land as the farmer who was building up the country." Nevertheless, in 1908 the state board of equalization slashed the assessed value of patented lands in Twin Falls County by 50 percent, and compensated by raising taxes on improvements. Not until 1911, when Idaho's governor called for a system of taxation known as "full cash valuation," was property assessed at rates even remotely close to actual value. The new system increased Twin Falls' per-acre assessed value from thirteen dollars to more than forty-nine dollars per acre, but by that time the company had sold most of its land and the farmers operated the water system.[33]

Not surprisingly, the city of Twin Falls looked for "painless" alternatives to property taxes. In 1905, the village trustees imposed an annual license fee on saloons, and for years thereafter, one-third to one-half the cost of public services came from these licenses. Other sources of revenue included fines, dray licenses, building permits, road taxes, and a poll tax. Once the state legislature designated Twin Falls as a city in 1907, the town council limited annual expenditures to ten thousand dollars. In 1908, it approved a budget of fifteen hundred dollars in salaries for city officials, two thousand dollars to maintain streets and alleys, twenty-five hundred dollars for police protection, twenty-four hundred dollars for sewer bonds, five hundred dollars for the fire department, another five hundred for public grounds and buildings, and a six-hundred-dollar miscellaneous fund. City officials considered these expenditures inadequate, but voters consistently rejected bond issues, even for such necessities as a county jail.[34]

In 1907, the city lacked the money to water the streets to keep dust down, so businessmen paid to spray the two most heavily used thoroughfares, Main Street and Shoshone Avenue. Nevertheless, Main and Shoshone were so poorly graded that they collected large puddles of water that flooded basements. Two years later, voters approved a bond issue to pave major intersections, but only on condition that property owners pay the cost of paving the streets in front of their lots. Contributions from businessmen, and from those who owned property fronting the street, paid most of the bill. Funding public improvements by subscription fragmented the town into distinct districts, each of which sought to promote its growth at the expense of other neighborhoods.[35]

Sanitation posed comparable problems. Most cities without garbage collection and sewers were "shack towns" that projected an image of modest ambitions and impermanence. Piles of garbage made a poor impression on potential investors. The *News* warned that there were "enough tin cans on the townsite to put a tin roof on the Snake river canyon."[36] "The odor of cesspools will scare away more capital in a minute than would a sewer tax in a decade," it proclaimed, but voters opposed citywide garbage collection as well as a comprehensive sewage system. In 1906, the city assumed the responsibility for building the main sewer line, but the bond issue passed only because it required individual property owners to pay for a large part of the work—*if* they chose to use the service. Since the most valuable lots were downtown, the business district, where property values were high, subsidized the residential districts, where many lots were vacant. In the absence of a *mandatory* citywide system, those who held lots purely for speculation frequently blocked the construction of lateral sewers in districts where a majority of residents wanted them and were willing to pay for them. A 1907 scheme to require each lot owner to pay for sewer service, including the Twin Falls Townsite Company, encountered the wrath of the company and speculators alike.[37]

Limitations on taxation and spending shaped the politics and society of Twin Falls in countless ways. For example, Twin Falls' schools became dependent on liquor taxes, and for that reason many local businesses, as well as the *Twin Falls News,* opposed local and statewide prohibition. Within two years of its construction in 1905, the first school—designed for 550 children—housed 700, and the school-age population increased by 50 percent in 1907 alone. Even so, the campaign for a second school met substantial opposition from those who feared that it had been orchestrated by landowners near the potential site of the new school. In the spring of 1907, increasing revenue from liquor licenses permitted the school board to cut property taxes by one-third, paving the way for the construction of new schools through bond issues. Despite the city's relatively large population, the Twin Falls High School was not completed until 1913.[38]

Almost every other civic issue in the early history of Twin Falls—from establishing a fire department to building a courthouse—hinged on the power of the Twin Falls Land and Water Company. The editor of the *News* learned to appeal to financial self-interest rather than to civic virtue. In urging voters to approve a bond issue to build the courthouse, for example, he suggested that if land and tax records were destroyed by fire, "not a farm loan could be made in this county for years. The loan companies would not do business in a county where the records were cloudy. Moreover, the transfer of city and farm property would be greatly retarded if not totally stopped for an indefinite time." As always, the newspaper favored long-term bond issues that deferred as much of the tax burden as possible, transferring the financial obligation from the present to the future. "Let us have a court house which will answer the county's needs when we are all under the sod and for which posterity will pay. We pioneers have done our part, and it is right that those who follow should do theirs."[39]

THE POLITICS OF IRRIGATION ON THE TWIN FALLS PROJECT

The $25.50 an acre the first settlers paid to the Twin Falls Land and Water Company was just the beginning of their expenses. The cost of clearing, leveling, grading, fencing, and seeding land easily matched that amount. Farmers also had to find markets for their crops. Neighboring towns could absorb only a small share of Twin Falls' production. The closest market of any size, Salt Lake City, was well stocked by Utah's small farms, and Twin Falls' farmers lacked direct rail access to California until World War I. Potatoes grew well at Twin Falls, but Yakima already supplied Tacoma and Seattle with that food. Therefore, the first generation of Twin Falls farmers raised the same crops they had before they reached the Snake River Valley: wheat, oats, barley, hay, and alfalfa—which they fed to sheep or cattle. It took nearly two decades for Twin Falls to find an agricultural niche by specializing in dairy products and sugar beets (processed by local beet factories, then exported as sugar).[40]

Water proved to be the most difficult problem. From the project's beginning, farmers had questioned when they should begin paying the company—at the time they entered the land, at the time water first became available, at the time they were ready to use the water, at the time they diverted water, or at the time the state declared the project completed. Equally important was the question of when the canal should be turned over to the settlers. They could not secure patents to their land until the transfer of ownership, and, therefore, could not negotiate loans that required a mortgage on their land.

Farmers demanded a predictable supply of water year-round, but the company acknowledged a legal responsibility to deliver water only during the spring and summer growing season. Farmers suffered frequent crop losses because the company promised more water than it owned or could supply, failed to provide water when promised, and reneged on a tacit promise not to charge maintenance and operation fees on the ditches for two years after water first became available. As early as 1904, the company furnished water to a handful of farmers, but few irrigated until 1906. Therefore, the question of whether maintenance charges should begin in 1906, 1908, or even later became a hot issue. Meanwhile, speculation punished those who farmed, and not just because they were forced to pay higher taxes on improved land. The cost of maintaining ditches fell entirely on irrigators, not on the unoccupied land owned by nonresident speculators, and the weeds that thrived on vacant land—including Russian thistle (tumbleweed)—infested their crops. The first maintenance charge was imposed in March 1906—eighty cents per irrigable acre, payable in advance. In the following year, the company shut off the water of those who refused to pay.[41]

Farmers compiled a long list of grievances against the company. The company cut corners on hydraulic works. For example, its contract with the state specified headgates of masonry or concrete, but the company installed wooden gates and failed to provide measuring devices to determine how much water each farmer used. As a result, some took more than their fair share—to the detriment of their neighbors. Part of the canal was constructed through lava, which resulted in a substantial loss of water via percolation. Elsewhere, the company relied on natural coulees and ravines for lateral canals, which led to substantial losses from seepage and evaporation. This expedient also permitted wastewater from barnyards and pastures to contaminate water used for domestic purposes. To make matters worse, the grade of the main canal was too steep; banks washed out, adding a large quantity of silt to the water.[42]

In November 1906, the Twin Falls Land and Water Company proclaimed the canal complete. The company still owned between fifty thousand and a hundred thousand acres within the project's boundaries, however, and project farmers refused to take over the canal until all defects had been repaired. The transfer of control would end the company's financial liability, and farmers feared that they would inherit the responsibility of paying off outstanding liens or mortgages on the hydraulic works. At the least, they would have to hire a watermaster to make sure the water was fairly distributed.[43]

The conflict between settlers and the company spawned many lawsuits. Of fifty cases on the docket for the autumn 1907 session of the district court, twelve involved the Twin Falls Land and Water Company. The most expensive and protracted contests pertained to water rights. In 1904 and 1905, the company promised settlers who took up land under the Twin Falls South Side Project a secure, virtually unlimited water supply. Subsequently, the construction of competing water projects, such as the Twin Falls North Side Project, made that supply far less certain. Farmers south of the river were understandably apprehensive. They pressed a series of suits against the company for continuing to sell water rights when the company's supply had been exhausted. In 1909, the courts began to rank more than four thousand individual rights to the Snake River so that control of the canal could be transferred to the farmers.[44]

In 1905, project residents formed a union to negotiate with the Twin Falls Land and Water Company, but many farmers refused to join. Lawyers, businessmen, and nonresident landowners dominated the organization, and they had little knowledge of agriculture. Farmers suspected their motives, and the company quickly targeted the leaders. For example, in 1906, F. D. Kimball, the manager of a Twin Falls bank, protested to the Idaho Land Board that it should not transfer control over the canal until the farmers were satisfied that the company had met its obligations. In private correspondence, the secretary of the Twin Falls Land and Water Company reported that "to retaliate I withdrew all our deposits [in Kimball's bank] and will henceforth, unless his attitude is fairer and more just, give him no further business. He is simply playing politics and at [the] present writing is extremely sorry he took the action he did." Farmer or businessman, those who opposed the company faced serious economic reprisals.[45]

The settlers themselves were deeply divided among those who resided on the land and irrigated, those who dry-farmed rather than pay the expense of grading, furrowing, and digging ditches, and those who simply speculated. There was also friction among those who were the first to take up land on the project and those who came later, those who lived near the head of a lateral canal—and diverted as much water as they wanted—and those who farmed land near the end of the lateral, and between those who resided on farms or in town. The settlers' union was neither representative nor effective.[46]

THE MINIDOKA PROJECT

In 1890, the U.S. Geological Survey investigated potential irrigation projects in Idaho, including what would become the Reclamation Service's Minidoka Project, fifty miles east of Twin Falls. In the words of one USGS official, "the possibilities of storage are vast, far exceeding that of any other known river in the West, and . . . the cost [of irrigation], though absolutely considerable, will be small relatively [sic] to the value of the stored water." Government engineers also inspected the land around what would become Twin Falls, but they considered it isolated and inaccessible.[47]

The Snake River Valley attracted the Reclamation Service for several reasons: the river carried a large volume of water, there were few established water rights, and most land adjoining the stream remained part of the public domain. At the end of 1902, the secretary of the interior withdrew from entry a huge block of public land along the Snake River, and Minidoka Project surveys began in March 1903, in the same month that construction began on the Twin Falls Project. The secretary approved the project in April 1904 and set aside $2.6 million to pay for construction. The *estimated* cost of watering land within reach of the planned gravity canal averaged thirteen dollars an acre. By the time the project opened, that amount had increased to twenty-two dollars an acre—still three dollars cheaper than the charge on the Twin Falls South Side Project. The original project was smaller than government engineers had wanted—only one-third the size of the Twin Falls South Side Project—but the Reclamation Service forged ahead for two reasons. The spread of Carey Act projects downstream made it imperative for the federal government to launch a project as soon as possible—or run the risk of losing out entirely as private companies claimed all the water in the Snake River. Equally important, power companies wanted to use the river to generate electricity. The Reclamation Service demanded sufficient water to irrigate 180,000 acres, but the United States had no special water rights and no way to reserve water for anticipated future needs.[48]

The secretary of the interior set the size of most Minidoka Project farms at eighty acres, but those within a half mile of project towns were forty acres. As on other government projects, settlers took up land long before the construction of dams and canals began. The first filings were made in May 1904, and by the end of 1904 most of the public land had been claimed, including thousands of acres *south* of the river, beyond reach of the planned gravity canal. Eventually, government engineers promised, the diversion dam planned for the Minidoka Rapids, ten miles east of the town of Rupert, would develop sufficient power to pump water onto fifty thousand acres south of the river at a cost of only $17.47 per acre. At the end of 1905, the *Rupert Record* reported, "Every acre of desirable land on the north side of the river has been taken, and a great deal on the south side, but some of it is being held by people from whom relinquishments can be secured, and again some has been abandoned and is subject to refiling. Homes can yet be secured here." Tar-paper "squatters' shacks"—erected to conform to the Homestead Act, which governed entries on federal reclamation projects—dotted the countryside.[49]

In 1905 and 1906, harsh winters slowed work on the diversion dam, and farmers received no water from the gravity canal until 1907—three years after the first settlers arrived. Meanwhile, the Reclamation Service tabled plans to pump water onto land south of the river—much of which had been occupied in the months after the project was announced. The Minidoka Project competed for funds with the government's Boise-Payette Project, near the western border of Idaho. At the beginning of 1906, the secretary of the interior transferred $1.3 million from the Minidoka account to the Payette account, which prevented the government from constructing the Minidoka pump system. The shortage of funds also forced the Reclamation Service to cut construction costs. Rather than carry water to each homestead, for example, the service constructed distribution canals to within a mile and a half of each farm, leaving the farmers to do the rest of the work.[50]

Government circulars and pamphlets described the Minidoka Project as level, easy to clear, and capable of growing almost anything—from four cuttings of alfalfa a year to watermelons, peanuts, and sweet potatoes. But making a home on the Minidoka Project demanded hard work, patience, and endurance. Sagebrush from two to six feet high covered the land, and loose volcanic rock had to be cleared before plowing. Water was often two hundred to three hundred feet below the surface, and few settlers could afford to dig deep wells. They hauled water from Rupert in barrels for stock, gardens, and domestic purposes. Lumber was equally scarce, and some farmers used old railroad ties as fence posts. Tar-paper shacks offered little protection from the cold and wind, and many of the earliest settlers ate a steady diet of beans and jackrabbits. Some sold coyote, badger, or bobcat pelts, but most sought work off the land, helping to build and maintain local railroads (particularly the Oregon Short Line), erecting the Minidoka Dam, laying out the first roads, or excavating ditches in the Twin Falls region. The pioneers suffered countless hardships, from heavy winds that blew crops out of the ground, to dust storms, to swarms of flying red ants, to rabbits that ate crops and girdled young trees, to disease, malnutrition, poverty, and chronic hunger—if not starvation.[51]

Like any frontier newspaper, the *Rupert Record* emphasized progress, particularly the passing of the wilderness. In October 1905, the editor proclaimed a new day:

> The change has been so great and so swift that those whose eyes have not been trained upon this section of the state have absolutely no conception of what is going on here. Where a few months ago stood nothing but sage brush and the only sounds greeting the ear was *[sic]* the lonely cry of the coyote as he doled out his mournful tune from the fastnesses and solitude of the centuries past, now shrieks the locomotive's whistle in accompaniment to the song of the saw and the hammer, a spirit of real life animates the soul and farm houses are dotted everywhere in anticipation of the fulfillment of the government promise to supply the land with water, and at convenient points for the centralization of trade towns have sprung up like magic, and the scene is one delightful to behold.[52]

The principal advantage of the government project, according to the *Caldwell Tribune*, was that the construction work would be done "for all time":

> There will be no temporary structures, no makeshifts; there will be no breaking away of dams, no washouts, no sidebill sloughs. When the spring comes and the full heads [of water] are turned into the great canals, the flow will be constant to the end of the season. What a country this will be when this vast system of works is completed, and the development of the thousands of new farms is begun! Then will come the building of new homes, the erection of churches and school houses, the spring up of hamlets, the inauguration of new industries—all the life and activities of a great and prosperous community.[53]

These exuberant hopes quickly dissipated. The first crisis came over the construction of sublateral canals. Settlers on the Minidoka Project had the same expectation as settlers on the Twin Falls South Side Project: that ditches would be constructed to the edge of individual farms. But the transfer of money to the Boise-Payette Project, and higher than expected construction costs, forced the farmers to dig their own sublaterals. They pleaded that they had neither the time nor money to bear this additional burden when they lacked a steady income and were preparing their land for cultivation. How could they plant crops and excavate ditches at the same time?[54]

In June 1907, the project consisted of 1,211 farms. The Reclamation Service could provide water to more than 80 percent of them, but little more than 40 percent were ready to receive it. Project residents irrigated only 15,000 acres in 1907 and 24,500 in 1908. Many waited three years for water, because of the delay in constructing sublaterals. They implored the secretary of the interior to bring water to the edge of their farms and provide credits against construction charges for those who did the work themselves. Unfortunately, the farmers lacked the engineering skills to excavate reliable ditches. The flimsy banks washed out repeatedly, wasting water and creating stagnant ponds and other drainage problems. Therefore, the Reclamation Service was forced to rebuild many of the smaller ditches at its own expense.[55]

In March 1907, the secretary of the interior announced that the first of ten payments would be due at the end of that year. But the Reclamation Service did not finish installing headgates on the ditches until the late spring and summer, and farmers who planted crops in anticipation of being able to irrigate suffered heavy losses. At a mass meeting held in Rupert on September 7, 1907, the farmers asked the Reclamation Service to postpone the first construction payment a year, but project manager and former state engineer D. W. Ross refused. The delay had not been the government's fault, according to Ross. Labor shortages and a rapid increase in the cost of building materials had been unavoidable. After December 1, 1907, Ross noted, every new applicant for project land would be required to make the first payment *on entry*, regardless of whether the land had received water in 1907 or not. And since the Reclamation Service had decided that no entry would be cancelled until *two* payments had been missed, the first installment would not be overdue until December 1908, at which time any farmer who chose to make two payments would be right on schedule. Further delay in payments would play into the hands of speculators, and the Reclamation Service would have no money to build the pumping plant or drainage ditches, or to improve project towns, until farmers began to repay their debt to the government.[56]

Reclamation Service officials showed little sympathy for the settlers. The Minidoka Project's per-acre construction charge was the lowest of any federal reclamation scheme, and Minidoka was the only project on which farmers had been permitted to raise a full crop before making their first payment. Reclamation Service director Frederick H. Newell observed that "the settlers went upon these lands in the face of definite notice that water could not be furnished for a considerable time. They took the risk." Many of the first wave were not farmers, according to Newell, and had no right to the land. It might be "hard-hearted . . . to turn out the first man," Newell noted, "but the second man is just as deserving of aid from the Government as the first one."[57]

For project farmers, 1908 was no brighter than 1907. The most popular crops—wheat, oats, and alfalfa—returned only a modest income. To make matters worse, the spring was windy and cold, and seed blew out of the sandy soil as fast as it could be planted. As the year closed, between 20 and 25 percent of settlers had fallen behind in their payments to the government. The figure would have been far higher had the Reclamation Service not hired the farmers as construction workers and paid them in scrip called "cooperative certificates," which could be applied against their debt. By 1910, less than 10 percent of the total paid to the government was in cash.[58]

Building dams and canals was only part of the government's job. Maintaining them proved far more costly than the Reclamation Service had anticipated. In an attempt to limit speculation, the government imposed maintenance charges on *all* land that had been entered, not just that under cultivation (as at Twin Falls). Nevertheless, the per-acre charge increased from 40 cents in 1908—less than 20 percent of the annual payment for construction and half the maintenance charge on the Twin Falls South Side Project—to 60 cents in 1909, to 75 cents in 1910, and to $1.75 in 1911. Government engineers pleaded that they could not have anticipated the buildup of alkali in the soil, the need for drainage to prevent pools of wastewater, or the large increase in the cost of labor and materials. Nevertheless, the farmers considered such cost increases deceitful and unwarranted. They argued that since the construction debt was fixed by contract, the Reclamation Service used maintenance charges, which were adjusted annually, to cover unanticipated *construction* costs.[59]

A host of other grievances alienated Minidoka settlers from the government. For one, they considered the project demonstration farm an unnecessary extravagance. In March 1906, long before the demonstration farm had been cultivated, the *Rupert Record* observed, "Probably one half of the settlers on this project never saw an irrigation ditch until they came here. Fully three-fourths of them are without practical experience or knowledge of the subject of preparing the land and laying out the ditches so that water can be carried over their claims. If the government were in a position to furnish water today they would not know what to do with it. They are unfamiliar with agricultural conditions in this region and do not know what crops will be most profitable under these particular conditions."[60] Clearly, a model farm would have been helpful. At first, the Reclamation Service pleaded that it had no money to establish one. Finally, at the insistence of the project manager, the service in 1910 sowed fifty acres to alfalfa and various experimental crops. But by that time, the farmers were already self-educated, and as the project's historian, P. M. Fogg, remarked: "There appeared to be an entire lack of interest on the part of the farmers as to the results secured in this work[,] and the following spring, operations were discontinued."[61]

This barely scratches the surface of the mountain of complaints that had piled up by 1910 and 1911. Most farmers built shacks or cabins as symbols of possession. But few complied with the requirement that they take up residence on the land within six months of filing—that is, eat, sleep, and work continuously on their farm. In theory, living away from the land was cause for forfeiture, even if the land was cultivated.[62] Some farmers discovered that all or part of their land was too high to be irrigated from gravity ditches. Others found that their land was too low. After a few years of irrigation, poorly constructed canals and inadequate drainage turned some farms into swamps.[63] (Ultimately, the cost of drainage was assessed against the entire gravity project, not just the lands that needed it.) Government farmers expressed bitter disappointment when the Reclamation Service stopped issuing scrip in exchange for work in March 1909 (by which time more than two hundred thousand dollars in "cooperative certificates" had been issued, all of which were redeemed by 1912). And, finally, the settlers and Reclamation Service often battled over who should construct various public works within the project, such as roads and bridges over the main canals.[64]

The farmers shared responsibility for the turmoil on the Minidoka Project. They were not helpless victims of a remote, uncaring federal bureaucracy. As on the Twin Falls South Side Project, conflict among them was more apparent than cooperation. "At no time during the troubles on this project," the *Record* candidly observed in 1911, "has there been a unanimity of action or purpose. One section wants one thing and another wants something else and none seem willing to lay aside their own personal wants so that all can unite."[65] For example, the Snake River separated those farmers served by the gravity canal to the north and those who awaited a pump project to the south. The latter were the poorest on the project. In 1911, the Oregon Short Line provided them with twenty thousand dollars in seed and took mortgages on crops to ensure repayment. North-side farmers argued that the south-side settlers had been warned that they might not receive water for eight or ten years and, poor or not, had entered the land purely for speculative reasons. Those on the south side opposed project expenditures outside their district and consistently called for settlers on the north side to make construction payments on time. Since Idaho returned little to the Reclamation Fund from the sale of government land, all money likely to be spent on a pump project had to come from payments made by farmers on the Minidoka and Boise-Payette projects.[66]

Unlike the Twin Falls Land and Water Company, the Reclamation Service encouraged the formation of water users' associations to provide a forum to discuss common problems, a collection agency to guarantee the payment of construction and maintenance charges, and, eventually, a set of leaders who could supervise the transfer of control over hydraulic works from the government to the settlers. On some government projects, these organizations also supervised the allocation of water and acted as boards of arbitration to settle disputes among individual irrigators. Yet attempts to form a water users' association on the Minidoka Project failed. Membership and dues had to be mandatory so that collective decisions had the force of law, and so that money could be raised to pay lawyers, engineers, and watermasters. But Minidoka Project residents refused to make dues a lien on project land. Most already carried a heavy debt, and they feared that one faction would dominate the organization to the detriment of others. Moreover, while the Socialist Party did not exist in Twin Falls, it was strong on the Minidoka Project, and the socialists argued that the federal government should pay the entire cost of reclamation, including the expenses of the farmers' union. The Reclamation Service, not surprisingly, ignored this demand.[67]

RUPERT: THE GOVERNMENT TOWN

Irrigation promoters had powerful incentives to develop urban as well as rural land, to boost the price of farms adjoining the town, to sell town lots, and to provide markets. The *Rupert Record* put it well: "Build up a few thriving towns on the tract, accessible from every side and not more than six to ten miles distant from any point, and every farm on the tract will be enhanced in valuation from double to ten times its present value, owing to the nearness of the location to the trade center; kill the towns, take them away, and your farm values will never be any higher here than are the values of other remote settlements where distance from marketing centers renders their farms well nigh valueless except for raising stock." But how many towns was too many? In the relentless competition for residents, businesses, and the trade of the countryside, promoters inevitably thought big, setting the stage for intense conflicts among towns and between those towns and their hinterlands.[68]

The Reclamation Service initially touted Heyburn, a rail stop on the Snake River, as the Minidoka Project's leading city. Not surprisingly, the *Rupert Record* eagerly pointed out Heyburn's inadequacies and failures. When the first Heyburn town lots went on sale in August 1906, the *Record* covered the event. Four people attended the auction: three local farmers and a visitor from Twin Falls. Not a single buyer lived outside the community; the only bids came from local businessmen. "And this was the vaunted City of Destiny!" the *Record* crowed. "The future metropolis, 'Where rail and river meet!' The town touted by the reclamation officials at Washington as the real thing, the only town on the Minidoka project."[69] Subsequently, the Reclamation Service situated its headquarters at Rupert, at the geographical center of the project, and Rupert became the project's construction and supply depot. By 1911, a bridge across the Snake River east of town made it the only project settlement with easy access to Cassia County, across the river.[70]

Residents of frontier towns assumed that economic development followed a predictable pattern. The *Record*'s editor observed at the end of December 1905:

> Only a short time ago, less than 18 months, this entire country was but a stock range. . . . Then came the railroad [the Oregon Short Line] and the telegraph, next farm houses began to dote *[sic]* the homesteads of the entrymen, then followed the business men headed by that stalwart pioneer, W. N. Shilling and his son as the Rupert Mercantile Co., and on the 2d of May, 1905, commenced selling goods. They were immediately followed by John Vincent and C. C. Lorentz with restaurants, and the building up of a town was on. Lumber yards and hardware establishments and every other conceivable line followed in rapid succession like a panorama passing before the eye, until now there is scarcely no line left unrepresented here, and more business concerns coming every week.

In the same December issue, a banner that splashed across four columns proclaimed: "Rupert, The City of Destiny. Eight months ago a sagebrush plain, inhabited only by coyotes and long-eared jacks [rabbits]; now, at the close of eight months, a city of 400 inhabitants, a school of a hundred scholars, a business aggregation of 64 concerns, an opera house, two secret orders, a Methodist church, a Sunday school, a lawyer to get the people out of trouble, a dentist to keep the 'grinders' in shape, a doctor to cure the people of their ills and a glorious future that no man can doubt."[71]

Rupert was a government town just as Twin Falls was a company town. Carved out of the public domain, the townsite covered 320 acres. In the fall of 1905, the General Land Office surveyed both Rupert and Heyburn, but Rupert lots did not go on sale until a year later. Therefore, those who established homes and businesses in Rupert in 1905 and most of 1906 were technically squatters, and the original lot occupants enjoyed no preemptive right from the federal government. To limit speculation, the secretary of the interior set lot prices relatively high, demanded that buyers pay the entire cost at once, and sold the land at auctions spread over several years. Residential lots sold for a minimum of a hundred dollars, corner lots in the business district for seven hundred dollars. By the end of 1907, 371 lots had been appraised, but only 128 had been sold—at an average of four hundred dollars per parcel. The last were not put on the market until April 1910, when seven hundred lots covering two hundred acres went on sale at much reduced prices ranging from twenty-five to seventy-five dollars.[72] An early project resident recounted that even residential lots sold during the first auction remained vacant for many years: "Lots of people bought lots to speculate but there was a period of time when people were not building on the lots so a great many of the lots went back for taxes and a few people made money out of it because they bought the tax deeds and made a good profit. The lot I bought myself later on and the man that bought it he got it for about $50 for back taxes and I paid him $150 for it. And I bought a few lots and I let 'em go for taxes because there wasn't any building going on."[73]

For years the Rupert townsite was little more than a sagebrush and weed-infested public pasture, and at one time the city government offered twenty-five cents for each head of loose livestock driven to the pound. In an attempt to profit from the "unearned increment," the Interior Department withheld lots from sale in the hope that completion of the irrigation project would drive up their value. But the requirement that government farmers live on their homesteads reduced the demand for residential property, as it limited interest in civic affairs. Rupert's tax revenue suffered, along with its public services. Local businessmen refused to make substantial improvements be-cause they ran the risk of being outbid when the lots they occupied went on sale. The *Record* saw no harm in town lot speculation, because most of the profits would stay within the community. It was unjust, the editor reasoned, to give homesteaders free land but fix the price of town lots artificially high. Both the town and the farms that surrounded it had been carved out of the public domain, and setting the price of town lots too high would deprive farmers of an important source of capital.[74]

Hostility toward the lot-sale policy would have been greater had local res-idents not expected the government to use at least part of the proceeds to provide Rupert with essential public services, helping to keep taxes low. If the Reclamation Service laid water mains, constructed sewers, and built schools, then the value of privately owed land would soar, and everyone would gain.[75] The Reclamation Service drafted many townsite bills, but few surfaced in Congress. Most permitted "squatters" who erected permanent buildings to purchase lots at a price determined in advance by the secretary of the in-terior rather than face the uncertainty of a bidding war at the auction. Some of them applied to all government townsites, others only to Rupert and Heyburn. Some called for payment in cash, others in ten or even twenty in-stallments. Some pledged all revenue from lot sales to public improvements, others as little as 20 percent. Congress ignored the Reclamation Service's suggestions.[76]

Reserving money from lot sales to pay for basic services won little support outside a few project towns. To permit the federal government to build schools or sanitation systems would increase the Reclamation Service's power vis-à-vis the states, threatening home rule and local autonomy. The states, not the federal government, should determine educational policy. Once the schools had been completed, federal agencies would be tempted to meddle in the curriculum, and if the central government could construct educational institutions, it could build anything. Moreover, model govern-ment communities would constitute intolerable favoritism and paternalism. As Senator Jacob Gallinger of New Hampshire put it on the floor of the Sen-ate in 1908: "[I]t seems to me rather remarkable that . . . we should proceed to divert a portion of the money [from the reclamation fund] to build up towns and give people all the benefits that other people enjoy after they have earned their money. . . . I have in mind some communities in New England, where they are struggling to get a living on farms that are mostly rocks, that would be glad to have the Government step in and build schoolhouses and sewers for them and make them as comfortable as the people are out on the prairies of the West; but we have never thought that we had a right to come to Congress and ask for help of that kind."[77]

Rupert's dreary appearance—in notable contrast to that of Twin Falls—was in large part due to the Reclamation Service's lack of money to grade streets and plant trees, let alone to build domestic water and sanitation systems. Only after the government sold the last of the town lots did voters bond themselves for public improvements.[78] "Government promotion of townsites has proved to be a failure," the *Record* candidly observed in 1908, "owing to the inexperience of public officials in these matters and the many red tape restrictions which surround them. These government towns have made practically no progress, while towns handled by private enterprise on adjacent tracts [i.e., Twin Falls] have advanced by leaps and bounds."[79] It should also be said, however, that Minidoka farmers opposed the application of proceeds from town lot sales to public improvements. Instead, they supported those in Congress who asked that all lots sell at the highest price possible, with the proceeds paid into the reclamation fund. The reclamation fund should be used to construct irrigation works, not model towns.[80]

In 1906, Rupert's budget totaled $2,820: $1,500 for the village waterworks; $820 for the salaries of city officials and employees; $100 for police and fire protection; $100 for the maintenance of streets, alleys, and parks; and $300 in contingency expenses. As in Twin Falls, the town relied heavily on licenses and fees. Liquor licenses paid a large share of the cost of education. Schools got half of all proceeds from that source, and the income it brought in doubled between 1906 and 1908. In the latter year, saloon owners paid $300 for a village license and an additional $700 for a state and county permit. A $2 village poll tax, payable in cash or labor, went to improving the streets. Merchants paid $5 to $100 a year for business licenses, the amount determined by the capital they had invested. To some extent, county taxes compensated for the lack of municipal revenue. Minidoka County's biggest taxpayer was the Oregon Short Line, which shouldered two-thirds of the tax burden. In 1909, the *Record* noted that the railroad "is building more school houses and contributing more to the support of the schools than all other property owners combined. Of course the people 'pay the freight' and it is their own money that comes back to them. Still, it must be said of the Short Line that it is a cheerful taxpayer and chips in its share without a grumble."[81]

Direct taxes were seldom used, but, as in Twin Falls, task-oriented subscriptions were common. In 1908, fourteen businesses pledged five dollars apiece to grade the public square, plant grass on it, and erect a bandstand. When town leaders called for cement sidewalks on the four blocks that fronted the square, an improvement district was created—with power to tax only that property adjoining the sidewalks. Similarly, when streets required grading, the residents of those streets joined together to raise the money. Rarely did the entire community donate to a project.[82]

Not all public services could be funded through subscription. For example, initially each property owner was responsible for his or her own fire protection. In 1907, Rupert voters approved a bond issue of $250 to erect a fifteen-thousand-gallon water tower in the business district, but for many years the town relied on bucket brigades rather than a fire company. In 1910, a conflagration destroyed the Ferry Lumber Company. It began in a blacksmith shop separated from the lumber yard by a vacant lot covered with dry weeds. (The mayor and county Board of Health had frequently urged property owners to remove sagebrush, weeds, and debris from their property, but with little result.) The fire did not inspire the town to create a fire department. Instead, several businesses installed pump systems on their property—at a cost of fifty dollars apiece. The fire also prompted a campaign to sell the public park at the center of town and use the proceeds to pay for a domestic water system and a twenty-six-hundred-dollar fire engine. It took Rupert eight years to create a police department and ten to create a fire department.[83]

In 1905, the Reclamation Service drilled a well in the public square to furnish water for stock. For many settlers, however, it was the only source of water other than the Snake River, several miles from town. "It was no unusual thing to see teams with wagons lined up for a block," the *Minidoka County News* recounted years later, "women drivers of course, waiting for the chance to pump water by hand to take home in a barrel. The men folks at that time were working on the canals trying to earn money to develop their claims." In September 1905, Rupert residents raised sufficient money to purchase a gasoline engine to pump water from the well into a five-thousand-gallon storage tank. At first the water was free, but a year later it became necessary to charge at the pump to maintain the system. The Reclamation Service offered to provide domestic water to the city if each lot owner bore a proportionate share of the expense; most refused. Not until 1913 did work begin on a city water system, and not until 1917 did the city begin constructing a sewer system.[84]

Schools were a community's most powerful advertisement, as the promoters of the Twin Falls South Side Project realized. Twin Falls established a unified school district and used wagons to transport children from farms to schools in town. This system permitted graded education, expanded taxable property, increased the allegiance of farm families to urban institutions, and unified city and hinterland. By contrast, small, poor, and independent school districts characterized Rupert's educational system—along with widely scattered one-room shacks, ungraded classes, and poorly paid teachers. Therefore, Rupert was no more the educational center of Minidoka County than were its principal rivals: Heyburn, Burley, and Minidoka. In 1905 and 1906, the town's children attended classes in churches, the opera house, and the Odd Fellows Hall. The town's first school building went up in 1907, but it was too small to accommodate more than grades one and two. The school board appealed to the Reclamation Service for help, but Congress balked. The *Record,* nevertheless, continued to push for consolidated schools. "Under the central school system all could have the benefit of fine graded schools, with a school year of nine months," the newspaper observed in February 1909. "All progressive communities have adopted this system and we must come to it in time. It is easier to do it now than after permanent school buildings have been erected,"[85]

In 1909, Rupert voters bonded the Rupert School District to the maximum limit, twelve thousand dollars, to erect a new schoolhouse. The building— designed by Twin Falls architect C. Harvey Smith—consisted of two stories with eight rooms and an assembly hall. "It is a common occurrence for a new-comer to state that our school largely influenced him to cast his lot here," the *Record* reported in November 1910. "Who can say just how much it had to do with the rapid growth in this part of the project?" Nevertheless, the *Record* continued to complain about insufficient desks, inadequate supplies, and too few teachers. Rupert did not erect its own high school until 1914.[86]

The *Record* blamed the federal government for the town's problems. But those who settled the Minidoka Project were different from those who settled Twin Falls. Affluent settlers bypassed the government project and town. In 1909, Idaho's state engineer noted, "The majority of the settlers who file upon Carey Act lands come from the irrigated districts of Oregon, Washington, Colorado, and Montana. The following Central States also furnish a large number of settlers: Kansas, Nebraska, Iowa, North Dakota, South Dakota, and Illinois." The Minidoka Project drew farmers from the same states, but it also attracted a substantial number of impoverished recent immigrants to the United States—including Greeks, Italians, Russians, Irish, and Spaniards—who came to build canals or the Oregon Short Line and stayed to take up homesteads.[87]

Ethnic diversity made it more difficult for Rupert residents to organize. In November 1906, the *Record* reported that the Twin Falls Commercial Club counted seventy-three members and $524 in its treasury, while the Rupert Commercial Club had trouble getting a quorum for meetings and was likely to disband. Businessmen dominated the economic life of both towns, but Twin Falls' farmers had more friends in the business community, in part because many rural landowners not only owned property in town, but lived there. Twin Falls boosters promoted the unity of city and country because they had invested in both. In most agricultural towns, commercial clubs included farmers as well as merchants. Rupert's club consisted entirely of businessmen—in part because project farmers were too poor to afford the monthly dues of $1.50. The gulf between Rupert's farmers and merchants was all too apparent when its commercial club attempted to encourage the construction of an alfalfa mill. The prospective builder demanded a guaranteed supply of at least ten thousand tons of alfalfa before he was willing to erect the mill. The farms within four miles of town produced at least three times that amount, but the Rupert Commercial Club failed to secure the necessary contracts: project farmers preferred to bargain on their own and did not trust the club to represent their interests.[88]

PRIVATE ENTERPRISE AND FEDERAL RECLAMATION

In the first two decades of the twentieth century, Idaho's proportion of irrigated land increased by 400 percent, the largest percentage increase of any western state. In the Snake River Valley, the irrigation boom helped build a string of towns from Boise to Pocatello. Carey Act projects had lured fifty thousand people into Idaho, a massive number in a state whose total population was smaller than Denver's. In 1925, only two Idaho towns contained more than ten thousand people—Boise, with twenty-one thousand, and Pocatello, with fifteen thousand—and they were but larger versions of Twin Falls and Rupert. The six Snake River counties that benefited most from irrigation—Twin Falls, Cassia, Gooding, Lincoln, Jerome, and Minidoka—increased in population from fifty-seven hundred in 1900 to seventy thousand in 1920, and in irrigated acreage from forty thousand in 1900 to more than six hundred thousand in 1920.[89]

The Carey Act served thinly populated states like Idaho and Wyoming well. The irrigation district—an institution first used extensively in California—better suited relatively densely populated parts of the West. It was the most efficient way to consolidate small, inefficient delivery systems into larger units. And since it bonded both irrigated and unirrigated land to raise the money to build dams and canals, it avoided the injustice of levying all or most taxes on farmers just getting started. By imposing a uniform tax, and using the land as collateral for the bonds, it discouraged speculation and enabled districts to borrow money at lower interest rates than private reclamation projects could. Finally, the creation of an irrigation district *forced* farmers to organize, elect a board of directors, and participate in their own governance. Thirty irrigation districts were formed in Idaho between 1899 and 1916, but few if any were formed to construct new dams and canals.[90]

State officials exercised little effective control over Carey Act projects. From 1909 to 1919, California expanded state supervision over irrigation and demanded greater accountability from corporations that provided water to the public.[91] But Idaho's Carey Act projects were free enterprise dressed in new clothes, not a partnership between private enterprise and government. Idaho took little responsibility for companies that failed to honor contracts with land buyers. It put up no money, nor did it create the bureaucracy needed to investigate the health of private water companies, the availability of water, or the fairness of charges for water rights. Not until 1917 did Idaho assume regulatory control over water companies, and by that time the irrigation boom had abated.[92]

The Twin Falls *North* Side Project exemplified the failure of state supervision. Pittsburgh capitalist William Kuhn so dominated Idaho's State Land Board that the board not only granted his initial request for 185,000 acres, but added an additional 100,000 acres even before the irrigation works were completed. The sale of water rights promised Kuhn and associates from $8.6 million to $12.8 million—three to six times the cost of the project. The board accepted Kuhn's engineering plans on faith, along with his wildly optimistic estimates of the available water supply. The first drawing for land on the North Side Project yielded more than $2 million, nearly the cost of construction.[93]

Before 1909 or 1910, public criticism of Carey Act promoters was rare. Kuhn and his associates dismissed the law's detractors as stockmen who opposed reclamation on principle, or as friends of federal reclamation who wanted to torpedo the North Side project so that the government could take it over. As long as North Side settlers who purchased the land reaped speculative profits along with the Kuhn syndicate, the fact that Carey Act water rights more than doubled in price between 1905 and 1910 seemed almost irrelevant. Only when the tide of new settlers began to abate did criticism mount. Short of water and settlers, the Twin Falls North Side Project never produced the profits of the Twin Falls South Side Project, as many investors learned the hard way.[94]

From 1894 to 1922, the secretary of the interior withdrew nearly 4 million acres from the public domain under the Carey Act. Only 1 million acres were patented, most of which were in Idaho and Wyoming. The projects created many new farms, but only one in twenty of these projects returned a profit to investors. In 1912, the secretary appointed a committee to investigate the Carey Act projects. The committee concluded that those ventures suffered from the same problems that had plagued virtually all irrigation enterprises in the past, private or public. The companies promised more water than they could deliver, promoters underestimated the cost of irrigation works, and state officials did little to supervise construction or settlement. By 1913, Idaho irrigation bonds sold at such a steep discount that the cost of borrowing money was far higher than the 6 percent interest the bonds usually carried. The construction of reclamation projects had become so expensive that neither the government nor private enterprise could break even unless the project produced high-value crops and generated electrical power.[95]

Carey Act boosters argued that federal reclamation should be restricted to projects beyond the reach of private capital. But the Reclamation Service launched the Minidoka Project as a direct challenge to the Twin Falls South Side Project—as a testament to the superiority of government planning and engineering. The service filed for far more land and water than it could use— 3 million acres in Idaho alone. The Minidoka Project blocked a private company's preliminary plan to water the same land under the Carey Act, and the Reclamation Service attempted unsuccessfully to reserve the Twin Falls townsite from entry *after* the Twin Falls Land and Water Company began to sell lots.[96] Not surprisingly, the leading Twin Falls newspaper painted the Reclamation Service in the darkest colors. "The reclamation service . . . has hampered legitimate private enterprise," the *Twin Falls News* observed in 1907. "The Minidoka south side project is a disgrace to the administration. Newell is a failure. He has done his utmost to harm Carey act projects and the west owes him a grudge which it will pay some day when the reclamation service gets its due. . . . Granny Newell will eventually get what is coming to him."[97]

Within a decade of their creation, however, the line between government and private projects in the Snake Valley began to blur. Drought and chronic water shortages forced Minidoka and Twin Falls South Side farmers to join together to build new storage reservoirs and to adjudicate Snake River water rights. The Warren Act (1911) permitted the Reclamation Service to sell surplus water to farmers *outside* federal projects. Therefore, the federal government contracted with Carey Act promoters and Twin Falls farmers to enlarge the dam at the outlet of Jackson Lake, at the headwaters of the Snake River, which was completed in 1916. Subsequently, the government built more dams that served both private and public projects, including the American Falls Dam (1925–27) and the Upper Snake River Storage Project (1935–39). These watered nearly a million acres of private land, many times the number of acres within the Minidoka Project. The most significant addition to the Minidoka Project, the Gooding Division, which opened at the end of the 1920s, served only eighteen thousand acres of public land. The Twin Falls North Side Project could not have been opened without this additional water. Ironically, dams built by the Reclamation Service eventually contributed more to the growth of the Twin Falls region than to the Minidoka region.[98]

Expenditures on the Twin Falls South Side Project and the first phase of the Minidoka Project were comparable. The Minidoka Project cost 50 percent more per acre, but the government project added the cost of storage and drainage to the per-acre reclamation cost. It was more expensive, but not because government work was poorly planned or inherently more costly. The government project attracted many virtually penniless settlers who believed the General Land Office when it predicted in July 1904 that the cost of government reclamation would be as little as twelve dollars an acre—about half the charge at Twin Falls.[99]

The General Land Office, not the Reclamation Service, supervised land claims within the first federal reclamation projects. The Reclamation Act, it decided, did not require the federal government to screen entrants according to their likelihood of succeeding. The land office assumed that everyone should have an equal chance to secure government land. Carey Act settlers had money to gamble, on both urban and rural real estate. As a rule, Carey Act promoters built hydraulic works more quickly than the government because they could not collect from the farmers until the work was finished. Moreover, while the Reclamation Act of 1902 required five years' continuous residence following entry, and half of each homestead had to be cultivated before a patent could be obtained, Carey Act farmers could secure title in a year or less. Equally important, they could sell or assign their entry right before final proof was made, and only one-eighth of the land had to be reclaimed. On government projects, even settlers willing to pay construction charges in one lump sum could not secure clear title in less than five years—the residency requirement stipulated in the Homestead Act of 1862—and in most cases it was ten or more. Meanwhile, the land could not be taxed, or used as collateral.

Initially, Rupert's leading newspaper lavishly praised the Minidoka Project. Dams and canals built by the government were more substantial than those built privately, it argued, and in the long run they were less costly to maintain. And since the Twin Falls Land and Water Company charged interest to those who paid for water rights on time, the *Record* predicted that the per-acre cost of reclamation at Twin Falls would run 30 percent higher than upstream around Rupert. Rupert and its hinterland, the editor maintained, would be better off without the speculation that prevailed at Twin Falls. The government town would grow slowly and steadily, immune to the boom-and-bust cycles that plagued most new agricultural districts. The Minidoka Project would attract and welcome the homemaker, not the large-scale gambler. In January 1907, the *Record* reported that there were few claims on the Minidoka Project available for sale, which it interpreted as evidence that "the settlers are here to make permanent homes and . . . they realize there is more money to be made in improving and holding their claims than in selling them."[100]

Within a few years of the project's opening, however, the *Record* had second thoughts. The absence of a speculative boom, it now reasoned, had *retarded* the project's growth. The residents of Twin Falls brought money with them, and they spent it, creating an initial wave of prosperity Rupert never experienced. For example, more than four hundred imposing homes were constructed in Twin Falls in 1908 alone—many with two stories and electricity. Twin Falls found it difficult to raise money to pay for public services, and its residents voiced the same complaints about the dictatorial policies of those who built water projects as the citizens of Rupert, but the similarities ended there. "The government requirements operate as a wet blanket on the speculative public," the *Record* observed in 1908, "and we have no organized publicity bureau to spend thousands of dollars in flooding the east with alluring advertisements. Few home seekers coming west have ever heard of the Minidoka project, and that is why they invest in less inviting fields at double the money it would cost here." Constraints that once seemed a blessing now appeared a curse: "it is quite possible to impose so many limitations, restrictions, and obligations that not only the speculator, but the bona fide settler as well, will take to the woods."[101]

In 1910, Rupert was a struggling village of about five hundred, tributary to 120,000 acres of cultivated land; Twin Falls contained more than five thousand people surrounded by nearly six hundred thousand acres of farmland. A 1910 state business directory referred to Rupert modestly as a "growing town," but characterized Twin Falls as a "favored city" with "all the modern city conveniences"—"a most desirable place for residence." By 1930, Twin Falls exhibited a flourishing chamber of commerce, Rotary Club, Kiwanis Club, Business Women's Club, Gun Club, chapters of the Masons, Eagles, Odd Fellows, and Elks, and "numerous other civil and patriotic societies." It was home to two daily newspapers, three modern hotels, two theaters, eleven garages, candy stores, jewelry stores, movie houses, a business college, and five up-to-date school buildings valued at more than eight hundred thousand dollars.[102]

By almost any measure, the promoters of the Twin Falls South Side Project did far more than the federal government to encourage settlement and a spirit of industry.[103] Surrounding towns bore the names of the capitalists who invested in the region's agricultural future, including Kimberley, Filer, and Buhl. Imposing brick structures quickly replaced Twin Falls' original false-front buildings—the wooden boxes characteristic of frontier towns. As a promotional pamphlet prepared by the Oregon Short Line noted in 1909: "It is but five years since the first temporary dwelling was erected on the sage-brush-covered tract whereon now stands the up-to-date thriving city of Twin Falls. With astonishing rapidity, these temporary structures have been replaced by handsome and well-constructed business blocks, until today it is questionable if any city of like population in the Pacific Northwest can boast of as handsome a residential area, as substantial and well-constructed a business district or any better features of civic life and progress."[104] Several years later, a booster publication applauded the "high type of citizenship" in the Twin Falls region. "The majority of the settlers are from the Eastern and Middle West states," it observed, "and there are over three hundred college graduates engaged in irrigated farming on the Twin Falls tract. The piano, automobile, daily newspaper, electric light and heat, telephone and other similar present day conveniences are deemed a necessary part of the equipment for the Twin Falls farmer."[105]

A cursory reading of the 1930 census confirms the anecdotal evidence. In that year, Twin Falls County contained a population 3.6 times larger than Minidoka County's. Its farmland and buildings were worth six times the same property in Minidoka County; its crops were worth five times as much, and the cropped acreage was four times greater. Wealth and productivity are only two measures of prosperity; they tell us little or nothing about the quality of life of the 29,828 people who resided in Twin Falls County and the 8,403 who resided forty or fifty miles upstream in Minidoka County. But such indices do suggest that the economic advantages Twin Falls enjoyed from the beginning of its life were hard for rival communities to overcome.[106]

CONCLUSION

As noted in chapter 1, the popular writer and publicist William Ellsworth Smythe thought that irrigation would transform the West from a backward region into a model society characterized by small towns, a large middle class, and uniquely democratic institutions. Irrigation would bridge the gulf between the haphazard nineteenth-century society built on individualism and self-interest and a planned society characterized by cooperation and interdependence.[107]

Irrigation was never the panacea Smythe promised, as the history of Twin Falls and Rupert demonstrate. Nevertheless, it helped shape rural economies as well as western communities. In his classic study of Kansas cattle towns, Robert Dykstra observed a strong antagonism between town and country, and between commerce and agriculture. The typical cattle town, in his words, was "anxious to embrace local agriculture only when a more dynamic economic base failed to materialize." Yet Kansas is not a good model for the West as a whole. As a rule, irrigation farmers were *not* antagonistic to the development of towns or to their business community.[108]

Neither Twin Falls nor Rupert exhibited the sharp division between farmers, stockmen, and businessmen so evident in the cattle towns of Kansas. In Idaho, conflict *within* these groups was just as important as conflict among them. The city and countryside were connected in far more ways than in the older agricultural regions of the nation, and since irrigation demanded huge amounts of outside capital, it created leadership elites whose interests were no more synonymous with local businessmen than they were with local farmers. In Rupert, that faction consisted of government bureaucrats; in Twin Falls, it was the officers of the Twin Falls Land and Water Company.

Early in their lives, Twin Falls and Rupert were *less,* not more, democratic than towns in other parts of the nation. Initially, at least, irrigation *discouraged* cooperation and the formation of voluntary organizations. The sociologist John Walton examined California's Owens Valley—a region highly dependent on irrigation—and found voluntarism everywhere, from vigilantism to the construction of schools and roads. He concluded that "rudimentary institutions of local government were constrained less by individualism or aversion to social restraint than by the sheer cost of public services in a cash-poor economy." Walton is right about the limited revenue available to frontier towns, but he does not draw enough distinctions among the kinds of "voluntarism" exhibited in small towns. Both Rupert and Twin Falls contained a wide variety of volunteer organizations, from literary guilds to fraternal orders to baseball teams and brass bands. Yet in both communities it took years for farmers to come together in cooperatives and water users' associations, and divisions among farmers profoundly affected the political and social life of the new towns.[109]

Twin Falls and Rupert began life during a period of unparalleled economic prosperity. But their leaders looked back to the 1890s and to a Midwest and West in which most towns died—those spawned by agriculture as well as those generated by mining, railroads, or the cattle and timber industries. The impermanence of western communities helps to explain irrigation's appeal, to speculators in rural land and to town builders alike. From the time Iowa became a territory, in 1838, until 1930, 2,205 towns and villages were abandoned within its boundaries, and Kansans saw more than 2,500 settlements deserted between 1852 and 1912. Mining towns suffered the most abrupt and precipitous decline; agricultural communities often clung to life for decades before fading away. Yet protracted wheat farming and extended droughts had an economic impact similar to the exhaustion of mines or forests.[110] Persistence rates are difficult to determine, because some communities changed their names or were disassembled and moved to new locations. But only half of all towns founded in the nineteenth-century West survive today, ranging from 33 percent in Montana to 75 percent in Utah. If irrigation produced more valuable crops, it also represented a "permanent" investment in the land. Dams and canals could not be moved, irrigated fields would produce their wealth forever, and the towns that depended on irrigation would persist.[111]

Ghost towns dotted the western landscape at the beginning of the twentieth century, towns that began life with the same high hopes as Twin Falls and Rupert. They symbolized blighted dreams as well as the impermanence of community. What westerners of the time longed for was not just a renewal of opportunity following the depression of the 1890s, but economic and social stability.

4

An Administrative Morass

Federal Reclamation, 1909–1917

During the presidency of Theodore Roosevelt (1901–09), the Reclamation Service led a charmed life. Most of its irrigation projects were planned or designed during Roosevelt's first term, but few were finished before he left office. The problems that were to plague federal reclamation over the next few decades did not become public until 1908 or 1909. Tension developed between advocates of centralized and local control and affected all facets of reclamation, from the selection of projects, to the awarding of construction contracts, to the creation of filing and bookkeeping systems. Like the Forest Service, the Reclamation Bureau attempted to insulate itself from public criticism by controlling the press. It did so effectively during Roosevelt's administration, but William Howard Taft's secretary of the interior, Richard A. Ballinger, considered the bureau independent, duplicitous, and recalcitrant, and so did Woodrow Wilson's interior secretary, Franklin K. Lane. By the second decade of the twentieth century, the administration of the Reclamation Bureau had fallen under heavy fire.

EARLY HISTORY OF THE RECLAMATION SERVICE

Federal reclamation suffered as much from the inexperience of its leaders as from their lack of vision and idealism, defects in the Reclamation Act of 1902, and conditions in the West. When the program began, Frederick Haynes Newell had never designed or supervised the construction of an irrigation project. He had measured streams and surveyed potential canals as a member of the U.S. Geological Survey's Irrigation Survey (1888–90), and after 1895 he headed that agency's Hydrographic Division. But he was a Washington bureaucrat with limited knowledge of the West and its political leaders. "If ten or twelve years' work gauging streams makes a civil engineer of a geologist and mining engineer," the editor of *Irrigation Age* observed, "we are greatly deceived as to the character of the apprenticeship under the Geological Survey." Newell craved flattery, according to *Irrigation Age,* and "surrounded himself with a coterie of men of more or less ability, but whose servility is pitiable and degrading."[1]

Indeed, *Irrigation Age* suggested that George Maxwell—the man most responsible for passage of the Reclamation Act—had favored Newell's appointment precisely because Newell *lacked* skill and experience. "It would be presumed that Mr. Maxwell would want a man at the head of the reclamation service who did not know too much about irrigation or engineering construction work. A man that was thoroughly qualified in such work would not be liable to take the advice of a professional lobbyist [working on behalf of the railroad], and Mr. Maxwell knew this when he published Mr. Newell's record far and wide during the spring of 1902 [prior to passage of the Reclamation Act]."[2]

Irrigation Age was only partly right. Newell secured control of the new program because the USGS exercised great power in Congress, because he was a prominent figure in various Washington scientific societies, and most important, because he had advised Theodore Roosevelt in conservation matters before T. R. became president. Newell's second-in-command, Arthur Powell Davis, also knew the right people: his uncle was the longtime director of the USGS, John Wesley Powell. Davis was from Kansas, but his education and administrative experience were distinctly eastern. He graduated from George Washington University (then Columbian College) in 1888, joined Powell's Irrigation Survey for two years, then headed the Geological Survey's topographic work in the southwestern United States. In the mid-1890s, Davis transferred to the agency's Hydrographic Division, where he joined Newell in measuring streams. He became chief engineer of the Reclamation Service in 1902 and oversaw the construction of many important dams, including the Roosevelt, Shoshone, and Arrowrock structures. His crowning achievement was locating the site and drafting some of the preliminary plans for Boulder Dam. He was a fellow of the American Geographical Society and a member of the Washington Academy of Sciences, the American Philosophical Society, and the American Academy of Political and Social Sciences. Both Newell and Davis eventually became well-respected engineers and leaders in civil engineering societies, but in 1902 many engineers had just as much administrative experience, and a greater knowledge of hydraulic engineering and irrigation agriculture.[3]

The historian Donald Jackson has shown that the inexperience of Newell and Davis had far-reaching consequences. The Reclamation Service used consulting boards to review its engineering plans. These boards consisted entirely of engineers, often easterners with little dam-building experience in the West. When it came time to plan the Salt River Project, for example,

Newell chose George Wisner to head the board and passed over James D. Schuyler, a former assistant state engineer in California who had designed the Sweetwater Dam, near San Diego, in the 1880s. A. P. Davis and W. H. Saunders completed the board. Wisner's experience, *Irrigation Age* pointed out, was limited to "sanitary engineering, harbor development, and water transportation on the Great Lakes and the Mississippi River."[4]

The Reclamation Service produced competent designs, but politics took precedence over innovation. For example, Roosevelt Dam, in Arizona, harked back to structures built in France as early as the mid-nineteenth century. It depended for stability on massive size, and it conveyed an image of durability and permanence. As the first major dam constructed by the federal government, and as one of the government's most visible monuments prior to the high dam era, public perception mattered more than technical innovation. "As reflected in his concern for monumentality in dam design," Jackson has observed, "Newell was driven to oversee the erection of huge structures that would visually testify to the power of his vision."[5] Solid dams conveyed the image of a solid bureau, and appearance counted for more than substance. After all, the Reclamation Service had to *sell* the public on federal reclamation, not just build safe dams.

In 1909, Newell observed that although the engineers who designed the bureau's dams considered cost, safety, and efficiency, the most important requirement was that the dams *look* durable to the public. "People must not merely be told that they are substantial," Newell wrote, "but when the plain citizen visits the works he must see for himself that there is every indication of the permanency and stability of a great storage dam. . . . [H]e must feel, to the very innermost recesses of his consciousness, that the structure is beyond question." Newell freely admitted that the Reclamation Service preferred "the older, more conservative type of solid [masonry] dam . . . because of the desire not only to have the works substantial but to have them appear so and recognized by the public."[6]

Some engineers feared gravity dams, which relied on their sheer mass and weight to keep them in place. If water eroded the foundation, such large structures could slide. But that danger counted for less than the overall impression such a structure conveyed, especially because photographs of notable dams and canals taken by Reclamation Service publicists appeared in newspapers and magazines across the country. The collapse of dams was common in the nineteenth and early twentieth centuries. In 1889, an earthen dam in the Little Conemaugh River Valley in southwestern Pennsylvania gave way, and the resulting flood killed more than twenty-two hundred people. That event, along with the reputation private water companies developed in the arid West for cutting corners in the construction of dams and canals, prompted widespread concern for public safety. The Reclamation Service sought to convince a wary public that its designs were more reliable than those used by engineers outside government—one of the many ways in which politics influenced engineering.[7]

Rarely was there one correct, "objective" dam design for a given locality. Indeed, the constant-angle arch dam of Lars Jorgensen, and the multiple-arch design of John S. Eastwood (introduced in 1908–9), had distinct advantages over the more traditional structures built by the Reclamation Service. Constant-angle arch dams used the same angle at every elevation of the dam to reduce the amount of concrete needed without increasing stress on the arch. Multiple-arch dams employed a series of buttresses to reinforce a relatively thin dam face. Some government engineers worried that the stress transferred to the arches was too great, and by the late twentieth century, the high cost of labor made such dams impractical. Yet early in the century they had distinct advantages. They were less likely to shift, and since far less concrete was used, they were cheaper to erect. A multiple-arch dam constructed near Salt Lake City in 1917 cost less than half the price of a comparable gravity dam.[8]

Newell and Davis had been based in Washington for thirteen or fourteen years prior to passage of the Reclamation Act. Their Washington connections helped them deal with Congress and secure the support of scientific and engineering organizations, but those ties made them suspect in the West, where federal policies related to the public domain were often perceived as unrealistic or unjust—conceived by people who knew little or nothing about conditions in the region. Little wonder that Elwood Mead posed such great danger to Newell and Davis. Mead had few ties to the East. But on paper, he was far more qualified to direct the federal reclamation program than Newell, and Newell knew it.[9] That the Reclamation Service refused to recruit many important western engineers, or offered them positions that did not take full advantage of their talent and experience, suggests that Newell shied away from appointing engineers who might question his judgment, upstage him, or seek his job.

THE STRUCTURE AND ORGANIZATION OF THE RECLAMATION SERVICE

Theodore Roosevelt assigned federal reclamation to the U.S. Geological Survey. Frederick H. Newell was a friend and adviser to Roosevelt, and T. R. also had close ties to Charles D. Walcott, who had succeeded Powell as head of the USGS in 1894 and was a prominent figure in Washington scientific circles. As noted in chapter 2, the U.S. Geological Survey had conducted the only major examination of irrigable land and potential dam and canal sites in the West (1888–90). As director of the Geological Survey's Hydrographic Division, Newell had studied rivers throughout the nation. Equally important, Newell had compiled surveys of irrigation agriculture for the 1890 and

1900 national censuses, which, presumably, gave him a broad knowledge of economic conditions in the West.

Despite its sterling reputation for scientific work, the USGS faced a formidable job in staffing the Reclamation Service. From little more than a dozen men in 1902, the service's engineering corps grew to more than 360 by 1905. The USGS provided most of the service's administrators, but it was not easy to find hundreds of engineers experienced in the construction of dams and canals. Construction sites far removed from cities and towns took field crews away from their families for months on end, and extremes of heat and cold made the work arduous. To compound the problem of assembling a staff, the Reclamation Service competed for talent with two other projects that used large numbers of hydraulic engineers: the Panama Canal and New York Barge Canal. The first engineers hired by the Reclamation Service were recent graduates of engineering schools or former employees of private water companies. Partly because the salaries it offered were too low to attract a sufficient number of older, more experienced professionals, and partly because it preferred young men with university training and new ideas, the Reclamation Service favored younger engineers who knew how to follow orders.[10]

In the beginning, the Reclamation Service's power flowed from the top down. Engineers familiar with conditions in different parts of the West prepared preliminary construction plans at the instigation and direction of Reclamation Service officials in Washington. Nevertheless, the scattered nature of the service's work soon demanded a more decentralized administrative structure. A. P. Davis wanted to divide the West into northern and southern divisions, so that supervising engineers could work in the northern states in the summer and the southwest in the winter. Newell, however, favored smaller districts defined by major rail lines rather than climate. By 1912 there were six: the Pacific, Washington, Idaho, Northern, Southern, and Central Divisions.[11] They were abolished in 1919 as too expensive and inefficient. The nine field offices survived, but thereafter each project manager reported straight to the director in Washington.[12]

Despite family ties to the USGS, the Reclamation Service was a remarkably independent child. In Washington, the Hooe Building served as home to the USGS, but the service was headquartered in the Munsey Building. Newell prepared the important correspondence, and messengers carried it to the Hooe Building for Walcott's signature. All letters that originated in the Reclamation Service were filed in Newell's office. Walcott sought to conduct the affairs of the Reclamation Service "as nearly independent as possible from [those] of the Geological Survey, so that there shall be no tendency toward mingling of appropriations or increase of one item at the expense of another." Not all functions could be neatly separated, however. The service, for example, depended heavily on the Geological Survey's drafting and photographic staff.[13]

The Reclamation Service blamed many administrative problems on its relationship with the Geological Survey. The USGS accounting system was inadequate, Newell insisted, because the Geological Survey had never constructed public works. From June 1902 to March 1905, the USGS used quarterly projections to allocate money to surveys and projects. But it assigned no accountants or bookkeepers to the projects, and the various engineers used different methods of tallying costs as they paid their contractors, suppliers, and workers. They did not itemize construction costs and made no effort to distinguish between money spent on construction and money spent on administration. After a million dollars had been spent and another million committed, the Treasury Department ordered the service to do all vouchers over to separate or distinguish between construction and administration. Not until 1904 did the USGS authorize the Reclamation Service to hire a bookkeeper of its own, and not until 1906 did the service devise a bookkeeping system for its field offices. In 1909, Newell asked the service's bookkeeper to prepare a history of the accounting system. The director admitted that the early methods were "beginning to appear absurd in view of later experience. Also please note the fact that for some months or years we were compelled to have all disbursing done in Washington to the detriment of work in the field."[14]

Only after 1907, when the Reclamation Service became an independent bureau in Interior, did the agency modernize its office procedures. Filing was no less a concern than accounting. The engineering staff began field work without adequate clerical support to maintain records, and engineers in the field wrote long letters covering many different subjects. These letters defied easy classification, so they were placed in a file bearing the author's name. Other letters and telegrams were segregated by subject, according to an index card system maintained in Washington. Over time, subjects proliferated and overlapped. To complicate matters, individual projects devised their own filing systems. As a result, office staff could not transfer easily from one project to another, and new clerks had to learn not only the Washington system, but also all previous systems used on an individual project, along with the one in use at the time they were hired. In 1919, the Reclamation Bureau, which was still called the Reclamation Service by many for decades after 1907, adopted a Dewey decimal filing system. Numbers in the 100s pertained to administration, those in the 200s to finance and accounting, those in the 300s to construction and engineering, those in the 400s to lands, and those in the 500s to miscellaneous subjects. The first folders under an assigned number related to the subject in general, and the remainder pertained to that subject on individual projects. The Reclamation Service did not innovate; it copied its filing system from other bureaus, particularly the Bureau of Mines and the Forest Service.[15]

The triumph of publicity—not the conquest of science, engineering, or administrative efficiency—best defined the Reclamation Service in its early years. The USDA had long been an information department. In 1894, for example, nearly half its budget went into publishing 205 titles with a total press run of 3.1 million copies. After 1905, when the Interior Department's Forestry Office moved to the USDA, Gifford Pinchot, chief of the Forest Service, greatly expanded its publication program. A staff of five contributed articles to newspapers and magazines, and professional lecturers carried the story of government forestry from city to city, appearing before groups ranging from chambers of commerce to elementary school classes. Newell learned from Pinchot. The two men turned such magazines as *National Geographic* and *Forestry and Irrigation* into house organs, and they encouraged and subsidized writers sympathetic to federal reclamation.[16]

The Reclamation Service fed the public an endless stream of stories about the construction of hydraulic works, the retreat of the desert, and the transformation of nature. In 1903—ostensibly in response to appeals from home seekers for information about the government irrigation projects—the service created an Information Section directed by a "chief statistician." The first person to hold that office, C. J. Blanchard, recounted years later, "Publicity work of this kind was new in the departments, and the plans worked out in the Reclamation Service may be said to have been the first attempt by a Federal Bureau to systematically and thoroughly present its activities and its methods to the public." Blanchard denied that the Reclamation Service maintained a mailing list comparable to the Forest Service's, which contained 750,000 names. But he did submit stories about the triumphs of federal reclamation on request, and a field photographer provided "before and after" project photos to such magazines as *World's Work, Harper's, Century, Review of Reviews,* and *Collier's.* Blanchard justified this work as necessary to attract settlers—one article prompted six thousand letters to the Reclamation Service from would-be government farmers—and the photographs were also used to illustrate presentations to congressional committees.

"Statistician" Blanchard prepared nearly a thousand slides to enliven his lectures. He explained federal reclamation at the Union League Club, Friars' Club, Lotus Club, Quill Club, and eight different churches in New York City, as well as at colleges, geographic societies, men's clubs, the Daughters of the American Revolution, and many other organizations. He was also behind the Reclamation Service's efforts to use film to publicize its work—apparently the first federal agency to do so. In 1914, the service made a motion picture whose central characters were Judson Strong and Marian Weatherbee. Marian was an Illinois schoolteacher who decided to escape city life and move West. With little money and no knowledge of farming, she visited a government reclamation project and settled on a forty-acre farm. Strong, who owned the homestead next to hers, helped Marian tame the land. Romance had its way, and eventually the two married. The film ended with the newlyweds tearing down the fence separating their land. A new family had been formed in the freedom and prosperity of the West.[17]

Equally important was the bureau's magazine. The *Monthly Bulletin of the United States Reclamation Service* first appeared in 1907, but in May 1908, it was renamed *Reclamation Record*. At first, the *Record* focused on the construction of projects, not the farmers; it was designed to build camaraderie within the Reclamation Service. Beginning in 1914, however, the *Record* paid increasing attention to matters of interest to project residents. For example, C. J. Blanchard began writing an upbeat column on news from the various projects. At about the same time, he began sending the publication to politicians, newspapers, magazines, and freelance journalists. Newspapers that served project towns often copied articles directly from the *Record* and used them as filler. Given the Reclamation Service's monopoly on project data, its laudatory material often influenced editorials.

Project residents and bureau employees received *Reclamation Record* free. Nominally, the subscription rate to nonfarmers and nonemployees was fifty cents a year. But in 1915 the bureau published 145,000 copies, most of which were distributed without cost to politicians and potential settlers. *Reclamation Record* was designed in part to influence pending reclamation legislation; all members of Congress, and all clerks of legislative committees, received copies. In 1917, A. P. Davis ordered that the magazine be sent to all governors and state legislatures in the seventeen reclamation states as well. He refused to provide governors and state legislatures outside the West with gratis copies, ostensibly because the cost of publication fell on the farmers.[18]

Many westerners considered the Forest Service and Reclamation Service threats to the autonomy and authority of their state governments. They resented the two agencies' press bureaus, which not only publicized federal conservation efforts, but, in the words of a resolution passed by the Colorado legislature in 1913, "create a sentiment against the West." That is, the Forest Service and Reclamation Service undermined state authority in the quest to increase their own power over land, water, and forests. Not surprisingly, from 1905 to 1913, Congress debated ways to cut federal spending on publicity, including a ban on the hiring of publicity agents by federal agencies.[19]

RECLAMATION IN THE INTERIOR DEPARTMENT AND CONGRESS, 1909–1912

From the beginning of the federal reclamation program, members of Congress from both the West and East worried that the Reclamation Service enjoyed too much autonomy. In January 1904, Senator Henry Hansbrough of North Dakota introduced legislation to create an office of "supervising engineer" directly under the secretary of the interior and independent of the Geological Survey or Reclamation Service. Newell would remain the nominal administrative head of the Reclamation Service, but the new official would take direct charge of all construction work. The bill specified a salary of ten thousand dollars a year—far higher than Newell's. Hansbrough probably had Newell's old rival, Elwood Mead, in mind. Senator Thomas R. Bard of California, a good friend of the Reclamation Service who chaired the Senate Committee on Irrigation, advised the secretary of the interior, "If this were done the surveys and investigations would be carried on in accordance with the views of one man, while the construction would be carried on in accordance with the views of another. Unless the two men were in the closest co-ordination, many difficulties would result . . . and it might be even disastrous results." Bard saw such legislation as part of a campaign "to break down the confidence of Congress in the personnel and management of the reclamation service," and to turn the Reclamation Service over to "the politicians of the country." Secretary of the Interior James R. Garfield also opposed the legislation. The secretary, not Congress, should recommend the appointment of engineers and set their compensation, he insisted.[20]

William Howard Taft was far less enthusiastic about federal reclamation than Theodore Roosevelt, and the year 1909 marked a turning point in the relationship between Congress and the Reclamation Service. Congress had examined the irrigation projects before, but not as systematically as in 1909.[21] In the summer and early fall, the Senate Irrigation and Reclamation of Arid Lands Committee covered twelve thousand miles, inspecting all thirty projects and taking testimony at most of its stops. Conditions varied from project to project, but the lawmakers heard many common complaints: that ten years was not enough time to repay construction costs; that bloated administrative expenses had been hidden in construction charges; that government engineers refused to solicit or consider the advice of project farmers; that the federal government should lend money to farmers to help pay for houses and barns; that access to transportation and markets was poor on most of the projects; and that since farmers could not secure clear title to their land for at least five years, good schools could not be built because local governments were unable to tax land owned by the federal government.

The senate committee concluded that the Reclamation Act prevented the Reclamation Service from "resisting . . . local demands." Too many projects had been undertaken too soon—far more than the revenue in the reclamation fund warranted—and some should not have been undertaken at all. Nevertheless, a majority of the committee concluded that "the mistakes made involve but a small fraction of the total sum expended," and the minority report filed by Francis G. Newlands of Nevada—who had been elected to the Senate in 1903—and William Borah of Idaho insisted that the "great majority of the settlers are successful and the percentage of irrigators who have not been able to succeed is remarkably low."[22]

In the summer of 1909, Richard A. Ballinger, William Howard Taft's new secretary of the interior, joined the Senate Irrigation Committee for part of its western tour and participated in public hearings. Ballinger was a westerner—which was unusual for secretaries of the interior in the late nineteenth and early twentieth centuries. He had practiced law in Port Townsend and Seattle (1889–94, and 1897–1904); sat as superior court judge of Jefferson County, Washington (1894–97); and served as a reformist mayor of Seattle (1904–06). His honesty and administrative skills so impressed Theodore Roosevelt and Secretary of the Interior James Garfield—Ballinger's classmate at Williams College—that in 1907 Roosevelt chose him to clean up and reorganize the General Land Office.[23]

Richard Ballinger's conception of bureaucratic responsibility, although not in opposition to the Roosevelt conservation program per se, prompted the famous 1909–10 battle between Ballinger, Gifford Pinchot, Frederick Newell, and other federal officials over the management of the nation's natural resources. Having rendered the notoriously decentralized General Land Office accountable to the secretary of the interior, Ballinger wanted to do the same with the Reclamation Service. During the Roosevelt administration, Secretaries of the Interior Ethan A. Hitchcock and James R. Garfield rubber-stamped decisions made in the Reclamation Service and U.S. Geological Survey. Neither had rejected a single irrigation project recommended by Newell, nor did they ever express substantial reservations. As interior secretary, Ballinger brought a new style of leadership to the department. He stood for two principles: a well-defined chain of command and a commitment to following the statutory will of Congress. Bureau chiefs should defer to cabinet secretaries and provide the latter with the facts needed to make wise and just policies. They should also cooperate in the name of administrative order and efficiency. In particular, Secretary Ballinger hoped to coordinate the department's land and water policies by forcing the General Land Office, the U.S. Geological Survey, and the Reclamation Bureau to work together. He proposed many other radical reforms, including transferring to the states control over federal reclamation projects that served private land.[24]

A vocal group of western senators, led by Thomas Carter of Montana, strongly supported Ballinger. Responding to complaints from settlers on the northern projects, as well as to constituents who thought that their state had been short-changed by the Reclamation Service, these senators demanded Newell's dismissal.[25] As Ballinger's secretary put it: "When Mr. Ballinger became Secretary of the Interior it was found that the Reclamation Service was, generally speaking, a department unto itself, and the Secretary of the Interior, who is charged by the [Reclamation] Act with the responsibility in connection with the Reclamation Service, was a mere figurehead. There was and has been a disposition on the part of the officials of the Reclamation Service to maintain this relation, which, to a certain extent at least, has handicapped the secretary in his supervision of the administration of the affairs of this service."[26] Ballinger had good reason to worry, and President William Howard Taft shared his concerns. Speaking in Spokane in the fall of 1909, Taft suggested that "prudence was not observed by those engaged in executing the Reclamation act." The Reclamation Service, he complained, had tackled far more projects than proceeds from public land sales warranted.[27]

Soon after taking office, Ballinger met with Newell and A. P. Davis to discuss problems on the reclamation projects. "I was particularly urgent with Mr. Newell to give me data by which I could find out what the estimated cost of these various projects had been at the time they started in on them, and what variance and differences there were between the estimated cost and the actual cost of construction, and I was not able then, and have not been since, to get this data." Newell opposed any attempt to reorganize the Reclamation Service to make it more efficient and accountable to the secretary, and he denied that the Reclamation Service had made *any* mistakes in administering the reclamation program.[28]

Officials in the Reclamation Service insisted that their problems resulted from defects in the Reclamation Act and from cost overruns fully justified in a time of rising prices. Ballinger disagreed. The Reclamation Service had constructed projects in too many phases, he insisted. The secretary of the interior had permitted the service to set the per-acre construction charge anytime *before* completion of a project—which could be years after the first settlers filed for their land. The Reclamation Service issued so many contracts for each project that it was impossible at the outset to predict the ultimate cost. Ballinger argued, however, that no project should have been launched until plans were complete, and one construction contract should have covered each project. The Reclamation Service, he said, should fix the per-acre cost *before construction began,* at the same time the government selected the construction company or companies.[29]

Ballinger did not want to turn all reclamation over to private enterprise. Nevertheless, he did think that the Reclamation Service had violated the spirit of the Reclamation Act by including so much private land within the projects. Some projects, he acknowledged, had to include private land, but *most* of the land should be public. Ballinger also resented that Secretary James Garfield, at the insistence of Newell and Pinchot, withdrew from entry nearly 3.5 million acres in 1909, just before Roosevelt left office. Ballinger rescinded this order. Congress had passed the Reclamation Act in the hope that the legislation would *encourage* private development, Ballinger insisted, not retard it. Over half the land withdrawn by Garfield was reserved for federal reclamation projects at a time when the reclamation fund was exhausted and new construction was unlikely. In effect, the secretary's power to reserve public land had been used to serve a completely different purpose from that intended by Congress.[30]

Newell refused to supply Ballinger with reliable information, so the secretary found "spies" within the Reclamation Service, including E. T. Perkins, a disaffected engineer. Federal reclamation was in trouble, Perkins reported, because neither Newell nor Davis had the necessary experience as a hydraulic engineer. "[Newell] is of a weak and vacillating nature," he claimed. "[S]wayed by the various influences brought to bear on him, he is disloyal to those above him and to those below him, he has not the confidence or esteem of the engineers of the Reclamation Service, he fears to assume responsibility of any kind—self preservation is the first and only law of his cowardly nature and to this he sacrifices all men and all things."[31]

Newell and Davis had refused to adopt proper systems of auditing expenditures and systematizing purchasing, Perkins said, and they continued to "justify previous action even when declared illegal by the Attorney General and other law officers of the Government." In New Mexico, the Hondo reservoir would not hold water because the ground upon which it was built was too porous; work began on the Belle Fourche and North Platte Projects before the necessary dam sites had been secured; and the Williston, Buford-Trenton, and Garden City Projects had been constructed before private landowners within their boundaries had signed contracts to use the water promised by the government. Conditions on the Truckee-Carson Project, in western Nevada, were particularly disturbing. The first government project to open, it attracted great attention from the press. But the Reclamation Service launched the project before securing control over Lake Tahoe, which, initially, served as the project's storage reservoir. Consequently, the Reclamation Service was able to secure water for only one-seventh of the land it hoped to irrigate in western Nevada. "No wild cat stock-jobbing land scheme was ever so disastrous and expensive to the investors," Perkins concluded. The thirty thousand acres under irrigation within the Truckee-Carson Project cost an average of nearly fifteen hundred dollars per acre to reclaim. As the engineer responsible for supervising construction, the fault rested with Davis, as well as with Newell. Had Davis been the chief engineer of a private company, Perkins insisted, he would have been fired, because "there is hardly a [national] project built or in process of building that will not show a like history of engineering and financial bad administration and failure."[32]

Ballinger tried to force Newell to resign by expressing his concerns to friendly journalists. Throughout the summer of 1909, rumors abounded that Newell would be replaced by Seattle's city engineer, R. H. Thompson, as part of a wholesale reorganization of the Reclamation Service.[33] In August 1909, Ballinger informed an editor at the *New York Sun* that he had seen enough to know that Newell "suffered from a lack of breadth of view, business capacity and tact in handling public interests. . . . Enough has developed to satisfy me that Mr. Newell has been from the beginning, in order to fortify himself, absolutely disloyal, and I believe that is his attitude to-day." In a letter to the editor of the *Outlook*, Ballinger declared himself "strongly of the opinion that he [Newell] has not the capacity as an executive officer to handle this important service, and that if he had had this capacity a different condition would exist in the various reclamation projects."[34] These threats had no effect; Newell continued to treat the Reclamation Bureau as a private fiefdom.[35]

Despite mounting complaints from farmers, in the summer of 1910 Newell informed Ballinger that *all* the government projects were "feasible and worthy." "The only project which has been publicly mentioned as of questionable character," Newell advised, "is the simplest and the cheapest of all, namely, the Hondo in New Mexico, where there has been an abnormal deficiency in rainfall since the works were completed." All projects had "advanced to a stage where their success may be considered as assured." Pump systems in Kansas and North Dakota would require "patient and skillful administration," Newell admitted, because farmers on those projects preferred to dry farm rather than to irrigate. Otherwise, he was optimistic.[36]

Ballinger was not persuaded. He asked A. P. Davis to shut down the service's publicity mill and take a desk near his office to keep him informed. Ballinger exhibited little sympathy for project settlers, and on one point he agreed wholeheartedly with Newell and Davis: those who called for a debt moratorium were mainly private landowners driven by the promise of speculative profits. He saw no reason to delay, extend, or graduate payments. Changing repayment terms would encourage settlers to press for cancellation of the entire debt, thereby reducing the size of the reclamation fund. Ballinger and Taft did favor a $10 million bond issue to finish the work already under way as rapidly as possible. Otherwise, water rights filed under state law—which required use within five years of the original claim to perfect title—might be lost.[37]

Newell's job was at stake, and he fought back hard. One of the Interior Department's chief legal officers warned Ballinger that Newell and Forest Service director Pinchot had organized a propaganda campaign "to spread the idea that the Interior Department is against Reclamation development and [is] falling into the scheme of power companies to monopolize streams on public lands." Many editorials appeared expressing support for the Reclamation Service, such as this one, in *Engineering News:* "The fact is—and we wish to emphasize it—that the leaders of the Reclamation Service are entitled to quite as much credit for their success in *administration* as for their success in solving purely engineering problems." Ballinger, the *News* suggested, was intent on destroying a skilled, dedicated, and blameless public servant.[38]

Other Reclamation Service officials also criticized Ballinger, at least in private. Morris Bien—the service's legal officer—claimed that Ballinger wanted to remove both Newell and himself. Newlands and other senators blocked the firings, but rumors of a shake-up disrupted the Reclamation Service, for, in Bien's words, "our best men seeing the direct promise of the injection of politics in the administration of the service were [are] looking about for other places. . . . Ballinger is mentally incompetent for the place & is totally out of sympathy with the objects of the Reclamation act. The word Reclamation is like a red flag to a bull for him. . . . [H]e is . . . a menace to our unusually strong engineering & technical organization."[39]

The conflict between Ballinger and Newell reached white heat in late 1909 and became swept up in the famous Ballinger-Pinchot affair, in which Pinchot claimed that Ballinger opposed the entire Roosevelt conservation program and, more significantly, questioned the legality of leases awarded by Secretary Ballinger to mine public coal lands in Alaska. In response, Taft in January 1910 fired Chief Forester Pinchot for insubordination, and in the same month Ballinger invited Congress to investigate the Department of the Interior.[40]

A joint congressional committee conducted hearings from January to April 1910. Its investigation revealed how the Reclamation Service had stretched and evaded the 1902 law. In 1908, for example, the service had begun issuing "cooperative certificates"—also called reclamation scrip, or "Garfield currency"—to settlers who constructed irrigation ditches and performed other project work. In some cases, particularly on the Grand Valley Project, in Colorado, farmers had contributed money and materials as well as labor. In all, the Reclamation Service distributed between $2 million and $3 million worth of IOUs. Officials of the service insisted that the certificates had not been designed to pad the reclamation fund, but to ease the suffering of settlers who moved onto projects years before water could be delivered. The scrip became a form of money, and by the time of the congressional investigation, little was held by the farmers who originally had received it.[41]

During a May 18, 1909, meeting of the president's cabinet, Ballinger warned Taft about the certificates, and the president asked the Justice Department to determine whether the Reclamation Service had acted within the law. The attorney general responded that nothing in the Reclamation Act authorized the federal government to issue what amounted to promissory notes. The legal staff of the Interior Department agreed. "I am a most firm believer in the Reclamation of Arid lands and Forestry protection," one of the department's chief legal officers informed Ballinger, "but [I] cannot of course permit my views of the law to be trimmed to suit the notions of anyone who wants to do something in contravention thereof." In September 1909, Ballinger ordered Newell to stop issuing the certificates and to pay off the existing scrip from the reclamation fund. He worried, however, that much of the scrip had already fallen into the hands of speculators.[42]

What was wrong with federal reclamation? Roosevelt, Newell, and former interior secretary James Garfield argued that most settlers on government projects had failed to anticipate the problems of irrigating virgin land, including the shortage of income during the long period of preparation before the first crops came in. Project farmers expected the government to do too much, and some assumed that if they complained loudly enough, they could reduce or eliminate their debt to the government. Ballinger, in contrast, thought that too many projects had been opened too soon. While $63 million had been expended on federal reclamation by the summer of 1910, $30 million more was needed to complete the work under way—far more than the reclamation fund could provide. Of the thirty projects undertaken in fourteen states and two territories, water was available for little more than seven hundred thousand acres, and only two small projects had been completed. Had fewer projects been undertaken, Ballinger reasoned, they would have been completed more rapidly and repayments from satisfied farmers would be flowing into the bone-dry reclamation fund. Moreover, the interval between canal and reservoir surveys and the first application of water to the land would have been shortened, reducing the number of impoverished settlers.[43]

In December 1909, Ballinger wanted to demote Newell from director to division head, but the Ballinger-Pinchot congressional investigation forced him to drop that plan. A few months later, Taft and Ballinger considered replacing Newell with an army engineer. "The eminent success of Lieut. Col. Goethals at Panama, in the construction of the big canal," the *Washington Post* reported, "has deeply impressed the President with the possibilities to be obtained by an extension of the duties of the army. Therefore, with this medium, he proposes to inject both speed and business-like precision into the immense amount of work still to be done toward the completion of the many dams, reservoirs and canal systems which the government is furnishing the settlers in the West." Nevertheless, by the summer of 1910, the *New York Times* reported that Taft had decided to replace Newell with L. C. Hill, the government engineer in charge of the Salt River Project in Arizona. In the end, the president abandoned plans to reorganize the Reclamation Service and replace Newell, fearing that he would further alienate the Roosevelt wing of the Republican Party.[44]

Instead, Taft appointed a board of army engineers, headed by General William L. Marshall, to inspect the government water projects. As Roosevelt's secretary of war (1904–08), Taft had developed great faith in the Army Corps of Engineers, but in truth they knew little about irrigation agriculture, and the corps was unsuited to conduct the 1910 investigation.

The army board concluded that the dams and canals were well built—though often at an excessive cost that drove up the settlers' debt to the government. Ballinger had hoped that the corps report would justify reorganizing the Reclamation Service, but it did not. Following the army's survey of the projects, Ballinger created the office of consulting engineer for the Reclamation Service—an adviser who reported directly to the secretary—and named Marshall to the post. Marshall had just retired from the army, and as a pensioner, federal law prohibited his appointment as director of the Reclamation Service. And, given the tension that existed between the Corps of Engineers and Reclamation Bureau, Marshall warned that it would be dangerous to place a former military officer in charge of civilian engineers.[45]

The army report dodged the question of where money could be found to finish the projects. As early as 1905 or 1906, a handful of western politicians favored fattening the reclamation fund with a direct appropriation of $1 million. Initially, Newell opposed such a bailout, because "the various projects in hand are sufficiently well distributed and typical of such a wide range of conditions that it would seem to be wise to wait the results of the present expenditure before asking for more money."[46] By 1910, however, his opposition had softened. In that year, Congress debated an administration measure drafted by Ballinger or Marshall to lend the reclamation fund $30 million to complete construction then under way. The proposed loan was substantial; as of 1910, about $49 million had been spent on federal reclamation.[47]

The loan bill prompted the first extended congressional debate over federal reclamation since 1902. Newell resented that he had not been asked to prepare the legislation—which he took as yet another sign that his days in Washington were numbered. In testimony before the House Ways and Means Committee, he suggested that $7 million annually would finish the projects, implying that Taft and Ballinger favored the larger amount to curry favor with western senators and that the extra money would be used to build *new* projects, not finish old ones.[48]

Supporters of the loan emphasized the hardships faced by settlers who, in some cases, had waited as long as five years for water. "Out on the desert in the west," Senator William Borah of Idaho lamented, "are men and women from every state in the Union . . . struggling in every way which their ingenuity can devise to protect their homes until the water which they stand ready to pay for and which the government promised to deliver reaches them. . . . Gradually through delay of the government they are being forced into absolute need. To leave them in the situation of victims of the government's invitation and dilatory methods when they offer to pay every dollar of expense would be a shameless betrayal of public duty which no congress will do when it fully understands the situation."[49] Senator Weldon Heyburn of Idaho blamed the Reclamation Service's money problems on the more than two hundred million acres of western public land reserved since 1891, which action "starved the [reclamation] fund by destroying the source from which the fund was to come. . . . You can not withdraw the lands from sale and at the same time derive a fund from the sale of the lands." Congressman Frank Mondell of Wyoming maintained that soaring construction costs dictated the loan—costs that had increased by more than 60 percent during the first decade of the century. Congressman Atterson W. Rucker of Colorado noted that at the rate farms were being abandoned in New England, the West would once again serve as a "safety valve": "You of the East want homes for your very congested population; we in the West can accommodate you, and this measure is calculated to do so." Mondell, Newlands, and others reiterated that the existing projects had been wisely selected and well built.[50]

The 1910 loan bill stood a much better chance of passing as an administrative measure than as an initiative by western legislators or the Reclamation Service. Strong opposition to federal reclamation had emerged in the Democratic South. Disappointed that the Reclamation Service had not expanded the reclamation program to include swamp and cutover land in their part of the country, by 1910 southern politicians had reverted to the states' rights arguments commonly used to oppose national public-works programs. Senator Alexander S. Clay of Georgia considered the loan bill as an opening wedge. The time would come, he predicted, when the Reclamation Service would demand an annual appropriation of $50 million or $60 million to carry on its work—a sum comparable to that expended each year on rivers and harbors.[51]

Representative Oscar Underwood of Alabama, a strong advocate of federal reclamation in 1901 and 1902, now argued that the reclamation program was unconstitutional, because it used public money to develop private land:

> If you think it is right to take money out of the Treasury and loan [it] through the Reclamation Service to individuals to develop irrigation projects, where it is entirely private land and all the benefits to accrue to private persons and all the risk [is] to be taken by the Government, why is it not just as right and just as constitutional to create great public parks in the States for the health of local communities? Why is it not just as right and meritorious to establish hospitals throughout the country for the aid of the sick and those in distress? Where are you going to draw the line when you pass beyond the limitations prescribed by the constitution[?] . . . If it is right to go into the Public Treasury and use the public funds for the promotion of irrigation enterprises on private property, is it not just as legitimate to go into the hills of Pennsylvania and build furnaces out of money borrowed from the Public Treasury to develop the coal fields of that State for the benefit of private individuals? I can see no distinction, and I believe there is none.[52]

The Reclamation Service needed the additional money, Underwood contended, because it had unlawfully decided on its own to build lateral canals and drainage works in addition to the dams and main canals Congress had authorized in 1902. He considered many of what the Reclamation Service called "project extensions" as entirely new projects launched next to existing ones.

In July 1910, on the recommendation of Senator Thomas Carter of Montana and Senator Reed Smoot of Utah, the size of the loan was reduced from

$30 million to $20 million; it was to be repaid at the rate of $1 million a year beginning in 1920. The House passed the legislation without a formal roll call vote. Few of its members understood what the measure was all about; it was enough that Taft endorsed it. No money could be spent without the approval of the army panel that had investigated the projects. In effect, Marshall assumed veto power over the recommendations of the Reclamation Service. The legislation also stipulated that no new projects could be launched without the approval of the president; that on *new* projects no entry would be permitted until the secretary of the interior determined that water was available; and that settlers could leave their land for extended periods during the construction phase. Most important, it rescinded the requirement that at least 51 percent of the money raised from land sales be spent within the state or territory where the land had been sold.[53]

The Warren Act, sponsored by Wyoming senator Francis E. Warren and passed by Congress in February 1911, completed the major reforms of federal reclamation adopted during the Taft administration. The Townsite Act of 1906 permitted the Reclamation Service to sell surplus *power* generated at government dams to private companies and municipalities in the vicinity of government projects. But since most of the projects were designed to serve far more land than the Reclamation Service irrigated in 1910, Ballinger and the army board urged Congress to permit the sale of surplus *water* to the owners of private lands outside the projects as well.

Construction of the Jackson Lake Dam at the head of the Snake River, and the Pathfinder Dam in Wyoming, prompted the Warren bill. The West's major rivers contained few prime reservoir sites, and in some cases the government could build dams twice as large as a project needed for little more money. It made sense, therefore, to construct the largest dams possible. Secretary of the Interior Ballinger warned that unless he could "cooperate and contract with companies, associations, or districts to the end that reservoirs may be erected of such dimensions as to irrigate larger areas than the Government has included within its own project[s], great quantities of arid lands capable of irrigation will necessarily remain barren." Warren expected Carey Act projects, private corporations, and irrigation districts to pay the difference in cost for the larger dam either at the time of construction, or as they purchased the additional water. In either case, the money would be paid into the reclamation fund, providing an additional source of revenue.[54]

The Warren bill had critics. Senators Heyburn of Idaho and Frank Flint of California, as well as Congressman Edward T. Taylor of Colorado, worried that the Reclamation Service might use the construction of large dams to destroy state control over water. Nevertheless, a far more common complaint was that federal reclamation had drifted far from its original ideals. Senator Elmer Burkett of Nebraska worried that the Warren legislation would shift the focus of federal reclamation from public to private land and permit "the

Secretary of the Interior in the future, with practically no let or hindrance, to go in with private organizations or corporations anywhere in building a dam for an irrigation project that may be only of private concern." Private companies might persuade the Reclamation Bureau to construct costly parts of their irrigation systems at public expense.[55]

The Warren Act compromised the original goal of federal reclamation—to use the West's surplus water to carve new farms out of the public domain. It permitted the secretary of the interior to sell water at cost, plus a reasonable charge for delivery. No individual could buy water for more than 160 acres. Like the Reclamation Act itself, the new law was ambiguous. Surplus water from government dams might be sold year by year, according to variations in stream flow and the amount stored, or it could be allocated by contract, which would allow private interests to create *permanent* water rights. But if rights to surplus water were fixed by contract, then the future growth of government projects might be severely hampered. Another interesting feature of the legislation was that it applied to future as well as to existing private water projects. Therefore, it permitted the government to design storage works *primarily* to serve virgin land in the hands of speculators instead of simply to provide supplemental water for private land already under irrigation.[56]

The Warren Act offered hope to the Reclamation Service at a time when it faced mounting criticism in the West. Private interests demanded a uniform water supply, not one that expanded and contracted. Only if it could store and deliver a certain quantity of water at a fixed price could the service broaden its constituency. Selling storage rights became a way to "adjudicate" water rights by augmenting the existing supply. But the question of whether Warren Act contracts superseded previous water rights, or whether private storage rights should be subordinate to government rights, lingered on for decades. By 1925, farms supplied with water under the Warren Act returned $53.7 million to their owners, while government farms yielded $77.6 million, and in 1931 the bureau watered almost as much land outside government projects as within. Once, the Reclamation Bureau had attempted to block or torpedo private reclamation schemes that competed with government projects. After 1911, it eagerly embraced them.[57]

The last reform enacted during Ballinger's short term as secretary of the interior also came in February 1911, when Congress gave the secretary power to negotiate new contracts with delinquent farmers. Government farmers could now start their ten-year repayment cycle over by lumping past due payments into a new debt and accepting the increase in construction charges that had occurred since they had signed their original contracts. Most settlers, however, considered this measure part of a plot to shift the cost of bad management onto the farmers, not an effort to provide a more equitable repayment schedule.[58]

Richard A. Ballinger resigned in March 1911, and Taft's second secretary of the interior, Walter Fisher, did little to alter reclamation policy. As noted previously, in June 1910, Congress softened the residency requirement by permitting farmers who made initial improvements to live elsewhere while they waited for water to become available. Then, in April 1912, it excused homesteaders who had entered reclamation projects prior to June 25, 1910, from the continuous residency requirement. No action would be taken to evict settlers who had not improved their land. Nevertheless, claimants still had to live on the land year-round for five consecutive years to gain clear title.[59]

FRANKLIN K. LANE AND FEDERAL RECLAMATION, 1913–1917

The election of Woodrow Wilson to the presidency brought Democratic secretary of the interior Franklin K. Lane to Washington in March 1913. Raised in northern California, Lane served as San Francisco's city and county attorney before Theodore Roosevelt appointed him to the Interstate Commerce Commission. Lane valued individual enterprise as much as efficiency and order. In a speech at the Pan-Pacific Exposition in 1915, he said of the western pioneer: "Without him we would not be here. Without him banners would not fly, nor bands play. . . . Here he stands at last beside this western sea, the incarnate soul of his insatiable race—the American pioneer. Pity? He scorns it. Glory? He does not ask it. . . . In his long wandering he has had time to think. He has talked with the stars, and they taught him not to ask why."[60]

Lane regretted that to many Americans, conservation suggested "stinginess and a provincial thrift, spies in the guise of Government inspectors, hateful interference with individual enterprise and initiatives, governmental haltings and cowardice, and all the constrictions of an arrogant, narrow, and academic-minded bureaucracy which can not think largely and feels no responsibility for national progress." He regarded nature as inherently disorderly, wasteful, and capricious. The instinct to dominate, manage, and control—to render the world a more predictable place—characterized his brand of conservation. At a June 1916 commencement address at Brown University, he stated his philosophy concisely: "Every tree is a challenge to us, and every pool of water and every foot of soil. The mountains are our enemies. We must pierce them and make them serve. The sinful rivers we must curb." Water ran unused to the sea, lightning fires consumed vast forests, and floods washed away millions of acres of topsoil. In his first annual report as secretary of the interior, Lane promised a plan to lease public mineral lands—the lack of which had triggered the Ballinger-Pinchot controversy—as well as comprehensive waterpower legislation and a new reclamation act. Federal reclamation was central to Lane's vision of a managed environment.

He was willing to spend an additional $100 million on federal reclamation, but only if the administration of the program improved and the states contributed to it.[61]

By 1909 or 1910, project newspapers bristled with savage attacks on Newell. Nevada's *Fallon Standard* called him "an illogical, uncompromising and extremely narrow individual, who is not fit to hold down the position of director of Uncle Sam's reclamation operations." Idaho's *Rupert Pioneer-Record* proclaimed, "Newell is the cancer in the body of the Reclamation idea. It is he who is eating away the vitals of the whole structure and driving it to certain ruin. . . . It is a pity Newell cannot find a job in Russia or some other country like it, where his methods would be appreciated, as he is certainly out of place in the United States." Lane had no sympathy for farmers who sought to repudiate their debt to the government, but, in the words of A. P. Davis, the secretary believed that "there must be a great deal more behind the complaints against Mr. Newell, and that he [Newell] seemed to be lacking in tact, or in some quality which was essential for the office [of director]. [Lane] stated that the condemnation of the Service was so great that undoubtedly Congress would shortly stop the work unless criticism could be checked."[62]

Lane was the first interior secretary to recognize that the problems of federal reclamation were psychological as well as economic. In May 1913, he invited representatives from the irrigation projects to Washington to air their grievances. For seventeen days, Lane presided over the hearings. The most common complaint was that the Reclamation Service intentionally obscured the per-acre cost of reclamation by predicting that far more land could or would be irrigated within each project than was realistic. Project representatives pleaded for a moratorium on payments until the farmers had had time to clear and level their land. They also asked for an extension of the ten-year repayment period; that no work be undertaken without the full cooperation of those affected; that water users' associations be informed of all changes in construction plans and contracts; that contracts for the sale of power or for surplus water from government dams be approved by the relevant associations; that revenue from sales of power or surplus water be credited against construction or operation and maintenance costs; that the associations be consulted when project employees were hired; that itemized statements of all charges and expenditures be furnished quarterly to the associations; that the plans, maps, and books of all projects be open to project farmers; that land entries under the Reclamation Act not be reduced by the secretary of the interior after bona fide entry; and that the secretary push for legislation to transfer the irrigation works to water users at the earliest possible date. The delegates also wanted to adopt a formal resolution denouncing Newell and demanding his removal, but Lane pleaded against it.[63]

In July and August 1913, following completion of the hearings, Lane toured reclamation projects, Indian reservations, and national parks, beginning in Minnesota and continuing through Montana, Wyoming, and Washington. He quickly became, in his words, "overwhelmed" with "curses upon the Reclamation Service," both by government farmers and by western politicians. In a May 1913 letter to the editor of the *Great Falls Tribune,* Lane observed that the Montana projects had made "a very bad showing." "It was disheartening to feel that we had spent so many million dollars and that the Government was looked upon as a bunko shop who *[sic]* had brought people into Montana where they were slowly starving to death. . . . I certainly am not going to be a party to gold-bricking the poor devil of a farmer who has been told by everybody that he is being charged twice as much as he ought to be charged by the Government."[64]

Lane recognized that federal reclamation had become a benefit program for well-to-do farmers and speculators. Farmers with limited means had acted as shock troops to clear the land and make it productive. When economic necessity forced them to abandon their homesteads, a more affluent class purchased their farms at bargain prices and profited from their labor. The spirit and intent of the Reclamation Act had been perverted. An editorial in the *Independent* magazine told the story of an immigrant returning to his homeland who met an immigrant who had just landed in New York. "Tell me, now, is it true that Uncle Sam gives every man a farm?" the newcomer asked. "No," said the former resident of the West. "You ain't got it quite right. Uncle Sam bets you 160 acres agin $200 that you can't live on the land five years, and the old man wins every time."[65]

Like Ballinger, Lane quickly decided that the Reclamation Service was more loyal to Newell than to the secretary of the interior—or to the mission of providing homes in the desert. Threatening that Congress would abandon the federal projects, completed or not, the secretary followed a strategy of divide and conquer when dealing with the service. He asked Davis to explain Newell's mistakes and weaknesses as director—with the promise that if Davis complied, he would become the next director.[66]

Davis refused, but at the end of May 1913, Lane created a five-man reclamation commission to dilute Newell's authority. Commissions offered an alternative to hierarchical lines of authority. As a former member of the Interstate Commerce Commission, Lane believed that divided authority promoted new ideas and cooperation. Newell retained the title of director, but he shared authority with the chief engineer (Davis), chief counsel, comptroller, and supervisor of irrigation—the heads of the departments into which the Reclamation Service was divided. He was a poor first among equals; the department heads answered only to Lane. Although its size varied, the board lasted until 1918, when complaints from Davis that it hampered the Reclamation Bureau's ability to respond to the needs of World War I resulted in its abolition.[67] Shortly after the 1913 reorganization, Davis recounted that "the Secretary assured us in Mr. Newell's absence, that this [Newell's title as director] meant nothing; that he had no more authority than the rest of us, and [Lane] indicated in a very emphatic manner that he did not value Mr. Newell's services, and more and more the evidence accumulated showing that he had no confidence in Mr. Newell."[68]

When Newell finally "resigned" from the Reclamation Service in early 1915, and A. P. Davis took his place, his authority had long since been stripped away. His unpublished memoirs complained that the 1913 reorganization resulted in "almost interminable talk." Aside from Newell and Davis, the commission "knew nothing about the subject but felt they must interpose some objection. It was of course impossible to function long in this way and while Davis and myself made every concession in the effort to promote harmony and at the same time carry on the work efficiently, I was compelled to tell the Secretary frankly of the difficulties and impossibilities." On May 1, 1915, at the age of fifty-three, Newell became the head of the Civil Engineering Department at the University of Illinois.[69]

Meanwhile, Congress had stripped the Interior Department of much of its authority over the government irrigation projects. Newell complained that congressional arrogance had compounded Lane's vindictiveness: "The politicians . . . discovered that this work had certain possibilities for them," he explained, "and for various reasons, mainly founded on ignorance, were anxious to get control of the larger expenditures which had been justified by the results achieved." In August 1914, several months before Newell resigned, Congress adopted the Reclamation Extension Act, which doubled the repayment schedule from ten to twenty years—as Lane had proposed in his annual report at the end of 1913. Payments were graduated so that only 2 percent of the total cost of construction was due during the first four years after entry, then 4 percent for two years, then 6 percent for the last fourteen years.[70] The 1902 law provided that reservoirs built by the government would forever remain under national control, but the 1914 act authorized the secretary to turn over to water users' associations or irrigation districts "the care, operation and maintenance of all or any part of the project works," even before construction charges had been paid. The same legislation gave Congress new power over federal reclamation. It required the secretary of the interior to send Congress detailed estimates of the cost of completing existing projects. After July 1, 1915, the secretary could no longer select projects without congressional approval, and the reclamation fund was no longer under his exclusive control. Thereafter, Congress reviewed appropriations year by year. While the Reclamation Service presented Congress with a menu of reclamation options, Congress now decided where projects would be built and which ones would be expanded.[71]

The last of Lane's reforms came in 1915, when he created a three-person "Board of Revision" for each project: one member selected by the water users, one by the Reclamation Service, and one by the secretary of the interior. The local boards recommended construction charges on new projects and adjustments to construction charges on old ones. But their decisions were purely advisory. A Central Board of Cost Review, composed of Elwood Mead, General William Marshall, and I. D. O'Donnell (the Reclamation Service's supervisor of irrigation), reviewed all recommendations from the projects. Mead, who had just returned to the United States after serving as chair of the State Rivers and Water Supply Commission of Victoria, Australia, from 1907 to 1915, chaired the board. His panel did not regard soaring construction costs as the main problem facing federal reclamation. Far more important, in Mead's eyes, were inflated land prices, high interest rates, and rampant land speculation. Reducing construction charges, he warned, would simply encourage speculation. Some settlers would benefit, but the inevitable increase in the price of private land within the projects would more than offset any reduction in each farmer's debt to the government.[72]

The 1914 and 1915 administrative changes did not go far enough for Mead, who proposed fundamental changes in the Reclamation Act and the Reclamation Service. "If there ever were an institution, public or private, that needed overhauling, it is the Reclamation Service," Mead wrote to U.S. senator John Works of California. Mead found it "difficult to conceive of anything more crude, wasteful and unscientific than the present method of settlement under Government Irrigation Projects." Some reclaimed tracts were worth three or four times others nearby, but land within each project was thrown open at the same price. No distinction was made between settlers, so that "the man already rich in land can come in and absorb opportunities that ought to go to the land-less." Yet those with no capital or experience could also secure a farm, which almost guaranteed failure. As a result, "there is economic waste, wrong and injustice, all of which could be prevented by adequate oversight of settlement."[73]

Mead thought that the interest-free provision of the Reclamation Act undermined the "sense of financial responsibility that would be felt if the ordinary commercial obligations of business were imposed. It makes all concerned in these payments feel that they are the objects of special privilege; it whets the appetite for further concessions; it has in it the seeds of repudiation." Many settlers on government irrigation projects resented having to pay anything. The sting of debt was interest, not the size of the debt itself. It would be far better, Mead thought, to charge 4 percent interest but reduce the financial burden during the early years of a project by extending the period of repayment to thirty or forty years.[74]

Mead also wanted to classify and divide all land within government projects according to its productive potential. Farm sizes should vary from five acres for farm laborers to two hundred acres, and the Reclamation Bureau (not the General Land Office) should have sole authority over project entries—

and the right to reject applicants who seemed unlikely to succeed. The poorest farms should be larger and carry a lower per-acre construction cost. All settlers should be required to make a substantial cash deposit at the time they entered the land to protect the government from loss through failure or abandonment. No one who already owned private land within a project should be permitted to acquire additional land by homesteading, and no hydraulic works should be built to reclaim that land *until* the government set a maximum price and acquired title to at least 50 percent of the private holdings within project boundaries. Some of Mead's ideas were radical. For example, he called for the abandonment of the rectilinear survey so that government farms could be laid out according to the route of the main ditches, and he proposed that the government should either prepare farms for settlement or provide loans to enable settlers to grade and fence their land, build homes, and construct distribution ditches. That would encourage farmers to cultivate the land as rapidly as possible. Mead's proposals anticipated those of the famous Fact Finders' Commission, which he would head a decade later.[75]

In little more than a decade, the Reclamation Service had been transformed from a relatively autonomous agency with virtually full control over the reclamation fund into a bureau subject to keen congressional oversight. Now the ethics of science and efficiency—which had been compromised from the beginning—formally became captives of the political process. George Maxwell bitterly complained that Franklin K. Lane had "undone the work of twenty years":

> His policy has made it certain that the reclamation fund will never be replenished by re-payments. Long before the extension which he has approved has expired, another movement will be organized by local grafters and politicians to get another extension or in some way avoid or delay re-payment of its advances to the National Government. Nothing will work if it is based on the idea of making the government a philanthropic institution to provide money for weaklings who have shown themselves to be such by their failures. That may have been the fault of their environment and lack of proper training, but that is their misfortune, and neither the government nor anyone else can make a successful community out of such material.[76]

Later, Newell traced the failure of federal reclamation to the 1914 law. The legislation might have worked, he argued, had it imposed an interest charge during the second ten years of repayment. Instead, it served as a touchstone for settlers who wanted to repudiate all or part of their debt to the government.[77]

By the time the United States entered World War I in 1917, half the federal projects had been completed, including a hundred storage and diversion dams and eleven thousand miles of canals. Virtually all the projects had been approved during the Roosevelt administration, before the reclamation fund dried up. Federal reclamation accounted for little more than 10 percent of the more than 6.2 million acres opened to irrigation during the first decade of the twentieth century, and for less than one-third of the money invested in new dams and canals. More ominous still, while the per-acre cost of irrigation increased little between the 1880s and 1890s, it climbed by 250 percent between 1900 and 1910. That alone suggested that federal reclamation was unlikely to become a self-supporting program.[78]

CONCLUSION

When he assumed the directorship of the Reclamation Service, Frederick H. Newell had little experience designing and building irrigation projects, and his knowledge of political conditions within the West was limited. After Theodore Roosevelt left the presidency, Newell became highly sensitive to criticism—and apprehensive about being replaced. Elwood Mead was the person best qualified to head the federal reclamation program, and Newell knew it. Mead left for Australia in 1907, but by 1909 the Reclamation Service was facing a series of pretenders to the throne who won the support of the secretary of the interior, western politicians, and project farmers. Richard Ballinger and Franklin K. Lane found it difficult to render the Reclamation Service accountable. Newell refused to admit that *any* serious problems existed on the government irrigation projects, let alone accept responsibility for them. He was evasive, if not duplicitous, and he developed a siege mentality. Proposed administrative solutions included turning the service over to a director selected from the Army Corps of Engineers or the Department of Agriculture; rule by commission, which would dilute the director's authority; and the appointment of special assistants to the secretary, who would serve as de facto agents within the service. But it proved impossible to balance power between the secretary of the interior and the Reclamation Service.

The Reclamation Extension Act of 1914—favored by both Lane and Congress—was a serious blow to the Reclamation Service. Not only did Congress demand the right to pass judgment on projects and project extensions proposed by the Reclamation Service, it also wanted to pick and choose projects on its own, regardless of recommendations by the director of the service or the secretary of the interior. Nevertheless, the resignation of Newell early in 1915 and the patriotic appeal of feeding Europe during World War I gave the Reclamation Service a reprieve. In 1915, Mead—Lane's chief adviser on reclamation and the service's harshest critic—left Washington to head California's Commission on Land Colonization and Rural Credits. It would be a decade before he returned.[79] Crop and land prices rose throughout the United States, and the Reclamation Extension Act bought peace on the projects until 1920, when the Reclamation Bureau faced a new wave of appeals for relief.[80] As the war ended, officials in the Reclamation Bureau hoped that it had outlived its prewar problems and would now enter an era of growth and prosperity. The homestead ideal was not dead in the United States. The anticipated demand for land among veterans returning from Europe promised to fill vacant farms on government projects and revive the dream of 1902.

5

Boom, Bust, and Boom

Federal Reclamation, 1917–1935

During the 1920s, federal reclamation clashed with powerful trends in American agriculture. In many parts of the nation, mechanization and new methods of cultivation resulted in the withdrawal from production of marginal and inferior lands. The abandonment of farms continued. From 1900 to 1920, the nation's agricultural products increased in value by 300 percent, and the value of its farmland by nearly 400 percent. Nevertheless, the urban population grew three times faster than the rural population in the first decade of the century, and in the second decade of the century nearly five times faster. In the third decade of the century, rural America experienced a population *decline* of 1.2 million people.[1]

During the 1920s, Congress rejected as paternalistic or socialistic measures introduced to help debt-ridden farmers in the East, yet it postponed or excused much of the debt on the western irrigation projects. Those projects contained an abundance of vacant land, and there was no need for new farms anywhere in the country. Nevertheless, at a time of crop surpluses, depressed prices, and rising debt, the friends of federal reclamation in Congress pushed for new projects and the extension of old ones, and virtually all the targeted land was privately owned. Simultaneously, the Reclamation Bureau renewed its campaign to cultivate swamp and cutover land, particularly in the South. It was eager to reclaim land anywhere in the country—with the assistance of the states or irrigation districts. Federal reclamation contributed to a dramatic increase in land prices during World War I, but it also created a new class of working poor in the 1920s. Set against the rising wages and improved working conditions of factory workers, the plight of residents on the government projects was all the more poignant.[2]

From 1913 to 1920, crop prices soared on government irrigation projects. On Nevada's Truckee-Carson Project, for example, the yield per acre averaged $12.83 in 1912 but reached $38.43 in 1918. Cultivated land within the projects increased by 241 percent, from 923,000 to 2,229,000 acres, and irrigated land increased by 77 percent, from 694,142 acres to 1,225,480 acres. Yet all the news was not good. The war sharply increased crop prices, but it also doubled the price of turning raw land into farms. Therefore, the expansion of irrigation on existing projects did not lead to the construction of new dams and canals. Congress authorized two additional reclamation projects in 1917, but refused to fund them for fear of increasing the federal deficit. In 1919, it rejected bills to add $50 million to $100 million to the reclamation fund, and to build the All-American Canal, linking the Colorado River and the Imperial Irrigation District in Southern California.[3]

THE POSTWAR "RECONSTRUCTION"

In 1919, A. P. Davis, who had become the Reclamation Service's de facto director in 1915, following Frederick Newell's resignation, proclaimed that the primary purpose of the Reclamation Act of 1902 was "to create homes, and . . . its purpose has been fulfilled richly and abundantly. . . . [N]ational reclamation has amply justified all [that] its exponents declared for it." The nation's investment in reclamation had returned indirect, as well as direct, benefits. The $122 million spent on western water projects had generated more than $550 million in new wealth. In fiscal year 1920, the government farms yielded an income of $70 million, twice the value per acre of nonirrigated land, and crops on the Salt River Project returned more than double the cost of constructing the entire project. In 1902, project land sold for an average of $10 an acre; by the end of World War I it commanded $200 an acre. The appreciation in land and crop values, Davis insisted, dwarfed the cost of reclamation. The amount needed to complete the existing projects—$49 million—was less than the value of one year's crop.[4]

Forty thousand families had found new homes, and the livelihoods of four hundred thousand people depended directly or indirectly on the projects. Hundreds of western towns and cities benefited from the Reclamation Act, which had particularly far-reaching effects on poor states such as Arizona and Nevada. Largely because of the Salt River Project, for example, the population of Phoenix increased by more than 400 percent from 1905 to 1917. By the end of the 1920s, six hundred thousand people lived on or near government projects.[5]

Reclamation took center stage in the debate over demobilization at the end of World War I, when an old crusader took a new job. Secretary of the Interior Franklin K. Lane hired William Ellsworth Smythe to study what was likely to happen now that peace had been achieved. Aided by officials in the Reclamation Bureau, Smythe drafted a long memorandum entitled "Reconstruction," which reflected the anachronistic homemaking ideal that had dominated American land policy in the late nineteenth and early twentieth centuries. In 1919 and 1920, revolution and social unrest swept through Europe. The United States would be next, Smythe predicted, unless Congress could decentralize the nation's population. "In nearly every country where revolution has occurred, or threatened, the land question was at the bottom of it," Smythe observed. "The instinct of ownership is planted deep in the hearts of men, and its commonest expression is the desire for homes of their own. There can be no assured stability of political institutions in a country where an opportunity to gratify this desire is denied."[6]

That "instinct of ownership" could not be satisfied by rewarding former soldiers with "virgin land," as the nation had done after the Civil War; little arable land remained within the public domain. To make matters worse, farmers fled marginal or exhausted farmland at an alarming rate. Abandoned land had once been confined to New England and parts of the South; now every state in the Midwest, save for Minnesota and Wisconsin, experienced the problem.[7] At one time, New England had been agriculturally self-sufficient, but by 1920 it imported 75 percent of its food. Was the United States destined to lose its agricultural self-sufficiency in the same way? To some extent, labor-saving machinery and better methods of cultivation compensated for fewer farms and farmers. But the 2 percent annual growth in the nation's population, Smythe reasoned, called for an additional 6 million acres of farmland each year.[8]

Smythe's fears help explain the popularity of soldier-resettlement legislation at the end of the war. Woodrow Wilson supported it in two messages to Congress; Theodore Roosevelt embraced it in the last article he published before his death in 1919; and General Mark L. Hersey, commander of the Fourth Division, Allied Expeditionary Force, found that 20 percent of his soldiers hoped to find a farm when they mustered out. (One-third to one-half of all men who served overseas came from rural America, although many had been hired hands or tenants.) A demobilization officer at Camp Shelby, Mississippi, claimed that nearly 90 percent of the veterans who passed through his station preferred land to a cash bounty. Lane predicted that veterans would turn to farming after the war because it was consistent with the habits of soldiering—healthful physical activity in the open air.[9]

Lane was no less a Jeffersonian than Smythe. He recognized that the nation's cities were growing much faster than its rural communities.[10] He thought that the war had "purified" American business, and he predicted that an era of democratic planning would follow in its wake. Returning soldiers could build dams and canals as public works projects, then till the soil watered by those dams and canals. Reclamation would help shape the new America as it reinforced traditional values. Secretary Lane echoed Smythe's warning: "There is a much larger thought behind this plan than the furnishing of farm homes to war heroes. The stability of the country is in no slight measure measured by the number of those who have an interest in its lands. Present industrial tendencies are anti-national. They make for the breaking of allegiances which are fundamental to a potent and self-sufficient nation."[11]

Lane considered soldier settlement the best chance ever offered to the nation to achieve a planned society. Technology—particularly the automobile, telephone, and a wide variety of electrical appliances—made possible a new kind of rural existence. The United States could support a population three or four times as large as it contained in 1918, but not in its large eastern cities. Since the easily cultivatable public domain was gone, the nation would have to turn to arid lands in the West; to cutover lands in the Pacific Northwest, the Great Lakes States, and the South; and to swamplands in the Midwest and the South. There were, Lane estimated, 150 to 200 million acres of cutover land and 50 million acres of swampland suitable for farming, along with at least 15 million acres of arid public land. Urbanization and the nation's normal population growth would require an additional 6.3 million acres of cropped land annually. The postwar reconstruction would extend the Progressive Era conservation policy from natural to human resources, which Lane characterized as "the most neglected of our resources." For example, 25 percent of the 1.6 million men between twenty-one and thirty-one years of age who had been drafted during the war could not read or write English.[12]

In July 1918, Lane asked Elwood Mead to write the administration's postwar reclamation bill.[13] Congressman Frank Mondell of Wyoming introduced the legislation early in 1919. It called for an initial appropriation of $100 million to establish twenty-five thousand farms on 1.5 million acres. (Later in the year, the amount was raised to $500 million.) Lane predicted that fifty thousand returning veterans would find work clearing stumps, excavating drainage ditches, leveling land, laying out townsites, building houses, barns, and roads, and erecting town halls, schools, and churches. "You have a responsibility to these boys," Lane told Congress. "We cannot tell what labor conditions will be in three months, but we should be prepared as we do not want tramps. . . . No one has suggested any plans except this one for relieving conditions. . . . No man who is willing to work should be out of a job."[14]

The Lane-Mondell Bill—as it came to be called—advocated a partnership between the states and the central government. The states had two choices. They could donate unimproved land to the federal government, leaving reclamation and settlement to the Reclamation Bureau, or they could pay at least 25 percent of the *entire* financial burden—from purchasing the land to building houses, barns, and roads. The states were also required to create soldier settlement boards to screen applicants and administer the completed projects. The farms would average sixty acres and cost five thousand dollars. Only soldiers with financial assets of less than fifteen thousand dollars could participate, and they were required to repay the cost of land and reclamation in forty years or fewer, at 4 percent interest, and the cost of improvements in twenty years or fewer. To prevent or limit speculation, no farm could be sold or transferred without the state board's approval—and then not until the farmer had repaid his debt to the federal government. Though all plans had to be approved by federal authorities, state boards would share in every detail of design and construction. The states would also provide returning soldiers with agricultural training, sharing that cost with the federal government. In late 1918 and early 1919, Lane and Mead lobbied hard for the legislation, and the Interior Department promoted the plan among American servicemen in France. The department distributed 900,000 copies of a pamphlet entitled, *Hey There! Do You Want a Home on the Farm?* and received 140,000 inquiries in response.[15]

Initially, Lane tried to sell the Mondell legislation *mainly* as a jobs bill.[16] But the war ended in November 1918, and the economy readily absorbed the first wave of returning veterans. A fear of socialism replaced the specter of unemployment, and the planning ethic so popular during the war fell into disfavor. Veterans' bills flooded Congress in 1919, but only the Lane-Mondell Bill reached the floor of either house.[17] Legislation that promised veterans land clashed with other bonus bills. The American Legion had included the Lane-Mondell scheme in an omnibus bill to provide veterans with vocational training, low-interest home loans, and cash awards, as well as reclaimed land. No legislation could be passed without the Legion's help, or at least acquiescence. Reclamation was, therefore, held hostage to a wide variety of proposed benefit programs. Given the budget deficit at the end of the war, the "grab-bag" nature of veterans' legislation gave Congress the perfect excuse to do nothing.[18]

The Lane-Mondell Bill encountered many other obstacles. It promised reclamation in almost every state—in the West, South, and North—and given the uncertain number of soldiers who might settle on one of the proposed projects, critics claimed that the bill's suggested $500 million appropriation would be inadequate.[19] Moreover, if farmers on government irrigation projects had refused to repay their debt to the government, would those who purchased reclaimed swamp or cutover land be any different? The bill also raised the old question of constitutionality. "[I]f the Reclamation Service, with its vast personnel which has been built up at the expense of hundreds and thousands if not millions of dollars, may be used for private purposes," Senator William H. King of Utah warned, "why may we not use any organization of the Government and any technical skill of government employees and Government instrumentalities to aid in any undertaking or enterprise in which private individuals may engage?" If the federal government could develop private lands, it could develop private mines or factories. Since the states were likely to issue bonds to raise their share of the cost of reclamation, King also worried about the federal government's obligation to investors. Would the bondholders blame the federal government if the land did not sell and their investment went sour? Would they demand restitution from Uncle Sam?[20]

Eastern and Midwestern farm groups, meanwhile, argued that no new farmland was needed—or that the government should restore the fertility of existing farms rather than open new ones. A national policy of *keeping people on the land,* their spokesmen claimed, made more sense than trying to reverse the migration from farm to city. The best way to resurrect rural America was to lend each returning veteran five thousand dollars and allow him to purchase a farm where he wanted.[21]

The Lane-Mondell Bill also generated sectional tensions. Western politicians feared that reclamation projects in the humid half of the nation would lure prospective settlers away from the West and reduce Congress's commitment to building up that region. Many who had helped push the 1902 law through Congress—including George Maxwell—argued that the West should "go it alone" and not pin its hopes on such a sweeping program. Congress was far more likely to appropriate $10 million or $20 million for western irrigation projects than $500 million for a national program.[22]

Congress considered more than seventy veterans-aid bills in 1918 and 1919, but by the time the second session of the sixty-sixth Congress convened in December 1919, support for both the Lane-Mondell and American Legion bills had waned. In the words of William Ellsworth Smythe, Lane's plan "received a shower of brickbats from every side." Idaho senator William E. Borah introduced a variant of the Lane-Mondell Bill that dispensed with state reclamation boards and gave the secretary of the interior authority to select and construct the projects; it provided for an appropriation of $300 million. A bill proposed by Senator Duncan Fletcher of Florida limited the federal government's financial liability to backing the bonds of local improvement districts. The Treasury Department would issue up to $350 million in government bonds, but only if reclamation districts in the South or West issued bonds of their own that could be used as collateral. Senator Reed Smoot of Utah introduced legislation that carried no federal appropriation at all. Under his bill, landowners within existing or proposed reclamation districts could ask the secretary of the interior to investigate proposed projects, and the Reclamation Service would build them—*after* the landowners deposited the cost of the surveys and projected works in the U.S. treasury. Smoot's bill passed the Senate unanimously in April 1920 but failed to find a slot on the House calendar before adjournment.[23]

At the end of February 1920, poor health prompted Franklin K. Lane to resign as secretary of the interior. He lamented that Congress had not accepted his soldier settlement plan.

It was not just the demand for economy, or the fear of government paternalism, or even sectional rivalries that killed the Lane-Mondell Bill and other
reclamation legislation introduced after World War I. More important, there
was no groundswell of grassroots support for reclamation or planned settlements, and what support there was evaporated when crop and land prices
collapsed. The homemaking arguments of 1902—so effective following the
depression of the 1890s—generated little passion or enthusiasm in 1919.[24]

HARD TIMES

By 1920, only one large government reclamation project had been completed: Arizona's Salt River Project. Many were 80 to 90 percent finished,
but the Newlands (Nevada), Klamath (California-Oregon), and Shoshone
(Wyoming) Projects were little more than half done, and the North Platte
Project (Nebraska-Wyoming) was only 30 percent complete. Nevertheless,
the 1920 agricultural census revealed that cropped land in the West could
be increased by more than one-third without constructing any new dams or
canals.[25] Even with the expansion of irrigation during World War I, less than
half the sixty thousand farms on government projects were irrigated. Much
of the land was dry-farmed—including 75 percent of the acreage on Montana's Milk River Project and 80 percent on the Williston Project, in North
Dakota. Much of the rest had never been cultivated. Only 3 percent of the
public land within the projects was untilled, but on many projects *most* of the
privately owned land was unused. In 1925, one-sixth of all government farms
were vacant; some had been abandoned, but others had never been occupied.
Sixty-five percent of land within Oregon's Owyhee Project was unoccupied,
and only five hundred of sixty thousand acres on Wyoming's Riverton Project
had been entered.[26]

Average crop values on government projects fell by nearly half from 1919
to 1922. During the years of boom and bust stretching from 1917 to 1926,
returns ranged from a high of eighty-nine dollars an acre on the Yakima
Project to less than ten dollars an acre on the Huntley, Milk River, Sun River,
and Lower Yellowstone Projects, in Montana. As crop prices plummeted,
so did the price of land. From 1920 to 1930, the average farm in Montana
lost 50 percent of its value, and 20 percent of the area farmed went out of
production—more than all the land farmed in Montana in 1900.[27]

Even as crop prices fell, the cost of irrigation increased. By 1923, the per-
acre construction cost on existing projects averaged eighty-four dollars an
acre, nearly three times the original estimate of thirty-one dollars, made when
the first projects opened. The North Platte Project, in Wyoming and Nebraska, cost four times what government engineers had once estimated, the
Minidoka (Idaho) and Yuma (California) Projects more than three times,
and the Uncompahgre (Colorado) Project 2.7 times. To make matters worse,

per-acre cost and per-acre return did not correlate. The Yakima Project, in Washington, took an average of fifty-two dollars an acre to furnish with water but produced an average annual income of eighty-nine dollars per acre. But the Frannie Division of Wyoming's Shoshone Project cost eighty dollars an acre to reclaim and returned only seventeen dollars per acre. Even different units of the same project showed large variations. As a rule, however, projects on the northern Great Plains, and in Wyoming and Montana, returned far less per acre than projects in states or territories where irrigation was a necessity and the growing season was longer. Measured by the ratio of debt to productivity, the most profitable projects were in Arizona, Washington, and Idaho, and the least profitable in Wyoming, Montana, and North Dakota.[28]

One symptom of hard times was the growing number of tenants on government projects. By 1920, renters operated 37 percent of American farms. Tenancy on government irrigation projects was lower than the national average, but it increased from 20 percent in 1912 to 33 percent in 1924. So great was the demand for farmland during World War I that many farmers rented out their less desirable acreage. The sharp increase in tenancy during the early 1920s occurred in large part because those who purchased land at inflated prices during the war could no longer make a profit farming, nor could they sell the land for enough to pay off their mortgage. Therefore, they rented it as a stopgap. Banks and insurance companies that foreclosed on mortgages during the 1920s also leased much of the land they acquired.[29]

Tenancy is a slippery word. Census figures do not reveal the number of renters who owned one or more farms and rented others, or *part* owners who paid rent. To assess its impact, moreover, one has to consider whether the land in question was improved or unimproved, the value of crops, and whether it was rented year by year or held on long-term leases (as was common in Illinois, Oklahoma, and South Dakota). A far lower percentage of tenants resided in the West than in Appalachia or the southeastern United States. When the USDA surveyed tenantry in 1926, it discovered that half of all landlords in the West had once been tenant farmers themselves. Nine out of ten were or had been farmers—they were not absentee investors—and only one-sixth of the land in question had been inherited. Moreover, a large percentage of tenants were sons or sons-in-law of those from whom they rented. In the West, the owner often rented to relatives, who were far more likely to treat the land kindly and participate in the community than those unrelated to the owner. In the West, landlords and renters did not constitute self-conscious "classes," nor were their interests necessarily inconsistent or antagonistic.[30]

On the most prosperous government projects, tenancy was rare. But on the poorest projects, the number of renters more than doubled between 1920 and 1925. In the latter year, tenants exceeded 40 percent of the farm operators on the Uncompahgre, Yuma, Minidoka, Milk River, North Platte, Yellowstone, Sun River, Klamath, Huntley, and Carlsbad Projects. These figures were chilling. "I do not believe that tenantry carries out the ideals of the reclamation act," the director of the Reclamation Bureau's new Division of Settlement and Economic Operations noted in a memo prepared for Elwood Mead in 1925. "Naturally the renter of a farm invests his limited capital in the most productive manner, which is in getting all he can out of the land during the time of his lease. As a rule it matters little to him whether the buildings and fences of the farm are kept in good repair, or whether the fertility of the soil is maintained. It is also true that the social life in many neighborhoods is poor because of a population that is shifting [i.e., transient]." Tenants were more likely to overirrigate and plant crops destructive to the soil. They were also less likely to cooperate with other farmers and participate in the affairs of the community.[31]

Tenancy and land monopoly increased as successful farmers and speculators bought land from farmers who failed. Despite the Reclamation Bureau's efforts to discourage large estates, on the Lower Yellowstone and Belle Fourche Projects many individuals held a thousand to three thousand acres.[32] The enabling legislation for several new projects authorized during the 1920s—including the Owyhee-Vale in Oregon and Idaho and the Kittitas in Washington (an extension of the Yakima Project)—prohibited the sale of surplus private land before the secretary of the interior fixed the purchase price and the owner paid half the anticipated construction charges. If a landowner sold surplus land for more than the appraised price, he or she would be required to turn half of the money received over to the government, to be applied against construction charges. The secretary could also cancel the water rights of landowners involved in illegal transactions. But this law was never enforced. Farmers complained that prices set by Interior Department appraisers were so low that the land's value as collateral for loans was sharply reduced.[33]

In 1925, the bureau proposed that when the owner of surplus land within a project sold that land, or any part of it, he or she should pay 5 to 10 percent of the purchase price toward the construction charges due on that parcel. Landowners protested, and the plan was shelved. In the following year, the Omnibus Adjustment Act of 1926 stipulated that excess lands could receive water only if the landowners signed a contract to sell them at a price set by the secretary of the interior. However, while the law required the owner to enter a contract to sell the land, it did not set a deadline for doing so. At the end of the 1920s, the bureau asked holders of excess lands on *new* projects to organize irrigation districts and pledge to sell the land at the undeveloped price, regardless of any increase in value created by the government irrigation works. The irrigation district would serve as an enforcement agency. Landowners had three years to dispose of the land after water became available, at a price of one to twenty dollars an acre, depending on the quality of the soil. If they refused, their water supply could be cut off. Land could be sold for more than the appraised value set by the secretary of the interior, but only on condition that 50 percent of the excess apply toward the cost of construction. This plan did not apply to existing projects, and it worked no better than previous attempts to limit the size and sale of private holdings.[34]

PAYING FOR RECLAMATION: THE COOPERATIVE ALTERNATIVE

Proceeds from public land sales fell from an annual average of $4.5 million in 1911–15 to a negligible $631,000 in 1926–30. Since 1902, Reclamation Service officials had eyed additional sources of revenue independent of Congress. As noted in chapter 4, in 1910 Congress agreed to lend the reclamation fund $20 million, to be repaid at the rate of $1 million a year beginning in 1920, and in the following year the Warren Act pledged all income from the Reclamation Bureau's sale of surplus water to the fund. In 1917, Congress dedicated all royalties and rentals from federal potassium lands to irrigation, at least until the uncompleted projects had been finished. The Oil Leasing Act of 1920 pledged 52.5 percent of future proceeds from the sale and rental of petroleum or mineral lands to reclamation, and the Water Power Act of the same year committed 50 percent of all license fees to the same purpose. From 1902 to 1923, $106 million of the $186 million spent by the Reclamation Service came from the sale of public lands. (The next-largest source of income, $46 million, came from project collections, including construction charges.) By 1929, however, oil leases contributed to reclamation three times more revenue than land sales.[35]

The more money that poured into the reclamation fund, the more likely project farmers were to see federal reclamation as a giveaway or welfare program. The states, which now profited from gasoline taxes, motor vehicle registration fees, and other new sources of income, were an alternative source of revenue. The unsuccessful Lane-Mondell soldier settlement bill had emphasized cooperation between the federal government and states in postwar veteran resettlement efforts. That set a precedent for much of the cooperative legislation considered during the 1920s.[36]

Cooperation was not a new idea. For example, in 1900, following a major drought, the California Water and Forest Association—composed mainly of San Francisco banks that held mortgages on land in the Central Valley—raised ten thousand dollars to help pay the cost of a hydrographic survey of water rights and reservoir sites conducted by Elwood Mead's Office of Irrigation Investigations in the U.S. Department of Agriculture. The State of California also engaged in cooperative investigations with both Mead's office and the Forestry Bureau, matching federal appropriations dollar for dollar.[37]

As early as 1904, William Ellsworth Smythe, Francis G. Newlands, and other friends of national reclamation proposed using irrigation districts to supplement the budget of the Reclamation Bureau, particularly where opportunities to construct large projects on the public domain were limited, as in California. Irrigation districts could use the Reclamation Service to assess the feasibility of potential irrigation projects, and to design and construct the hydraulic works. This would reduce the cost of construction, ensure the quality of dams and canals, and provide the impartial supervision that districts had lacked in the past. If government engineers rejected a proposal sponsored by local landowners, it would be impossible to sell the bonds; bad schemes would be killed in their infancy. But if the Reclamation Service agreed to construct a project, that, in itself, would give the project credibility.[38]

Smythe persuaded the 1904 Irrigation Congress to endorse his idea, but the Reclamation Act of 1902 gave the secretary of the interior no authority to undertake such hybrid projects, and Congress showed no willingness to amend the law. Easterners and midwesterners were in no mood to expand federal reclamation, and many westerners feared that Smythe's scheme would give the national government too much *direct* control over their water—and their economic development. Any partnership between the national government and local water users threatened to undermine the authority of the states.[39]

Despite Congress's reluctance to permit the Reclamation Service to enter contracts with irrigation districts, the district form remained very attractive. Districts could sell bonds and use the proceeds to repay the federal government *immediately* for the cost of construction. They seemed ideally suited to administer water projects in which the national government built dams and main canals and the district constructed the distribution and drainage systems. And while the Reclamation Service found it difficult to collect charges from uncultivated or dry-farmed land within its projects, irrigation districts had the power to tax *all* land within their boundaries, including urban real estate, whether the owners chose to irrigate or not.[40]

The irrigation district offered great advantages over water user associations, which prevailed on most of the projects. Water user associations were inherently "undemocratic." They operated on the principle of one acre, one vote, rather than one man, one vote, and they had little authority to discipline members. They were not collection agencies. Every water user had a separate contract and account with the government, which drove up the Reclamation Service's administrative and bookkeeping costs. When farmers refused to repay construction debt, the government filed suits against every farmer in arrears. Nor could water user associations compel project landowners who refused to apply for water rights to pay operation and maintenance charges. By transferring administrative responsibilities to local officials elected by the farmers themselves, it was hoped, much criticism could be diverted away from the Reclamation Service. The Warren Act, which permitted the Reclamation Service to sell surplus water stored in government reservoirs to landowners outside project boundaries, renewed interest in the irrigation district. In many parts of the West, farmers who worked land adjoining federal projects organized irrigation districts with the express purpose of purchasing water.

In 1915, a Reclamation Service official drafted a plan to create a *second* reclamation fund exclusively to construct dams and canals within irrigation districts. (The original fund would be used to complete existing projects.) To reduce interference from state officials, the Reclamation Bureau would pay the entire cost of investigating proposed projects, and the secretary of the interior could veto any project. Each state would establish its own reclamation fund, and the secretary would draw on that money to match federal contributions, dollar for dollar. District taxes would replenish the state fund, plus interest. The federal government would operate the hydraulic system until the state had recovered its investment. Then control over dams and canals would pass to the water users.[41]

The author of the 1915 district plan recognized that it would not be easy to implement. Large landowners opposed water districts that imposed too many restrictions on their property. They feared being forced to shoulder the construction debt of poor and "improvident" neighbors. Congress would have to find a way to include public lands within irrigation districts while title to that land remained with the national government. And the states would have to enact district laws consistent with the Reclamation Act of 1902, which required landowners to reside on or near the land irrigated; imposed a limitation of 160 acres on the amount of land that could be watered; and attached water rights to individual parcels (rather than allowing rights to "float" within the district). Simultaneously, the states would have to amend their constitutions to permit the federal government to spend money they had raised, and state officials were likely to demand a say in deciding which projects were built and how they were managed. Moreover, state legislatures were unlikely to approve schemes to build up one community at the expense of another; competition within states was often as intense as competition among them. The state mercantilism that crippled public policy in the nineteenth-century West survived well into the twentieth century. Nothing came of the 1915 district plan.[42]

Following World War I, Congress placed renewed emphasis on federal-state cooperation. In 1922, the postwar agricultural slump finally persuaded Congress to authorize the Bureau of Reclamation to enter contracts with irrigation districts. The legislation's main purpose, according to Congressman Moses P. Kinkaid of Nebraska, was "to afford farmers under Government reclamation projects equal opportunity with farmers in the humid regions to secure a loan of the federal farm land banks [created in 1916]." Before making a loan, the Federal Farm Loan Board required a first mortgage on the land, which was impossible to secure within federal irrigation projects, where the title to public land remained with the federal government until the cost of constructing irrigation works had been repaid. The 1922 legislation was also designed to give water users more say in the administration of federal reclamation projects, but the main advantage to the Reclamation Bureau was that *all* lands within a project could now be made liable for the cost of construction.[43]

The 1922 law was designed to facilitate the transfer of power over dams and canals from the federal government to local water users rather than to expand water projects or build new ones. Therefore, during the mid-1920s, the Reclamation Bureau tried a new approach. The western states were no longer as poor as they had been in 1902, as the cooperation by federal, state, and local governments in road construction had demonstrated. By 1924, the federal government had spent more than $400 million on road building, twice the total amount invested in federal reclamation. Under 1916 and 1921 laws, the states proposed the roads to be built and paid for construction, but they received a rebate of half the cost from the Bureau of Public Roads in the USDA. Congress limited financial aid to no more than 7 percent of a state's roads, measured by total mileage. To secure aid, the states were required to create highway departments and take over maintenance of completed roads from the counties. Federal highway construction represented shared responsibility, not a consolidation of power in Washington. The Bureau of Public Roads grew in size, but so did state engineering offices. All the western states participated.[44]

If the federal government and states could cooperate in road building, why not in reclamation? The states had raised constitutional objections to sharing the cost of *construction*. But what if the federal government took the responsibility for construction and the states for settlement? Bad projects—those advanced simply to secure federal revenue—would disappear because the state governments would serve as a buffer between local water users and their congressional representatives. Congress had balked at planned colonization and direct financial aid to settlers, so why not ask the states to undertake that work? Such a plan would make eastern members of Congress more likely to support future appropriations for irrigation. Little could be done with projects already under construction, but in 1925 Congress required that on new projects pending in Washington, Oregon, and Montana, the state should select and finance settlers.[45] Under this plan, Washington, Oregon, and Montana would be required to investigate the cost of setting up the farms, how much revenue those farms would produce, where settlers could be found, and how much capital and additional assistance settlers would require.[46]

The plan became law, but not a single member of the West's congressional delegation voted for it. Western politicians claimed that their states had already exceeded bonded debt limits; that their constitutions forbade such cooperative arrangements; that it would be impossible to administer such public works because state bureaucracies were much more susceptible to changes in administration and policy than the Reclamation Bureau; that a system of dual authority would not work; and that the federal government had withdrawn so much public land from taxation in the West that it had an obligation to pay the entire cost of reclamation to compensate for the lost revenue. There was also a matter of equity. Senator John B. Kendrick of Wyoming noted that while mineral leases and land sales in his state had returned $26 million to the reclamation fund, the federal government had spent only $16 million in his state. Wyoming had, in Kendrick's judgment, subsidized the agricultural development of other states. The federal government had a moral obligation to water the West. "The Government should not consider abdicating its position and leaving the real and final work of completing the task to the states with their doubtful capacity, their limited abilities, and changing personnel of State administrations," Kendrick observed. The cooperative schemes of the 1920s demonstrated that the Reclamation Bureau wanted greater involvement by the states, but the states refused to share the financial and moral burden of reclamation.[47]

RECLAMATION REFORM IN THE 1920S

In the early days of federal reclamation, an employee of the Reclamation Service encountered a shack in the desert that bore the sign: "Taint much but its our'n." That spirit of independence and autonomy had largely disappeared by the 1920s. Problems of construction gave way to problems of settlement, and the friends of federal reclamation began to study rural society. The Bureau of Reclamation's magazine *Reclamation Record*—which became the *New Reclamation Era* in 1924—reflected the change. A host of new concerns emerged in the 1920s, including the health of children, the quality of rural schools, opportunities for recreation, and the rate of participation in local politics. Once, *Reclamation Record* had focused almost entirely on the contest between farmers and the land. Now it discussed diet and nutrition, how to make curtains, how to purchase a washing machine, how to fit shoes properly, and how to eradicate rats and mice. The publication educated farm families about home beautification and modern conveniences—particularly indoor plumbing and heating. Farmers on government projects now wanted a *comfortable* living, not just a living.[48]

Reclamation had become a family affair. *New Reclamation Era* addressed farm women in the regular feature "Reclamation Project Women." Secretary of the Interior Hubert Work acknowledged that lack of attention to women's needs was one of the main reasons that the government projects contained so many abandoned farms. "There is no exhausting monotonous drudgery known to civilization that is comparable to that the average farmer's wife endures," he observed. Cooking, cleaning, washing, and child rearing took a toll, but farm women were much more than homemakers. In the mid-1920s, a government survey revealed that 89 percent of project women raised poultry (which produced an income almost as great as dairying on many projects); 93 percent washed milk pails; 66 percent made and sold butter; 66 percent maintained gardens; 26 percent tended livestock; 22 percent worked in the fields an average of five weeks or more per year; and 45 percent helped with the milking.[49]

By the end of the 1920s, project women had begun to organize. Women on the Uncompahgre Project in Colorado formed both a women's club and a community club. After securing a telephone system, rural mail service, and enclosed school buses, they decided to build a community center. By selling fruits and vegetables from their gardens, and by hosting chicken dinners, the women raised twenty-five hundred dollars for building materials. The men excavated the foundation, hauled sand, gravel, and lumber, and constructed the furniture. Only a carpenter—hired mainly to instruct and direct the volunteers—received wages. Construction lasted six months and promoted sociability and community spirit among Uncompahgre residents. Subsequently, the women's club raised money to equip the building with acetylene lighting, a piano, a kitchen range, and dishes. The community center was heavily used by the Business and Professional Women's Club of Grand Junction and by the Mesa County Women's Extension Club. It was open to the public "on all occasions except dances," according to the *New Reclamation Era*. "Such entertainments [the dances] are strictly by invitation, assuring reputable guests." The message was clear: A common purpose, cohesive community, and active social life produced happy women and a successful agricultural project.[50]

Unfortunately, many problems faced by federal reclamation in the 1920s could not be solved by project residents. The settlers on one project included a former deep-sea diver, a one-time missionary to China, and the wife of an itinerant baseball player. Nonresident owners included a painter, a plumber, a carpenter, and a nurse—all of whom lived in distant cities and refused to pay either local taxes or their debt to the government. As Mead noted: "Creation of a great agricultural community or the solvency of an irrigation project cannot be secured with this kind of human material. On projects like this the fundamental problem is to get real farmers to replace these derelicts who have given up hope but linger on, like Micawber, waiting for something to turn up."[51]

In March 1923, Hubert Work succeeded Albert B. Fall as secretary of the interior. A medical doctor and former postmaster general, Work had few ties to the West. Soon after taking office, he found himself deluged with complaints from the government reclamation projects, much as Franklin K. Lane had been when he became secretary in 1913. Delinquent construction payments had increased from 14 percent in 1919 to 40 percent in 1922. Despite protests from the Reclamation Bureau, Congress had excused both construction and operation and maintenance payments in 1921, 1922, and 1923, and it seemed likely to do so for the foreseeable future—or write off the entire debt, if a strident group of westerners in Congress had its way.[52] Work promised to apply to the Interior Department the "same strictly business methods that prevailed in the Postoffice Department during my incumbency as Postmaster General." He questioned whether project farmers were as financially destitute as they claimed. He observed that on one project, where fifty-five irrigators had paid nothing for four years or more, a 1925 order to turn off water resulted in collection of the previous year's charges from more than 80 percent of those in arrears. They stalled, he believed, because they felt little pressure to pay.[53]

One of Work's first acts as secretary of the interior was to appoint D. W. Davis—president of the Western States Reclamation Association, a banker in Idaho Falls, and twice the governor of Idaho—as a special adviser on reclamation, responsible to him alone. (D. W. Davis was not related to A. P. Davis, the commissioner of reclamation.) Then, at the beginning of April 1923, Work ordered his new adviser to investigate each federal reclamation project in company with A. P. Davis. Unable "to get figures that appear to be dependable as to the cost of individual projects or the total money expended on all projects"—a problem Ballinger and Lane had complained about a decade earlier—Work soon decided to reorganize the Reclamation Service. "If the Reclamation Department had taken the time to test a single experiment to its conclusion before starting on the big programme," Work recounted in 1925, "many, many millions would have been saved, but our enterprising Westerners would not have been satisfied." Not only had construction costs run as much as ten times more than original estimates, but overhead expenses had been hidden in operation and maintenance charges. Like Ballinger and Lane, Work became convinced that the Reclamation Service had engaged in willful deception.[54]

In June 1923, Work fired A. P. Davis and replaced him with D. W. Davis. In a deliciously ambiguous press release, the secretary remarked that "the reclamation service of the Government has had but two directors in its history of 21 years, both engineers and each with 10 years' service. They have erected their own monuments and the different projects are writing the inscriptions for them."[55]

A. P. Davis had been responsible for the construction of many of the Reclamation Service's most notable works, including the Shoshone, Arrowrock, and Elephant Butte Dams, and the four-mile Strawberry Tunnel and the six-mile Gunnison Tunnel. His removal caused a firestorm of controversy within professional engineering societies. Work claimed to represent the ethics of business, but he was a medical doctor, and D. W. Davis was a politician and businessman, not an engineer or agricultural scientist. D. W. Davis was the first non-engineer and the first non–civil service employee to head the Reclamation Service, and he had even less experience designing or administering reclamation projects than Newell or A. P. Davis had when they had taken office. Engineering organizations resented the suggestion that engineers could not be effective administrators or businessmen, particularly when the nation's most prominent engineer, Herbert Hoover, then served with great distinction as secretary of commerce.

A. P. Davis claimed that he had been the victim of a cabal of project farmers and land speculators who sought to repudiate their debt to the government, along with western politicians; boosters who wanted the Reclamation Service to build new projects, which Davis considered infeasible at a time the reclamation fund was impoverished; boosters in the Columbia Basin who resented Davis's support of the Colorado River Project; and private power companies in Colorado and California. (A. P. Davis favored the construction of a series of high dams on the Colorado River—dams that could generate electricity. The Reclamation Service's plans to develop the Colorado River threatened applications from private companies to build dams—applications then pending with the Federal Power Commission.)[56]

Work denied that he had any motive for firing Davis other than to rescue the Reclamation Bureau. Soon after taking office, the secretary formed a commission to study the problems of federal reclamation, in part to shield the Harding administration from mounting criticism of the Interior Department following the March 1923 resignation of Albert B. Fall, who had been caught secretly leasing oil reserves at Teapot Dome, Wyoming, and Elk Hills, California, to private companies in exchange for bribes. The Interior Department, or the "Great Miscellany," as it was derisively called, was a favorite target for budget cutters and those who wanted to reorganize the cabinet departments. Reclamation contributed to its reputation for inefficiency. "No comprehensive, independent, and comparative study of the success, partial success, or failure of reclamation projects . . . has ever been made by investigators who have had original official records opened to them," Work explained. The commission consisted of D. W. Davis; John A. Widtsoe, an internationally known agronomist and former president of Utah State College; Thomas E. Campbell, former governor of Arizona; James R. Garfield, Theodore Roosevelt's secretary of the interior; Oscar E. Bradfute, president of the American Farm Bureau Federation; Julius Barnes, president of the U.S. Chamber of Commerce; and the group's guiding light, Elwood Mead. The commission first met in October 1923, but public hearings did not begin until January 1924.[57]

Mead's committee came to be called the Board of Special Advisers, or the Fact Finders' Commission. It pored through Interior and Reclamation Bureau records, interviewed project managers, and heard testimony from 124 witnesses, including the leaders of many of the federal government's natural resource bureaus. The committee's formal report was inspired, if not written, by Mead, who became head of the Reclamation Bureau when D. W. Davis resigned in April 1924, around the time the document became public.[58]

The Fact Finders' report symbolized federal reclamation's new focus on agriculture rather than hydraulic engineering, but most of its recommendations dated to the critique of bureau policies Mead wrote for Franklin K. Lane in 1915.[59] The Fact Finders recommended that project lands should be classified according to their productive capacity *prior* to the construction of dams and canals. The land's income-producing potential, not the pro rata cost of constructing dams, canals, and drainage ditches, should determine the per-acre debt. Before opening any new project, the government should determine not just the cost of developing the land, but also how much capital farmers would need to get started. It should then secure control of all private holdings to limit farm size and prevent speculation. It should also screen settlers to ensure that they had the temperament, experience, industry, and capital needed to succeed at desert farming. No project should be authorized before a thorough study of available markets had been completed, and no payments should be required until the land began to produce crops.

Each project should include an experienced "farm adviser" to furnish new settlers with plans for houses and barns and to teach them what machinery to buy, what crops to plant, and how to market those crops. Before the project opened, a demonstration farm of ten thousand to fifteen thousand acres should be cleared, leveled, and planted to fodder crops. Not only would the demonstration farm show farmers the best crops to grow, it also would teach them how to supplement their agricultural income by dairying, bee keeping, or raising livestock or poultry. In addition, the Fact Finders' Commission proposed the establishment of a fund to loan farmers money at low interest so that they could build houses and barns, purchase equipment and livestock, and support their families until their land produced an adequate income.[60]

The Fact Finders' report was a tract for the times—consistent with the ideals of the 1920s, which emphasized scientific agriculture, land-use planning, and social engineering. The frontier phase of haphazard economic development—development driven by speculation and the ethics of localism—had passed. The era of "free land" and cheap irrigation was over. The report recognized that under the best conditions, reclamation could not become self-supporting for thirty to forty years, if ever.

What the Fact Finders' Commission left unsaid, however, was as important as the reforms it proposed. The high cost of constructing irrigation works and languishing crop prices suggested that in the future, reclamation would become even more dependent on federal aid; desert agriculture could no longer pay for itself. As Mead noted in a memorandum prepared for Senator Charles McNary of Oregon in 1926, "Adequate capital from private sources can not be secured. The country is undeveloped; the capital is not there." Without government loans of *substantial* amounts of money to new settlers at low interest, there was no way to populate the existing projects, let alone expand the amount of land irrigated.[61]

"I feel sure," Mead hopefully wrote to a friend in October 1924, "that with a properly aroused public opinion, Congress will be induced to rewrite the social and economic features of the reclamation act, and if they do, we can create some western communities that will be landmarks like Greeley, Colorado." Many nations had demonstrated the desirability and effectiveness of aiding farmers directly. The governments of England, Holland, Denmark, France, Germany, and Italy lent farmers money at interest rates of 2.5 to 5 percent, with repayment stretched over forty years or more. Mortgage banks in Europe lent up to 90 percent of the value of a farm—far more than in the United States, where a 60 percent loan was unusual. Australia's provincial governments tapped deposits in postal savings banks to provide settlers with low-interest loans. "If the United States would increase the interest rate on postal savings to 3 or $3\frac{1}{2}\%$ and lend that money to the states to be reloaned to settlers at 4%," Mead observed, "two classes of people whose contentment and success are vital to democracy would be working for each other."[62]

The parsimonious mood of Congress in the 1920s, and its refusal to aid distressed farmers anywhere in the nation, reduced the impact of the Fact Finders' Commission. Nevertheless, in December 1924, Congress enacted major changes in federal reclamation. It authorized the secretary of the interior to write off unrealistic construction charges. The debt burden was also reduced by eliminating administrative costs from the charges levied against settlers. The Reclamation Act of 1924 temporarily suspended the existing twenty-year repayment schedule. In lieu of an arbitrary per-acre construction charge, it imposed an annual charge of 5 percent of gross income per acre. In years of poor crops, or in years when prices fell sharply, payments could be deferred.[63] (By 1926, the cost of construction had been recalculated on twenty-one projects, and the repayment period had been doubled to forty years.) In theory, potential projects could no longer be undertaken until studies demonstrated an adequate water supply, fertile soil, and a capacity to repay the cost of construction. The legislation also permitted the Reclamation Bureau to screen potential settlers, and it required those selected to have at least two thousand dollars in capital. Nothing, however, was done to implement the more ambitious recommendations in the Fact Finders' Report, such as providing low-interest loans.[64]

Federal reclamation faced a dilemma: despite the fact that the program was not paying for itself as originally intended, Congress could not abandon the projects, because many poor western states had come to depend on them. Having made an economic commitment to develop the West, the federal government could not back out. Yet without providing the West with a great deal more aid, it could not move forward. Simply to stay afloat, federal reclamation would have to go far beyond the objectives of the Reclamation Act of 1902. There was also a second dilemma. Mead acknowledged that "it was never the purpose of that [1902] act to subsidize private owners by furnishing interest free money to develop their excess land holdings, leaving them free to capitalize the Government's investment in reclamation works and add it to their price at which they sell their excess holdings to actual settlers."[65] Yet the government's efforts to help needy farmers were likely to increase speculation rather than reduce it.

"Future reclamation . . . has to deal almost entirely with privately owned land," Mead observed in 1924. "The iniquitous grazing homestead act (1909, 1912, 1916) has been employed to secure title to every quarter section that there is hope of having included in a future Government project. A few weeks ago I went over the proposed Casper-Alcova project [in Wyoming]. When we came to the area that was to be watered it was dotted over with tar paper shacks, placed there by the speculative grazing homesteaders who probably had never stayed in the place a night." Despite the 1924 reforms, federal reclamation could not be rescued from the mistakes of the past. The Fact Finders' Commission proposed a dramatic increase in the power of the Reclamation Bureau at a time when Congress refused to expand the responsibilities of any federal bureaucracy.[66]

FEDERAL RECLAMATION, 1924–1935

Elwood Mead brought impressive credentials to the Reclamation Bureau, including a breadth of experience unmatched by any chief executive of the bureau before or since. Born on an Indiana farm in 1858 and educated as a civil engineer at Purdue and Iowa State Universities, he in 1882 joined the faculty of what became Colorado State University as the first professor of agricultural engineering in the United States. He also served as Colorado's assistant state engineer before moving across the border to Wyoming, where he became territorial engineer in 1888 and state engineer in 1890. From 1898 to 1907 he headed the USDA's Office of Irrigation Investigations. Early in the twentieth century he also created a department of irrigation within the Agriculture College at the University of California, Berkeley, where he remained on the faculty until 1928, though often on leave to advise officials in Washington, Australia, or Palestine.

From 1907 to 1915, Mead directed the State Rivers and Water Supply Commission in Victoria, Australia, where he supervised the planning and settlement of thirty-two irrigation projects. The Australia experience strengthened his vision of planned agricultural settlement. Victoria's government planted the land, constructed roads, laid out towns, and even built homes for settlers—all in advance of their arrival. After returning to the United States, Mead worked briefly as an assistant to Secretary of the Interior Franklin K. Lane before he persuaded the California legislature to create irrigation colonies at Durham and Delhi. He administered those colonies from 1915 to 1923. They collapsed in the postwar agricultural depression and exhibited many of the same problems as government reclamation projects. Nevertheless, they stood as bold experiments in colonization, with their careful selection of settlers, preparation of the land in advance of cultivation, and long-term loans for improvements.[67]

Mead became commissioner of reclamation in April 1924, following the resignation of D. W. Davis. "I have said," Mead wrote to the editor of the *Yakima Republic* in 1926, "and I believe you will agree with me, that the procedure we have followed [in federal reclamation] is exactly analogous to expending huge sums of money erecting factory buildings, without any idea of what particular product the factory was to make, what kind of machinery was to be installed or its cost, or what kind of workers were to be employed."[68] "The pioneer believed that every man should hoe his own row and take care of himself," Mead observed on another occasion. "It [the pioneer spirit] created a confident and hopeful people but made them migratory and speculative. The pioneer was not a good farmer. He was ready to move on when there was a chance to sell out at a profit, and gave little thought to the needs of the rural civilization he was helping to create."[69] It was, according to Mead, "simply throwing money away to build more canals without some provision for peopling the land."[70]

Mead was not as "modern" as he appeared; he was as much a nineteenth-century man as Frederick H. Newell. What set him apart from Newell was the recognition that the pioneer phase of settling the West was over. Mead understood that there was no room for the independent farmer in the 1920s—an era characterized as the "age of organization" or the "age of association." In his judgment, reclamation had to become more scientific, planning had to become more comprehensive, and farmers had to learn to work together. He doubted that western agriculture could be made profitable enough to attract capable farmers, but he never questioned the *need* to maintain the family farm, nor did he doubt that under the right conditions most Americans would choose rural over urban life. Like Newell, Smythe, Maxwell, and Davis, Mead was a romantic and a stern moralist. He did not see the economy as a series of interconnected parts, and he rarely considered the agricultural implications of industrial capitalism. In an age dominated by large economic units—particularly the manufacturing corporation—Mead clung to an antiquated Jeffersonian view of society. That was his dilemma: he understood the need for planning and efficiency but could not escape the ancient, outmoded agricultural models of the New England village and the family farm.

Mead had five goals when he took office at the Reclamation Bureau: to promote greater cooperation among the federal government, states, and local groups of water users so that all levels of government would address the rising cost of reclamation; to limit land speculation; to colonize government projects in a systematic manner; to reduce the number of settlers with inadequate capital or experience; and to provide them with more financial and educational aid. Despite Mead's best efforts, none of these goals was accomplished.[71]

In June 1924, Mead visited government irrigation projects in nine western states, inspecting six proposed and thirteen existing projects. He then established a test for prospective settlers. Since the beginning of federal reclamation, all who had filed for a government farm had been accepted, regardless of experience or financial resources. When the number of applicants exceeded the number of available farms, the Reclamation Service used a lottery to select the winners—an open-door policy that had powerful appeal because it gave *all* citizens a chance to share in the benefits of the program. Since some people were destined to fail in whatever career they choose, it seemed fairer to let the person eliminate himself or herself rather than to assign that job to a committee of settlers or to a government bureau.[72]

In keeping with the Reclamation Act of 1924, the Reclamation Bureau in 1925 applied the first minimum requirements to applicants for vacant farms on existing projects and appointed local examining boards to consider the industry, experience, character, and capital of prospective settlers. These settlers had to have at least two years of agricultural experience, enjoy vigorous health, and possess a minimum of two thousand dollars in money, land, farm equipment, or livestock. Since 70 percent of the applicants for government farms had less than fifteen hundred dollars in assets, that was a substantial restriction. Nevertheless, the policy had little effect. Most unsettled land within the projects was privately owned, and the Reclamation Service had no authority to screen those who bought private land.[73]

Mead also wanted to set aside part of the vacant land on each existing project to demonstrate the advantages of planned group settlement. The area had to be large enough to provide a hundred farms and at least five farm laborers' allotments. Where public land was insufficient, the secretary of the interior could purchase land from private owners at no more than ten dollars an acre. He would then classify the soil, appraise its productivity, determine reasonable construction costs, and sell it in small parcels, offering buyers forty years to repay at 4 percent interest. Applicants for these farms would be required to have at least one year's experience in farming and financial resources equal to 25 percent of the farm's appraised value. To protect against nonresident owners, and to limit speculation, he or she was required to reside on the farm for at least eight months a year, and the land could not be sold or leased without the secretary's approval. The secretary could lend each settler up to three thousand dollars for improvements, and each farm laborer up to eight hundred dollars, but the total could not exceed 60 percent of the value of the improvements or livestock for which the money was requested. The loan could run no more than twenty years and would carry 4 percent interest.[74]

In 1925, Mead drafted a planned settlement bill, but Congress rejected it. In 1926, he proposed a more modest measure that would have created two demonstration colonies, each containing a hundred farms. The Senate approved the legislation, but in the House it ran into the Midwestern "farm bloc," the economy-minded, and those to whom government planning of any sort smacked of socialism. The failures of Mead's Durham and Delhi colonies in California made Congress wary of even the two-project scheme.[75] The more ambitious planned-settlement legislation that first appeared in 1924–25 was reintroduced in 1928, but with no greater success.[76]

In 1924, settlers on government projects paid less than half their scheduled construction charges and little more than half their operation and maintenance charges. Residents of the Okanogan and North Platte Projects remitted only 6 percent of what was due, and those on the Umatilla only 3 percent. The Lower Yellowstone and Williston Projects returned nothing. Many families lost their farms to mortgage holders. On the Fort Laramie Division of Wyoming's North Platte Project, for example, 3,300 veterans filed on eighty farm units in 1920. Of the eighty "winners," only twenty-five remained in 1923, and only twelve stayed on their land through the end of the decade.[77]

Mead's dilemma was that he wanted to provide loans and other assistance to government farmers, but not postpone or excuse the repayment of construction costs. Conditions on the poorest projects warranted special consideration, but any concessions would encourage defaults on the most prosperous projects—where farmers could easily make their payments. "If the reclamation fund is to be used as a credit fund and collections are not to be pressed whenever there are poor crops or low prices," Mead observed in 1926, "then . . . a complete separation [should] be made between operation and development and credits and collections." The latter function, he thought, could be transferred to the Treasury Department.[78] Once again, Congress ignored Mead's advice. In 1926 it wrote off the entire cost of the Buford-Trenton and Williston Projects in North Dakota, cancelled nearly $15 million in construction debt, and deferred the repayment of another $13 million—which debt seemed likely to be excused in the future.[79]

The poor record of repayment persuaded Mead that no new projects should be considered until the twenty-two yet unfinished had been completed—at an estimated cost of $100 million. Nevertheless, in 1924 Congress voted $7.1 million to launch several new schemes, and from 1924 to 1926 it approved five new projects and the expansion of three old ones—at a cost of $60 million. The per-acre cost ran four or five times that on the original government farms. "The land that is to pay these costs is unimproved, unpeopled, unleveled sagebrush, most of it remote from markets, and in some instances having such broken surfaces that preparation for irrigation will be expensive," Mead warned. Establishing an eighty-acre farm within these projects would cost from sixteen thousand to twenty thousand dollars. Since improved land with buildings and crops could be purchased for $150 an acre in many parts of the West, these projects were wildly impractical.[80]

The U.S. attorney general ruled that the Reclamation Act of 1924 gave the secretary of the interior power to reject projects approved by Congress. In any case, Congress had authorized the expenditure of money only from the reclamation fund, not from the general treasury. It was committing anticipated revenue, not spending available money. With proceeds from oil royalties and land sales falling rapidly, the construction plan was meaningless. Oil royalties poured about $7 million into the reclamation fund in 1924, but only $2.5 million in 1928.[81]

With its best efforts at social planning blocked in the West, the Reclamation Bureau again looked to the South. That region had advantages over the West, including a long growing season, flat or gently rolling land, productive soil (if adequately fertilized), and a good transportation system. As the poorest part of the nation, the South would demonstrate the greatest benefit from planned agricultural development. And since it specialized in crops such as tobacco, rice, and cotton, grown exclusively in that region, midwestern farmers were less likely to oppose reclamation there than in the West. During World War I and the 1920s, a new spirit prevailed in Dixie; boosters wanted to discard the image of "cotton country" and to woo new residents and industry. "Its people no longer look indifferently upon the rich and vitalizing flood of immigration that swept to the West . . . while passing by the greater opportunities in the South," the *New Orleans Times-Picayune* observed. "[T]he future development and progress of the United States lies in the South." The West-South gap in land prices narrowed throughout most of the 1920s, but in 1928 an eighty-acre farm in the West still cost twice as much as the same farm in the South.[82]

Given the South's economic "backwardness," no part of the nation had greater potential to demonstrate the transformation wrought by reclamation. Its farmers had little familiarity with scientific agriculture, much of its agricultural land had been exhausted, and rates of tenant farming were far higher there than in other regions. As Elwood Mead put it: "The negro, the mule and the single-crop farm must give way to mixed farming, to the introduction of improved breeds of livestock, to the use of costlier and more complicated farm implements"—and, of course, to irrigation.[83]

From 1920 to 1925, farmland decreased by 3.5 million acres in Georgia, 3 million acres in Alabama, 2 million acres in South Carolina, and 1.5 million acres in North Carolina. Unlike in the West, therefore, planned agricultural communities in the South could be sold as *replacement acreage* rather than as an addition to the nation's stock of farmland. Both abandoned and swamp land would be much cheaper to reclaim than arid land, and such land was more likely to be near large cities and markets. "It is my belief," Mead wrote to a friend at the beginning of 1922, "that there is a wider opportunity and greater need for the creation of organized rural communities on the waste lands of the older states . . . than there is in the reclamation of land [in the arid West,] where people will have to live under pioneer conditions and where they are remote from markets." A few years later, Mead observed, "I believe that a few organized colonies will have a lasting effect on rural life and agriculture in the South, . . . [and] that success there will react on other parts of the Nation."[84]

In 1918, with the Reclamation Bureau's encouragement, Franklin K. Lane had persuaded Congress to appropriate a hundred thousand dollars to investigate the reclamation of marsh, swamp, and cutover lands in the South. A. P. Davis had estimated that three times more swampland could be turned into farms than arid land—and more quickly. In his message to Congress at the end of 1918, President Wilson had heartily endorsed Lane's reclamation plan. The Reclamation Bureau then combed each state for unoccupied blocks of land containing at least ten thousand acres.[85] The hundred thousand dollars appropriated in 1918 was followed by additional expenditures in 1926, 1927, and 1928 that funded a series of national-state cooperative investigations. In November 1926, Interior Secretary Hubert Work appointed a committee headed by Howard Elliott—chair of the Northern Pacific Railroad's board of directors—to select potential reclamation projects in the South.[86] Work asked each southern governor, in consultation with representatives of the USDA and state agricultural colleges, to designate between ten thousand and thirty thousand acres of land—a tract sufficient to provide homes for one hundred to three hundred families. The committee visited these sites in December 1926 and two months later recommended four projects to Congress. In 1928, legislation was introduced to authorize construction. The bill carried an appropriation of $10 million, with the stipulation that no more than $2 million could be spent in any one southern state. The secretary of the interior, through the Reclamation Bureau, would purchase and subdivide the land, and the beneficiaries would repay the cost over forty years at 4 percent interest. The legislation permitted the secretary to loan up to three thousand dollars per farm for improvements and up to a thousand for farmworker allotments.[87]

The plan strongly resembled Mead's western land settlement legislation. Not surprisingly, it won little support in Congress and severe criticism in the Department of Agriculture. In his annual report for 1927, Secretary of Agriculture William Jardine chastised federal reclamation and strongly opposed extending it to swamp or cutover land. Between 1919 and 1924, the secretary argued, the amount of cultivated land east of the Mississippi River declined by nearly 16 million acres, and less than 40 percent of the reclaimed swampland in the lower Mississippi Valley and the South Atlantic states was under cultivation. Federal reclamation had already brought more land into cultivation than market conditions warranted, which, he claimed, contributed to the agricultural depression, and Congress had unwisely approved new projects in the West. "When farming is sufficiently profitable," the agriculture secretary noted, "there will be plenty of land forthcoming. Much of the needed increase will be made available from the larger areas of cut-over land and semiarid land not requiring extensive reclamation, much of it already within the boundaries of farms. Indeed, experience has shown that when the outlook is sufficiently promising private enterprise can be depended on to reclaim new areas. . . . [I]t hardly seems necessary or desirable to employ Federal funds, except under very unusual conditions, to accomplish what private capital will not venture to undertake on account of the doubtful profitableness of the enterprise."[88]

For all its advantages, the South had many perceived liabilities. Tenancy averaged 45 percent for the entire region but as high as 65 percent in South Carolina and 64 percent in Georgia. The memory of the Civil War made northerners wary of settling there, and, as one Reclamation Bureau official put it, the "Negro's anomalous place in the social, industrial, and agricultural life of the region" suggested that "the white manual laborer's social caste is lower in Dixie than elsewhere in the country." The South, moreover, was subject to enervating summers, fevers, and malaria. In much of the region, heavy rainfall produced pools of water and swamps that served as the domicile of deadly mosquitoes.[89]

By the end of the 1920s, Mead's attempts to reform federal reclamation faced criticism from all parts of the country.[90] In 1928, a committee of the American Society of Civil Engineers recommended that no new irrigation projects be approved until the agricultural depression lifted, and the U.S. Chamber of Commerce and National Grange took similar stands. The problem was more than economic; Americans disliked planning. They were, in Elwood Mead's words, "so wedded to the pioneer doctrine of every man for himself and the devil take the hindmost that it is almost impossible to get people to think of cooperation or coordination in the action of rural communities." A faculty member in the department of mechanical engineering at the University of Iowa reacted to Mead's first planned settlement bill with typical disdain:

> My first reaction in consideration of a measure so paternalistic in its general aspects is unfavorable. We who were brought up in that region of our arid west where all material development reflected the result of individualistic, or in some

cases mildly communistic effort, and where the sacrifices and privations of the pioneers who wrested the country from the wilderness had become a sort of glorified tradition, cannot help but feel an impatience with a class of people who in these days with infinitely more of material aid seem to have neither the courage, the skill, nor the patience to win a competence or at least a living out of irrigated agriculture.[91]

Critics of federal reclamation believed, with Frederick H. Newell, that a breakdown in the character of settlers had doomed the national irrigation program. No federal policy would work if farmers were unwilling to take responsibility for their own destiny.

Much to Mead's dismay, the most strident opposition to his policies came not from farmers in the eastern half of the nation but from the West. "Secretary Work is unwilling that we should have anything to do with legislation in aid of [planned] settlement unless we know there is practically unanimous support for it in the West," Mead noted in 1927. "We have advocated three bills of that character only to be ridiculed by western senators and congressmen. The Secretary is not willing to undergo that experience again." Two years later Mead predicted that "there will be no legislation this Congress, nor until the speculative element in the West becomes convinced that it is not possible to get money for new canals unless there is assurance that the water will be used after they are built." Save for postponing or excusing their debt to the national government, most westerners opposed any change in the Reclamation Act of 1902.[92]

Herbert Hoover and his secretary of the interior, Ray Lyman Wilbur, applauded Mead's demand that the states play a larger role in reclamation. Wilbur proposed that the central government relinquish control over the two hundred million acres of remaining unreserved public land to the states. Instead of laying out additional reclamation projects, the Reclamation Bureau should build dams and turn them over to the states—after the cost had been repaid from sales of power and water. The states would excavate canals and colonize the land. This proposal suggested that the federal government's role in the agricultural development would be much smaller in the 1930s than it had been in the first three decades of the twentieth century.[93]

In the early 1930s, federal reclamation hit rock bottom. Cultivated acreage on the government projects rose from 1.15 million acres in 1921 to 1.6 million in 1930, and crop prices showed a modest increase in the second half of the 1920s. But when the depression hit, prices plummeted, losing 50 percent of their value between 1930 and 1932. In the latter year, the average value of crops fell to $20.69 an acre, the lowest in the history of federal reclamation. Abandoned farms testified to the hard times. So did the number of renters. On the Carlsbad and Rio Grande Projects, in New Mexico, more than one-third of all farms were operated by tenants, and that number exceeded 50 percent on the Huntley Project, in Montana. The Reclamation Bureau's income from repayments and other sources of revenue dried up. In 1930, Elwood Mead predicted that the modest ten-year construction program adopted by the bureau in 1927—a program that contemplated spending $80 million to finish old projects and launch a few new ones—would now take at least fifteen years to complete.[94]

Mead continued to push for reform. His annual report for 1930 summarized his main goals. Where possible, he wanted the projects turned over to water users to reduce the cost of administration. (The Salt River and Minidoka Projects had changed hands in 1917, and by the end of the 1920s the Reclamation Bureau administered only the Rio Grande, Carlsbad, Yuma, Orland, and Klamath Projects.) He also wanted all surveys of new projects, or extensions of old ones, to include an economic appraisal of the benefits *outside* the project boundaries. Such surveys would give the Reclamation Bureau data it could use in asking the states and local communities for financial help. No project should be undertaken unless *all* water users signed binding contracts to repay their debt to the government. This was part of the Reclamation Bureau's attempt to move away from individual contracts so that it could negotiate exclusively with institutions that represented the farmers, such as irrigation districts. Mead repeated that the only way to protect against land speculation—which robbed the bureau of any chance to predict what a project would cost—was for Congress to authorize it to purchase all surplus land within a proposed project. Finally, he urged Congress not to make special appropriations for reclamation. Construction expenditures should be restricted to revenue from sales of public lands, oil royalties, repayment of construction costs, and profits from hydroelectric power. The only exception was that in the case of the most distressed government projects, they should be refinanced using government funds—at 4 percent interest to the farmers.[95]

The Great Depression added to the dilemmas Mead and the Reclamation Bureau had faced in the 1920s: how to balance costs and benefits; how to assist states desperately in need of federal aid without worsening conditions on the existing projects; how to maintain some semblance of rational management in a political system that encouraged waste, greed, and shortsightedness; and how to plan for the future in a constitutional order that dispersed rather than concentrated power. In a nation desperately seeking work, how could the bureau prevent the approval of unnecessary projects when it had been unable to control western politicians during the 1920s, a decade known—perhaps inaccurately—for "fiscal restraint"?

From the beginning of its life, the Reclamation Bureau had tried to balance the competing goals of opening new land to irrigation and providing additional water to land already cultivated. When drought hit the West in 1929, a drought that in some places lasted until 1935 or 1936, the cries for supplemental water became shrill in communities scattered from the Central Valley of California, to the Salt Lake Valley of Utah, to the Platte and Arkansas Valleys of Colorado, Wyoming, and Nebraska.[96] Nevertheless, the drought and the abandonment of land on the Great Plains also provided the bureau with a powerful excuse to open new land for the first time since World War I. Elwood Mead claimed that most farmers who fled the Great Plains took up irrigated land father west, such as on the Shoshone Project, in Wyoming. Therefore, two acres of dry-farmed land were abandoned for every acre of new irrigated land. No longer could critics of federal reclamation claim that government irrigation projects increased the amount of farmland. Moreover, irrigation farmers did not raise the crops that glutted agricultural markets in the early 1930s, such as wheat, corn, and cotton. Instead, they produced crops consumed within the West, particularly alfalfa, barley, and oats fed to livestock raised on the projects, or they cultivated crops not raised outside the West, such as sugar beets and potatoes. Because the drought hit the West's public grazing lands particularly hard, a new market opened for farmers to provide stockmen with alfalfa, at least as winter feed.[97]

Often overlooked because of Boulder Dam and the other high dam projects authorized at the beginning of the first administration of Franklin D. Roosevelt is the fact that the New Deal also stimulated the construction of smaller government reclamation projects, in part to provide jobs and in part to furnish homes to farmers displaced by dust storms on the Great Plains. In 1933 or 1934, the Public Works Administration allocated $103,535,000 to complete the bureau's existing water projects and begin a few new ones. To put this figure in perspective, it was more than twenty times the income that entered the reclamation fund each year at the beginning of the 1930s, and 39 percent of the total amount spent on federal reclamation since the inception of the program, in 1902. The bureau now had more to do than at any time in its history, and its Denver office staff increased from 250 to 700 almost overnight. By the middle of the 1930s, the first work had been done on the Columbia Basin Project, but work was also under way on many smaller projects, such as the Casper-Alcova Project, on the North Platte River near Casper, Wyoming, and the Owyhee-Vale Project, in Oregon and Idaho. At least seven projects were launched in Utah alone.[98]

In 1934 or 1935 the Reclamation Bureau received another $100 million, this time from the Works Progress Administration. In 1934, twenty-five new farms covering nearly two thousand acres were thrown open to settlement on the Yakima Project, in Washington. In the following year, the bureau offered a hundred thousand acres of new land on the Riverton Project, in Wyoming, and on the Owyhee-Vale Project, in Oregon and Idaho. Crop prices still lagged behind their 1929 value, but they had increased dramatically since 1932. "The Bureau is now engaged in the largest construction program in its history," Elwood Mead proclaimed in 1935. "The program makes up the greatest conservation campaign as yet undertaken by a single agency of the United States Government."[99]

CONCLUSION

The 1920s were not kind to the Bureau of Reclamation, which became increasingly unpopular in the West owing to low crop prices, resistance within the bureau to excusing or delaying the repayment of all or part of the construction debt, and the refusal of Republican administrations to approve new water projects until the old ones had been settled and agricultural conditions improved. As opposed to the Newell and Davis years, after 1924 Elwood Mead and other bureau leaders freely admitted the weaknesses and shortcomings of federal reclamation. They proposed sensible remedies, such as providing settlers with low-interest loans and laying out farms in advance of actual settlement—remedies resisted in the West and in Congress. Yet it is uncertain that any reforms could have rescued a program that seemed increasingly anachronistic. Doing too much offered as many risks as doing too little. Would any amount of money make federal reclamation "successful"?

Westerners often complained that the federal government exercised too much authority over natural resources. Yet when invited to share in paying for and administering reclamation, most states did nothing. They balked at providing the land, or recruiting the settlers, or training settlers in desert agriculture, or providing low-interest loans to new farmers. Westerners saw federal reclamation as more welfare than conservation. They claimed that their states were too poor to participate in a joint program and that they already carried too much debt. They also feared that shared authority would prove unworkable.

As the Reclamation Bureau's popularity and prospects waned during the 1920s, it turned South. In many parts of that region, economic conditions resembled those in the frontier West in 1902. Southerners sought to replace plantation agriculture and cotton culture with diversified agriculture, and land was much cheaper there than in the West. Moreover, southern politicians eagerly cooperated with the Reclamation Bureau, which attempted to institute the same cooperative program in Dixie that it had offered the West, with the states providing some combination of money, land, and directed settlement in exchange for federal construction of drainage and irrigation works. Once the Great Depression hit the region, however, the southern states lost interest in this program. And once Congress approved the Flood Control Act of 1928, discussed in chapter 9—an act whose major benefits went to the Deep South—the lawmakers were unwilling to support a new program of drainage and reclamation.

Government farmers complained that they had little say in formulating reclamation policy, but they were well represented in Congress by sympathetic and knowledgeable politicians. Indeed, in some ways federal reclamation suffered from too much democracy, not too little. However, one group of Americans, Native Americans, had far less influence on federal water policy than white residents of the national irrigation projects. Many Indians were farmers, and they saw the pitfalls of the family farm more clearly than those who administered the Reclamation Service or the Bureau of Indian Affairs. Their story demonstrates that federal reclamation was not just the engine of agricultural expansion and homemaking, but also an instrument of cultural imperialism.

6

Uneasy Allies

*The Reclamation Service and the
Bureau of Indian Affairs*

Irrigation was sold to the nation as a cure-all for the social and economic problems that afflicted the United States during and after the depression of the 1890s, but it also played a large part in the campaign to amalgamate Indians into white society. The leaders of the Bureau of Indian Affairs, the first agency to construct irrigation projects on federally managed land, hoped that irrigation would keep agricultural Indians on their land and persuade nomadic Indians to settle in one place. Small irrigated farms would strengthen the nuclear family by utilizing the labor of children as well as parents. By driving up the value of land, irrigation might also help develop an "instinct" for private property. And since irrigation would attract a large population of whites to former Indian lands, it would encourage the mixing and interaction of the two groups. Whites would teach Indians by example. They would serve as models of industry, self-discipline, and thrift. Such, at least, was the promise of reclamation.

The BIA deferred to the Reclamation Service, which by the end of Theodore Roosevelt's second administration built and directed Indian water projects and used the Justice Department as well as the Interior Department to limit Indian agriculture and water rights. The Reclamation Service had little real interest in the welfare of Native Americans, but it needed Indian land and money. As the arable public land rapidly disappeared during the early years of the twentieth century, Indian reservations and former reservations offered agricultural opportunities coveted by whites. The assumption that virtually any desert land could be rendered productive given enough water made Indian land in Montana as attractive as Indian land in Arizona. And leaders in the Reclamation Service recognized that transforming "savage" Indians into peaceful farmers had no less appeal than transforming the wilderness into a garden. In short, it used every argument available to sell federal reclamation to the public.

The relationship between the Bureau of Indian Affairs (often called the Indian Office) and the Reclamation Service compounded the Indian Office's lack of consistent objectives. The service had a clear objective: to provide as much land to white farmers as it could, using money from the sale of Indian land as well as from the reclamation fund. But the Bureau of Indian Affairs was never as committed to agriculture as the Reclamation Service. Its leaders were torn between competing visions of agricultural and industrial America. Transforming Native Americans into autonomous family farmers imbued with a strong sense of private property clashed with the dream of integrating Indians into the expanding economy outside the reservation. Wage labor was more consistent with Congress's professed goal of assimilation than was subsistence farming, which implied separation, if not isolation, from white society.

IRRIGATION AND INDIAN POLICY

In the years after the Civil War, military leaders looked for ways to concentrate and subjugate the Indians. For example, in 1871, General William Tecumseh Sherman predicted that irrigation would prevent Apaches from raiding white settlements and from leaving reservations in search of water and forage for stock. The cultivation of hay and alfalfa would supplement government rations and permit the Indians to pursue their traditional livestock industry on much less land. In the decades that followed, settled agriculture became synonymous with the goal of getting the federal government out of "the Indian business." "It has been asserted that with a proper system of irrigation on the Navajo Reservation adjacent to the San Juan River," the commissioner of Indian affairs observed in 1902, that "two-thirds of the families occupying that reservation could make homes and become self-supporting." Irrigation would eventually eliminate the cost of rations.[1]

The construction of dams and irrigation ditches provided Indians with valuable work experience and a discretionary income that taught the virtues of thrift and careful money management. More than one-third of the cost of the Zuni dam at Blackrock, New Mexico, begun in 1903, was paid out in wages to Indians. As the commissioner of Indian affairs noted in 1906: "The lesson taught by the experiment with Indian labor at this dam is unquestionably that if the Indian can be weaned from his habits of irregularity of days and hours, induced to postpone or rearrange his religious festivities so that they shall not interfere with the demands of his employment, and taught the white man's idea of laying something aside for to-morrow instead of spending all to-day, he can be made into a very valuable industrial factor in our frontier country." In fiscal year 1910, the Indian Service spent $145,000 on wages to Indians—more than 10 percent of its total budget.[2]

Congress appropriated the first money for Indian irrigation in 1867—to build a canal on the Colorado River Reservation—but annual expenditures did not begin until the 1890s. The Dawes Act (1887) provided both the justification and the revenue to construct irrigation systems on Indian land. Providing water to the reservations would drive up land values; the sale of surplus lands would pay for dams and canals. The severe drought that hit large parts of the West at the end of the 1880s underscored the need to furnish the reservations with a more dependable water supply than nature delivered.

In 1890, a special commission promised Indians on Montana's Crow Reservation that the federal government would spend two hundred thousand dollars irrigating land adjoining the Big Horn and Little Big Horn Rivers *if* the Indians accepted a smaller reservation. "Plainly, then," the commission concluded, "if it is the object of the Government to make the Crows self-supporting, one of the first steps to be taken is to make the land allotted to them productive by means of a thorough system of irrigation." Without irrigation, the allotment of Crow land could not be justified. The Indian Office sent Walter H. Graves, a civil engineer, to Montana to supervise ditch construction. By 1896, a hundred miles of main canal had been constructed, capable of watering about twenty-five thousand acres. The irrigation system, it was hoped, would replace with individual freeholds the common farms that supplied wheat and hay to Fort Custer and other local markets.[3]

The construction of canals provided steady employment, and 80 percent of the money spent on the Crow project went to Indian workers. Graves informed the commissioner of Indian affairs that the Crow were "excellent workmen and in the handling of earth in the construction of channels and embankments some of them can be easily classed as skilled workmen." They did not like pick and shovel work, and they easily became discouraged when harnesses snapped or wagons broke down, but they were adroit at directing horses and manipulating the scrapers used to excavate ditches. Equally important, they appreciated the opportunity to earn sufficient money to buy livestock, wagons, and farm machinery, and a few used their wages to build houses. Unlike the six-dollar payment each Indian received twice a year for land ceded to the federal government, the wages came in lump sums large enough to matter. "It is remarkable as it is gratifying," Graves reported, "to see how quickly the ideas of individuality, in responsibility, in ownership, in labor, of conservation of their resources, of emulation, etc. are growing and developing among them."[4] By 1910, nearly a million dollars—mostly Crow money—had been spent to excavate ditches with the capacity to water about seventy thousand acres. Little more than twenty-seven thousand acres were actually irrigated, however, and most of that land was flooded to increase the growth of native grasses for stock.[5]

Shortly after work began on the Crow Reservation, the BIA launched water projects on the Fort Peck, Blackfeet, Fort Hall, and Navajo reserves. Experienced engineers supervised the Crow and Navajo work, but most projects remained under the control of local Indian agents who hired "engineers" who lived near the reservations to design the works. As a result, many canals were poorly conceived and badly constructed, and there was little consistency in design or materials from one project to the next. During the 1890s, the Indian Office and secretary of the interior repeatedly asked Congress to authorize the BIA to hire a supervising engineer to oversee the construction and maintenance of Indian public works. This was finally done in 1898, when Walter Graves assumed the new position.[6] Meanwhile, the expansion of reservation agriculture during the 1890s prompted one writer to observe that "the plow and the sickle have, to a great extent, driven the tomahawk and the scalping knife from the field."[7]

Appropriations for Indian irrigation projects steadily increased during the first three decades of the twentieth century, from $670,000 in 1907, to $1,065,000 in 1910, to $1,957,700 in 1917, to $2,408,750 in 1924.[8] The Indian Irrigation Service also grew. The 1900 budget provided for two "superintendents of irrigation." By 1911, that number had increased to seven. Nevertheless, the Indian Office did not require that these men be trained as hydraulic engineers, and the Indian Irrigation Service was no match for the Reclamation Bureau in numbers or expertise. Employees of the Indian Irrigation Service, according to historian Douglas Hurt, "received the lowest salaries of any in governmental service, and its work suffered from shoddy planning and lack of coordination and standardization among the reservations." "Irrigation projects on reservation land became ends in themselves," according to Hurt, "and their benefits were only of secondary importance to the Irrigation Service."[9] Nevertheless, the Jeffersonian ideal remained powerful. A 1903 editorial in the periodical *Forestry and Irrigation* proclaimed that irrigation was "one of the greatest factors for education and civilization of the American Indian."[10]

INSTITUTIONAL IMPERIALISM:
THE RECLAMATION SERVICE AND THE INDIANS

The Dawes Act of 1887 sought to break up Indian reservations in the American West and convert most tribal property into individual freeholds. It promised single Indian men 80 acres of agricultural or 160 acres of grazing land. Heads of households would receive twice those amounts. The act was meant to reduce the dependence of Native Americans on the federal government. It did the opposite. A large bureaucracy was needed to supervise the allotments and leases provided for in the act during the twenty-five-year trust period when Indians could not sell, transfer, or encumber their land,

and few government bureaucrats saw themselves as stewards of Indian property. Their mission was to supervise the transition from reservation to freehold, and the demise of the reservation was seen as both inevitable and desirable. The central government's custodianship of Indian land took second place to economic growth.[11]

Federal Indian policy blended faith in material progress with social Darwinism. William A. Jones, commissioner of Indian affairs from 1897 to 1904, and Francis E. Leupp, commissioner from 1904 to 1909, shared a similar worldview. In 1901, Jones predicted that "there will be many failures and much suffering" in the process of civilizing the Indian. Suffering was "inevitable in the very nature of things, for it is only by sacrifice and suffering that the heights of civilization are reached." Two years later he wondered whether "the American Indian shall remain in the country as a survival of the aboriginal inhabitants, a study for the ethnologist, a toy for the tourist, a vagrant at the mercy of the state, and a continual pensioner upon the bounty of the people."[12]

According to Jones and Leupp, Indian reservations, along with government stewardship of Indian land, were doomed by social evolution. The elimination of the reservations would inevitably result in some Indians losing their property, but, in Leupp's words, "you never saw the man, red, white, or of any other color, who did not learn a more valuable lesson from one hard blow than from twenty warnings." He continued:

> Perhaps, in the course of merging this hardly used race into our body politic, many individuals, unable to keep up the pace, may fall by the wayside and be trodden underfoot. Deeply as we deplore this possibility, we must not let it blind us to our duty to the race as a whole. It is one of the cruel incidents of all civilization in large masses that some—perchance a multitude—of its subjects will be lost in the process. But the unseen hand which has helped the white man through his evolutionary stages to the present will, let us trust, be held out to the red pilgrim in his stumbling progress over the same rough path.[13]

Reformers who attempted to shield Indians from the harmful influences of white America merely postponed the inevitable.[14]

Leupp promoted allotment and leasing in part so that Indians could exercise greater control over their property. He encouraged them to mix with "other races in competition for a livelihood." He favored the intermingling of whites and Indians in schools on and off the reservations, and he set up an employment bureau where whites could hire Indian laborers. He fancied himself a conservationist and welcomed the Reclamation Act of 1902. In 1906 he noted that "this office is anxious, for the sake of the Indians, to have the surrounding country settled up by a good and thrifty class of white farmers, and to that end stands ready, as it has stood ready from the start, to see that every drop of water not needed by the Indians for the development of their farms shall be allowed to go to the white settlers."[15] Shortly after he left office, Leupp observed that his administration had taken great pride in "[e]ncouraging the development of the natural resources on reservations, such as water powers, mineral deposits, timber, reservoir sites, peculiar soils and climates, and the like, and to this end establishing co-operative agreements with other bureaus of the Government." The Reclamation Service headed the list of "other bureaus."[16]

Jones and Leupp were witting and unwitting accomplices of the fledgling Reclamation Service. By 1900, the sale of "surplus" lands left over after allotment, along with lease proceeds, swelled to $34 million, the money held in trust for Indians. The fund continued to grow during the first decade of the twentieth century as the process of allotment picked up pace.[17] Frederick H. Newell thought that this money could be put to good use, as could the large blocks of land left over after allotment. Most important, Indian irrigation projects could serve as an entering wedge by which the USGS might persuade Congress to adopt a reclamation program for the entire West. In a 1900 letter to George Maxwell, Newell noted that the Indian Office spent forty thousand dollars a year to build dams and canals, and that the amount was likely to increase. "If a good engineering division were created in the Department of the Interior to handle such matters as this," Newell mused, "there would be a natural growth toward the construction of works for the benefit of the whites and Indians combined and from this, for the whites alone. This would come about naturally without the vigorous fight which would doubtless follow the injection of irrigation matters into the river and harbor bill."[18]

Senator Henry Dawes of Massachusetts, sponsor of the Dawes Act, insisted, "No English baron has a safer title to his manor than has each Indian to his homestead."[19] The Dawes Act did promise farm or grazing land to the Indians, but after passage of the Reclamation Act the allotment policy took a new turn. The West's supply of arable public land was limited, so the Reclamation Service drew project boundaries to include potential farms within reservations. In 1904, for example, Congress authorized the secretary of the interior to allot land within the Yuma and Colorado River Reservations in five-acre tracts. The Yuma Reservation constituted the largest block of irrigable "public" land within the Yuma Project, and the board of engineers responsible for approving the project did so only after Congress accepted the reduced Indian allotments. White settlers bought the remaining land at bargain-basement prices—the price of the land prior to the construction of irrigation ditches. The government sold nearly half the reservation to white settlers, then deducted the cost of irrigation works from the revenue credited to the Indians. The same law permitted the interior secretary to decide where the irrigated Indian tracts would be located. Farms of white settlers on the project varied from forty to a hundred acres, many times the size of the Indian holdings. (One justification was that the Indians had little experience with desert agriculture, and an average-size Indian family could parlay its allotments into a much larger farm.)[20]

In Nevada's Carson Sink Valley, 196 Paiute Indians had been granted allotments covering thirty thousand acres *prior* to 1902. Under pressure from the Reclamation Service, the secretary of the interior confiscated twenty-seven thousand of those acres by reducing the allotments to ten acres. Even before the cancellation of the original allotments, white squatters invaded the former reservation. In 1906 Commissioner Leupp commented: "The newspapers of Nevada are . . . urging white settlers to go upon the lands, take their choice, build homes, and make improvements, assuring them that the Reclamation Service will supply them with water and the Indian Bureau must give way."[21]

The allotment of reservation land coincided with the Reclamation Service's effort to assert control over government irrigation throughout the West. Efficiency and economy dictated one federal irrigation agency, not two; it followed that the Indian Irrigation Service should give way. Some officials in the Indian Office agreed. Two years before passage of the Reclamation Act, an inspector for the Indian Office advised the commissioner of Indian affairs: "As carried on at present large sums are annually expended [by the Indian Irrigation Service] in the construction of ditches dug mostly at random without intelligent plan or system. Most of the money so expended is absolutely thrown away and wasted so far as any practical results are concerned. Those reservations that I have visited and upon which some attempt has been made to construct an irrigating system show ample evidence of the folly and waste resulting from the present extravagant and haphazard method of conducting this branch of the service."[22]

As the construction of canals on Indian land expanded during the first decade of the twentieth century, the duplication of effort became obvious. Many Indian irrigation projects adjoined white projects, and in some cases tapped the same water supply.[23] On the other hand, the Reclamation Service walked a tightrope. If it completely displaced its counterpart in the Indian Office, Congress might decide that Indian dams, ditches, and canals should be paid for out of the reclamation fund, limiting the amount of money available for white projects.[24]

In April 1907, Secretary of the Interior James Garfield demanded that the Reclamation Service and Indian Office reach a formal accommodation. The two bureaus made a momentous decision: the Reclamation Service would build the largest "Indian" irrigation projects and the Indians would pay for them. Nominally, the BIA would decide where to situate the projects, but only on the "advice" of the Reclamation Service. In the same year, control over the three largest Indian projects—all in Montana—passed to the Reclamation Service.[25] The Fort Peck, Blackfeet, and Flathead Reservations were near the Great Northern and Northern Pacific Railroads, and the Reclamation Service promised to reclaim more than four hundred thousand acres on those reservations. Montana had experienced a land rush in the opening years of the twentieth century, and these projects were clearly designed mainly to serve whites.[26]

INDIAN WATER RIGHTS: THE WINTERS CASE

Despite the Indian Office's eagerness to encourage contact between whites and Indians, the Reclamation Service needed judicial help to dominate reservation water policies. Six months after passage of the Reclamation Act, the U.S. Supreme Court issued a pathbreaking decision in *Lone Wolf* v. *Hitchcock,* which had far-reaching implications for Native Americans and their access to water.[27]

The Treaty of Medicine Lodge Creek (1867) stipulated that no part of the Kiowa and Comanche Reservation in southwestern Oklahoma could be sold or given away without the consent of three-fourths of the adult males in those tribes. In 1892, a minority of these Indians agreed to allotment. Despite protests from many Indians that the 1892 agreement had been secured through fraud and deception, Congress ratified their decision in 1900. Encouraged by the Indian Rights Association, the Kiowa chief Lone Wolf turned to the courts. The case reached the U.S. Supreme Court in 1903, and lawyers for the Indians were optimistic. The high court had long regarded Native Americans as wards of the federal government, subject to protection as well as supervision. Moreover, Congress had always paid at least lip service to treaty rights. Nevertheless, in *Lone Wolf* the high court refused to challenge the prerogative of Congress to deal with Indian property as it wished, so long as it acted as a responsible steward. Congress could abrogate treaties when it deemed necessary *even without the consent of the Indians,* and its trust responsibility was not subject to judicial review. Whether or not the 1892 agreement had been obtained through fraud was irrelevant; the legislative power was supreme. Indians whose land had been allotted were no longer wards of the state, the high court decided, and, hence, had no right to protection.[28]

Lone Wolf rendered Indian natural resources even more vulnerable than they had been in the nineteenth century. The Supreme Court had severely limited the judiciary's power to define and protect Indian rights and interests. Congress took full advantage by enacting a series of bills that appropriated Indian land without Indian consent. Nevertheless, the notion that treaty rights deserved special protection did not disappear. In 1905, in a case testing the fishing rights of Yakima Indians under the 1855 treaty that created their reservation, the Supreme Court declared that treaty rights had to be defined as the Indians understood them at the time a treaty was negotiated, "as justice and reason demand." In other words, "the substance of the right" had to be honored "without regard to technical rules." In interpreting Indian treaties, the intent of both parties had to be considered. Moreover, "the treaty was not a grant of rights to the Indians, but a grant of rights from them—a reservation of those not granted." This case had ominous implications, because neither Congress nor the federal courts were equipped or disposed to determine what the Indians had in mind when they negotiated treaties.[29]

Since the end of the 1880s, Congress had recognized the need to reserve and protect a *future* water supply for the Indians. Section 7 of the Dawes Act granted the secretary of the interior the right to distribute water within the reservations, regardless of state law. This implied the existence of Indian water rights beyond state authority. In 1891, Congress granted a private water company the right to run a canal across the Umatilla Reservation in Oregon, but stipulated that the company could not "hinder or prevent the occupants of lands on said reservation the full enjoyment of said streams [that flowed into the reservation] either for power, irrigation or domestic purposes." An 1894 right of way law pertaining to the Yakima Reservation required a private ditch company to provide free water to each allottee along the course of its canal. And an 1899 statute covering the Uintah Reservation in Utah stipulated that "all such grants shall be subject at all times to the paramount rights of the Indians on said reservation to so much of said waters as may have been appropriated or may hereafter be appropriated or needed by them for agricultural and domestic purposes." The 1899 law left it up to the secretary of the interior to determine the amount of water needed by the Indians. Congressional recognition of an implied Indian water right antedated the Winters case by a decade.[30]

The first major legal contest over Indian water rights came in Montana. By treaty, Congress set apart the Milk River Reservation in 1855 and 1856. In 1874, the reservation was reduced to that portion of Montana north of the Missouri River, stretching from the Rocky Mountains to the Dakota Territory. Then, in May 1888, Congress carved the land into ten units, including a million acres near Fort Belknap, bordered on the north by the Milk River. More-compact reservations, the 1888 treaty declared, would enable the Indians to become "self-supporting as a pastoral and agricultural people, and to educate their children in the paths of civilization," but it did not mention irrigation. It did promise that the United States government would purchase livestock, farm equipment, and other implements to help the Indians farm and build homes, however, and both Indians and whites understood that the land in question could not be made productive without water. Since there were no white settlements on the Milk River in 1888, the treaty-makers had no need to mention water rights directly. They did not anticipate the white pressure on Indian natural resources that would develop during and after the 1890s and would culminate in the famous Winters case.[31]

The Indians began to irrigate during the drought of 1889, but the reservation agent did not file a formal water claim under Montana law until 1898. The claim was entered in his name rather than that of the United States, or those of individual Indians within the reservation. In 1899, a new drought and the completion of the Fort Belknap Reservation's first major canal resulted in a tenfold increase in the amount of water used on the reservation. By 1905, the Indians were watering five thousand acres planted to hay, grass, grain, and vegetables—about one-sixth of the irrigable land within the reservation.[32] In that year, drought returned. The water shortage, as well as rapid white settlement adjoining the reservation, precipitated the test of water rights that resulted in the Winters case.[33]

The first white farmer appropriated water from the Milk River in 1895, but most claims upstream from the reservation dated to 1900 and 1903. In the spring of 1905, these diversions, compounded by a dry winter in 1904–05, suggested that the reservation would receive no water that coming summer for livestock or crops. W. R. Logan, the Fort Belknap agency superintendent, warned the Indian Office that the Indians faced starvation and destitution. He asked the Justice Department to defend Indian rights *against encroachment by subsequent appropriators.* On June 13, 1905, the United States attorney general wired the U.S. attorney for Montana, Carl Rasch, asking him to take immediate action. Rasch filed suit on June 26 and won a *preliminary* restraining order against twenty-one defendants.[34]

Rasch faced a dilemma. The Indian Office had asked the Justice Department to treat Indian rights as senior appropriations under Montana law. Rasch recognized, however, that this legal strategy posed problems. As mentioned earlier, the 1898 Indian claim had been filed in the name of the reservation agent and remained in his name. No Indian claimants were listed. The *intent* of that claim was clear—to water reservation land along the south bank of the Milk River—but the blanket title might well be contestable in court. Furthermore, the Indians had never used more than half the water claimed in 1898. Under the doctrine of prior appropriation, titles to water were defined by "full" and "continuous" use, as well as by the date of first use. No white claims dated to 1889, the year the Indians first tapped the river for irrigation, but a small number had been established prior to 1898. For these reasons, Rasch took a novel approach. "In my presentation of the matter to the Court here," Rasch explained to the attorney general, "I relied most strongly upon the riparian rights of the Government, and in my humble judgment that is the strongest point in the case."[35]

Montana had never abrogated the riparian doctrine. Therefore, like any riparian claimant, the government could insist that the Milk River flow undiminished in quantity or quality past its "property" (the Milk River Reservation). However, this argument posed dangers of its own. For example, what if future agricultural development *downstream from the reservation* prompted white farmers to take the same action? In view of that possibility, Rasch added two more legal arguments to his arsenal: first, the Milk River was part of the Fort Belknap Indian Reservation and, therefore, not subject to appropriation under either state or federal laws, and second, the Indian water supply was protected by the treaty that created the reservation.[36]

The federal judge for Montana, William H. Hunt, heard the case on July 17, 1905, and issued a formal injunction against the white farmers on August 8. He agreed that the reservation had been created in part to promote agriculture and that federal officials were legally obligated to protect treaty rights. But Hunt went further. "In my judgment, when the Indians made the treaty granting rights to the United States they reserved the right to the use of the waters of Milk River, at least to an extent reasonably necessary to irrigate their lands. The right so reserved," Hunt declared, "continues to exist against the United States and its grantees as well as against the State and its grantees." In short, no water rights could be acquired by whites that violated the "reasonable" needs of the Indians. A week after Hunt issued the injunction, Henry Winter, representing the white farmers, launched an appeal in the Ninth Circuit Court of Appeals.[37]

The brief Rasch prepared for the appeal employed several legal strategies. One concerned intent. The 1888 treaty suggested that the Indians considered water and land inseparable. So did subsequent federal policy. The land had little value without water, and the largest expenditure on the reservation had been for the construction of dams and canals. Second, Rasch argued, the federal government had never divested itself of the riparian right it enjoyed as the owner or trustee of government land, nor had Montana formally abrogated riparian rights. The federal government or the Indians— Rasch did not make clear which—were riparian owners. Whether the government had inherited riparian rights incidental to its *original* ownership of the public domain was not at issue. The question was much narrower: the right of the government to irrigate land adjoining a stream when that land had been set aside for a particular purpose. Montana had long recognized the primacy of prior appropriation, as had Congress, but it had never claimed state sovereignty over water (as had Colorado and Wyoming). Thus, Rasch reasoned, if a patent to government land adjoining a stream vested *before* any water had been diverted from that stream under prior appropriation, then subsequent uses occurred only at the sufferance of the riparian proprietors. And since the Fort Belknap Reservation was established before any appropriative claims had been filed to the Milk River, the federal government, as trustee for the Indians, could block all appropriative claims. As the only riparian owner on the stream, it could claim the entire river.[38]

Rasch regretted that Judge Hunt had spent so little time considering the rights of the United States in issuing his injunction. The riparian right, Rasch maintained in a letter to the U.S. attorney general, was "the strongest point in the [government's] case." Yet like any good trial lawyer, Rasch was reluctant to rely too strongly on an untested legal theory. Government ownership of land conferred riparian rights, he believed, but the Indians' treaty rights and senior appropriative rights also guaranteed an adequate water supply for the reservation's irrigable land. Rasch sued only the twenty-one largest water users, who were "unquestionably subsequent in time of appropriation to the Government appropriation in 1898"; he did not contest the rights of all the 225 to 250 people and corporations who used the Milk River. That Rasch raised the issue of riparian rights at all was because at a hearing held on July 17, an unexpectedly large number of defendants had demonstrated rights older than 1898.[39]

In 1906, the Ninth Circuit Court of Appeals heard two requests to overturn Hunt's ruling. In both, the district judge ignored Rasch's argument for riparian rights and proclaimed that treaty rights *guaranteed* the Indian water supply.[40] In 1908, the Supreme Court followed suit and decided the case almost entirely on treaty rights. The long string of decisions that required the court to interpret treaties as the Indians understood them played a large part in shaping the decision. The 1888 treaty had many purposes—such as providing land to whites and isolating the Indians—but the *main* purpose was to allow the Indians to become self-sufficient. There was no need to go beyond the intent of that treaty.[41]

The Supreme Court did little to define the precise nature of the federal right, and no Supreme Court water decision has raised more questions than *Winters*. "The power of the Government to reserve the waters and exempt them from appropriation under the state laws is not denied," the court noted in a sentence that was to become famous (or infamous) to water lawyers in the 1960s and after, "and could not be. That the Government did reserve them we have decided, and for a use which would be necessarily continued through years."[42] But were the Indian rights created by treaty, or had they existed from time immemorial? (In other words, who had reserved the water, the Indians or the United States government?) Did the same rights apply to reservations created by statute, proclamation, and executive order as those created by treaty? Did they apply to both unallotted and allotted lands? Did *Winters* rights apply to reservations not specifically created to promote agriculture (as stated in the 1888 treaty)? Could the water be used only for the purposes intended at the time the reservation was created, or for any purpose that contributed to "civilizing" the Indians and making them self-sufficient and independent? Was the agricultural water supply limited to the amount needed at the time the reservation was created, or could it be increased to meet new needs? Assuming that the water rights were held by the Indians rather than the federal government, could those rights be leased or sold to non-Indians? And finally, were those rights the subset of a larger category of federal rights attached to government lands used for other purposes, such as national parks, forests, and military posts? Many lawyers have agreed with the assessment California's deputy attorney general made in 1957: "It [the *Winters* decision] is a cryptic and obscure opinion, incapable of being understood, if at all, without reference to the prior opinion in the Ninth Circuit Court of Appeals."[43] The Supreme Court did not consider Indian water rights again until 1939.[44]

THE BUREAU OF INDIAN AFFAIRS AND INDIAN WATER RIGHTS

The *Winters* decision proved to be a hollow victory for Native Americans. Officials in the Reclamation Service tracked the case through the courts and protested the Justice Department's arguments to Theodore Roosevelt.[45] The government's defense of riparian rights, they insisted, ran counter to the anti-riparian arguments in *Kansas* v. *Colorado,* then pending before the Supreme Court. In January 1906, Secretary of the Interior Ethan Allen Hitchcock informed Roosevelt that if the U.S. Supreme Court upheld Rasch's pro-riparian argument in *Winters,* "and the same be strictly enforced throughout the arid region, [then] the policy of the Government as indicated in the Reclamation Act would be defeated and the development of the entire arid West be materially retarded, if not entirely destroyed."[46]

Unlike *Lone Wolf,* the *Winters* decision suggested that Indian water rights could be quantified only by administrative decree or by litigation. But the 1908 Supreme Court decision was ambiguous. As the head of the Indian Irrigation Service noted in a 1911 letter to a subordinate:

> I do not see how the Government can open the Reservation [to allotment] and then hold onto the waters of the same for the Indians. . . . If the reservation is opened, presumably the waters are subject to appropriation under the laws of the state, and it would take an Act of Congress to hold such waters for the Indians for all time subsequent to the opening of the reservation. Such an Act would be a very difficult one to obtain. Of course as long as the reservation remains intact, the Government can control the water, but after it is opened up it is difficult to see how the Milk River decision could be made to apply. . . . I think we should make all the investigations necessary to enable us to report on what work should be done in the way of canal construction and storage, in order that the waters might be acquired in the regular manner [under state water laws] for the benefit of the Indians.[47]

The Indian Office could find no practical way to apply the *Winters* decision, especially once allotment had begun.

The Indian Office employed few lawyers, and none trained in water law. As late as 1913, no one in the Indian Office or in the Justice Department had the job of protecting Indian property rights, and United States attorneys relied on information collected by federal and state agencies antagonistic to Indian claims. Seldom were these agents of the Justice Department experts in irrigation, and rarely did they understand the federal government's responsibility as a trustee. More often than not, they sympathized openly with those who demanded access to Indian natural resources. The Indian Office repeatedly asked for money to hire a water lawyer. Congress balked because the Reclamation Service wanted to monopolize the interpretation of water law and the lawmakers wanted to keep the Indian Office as small as possible. By contrast, seven specialists in water law assisted the chief legal officer of the Reclamation Service, and a lawyer schooled in water rights served each of the eight or nine supervising engineers who headed the Reclamation Service's regional offices.[48]

The Bureau of Indian Affairs drew a sharp distinction between *theoretical* and *defensible* Indian property rights. What was just was not necessarily practical. The Uintah Reservation was a case in point. Its isolation in northeastern Utah, one hundred miles from the closest railroad, discouraged farming. Few Indians were ready to use water following allotment in the first decade of the twentieth century, but the BIA filed claims on their behalf, fearing that white farmers would appropriate the entire supply before the Indians were ready to irrigate. Utah law dictated that all water claims had to be put to use within five years, on pain of forfeiture. Therefore, BIA officials claimed the water and repeatedly met with Utah's political leaders to request extensions of the original time limit. They did not assert special Indian rights, nor did they threaten to sue. In 1909, the director of the Indian Irrigation Service, W. H. Code, observed, "In my opinion the State of Utah will be treating the Indians very fairly if the Government, acting in behalf of its wards, is given an additional period of four years for making formal proof to the waters of the former Uintah Reservation." Utah lawmakers complied by extending the time limit first to 1915, then to 1919. If the Indians did not put the water to use within the prescribed period, Code reasoned, then they deserved to lose it. If they so lacked initiative, then the water *should* be granted to white farmers and private water companies. Meanwhile, Code hoped that a railroad would be built across the reservation, opening new markets and making the Uintah land more attractive to white lessees.[49]

Under Utah law, one year's irrigation of a plot of land reserved a water right for seven years. Since the Indian Office had failed to persuade more than a handful of Indians to cultivate their allotments, it made every effort to lure whites onto Indian land. In 1913, the commissioner of Indian affairs reported that "a vigorous advertising campaign has been inaugurated offering to lessees very favorable terms for . . . the next two years. In some cases [no charge is levied and] it is only required that the lessee clear the land of sage brush, level it, and leave buildings on the . . . premises to the value of about $500 at the expiration of the lease."[50] The advertisements were enticing. One candidly admitted: "Our WATER FILING . . . expires in 1919 and it is necessary for us to make beneficial use of our water prior to that date." Another encouraged white farmers to lease up to 640 acres of land, promising *free* use of both the land and water for five years as well as the right to graze cattle on a 250,000-acre commons at fifty cents per head per season. But the best government offer was forty acres of land, free water for five years, free logs to build a cabin, and a small cash stipend for reclaiming the land.[51]

The Indian Office hoped that white lessees would eventually buy Uintah land and settle permanently on the former reservation, but the ads did not attract the sober, responsible citizens that the bureau hoped to see. Lessees treated the Indians and their allotments with contempt. They wasted water and waterlogged the land; they broke locked headgates and stole water from their neighbors; they threatened Indians who tried to divert water; they routinely dug ditches across allotments used by Indians without securing a right of way; and they ignored the efforts of Indian policemen to keep the peace. By 1919, there was ten or twenty times more land farmed in the Uintah Valley by those who had purchased or leased Uintah land than by the Indians themselves. The land irrigated by the Indians had decreased since allotment. The Indian Office's attempt to protect Indian water rights had contributed to a state of anarchy on the Uintah Reservation, and similar conditions prevailed on many other reservations.[52]

INDIAN WATER RIGHTS IN CONGRESS, 1913–1914

Members of Congress from outside the West showed little interest in or understanding of water rights, and few western water lawyers considered the *Winters* decision a serious threat to vested rights or to the principle of state control over the allocation of water. *Lone Wolf* gave Congress the responsibility to oversee Indian property, and Congress had granted the secretary of the interior the right to allocate water on Indian reservations and former reservations.[53] In bills appropriating money to pay for Indian irrigation works in Utah, Montana, and Wyoming, Congress ordered the BIA to comply with state water laws. Moreover, the 1906 Jones Act—discussed in chapter 7—suggested that Indians had no special rights to the streams that bordered their reservations, or to sufficient water to serve *all* allotted land. Indian water needs, the Reclamation Service contended, should be met by the construction of new storage reservoirs, not by taking water away from white farmers. The Indian Office, no less than the Reclamation Service, assumed that "construction work by the Reclamation Service means the abandonment of any special [water] right reserved to the Indian."[54]

By the time Roosevelt and Leupp left office in 1909, it had become clear that the government water projects built for whites would not grow as rapidly as expected in 1902. Therefore, Taft's BIA considered it reasonable and prudent to save some water for the Indians. Robert G. Valentine, the commissioner of Indian affairs from 1909 to 1913, was more sympathetic to Indian water rights than any commissioner from 1902 to 1933. In late 1911, he informed the secretary of the interior that *Winters* "would be controlling in an [anticipated] action brought by the Government to recover the water rights of the Pima Indians." White farmers might suffer from such litigation, but the federal government "should be just to the Indians . . . before it is generous to the subsequent appropriators of the waters in question, and at the expense of these Indians." A few months later, Valentine informed the secretary that the *Winters* decision also applied to the Yakima Reservation, and that Yakima water rights were "not subject to alienation by any existing law, or by Departmental action." In his report for 1913, Valentine cited *Winters* as evidence that "prior appropriation by the United States and beneficial use by the Indians is not necessary, because of an implied reservation of water with and at the time of the reservation of the land sufficient for the irrigation thereof."[55]

In 1912, the chair of the House Committee on Indian Affairs asked the Justice Department to adjudicate Pima and Yakima water rights, but the secretary of the interior blocked that effort.[56] In the following year, however, a new secretary, Franklin K. Lane, took office with the Wilson administration. Lane warned that "the pressing [white] populations of the West will not long look upon [Indian natural] resources unused without strenuous and effective protest." The fate of the Indians, he insisted, depended on their ability to use those resources. But he also believed that the Interior Department had a moral obligation to protect Indian property, and he recognized that Indian water projects benefited whites far more than Indians.[57]

After the Wyoming state engineer refused to recognize any special Indian water rights on the Wind River reservation, Lane urged Congress to enact legislation to "provide for confirmation and protection of the prior reserved rights for such lands," as stipulated in the *Winters* decision.[58] The Indian Office drafted a bill that rescinded all previous statutes that reserved sufficient water for existing or *future* agricultural and domestic needs on land held in trust by the federal government, allotted or not. When the trust period had elapsed, however, the water right would pass with title to the land. Once vested, a right secured under the *Winters* ruling would be no different from those acquired by prior appropriation.[59]

Given the West's power in the U.S. Senate, the BIA bill had little chance in Congress. The debate over Indian water rights crested in the Senate in June 1914 during discussion of the Indian appropriation bill.[60] Year after year, the Senate had appropriated money for irrigation on Indian reservations, yet that money had provided little or no immediate benefit to the Indians. Senator Joseph T. Robinson of Arkansas—a prominent member of the Indian Affairs Committee—suggested that the *Winters* decision reserved sufficient water to carry out the basic purpose of setting up the reservations. Non-Indian irrigation projects that diverted water from streams bordering or crossing a reservation ran the risk that the federal government would *reassert* control over the water when it was needed by the Indians.[61]

Robinson directed his fire at the "Indian" reclamation projects administered by the Reclamation Service. The Indians had never been asked if they wanted these projects, even though the sale of their surplus land had paid for them. The principle followed on non-Indian irrigation projects administered by the Reclamation Service—that the land irrigated should bear a pro rata share of the cost of reclamation—had never been applied to the Indian projects. The reason was obvious: on the Indian projects those who paid to construct the hydraulic works and those who benefited were entirely different groups of people; the Indians subsidized white farmers and land speculators. As Robinson noted, "It is a great wrong that is being perpetrated on [the Indians]. . . . It is wicked."[62]

The 1914 Senate debate occurred six years after the *Winters* decision, but few U.S. senators had heard of the case, and fewer still took it seriously.[63] Senator William E. Borah of Idaho considered the opinion vague and unenforceable. Senator John D. Works of California, a former judge and an expert in western water law, regarded it as an aberration. The federal government had control over a territory's surplus water, he argued, but that authority ceased when the territory became a state. And since Montana became a state *after* the treaties creating the Milk River Reservation, and since *Winters* v. *United States* did not test the relative rights of states and the central government, whatever inchoate rights the Indians once enjoyed had been lost. In addition, *Winters* ran counter to *Kansas* v. *Colorado* and many other decisions that upheld the doctrine of "beneficial use"—that is, the principle that water rights could be perfected and maintained only through "continuous" application of water to the land. Beneficial use was the linchpin of western water law, and it was closely linked to state sovereignty over water.[64]

Many other senators raised questions about what Congress could do to protect Indian water rights. If state water laws were supreme, then what could Congress do to help? If the Indians had a special right to water, only the courts could define it. In any case, application of the *Winters* decision across the West would result in the loss of the money spent on Indian irrigation systems. Without secure water rights, whites who had taken up land within the allotted reservations would flee, leaving no one to establish rights by prior appropriation. Like it or not, the future of the Indians was inextricably linked to the success of white farmers.[65]

In a vain effort to protect Indian rights, Senator Robinson offered two amendments to the 1914–15 Indian Appropriation Act. One would have curtailed federal appropriations on the Flathead Project until the State of Montana guaranteed forever a sufficient water supply to irrigate *all* the allotments.

The other promised one hundred thousand dollars to pay for suits to protect Indian water rights. The first measure never came to a vote. The Senate initially approved the second by a 29 to 20 vote, but a month after that vote, in Robinson's absence, Thomas J. Walsh of Montana moved to rescind the appropriation, and his motion carried 45 to 7.[66]

Neither the *Washington Post* nor the *New York Times* took note of the lengthy Senate debate over Indian water rights. Robinson—serving his first term in the Senate—refused to jeopardize a promising career for such a doubtful, if not hopeless, cause. Arkansas contained few Native Americans, and that state's newspapers paid no more attention to the debate over water rights than the *Post* or *Times*. In the Senate, Robinson was part of a coalition of Democratic Progressives that included Henry F. Ashurst of Arizona and Thomas Walsh of Montana. A loyal supporter of Woodrow Wilson, Robinson hesitated to push an issue that might alienate Western Democrats from the party. He decided to save his political ammunition for bigger issues—battles over banking, currency, railroads, trusts, the tariff, and other matters of importance to his constituents. His seat on the Interstate Commerce Committee took precedence over his service on the Indian Affairs Committee. "I do not desire the chairmanship of the Indian Affairs Committee," he observed in a letter to a friend in 1915, "and in all probability it may become necessary to discontinue further service on that committee on account of other labors."[67]

The 1914 Congress created a joint committee chaired by Robinson to investigate the Blackfeet, Flathead, Fort Peck, and other Indian reclamation projects under the direct control of the Reclamation Service, but it refused to appropriate money to define, adjudicate, or protect Indian water rights.[68] Congress did transfer the cost of Indian irrigation projects from tribal funds to individual parcels of irrigated land, but not until 1920 did it specify the term of repayment (twenty years), and only then did it make construction charges a lien against the land. The secretary of the interior did not issue the actual terms of repayment until the following year. Therefore, a seven-year delay followed the 1914 congressional reforms.[69]

Congress had many reasons for shifting the cost of Indian irrigation from the tribe to individuals. Not all Indians held irrigable allotments, and not all allotments were equally productive. Taxing some Indians to benefit others, therefore, was a great injustice. The desire to free up additional Indian funds to pay for livestock, farm equipment, and other needs also motivated the legislation.[70] Unfortunately—at least from the perspective of the Indian Office—this also made Indian land far less attractive to white settlers.[71]

The controversy over Indian water rights abated during World War I, but it reappeared after the war. In 1919 and 1920, for example, a proposed adjudication of water rights on the Uintah Reservation prompted Commissioner of Indian Affairs Cato Sells to warn the secretary of the interior that the *Winters* decision not only guaranteed water for *irrigable* allotments, but also established that the Indians held a "naked *legal* right" to sufficient water to serve the reservation's 250,000 acres of common *grazing* land. John F. Truesdell, a legal specialist in the Department of Justice, agreed, noting that a case decided in a Montana federal court soon after *Winters* "left the matter of the extent of their future needs open, thus permitting a larger use [of water] by the Indians in the future if that should be desirable." The Montana decision suggested that *Winters* rights were elastic. Nevertheless, Truesdell proposed that the government set aside a water supply that the Indians could depend on, rather than relying on federal court rulings or the Supreme Court's vague 1908 promises.[72]

INDIAN IRRIGATION, WORLD WAR I TO THE 1930S

World War I proved a mixed blessing to Native American farmers. Crop prices on Indian irrigation projects quadrupled during the war, and that did more to encourage Indian agriculture than any previous federal policy. According to historian Janet McDonnell, 24,489 Indians farmed 383,025 acres in 1911, but by the end of the war 37,000 Indians tilled 1 million acres. As the commissioner of Indian affairs noted in 1919, the reservation water systems permitted the Indians to respond "nobly to the call for greater production and materially increased the acreage cultivated and the yield per acre." Not only did irrigated land yield a far greater return per acre, it also allowed reservation farmers to survive and prosper during the drought of 1917–19. Nevertheless, on many reservations the number of Indian farmers declined. On the Blackfeet Reservation in Montana, Indians operated nearly 90 percent of the farms in 1915 but only 30 percent at the end of the war. And on the Wapato Project, in the Yakima Valley, only 6 percent of the Indian allotments were farmed by their owners. Despite inflated wartime prices, most Indians still rented their irrigable land to whites, and the remainder raised forage crops. Indians lacked the training and equipment to raise high-value crops; many lacked access to cooperatives and markets, and some lacked water to irrigate, particularly during the summer, when whites who lived on Indian land took more than their fair share of streamflow.[73]

In 1917, Commissioner of Indian Affairs Cato Sells remarked, "The Indian's transformation from a game hunter and a wanderer to a settled landholder and home builder is everywhere evident."[74] Despite the agricultural glut of the 1920s, the construction of irrigation works went forward, and Indians still had little say in the construction of new projects. In 1922, reservation irrigation systems had the capacity to water 600,000 acres. By 1930, this figure had climbed to 775,000 acres, even though less than half the land was cropped.[75]

The number of Indian farmers declined during the 1920s. In a vain attempt to avoid repaying the cost of irrigation works, many stopped farming when prices plummeted. Those who defaulted on their debt to the government—and most did—had their water cut off, resulting in more abandoned land. White lessees were unable to make their rental payments when wheat and livestock prices fell, and potential lessees feared that they—rather than the actual owners—would become liable for construction charges. (Most Indians thought that the lessees should pay all construction, as well as operation and maintenance charges.) It became difficult during the 1920s, therefore, to find whites willing to lease Indian land. In 1932, at the depth of the Great Depression, Congress empowered the secretary of the interior to reduce or rescind the reimbursable charges—as they had been postponed on the Reclamation Bureau's non-Indian projects—but the damage had already been done.[76]

Conditions were particularly grim in Montana, home of the largest Indian irrigation projects. Through sale or lease, more than 80 percent of the land allotted in Montana ended up in the hands of non-Indians. On the Blackfeet Reservation, Indians refused to settle on agricultural allotments, preferring to live along streams close to the mountains and traditional grazing lands. The Reclamation Service originally anticipated that the Blackfeet Project would water more than 100,000 acres. In 1921, more than 75 percent of the reservation's irrigable land remained in Indian hands, but only 14,650 acres were irrigated. Within two years, that acreage fell to 1,873 acres, and during the same period, operation and maintenance charges increased by more than 300 percent. In 1928, W. M. Reed, head of the Indian Irrigation Service, advised the secretary of the interior: "I believe it is time for all connected with the project to finally admit that the inception and construction of the unit was a failure, and that a great loss must be acknowledged and accepted."[77]

The BIA opened Montana's Flathead Reservation Project to white settlers in 1910. Thereafter, the acreage irrigated by Indians steadily declined. By the end of World War I, Indians cultivated little more than 1 percent of all land watered on the reservation. In 1914, the chief engineer of the Indian Irrigation Service admitted that the project would cost at least $6 million to complete, $1 million more than the tribal fund contained. In an attempt to reclaim far more land than the Indians could use, reservoirs and pump systems were added to the cost of canals and ditches, and the cost of the project soared.[78] "According to some accounts," historian Janet McDonnell has written, "Indians on the Fort Peck and Flathead reservations survived largely on prairie gophers and horsemeat, and were close to starvation." Those accounts may have been exaggerated, but it is incontestable that allotment in small parcels for irrigation limited the Flatheads' opportunity to purchase livestock.[79]

During the Progressive Era, the Reclamation Service repeatedly attempted to take over *all* Indian irrigation projects. Beginning in 1913, the Indian Office created its own engineering corps—on a much more modest scale than the Reclamation Service—and Congress transferred control of all Indian water projects back to the BIA in 1924.

In 1928, two surveys of conditions on the Indian reservations underscored the problems of transforming Native Americans into farmers. In 1926, Hubert Work had asked the independent Institute for Government Research to conduct a comprehensive survey of federal Indian policies. Lewis Meriam, a staff member of the institute, supervised the study in administration. Over seven months, the Meriam Commission's staff visited ninety-five reservations, agencies, hospitals, and schools. The commission, composed of specialists in law, health, education, agriculture, and sociology, but none in irrigation, concluded that attempting to teach Indians diversified market agriculture had been a mistake. Indian tribes were no longer nomadic, but many Indians regularly abandoned their farms during the summer to hunt or to visit relatives. Such habits, the commission concluded, were inconsistent with market agriculture.[80] But since many reservations were remote from markets and poorly served by transportation anyway, and since the Indians had little experience with commerce, it seemed proper that subsistence agriculture should take precedence over market agriculture. The Meriam Commission recommended the creation of a Division of Planning and Development in the Indian Office, composed of specialists in agriculture and grazing, to draft economic blueprints for each agency or region. Like white farmers, the Indians needed much more than land and water. The commission recommended that the government also provide teachers, tools, livestock, lumber, and reimbursable loans.[81]

The Meriam Commission questioned the wisdom and justice of launching the Indian irrigation program using congressional appropriations, then making the charges reimbursable from Indian funds. In many cases, the land was too poor to bear the cost of dams and canals. Like the Fact Finders' Commission of 1924, the Meriam Commission proposed that many irrigation charges be excused—and ultimately they were. It also recommended the organization of a legal force within the Indian Service, and the appointment of nine or ten district counsel "situated in the centers of Indian population," to protect Indian property. "The nominal conduct of litigation would remain with the United States district attorneys," the report explained, "but these district counsel of the Indian Office, acting under the supervision of the general counsel in Washington, would actually prepare the cases and actively assist in the trials." The report paid no attention to Indian water rights, though it acknowledged that the legal system worked against the Indians, "particularly in irrigation matters."[82]

Given the composition of the Meriam Commission, with its lack of irrigation specialists, Secretary of the Interior Hubert Work asked the secretary of agriculture to form a second committee to look strictly at water policy. It consisted of Porter J. Preston, an engineer from the Reclamation Bureau, and Charles A. Engle, a supervising engineer from the Bureau of Indian Affairs.

The Preston-Engle survey was even more critical of Indian policies than the Meriam report. As of 1927, 150 irrigation projects included land that was or had been part of an Indian reservation. They ranged in size from a few acres to the 89,000 acres under ditch on the Yakima Reservation. The Bureau of Reclamation and Indian Irrigation Service had rendered 700,000 acres of Indian land irrigable at a cost of twenty-seven dollars an acre for construction and nine dollars a year for operation and maintenance. About 450,000 acres were actually irrigated. Seventy percent of that land belonged to the Indians, and 30 percent to whites. However, the Indians irrigated only 16 percent of their irrigable land, while non-Indians watered about 66 percent of the former Indian land they owned. "The continual decrease in the acreage farmed by Indians is the natural and logical result of the leasing system," Preston and Engle concluded, "and the leasing system in turn is the inevitable result of the allotting system."[83]

The average Indian farm returned twenty-one dollars an acre, as opposed to the forty dollars an acre generated by non-Indian farms within the reservations. This income was inadequate:

> On a few of the projects the income or annual crop return is so low as to make it a matter of speculation how the Indian exists. It can be explained only by the fact that some members of the family occasionally find outside employment, sell a few cattle, or some may receive rations. On some projects the farm income for those families actually engaged in farming ranges from $60–$80 each [per year] or only $15 or $20 for each individual. In view of this it seems probable that undernourishment may be a principal cause of the unsatisfactory health conditions among Indians.[84]

Little wonder that even Indians with a strong desire to irrigate were demoralized.

As for water rights, Preston and Engle favored using the *Winters* decision only in cases where it did not encroach on rights established by white farmers. It was safer for the federal government to buy up conflicting water rights, or pay for new reservoirs to store a supplemental water supply, than to rely on the vague and contradictory opinions of the Supreme Court. "Any other course, in our opinion, would be penalizing the rights of [white] private citizens for the failure of the Government to properly protect the Indian in his water rights." Although it did recommend securing tribal consent before launching new water projects, along with the appointment of instructors to teach Indians how to farm, the Preston-Engle Report suggested that "justice" was less important than maintaining peaceful relations between Indians and the whites who surrounded and lived among them.[85]

The Indian Office nominally approved most of the Preston-Engle recommendations, but little changed. Eventually, Secretary of the Interior Ray Lyman Wilbur, who became secretary at the beginning of 1929, predicted that all land irrigated within the former reservations would be owned by whites, "due to the death of the original allottees and sale of the unallotted lands. Most trust restrictions are mandatorily removed under the law on the death of the original allottee."[86]

The Great Depression and drought of the early 1930s created new problems for Indian farmers. Cotton produced on the Gila River Reservation fetched seventeen cents a pound in 1929, but only four cents a pound in 1931. In parts of the West, wheat prices fell by 60 percent and alfalfa prices by two-thirds.[87] The New Deal ended sales of Indian land in August 1933, and the Wheeler-Howard Act (1934) reversed the allotment policy. "Civilizing" the Indian gave way to Indian cultural autonomy. The new irrigation policy adopted by the Indian Irrigation Service cancelled, in the words of Franklin D. Roosevelt's secretary of the interior, Harold Ickes, "unjust and uncollectible reimbursable indebtedness on Indian irrigated lands," and it attempted to decentralize Indian irrigation by giving more power to local superintendents and to the Indians themselves.[88]

Irrigation was no longer seen as a way to transform the lives of Native Americans; in the mid-1930s, as in the 1890s, it provided "make work" on the reservations. The BIA launched a ten-year program to add 430,000 acres to the 730,000 acres already capable of irrigation by the Indian Office—virtually all the remaining irrigable land within the reservations. Public Works Administration (PWA) money poured into the reservations, but the new dams and canals did not result in a coherent Indian agricultural program. For example, Indian farmers still needed a system of government financial assistance, which Congress refused to provide. Despite enormous changes in American society, the Indian Office remained committed to developing a subsistence, if not market, economy on what remained of the reservations. As the commissioner of Indian affairs observed in 1938, "The orderly expansion of Indian irrigation is essential to afford means and opportunities for self-support, as well as to preserve Indian water rights, which are increasingly being jeopardized as development of the country takes place."[89]

CONCLUSION

The secretaries of the interior and commissioners of Indian affairs who held office between 1902 and 1935 promoted Indian irrigation for different reasons: to prevent Indians from straying off reservations; to develop a love of private property; to create work; to protect water rights; to enhance the value of Indian land; to free up land for white settlers; to attract white farmers who would give Indians jobs and serve as models of industry; to supplement tribal funds; and to reduce the cost of maintaining the reservations. By the 1930s, however, the dream of turning Indians into farmers had faded. President Herbert Hoover's secretary of the interior, Ray Lyman Wilbur, claimed that Indians were communists "with no incentive to personal endeavor, to accumulation of any sort." They could better develop a sense of private property by "working for hire, under direction" than through farming. "The Indian still seems to lack adjustment to the prevailing civilization," Wilbur observed, "and it is now found that this lack of adjustment is due to the fact that the prevailing civilization works and the Indian does not." Officials in the Bureau of Indian Affairs agreed: most Indians would be better off drawing a regular paycheck than farming.[90]

Yet Wilbur was wrong. Not all Indians were "communists." Some worked hard at farming, and one historian has concluded that "substantial progress in Indian farming was made before allotment."[91] Nevertheless, on one point Wilbur was right: the federal government's Indian agricultural policies did not accomplish their objectives.[92] The Indians had to take responsibility for their own destiny, the BIA argued, but seldom were they consulted in the formulation of federal policies. Nothing better illustrated what Franklin Roosevelt's commissioner of Indian affairs, John Collier, called the "ruthless benevolence" or "benevolent ruthlessness" of the Indian Office than reclamation.[93] Native Americans flooded the Indian Office and Congress with protests, but whites who lived on or near reservations had far more influence within the Indian Office than Indians, who could not be blamed for concluding that reclamation was just another scheme to evade treaty obligations and transfer control over their land to whites.[94]

The policy of using agriculture to "civilize" the Indians had many flaws. First, it ignored the fundamental lesson of frontier farming: with few exceptions, the generation that plowed "virgin land" rarely enjoyed financial success and seldom put down permanent roots. White pioneers usually moved on after five or ten years of frustrating, poorly rewarded labor. How could Native Americans succeed when so many whites had failed?[95] Second, at a time when the Reclamation Service urged white farmers to organize and cooperate, Native Americans were asked to give up collectivism in favor of individualism and autonomy. As white farmers created collective organizations such as the National Grange and the Farmers' Alliance, the ideal of the yeoman farmer became an anachronism in most parts of the United States. Yet it was deemed a suitable model for Indians well into the 1920s. Finally, irrigation encouraged speculation in Indian lands, and one way to protect land from whites was by doing as little as possible to improve it. To become a good farmer was to invite non-Indians to invade what was left of the reservation. The more valuable the Indian land became—and irrigation did more to increase its value than any other improvement—the less secure became the Indian's title.

The Indians faced many agricultural barriers. At the beginning of the twentieth century, officials in the Reclamation Service assumed that all desert soil was productive, but the Indians knew better. Years of observation had taught them that no amount of water could make sterile land, or land impregnated with alkali, fertile. Most reservations suffered from short growing seasons as well as poor soil. Tribes in the southwest relied heavily on agriculture, but the Indians of the northern plains adapted to a harsh environment by hunting, fishing, gathering, and raising stock. Depending entirely on agriculture, experience had taught them, was unwise, if not irrational. By the 1920s and 1930s, furthermore, farming required a much more specialized knowledge of agriculture and far more costly equipment than it had in the 1870s or 1880s. To buy that equipment, and to use land "productively," Native Americans needed capital. Yet they could not mortgage land or borrow money while title to their land remained with the federal government. Even Indians who owned their allotments outright were reluctant to pledge them as collateral.

The Indian Office made the same mistake as the Reclamation Service: it assumed that reclamation was essentially a matter of engineering. As spending on dams and canals increased, appropriations for nonreimbursable agricultural purposes and for the purchase of livestock declined.[96] The thirty thousand dollars Congress appropriated for seed and farm equipment in 1888—a modest amount, considering the goal of the Dawes Act—was halved in 1891 and eliminated entirely in 1894. After 1911, tribal funds could be tapped for such purposes, but never to the extent needed by would-be Indian farmers. "We did not give him [the Indian farmer] a penny with which to buy a plow, or a harrow, or a grubbing hoe, or anything at all with which to work the land," Senator Harry Lane lamented on the floor of the U.S. Senate in 1914. "He was left with his bare hands. The white man could not make a success under such circumstances."[97]

Native Americans and reservation agents pleaded with the Indian Office to free up tribal money for livestock, seed, lumber, farm machinery, and other agricultural necessities. Those appeals fell on deaf ears. Congress might have subsidized the growth of certain crops, encouraged the Indians to form cooperatives, helped locate markets, furnished free livestock, or at least paid for irrigation projects with nonreimbursable funds from the general treasury. Had the reservations been closed to whites; had the federal government provided sufficient money to clear, level, fence, and irrigate the land and purchase farm equipment, seed, and livestock; and had it provided marketing cooperatives and processing facilities (such as canneries), the story *might* have been different.[98]

The social isolation of the individual freehold and the Indian Office's lack of sympathy for traditional gender roles also stood in the way of success. White farmers bitterly complained about the isolation and loneliness of farms and ranches in the West. Yet how much worse such farms must have seemed to Native Americans, most of whom considered solitude a cruel punishment and put the health of their community before individual success. In many tribes, farming was a common enterprise, or women's work; men regarded it as demeaning or degrading. The Meriam Commission recognized that truth and urged that Indian women be trained to tend gardens and raise poultry. On the other hand, on most Montana reservations Indian men took to raising livestock, perhaps because that vocation was consistent with the hunt. After 1914, some federal and Indian money was used to purchase livestock, but it was too late for many tribes, whose best grazing land already had been leased to whites.[99]

Indian policy was filled with inconsistencies. The Bureau of Indian Affairs promoted both the autonomous Jeffersonian freehold and cultural assimilation, and individual acquisitiveness as well as the cooperation necessary to make one's way in the new corporate order. Was the paramount goal of Indian policy to help Indians adapt to a harsh desert environment, or to produce "imitation white men"? Was its basic purpose to turn the Indians into farmers, or to promote individualism? The Indians had to learn that both land and crops were commodities to be bought and sold. It was not enough to make the Indians self-sufficient; they had to find the "way to wealth." But was agriculture the best way to teach that lesson? It was widely perceived as the foundation of civilization—a stage through which the Indians had to pass on their way to merging with the larger society. But could it teach Indians how to live by a schedule or understand markets and contracts?

Transforming Indians into farmers was unlikely to break down the reverential view of land at the heart of many Native American cultures. Therefore, as early as the 1880s and 1890s, the Indian Office encouraged Indians to leave the reservation in search of work. Working for wages, it was hoped, would promote thrift, punctuality, and acquisitive instincts. One goal of leasing Indian land was to encourage white farmers to hire the Indians from whom they rented. Not only would Indians derive another source of income and help improve their own land, they could also pattern their behavior after the white farmers.

In 1933, nearly two-thirds of all Indian men worked in agriculture, but half of them worked as farm laborers rather than farm operators. Some jobs complemented agriculture, but few Indians had the energy to harvest or plant crops for whites as well as themselves. Then, in the 1930s and 1940s, wage labor increased rapidly as the federal government became a major employer in the West. In 1935, wages paid to Indians enrolled in the Civilian Conservation Corps on the Rosebud Reservation exceeded all other sources of income. When the program ended in 1942, 85 percent of the Rosebud men had worked in the CCC or on other federal work relief projects. As is well known, after World War II, large numbers of Native Americans continued on the federal payroll. We should not forget, however, that Native Americans participated in the white economy in the nineteenth century as well as the twentieth. They did not become wage laborers solely in response to the loss of their land, or because they moved in large numbers to cities during and after World War II. Wage labor and agriculture were often compatible, and many Native Americans blended the two—as did white farmers. But the two goals were less consistent to policy makers in the Bureau of Indian Affairs, who until after World War II failed to acknowledge that an urban, industrial order had triumphed over the agricultural society of the nineteenth century.[100]

Having looked at Indian policy from the top down, we now turn to the study of federal water policy in the lives of two particular groups of Indians, the Yakima (or Yakama) of Washington and the Pima of Arizona.

Figure 1. Frederick H. Newell. Chief Engineer and Director of the United States Reclamation Service, 1902–14. By the 1930s, Newell had conceded that the federal reclamation program conceived at the beginning of the twentieth century had been unneeded and unwise. Photograph courtesy of the United States Bureau of Reclamation, Denver, Colorado.

Figure 2. Arthur Powell Davis. Director of the United States Reclamation Service, 1914–23. Davis paid the price of being second in command to Newell in the Reclamation Service from 1902 to 1914, and for the downturn in farm prices on federal reclamation projects in the early 1920s. Photograph courtesy of the United States Bureau of Reclamation, Denver, Colorado.

Figure 3. Elwood Mead. Commissioner of the United States Reclamation Service, 1924–36. More sympathetic to government farmers than Newell or Davis, and more of an idealist, Mead was no more successful than his predecessors in dealing with Congress or in making desert agriculture profitable enough to lure families with capital onto the projects. Photograph courtesy of the United States Bureau of Reclamation, Denver, Colorado.

Figure 4. The dedication of Derby Dam, June 1905. Thirty miles east of Reno, Nevada, the first major work completed by the Reclamation Service permitted the diversion of half the Truckee River south into the Carson basin, where it irrigated farms on the Truckee-Carson, or Newlands, Project, the first government project to open. Because the Reclamation Service failed to secure the source of the river, Lake Tahoe, however, government farmers on the project faced chronic water shortages. Photograph courtesy of the United States Bureau of Reclamation, Denver, Colorado.

Figure 5 (right top). The Truckee Canal. The Reclamation Service completed the thirty-one-mile Truckee Canal, connecting the Truckee and Carson Rivers, in November 1906. It became one of the service's highly publicized early irrigation works, a symbol of the triumph of civilization over the wilderness. But the Truckee-Carson Project never succeeded as grandly as the fanfare predicted. Five years after the project opening, only a quarter of the original homesteaders remained. Photograph courtesy of the United States Bureau of Reclamation, Denver, Colorado.

Figure 6 (right bottom). The first building in Twin Falls, Idaho, 1905. Irrigation created a land boom in the Snake River Valley, and the Twin Falls Investment Company was there to cash in on it. The capital that flowed into the town of Twin Falls permitted it to eclipse other agricultural communities in the area. Photograph no. 73.221.224; photographer: Clarence Bisbee; courtesy of the Idaho State Historical Society.

Figure 7. "Twin Falls: A Six-Month Town." The tents, claim shacks, and vacant land between "houses" demonstrate the speculation in town lots that fueled the early growth of Twin Falls. Photograph no. 73.221.774, courtesy of the Idaho State Historical Society.

Figure 8. Main Street, Twin Falls, 1910. In this and the next photograph, note the substantial brick buildings and the electric lights. Photograph no. 73.221.203; photographer: Clarence Bisbee; courtesy of the Idaho State Historical Society.

Figure 9. Twin Falls Civic Center, c. 1915. The domed Twin Falls Civic Center presides over the downtown park. At left is the city courthouse. Photograph no. 73.221.775, courtesy of the Idaho State Historical Society.

Figure 10. Street scene, Rupert business district, 1906. Many civic planners hoped that the towns within and adjoining federal reclamation projects would become models for new rural communities throughout the nation—and certainly the local newspaper shared that enthusiasm. But the government's policy of spreading lot sales in Rupert over several years, and charging relatively high prices, did nothing to encourage investors. Although founded at roughly the same time as Twin Falls, Rupert became a poor cousin of its competitor fifty miles to the west. Photograph courtesy of the United States Bureau of Reclamation.

Figure 11. Rupert business district, 1915. Rupert lacked the substantial brick structures that characterized Twin Falls. Nor did it contain the notable public buildings of its rival community. Photograph no. 77.127.34, courtesy of the Idaho State Historical Society.

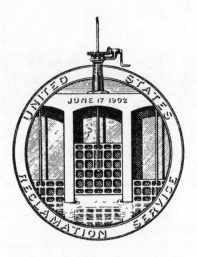

Figure 12. Before: The original seal of the United States Reclamation Service. The emphasis on engineering was characteristic of the early years of federal reclamation. Photograph courtesy of the United States Bureau of Reclamation, Denver, Colorado.

Figure 13. After: The seal of the United States Reclamation Service, July 1908. Note the renewed emphasis on homemaking as criticism of the service intensified on the projects and within Congress toward the end of Theodore Roosevelt's second administration. Photograph courtesy of the United States Bureau of Reclamation, Denver, Colorado.

Figure 14. Farm dwellings: Minidoka Project near Heyburn, Idaho, 1905. The heavy investment in land, machinery, and irrigation left most government farmers little money for housing. Their homes exemplified their tenuous hold on the land. Photograph courtesy of the United States Bureau of Reclamation, Denver, Colorado.

Figure 15. Farm dwellings: The Hill residence, Klamath Project, Oregon, 1916. Many farmers ultimately succeeded in building larger and more substantial houses, but note the original family residence to the right. Photograph courtesy of the United States Bureau of Reclamation, Denver, Colorado.

Figure 16. Farm dwellings: Truckee-Carson Project, Nevada, 1930. The dugout on the left of the main building served as living quarters for many years. Photograph courtesy of the United States Bureau of Reclamation, Denver, Colorado.

Figure 17. Farm dwellings: "Desert Ranch," Boise-Payette Project, Idaho, 1940. As late as 1940, living conditions on most government projects remained primitive, as they were in many parts of rural America. Federal reclamation had done little to change the way farm families lived. Whether this hardy couple recognized the mixed message conveyed by the sign is unclear. Photograph courtesy of the United States Bureau of Reclamation, Denver, Colorado.

Figure 18. Farming "virgin land." Clearing, leveling, and fencing constituted a substantial part of the cost of farming virgin land. In this photograph, a farmer clears sagebrush on the Yakima Project in 1929. Photograph courtesy of the United States Bureau of Reclamation, Denver, Colorado.

Figure 19. Flood irrigation, Truckee-Carson Project, Nevada, 1910. Initially, many government farmers found it cheaper to flood their land, rather than use furrows. This created severe environmental problems, from waterlogged farms, to the buildup of alkali in the soil, to stagnant pools of water that served as breeding grounds for mosquitoes. Photograph courtesy of the United States Bureau of Reclamation, Denver, Colorado.

Figure 20. Haying scene, Truckee-Carson Project, 1914. This picture was probably posed. Women carried a heavy workload on government farms, but Reclamation Service photographers portrayed their lives as adventurous, healthy, and joyful. This photograph also illustrates that, with a few notable exceptions, federal reclamation projects produced low-value crops fed to livestock, such as hay and alfalfa, not high-value vegetables, nuts, and fruits. Photograph courtesy of the United States Bureau of Reclamation, Denver, Colorado.

7

Case Studies in Water and Power

The Yakima and the Pima

Prior to contact with whites, few Native Americans depended exclusively on hunting, farming, or gathering. Most practiced a mixed or balanced economy, which gave them at least limited agricultural experience. Compared to Indians living in the Dakotas, Montana, and Wyoming, the Pima of southern Arizona and the Yakima (or Yakama) of south-central Washington enjoyed nature's favor. Native Americans who lived in Arizona's forbidding Sonora Desert required irrigation to survive, but the desert soil was rich and productive, capable of cultivation all year long. Residents of the Yakima Valley enjoyed a temperate climate and diverse flora and fauna. Nearby mountains and forests contained abundant wild food plants and game, and the valley's streams held plenty of fish—as did the Columbia River, to the east. Indeed, the Yakima had less incentive to practice settled agriculture than the Pima. The Pima had been irrigating since long before their first contact with Spanish explorers and missionaries, but the Yakima began doing so only after the creation of their reservation in the mid-nineteenth century. Nevertheless, in many ways the two groups of Indians were similar. Both were highly adaptable. Both readily saw the value of irrigation. And both found that success at farming was no less to be feared than failure.

In the Gila and Yakima Valleys, the Bureau of Reclamation consolidated old irrigation systems into larger unified networks of canals—as it did on most of its projects. Nominally, the bureau represented *all* residents of the two valleys, Native American as well as white. And given that both the Yakima and Pima had been successful cultivators before white farmers appeared in the 1880s and 1890s, the Indians had a superior moral and legal claim to the local water supply. They were self-supporting and peaceful, and many of them showed an interest in market agriculture. If any Indians could serve as successful agricultural models to other Native Americans in other parts of the

West, these were the ones. Instead, the bureau catered exclusively to white farmers and land speculators. It permitted whites to use more and more of the Yakima and Pima water supply, then promised to fill the Indian canals with stored or underground water, then used Indian money to help pay for reservoirs and pumps that served whites as well as Indians.

THE YAKIMA

The Yakima Basin varies in elevation from over twelve thousand feet above sea level at its western boundary, the crest of the Cascade Mountains, to about six hundred feet at the Yakima River. Storms from the Pacific Ocean lose most of their moisture as they pass over the Cascades, so the Yakima Valley averages only seven or eight inches of rainfall a year, most of which falls during the winter and spring. Agriculture is virtually impossible without irrigation.[1]

In the mid-nineteenth century, the region's rivers provided a large share of the food consumed by local Indians. At the heart of their diet was salmon: king salmon caught between late May and early July; sockeye, chinook, and coho taken in the early fall. The Yakima River provided trout and freshwater mussels along with salmon, but the region's largest fisheries were on the Columbia at Celilo Falls (Great Falls) and at the Dalles. Dried and pulverized salmon provided a powder that could be mixed with other foods in the off-season. Roots, berries, nuts, and game supplemented the fish. The Yakima collected "Indian celery" (lomatium) in the middle of February, using it for insect repellant and medicines as well as greens. In mid-April, Yakima women began harvesting bitterroot, and in the summer and fall dug balsam root, yellow bells, onions, carrots, and potatoes. Most villages were situated near fishing sites, but the Indians of the Yakima Valley followed their food supply from season to season.[2]

The 1855 treaty that established the Yakima Reservation nominally created the Yakima "nation" out of the fourteen groups of Native Americans assigned to the reserve. Some bands loosely affiliated with the Yakima before 1855 now became full partners. (Opposition to the treaty came as much from Indians reluctant to share their reservation with bands from outside the Yakima Basin as from those who resisted ceding the land.) The thirty-five hundred "Yakima" surrendered 10 million acres for two hundred thousand dollars, paid over twenty years; the money could be spent only for purposes deemed useful by the president of the United States. The Indians retained 1.25 million acres, bounded by the Cascade Range to the west, Ahtanum Creek to the north, the Yakima River to the east, and Satass Creek to the south. They were "granted"—or "retained," depending on how the agreement was interpreted—the right to fish and process fish in accustomed places in customary ways, both within the reservation and without. They also secured or retained the right to hunt on, forage over, and pasture cattle and horses on the public domain. Unlike later reservations on the Great Plains, the Yakima reserve was not designed to alter the Indians' way of life; they were expected to feed themselves.[3]

Other than fish, timber and grass were the Indians' most valuable resources. The Bureau of Indian Affairs built a sawmill to supply the reservation with lumber, but the structure burned down under mysterious circumstances during the 1880s, and white lumber dealers successfully lobbied against rebuilding it.[4] The Yakima had better luck raising cattle and horses, which they first acquired in the 1840s and whose numbers peaked in 1880 at seventeen thousand and five thousand, respectively. In the mid-1880s, however, whites began to encroach on traditional Yakima summer grazing land outside the reservation. The promotion of agriculture on the Yakima Reservation by the Indian Office was, ironically, designed partly to replace the declining grazing industry.[5]

As early as the 1850s, the Yakima raised potatoes, fruit, melons, squash, barley, and Indian corn in small gardens and sold the surplus to non-Indians who passed through the valley. The traditionalists among them—the "Wild Yakima," as they were termed by whites and Indians alike—refused to farm, in part because they considered the earth a living thing. Most Yakima, however, resisted commercial farming because they lacked the machines needed to clear the sagebrush, level the fields, and plow and harvest them. Even more important, they balked at abandoning a diversified diet that could be adjusted to lean and fat years; they were loath to gamble as white farmers did. It made no sense to specialize in one crop when a year's hard work could be wiped out by drought, an extended freeze, or a plague of insects.

The Yakima first encountered irrigation in the 1830s at the first white settlements in the Pacific Northwest, the Whitman, Spalding, or Catholic missions. These were religious outposts dedicated to converting Native Americans to Christianity. In his diary entry for June 1, 1841, Lt. Charles Wilkes wrote: "Dr. Whitman . . . has had difficulty with the Indians as respects his . . . [water] rights for irrigating the soil. The Indians after granting him the priority and becoming aware of the use he made of it diverted it from him for their own use. They are intelligent and when they see an important improvement readily adopt it."[6]

With the encouragement of the reservation agents, the Indians excavated the first crude ditches in the 1860s. Cultivated acreage grew from about a thousand acres in 1865, to ten thousand in 1884, to eighteen thousand in 1899. During the 1890s, the Bureau of Indian Affairs commandeered money paid to the Indians for relinquishing a traditional fishing area at Wanatshapum to expand the water "system." By 1897, fifteen miles of canal had been constructed using Indian labor. The Indians who favored irrigation did so because the growth of white settlements in the Yakima Valley restricted their fishing, hunting, and gathering. They also wanted to render themselves less dependent on government rations, earn money by digging ditches, and drive up the value of their land.[7] The Bureau of Indian Affairs supported the expansion of irrigation to prevent Indians from straying off the reservation, and many Indians who opposed it did so because it interfered with traditional patterns of gathering food. Irrigated crops demanded care during the spring and early summer salmon runs—and later during the hop harvest in September. (Indians predominated among hop pickers on land farmed by whites west of the Cascades. The annual harvests became communal get-togethers as well as opportunities to earn money working for wages.)

At any given time, *most* Indians were absent from the reservation, and those who lived there year-round and farmed constituted a small fraction of the total population. In 1881, the Yakima agent noted that less than 30 percent of those assigned to the reservation could be classified as full-time residents. Nearly as many Paiute exiles lived there as Yakimas, banished from their Idaho home to the Yakima Valley following the Bannock War (1878).[8]

Until the 1880s, the Yakima Basin was relatively isolated. Then, in 1883, the Northern Pacific Railroad opened its line through the valley. During the 1880s, the white population of Yakima County grew from 2,811 to 4,429, and it reached 13,462 in 1900. Now the pressure to expand irrigation came not from the Indians, the BIA, or reservation agents, but from white farmers and land speculators interested in the government's allotment and leasing policies. As early as the 1860s, a handful of Indians *voluntarily* took up individual allotments along Simcoe and Toppenish Creeks, in part because Yakima agent Jay Lynch promised that their fee simple titles would be more secure and easier to protect in court than land held in common. Most Indians opposed forced allotment, however.[9] Some feared the loss of government protection once the reservation had been divided up. Others— including a handful of Indians who had fenced off tracts of pasture as large as a thousand acres within the reserve—feared that they would lose their exclusive, traditional rights.[10]

Congress first applied the 1887 Dawes Act to Yakima land in 1892. In that year, about half the arable reservation land was allotted, and by 1905 all the land suitable for irrigation had been parceled out. That was little more than one-third of the reservation established in 1855, and the Yakima held most of the remaining pasture and timberland in common use until 1904 or 1905. When the last allotment was made in 1915, 450,000 acres had been distributed to forty-five hundred Indians.[11]

In 1871, the commissioner of Indian affairs called the Yakima Reservation "the model agency of the Pacific slope." He attributed its success to the Indians' lack of contact with morally debased frontier whites. The Yakima could, therefore, advance along the path of civilization at their own pace.[12]

By the 1890s, however, most Bureau of Indian Affairs officials thought that segregation was a bad idea and encouraged whites to settle on Indian land. Lessees would clear the land of brush, level it, and perhaps erect houses, barns, and fences. Rental money would provide the Indians with a "nest egg" to purchase seed, plows, stock, lumber, and other agricultural necessities. Everyone would gain.[13]

Congress first authorized leasing in 1891, but few whites took up Yakima allotments during the depression-ridden 1890s. The end of the depression in 1898, and an increase in the length of leases from five to ten years in 1900, made renting the land more attractive. In 1901, the Indian Office approved 76 leases. In the following year, the number nearly doubled, and in 1904 it reached 335. By 1920, the government had rented out nearly ninety thousand acres of the reservation's best agricultural land. Revenue averaged a scant $1.75 per acre per year, but that constituted 60 percent of the total income of the Indians and *twice* the net return from their crops.[14]

The demand of white settlers and speculators for Indian land proved insatiable. The Commercial Club of North Yakima petitioned Congress to sell the "surplus" within the reservation and give all Indians immediate fee simple titles to their allotments. Unless that was done, the club's directors argued, the property could not be mortgaged and would remain unproductive during the twenty-five-year trust period specified in the Dawes Act, retarding the Indians' agricultural progress. Furthermore, the "club" recommended that all unused allotments be sold instead of leased. Invested at 6 percent interest, the proceeds would return more revenue to the allottee than annual rental fees.[15]

Until the drought of the late 1880s, the water supply of the Yakima Basin was adequate to serve both whites and Indians. In 1889 and 1891, however, diversions by white farmers from Ahtanum Creek, the northern border of the reservation, dried up that stream in midsummer. At the same time, the Northern Pacific Yakima and Kittitas Irrigation Company—a subsidiary of the railroad—claimed the entire flow of the Yakima River and began diverting most of it onto private land through its Sunnyside Canal. Indian fishing rights suffered, as did the supply of water available to reservation land. Yakima agent Jay Lynch protested, but without success. In 1896–97, the Indian Irrigation Service constructed the first canal from the Yakima River onto the reservation. Lynch, however, failed to file for water under Washington law until 1903.[16]

By the turn of the twentieth century, the Yakima Valley contained 80 percent of the state's irrigated land, and the privately constructed Sunnyside Canal was the largest in the state. All the valley's water had been claimed by private land and water companies, and no expansion of irrigation could occur without consolidating smaller ditches and constructing new storage reservoirs. Therefore, the Reclamation Act of 1902 offered new hope to white residents of the Yakima Basin. In 1903, fifty ditch companies deeded their water rights to the federal government in anticipation that the Reclamation Service would undertake a comprehensive water project. (The goal was to free old water rights from lawsuits by putting them all on an equal footing.) That done, the secretary of the interior authorized the Reclamation Service to buy the water rights and property of the Washington Irrigation Company— which had purchased the Sunnyside Canal from the railroad in the 1890s.[17]

The Indian Office had plans of its own. In 1903, it began excavating a new canal upstream from the Sunnyside Canal's headgate.[18] Shortly thereafter, two private irrigation companies filed an injunction suit against the Indian Office, forcing it to suspend work on the new canal, and the Washington legislature passed a bill allowing the Reclamation Service to withdraw virtually all unappropriated water in the state for up to three years if it contemplated using that water on one of its projects.[19] The Reclamation Service now exercised de facto control over all the Yakima Basin's "surplus water"— including the spring runoff. It bought out the Washington Irrigation Company, owner of the Sunnyside Canal, in June 1905. The government takeover constituted a tacit promise to provide a dependable supply of water to the owners of forty thousand acres of private land served by the canal.[20]

In 1905, the BIA opened eight hundred thousand acres of unallotted land on the Yakima Reservation to white settlement, making a division of the Yakima River imperative.[21] Now the demand for irrigating Yakima land came as much from whites as from Indians. At the beginning of 1906, Secretary of the Interior Ethan Allen Hitchcock arbitrarily allocated the minimum annual flow so that the Sunnyside Canal, the government's main ditch, received 650 cubic feet per second (c.f.s.) for the forty thousand acres it served, while the Indians received only 147 c.f.s. to service a much larger irrigable area. Hitchcock's 1906 division of water became a turning point in the history of the Yakima Reservation. Later in the same year, Washington congressman Wesley Jones sponsored legislation to transfer control over irrigation *within* the reservation from the Indian Office to the Reclamation Service and to reduce the size of irrigated Indian allotments from eighty to twenty acres. All irrigation works previously constructed for the Yakima Indian Reservation by the Indian Irrigation Service could be included "in any project developed under the provisions of the reclamation act [of 1902]."[22]

The "Jones Bill," as it quickly came to be called, dedicated proceeds from the sale of the sixty "surplus" acres in each of the original eighty-acre allotments to the construction of a new storage reservoir and other irrigation works by the Reclamation Service, and it guaranteed a "perpetual water right" to each Indian who accepted the reduced allotment. Proponents of the legislation argued that eighty-acre allotments doomed the Yakima to failure. No Indian could intensively cultivate that much land, and irrigation would make the twenty acres more valuable than the original eighty. The average

Yakima family would still have roughly eighty acres by consolidating the allotments of individual family members, and the crops raised through irrigation would be of much greater value. Moreover, it was, in the words of the House Indian Committee, "a good thing to allow the Indians to dispose of a portion of their allotments and thereby surround themselves with energetic, industrious [white] farmers." In his report for 1906, the commissioner of Indian affairs noted that the Indian Office favored the legislation even though it had been "drawn to meet the needs of the Geological Survey [i.e., the Reclamation Service]." He feared that litigation would delay the expansion of irrigation within the reservation as well as without. "The purpose of the act of March 6 [the Jones Act]," the commissioner concluded, "is to extinguish certain tribal [water] claims and give the Indians in exchange individual [water] rights apparently more substantial."[23]

The Reclamation Service had many reasons for supporting the legislation. If the federal government provided water to eighty acres, Indian families would be scattered over a much larger area. Canals would have to be longer, driving up construction and maintenance costs. As Frederick H. Newell put it: "The condition, I believe is as absurd as though the Government insisted on building for each man, woman and child a 10-room house, so big and expensive that no individual could afford to occupy it, and the annual repairs so great that it would soon fall to ruin. This is my conception of the present policy regarding irrigation on the reservations."[24] The Bureau of Indian Affairs had no choice but to accept the dominance of the Reclamation Service in the Yakima Valley. Nevertheless, months before the Jones Bill was introduced, W. H. Code, head of the Indian Irrigation Service, had recommended that the construction of a storage reservoir in the valley be assigned to the Reclamation Service and that the dam be paid for by selling part of the irrigable allotments.[25]

Whites who owned or leased land on the reservation, along with the residents of towns adjoining the reservation, thought that litigation over water would cease once the Reclamation Service exercised complete control over all ditches and canals within the Yakima Basin. Unified authority, they believed, would in itself increase the price of land and lure new settlers into the valley. Even the Indians had an incentive to support the 1906 legislation. Typically, money from the sale of Indian land went into a common fund over which they exercised little control. But the Jones Bill provided that if the land left over after the allotment of irrigable parcels sold for more than the cost of watering it, the extra money could be paid *directly* to the Indians, "if in the opinion of the Secretary of the Interior, such payments will tend to improve the condition and advance the progress of said Indians."[26]

The Indian Office nominally favored the Jones Bill, but the Yakima agent, Jay Lynch, did not. Congress adopted the Jones Bill two years before the U.S. Supreme Court issued its ruling in *Winters* v. *United States,* but Lynch thought that existing laws, if enforced, adequately protected Indian rights. The State of Washington recognized riparian as well as appropriative water claims. The reservation was downstream from the white diversions, and 28 percent of the Indian allotments were riparian. Therefore, Lynch argued, riparian rights alone would permit the Indians to block any upstream diversions. In addition, both Ahtanum Creek and the Yakima River were reservation boundary streams, and Lynch assumed that the reservation *included* these waterways. Therefore, their water could be used only with congressional approval. Finally, the treaty that created the reservation clearly protected the fishing rights of the Indians, and white diversions seriously reduced the value of the fisheries.[27] "Supt. Lynch," W. H. Code noted in a 1905 letter to the Secretary of the Interior, "has always been of the opinion that the original treaty rights of the Yakima Indians, giving them exclusive fishing privileges in the reservation boundary streams . . . would also give them the right to appropriate half of the water of said boundary streams for irrigation purposes."[28]

Whether or not the Indians held special water rights was irrelevant to Commissioner of Indian Affairs Francis E. Leupp. On September 12, 1906, Leupp informed Secretary of the Interior Hitchcock that he was confident "the Indians of the Yakima Reservation can, if permitted to do so, establish a paramount right to sufficient water to irrigate all their irrigable lands; but I realize such a course would be attended with a great deal of difficulty and expense." The best alternative, Leupp decided, was "conceding something in return for the advantage gained by avoiding a legal contest."[29]

The Indian Office acknowledged the "superior" water rights of whites, and Lynch was forced to accept the 1906 division of the Yakima River, which gave more than 80 percent of the minimum seasonal water flow to white landowners. In a June 8, 1908, letter to Commissioner Leupp, Lynch bitterly complained that "it seems unjust to the Indians that the proceeds of the sale of their land should be expended in the construction of reservoirs to furnish water. It is my opinion that if they are entitled to even one-half of the flow of the Yakima River, they would not need any storage water." On January 1, 1909, Lynch was fired and replaced with a more tractable agent.[30]

The 1906 Jones Act required three-fourths of adult allottees to approve reducing the size of their parcels from eighty to twenty acres before the Reclamation Service could begin constructing a storage reservoir. Half the Indians refused to accept the smaller holdings. That prompted the new reservation superintendent to promise to waive the trust period specified under the Dawes Act for all Indians who approved the smaller parcels. They could then sell or lease their land at will. Of those who agreed to the Jones Act, the vast majority were minors or deemed legally "incompetent" by the secretary of the interior, or were whites who had acquired reservation land. Meanwhile, the Reclamation Service pressured opponents of the storage project by cutting off their water or raising its price.[31]

The Yakima had good reason to mistrust officials in the Indian Office and Reclamation Service. In 1911, without consulting the Indians, Congressman Jones sponsored another bill, this time to use one hundred thousand dollars from the sale of surplus Indian land to pay for constructing wagon roads on the reservation—roads designed primarily to benefit whites. Moreover, the Indian Office permitted nine or ten "mixed bloods" (Indians who intermarried with whites or members of other tribes) to monopolize two-thirds of the Indian rangeland, and it imposed few restrictions on the whites who leased grazing land.[32] Most important, as historian Barbara Leibhardt has shown, the Bureau of Indian Affairs did little to protect Indian fisheries. At the same time it urged the Yakima to expand agriculture, it sharply restricted hunting and fishing. Both were protected by U.S. Supreme Court decisions. But just as the BIA insisted that Indians file for water rights under state law, it pressured Indians to purchase fishing licenses and follow state fish and game laws. In the 1880s, whites stole salmon from Indian traps, and by the end of that decade all riparian land at the Dalles was under the control of white settlers, whose barbed-wire fences prevented Indians from reaching the river. To make matters worse, timber companies floated logs down the Yakima River, towns such as Ellensburg dumped raw sewage into tributaries of the river, and irrigation diversions sharply reduced the stream's volume. Each of these activities hindered fishing.[33]

Factions within the "Yakima Nation" prevented the Indians from presenting a united front. "There were originally fourteen tribes or bands assigned to this reservation," agent Jay Lynch observed in 1897, "and, while many of them have lost their identity, there still exist several distinct tribes, and however careful an agent may be in making contracts and distributing supplies, he is almost sure to incur the ill will of a part of the tribes. They are apt to have the idea that one tribe is being favored, and this arouses their jealousy and brings to light their natural suspicions and hatred for the white man. When this occurs, they immediately begin to slander the agent, file charges, and call for a new man." Not all Indians on the reserve were Yakima, but the Yakima monopolized the best riparian land, to the consternation of the many Indians who had moved onto the reservation after 1855. Divisions deepened as intermarriage increased the number of mixed bloods.[34]

As in white communities, irrigation did much to promote conflict. The Indians who dominated council meetings and wrote letters to politicians generally favored resource development on the reservation, if only to enhance the value of their property. They embraced the spirit of capitalism, even if they enjoyed few of its benefits. On the other hand, the traditionalists, the Wild Yakima—most of whom occupied riparian lands along the Yakima and Toppenish Creeks far removed from the agency—resisted allotment and continued to hold land in common. They declined all government aid, wore their hair long, dressed in their traditional fashion, refused to send their children to the agency school, and ignored orders issued by the reservation agent. They lived, so far as it was possible, as if the whites did not exist.

Many Yakima—perhaps half of all adults—favored an expansion of irrigation. By driving up the value of the land, irrigation increased lease revenues. Who should pay for the hydraulic works, not whether Indian land should be irrigated, remained the paramount question. Some Indians wanted to use proceeds from timber sales on common lands to build dams and canals, but few were willing to relinquish any part of their individual allotments.[35] Kla-toosh, a hereditary chief, put the matter succinctly when he addressed the new Yakima agent at a Fort Simcoe council in 1909: "This country is ours. The water is ours. The law knows this. Who gave you the right to take from us our water which is life, and then offer it back to us in exchange for our land? Why should we pay for that which always belonged to us?"[36]

Yakima protests became more strident during the William Howard Taft and Woodrow Wilson administrations.[37] Robert Valentine, the commissioner of Indian affairs in 1912, admitted that the Roosevelt and Taft administrations had let the Yakima down. Eighty thousand acres within the reservation were "under ditch"—twenty thousand acres more than off the reservation—but the Indians received only a small fraction of the water used by whites and less than half the water they needed. In a March 15, 1912, letter to the secretary of the interior, Valentine noted that "this Office has pursued a quiescent and conciliatory policy of not encouraging any belief that their [Yakima] rights would be asserted and protected, as a result of which the reservation has borne the hardships incident to the shortage of water." Valentine wanted to provide the reservation with sufficient free water to irrigate *all* arable eighty-acre allotments. He also urged that control over reservation irrigation works be removed from the Reclamation Service and restored to the Indian Office, as the Yakima had frequently requested.[38]

One week after Valentine wrote that letter, he met with Secretary of the Interior Walter L. Fisher, Frederick H. Newell, Wesley Jones (who had graduated to the U.S. Senate), and white landowners on the Yakima Reservation. No Indians were present. Valentine argued that the 1908 *Winters* decision (discussed in chapter 6) guaranteed the Indians a right to irrigate all their arable land. Newell responded that whatever their *theoretical* rights, the Indians could not abrogate the rights of white farmers that had already vested under state law. By default, the Indians had lost whatever inchoate rights they once held. And since the courts had never quantified Indian rights, the secretary of the interior was the logical authority to determine each tribe's entitlement, as Secretary Hitchcock had done in 1906. In any case, Newell insisted, the *Winters* right was solely to *natural* stream flow, not to floodwater. Therefore, the Yakima had no claim on the new water supply the government would make available once a storage reservoir had been built.[39]

Following the 1912 meeting, Secretary Fisher reaffirmed Hitchcock's 1906 allocation. All water rights, the secretary insisted, should be contingent on beneficial use. The idea that Indians had an open-ended or indeterminate right was unthinkable. Such claims amounted, in Fisher's words, to "a reservation of the total flow of the river without any obligation on the part of the Indians to utilize the water which might thus flow forever unused to the sea." There were limits to the amount of water that could be stored, and it was not possible for the federal government to provide water to *all* the arable land within the reservation. Promising the Indians an open-ended water right was infeasible for another reason: it was impossible to predict what crops or land the Yakima would irrigate in the future. Water needs would change from year to year. Some plants were thirstier than others, and future allotments on benchlands well above the river might require more or less water than the land then under cultivation. Since the Indian refusal to accept the 1906 Jones Act had stalled the construction of the long-delayed storage reservoir on the Yakima River, Fisher asked Wesley Jones to introduce new legislation to authorize construction.[40]

The 1912 Jones Bill received much more public scrutiny and criticism than the 1906 legislation. By 1912, the national Indian Rights Association closely monitored conditions in the Yakima Valley. It discussed the plight of the Yakima at its annual meetings, fed articles to national magazines, and maintained a lobbyist in Washington.[41] A month after the new legislation was introduced, the Yakima Nation protested to Congress, calling it "grossly unjust." The Indians particularly resented the bill's requirement that they abandon all previous water claims before they could receive any water from the proposed reservoir:

> Our riparian rights are older than those of the white man. This reservation we were permitted to hold when the Government took our other land. Water is life and belongs to the earth. . . . The Government has set still and let our water be stolen. . . . White man is better farmer than Indian. Indian only understands horses and cattle. Reclamation [Service] make high cost water, high cost drainage; Indian can not pay, and land be sold from him. This is what white man want. . . . We own half of Yakima River and all water in reservation, but we are not protected in any rights.

The Indians urged the U.S. attorney general to file suit to settle the Indian rights. If he refused, they promised to carry their case to a federal court.[42]

With the Indians mobilized and the Indian Office demanding sufficient free water to irrigate every acre of allotted land, a federal suit to adjudicate rights to the Yakima River appeared imminent.[43] Congress created a joint commission to study Yakima water rights in June 1913. It visited the Yakima Reservation in September 1913. After hearing testimony from representatives of the Yakima, Indian Office, and Reclamation Service, it concluded that the 1906 Hitchcock allocation was "inadequate, inequitable, and unfair to said Indian reservation." The congressional commission, however, did not acknowledge any special Indian water rights. Congress, it proposed, should compromise between providing water for the twenty acres specified in the 1906 Jones Act and irrigating the eighty acres demanded by the Indian Rights Association. Moreover, Congress should approve no appropriation for a dam unless at least 80 percent of the allottees favored the project. The prospects for compromise were slim. Even enough water to irrigate forty acres, half of each allotment, would require five times the supply promised to the Indians by Secretary Hitchcock in 1906.[44]

The congressional commission's recommendations were largely ignored. In 1917, the Reclamation Service completed the Wapato Dam at Union Gap on the Yakima River. In the opinion of Cato Sells, who succeeded Robert Valentine as commissioner of Indian affairs in 1913, congressional approval of the Wapato Project had "disposed of" all Indian water claims to the Yakima River and other streams. The Indians still had no voice in federal water policy, and Louis Mann, the Yakima Council's recording secretary, suspected that the Yakima had been "downed by the law." The reservation superintendent, Indian Office, and Reclamation Service, in his judgment, had conspired to "steal Indian Rights."[45]

Congress spent more money on the Yakima Reservation's water system than on any other Indian irrigation project. The additional supply of water from Wapato reservoir doubled the fifty-seven thousand irrigated acres within the reservation. But the water went to whites, not Indians. Before Congress curtailed the sale of Indian land in the 1930s, sixty thousand acres of the best Yakima allotments had been acquired by non-Indians. Indians cultivated less than 10 percent of the land irrigated on the reservation in 1919, and less than 6 percent in 1930—when 108 Indian families tilled about forty-six hundred acres. In 1935, land cultivated by the Yakima returned an average of $31.15 per acre; that *leased* by whites from the Yakima provided a gross income of more than $47 an acre; and land formerly part of the reservation but *owned* by whites earned nearly $85 an acre.

Only one in five Yakima allottees benefited from reservation irrigation works, and the Reclamation Service often discriminated against even them in the distribution of water. The Indians received most of their supply early in the irrigation season, when the Yakima River ran full. For that reason, they were restricted to low-value crops such as alfalfa, crops that did not require the heat of middle and late summer to mature. The Yakima seldom grew sugar beets, hops, or fruit, and the alfalfa was used to feed cattle, not sold outside the reservation. Whites controlled the Yakima Valley's marketing and processing facilities—whites who had a vested interest in limiting competition from Indian farmers.[46]

THE PIMA

The Pima live in south central Arizona, where annual precipitation is erratic, varying from five or six to more than twenty inches. Most rainfall comes from summer thunderstorms, whose value is lost as the moisture evaporates in the intense heat, and the remainder drains off into culverts and gullies. Rain is least likely during the spring, when farmers plant most of their crops. The Pima, Papago, Zuni, New Mexico Pueblo, and other tribes of the Southwest practiced irrigation long before they encountered Euro-Americans, and the Pima historically had a much stronger sense of private property than most other tribes.[47]

The Pima spread out in small villages along the Gila River and adapted to cycles of abundance and scarcity. The river carried nutrient-laden silt that prevented soil exhaustion and obviated the need for crop rotation, and the desert was far from barren. The Indians used the seeds or nuts of twenty-four plants; the stems, leaves, and flowers of twenty-two; the fruits or berries of fifteen; and the bulbs or roots of four. Mesquite beans, saguaro fruit, and cholla buds were particularly important. The first Spanish explorers reached central Arizona in 1533, bringing European crops and domestic animals. Thereafter, the Indians planted indigenous crops in the summer, such as maize, beans, and pumpkins, and European plants from November to January, particularly wheat and barley. The wheat ripened in May, by which time the supply of food from the fall harvest had been exhausted and cactus fruit was not yet available. Once whites appeared in large numbers, wheat and barley became good cash crops, and since natural forage was insufficient in central Arizona, the introduction of cattle, horses, and sheep required an expansion of cultivated land. Like most agricultural Indians, the Pima did not depend entirely on agriculture. About half their food came from fishing, hunting, and gathering.[48]

In 1846, Major W. H. Emory of the United States Army encountered the Pima on a military reconnaissance mission. He camped in one of their cornfields and later noted:

> We were at once impressed with the beauty, order and disposition of the arrangements for irrigation and draining the land. Corn, wheat and cotton are the crops of this peaceful and intelligent race of people. All the crops have been gathered in and the stubbles show they have been luxuriant. . . . The fields are subdivided by ridges of earth, into rectangles of about 200 × 100 feet for the convenience of irrigating. The fences are of sticks, wattled with willow and mezquite, and, in this particular, set an example of economy in agriculture worthy to be followed by the Mexicans, who never use fences at all. . . . To us it was a rare sight to be thrown in the midst of a large nation of what is termed wild Indians, surpassing many of the Christian nations in agriculture, little behind them in useful arts, and immeasurably before them in honesty and virtue. Dur-

ing the whole of yesterday our camp was full of men, women and children, who sauntered amongst our packs unwatched, and not a single instance of theft was reported.[49]

The Pima seemed well on their way to civilization.

For three centuries after first contact with the Spanish, the Pima remained relatively isolated. That changed during the Mexican War (1846–48), when the U.S. War Department surveyed a wagon road to California via Tucson, the Gila River, and Yuma. Subsequently, the Pima villages became a way station between Tucson and Yuma, the only place where argonauts bound for California could secure water, food, horses, and supplies. In September 1857, traffic through Pima country became even heavier when the Butterfield Overland Mail Company launched a semimonthly stage line between St. Louis, Memphis, Fort Smith, San Antonio, and the Pacific Coast. The discovery of gold and silver near present-day Prescott and Wickenburg in 1863 increased traffic between Tucson and the Salt River Valley.

During and after the Civil War, the Pima fought side by side with whites against their traditional enemy, the Apaches, and sold the U.S. Army wheat, cattle, and other supplies.[50] At that time, most of the four thousand Pima lived in seven or eight villages scattered along a thirty-mile stretch of the Gila River between Casa Grande and present-day Phoenix. In 1859, Congress designated a sixty-four-thousand-acre reservation for the Pima and provided them with ten thousand dollars' worth of agricultural implements. The Indian population soared, wheat production more than doubled, and the size of farms—most of which had been from one to five acres—increased. Trade with neighboring tribes largely disappeared as whites purchased or bartered for surplus crops. Since the reservation included only existing villages and cultivated land, the Pima, who often changed the site of their villages, clamored for the inclusion of previously cultivated land outside the reservation. By executive order, the president enlarged the reservation in 1869, 1876, 1879, 1882, and 1883. By the 1880s, it contained more than 150,000 acres.[51] The hot, dry desert environment contributed to the concentration of Pima in villages, but aridity did not act alone. Frequent raids by the Apaches dictated patterns of settlement as much as the climate. The denser the concentration of people—and irrigation permitted much smaller farms than those of Indians who specialized in raising stock (such as the Papago)—the safer the community was from attack.[52]

In 1864, the construction of Forts McDowell and Grant ended the Apache threat and permitted the Pima to turn their full attention to agriculture. Commercial ties to the outside world became even stronger when the Southern Pacific Railroad crossed southern Arizona at the end of the 1870s. Economically, there was no turning back. In 1870, the Pima and Maricopa farmed fewer than three thousand acres; by the end of the 1880s they cultivated more than nine thousand. Decades before whites began to reduce the Indian water supply, market farming had substantially altered the relationship of the Pima to the land.[53] Most of the Indians dressed in the fashion of whites, and many converted to Catholicism or Presbyterianism. Few gambled or used peyote or mescal, and a majority abandoned traditional ceremonies, songs, and games readily and without apparent regret. During the 1880s, the Pima built more than a hundred adobe houses and purchased forty sewing machines. Nor were they wards of the state. After the reservation was established, they received little assistance from the federal government. "The Pima Indians are a fine people," an official in the Bureau of Indian Affairs wrote in 1917. "[T]hey are sober, law abiding, not given to tribal dances and are religious and they are legally married and divorced."[54]

Increasing reliance on commercial agriculture, however, made the Pima more dependent on the Gila River's meager water supply and less capable of adjusting to "seasons of want." Ditches built by the vanished Hohokam centuries earlier helped convince the region's first white settlers and land speculators that the region around present-day Phoenix was immensely fertile and productive. The first ditch built by non-Indians, the Swilling Canal, excavated in 1867, tapped the Gila using an old Hohokam watercourse near present-day Florence. Larger diversions followed, particularly in the 1880s, and Indian land downstream suffered frequent water shortages. In 1870, the Pima refused a proposal by the Bureau of Indian Affairs to move them to Indian Territory, but 25 percent of the tribe did voluntarily relocate to the Salt River east of present-day Phoenix to relieve pressure on the Gila water supply. In 1879, Congress created the Salt River Pima Reservation.[55]

Despite the construction of the Swilling Canal, nature provided Indian farmers with enough water during the early and mid-1880s. But in 1887 the Florence Canal Company erected a diversion dam capable of turning the entire river into its ditches thirty miles above the reservation. To make matters worse, drought visited the valley at the end of the decade, lasting with brief respites into the mid-1890s. Eight thousand Indians lived on the Gila River Pima Reservation, which contained nine thousand acres of irrigated land and another thirty thousand acres capable of becoming highly productive with irrigation—the best land in the Gila River Valley. The Florence Canal Company watered seven thousand acres. The Pima agent urged Washington officials to file suit to protect the Indians' water supply, but the Justice Department refused. The drought made it difficult to determine whether nature or the ditch company was responsible for the Indians' plight. And although the Pima and Maricopa had used the Gila long before white farmers began to irrigate—and thus held the oldest rights to the river—it was not certain how much land they had cultivated in the past or how much water they were entitled to. Fearing an injunction, the Florence Canal Company promised not to reduce the quantity of water used by the Indians, but it went bankrupt during the depression of the 1890s.[56]

During the 1890s, the land cultivated by the Pima decreased by 60 to 70 percent, and in some years the Indians harvested no crops at all. For the first time, the federal government issued rations to the Pima to prevent starvation, and Indian villages began to disintegrate as more and more of their inhabitants wandered into towns and cities in search of food and jobs. In September 1899, the reservation agent at Sacaton observed that the river carried insufficient water to irrigate even a thousand acres of Indian land: "I notice in the Indians a restlessness as they realize their helpless conditions, and am often confronted with the solicitous queries, What are we to do? If we plant what [seed] we have, what assurance have we of getting it back?" He was confident that, under favorable conditions, the Indians "would soon become independent, prosperous, civilized citizens." But deprived of water, "hunger . . . and destitution are their lot. A nomadic life being taken on, their old tribal nature asserts itself, and the expenditures hitherto made and being made by the Government for their educations and improvement prove a curse to them rather than a blessing."[57]

In 1896, at the request of the Indian Office, the U.S. Geological Survey examined the Gila River and concluded that the water supply could be expanded either by pumping underground water or by building a storage reservoir. Officials in the USGS Hydrographic Branch favored government construction of a dam at San Carlos, fifty miles east of Florence, using Indian labor. Sales of water to white farmers would pay for the structure; the Indians would receive free water for all their arable land. The motives of the USGS were not altruistic. The depression of the 1890s prompted Congress to consider many public-works schemes as jobs measures. If the plight of the Pima persuaded Congress to pay for a reservoir, that precedent might pave the way for the Geological Survey to build reservoirs throughout the West, for whites as well as Indians. The San Carlos site was one of the best in the West. Situated on Indian land, it could not be claimed by a private water company. Not surprisingly, the Pima won the congressional support of such dubious champions as Senator William Morris Stewart of Nevada—who since the late 1880s had been trying to get Congress to pay for storage dams in his impoverished state.[58]

In 1897, F. H. Newell, then head of the Hydrographic Branch in the Geological Survey, noted that the Pima "have been rapidly losing their capabilities for self-support and are becoming a permanent charge and source of annual expense. If they are to be kept from further degradation it is necessary that prompt action be taken." He favored construction of the San Carlos reservoir, nominally because it would cost seventy thousand dollars a year to feed the Indians but only an estimated million dollars to build a dam that would permit them to feed themselves. In 1901, the Senate added a hundred thousand dollars to the Indian Appropriation Bill to complete surveys for the dam, but the House eliminated this item from the budget.[59]

After passage of the Reclamation Act in 1902, the Geological Survey quickly lost interest in the Indians. As one of the chief architects of the Reclamation Act observed privately in 1903, "Both the Tonto [Salt River] and the San Carlos [Gila River] projects . . . must stand or fall on their merits as projects for the creation of homes for 'white people.'" The Pima Reservation contained the largest block of irrigable "government" land in southern Arizona, but the strongest white support for federal reclamation came from farmers and land speculators around Phoenix, who wanted the government to build a dam on the Salt River rather than on the Gila. There was also efficiency to consider. Since the Indian farms were far downstream from most white irrigators, much water was lost to seepage or evaporation before it could be turned into canals on the reservation. If Indian needs took precedence over those of whites, Newell observed, "several acres well-tilled by white men would be destroyed for the benefit of one acre poorly worked by the Indians."[60]

As in the Yakima Valley, the Reclamation Service had little trouble winning the cooperation of the Bureau of Indian Affairs. In 1900, Congress appropriated thirty thousand dollars to construct irrigation canals on the Pima Reservation—even though there was no water to fill them. The commissioner of Indian affairs candidly commented: "While the ditches may not be of use, it is certainly wise to require the Indians to perform labor in return for the appropriation [instead of doling it out in assistance], as otherwise they might be led to abandon their former habits of industry and become pauperized."[61] In an effort to fill the empty ditches, the U.S. Justice Department pressed suit to adjudicate all rights to the Gila River, but it dropped the case a few years later. The reservation superintendent feared that a court decree dividing up the stream would be unenforceable, because 960 people tapped the river above the Pima diversion. The Indian Irrigation Service also nixed the San Carlos storage project on grounds that the dam would be too far above the reservation to provide the Indians with a dependable water supply. The water would be subject to seepage, evaporation, and pilferage by whites, and the Indian Office's engineers questioned whether the Gila's flow would be sufficient to fill the reservoir. And the river carried so much silt and mud that nature might, within a few years, render the structure useless.[62]

The Indian Office and the Reclamation Service favored the use of underground rather than stored water on the reservation, and in 1903 the two agencies agreed to install a pump system capable of irrigating twelve thousand of the reservation's two hundred thousand arable acres—financed, of course, by the sale of "surplus" Indian land.[63] The system was completed in 1910. Meanwhile, in 1907, authority over Pima irrigation works passed from the Indian Office to the Reclamation Service. The Pima project became the poor cousin of the Reclamation Service's Salt River Project, which served land near Phoenix.[64]

Officials in the Indian Office and the Reclamation Service claimed that underground water was immune to theft by white farmers and beyond seasonal or annual fluctuations in volume. It would also permit the Indians to cultivate fertile land far removed from the Gila River.[65] As on the Yakima Reservation, federal reclamation opened the best Indian land to white settlers. The pump project made it possible to divide the Pima Reservation into five- or ten-acre parcels distant from the river, freeing up 180,000 acres of the best Pima land at Casa Blanca. Sale of that land to white farmers more than paid for the pumps. Equally important, the pumps required an enormous amount of electricity from the Salt River (Roosevelt) Dam. Not only did Congress charge the Indians for installing the pumps—without their consent—but until 1912 it charged for the electricity to operate them. And since revenue from that source helped pay for constructing the Salt River Project, the proceeds from power subsidized white farmers at the Indians' expense.[66]

Like the Yakima, the Pima pleaded that they should be consulted in the formulation of government policy. They opposed the pump project on grounds that the wells could not produce sufficient water, that they would be too costly to operate and maintain, that underground water lacked the silt that enriched alluvial farmland, and that it was poisoned with alkali—which made crops wither and die. Experience taught the Pima that underground water was inferior to surface water. The pump project would, in the words of one Pima protestor, "make our land sick & worthless & kill it in less than ten years." Most Indians refused to use underground water and continued to rely on surface flow—in those years that the Gila reached the reservation.[67]

The process of allotment began in 1908. The Pima wanted ten-acre allotments, but the pump system was inadequate to serve even five-acre farms. Only if the government built the San Carlos reservoir could the Pima Reservation be divided into ten-acre parcels.[68] The Indian refusal to use the pump system was, in large part, a protest against reservation water policies. Nevertheless, F. H. Newell attributed it to greedy whites who bought Indian land in the hope that if the Indians refused underground water, Congress would be forced to approve the construction of the San Carlos reservoir—providing water to whites and Indians alike.[69] By 1911, the Presbyterian Church of America's Synod of New Mexico charged that white diversions had reduced the Pima tribe "to the verge of beggary."[70]

Not until 1924, and not without strenuous lobbying by such groups as the Presbyterian Synod, did Congress authorize construction of the San Carlos dam, which the Pima expected to provide water to fifty thousand acres on the reservation, or ten acres for every man, woman, and child.[71] At a mass meeting held at Casa Grande in 1924, the Pima Council urged every member of the tribe "to clear and fence his allotment as soon as possible so that our land may be ready for the water when it comes and [we] further urge that our homes be made models for cleanliness and morality. We believe that our tribe should set an example for the whole State in obeying the laws of God and man. And be it resolved that we believe it to be best for the welfare and progress of our tribe that all heathen dancing and drinking be abolished from our reservation." The San Carlos, or Coolidge, Dam was completed in 1930.[72]

When Congress authorized construction of the dam, it assumed that Arizona courts would approve an equitable division of the Gila River's surplus water before the new supply of water became available. A rough allocation between whites and reservation Indians was worked out in 1916, but a formal consent decree defining rights from the source of the Gila in New Mexico to its juncture with the Salt River near Phoenix did not appear until 1935. That decree gave the Gila River Pima a priority right to irrigate thirty-five thousand acres of reservation land.[73]

Ironically, the additional water had little effect on the Indian economy. During World War I, cotton replaced wheat on many Indian farms. Pima cotton sold for almost as much as Sea Island cotton, and not surprisingly the Indians took renewed interest in agriculture. Pima cotton was tougher and longer-lasting than any cotton fiber ever produced—even stronger than the Egyptian variety raised in the Nile Valley. It was suited for a wide range of uses, including automobile tires. "The future of the Pimas seems assured," the Indian Rights Association crowed, "a happy transformation from their condition a decade or more ago."[74] A 1917 BIA survey of the Pima reservation reported that "just now they are set on farm expansion and this strong desire, if skillfully handled by the superintendent, will make of them a prosperous, up to date, agricultural community."[75]

The slump in farm prices during the 1920s did even more than chronic water shortages and duplicitous federal water policies to undermine Pima agriculture. Working for wages beat the uncertainty of commercial agriculture, and fewer and fewer Indians saw themselves as farmers. For many Pima, the future was a menial job on the margin of white society.[76]

The Pima experience was similar to that of the Yakima: they could not participate fully in the new market economy, but they could not retreat to their traditional economy. "Primarily the Pima are agriculturalists," a writer observed in the *American Anthropologist* early in the twentieth century. "They say that formerly they hunted and fished and gathered many clams in the Gila, but owing to the settlement of the adjacent country, which began about twenty-five years ago, and the consequent diversion of water for irrigation farther up the river, most of the land and aquatic animals and birds, as well as the clams, have disappeared."[77] Once central Arizona had provided a wide array of game and plants. Now cities, mines, and farms—gigantic farms, by Pima standards—dominated a planned landscape.

CONCLUSION

Before stage lines and railroads brought them into close contact with large numbers of whites—in the 1840s and 1850s for the Pima, and the 1880s and 1890s for the Yakima—irrigation permitted these Native Americans to diversify and increase their food supply as a hedge against times of scarcity caused by fire, drought, or severe winters. The Yakima had less incentive to farm, both because their food supply was more extensive than that provided by Arizona's Sonora Desert and because they consisted of many different tribes or bands. Few Yakima, however, opposed watering gardens or raising irrigated crops to feed to livestock. Market agriculture was a deeply divisive force, and the Indians knew it. By making land far more attractive to whites, irrigation destroyed the isolation and integrity of the reservation. Yet irrigation also permitted the Indians to raise capital and to survive on less land. In the nineteenth century, the Pima began selling wheat, oats, and other crops to whites passing through Arizona, and during World War I they discovered cotton. Fewer Yakima sold their crops, but some raised apples and other high-value fruits and vegetables.

In both the Yakima and Gila Valleys, allotment resulted from threats to the Indian water supply as well as white demands for farmland. There was no correlation between the size of allotments and the eagerness of Indians to irrigate, or the income needed to sustain an Indian family. The number of acres each Indian received depended on the number of Indians, the size of the reservation, and the market for land among whites. The Reclamation Service and Indian Office worked to keep allotments as small as possible— five or ten acres in the Gila Valley and twenty or forty acres in the Yakima Valley. In this way, "surplus" land could be distributed to whites, and irrigators could be concentrated, permitting shorter canals and fewer diversions.

In Washington and Arizona, as throughout the West, the Reclamation Service used the suffering of Indians to win congressional appropriations, as the history of both the Wapato and San Carlos Dams indicates. Eventually, the Reclamation Service took over irrigation on both the Pima and Yakima Reservations, or what was left of those reservations, but it satisfied Indian water needs only after the demands of white farmers had been met—even if the Indian rights had seniority. When it could, the service encouraged the secretary of the interior to allocate water, as Secretary Hitchcock did on the Yakima Project in 1906. Never did the Reclamation Service file suit to adjudicate Indian rights, but it blocked several suits designed to define them. The service argued that the Indians could secure the water they needed only through the use of stored or underground water—water that augmented normal stream flow. The Indians paid for this water twice—by the reduction in the size of their allotments, and by the arbitrary use of money from the sale of their "surplus" lands to build dams and canals.

Irrigation undermined or destroyed the mixed economy that once sustained the Pima and Yakima. Their land base shrank, the land they retained was often leased to whites, and the white settlements surrounding them prevented the cultivation of the wild plants nature provided. To make matters worse, irrigation promoted discord between those Indians who sought to cooperate with reservation agents and those who did not, between those who lived on and off the reservation, between those who wanted to farm and those who wanted to raise livestock, and between those who practiced commercial and subsistence agriculture. The fall in crop prices during the 1920s and 1930s, along with the duplicity of both the Reclamation Service and the Indian Office, robbed both the Yakima and the Pima of much of their incentive to farm. If the Yakima and Pima, who already had farmed their fertile lands, at least part time, before the arrival of white settlers, found irrigation agriculture so destructive, what reason would Native Americans in less favored parts of the West—such as Wyoming, Montana, or the Dakotas—have to embrace it?

8

Wiring the New West
The Strange Career of Public Power

In 1902, most westerners embraced the Jeffersonian maxim that the expansion of cities inevitably led to the decline of the countryside. Yet they also assumed that industry could not develop without a sound agricultural foundation or base. For the West to "modernize," and for it to free itself from dependence on the East, it had first to become a land of family farms. By the 1920s, however, hydroelectric power held out the hope that industry could develop without small farms, or that the two could develop simultaneously. The West lacked significant deposits of high-grade coal, but it contained plenty of falling water. Cheap power might unify the city and country, to the benefit of both. Not only would it make rural life more attractive, but if dams could generate power for cities as well as store water for agriculture, then the profits from power sales could be used to offset the soaring cost of reclaiming desert land. The farmer and the industrialist would become equal partners in building the new West.

The concept of "multiple use"—using dams to provide flood control and power, as well as water for farms and cities—had been around since the early years of the twentieth century, but it was not put into use until the 1920s. By that decade, private utilities, the states, and municipalities all had the ability to build big dams—just like the federal government. But since most large streams were interstate, and since interstate streams contained the best remaining dam sites, the construction of such dams often hinged on the negotiation of interstate treaties or compacts by which the states acted in concert with the national government to divide the water, as Colorado River Basin states did in 1922, 1928, and 1944. The federal government, therefore, had a great advantage over its competitors for the West's surplus water.

Boulder Dam became a symbol of the West's new economy. It stored sufficient water to reduce or eliminate seasonal variations in stream flow, making possible the coordination of discharges of water for power, agriculture, flood control, and cities. The high dams authorized after 1928, which served far more water users spread over a much greater area than earlier dams, transformed the politics of water in the West. They posed new questions about what level of government should be empowered to allocate water and regulate its use. Who should get the power from these dams, under what conditions, and at what price, remained hot issues throughout the 1930s. Both the nation and the states addressed the question of hydroelectric power—more often in competition than cooperation—and easterners were just as likely to oppose the concentration of power in Washington, D.C., as were westerners.

THE ELECTRIFICATION OF THE WEST

The first large hydroelectric plant in the United States, constructed at Niagara Falls, New York, began generating power in 1895. The thirty-mile-long Niagara River connected Lakes Erie and Ontario and tumbled 160 feet at its famous falls. The stream carried an enormous volume of water, which varied little according to the seasons. Niagara Falls was an ideal power site that demonstrated the potential for sending alternating current long distances in large quantities. Few places in the United States, East or West, offered such opportunities. By 1904, Niagara Falls produced 20 percent of all the electricity used in the United States.[1]

Nevertheless, the future of hydropower was in the mountainous far West.[2] In 1890, John Wesley Powell observed that a system of irrigation dams and canals would also produce "power . . . unparalleled in the history of the world. Here, then, factories can be established, and . . . the violence of mountain torrents can be transformed into electricity." By the middle of the 1890s, *Irrigation Age* ran a regular column entitled "Water Power and Electricity." The editor, William Ellsworth Smythe, proclaimed that the construction of dams and canals would awaken "the latent possibilities of water falls, the mine, the factory and the ideal conditions of social life. Everybody is beginning to see that all these things are web of one woof." Water power would unleash the West's vast economic potential. "Let any fair-minded man compare the national endowments of western States with those of the East," Smythe gushed, "and he will have a sudden and startling revelation of future events." A writer in *Popular Science Monthly* predicted that one day the power sites of the West would "form the centers of manufacturing districts, thus gradually augmenting . . . industry in sections of the country that at present are principally agricultural."[3]

Hydropower would permit the West to revive and expand old industries as well as create new ones. Given its size, scattered population, and relatively high freight rates, no part of the country would benefit more from the electrification of railroads. Electrified trains would be cheaper, faster, more efficient, and less vulnerable to cold weather and mechanical breakdown than steam-powered trains, and they could be rigged to generate electricity on downhill slopes. The conversion of Montana's Butte, Anaconda and Pacific line to this new form of energy early in the twentieth century reduced fuel costs by nearly two-thirds. The chief of the Interior Department's Division of Power Resources claimed that "as a conservative estimate," 50 percent of the cost of railroad fuel could be saved by switching from steam to electricity.[4]

Transportation would be the cornerstone of the new western economy, but mining would also benefit. "The use of electric power in mining," one mine owner proclaimed, "will begin a new era in the industry. The expenses . . . will be cut down so much that poor mines may be worked at a profit, and besides, the ore can be got out with less work. No one can yet estimate the changes in gold and silver mining that will follow the introduction of electricity in the industry." Cheap power would permit the excavation of deeper deposits, poorer-quality ores, and minerals far removed from water. Hydraulic mining required the construction of dams, canals, and flumes, so often electricity could be produced as a by-product of mining itself. Not surprisingly, many of the earliest hydroelectric plants were constructed at such centers of mining as Telluride, Colorado, and Bodie, California.[5]

Western agriculture would benefit in countless ways from hydropower. To many observers, the development of irrigation in "Arid America" was but the first stage in building an economic empire that would one day monopolize the vast markets of Asia.[6] Hydroelectric power would take technology one step further, permitting electric pumps to compete with those driven by internal-combustion engines in such regions as California's San Joaquin Valley, where they freed farmers from seasonal variations in stream flow and rendered them relatively immune to litigation over water rights. Vast pools of underground water held out the promise of an unlimited supply—if the energy could be found to exploit them. Where crops could be raised all year long, underground water made agriculture far more productive—and far less dependent on the cycles of nature. By the second decade of the twentieth century, pumps also permitted farmers to raise water from surface streams carved deep into the earth onto farms hundreds of feet above the channels. That added 10 million acres of bench and mesa land to the West's supply of irrigable land. Finally, nitrogen—the basic ingredient in fertilizer—was for most of human history supplied by decomposing organic materials, such as garbage or sewage sludge. In the late nineteenth century a method was found to extract or "fix" nitrogen from the atmosphere using electricity, and hydroelectric power promised a cheap and abundant supply of fertilizer. European farmers used far more fertilizer than their American counterparts and reaped far larger crop yields. Synthetic fertilizers sold in the United States contained one-fifth or one-sixth the nitrogen content in European fertilizers produced by hydroelectric power.[7]

Not surprisingly, hydroelectric power developed much more rapidly in the West than in other parts of the United States. From 1902 to 1912, hydropower kilowatts increased by 451 percent in the eleven western states but only by 98 percent in the rest of the nation. Seventy-five percent of the nation's potential hydroelectric power was in the so-called public-land states. In 1908, New York produced twice as much hydropower as California. Within twenty years, California had eclipsed New York and was turning out 15 percent of the nation's total supply. Eighty-six percent of the power generated in the Pacific Coast states and 89 percent of the power produced in the Rocky Mountain states came from falling water. By contrast, only about 14 percent of the electricity generated in Ohio, Indiana, Illinois, Michigan, and Wisconsin came from that source. By 1920, California, Washington, and Oregon generated more than one-third of the nation's hydroelectricity.[8]

NATIONAL HYDROELECTRIC POLICY, 1902–1919

The Constitution of the United States granted Congress authority "to dispose of and make all needful rules and regulations respecting the territory or other property belonging to the United States," including the public lands, and many of the best dam sites were part of the public domain. It also granted the power to promote "interstate commerce" and the "general welfare," along with a treaty-making power to regulate international waters, such as the Great Lakes, Niagara Falls, the Columbia and Colorado Rivers, and the Rio Grande.[9] Nevertheless, if the congressional power to regulate commerce was unquestioned, the water itself either belonged to the states through which it passed or at least fell under their administrative control. It was difficult, therefore, to determine where the authority of the individual states ended and the power of the federal government began.

Electricity differed from other industrial products. The amount of capital required to build plants, string transmission lines, and maintain far-flung systems was enormous. Yet the demand for electricity was seasonal, and power companies could not store their output in warehouses, as manufacturing companies did. Utility companies enjoyed more stable markets than most factories, and they could depend on a relatively steady stream of revenue. Nevertheless, for years after the construction of a plant, most income went to pay interest on loans.[10]

From 1886 to 1911, Congress claimed jurisdiction over the power companies that used navigable streams or the public domain, and it dealt with them individually. It passed nearly a hundred bills granting individuals and corporations the right to dam navigable streams, and some of those dams generated electricity. During Theodore Roosevelt's administration, the Interior Department devised a permit system covering power sites on the public domain, but the transfer of control over the national forests from Interior to Agriculture in 1905 splintered authority, as did the famous Ballinger-Pinchot conflict over Republican conservation policies during the administration of William Howard Taft (1909–13). When Woodrow Wilson, a Democrat, succeeded Taft in 1913, his secretary of the interior, Franklin K. Lane, called for a uniform permit system covering navigable streams, national forests, and the remainder of the public domain.[11]

Many members of Congress wanted to continue licensing water power sites in the same way they doled out river and harbor improvements: project by project. By so doing, legislators could claim credit for bringing new public works to their districts and simultaneously protect the prerogative of the national legislature against encroachments from the executive branch. Nevertheless, there were deep divisions within Congress. One small group, led by Senator Francis G. Newlands of Nevada, believed that the nation's waterways had to be developed comprehensively, not according to the whims of private companies. Most power bills, according to Newlands, sought to regulate only "a detached portion of the waterway development of the country." He feared, therefore, that they would "put the full development of waterways in a strait-jacket in the future." Another small group of legislators supported "mixed" enterprise—government construction of dams and power plants according to a comprehensive plan, with private operation of the completed plants and transmission of power to consumers. The most vocal congressional minority—supported by the National Grange and other farm organizations—favored government ownership and delivery of power. "Public power" advocates worried that turning the nation's hydroelectric sites over to private companies would stunt the growth of industry and result in corrupt and inept regulatory institutions (particularly at the state and local levels).[12]

The vast majority of lawmakers preferred private enterprise regulated by local, state, or national utility commissions. They regarded public power as an entering wedge for government to engage in other economic activities—what came to be called "creeping socialism" in the 1950s. Government, they claimed, sold electricity more cheaply than private companies not because it was inherently more efficient, but because it borrowed money at lower rates of interest, did not have to make a profit, and paid no taxes. The promised benefits of public power, critics insisted, were illusory. Public power merely shifted the tax burden to consumers, and eliminating profits also eliminated the incentive to innovate—which was far more responsible for the sharp decline in the cost of electricity during the first two decades of the twentieth century than the threat of government regulation. Given the deep differences over the future of hydroelectric power, Congress could not decide which committee should review water power legislation—Public Lands, Interstate and Foreign Commerce, or Agriculture. Not until January 1918 did it break the impasse by establishing a special committee to review water power legislation.[13]

Within and without Congress, conservationists expected water power legislation to do three things: limit easements to a certain term (no award should be granted in perpetuity); require companies to pay for each unit of horsepower generated; and prevent speculation in dam sites. But profound legal questions complicated the debate over legislation. Should private companies be able to claim and reserve undeveloped sites until an actual market for power developed? Should leases run from the date of application or from the completion of plant construction? Should preference be given to companies that produced the greatest amount of power, or to those willing to offer the federal government the best terms? And should the *first* company that filed on a site be favored over other companies—even those willing to pay higher fees for use of that site? The Forest Service sold timber within the national forests to the highest bidder. Should power permits be auctioned off in the same way?

No one could predict changes in technology, population distribution, and the location of industries with any precision, so was it wise to use fifty-year permits to dictate terms "up front," or should all conditions be imposed ad hoc by regulatory commissions? Who could foretell what the service area of a particular plant might be in twenty or thirty years? Equally important, what purpose did lease and license fees serve, and to whom should those fees be paid—to the federal government or to the states? Should nominal charges be levied on private companies simply to acknowledge that the water and land belonged to the federal government, or should the charges be substantial? The fees could be considered compensation for the rental of the federal lands used for power sites, but they could also be used to administer the permit system, to defray the expense of maintaining navigation or administering national forests, to raise general revenue, or to force a company to reduce rates or improve service. Some bills readjusted royalties every few years; others fixed payments for the life of the lease.[14]

Another major issue was "recapture." Private utility companies worried less about the length of permits than the conditions under which federal agencies might reclaim power sites at the end of a lease. They wanted recapture clauses that maximized the value of plants and distribution systems, regardless of the profits and dividends received over the term of the lease. If the cost of purchasing plants could be set high enough, Congress was unlikely to appropriate the money to buy them back. Some legislation required the government to purchase transmission lines, sub-stations, and even urban distribution systems in addition to the main plant. Should the lease-end price be restricted to the "actual cost" of lands, rights of way, water rights, plants, and other improvements, or to "fair market value"? Those who opposed fair market value argued that private companies should not profit from the "unearned increment," or charge the government for water rights and other "intangible assets" the company had received for nothing. Those who favored "fair market value" claimed that power companies needed this incentive to undertake large water projects. Whether administrative officials or the courts should decide proper compensation was another difficult issue, as was whether the federal government should operate the plants it took over or assign that job to municipalities and public utility districts.[15]

Among the opponents of federal regulation in Congress, the defenders of states' rights in the Rocky Mountain states were the most intractable. To Senator William E. Borah of Idaho, for example, legislation to strengthen federal control over water power was part of "that same subtle, persistent, impudent effort upon the part of the [federal] bureaucrats to take possession of the natural resources of the country and dominate and control them from Washington." It would "result ultimately in putting hundreds of agents, inspectors and spies among us and upon us." "These power sites are our wealth," Borah noted in 1910. "They are part of the state's heritage. It is a violation of the Constitution to withhold them from our use. . . . We will deal with the monopolist [ourselves] when he comes within our border. We can tax his property, and we can regulate the charges he makes to the people, and, above all, we can disrobe nature of this mantle of idleness with which the theorists and dreamers would clothe her." It was not just the central government that Borah feared. The concentration of regulatory power in federal bureaus would, he assumed, invite large corporations to command the West's wealth—as the Interstate Commerce Commission had invited capture by the railroads. Any leasing system, he predicted, would *strengthen* the biggest utility companies, not weaken them.[16] Congressman Edward Taylor of Colorado argued that far more would be lost if the states could not tax the power plants within their borders directly than would be gained if the federal government rebated to the states all or part of the royalties or lease fees it collected.[17]

The arguments of Taylor and Borah masked a deeper issue. Water power was closely related to reclamation, and legislation to regulate hydroelectric sites reflected long-standing divisions within the West. Interior Secretary Lane promised to dedicate revenue derived from power leases to the Reclamation Fund, but where would that money be spent? The Reclamation Act of 1902 originally required that 51 percent of all money received from sales of public land be expended within the state or territory where that land was sold. Lane refused to apply that failed principle to power revenue, but it was uncertain how Congress and the secretary of the interior would apportion this new source of income. Since California, Oregon, and Washington contained most of the public domain's best power sites, the interior West feared that water power legislation would benefit the Pacific Coast at their expense.[18]

The East led in the development of state regulatory commissions. Supporters of states' rights in that part of the nation doubted that Congress could design legislation with teeth in it—or that the federal bureaucracy could administer a just law fairly and effectively. The strongest opposition came from New York and Wisconsin, states that contained no public land, were more than capable of regulating utility companies without federal help, and that needed every new source of revenue they could get to fund ambitious new programs. As early as 1907, they began charging for power franchises under their authority to charter corporations. The commissioner of New York's Water Supply Commission demanded that the federal government limit itself to the protection of navigation. The states should regulate power, he insisted, even on interstate and international streams.[19]

World War I contributed greatly to the campaign for water power legislation. No event in American history did more to underscore the relationship between organization, planning, and efficiency. The centralized operation of railroads and war industries promoted interest in a coordinated power network that most progressive reformers would have considered monopolistic during the Roosevelt and Taft administrations, and representatives from business and government formed special boards or commissions to manage the allocation and use of critical natural resources.[20]

War industries demanded huge amounts of power. From 1914 to 1918, the supply of electricity increased by more than 60 percent, but still there were shortages, particularly in the shipbuilding industry during the winter of 1917–18. The cost of coal and petroleum also increased. From 1915 to 1917, for example, the price of fuel oil rose 160 percent, and from 1913 to 1918, the price railroads paid for coal increased from $1.13 to $2.95 a ton.[21] "The scarcity and high prices of fuel and construction materials have increased the cost of steam [electrical] plants and those interested in power development are turning their attention more and more to water power as a source of supply," the secretary of agriculture observed. Even had the coal supply been unlimited, the shortage of miners and the rail cars needed to transport it to market suggested the wisdom of replacing steam with water power wherever possible.[22]

In the winter of 1917–18, Franklin K. Lane proposed the creation of one vast power grid from Boston to Washington, a coordinated network that he hoped would cut the price of electricity in half. The district's western boundaries would be Albany, New York, to the north and Harrisburg, Pennsylvania, to the south. On the East Coast, coal constituted a large share of the railroad freight. Electrifying overburdened lines would free up the fuel they carried for other purposes. Cheap power would also reduce the cost of mining coal, and the cost of producing iron ingots as well. Lane hoped to construct twenty hydroelectric power plants in the region, many near coal mines. He asked Congress for two hundred thousand dollars to survey the power needs and potential of the industrialized northeastern United States. (Congress eventually approved the survey in July 1920.)[23]

In 1918, the War Industries Board, led by the powerful industrialist Bernard Baruch, proposed that the central government take over *all* the nation's power plants and operate them for the duration of the war. Public power advocates called for government ownership *after* the war as well. Meanwhile, they opposed any permit system that would strengthen private utilities. The U.S. Geological Survey, acting through the Fuel Administration, forced the closing of uneconomical and redundant steam-power plants and in at least one instance—in the Albany, New York, district—forced competing power systems to connect. Nevertheless, the federal government regulated but did not replace private utility companies.[24]

The end of World War I added a new sense of urgency to the debates in Congress. Cheap power would influence the ability of the United States to compete in Europe's postwar markets, and Franklin K. Lane expected heavy investment in power companies after the war. It was imperative, therefore, that Congress enact legislation to keep investment dollars at home and prevent the possible loss of industries heavily dependent on cheap power to Canada, Norway, and Sweden, all of which relied heavily on hydroelectric power. (The expectation that investors would favor utility companies proved correct. The capitalization of the nation's power companies doubled between 1919 and 1927.)[25]

THE WATER POWER ACT OF 1920 AND THE FEDERAL POWER COMMISSION

At the beginning of 1917, Franklin K. Lane proposed that the secretaries of war, agriculture, and interior serve as a special commission to license new power plants on navigable streams and within the public domain. Congress did not act on his suggestion until after the war, but when it did, it was a major breakthrough that eliminated the cost of creating an entirely new bureaucracy at the same time that it reduced bureaucratic conflict among the existing agencies. Mandated by the Water Power Act of 1920, the Federal Power Commission (FPC) was the child of the Progressive Era regulatory commission and World War I oversight boards that coordinated and administered industrial production, transportation, and labor, boards that served as bridges from one department of the executive branch to another, and between government and private industry. Federal regulatory commissions had been around since the 1880s. Many in Congress resented their autonomy, but such agencies were, at least in theory, also independent of the executive branch. They were an alternative to existing administrative bureaucracies.[26]

The Water Power Act of 1920 assigned the Federal Power Commission a daunting set of responsibilities—forty-five specific jobs in all. It was to survey the power potential of the nation's streams. It was to review plans for hydroelectric projects conceived by both private companies and the federal government. It was to issue licenses for power plants and transmission lines on navigable streams, public lands, and other reservations of the United States. It was to inspect finished projects to see that they were properly maintained and administered. It was to supervise the issuance of stock by the power companies it licensed, and it was to assess the value of their property to determine fair rates of return.[27]

Leases were limited to fifty years. At the end of that period, the commission would audit the company's financial records. The federal government, or any state or municipal agency it named, could take over the power plant for the amount invested, less depreciation. "Excess earnings" would be deducted from the recapture price. Power companies had to submit to the regulation of rates and service by state authority or, in its absence, the FPC. They were also required to pay nominal fees for the privilege of generating power. States and cities received first claim to develop power sites, but Section 27 specified that nothing in the law "shall be construed as affecting or intending to affect or in any way to interfere with the laws of the respective States relating to the control, appropriation, or distribution of water used in irrigation or for municipal or other purposes, or any vested right acquired therein." This statement was almost identical to the assertion of paramount state control over water in the Reclamation Act of 1902.[28]

At first, the Water Power Act of 1920 inspired great hope among reformers. Indeed, the *New York Times* editorialized that the Water Power Act "contemplates, or makes possible, ultimate public ownership." In 1920, less than 10 percent of the nation's estimated capacity for hydroelectric power had been developed, and more than three-quarters of the *potential* supply fell under FPC jurisdiction. Twenty percent would be generated on the navigable streams and the remainder at sites within the public domain. O. C. Merrill, the new executive secretary of the commission, was a respected conservationist. As the Forest Service's chief engineer from 1913 to 1920, he had drafted many of the power bills considered by Congress. As the FPC began its work, Merrill predicted that the production of electricity by falling water was "destined to be the outstanding industrial fact of the next 25 years." Water power, he predicted, would gradually supplant the use of coal, gas, and oil.[29]

The FPC held its first meeting on July 1, 1920, and within five months it received applications to develop three times the hydroelectric power that the Interior, Agriculture, and War Departments had authorized during the previous fifteen years. On March 1, 1921, the commission issued its first license, permitting the Niagara Falls Power Company to build the largest hydroelectric project in the nation. In the next year, half the horsepower applied for was in two states—California and Arizona—and only one state outside the West, New York, showed any great interest in hydropower. Of the applications received, eighty were from California, eighteen from Washington State, sixteen from New York, thirteen from Arizona, and six from Utah. By 1928, the FPC had received 910 applications to generate about 25 million horsepower. One-third of the applications were rejected or withdrawn, one-third were approved, and one-third were pending.[30]

The new law did not provide for the recapture of power projects built under federal authority prior to 1920, nor—beyond modest fees to defray the cost of administering the act—did it ask utility companies to pay royalties on the power they generated. Fragmentation of authority and lack of vision were evident from the beginning. Top officials in War, Agriculture, and Interior had many other responsibilities, and the full Federal Power Commission rarely met. To make matters worse, the postwar recession contributed to calls for retrenchment by Congress, and the Republican administration had little sympathy for the new regulatory body. The FPC budget shrank by two-thirds from 1921 to 1927. The commission, in the words of historian Donald C. Swain, "did little more than act as a clearinghouse for water power licenses, making certain that duplications did not occur."[31]

Soon after passage of the 1920 law, the comptroller of the treasury ruled that the FPC lacked the authority to hire a staff of its own. Therefore, the commission "borrowed" field personnel from War, Agriculture, and Interior and farmed out applications to those departments for review. In 1921, the FPC consisted of eight engineers, two lawyers, two accountants, two draftsmen, and sixteen clerks—all paid and evaluated by their home departments. The commission's chronic shortage of lawyers and accountants prevented it from licensing power plants already in operation. It lacked the personnel to audit the books of the power companies and to determine how much they had invested in plants and distribution facilities. It could not make thorough reviews of proposed projects, let alone comprehensive surveys of the power potential of the nation's streams.[32]

The Federal Power Commission's responsibilities were so extensive that conflict with the states became inevitable. Since power projects on the tributaries of navigable streams could affect the flow in the main channel, the FPC decided that its licensing power extended to those tributaries. When several states protested, the U.S. attorney general ruled that the states had control of such streams, not the federal government. Inconsistencies in state laws, and their lack of conformity with federal legislation, also worked against a unified power policy—as did the tendency of Congress to exclude major streams from FPC authority, including the Colorado, Columbia, and St. Lawrence Rivers.[33]

The Federal Power Commission's story is a classic example of the powerful limitations Congress placed on regulation by the central government. The Water Power Act ordered the FPC to approve only comprehensive projects that integrated water power, navigation, and other uses of water. In theory, the FPC could restrict power companies to sites that allowed for the complete development of a stream instead of permitting those companies to choose the most profitable locations or the easiest to develop. But the commission could do nothing when a state granted water for irrigation or municipal uses, even if those grants impinged on or limited future power developments. Control over water rights remained with the states.[34]

The FPC had authority to regulate service in the eight states that lacked regulatory bodies, but the proliferation of holding companies—which in 1924 produced three quarters of the electricity generated in the United States—crippled the capacity of any arm of government, federal or state, to set rates. State utility commissions, the courts decided, could regulate only companies that marketed electricity, not parent companies, and utilities that imported power from outside the state in which it was sold could be regulated only by their home state.[35]

Within two years of the law's passage, the bright promise of the Water Power Act had faded. The State of New York brought suit in the U.S. Supreme Court to annul the 1920 law, and Henry Ford tried to make an end run around the FPC by asking Congress to lease to him the Muscle Shoals power plant on the Tennessee River, constructed by the government during the war. The most strident opposition to the FPC came not from private power companies but from the Republican administration, on the right, and advocates of public power, on the left. President Calvin Coolidge wanted to abolish the commission, and William Kent, one of the nation's staunchest advocates of public power, complained that Merrill, the executive secretary of the FPC, had "gone into publishing diatribes against public ownership, just as if he were bought and paid for, which I presume he is." In Kent's judgment, Merrill—who at one point characterized the Boulder Dam Project as "impracticable and undesirable"—showed far more sympathy for the private companies who sought to monopolize the Colorado and other rivers than for the public interest. Merrill resigned in 1929, and a 1930 Senate investigation concluded that the utility companies exerted undue influence on the FPC. In the same year, on President Herbert Hoover's recommendation, the FPC became an independent five-member body. No longer the captive of the War, Interior, and Agriculture Departments, its authority was limited by Congress to the 10 percent of power produced in the United States that was transmitted across state lines. Even though they had no authority over holding companies, state regulatory bodies took precedence over the FPC.[36]

BEFORE BOULDER DAM:
THE RECLAMATION BUREAU AND HYDROELECTRIC POWER, 1902–1928

The controversy over who would develop the power potential of the public domain, and whether the states or national government would regulate water used for that purpose, had a profound effect on the Bureau of Reclamation. Chronically strapped for money and faced with the soaring cost of reclaiming desert land, it quickly recognized the value of hydroelectricity. But the absence of large urban markets, the opposition of private power companies, and congressional resistance to all forms of social planning limited the generation of power on the government irrigation projects.

As early as 1902, Morris Bien—then an employee of the General Land Office but soon to become the chief legal officer of the Reclamation Service— noted in a letter to the secretary of the interior: "In a number of irrigation enterprises it is found that the water stored can be used for the development of power without any material interference with its use for irrigation purposes. I would therefore recommend that the Secretary of the Interior be empowered to permit the water to be used for that purpose. This would be a source of revenue and would be an addition to the reclamation fund, without interfering with the uses for which the water is developed." Two years later, an electrical engineer working for the Reclamation Service observed that the technology for transmitting current great distances was developing so rapidly that "water powers now apparently worthless" would soon find markets hundreds of miles from the place of production.[37]

The Reclamation Act of 1902 said nothing about electricity. But on many federal irrigation projects, especially those distant from towns and cities, private contractors refused to bid on construction jobs. Therefore, the Reclamation Service built hydroelectric plants to provide the power to quarry stone and mix cement. Following project completion, the same plants generated electricity to drain waterlogged farms, pump underground water, or lift it from surface streams onto highlands. The supply of electricity often exceeded demand, and in April 1906, Congress authorized the Reclamation Service to lease surplus electricity to private companies for up to ten years, with preference given to "municipal purposes." The 1906 law credited all revenue from power sales to the project from which it was derived. The power could be sold anywhere *outside* the project, and the Reclamation Service could string transmission lines to the point of sale. Frederick H. Newell urged Congress to amend the law so that the secretary of the interior could award unlimited franchises or grants of at least twenty-five years. In 1922, Congress permitted fifty-year power contracts on the Salt River Project, but it refused to do the same on the other projects. Even after passage of the Water Power Act of 1920, the Reclamation Bureau's standard power contract remained ten years.[38]

Neither the 1902 Reclamation Act nor the 1906 Townsite Act prohibited the Reclamation Service from selling power directly to consumers, and on occasion, the service did so. But stringing transmission lines was expensive, and money spent on electrical systems was money diverted from the construction of dams and canals. Moreover, using power revenue to reduce the cost of construction proved dangerous because the subsidy—usually applied against the cost of the irrigation works—discouraged farmers from paying their full debt to the government. And since some projects generated much more power than others, government engineers feared that farmers would refuse to settle where there was no substantial power rebate—or use its absence as an excuse to renege on their debt to the government. Still, in 1924 Congress decided that proceeds from sales of surplus power should be applied first to construction costs, then to operation and maintenance charges, then as the water users themselves specified. No money reached the general treasury.

The hydroelectric potential of western rivers varied enormously, making it difficult for the Reclamation Service to establish a uniform power policy. In 1914, a kilowatt hour of power cost 13 cents to produce on the Minidoka Project in Idaho, $1.12 on the Truckee-Carson Project in Nevada, and $2.87 on the Rio Grande Project in New Mexico. Eighty-five percent of the Colorado River could be used for power without interfering with irrigation, but only 50 percent of the flow of Oregon's Deschutes River could be so utilized. In many parts of the West, therefore, power development was restricted to the lower river, using water "returned" from irrigation upstream. In the era before high dams—dams that could store the volume of a stream for a year or more—seasonal variations complicated the use of reservoirs for irrigation and power. So did variations in temperature. Much of the Southwest was warm enough to raise crops all year long. Therefore, water flowed in ditches continuously, and the supply of water for the Salt River Project in Arizona was more consistent from season to season than on government projects in Montana, Wyoming, or South Dakota.[39]

Government irrigation projects were isolated, with their residents scattered over a large area. The Reclamation Bureau sold electricity for as little as 10 percent of the price charged by private companies. But that was for peak periods, not year-round, and the bureau cut off service when irrigators needed water or power. Water used to generate electricity in the winter was lost to crops in the summer. The production of power, therefore, was restricted to the growing season when water was released from reservoirs and flowed through canals. Other than for pumping, farmers needed electricity most for winter heating, when water was least available. Therefore, most private power companies regarded the power sold by the Reclamation Bureau as a supplement to the year-round output of their own plants, not as an alternative source.[40]

The Reclamation Service built its largest power plants on the Salt River Project, near Phoenix, and on the Minidoka Project, in southern Idaho. The Salt River facility obviated the need to haul oil or wood to the remote site of Roosevelt Dam, fifty miles east of Phoenix. It included a twenty-mile canal with a drop of 220 feet that electrified a concrete plant, sawmill, and quarry.

Long before completion of the canal, Arizona residents recognized that power revenue could make irrigation cheaper. "This power would be employed in carrying out the work upon the dam, and in cheapening the cost of its construction," a Tucson newspaper editor observed in 1903. "Whether or not this power would eventually be utilized for commercial purposes is a matter for the future to decide."[41]

Roosevelt Dam's generators began to turn in 1906, and the Salt River Project's chief engineer urged the Reclamation Service to sell surplus power at or near market value, to return maximum revenue. He also recommended that project farmers take over the plant as soon as possible, so that they could benefit from the cheap power by forming public utility districts. In June 1907, however, the Reclamation Service leased most of the power not needed for irrigation—and virtually all the power used within Phoenix—to the Pacific Gas and Electric Company, which held an exclusive franchise to distribute electricity within the city. This outraged many residents of Phoenix, but as it did so often on its reclamation projects, the Reclamation Service deferred to the status quo.[42] The power company had generated power from the forty-mile Arizona Canal, constructed mainly for irrigation in the 1890s, prior to authorization of the Salt River Project. The Reclamation Service had considered buying out the company, but the price was too high. Therefore, it offered the company virtually all the power generated by the original plant if it would turn its original rights over to the federal government at the end of the contract. While the Townsite Act of 1906 granted a preference to municipalities, the contract with PG&E expressly *prohibited* the government from selling power directly to the City of Phoenix. Frederick H. Newell insisted that the Reclamation Service had no choice, because the Pacific Gas and Electric Company's rights had vested before Congress authorized the Salt River Project.[43]

PG&E purchased power from the Salt River Project for 1.5 cents per kilowatt hour and sold it for as much as 20 cents per kilowatt hour. The City of Phoenix had the right to regulate rates, but it had no way to determine what PG&E paid for transformers, transmission lines, salaries, and other expenses—nor did the Reclamation Service. The utility company claimed that its profits did not exceed 5 percent of the appraised value of its "works," but there was considerable debate over whether those works included the contract itself. (Poors' Manual of Rail Roads listed the value of the contract at more than five hundred thousand dollars, even though it had been obtained from the government for nothing.) The Phoenix City Council, Phoenix Board of Trade, Maricopa County Commercial Club, and other organizations asked the government to abrogate the agreement as a conspiracy in restraint of trade that violated the Sherman Antitrust Act. The city council proposed that Phoenix build its own power plant, but Congress's

Committee on Territories turned down the city's application to do so in 1910. In July 1913, the U.S. attorney general upheld the contract.[44]

Within the Salt River Project, most of the power drove nine pump systems that delivered underground water to ten thousand acres of Pima land. There were four separate plants, with substations at Phoenix, Glendale, the Sacaton Indian Reservation, Chandler, Mesa, and Miami, all connected by a forty-five-thousand-volt transmission line strung on steel towers. The Salt River Project Water Users Association resented that most proceeds from power sales in Phoenix benefited a private company rather than project farmers. The expectation that power revenue would markedly reduce the cost of the Salt River Project spurred the association to pressure the Reclamation Service to install more generators—at the water users' expense—and eventually, power revenue paid most of the project's cost. As of 1917, one-third of the money spent on the project had been used to generate electricity—and this source of revenue contributed to soaring land prices and speculation.[45]

The Minidoka power system was very different from the Salt River Project's. The Snake River dropped rapidly as it crossed Idaho, and many of its falls afforded ideal hydropower sites. Underground water fed the stream, making its flow more consistent from season to season than that of rivers in the Southwest. As the irrigation of private land expanded downstream from the government project, the Minidoka Project's power potential increased, with storage reservoirs upstream releasing more and more water. In 1906, the project's leading newspaper predicted that "the power developed at the Minidoka dam will, within a very few years, pay for the construction of the entire Minidoka project. The same thing will be true of almost every other project which the government is building." Reclamation Service officials were not so optimistic, but A. P. Davis predicted that the profits would at least pay the project's operating expenses.[46]

The Reclamation Service dammed the Snake River, raising its water forty feet to the gravity canals that served land along the river. The size of the stream, and the release of water to satisfy older water rights downstream near Twin Falls, permitted the production of enormous amounts of electricity. This was fortunate, because forty-nine thousand acres within project boundaries on the south side of the Snake River fifteen miles from the dam could not be reached with gravity canals. At the end of the 1920s, 59 percent of the power produced on the Minidoka Project was used for pumping or drainage, 15 percent on farms and in towns, and the remaining 26 percent for winter heating.[47]

Power revenue did not provide a substantial subsidy to irrigation on the Minidoka Project, as it did in Arizona. The cities of southern Idaho were far smaller than Phoenix, and the region lacked large-scale utility companies, industry, and mining. Therefore, in Idaho the Reclamation Service sold most of its surplus power to mutual companies composed of farmers—delivering the electricity through 148 miles of power lines it had strung by the end of the 1920s—and in a few cases it carried power directly to individual consumers or industries.[48]

The Minidoka power plant opened in May 1909, and by 1920 it served the towns of Rupert and Burley, along with eleven hundred farms. Cheap power allowed project towns to tout themselves as progressive, modern communities. Restaurants used electric stoves, the Burley bakery used electricity to heat its ovens, and Rupert claimed to have built the first electrically heated high school in the United States. In Burley, which had about five thousand residents in the 1920s, a city-owned plant purchased power from the Reclamation Service at one cent per kilowatt hour and sold it for as much as seven cents per kilowatt hour—still half the rate private companies charged in the Pacific Northwest. Within five years, the city's power system had paid for itself. "Owning the plants enabled power to be furnished at a price the settler could afford to pay," the Department of the Interior boasted in a 1926 press release. "If settlers had been compelled to pay the rates which a private power plant would have had to charge," the release concluded, "the farmers' wives would now be using gasoline and kerosene."[49]

Hydroelectricity was employed to grind feed, separate cream, heat incubators and brooders, turn circular saws, and perform many other farm chores. In the home, it powered washing machines, vacuum cleaners, water heaters, sewing machines, hot plates, heater pads, flatirons, curling irons, percolators, toasters, waffle irons, and other appliances. Minidoka hydropower also permitted the creation of cooperative enterprises, such as creameries and cheese processing plants. During the 1920s, per capita use of power among the seventeen thousand Minidoka Project residents was four times greater than the national average. Half of all project homes were electrified—a far greater percentage than in most parts of rural America. Because of economies of scale, and as an incentive to industry, small consumers paid more per kilowatt hour than large users, and rates for lighting were higher than those for heating. The Minidoka power plant operated year-round, and in the winter the government sold power below cost to heat homes and barns and create a market among farmers. Given the government's fixed costs, it was better to receive some revenue during the winter than none.[50]

The Minidoka and Salt River Projects taught the Reclamation Bureau many lessons and established several important principles: that surplus power could contribute to urban growth; that the bureau should not sell power directly to consumers; that revenue from power should be retained by the project on which it was generated, not paid into the general treasury or used to build new projects elsewhere; and that the proceeds could and should reduce the soaring cost of irrigating desert land. The Idaho experience suggested that the rural West would offer few good markets for power, given its scattered population and erratic demands for electricity.[51] Using electricity to pump water, moreover, created two classes of farmers who came into conflict. The first took up the most easily irrigated alluvial land—and the cheapest to irrigate. Their debt to the government was much lower than those who came later and filed on bench or mesa land served by pumps. The latter group demanded that *all* government farms bear the same construction charge—or that the federal government pay for the pumps and the electricity needed to run them. On the other hand, the Salt River Project demonstrated that if a market could be found for electricity, almost any western land could be reclaimed, regardless of the productivity of the soil or the cost of ditches and canals. The Arizona experience suggested that the bureau might benefit more from an increase in urban than rural population. Phoenix grew by 12 percent in 1922 alone, and the government power policy contributed to that growth. Little wonder that the bureau took such a keen interest in the Southern California population boom of the 1920s.[52]

The Reclamation Bureau's leaders did not favor public power; indeed, given the political backlash against socialism and collectivism during World War I and the 1920s, it would have been suicidal to do so. Nevertheless, in the 1920s, as attracting farmers to government projects became more and more difficult, the Reclamation Bureau took a new look at electricity. Cheap power, it was hoped, would usher in a new age of labor-saving machinery that would banish boredom and monotony from government farms, reduce the drudgery of chores, and provide moral uplift, particularly to farm women. Electric washing machines would give women more time to read and reflect, more time to educate their children, and more time to socialize with friends. Electric lights would banish darkness, leaving evenings for relaxation and conversation. Electricity could help integrate rural and urban America.[53]

In the years after 1920—when the Water Power Act established fifty years as the standard lease period—the Reclamation Service repeatedly urged Congress to authorize contracts longer than the ten years specified in the 1906 Townsite Act. But Congress recognized that the Reclamation Bureau wanted to use the proceeds from power sales to create a second reclamation fund beyond the control of the lawmakers. Furthermore, in order to generate and market power on a large scale, the bureau would need to claim water for its own purposes, not just in the name of individual farmers, and such a policy might usurp the right of states to regulate water rights and the cost of electricity.

"Secretary [of the Interior Hubert] Work has expressed the desire to have the Bureau discontinue so far as may be practicable the sale of power to individuals in small amounts and to towns and other entities," a Reclamation Service official noted in a 1927 letter. "His desire is to lease power plants [to private companies] where this is feasible, and where the lease of the plant is not feasible . . . he believes electric energy should be disposed of by the

Bureau at the switchboard to one company, district or other organization. The desire is to avoid the construction and operation of transmission lines so far as possible." In any case, by the second decade of the twentieth century the Reclamation Service lacked the money to build large electrical distribution systems.[54]

In 1932, eleven of the twenty-nine federal reclamation projects contained one or more power plants, but their combined capacity was less than one of Boulder Dam's generators. (That dam's power plant cost more than six times the total spent on *all* previous Reclamation Bureau power plants.) The government operated less than half the facilities; the rest were owned and administered by groups of water and power users. Irrigation or drainage took 20 percent of the electricity; the remainder went to towns, cities, and commercial and industrial users. Despite Secretary Work's misgivings, by the end of the 1920s power sales had become an *indispensable* subsidy to irrigation, particularly on some of the expensive projects launched during that decade. On the North Platte Project in eastern Wyoming, for example, construction payments would have been twice as high without power revenue from Guernsey Dam. "With the increased cost of irrigation works in the future," a 1926 Department of the Interior press release noted, "the revenues from power must be depended upon to lessen the burden on the irrigator. It will make projects feasible that could otherwise be built only at a financial loss to the government." The Reclamation Bureau recognized the value of the power subsidy long before it designed Boulder Dam.[55]

MUSCLE SHOALS AND THE GENESIS OF LARGE-SCALE PUBLIC POWER

A consolidation movement swept through the utility industry during the 1920s; fifteen hundred mergers occurred in 1925 and 1926 alone. Vast holding companies came to manage apparently discrete, independent corporations.[56] Expanding power grids symbolized the decline of localism just as the radio—one by-product of cheap electricity—contributed to the nationalization of culture. The production and distribution of water power raised deep questions about the growth of industry, the concentration of wealth, the threat to democracy from monopolies and trusts, and the dangers of technology. Little wonder that the dams and power plants at Muscle Shoals and near Boulder City became emblems of modern America.

The great water projects of the late 1920s and 1930s, including Boulder Dam, the Tennessee Valley Authority, and Mississippi River flood control, make sense only when studied in relation to one another. As discussed in earlier chapters, federal water policies sought to link the economic fortunes of the South and West. The Reclamation Bureau tried to extend reclamation from deserts to swamps and cutover land, hoping to replace the plantation, tenant farmer, and sharecropper with prosperous middle-class communities. It failed to achieve that objective, but within the Tennessee Valley the experiment in regional planning and "public power" gave westerners an opportunity to demand massive new subsidies from Congress.

In the mid-1930s, Boulder Dam and the Tennessee Valley Authority offered planners two models of regional economic development. The TVA, whose roots reached back to the Muscle Shoals Project during World War I, was the first water project to cover an entire river and the only federal project to create an autonomous regional authority. The Tennessee River crossed Tennessee, Alabama, Georgia, Kentucky, Mississippi, North Carolina, and Virginia. Within its basin, the average farm was worth only 25 percent of the average farm nationwide, and during the 1920s and early 1930s more than half the region's farm families were on relief. The best timber had been cut and the soil was exhausted. Private enterprise had fled the region. The Tennessee Valley Authority attempted to transform the lives of those who lived within its boundaries by providing cheap hydroelectric power, flood control, navigation improvement, soil conservation, and reforestation. The project included thirty-two major dams, nine on the Tennessee River and twenty-three on its tributaries. TVA sold most of its power directly to municipal utility districts or cooperatives, preventing the creation of private power companies, and it worked as much as possible through municipal and county institutions, bypassing the states in favor of an alliance between national and local institutions.

The architects and directors of the TVA assumed that abundant power was indispensable to a modern economy. TVA provided farmers in the region with cheap hydroelectricity and cheap fertilizer, and its rates served as a "yardstick" to measure how much private companies should charge for electricity. It furnished a tool, therefore, to those who wanted more stringent federal and state regulation of private companies as well as to those who favored public power. Not only did the Tennessee Valley Authority inspire national interest in the hydroelectric potential of Boulder Dam, in the 1930s it became a model for planned economic development within the Columbia and Missouri Basins—economically backward parts of the West. If the federal government could assume the responsibility for saving the lives of impoverished southerners, Western politicians argued, then it was only just that the poorer parts of the West should receive comparable assistance.[57]

The Tennessee River is the fifth-largest river in the United States by volume. It drains an area with the greatest rainfall in the eastern United States, and it carries a volume comparable to much longer streams, such as the Ohio and Missouri. The river passes through seven states and covers 650 miles before it joins the Ohio. At Muscle Shoals, in northern Alabama east of Decatur, the river drops 136 feet in a stretch of thirty-seven miles, giving it tremendous potential to generate electrical power. It was also a navigable stream. Nevertheless, unlike the Niagara River, the Tennessee varied enormously in size from season to season. Only in the spring, when it carried the greatest volume, were the shoals navigable. By the early years of the twenti- eth century, the Army Corps of Engineers had begun to consider building a series of reservoirs—beginning with a dam at Muscle Shoals—to open the region from East Tennessee to Cairo, Illinois, to cheap water transportation. The Tennessee River had the potential to link Memphis, Nashville, Chat- tanooga, Birmingham, and Atlanta.[58]

In 1890, the corps completed a fifteen-mile bypass channel around the most dangerous part of the rapids, but the canal did not permit year-round navigation of the river. About the same time, Congress granted the Muscle Shoals Power Company a franchise to build a power plant, but the river was a mile wide at the rapids, and the company could not raise the money to be- gin construction. The Alabama Power Company inherited the franchise and pushed hard for a combined private-government power and navigation project consisting of three dams capable of maintaining a six- or nine-foot channel. Until the 1920s, however, no power company could find the capi- tal to undertake the job, and in 1914 and 1916 Congress rejected bills au- thorizing the federal government to construct the project.[59]

In the years before World War I, munitions makers in the United States relied heavily on nitrates imported from Chile, but during the war the Ger- man navy threatened this supply. Some members of Congress favored gov- ernment plants to extract nitrogen from the atmosphere. The manufacture of explosives required a great deal of energy. Cheap hydroelectric power could reduce the cost of many ingredients used in explosives, including gun cotton, dynamite, and smokeless powder, and explosives were also impor- tant in mining, road building, and construction.[60]

In 1916, after lengthy debate, Congress passed the National Defense Act, which authorized the president to select a site and begin constructing a hy- droelectric dam and nitrate plants. Justified as a wartime necessity, the project's appeal derived from the fact that after meeting military needs, the president could use the plant to manufacture fertilizer, as was done in Nor- way, Sweden, and at Niagara Falls. When Woodrow Wilson chose Muscle Shoals, no one anticipated that the project would one day become the foun- dation of the most impressive experiment in public power the country had ever known. Wilson was no friend of public power. Instead, he saw Muscle Shoals as important to national defense, regional economic development, and the Democratic Party's monopoly in the South.[61]

Construction of what came to be called Wilson Dam did not begin until the spring of 1918, and the first of two government nitrate facilities—a coal- burning, steam-powered plant near Muscle Shoals at Sheffield, Alabama— had been in operation only a few months when the European war ended in November 1918. Nevertheless, the dam quickly became a symbol. It was twice as high as the largest existing hydropower dam in the United States, the Keokuk

Dam of the Mississippi Power Company, and nearly as wide as the Assuan (Aswan) Dam across the Nile River.[62]

By the end of the war, Congress—anticipating that U.S. forces in France would peak in 1919 and 1920—had expended more than $116 million on nitrate production. Eventually, Wilson Dam was expected to power two nitrate plants, but it produced no electricity until several years after the war ended. Nor did it improve navigation on the Tennessee River. It provided slack water for only a few miles; another structure was needed to make the stream navigable year-round—Wheeler Dam, constructed as part of the Tennessee Valley Authority in the 1930s.[63]

At the end of the war, Congress faced two dilemmas, neither of which involved public versus private power. The first was whether to complete Wilson Dam, upon which millions of dollars had already been spent, or sell it for scrap. Put another way, should the government sell property of potentially great value at a loss, enriching private utility companies, or treat the dam and nitrate plants as a long-range investment? The second question was whether the cyanamide process of extracting nitrogen from the atmosphere—which by the end of the war many private chemical companies had abandoned for the far more efficient Haber Process—could produce fertilizer cheaply enough to undercut existing prices in the South, whose soils were impoverished from years of cotton cultivation. The cyanamide process, which was used at Wilson Dam, created a reaction between calcium carbide and partially liquefied air that yielded cyanamides, which could be ground up and used as fertilizer or employed to produce ammonia. The Haber process produced ammonia directly from nitrogen and hydrogen. By the 1920s, it had become the most efficient process, which made the plant at Wilson Dam inefficient, if not obsolete.[64]

Pending completion of the dam, the Wilson administration attempted to lease the nitrate plants to private companies, but given the questionable value of the cyanamide process and congressional reluctance to complete the structure, no bidders stepped forward. The Senate—where the South and West often joined forces—strongly favored completion of the dam. Just as strongly, the House resisted it. Work was stopped in the spring of 1921 and did not resume until the summer of the following year, at which time Wilson Dam was half-finished. Construction money came from appropriations for the nitrate plants, not for the dam itself.[65]

The Harding administration (1921–23) renewed efforts to lease the Muscle Shoals plant. The first formal bid came from Henry Ford in the summer of 1921. The offer was relatively simple. If the government completed Wilson Dam and promised Ford (or his company) use of it for a hundred years, along with the nitrate plants, the automobile tycoon would pay the government $5 million for the existing facilities, along with a fifty-thousand-dollar annual rental fee. He would also sell fertilizer to farmers at a profit of no more than 8 percent, furnish the federal government with free electricity to operate navigational locks, and build other dams and power plants on the Tennessee River, turning Muscle Shoals into a major industrial center where aluminum, cloth, steel, and auto parts would be manufactured—as well as fertilizer. As many as a million men would find work, transforming the Tennessee Valley from a backward agricultural region into a thriving center of commerce and manufacturing. Rumors circulated that Ford would sell fertilizer at half the prevailing market price.[66]

Henry Ford was an immensely popular figure in the 1920s, and his offer galvanized a strange assortment of supporters, including national and regional farm organizations, the American Federation of Labor, conservationists, and even Thomas A. Edison. Nevertheless, opposition to the Ford bid quickly mounted. Many Republicans were friendly to the utility companies, but the party also contained a vocal progressive wing and a Midwest farm bloc, both highly suspicious of corporate business. Despite Ford's popularity, his critics considered him a crackpot. The industrialist frequently attacked a purported conspiracy of bankers, investors, and the power trust. "International financiers" allied with the Alabama Power Company, he charged, held Muscle Shoals hostage.[67] Nebraska senator George Norris charged that the Ford proposal amounted to a hundred-year loan of $75 million at less than 3 percent interest with less than one-tenth of the principal to be repaid. The $5 million Ford promised to pay up front for the existing property was not only far below the more than $100 million invested in the site by Congress; it was less than one-third the estimated scrap value of the dam and nitrate plants. The length of the lease clashed with the fifty-year term stipulated in the Water Power Act of 1920. And since Ford opposed any form of government regulation at Muscle Shoals, critics charged that his offer would undermine the battle for federal oversight in other parts of the country. Congressional pressure would mount to dispose of other power sites independent of the Federal Power Commission. By 1924, Ford's bid also suffered from the Teapot Dome oil lease scandal, which suggested that the Interior Department could not be trusted to negotiate or administer any agreement by which a private company gained access to government property. Rumors abounded that the automobile maker had withdrawn from that year's presidential race in exchange for Calvin Coolidge's endorsement of the Muscle Shoals bid. Ford's offer also suffered because as government construction of the dam continued, and the nation's investment increased, Ford refused to increase his bid. The House voted to accept Ford's proposal in March 1924, but the Senate—led by George Norris—rejected it. Late in 1924, Ford withdrew the offer.[68]

Private power companies submitted additional bids, but Congress had reached an impasse. As the 1920s wore on, it became more and more difficult to decide whether the basic purpose of the Muscle Shoals Project was to salvage a bad investment, safeguard national defense, produce cheap fertilizer, stimulate the development of an economically backward part of the nation, or demonstrate the benefits of public power. It was no less difficult to decide who should approve the leasing of the works: Congress, the president, or the Federal Power Commission. The 1923 sale of the steam-powered nitrate plant at Muscle Shoals to the Alabama Power Company raised the prospect that the project might be disposed of piecemeal. Completion of Wilson Dam in September 1925 left the War Department no choice but to sell the power produced to the same company at a small fraction of its real value: there were no alternative bidders, and four-fifths of the plant capacity remained idle for the rest of the 1920s.

Hard hit by the postwar decline in crop prices, farmers in the South continued to demand that the government produce inexpensive fertilizer. In the late 1920s, however, national power projects faced plenty of obstacles. Senator Hugo Black of Alabama argued that people outside the Tennessee River Basin should not be called upon to subsidize flood control within the basin when they received no benefits from it. The Muscle Shoals project was inequitable for many reasons, Black insisted, but especially because the lands that benefited most, particularly those along the Mississippi River, would soar in value yet pay no tax to the federal government that had made this increase possible. There was also conflict between eastern and western Tennessee over whether a second major dam should be constructed on Cove Creek, a tributary of the Tennessee River. Another rift occurred because states such as Louisiana and Mississippi had far less potential to generate hydroelectric power from falling water than mountainous Tennessee. As in the nineteenth century, what benefited one state or region was often seen as robbing its neighbors.[69]

The battle lines between those who favored private vs. public ownership of the dam shifted many times during the 1920s, as did the tactics of Senator George Norris, who led the partisans of public power in the United States Senate. Norris advocated government ownership. As mentioned earlier, at first fertilizer and explosives took precedence over power in the debate concerning what to do with the Muscle Shoals Project—just as flood control would take precedence over hydroelectric power when Boulder Dam was first proposed. In 1922, as an alternative to a federal power project, Norris proposed the creation of a public *chemical* corporation administered by officials from the War, Treasury, and Agriculture Departments. The corporation would operate the dam and sell fertilizer to farmers at cost.[70]

Norris hoped that his limited plan would win votes in the states'-rights-favoring, Democratic South. His 1922 legislation did not mention flood control or navigation. It did call for a complete survey of the Tennessee River to discover additional hydroelectric sites to augment the power produced at Muscle Shoals, but it did not provide for a multiple-use project. The bill permitted the sale of surplus power to private companies, but states, counties, and municipalities would receive preference. It contained no provision for government transmission lines to carry the electricity to public utility districts, however. Originally, private power companies had sided with Norris and against Henry Ford. The support of these companies made many public power advocates suspicious of the legislation. When Ford withdrew his offer in October 1924, the battle lines reformed with the Alabama Power Company and later the American Cyanamid Company and Union Carbide on one side, and Norris and the advocates of public power on the other.[71]

In 1924, Norris presented yet another plan to separate the production of power and fertilizer at Muscle Shoals, giving the secretary of agriculture control over the nitrate plants and creating a government corporation to manage the power plants and string transmission lines to public agencies in the region. It also authorized the secretary of war to construct as many dams as necessary to provide power, flood control, and navigation. This bill, too, failed to become law, but it proved to be the genesis of what would become the Tennessee Valley Authority in 1933. In 1926, Norris made flood control as important as power, but in 1927 and 1928, he backed away from comprehensive development. He retained his faith in the multiple-purpose idea, but he did not believe Congress would accept it. He returned to a more modest plan to produce power and fertilizer at Muscle Shoals, but made it clear that he saw this as just a beginning.[72]

In March 1928, the Norris legislation—in the form of a resolution—passed the Senate by nearly two to one and the House by a similarly large margin, only to be pocket vetoed by President Calvin Coolidge, who opposed public power and government involvement in a realm he thought should be left to private enterprise.[73] No longer were large amounts of power necessary to extract nitrogen from the atmosphere, so advocates of the project began to focus on power and navigation, rather than explosives and fertilizer. To pacify southern critics of the Muscle Shoals Project who lived outside the Tennessee Valley, Norris amended his bill again in the following year, this time to offer both Alabama and Tennessee 5 percent of the revenue from power sales. Herbert Hoover vetoed this legislation in 1930. Meanwhile, in 1928 and 1929, the Army Corps of Engineers proposed a series of seven high dams to improve navigation, including a major dam on the Clinch River, along with 149 hydroelectric plants. The corps claimed the right to build hydroelectric plants because the operation of navigational structures required plenty of power. In 1930 the corps won permission to maintain a nine-foot depth in the entire Tennessee River.[74]

The 1928 vote on the Norris resolution reflected the alliance of West and South, as would the vote on the Boulder Dam Act in the same year: fifteen administration Republicans, most from the East, opposed the legislation, while twenty Republican senators from the West supported it. Muscle Shoals had become the symbol of multiple-purpose development in the East, as was Boulder Dam in the West. In both places regional economic development took precedence and cheap power subsidized other benefits; both projects profited from the groundswell of popular support for public power. Above all, aid to one section of the country justified aid to the other.[75]

BOULDER DAM AND THE CHIMERA OF PUBLIC POWER

Linked as it was to Southern California's growth in population and industry, Boulder Dam touched the lives of far more people than the multipurpose dams in the Tennessee Valley—and received far more publicity. As public power advocate George Woodruff wrote to Herbert Hoover at the beginning of 1930: "This Boulder Dam Law is an arrow aimed directly at the heart of the Power Trust. It not only hurts the Trust by freeing the municipalities in California, Nevada, and Arizona from its domination, but it will be an example leading gradually to nation-wide freedom. The future of the whole country is at stake." The intent of the law, Woodruff maintained, was "to have every kilowatt allotted to the States and municipalities. Allotment of any of the power to private companies is primarily against the law and the public interest." Boulder Dam's power should be marketed by public agencies for the common good.[76]

That Boulder Dam became a symbol of the struggle against corporate power is not surprising, but it was an ambiguous symbol. Republicans feared that if private companies took over the Colorado River, conflict would increase among those states bordering the stream. In 1915, the former state engineer of Arizona, James P. Girand, received a preliminary permit to build a 470-foot-high dam at the mouth of Diamond Creek, west of Grand Canyon National Park and upstream from the Boulder Canyon dam site, mainly to provide power to copper mines in central and southern Arizona. The Federal Power Commission confirmed the permit in June, 1921. By the time the first Swing-Johnson (Boulder Dam) Bill appeared in 1922, the FPC had received twenty applications to generate power from the Colorado River and its tributaries—all in the Southwest. The most important applicant, Southern California Edison, promised to spend $375 million to build a series of storage dams along the river from Glen Canyon to the Nevada-Arizona border that would serve the needs of flood control and irrigation and would generate power. In return, the company asked the FPC for a virtual monopoly over the river.[77]

At the insistence of Secretary of Commerce Herbert Hoover, Secretary of the Interior Albert Fall, and Reclamation Bureau Director Arthur P. Davis, in 1922 President Warren G. Harding ordered the FPC to stop granting permits to dam the Colorado River until upstream and downstream interests decided how to divide the river's surplus water. Wyoming, Colorado, Utah, and Nevada feared that the FPC would turn the stream over to private power companies in California or Arizona, preventing future agricultural and urban development upstream. Farmers within Southern California's irrigation districts worried that private control over the river would inhibit the expansion of irrigation. Residents of Southern California towns and cities anticipated that private companies would saturate the power market in an attempt to block construction of the dam by making it impossible for the government to sell power to municipalities at a high enough price to repay the cost of construction.[78]

Like other leading Republicans, Herbert Hoover had mixed feelings about the Colorado River legislation. He wanted to make peace among the states of the Colorado River Basin and spur economic growth in the Southwest, not promote public power. Electricity should be treated as a by-product of constructing dams for flood control, navigation, or irrigation, he insisted, not as an additional source of revenue to the federal government. It should be leased to private companies and municipalities at the lowest price necessary to recover the cost of generators and other power works. "I do not favor any general extension of the federal government into the operation of business in competition with its citizens," Hoover observed in an October 1928 speech in eastern Tennessee. "It is not the system of Lincoln or Roosevelt. It is not the American system. . . . There are local instances where government must enter the business field as a by-product of a great research or national defense, but that does not vitiate the general policy to which we should adhere." And in his March 1931 veto of the Norris Tennessee Valley legislation, Hoover insisted that the federal government should do no more than promote "justice and equal opportunity." If the central government generated and marketed power, it would "break down the initiative and enterprise of the American people" and negate "the ideals upon which our civilization has been based."[79]

Hoover regarded electrical power as an incidental benefit of Boulder Dam. The original Swing-Johnson Bill (1922) authorized the construction of a low dam whose main purpose was flood control, and in 1927, the secretary of commerce tried to scale down the size of the structure. Following congressional approval of the high dam and power plant in the Swing-Johnson legislation of 1928, Hoover recommended that the Federal Power Commission pass out licenses, rather than the Interior Department, "without imposing a new system of allocation." Both before and after he became president, Hoover seldom mentioned power in discussing Boulder Dam. Rather, he emphasized the need to protect the Imperial Valley from floods, provide a supply of domestic water to Southern California and Arizona, irrigate farms in those two states, and protect American rights to the Colorado River against the claims of Mexico.[80]

The decision to erect a high dam left the federal government little choice but to construct the power plant rather than leave that job to private companies or municipal utility districts. Since the federal government advanced the money to pay for the structure, and since the dam was tied to an allocation of the Colorado River between upstream and downstream states, most members of Congress insisted that the national government should decide who could purchase the power and at what price. Given resistance in the states to federal regulation of hydroelectric power, ownership of the generators was the only way to give the nation priority over the states in distributing the power. And if the United States did not build the generating plants, then they could be taxed by the states as private property, increasing the cost of the electricity to consumers.

The demands of Arizona and Nevada also contributed to the Reclamation Bureau's decision to install the generators. Neither state had any immediate need for the dam's water or power, but both wanted monetary compensation for the benefits Southern California received. The 1928 Boulder Dam Act called for repayment of the cost of the dam in fifty years, but it also promised Arizona and Nevada 18 percent of the power income apiece after the annual cost of constructing, operating, and maintaining the dam had been paid. Therefore, the legislation mandated selling the power at a price sufficient to generate the needed revenue. Senator Key Pittman of Nevada wrote to his state's engineer, "It is the duty of the Secretary of the Interior under the [Swing-Johnson] Act to sell the power generated at the project at the highest possible price that competition will permit in the markets where such power is sold . . . for the purpose of paying the States of Arizona and Nevada a compensatory revenue for the use of their property and their water rights and to repay . . . the United States Government." It was a given, therefore, that power from Boulder Dam could not be sold at rates that would result in the cheapest prices to consumers.[81]

The largest market for power in the Southwest was, of course, Los Angeles and its surrounding communities. The city's population increased by more than twelve times between 1900 and 1930, and the value of its manufactured products tripled in the 1920s alone. During the 1920s and 1930s, the city invested huge sums in water and power systems. Electrical use increased by an average of 15 percent annually between 1915 and 1922, in which year the chief electrical engineer of the Los Angeles Bureau of Power and Light predicted that if the boom continued, the city would need seven times more power in 1930 than it had used in 1915. He promised that "the City of Los Angeles would be perfectly willing and very glad of the opportunity to become wholly responsible for all carrying charges and operating expenses of the Boulder Canyon dam and reservoir and in return to receive from the Government the right of development of the power possible at that point." Already the city had annexed far more communities than its Owens Valley Aqueduct could provide with water, and real estate prices would plummet unless additional water and power could be found.[82]

Water had long been the city's principal tool of annexation, and among its neighbors public power was not an unquestioned good. The first wave of annexations, including the suburbs of Highland Park and Vernon, came from 1895 to 1913, following a decision by the California Supreme Court that the city's pueblo right required that the Los Angeles River be used exclusively within the town limits. To tap that stream, suburbs had to become part of the city. A second phase followed completion of the Owens Valley Aqueduct in 1913. As political scientist Vincent Ostrom explained, "Annexation was required as a condition for the sale of water. A vast expanse of territory, including most of San Fernando Valley, was annexed to the City of Los Angeles during the great annexation movement of 1915–1927." Many communities, including Santa Monica, Pasadena, Glendale, Burbank, and Beverly Hills, resisted incorporation by increasing their use of underground water, but the pressures of population growth, persistent drought during the 1920s, and a falling water table left them little choice but to join the Metropolitan Water District (MWD) in the late 1920s and support the construction of a 242-mile-long aqueduct from Parker Dam, on the border with Arizona, to a reservoir near Riverside. The third phase of annexation followed completion of that aqueduct at the beginning of World War II. The geographical size of Los Angeles doubled between 1930 and 1952, in large part because of water provided by the MWD.[83]

Power was no less an instrument of urban imperialism. Because the southern Sierra Nevada was much higher than the Los Angeles basin, the Owens Valley Aqueduct, completed in 1913, provided Los Angeles with hydroelectricity as well as water. But a high dam on the Colorado River promised sufficient power to serve the future needs of the city for decades to come — and pump water uphill from the river as well. The Boulder Dam Act prohibited the government from stringing transmission lines. Therefore, communities that lacked the financial ability to go to Boulder Dam for power, such as San Bernardino, feared that the dam would permit Los Angeles to sell electricity for less than their existing source of power, Southern California Edison. The lower prices would give the city a monopoly on new industries that migrated to Southern California. Eventually, communities surrounding Los Angeles would have no choice but to amalgamate with the queen city. In many parts of Southern California, therefore, private utility companies appeared less threatening than the region's largest city.[84]

The Boulder Dam Act gave preference to public utility districts, as had the Townsite Act (1906), Raker Act (1913), and Water Power Act (1920). When the Interior Department solicited bids for Boulder Dam power in 1929, it received twenty-seven applications, covering more than three times the power the dam could produce. The City of Los Angeles offered to purchase the entire supply. Secretary of the Interior Ray Lyman Wilbur followed two standards in allocating the power. First, he wanted to ensure repayment of the cost of the dam, so he selected those bidders least likely to default, and second, he tried to spread benefits from the power over as large a geographical area as possible. The price of electricity to consumers, and the uses to which it was put, concerned him little. As mentioned earlier, the Boulder Dam Act promised Arizona and Nevada 18 percent of the power apiece, but until they could put their shares to use, Wilbur granted 25 percent of the power to the City of Los Angeles, 25 percent to Southern California Edison, and 50 percent to the Metropolitan Water District. (The MWD allocation was necessary to transport water from its planned Colorado River Aqueduct at Parker Dam to the city and surrounding communities; ultimately, this took one-third of all power generated at Boulder Dam.)[85]

Ironically, the future power needs of the nation did not belong to water power, as many conservationists had hoped and expected in 1910 or 1920. Internal-combustion engines changed the power industry in many ways, and during the 1920s petroleum became an important energy source. A ton of oil produced far more energy than a ton of coal—and cost far less to ship. In the 1930s and after, when the nation suffered from an oil glut, petroleum replaced coal in the West's steam-powered power plants, making them far more efficient. Hydroelectric plants cost two to four times the price of steam plants, and the gap widened during the first three decades of the twentieth century. Much of the cost of hydropower had to be paid up front, regardless of the initial demand for electricity within the service area. Power companies generally issued bonds to pay for dams, canals, spillways, penstocks, transmission lines, water rights, and property rights-of-way. The large interest debt made such ventures highly susceptible to fluctuations in interest rates. Steam plants could be constructed close to markets. They did not require long transmission lines, they were less costly to maintain, and they were easier to expand than hydropower plants. During the 1920s and 1930s, hydroelectric plants also proved to be far more subject than previously thought to drought, seasonal variations in stream flow, and other conditions beyond the control of engineers.[86]

Prior to 1910, coal-fired steam engines generated most of the nation's electrical power. As a percentage of the total amount of power generated, hydroelectric power nearly doubled between 1902 and 1927. During the same years, however, the amount of that power used in manufacturing declined from 15 to 10 percent. Moreover, the number of municipally owned utility plants shrank from more than three thousand in 1924 to less than two thousand in 1930—in part because of the imperialism of such cities as Los Angeles and the consolidation of smaller utility districts, as well as the growth of private companies.

The efficiency of steam plants increased markedly during the early decades of the twentieth century, and at a much faster rate than the efficiency of water-powered turbines. From 1906 to 1910, Detroit's Edison Company used 3.3 pounds of coal to produce each kilowatt hour of electric power. That fell to 2.1 pounds from 1911 to 1920, 1.5 pounds during the 1920s, and 1.15 pounds in 1932. Not surprisingly, the ratio of hydropower to steam power declined during the same period. By the end of World War I, steam generators furnished 70 percent of the electricity sold to urban homeowners—as opposed to 29 percent by hydroelectric plants and 1 percent by gasoline-driven generators. Of the power used by manufacturers, steam generated 85 percent, falling water 9 percent, and gasoline engines 6 percent.[87]

The largest increase in hydropower occurred in the decade following the opening of Niagara Falls. In 1910, water power provided most of the power used from day to day in California, and the more expensive steam power was held in reserve for peak demands. After World War II, however, the equation was reversed. By that time, the best reservoir sites had been taken, which made petroleum and natural gas more attractive fuels to produce electricity. Hydroelectric plants met the variable seasonal load, and they supplied *new markets* not served by steam plants, but they did not compete for existing markets. Hydroelectric plants could produce several times as much power if used for a few hours a day, rather than in continuous use, although steam turbines required half an hour or more to warm up, and hydroelectric generators could produce power almost instantly. In 1920, hydroelectric power constituted 37 percent of all power generated in the United States. That percentage fell to 33 percent in 1940, and even the huge hydroelectric plants opened during World War II increased that number to only 36 percent in 1945. In 1958, only half of California's power was produced by falling water. Those who celebrated Boulder Dam's completion in 1935 did not recognize that in many parts of the country this symbol of the "mastery of nature" was already old technology.[88]

CONCLUSION

Franklin D. Roosevelt and others argued that once Boulder Dam had been constructed in the Southwest—along with a Columbia River power project in the Pacific Northwest, a St. Lawrence River Project in the Northeast, and the Muscle Shoals (Tennessee Valley) Project in the Southeast—"there will exist forever a national yardstick to prevent extortion against the public and to encourage the wider uses of that servant of the American people— electric power . . . in each of the four quarters of the United States." Yet if Boulder Dam (renamed Hoover Dam in 1947) set the pattern for the high dams that followed, it was a symbol of conservatism as well as reform, and decentralization as well as centralization. Boulder Dam did not limit the power of private utility companies, nor did it provide power to consumers at the lowest possible cost, nor did it suggest that the federal government would become the major generator of power on the West's interstate rivers. Geography imposed strict limitations on such power even in the West, where prime dam sites such as Black Canyon on the Colorado River and the Grand Coulee of the Columbia River were rare.[89]

The proponents of "public power" never agreed on a national power policy. A decade before the completion of Boulder Dam, such conservationists as Gifford Pinchot envisioned one vast national power grid in which cheap and abundant electricity generated in the mountain ranges of the West would be used to illuminate the streets and factories of Boston or New York. The sheer scale of such a system suggested national ownership. Yet few advocates of public power favored the government generation and sale of *all* power; many of them demonstrated greater faith in regulatory commissions than in *direct* government control. They hoped that a handful of government power projects—led by Muscle Shoals and Boulder Dam—would set standards for fair rates and efficient service that could be enforced by public utility commissions.[90]

Newspapers and magazines portrayed Boulder Dam as a symbol of national power—the federal government had done what the State of California, City of Los Angeles, and private power companies could not. But government at all levels, and private industry, cooperated much more than competed, and it is not easy to separate them. The creators of the Metropolitan Water District used the irrigation district as a model, and the irrigation district was as much a tool of private enterprise as public. Nor, given its close ties to the Reclamation Bureau, was the MWD simply an institution of local or regional government. A. P. Davis apparently got the idea of using power revenue to finance Boulder Dam from William Mulholland and E. F. Scattergood, who had designed and supervised the water and power systems of Los Angeles. Moreover, Homer Hamlin, who served as Los Angeles city engineer during the 1920s, was one of the first to conceive of a multiple-purpose dam in Boulder or Black Canyon. In 1929, F. E. Weymouth, who had been chief engineer of the Reclamation Bureau under A. P. Davis, was chosen to head the MWD, and he hired many former employees of the Reclamation Bureau who had left government service during the Harding scandals of the 1920s. Finally, the Reclamation Bureau constructed Parker Dam using funds provided by the MWD (even though the bureau operated the dam).[91]

Southern California Edison was, perhaps, the greatest beneficiary of "public power." From 1922 to 1928, the company resisted the construction of a high dam on the Colorado River. At first, it opposed any government dam. Then it attempted to limit the size. Later, when even most officials in the Coolidge administration came to favor a high dam, the company changed gears again, insisting that private enterprise install the generators. When it became clear that the federal government would build the generating plant, Southern California Edison asked for the right to carry the power to consumers. That accomplished, it sought to eliminate the preference given to municipalities and drive up the price of the power by urging that Arizona and Nevada be permitted to tax the power generated or receive a large share of the proceeds. Company officials understood that securing an additional supply of water from the Colorado River would permit cities on the coastal plain to grow in size, expanding opportunities for their company as well as the City of Los Angeles. The power company was in a "no lose" situation. The genius, as well as the curse, of Boulder Dam was the way in which it blended private and public enterprise.[92]

9

Gateway to the Hydraulic Age
Water Politics, 1920–1935

Federal water policy in the 1920s was a complicated mosaic. Chapter 8 considered water power. This chapter discusses irrigation, flood control, and transportation. Since the first administration of Theodore Roosevelt, conservationists had called for a comprehensive national policy that treated rivers as units rather than as disjointed parts of states, counties, or cities. Yet the old view of waterways died hard. River and harbor bills segmented water projects to reduce them to manageable size, to deliver benefits to the maximum number of constituents, to spread expenditures over many years, and to maintain strict congressional control over appropriations. Transportation and economic planning came second, and much of the money spent on discrete and uncoordinated "improvements" went to waste. Nevertheless, the 1920s were a "New Era," and 1928 represented a turning point in national water policy. Congressional approval of a massive flood control program on the Mississippi River at the beginning of the year, and the authorization of Boulder Dam at the end, symbolized the rapid erosion of constitutional reservations to water projects funded by the central government. Modern water politics was born in the 1920s.

THE CORPS OF ENGINEERS AND PROPOSALS
TO REORGANIZE THE CABINET DEPARTMENTS IN THE 1920S

European models of a centralized bureaucratic state won little favor in the United States. As political scientist Stephen Skowronek has remarked, "The United States was born in a war that rejected the organizational qualities of the state as they had been evolving in Europe over the eighteenth century. Indeed, it has been argued that an underlying cause of the [American] Revolution was the gradual development of a more concentrated, specialized, and penetrating state apparatus in Britain." The government of the United States became strongly antifeudal and antibureaucratic. Neither the Civil War, nor World War I, nor even the Great Depression resulted in a significant alteration of its *structure*. In 1933, political scientist Leonard D. White observed that the nation had seen no "agitation for a unitary as opposed to a federal system of conducting our public affairs; nor for a responsible or parliamentary government; nor is there much progress toward a new regionalism, although our administrative areas are obvious anachronisms."[1]

In the first two decades of the twentieth century, politicians rethought the functions of government, but they did relatively little to change its structure. The proliferation of independent agencies and commissions, not schemes to reorganize government, characterized the Progressive Era. These included the Civil Service Commission (1883), Interstate Commerce Commission (1887), Federal Reserve Board (1913), Board of Mediation and Conciliation (1913), Federal Trade Commission (1914), National Advisory Committee for Aeronautics (1915), Employees' Compensation Commission (1916), Tariff Commission (1916), Council of National Defense (1916), Shipping Board (1916), and Federal Board for Vocational Education (1917). By 1924, the number of independent bureaus, offices, boards, and commissions had reached thirty. These independent bodies existed in a twilight zone between the executive, legislative, and judicial branches.[2]

The executive agencies were the creatures of many Congresses, which had many concerns. Some Congresses had been interested in economy and retrenchment, some in efficiency, some in meeting the extraordinary needs of wartime, and some in limiting executive power and protecting congressional prerogative. The elastic system of dispersed power defied structural reorganization. Calls for reshaping the cabinet departments occurred because the number of agencies and commissions independent of cabinet departments proliferated during the Progressive Era; because some agencies—such as the Interstate Commerce Commission and Federal Trade Commission—exercised legislative and judicial as well as administrative functions; because lawmakers sought to reduce the costs of government after World War I; because the war had provided new models of government and a new enthusiasm for planning; because the work of many agencies overlapped; because departments performed too many unrelated jobs; and because the federal budget process adopted in 1921 suggested the need to centralize functions, such as purchasing supplies and hiring new personnel.[3]

The Interior Department was a popular target. It contained the United States Geological Survey, Bureau of Mines, Reclamation Service, General Land Office, National Park Service, and Bureau of Indian Affairs, all of whose work related to the public domain. But it also administered the Pension Bureau, Maryland School for the Blind, Washington Hospital for Foundlings,

Columbia Institution for the Deaf, St. Elizabeth Hospital for the Insane, Howard University, and all the territories and insular possessions of the United States. Little wonder that Interior had long been known as "The Great Miscellany."[4]

The established cabinet departments competed in 1920 much as they had in 1880 or 1900.[5] In his memoirs, Secretary of Agriculture David Houston complained that President Woodrow Wilson had asked Secretary of the Interior Franklin K. Lane to formulate a federal hydroelectric power policy "without consultation either with me or with the Secretary of War, although the Interior Department controlled only about 8 percent of the nation's water power, while Agriculture through the Forest Service controlled about 42 per cent., and the War Department . . . all our navigable streams." The Agriculture Department was "non-political," Houston recounted disingenuously, while Interior was "political and relatively inefficient. And, furthermore, the Interior Department's attitude and record on conservation have not been and are not now satisfactory." Houston believed that centralizing control over water power within Interior would produce "endless confusion and conflicts." Lane's plan, he feared, was partly a pretext to transfer control over the national forests back to Interior from Agriculture.[6]

Arid land reclamation contributed to the tension between Agriculture and Interior, as it had since the 1880s. As noted earlier, during the Roosevelt administration many westerners hoped that the job of building dams and canals would be transferred from the Reclamation Service to Elwood Mead's Office of Irrigation Investigations in Agriculture, opening the door to a reclamation program paid for entirely by the federal government, with no restrictions on the size of farms. During the 1920s the secretaries of agriculture catered to their traditional constituency in the Midwest. Nevertheless, the USDA posed a constant threat to the Reclamation Bureau, as when it designed and promoted drainage works in the South—into which region the Reclamation Bureau hoped to expand.[7]

The conflict between Interior and Agriculture seldom received the publicity of the rivalry between Interior and the Army Corps of Engineers. The corps was a well-entrenched institution long before Congress created the United States Geological Survey, in 1879. In the 1850s and 1860s, the army and the General Land Office served as the two arms of federal authority in the West, and in the 1870s the army attempted to consolidate the four scientific surveys of the West, headed by John Wesley Powell, Clarence King, F. V. Hayden, and Lt. George M. Wheeler. Congress frustrated that plan by assigning the work to the USGS. In the 1890s, some army officers, including Nelson Miles and Hiram Martin Chittenden, urged that the federal government use river and harbor appropriations to build irrigation works in the West. They viewed the expansion of the Geological Survey with trepidation. The creation of the Reclamation Service in 1902 raised the prospect that *all* waterways improvements, not just irrigation works, would end up eventually within the Geological Survey.[8]

Meanwhile, however, river and harbor appropriations jumped from $2 million in 1870, to $30 million in 1896, to $87 million in 1907.[9] Far more was spent on rivers and harbors than on the reclamation of arid land. Construction projects increased much faster than the number of military engineers turned out by West Point.[10] Consequently, the army hired civilian engineers, but not at a rate that satisfied the professional engineering societies, which became close allies of the Interior Department. Army officers monopolized the top jobs within the corps, so civilian engineers working for the army could not aspire to management positions.[11] As early as 1885, the nation's fledgling engineering organizations proposed the creation of a Department of Rivers and Harbors under a civilian commissioner appointed by the president.[12] In the following year, Congress considered legislation to establish a Department of Public Works to consolidate the construction work of the Coast and Geodetic Survey, the U.S. Geological Survey, the Topographical Survey, and other federal agencies. The House's new Rivers and Harbors Committee would decide what rivers to improve, but a Civil Engineering and Architecture Bureau would pass judgment on the feasibility of all projects.[13]

The depression of the 1890s, followed by the war with Spain and construction of the Panama Canal, muted criticism of the Corps of Engineers, and in 1907 extensive flooding on the Ohio River and other eastern streams contributed to demands for sharp increases in river and harbor spending. The Rivers and Harbors Congress—formed to lobby for larger appropriations—asked Congress to double the size of the corps and give it exclusive control over *all* waterways in the United States. Civil engineering societies strenuously opposed this proposal.[14] The army engineers were not united. Any expansion of the corps' responsibilities would require the army to hire large numbers of civilian engineers, and some officers preferred to abandon the river and harbor work rather than admit civilians into the corps. The creation of a Corps of Civilian Engineers might result in the eventual loss of all river and harbor work to the USGS or to the Reclamation Service.[15]

The reputation of the corps became even brighter during the presidency of William Howard Taft (1909–13). As noted in chapter 4, in 1909–10, Taft threatened to dismiss Frederick H. Newell and appoint an army engineer to administer the Reclamation Service. This deepened the rift between civilian engineers and the corps. "The civil engineering profession has looked upon the Reclamation Service with peculiar pride," *Engineering News* editorialized in 1910, "as the first great example of a government bureau of engineering construction carried on by an organization of civilian engineers, selected with merit and efficiency as the sole criterion and free to carry on their work without political interference or graft. To have this bureau now turned over to the army engineers will be felt, we are sure, as a most serious humiliation by every member of the engineering profession who has pride in its work."[16]

Taft did not carry out his threat, but the campaign to divest the corps of its civil engineering responsibilities revived during World War I. In 1915, George H. Maxwell, the nation's chief publicist for a comprehensive national waterways program, published a scathing indictment of the corps prompted by what he considered an inadequate response to floods in the Mississippi and Ohio Valleys during 1912 and 1913. The corps, he charged, opposed nationalizing flood control because it lacked the personnel to administer such a program. "The military caste of this country apparently think only of their own aggrandizement," Maxwell complained, "and persistently oppose any modifications of an evil system which would in the slightest degree involve a surrender of their autocratic authority or official prestige and power for the general welfare." Corps engineers were subordinate to the chief of engineers, and "[a]ll original and creative engineering genius is muzzled or chloroformed as soon as it is born. If by any Caesarian operation it chances to come into being it is promptly strangled." Army engineers had "a medieval contempt for everything non-military, and for all civil duties and affairs. . . . They lack initiative and originality because their whole education has operated to drill it out of them, and to make men who are mere machines, doing what they are told to do. . . . That is the exact opposite of the type of mind demanded in an emergency requiring initiative and the genius to originate and carry out new and better ways of doing things than those that have prevailed in the past." Corps officers frequently moved from post to post, and their transience, Maxwell claimed, prevented them from understanding complicated water problems.[17]

By the end of World War I, twenty-seven federal agencies participated in the construction of public buildings, sixteen in laying out roads, and nineteen in the design, construction, and maintenance of hydraulic works. The Department of State surveyed pollution of U.S.-Canadian boundary waters; the War Department contained the Corps of Engineers, the Great Lakes Survey, the Mississippi River Commission, and the California Debris Commission; the Interior Department was home to the Indian Irrigation Service and the Reclamation Service; the Agriculture Department included the Bureau of Soils, Forest Service, and Weather Bureau; the Department of Commerce encompassed the Bureau of Fisheries, Bureau of Lighthouses, and Coast and Geodetic Survey. These and countless other federal resource agencies competed far more than they cooperated with one another.

The war in Europe allowed Americans to study how other nations managed their affairs. Canada, France, Italy, Spain, and Sweden had departments of public works that could be turned quickly from peacetime work—such as the construction of post offices or levees—to war. Such departments also concentrated and focused engineering skills. "The war lesson as to the value of cooperation has had a telling effect," a writer in the *Engineering News-Record* observed in February 1919, "and the absurdity of scattering the Government's engineering and construction work through five administrative departments stands out stronger now than in the days of antagonistic individualism. A government which demanded of each industry that it mobilize in a single trade association or war-service committee does not find it so difficult now to see prospective benefits from combining under one head all its own functions of a similar character."[18]

In July 1918, a group of general contractors formed the Associated General Contractors of America to lobby for standardized government construction designs, specifications, materials, and contracts. "We have recognized for some time the loss in time and money and the annoyance in conducting business with 50 different departments or sub-departments having charge of construction work throughout the U.S. for the National Government," the organization's legislative committee observed in 1923.[19] Less than a year after the contractors formed their lobbying organization, delegates from seventy-four engineering, architectural, and business organizations gathered in Chicago to establish a federation with many of the same objectives. Originally named the Engineers, Architects, and Constructors Conference on National Public Works, within months it was renamed the National Public Works Department Association. Engineering societies were interested in more than administrative efficiency. A democratic nation, they argued, should oppose military control of any civil function, including the construction of public works.[20]

The campaign to centralize the planning and construction of national public works crested in 1919–20, winning the support of such prominent politicians as Democratic presidential candidate James M. Cox, former secretary of the interior Franklin K. Lane, and Herbert Hoover. Congress considered several bills to carve up the Interior Department and create a department of public works. The most popular legislation, the Jones-Reavis Bill, called for a secretary of public works and four assistant secretaries, one to manage architectural plans and construction; another to supervise matters of engineering, design, and construction; a third to administer scientific work and surveys; and a fourth to oversee the public domain. The work of the Interior Department unrelated to public works would be assigned to other departments.[21]

The Institute of Governmental Research, the National Public Works Association, and the American Engineering Council sponsored the legislation. Their leaders argued that a department of public works would promote efficiency and save money by standardizing government construction work.

It would also coordinate technical research and reduce the chronic rivalry and competition for authority and appropriations among different agencies. Equally important, it would expand the influence of civilian engineers and limit the work of military engineers. At the end of the war, 517 West Pointers—less than one-half of one percent of the nation's population of engineers—supervised the vast work of the Army Corps of Engineers. A department of public works would permit army engineers to work on a wide variety of public works *in addition to* rivers, harbors, and fortifications—better preparing them for war—but the work would be under civilian control.[22]

The reorganization bills were doomed. Proponents of a department of public works could not decide what shape that department ought to take, particularly the nature and number of its separate divisions. The department's primary job should be engineering, that much was clear. But should it also exercise control over the public domain, where the Reclamation Bureau built many of its dams and canals? And since most of the new department's bureaus would be inherited from Interior, what should be done with the bureaus that had nothing to do with engineering or public works? One bill answered this question by proposing a Department of Welfare to include the Bureau of Indian Affairs, Bureau of Pensions, Howard University, and other social welfare offices then in Interior.

In 1920, the Corps of Engineers led the opposition to reorganization. There was no evidence, according to its leaders, that a new department would reduce the cost of public works. Cost, in any case, was a secondary consideration. Public works could not be administered like a private business, because good government took precedence over efficiency. The army was above graft and far less subject to corruption than civilian agencies.[23] And if public service took priority, then engineering functions should be spread widely rather than consolidated in one department. There was no greater need to integrate engineering functions in one department than to concentrate all lawyers in the Department of Justice or all clerks in a department of clerical services. Centralization characterized the highly bureaucratized societies of Europe and Latin America; decentralization was the American way. The Department of Public Works suggested a European model that might lead eventually to the public ownership and operation of utilities. Such a department would set a dangerous precedent. Once reorganization began, where would it end? Create a Department of Public Works, and could a Department of Education, Department of Public Health, Department of Transportation, and Department of Public Welfare be far behind? Friends of consolidation argued that a department of public works would reduce the cost of government, but critics of the plan feared that reorganization could become an excuse to expand government.[24]

In December 1920, Congress established a joint legislative commission to study reorganization. It deliberated for three years and reached an impasse. President Warren Harding proposed his own reorganization scheme in 1923, and Congress held hearings on the Harding plan at the beginning of 1924.[25] They led nowhere. In the end, the Congressional Committee on Reorganization recommended no change in the responsibilities or administration of the Corps of Engineers. It concluded that "there is a measure of economy in using the personnel of the Corps of Engineers on necessary public works of a nonmilitary character." River and harbor work presented unique engineering problems that "would make it difficult to consolidate or amalgamate the organization maintained for its prosecution with other engineering agencies of the government." Furthermore, the committee suggested that the corps' responsibilities might be expanded to include road building in the United States—at least on roads paid for partly with federal money.[26]

By the middle of the decade, the Interior Department was widely considered to be the worst-administered department in the federal government—and the most corrupt. Secretary of the Interior Albert B. Fall resigned from the cabinet under a cloud of suspicion in March 1923 after being caught taking bribes in the Teapot Dome scandal. The Harding-Fall scandals—like the Ballinger-Pinchot controversy during Taft's administration—kept alive the possibility that the Reclamation Bureau would end up in Agriculture or a separate conservation or construction department.[27]

When he first took office, the new secretary of the interior, Hubert Work, wanted to divide Interior into a Bureau of Public Works, a Bureau of Education, a Bureau of Territorial Affairs, a Bureau of Public Lands, and a Bureau of Public Health (then in the Treasury Department). Instead, the Committee on Reorganization proposed stripping Interior of all functions except those that pertained to the public domain. The full Congress refused to accept that recommendation, but in November 1924, Work voluntarily cut Interior's staff by 8 percent. The biggest reductions came in the Reclamation Bureau, Geological Survey, General Land Office, and Pension Bureau. Interior Department budgets remained flat for the rest of the decade, and the annual expenditure for arid land reclamation was smaller in 1930 and 1931 than in 1915, even though materials and labor were more expensive. In 1931, Congress considered slashing Interior's budget by more than 20 percent over three years, but Herbert Hoover—fearing that the reduction would imperil spending on public-works job projects—blocked the reduction. "The principal change [in public works spending] between 1915 and 1930," an astute student of the federal government wrote in 1934, "was the decided drop in reclamation work, and the tremendous increase in road building." This, of course, enhanced the reputation of the Department of Agriculture, which managed the road-building program.[28] Legislation to reorganize the Interior Department reappeared in 1926, 1927, 1931, and

1932, but to no greater effect. The main result of the campaign to reorganize the Interior Department was to increase the power of the Army Corps of Engineers in Congress.[29]

HERBERT HOOVER AND THE "NATIONALIZATION" OF RIVERS

At the end of the American Revolution, George Washington visited Lakes George and Champlain in upstate New York, then explored a section of the Mohawk River. The New York waterways prompted him to ponder the future of the new nation. "I could not help taking a more contemplative and extensive view of the vast inland navigation of these United States," Washington later recalled in a letter to the Marquis de Chastellux, "and [I] could not but be struck with the immense diffusion and importance of it, and with the goodness of that Providence which has dealt her favours to us with so profuse a hand. Would to God we may have the wisdom to make a good use of them." Nearly a century and a half after Washington's journey, Herbert Hoover quoted the first president's words approvingly: "If we in our generation have so great a vision as the Father of Our Country we shall do it."[30]

Hoover was the first president of the United States from west of the Mississippi River and the first president to take a comprehensive view of the nation's waterways. Born on an Iowa farm in 1874, orphaned at the age of nine and raised by relatives in Iowa and Oregon, he graduated from Stanford University in 1895 with an engineering degree and soon became a leading figure in international mining. Hoover was a rare blend of idealist, pragmatist, statesman, administrator, negotiator, and consensus builder, and his career exemplified the tension between the progressive politician's moralism, the engineer's quest for order and efficiency, and the rugged individual's disdain for bureaucracy and paternalism. During World War I, he directed humanitarian aid to civilians in Belgium and France and served as Food Administrator of the United States. After the war, he supervised relief efforts for all of Europe. In each job, Hoover demonstrated moral vision and a sense of social responsibility. Warren Harding appointed him secretary of commerce, a position he held from 1921 to 1928.[31]

Herbert Hoover embraced the Progressive Era credo that Americans had an obligation to develop the nation's resources as fully and as rapidly as possible.[32] Water policy was the cornerstone of his conservation agenda. "We have need that we formulate a new and broad national program for the full utilization of our streams, our rivers and our lakes," Hoover remarked in a 1926 speech. "True conservation of water is not the prevention of use. Every drop of water that runs to the sea without yielding its full commercial returns to the nation is an economic waste." Years before the New Deal, Hoover argued that the nation should embrace "the coordinated long-view development of each river system to its maximum utilization." Every important river had the potential to increase the nation's wealth—through power, reclamation, or flood control, if not transportation.[33]

Government, Hoover argued, should not merely regulate business and referee economic disputes; it should direct, promote, and sustain economic growth. It should integrate and rationalize the nation's economy, making the marketplace as orderly and predictable as possible. Without water management, there could be no planned economy. And without a planned economy, the United States would remain vulnerable to boom and bust cycles. Hoover supervised negotiation of the 1922 treaty, or compact, by which the states of the Colorado River Basin divided that stream's surplus water as a prelude to construction of Boulder Dam. He also headed the American St. Lawrence River Commission in the mid-1920s, and in 1927 he directed the Mississippi River flood relief effort, which gave him a firsthand opportunity to study the problems of flood control.

Hoover was not just a disinterested engineer seeking to build an integrated, efficient transportation system, or a commerce secretary attempting to promote business. He was one of the Republican Party's most popular national figures and a likely presidential candidate. Any Republican who sought the nation's highest office had to pay close attention to the economy of the Midwest and the needs of midwestern voters. Since the Democratic Party monopolized the South and enjoyed great strength in the industrial states of the East, it was vital for the Republican Party to carry the Midwest and the West.

The Mississippi Valley was an important source of raw materials and manufactured goods. Including the Great Lakes states, the region turned out 50 percent of the nation's manufactured products, 80 percent of its coal, and nearly all of its iron ore.[34] But it also produced 70 percent of the nation's agricultural products. The Republican Party may have been the party of industry, but outside the South, rural America traditionally voted Republican, and the "farm vote" was particularly important in the Midwest. Crop prices had plummeted after World War I. Many midwestern Republicans favored the McNary-Haugen Bills of 1924 and 1926, which provided for the purchase of surplus farm commodities by a federal farm board that would sell them abroad at the prevailing world price, or store them until domestic prices rose. But both Hoover and Calvin Coolidge opposed the scheme as price-fixing and special-interest legislation. Hoover's inland waterways policy was intended, in part, to diminish support for the McNary-Haugen legislation. Instead of subsidizing farmers directly, Hoover proposed lowering their fixed costs.

World War I drove up railroad freight rates, and they remained high after the war, despite the return of oceanic freight rates to prewar levels. The railroad monopoly on transportation, according to Hoover, constituted a "row of tollgates around the Middle West." Despite their distance from the

United States, many farmers in Argentina, Australia, Eastern Europe, and even India were "closer" to agricultural markets on the eastern seaboard than were farmers in the Midwest. The cost of shipping a thousand bushels of midwestern wheat a thousand miles by rail ran $175 to $225, while the same distance on the Mississippi River cost $65 and only $20 to $30 on the Great Lakes. To compound the problem, completion of the Panama Canal in 1914 brought the markets of the East and West Coasts closer together, to the detriment of Chicago and the Mississippi Valley. It cost three times more to send iron and steel from New York to San Francisco by rail than by sea, via the Panama Canal. Hoover feared that the Midwest's inadequate transportation system would force the region's industries to move to the coasts.[35]

The 1928 Republican Platform included a plank stating:

> Cheaper transportation for bulk goods from the mid-West agricultural sections to the sea is recognized by the Republican Party as a vital factor for the relief of agriculture. To that end we favor the continued development in inland and intra-coastal waterways as an essential part of our transportation system. The Republican Administration during the last four years initiated the systematic development of the Mississippi system of inland transportation lanes, and it proposes to carry on this modernization of transportation to speedy completion.[36]

Hoover called for economic planning at least a quarter-century in advance of need. In a 1926 speech, as secretary of commerce, he proclaimed that "what we have missed is the idea that to make a really successful transportation system requires large interconnected systems of trunk lines from [the] seaboard with great feeders from our lateral rivers and its consequent widespread and diversified traffic. We have begun important works at the outer ends and worked back. We would not build a great railway system begun at the outer ends and building back toward the terminals and expect traffic to develop in the meantime." Haphazard river and harbor bills reflected the needs of individual communities, not river basins, regions, or the nation. Only seven thousand of the nation's twenty-five thousand miles of potentially navigable waterways had been "modernized," and that had been in segments. The nation needed a master plan to coordinate federal, state, and local water projects, to unify transportation and flood control, to prevent waste, and to determine which transportation routes were best served by ships, railroads, or trucks.[37]

Hoover proposed comprehensive water projects for the Mississippi, Missouri, Columbia, Colorado, Rio Grande, Hudson, Arkansas, Tennessee, and Cumberland Rivers; the Great Lakes; and the Central Valley of California, as well as an intracoastal waterway stretching from Boston to Corpus Christi, Texas. The capstone of his transportation plan was the maintenance of six- to nine-foot levels in two great, intersecting "continental systems" within the

Mississippi Valley. An east-west waterway would run from Pittsburgh to Kansas City, connecting the Ohio, Mississippi, and Missouri Rivers. A north-south waterway would channelize the Mississippi, linking Chicago, the Great Lakes, and New Orleans. The entire system would span nine thousand miles, providing farmers and manufacturers in twenty states with easy access to the sea. It would also connect New Orleans, Minneapolis, St. Paul, St. Louis, Chicago, Kansas City, Omaha, Cincinnati, Pittsburgh, Memphis, Chattanooga, Wheeling, Little Rock, and many smaller towns within the Mississippi Basin. Hoover was no less interested in the West than in the Midwest. Midwestern farmers had long opposed federal reclamation, but Hoover considered the crop surpluses of the 1920s temporary. Arid land reclamation should go forward in the West, he argued, particularly in the Central Valley of California and the Columbia Basin of Washington.[38]

Herbert Hoover recognized that by dividing power between Congress and the president, and between the central government and states, federalism all but prevented comprehensive waterway development. In some basins, as many as thirty governmental institutions supervised the use of water. Anticipating the New Deal, Hoover recommended that all drainage basins subject to multiple-use water planning be placed under an umbrella agency that would represent state, local, and federal agencies, but also include independent, and presumably impartial, technical advisers. These agencies would have no power to spend money, construct projects, or administer them. Instead, they would propose broad plans that could be executed by existing institutions of government. "These administrative suggestions are not proposals for centralization of government but decentralization," Hoover observed. "[T]hey are not proposals to displace the authority of Congress, but to assist an already overworked body; they are not proposals of more than trivial expense, but safeguarding from the waste of hundreds of millions in ill-planned development and loss of our full water resources."[39]

Hoover used the 1927 Mississippi flood, discussed later in this chapter, as an excuse to urge Coolidge to undertake a ten-year program to spend more than $30 million creating a uniform depth in the Mississippi and its major arteries. He wanted to enlarge the levees, construct bypass channels, and use swamps and land already subject to annual flooding as emergency overflow basins.[40] In 1928 and 1929, he continued to emphasize the need for comprehensive planning, and his first presidential speech on waterways noted: "We are reopening the great trade routes upon which our continent developed. This development is but an interpretation of the needs and pressures of population, of industry and civilization. They are threads in that invisible web which knits our national life. They are not local in their benefits. They are universal in promoting the prosperity of the nation." In his first address to Congress at the end of 1929, Hoover called for a five-year plan to improve the nation's rivers at the cost of more than $500 million, including an annual appropriation of $25 to $30 million for the Mississippi alone. Once Canada approved the St. Lawrence project, he was ready to recommend even larger appropriations.[41]

Hoover's waterways plans faced substantial opposition. Sectional jealousies remained paramount. The states of the Great Lakes wanted trade on the Mississippi to move north, through their ports and the St. Lawrence River to the Atlantic, rather than from Chicago or Minneapolis–St. Paul south to New Orleans and the Gulf of Mexico. And New York politicians hoped to turn trade away from the Great Lakes to New York Harbor via an "All American" canal across their state.[42] "If the country will be content to be moderate and patient and permit improvements to be made where they will do the greatest general good rather than insisting on expenditures at this time on secondary projects," President Coolidge warned in his message to Congress at the end of 1926, "our internal waterways can be made a success. If proposed [river and harbor] legislation results in a gross manifestation of local jealousies and selfishness this [Hoover] program cannot be carried out."[43]

Critics questioned the benefits of waterway improvements, and most railroads opposed Hoover's plan. During the war, railroad executives had welcomed the expansion of water transportation. By the mid-1920s, however, they regarded it as unfair competition. Ships and barges moved in channels maintained, if not created, by the federal government, and trucks moved on public highways. Railroads, on the other hand, paid for and maintained roadbeds and track, and the federal government regulated their rates much more closely than those charged by shipping or truck lines. If Hoover's plan was carried out, the railroads would lose revenue at a time when trucking had already cut deeply into their business. Railroad executives asked Congress to terminate the federal government's barge service on the Mississippi, impose the same rate restrictions on water transportation as on the railroads, and permit the railroads to engage in water transportation—which had been prohibited by the Interstate Commerce Commission. Meanwhile, Congress should limit river and harbor appropriations.[44]

Nevertheless, by the time Herbert Hoover left office in 1933, his great Mississippi Valley water project had become a reality. The "canalization" of the Ohio River, completed at the end of 1929, produced a nine-foot-deep east-west channel stretching a thousand miles from Pittsburgh, Pennsylvania, to Cairo, Illinois, on the Mississippi. The Ohio Valley was now as close to the ports of Baton Rouge and New Orleans as to those on the Atlantic Coast. And by 1933, the Mississippi River was navigable from New Orleans to Chicago (with help from several rivers within Illinois).[45]

Outside the Mississippi Valley, a ship channel was constructed from San Francisco Bay to Stockton. San Pedro Harbor was expanded. The Hudson River was opened to seagoing traffic from Albany to New York Harbor. And studies of comprehensive development for the Columbia, Tennessee, Cumberland, upper Missouri, and upper Mississippi Rivers were finished. In addition, sixty or seventy water projects, scattered throughout the West, were on the drawing board. In 1930, Hoover asked Congress to accelerate the construction of federal water projects to relieve unemployment, but most of those projects had long been part of his larger vision of planning, national economic development, and the impulse to manage nature.[46]

The Hoover administration was far more active in watershed management than any previous presidential administration. "A total of over $700,000,000 was expended during my four years in river projects," Hoover recalled in the second volume of his *Memoirs,* published in 1952, "advancing them further . . . than in the thirty years preceding." He took full credit for all the waterway improvements of the 1920s and 1930s, ranging from the Central Valley Project in California, to Boulder Dam, to the Flood Control Act of 1928, to the St. Lawrence Seaway. He also claimed to have "reoriented" the Reclamation Bureau toward "great multiple purpose water storage dams . . . all with a by-product of hydroelectric power." He called for an end to regionalism, an interdependent national economy, and new institutions to facilitate river basin planning. Herbert Hoover was not a modest man, but he was the first American president in the twentieth century to study the nation's rivers and the part they would play in the nation's economic growth.[47]

THE GREAT MISSISSIPPI FLOOD OF 1927

Floods occur during different seasons in different parts of the United States. Rivers within the Missouri and Mississippi Basins carry their heaviest volume in winter. In Oklahoma, Arkansas, central Texas, Oregon, and Washington, however, most floods occur in the early spring. In Northern California, high water comes in the late spring. In Southern California and Arizona, the heaviest runoff coincides with midsummer.[48]

Floods are not simply a matter of precipitation. The slope of the land, the straight or serpentine nature of river channels, the size of floodplains, the composition of alluvial soil, and the permeability of underground aquifers all play a part. So do the location of farms, towns, and cities: the greater the concentration of people along a stream, the greater the runoff from snow and rain. In the early twentieth century, the increasing number and size of communities within alluvial plains constricted river channels and reduced the land's capacity to absorb water. By the 1920s, more than 1.5 million people lived in farms, villages, and cities within the Mississippi's floodplain.

The Mississippi River drains 40 percent of the United States, from Canada to New Orleans, and from the Rocky Mountains to Pennsylvania. Its tributaries include some of the largest rivers in the nation, including the Missouri and the Ohio. Unlike rivers carved deep into the earth, such as the Colorado and Columbia, the Mississippi is relatively flat and hard to contain. During the last twenty-five hundred years, it has found five different outlets to the Gulf of Mexico, ranging from west of Bayou Teche, southeast of New Iberia in the Atchafalaya Basin, to the Breton Sound, southeast of New Orleans— a distance of 160 miles. The river's inability to decide where to meet the sea has created the largest semitropical marshland in North America.[49]

The Mississippi flood of 1927—the biggest in the history of the United States to that time—resulted from an implausible series of events. Nature has arranged the flow of the Mississippi's major tributaries so that in most years they deliver their peak flows seriatim rather than all at once. Spring floods on the Ohio come first, then the upper Mississippi makes its contribution, then the Missouri, then the lower Mississippi. But 1926 and 1927 were not typical years.

In the late summer and early fall of 1926, a time of the year when the Mississippi was usually shrunken and sluggish, heavy rains pelted the Midwest, saturating the land above Cairo, Illinois. During the last three months of 1926, the Ohio, Missouri, and Mississippi Rivers reached unprecedented heights for that season. Then, in December 1926 and January 1927, additional precipitation fell in the Ohio Basin, and in Oklahoma, Arkansas, and northern Louisiana. Precipitation upstream kept the Mississippi at flood stage throughout the winter. In March and April, it was the lower basin's turn. In mid-April, fifteen inches of rain fell on New Orleans in eighteen hours— about one-quarter of the average annual total—and water stood four feet deep in parts of the city.[50]

The first Mississippi River levees were constructed at the beginning of the eighteenth century to protect New Orleans. By 1735, they extended along both sides of the river thirty miles to the north of the city and twelve miles to the south. As cotton cultivation spread through the lower Mississippi Valley in the early nineteenth century, levee districts expanded the earthen embankments to protect the rich alluvial soil created by the river. The levees also served a second purpose. In the nineteenth century, most engineers believed that reducing the width of a stream increased its velocity, causing the water to scour out the channel and maintain the river at a uniform depth. Therefore, levees became the preferred method of constricting the Mississippi to maintain navigability.[51]

When Louisiana and Mississippi entered the union in 1812 and 1817, their legislatures formed new institutions of government to coordinate flood control across county or parish lines. "A typical bill required each county . . . to establish several levee districts and to appoint inspectors for each district," the sociologist Karen O'Neill has written. "Inspectors would plan levees and drainage ditches, would inform each landowner what work would be done, and could fine levee inspectors or landowners for neglecting their duties. When water threatened the levees, inspectors could order out the slaves of delinquent planters." Because levees served navigation as well as flood control, the Corps of Engineers helped to build and maintain them, and the federal role increased during the last decades of the nineteenth century.[52]

Natural levees were living monuments to the river's expansion and contraction over the centuries, and they interfered little with its ebb and flow. The Mississippi did not like to be constricted; it constantly searched for new channels and outlets to the sea. As the volume of water it carried increased, and as silt raised the river's bed, the stream spread out, abandoning its channel and forming new land. (For example, the river created the Mississippi Delta by depositing the sediment it carried at the mouth of the river.) Here, then, was the bargain: as human beings enlarged the levees nature had started, the river could no longer follow its natural inclinations. Silt concentrated in the main channel of the stream rather than over the entire riverbed, necessitating dredging and the systematic enlargement of the earthen embankments every few decades. The cycle was difficult to break.

By the second decade of the twentieth century, the levee system was complete. Huge walls of earth that averaged eighteen feet in height extended more than eighteen hundred miles along the lower Mississippi. Thereafter, maintenance concentrated on expanding the size of existing works and leveeing the Mississippi's tributaries. These levees, however, were no match for the 1927 flood. The first break occurred on April 16, near Dorena, Missouri. Then, on April 21, a much more serious crevasse opened at Mounds Landing, Mississippi. The escaping water swept over 735,000 acres before joining the Yazoo River. In the hope of saving homes and crops, landowners along the Mississippi dynamited levees upstream from their land. Before the flood subsided, the levees ruptured in 120 places, and armed guards patrolled the embankments as much to prevent sabotage as to search for leaks and weak spots. The flood lasted for two months and covered to a depth of as much as twenty feet nearly 17 million acres in seven states—an area twice the size of Maryland. It killed at least 443 people, and thousands more lost crops, livestock, and homes. More than six hundred thousand refugees took up residence at 149 Red Cross encampments, and seven months after the flood subsided, the Red Cross still was feeding twenty thousand people.[53]

In places, the high water lingered for months, and when residents of the lower Mississippi returned to what remained of their homes, farms, and towns, they found caked mud and swamps everywhere—along with the heavy, fetid stench of dead fish and animals and an imposing array of poisonous snakes. Those who managed to plant crops harvested little, and 1928 was not much better. Congressman William M. Whittington of Mississippi described the flood as "the greatest catastrophe that ever befell the United States. It is comparable only to war and in many cases it is more destructive than war. We know of Sherman's march to the sea. . . . But I have witnessed the death and destruction of a Mississippi flood. I know that the onrushing waters wrought infinitely more destruction in the Mississippi Valley than Sherman's march."[54]

The South was not alone. The year 1927 was unusually wet across most of the country. Following a rainy summer and fall, a tropical storm struck New England at the beginning of November, precipitating the worst flood in that region's history. The Connecticut Valley became a vast inland sea. Ten thousand people were rescued from the suburbs of Springfield, Massachusetts, and in Vermont the flood killed the lieutenant governor, halted all rail traffic, and isolated the capital. It took fifteen years for that state to pay off the debt left from reconstructing bridges, highways, and other public works.[55]

From all parts of the nation came calls for a special session of Congress to deal with the floods, but President Calvin Coolidge balked. He believed, as had most presidents before him, that the federal government could not and should not protect people from acts of God, nor should the whole country be called upon to pay for improvements that benefited a particular section. "The Government is not an insurer of its citizens against the hazard of the elements," Coolidge noted in his annual message to Congress. "We shall always have flood and drought, heat and cold, earthquake and wind, lightning and tidal wave, which are all too constant in their afflictions." The president's critics complained that at a time when the U.S. treasury contained a large surplus, the Red Cross directed the relief effort rather than the national government. After World War I, Congress had appropriated $100 million to relieve suffering in Europe, but in 1927 and 1928, Coolidge refused to lift a finger to help American citizens. Cynics observed that Coolidge led the Republican Party as well as the nation, and the South contained few Republican votes.[56]

Once it became clear that the federal government would not pay for relief, let alone reconstruction, pressure mounted in Congress to shield the Mississippi Valley from *future* flood damage. Advocates of a national program argued that the flood had exhausted the funds available to local levee boards. Farmers had no income, and tax revenue plummeted as vast tracts of land left the tax rolls. Residents of the lower Mississippi Basin faced the enormous cost of cleaning up and replacing lost homes, livestock, fences, and farm equipment—a financial burden that would last for years. Given the extensive damage to school buildings, it was doubtful that local taxes could even sustain public education. How, then, could these unfortunates afford to repair levees, let alone pay for a comprehensive flood control program?

The advocates of federal flood protection thought that the national government bore some responsibility for the tragedy. The levee system—which by 1927 extended from Cairo, Illinois, to the Gulf of Mexico—had been constructed *primarily* to promote shipping. It prevented the river from finding those natural reservoirs into which water had once emptied at flood stage, and it also increased the damage once floods broke through the embankments. Even more important, although President Coolidge regarded the flood as an act of God, the Mississippi drained thirty-one states, and a range of human activities upstream—from lumbering to urban growth—had contributed to the 1927 devastation. "The national problem arises," Congressman Edward Denison of Illinois proclaimed disingenuously, "by reason of the fact [that] the Federal Government has allowed the people of these various states to follow their own course and build their own levees as they choose and where they choose until the action of the people of one State has thrown the waters back upon the people of another State, and vice versa." Already, the South had spent nearly $300 million to protect itself from floods that originated upstream. It should not be required to pay more.[57]

The Constitution's Commerce Clause offered an equally potent justification for national flood control. By the 1920s, the various facets of the American economy were far more interdependent than they had been in 1900. What injured the residents of one section inevitably injured the nation as a whole. As Secretary of Commerce Herbert Hoover put it: "Our economic system is so interlocked that the loss of $1,000,000,000 in any one spot reflects over an enormous area. . . . The manufacturers of New England and Ohio, the orange grower of California, the wheat grower of Dakota, will all of them sell less goods in the flood area this year than last. There will be less products from the area this year than last. Every worker, every farmer, every investor in the whole United States will bear some part of the shock. . . . [W]hat we need for stable employment and stable agriculture is freedom from such economic shocks." Many politically conservative organizations, led by the United States Chamber of Commerce, strongly supported a flood control program completely funded by the central government.[58]

If a large-scale natural disaster in one river basin now harmed the whole nation, so the economic development of one section benefited the whole. *Manufacturers' Record,* a leading trade journal, promised that a national flood control program would "tremendously stimulate the progress of America" and make the Panama Canal "of small importance to the country as a whole as compared with the work that should be done in safeguarding the whole Mississippi Valley from any danger of an overflow." A comprehensive program to develop the Mississippi River and protect land from flooding "would result in a material advancement in that section such as the world has never before seen."[59]

The great flood of 1927 set the stage for a new era in the management of the nation's rivers and a new era in the history of the American West. It helped break down the states'-rights philosophy in the South. It demonstrated the relationship of rivers to the national economy. It suggested that managing waterways exceeded the capabilities of local or state institutions. And it proved that different regions could unite to push through Congress water projects far larger than anything considered by the central government prior to 1928. Central to the politics of water in the United States were a political alliance and vote trading between the South and West that would last well beyond the 1930s and World War II.

FROM THE MISSISSIPPI TO THE COLORADO

As early as the 1840s, bills appeared in Congress to protect land along the lower Mississippi River from floods, but critics denied that the central government had the authority to shield private property from acts of God: the nation could not afford such a vast program; it would exacerbate sectional tensions by encouraging competition among the states and localities for federal appropriations; the money spent would feed political corruption; and some property owners would benefit at the expense of others. The last argument was particularly persuasive, because northerners had little desire to aid the former Confederacy. In 1881, Congress stipulated that *no* federal money could be used to protect land from flooding, or for any purpose other than to deepen, straighten, or clear river channels.[60]

At the turn of the twentieth century, the strongest advocates of waterways legislation were organizations formed to push transportation improvements—such as the [Great] Lakes-to-the-Gulf Association—but by World War I, flood control had become the paramount concern. In April 1912, the Mississippi overflowed, driving more than thirty thousand people from their homes, and a second flood hit the Ohio River in January 1913, extensively damaging Louisville and Cincinnati. A third struck the Mississippi Basin in 1916. Critics blamed the Army Corps of Engineers for following a "levees only" policy, but Congress had left the corps little choice. It required local interests to match federal expenditures, and levee districts could tax only the land within their boundaries. Residents of the Mississippi Valley refused to pay for spillways, reservoirs, and other methods of flood protection far removed from their land. There were no basin-wide institutions and no system of shared authority.[61]

The floods of 1907, 1912, 1913, and 1916, and the expansion of government responsibilities during World War I, led to the Flood Control Act of 1917—the first federal law that explicitly appropriated money for river improvements other than navigation. It promised $45 million—at the rate of $10 million per year—to pay for flood control work between the mouth of the Ohio and the mouth of the Mississippi. It also appropriated $5.6 million for the construction of bypass channels and flood basins on the Sacramento River in California, expanding both the geographical scope and the nature of flood control—which previously had been restricted to levees. (The same two basins were favored in the 1928 Flood Control Act.) Local interests had to pay at least half the cost of constructing and repairing the levees.

The 1917 act further fragmented congressional authority over water. Flood control, navigation, and irrigation became the responsibility of different groups of lawmakers, just as they were the responsibility of different federal agencies. The House created a Flood Control Committee, taking that job away from the Rivers and Harbors Committee. (In the Senate, a subcommittee of the Commerce Committee reviewed flood control legislation.) Now three different groups of lawmakers passed judgment on water bills—the House Irrigation Committee was the third. The Flood Control Act of 1923 extended flood control to tributaries of the Mississippi and continued the appropriations authorized in 1917 for an additional six years.[62]

Although the 1917 Flood Control Act provided benefits to the West as well as the South, most of the West's congressional delegation thought it did not do enough for their region. Senator Francis G. Newlands of Nevada—who chaired the Senate's Commerce Committee but represented one of many inland western states with no navigable streams—claimed that the legislation exclusively benefited those who owned southern swampland. It did nothing to promote unified, comprehensive planning of waterway improvements. Senator George Norris of Nebraska tried unsuccessfully to amend the 1917 bill to permit the construction of irrigation dams in the West as well as flood control works in the South. Joseph Ransdell of Louisiana, the Senate sponsor of the legislation, strenuously opposed Norris's amendment for fear that it would serve as an entering wedge for legislators outside the Mississippi Basin. Ransdell's intransigence prompted Senator Thomas Walsh of Montana to warn that "it might be well to have a little regard for the desires and interests of other sections of the country." Southerners had asked the federal government to shoulder most of the cost of flood control. Why, then, Walsh wondered, was the federal irrigation program required to be self-supporting?[63]

Western opposition to the Flood Control Act of 1917 was significant, because the West and South had long been allies in Congress, and the two sections appeared to have much in common. Both considered themselves capital-starved provinces of the United States, and both claimed to have been slighted in river and harbor appropriations that favored the densely populated states of the East Coast and Great Lakes. Their representatives in Congress often traded votes. In 1902, the Reclamation Act passed the House by a vote of 146 to 55. The legislation won support in all parts of the country, but the margin of victory was greatest in the West and South—38 to 0 in the West, and 37 to 10 in the South.[64]

As noted earlier, from the beginning of its life the Reclamation Service had unsuccessfully attempted to expand into the Midwest and South, and between 1907 and 1917, Francis G. Newlands had sought to create a permanent Inland Waterways Commission in part to win greater public works appropriations for the two politically weakest sections of the country. The

alliance of West and South could be seen in resolutions passed by annual irrigation congresses in support of a national program to drain swamplands
in the South and protect alluvial lands from floods.[65] But by the second
decade of the twentieth century, the West-South alliance had begun to crumble. For example, when the Reclamation Extension Act of 1914 came up for
a vote—a bill to extend the period of repayment on western irrigation projects from ten to twenty years—Oscar Underwood of Alabama exhibited far
less enthusiasm for the irrigation of arid lands than he had in 1902. He supported the legislation, but only on the condition that Congress, rather than
the secretary of the interior, parcel out future appropriations for irrigation.
When the final vote was taken, the congressional delegations of Louisiana,
Florida, and South Carolina unanimously supported the Extension Act, but
support for the West had all but vanished from North Carolina, Tennessee,
Missouri, Texas, Alabama, and Georgia.[66]

The debate over the 1928 Flood Control Act revealed that if anything,
sectional differences in Congress had become even stronger than in 1917.
During lengthy hearings, the House Flood Control Committee pondered the
potential of reservoirs on the Missouri River to provide irrigation and hydroelectric power as well as flood control. Levees were by nature local improvements; reservoirs could be situated hundreds of miles from the land they
protected. The main stem of the Mississippi offered few sites for dams, but
the 1928 legislation permitted reservoirs to be substituted for other methods of flood control, and it appropriated $5 million for reservoir surveys by
the army engineers on Mississippi tributaries. This was a modest sum in a
bill carrying a total appropriation of $325 million, but in the West and up-
per Midwest it held out hope of massive future spending on new water projects. The Flood Control Act of 1928 was an entering wedge for legislators
outside the lower Mississippi. (The Flood Control Acts of 1936 and 1938
authorized the first federal flood control reservoirs on tributaries of the
Mississippi.)[67]

Interest in reservoirs came not just from those who thought reservoirs
might do a better job of protecting alluvial land than levees, but also from
lower Mississippi residents who feared that their land would be condemned
for use as overflow channels or basins.[68] The Flood Control Act of 1928 was
the most expensive act ever passed by Congress, exceeding even the Panama
Canal Bill. The legislation went far beyond the Flood Control Act of 1917
by eliminating local contributions to work on the main stem of the river. Nevertheless, it still required local contributions on the tributaries, and it asked
the states and levee districts to provide rights of ways and easements for levees and floodways—the national government would pay only for land that
had not flooded previously.

In both 1927 and 1928, the McNary-Haugen bill passed both houses of
Congress only to be vetoed by President Coolidge as special-interest legisla-

tion that authorized price fixing. By opposing the farm bill, Southern Democrats had lost favor in the Midwest. Drought had already fastened itself on parts of the Great Plains, and farmers there complained that crop losses from too little water were as important as property losses from too much. "The people of the Great Plains area are suffering from a lack of water," Congressman James H. Sinclair of North Dakota observed on the floor of the House, "while the lower Delta basins are suffering from too much water. Why permit this condition to exist when a comprehensive program of control can relieve both situations and provide additional economic benefits to all?" Some western and midwestern politicians also demanded that the federal government reforest the land adjoining the headwaters of Mississippi River tributaries to prevent soil erosion and evaporation.[69]

In his December 6, 1927, message to Congress, President Coolidge warned, "The recognized needs of the Mississippi should not be made a vehicle for carrying other projects. All proposals for development should stand on their own merits. Any other method would result in ill-advised conclusions, great waste of money, and instead of promoting would delay the orderly and certain utilization of water resources." Reservoir projects on tributaries of the Mississippi should be considered in discrete bills, Coolidge insisted, as public works had in the past. He denied that dams on the Missouri could serve the multiple uses of power and irrigation as well as flood control, and he saw the 1928 bill as a foundation for massive future expenditures on unnecessary projects.[70]

The 1928 Flood Control Act constituted a set of geographical compromises. The $5 million reservoir surveys bought votes in the Midwest, but the legislation also pledged that the federal government would pay one-third the cost of a $51 million flood control project in the Sacramento Valley (the State of California and local residents were required to split the remaining cost). Without that provision, the California delegation might never have voted for the act, nor would other states along the Pacific Slope that hoped to reap benefits from future flood control bills.[71]

As noted earlier, the formal marriage between the Mississippi and Sacramento Rivers dated to the Flood Control Act of 1917. Senator Hiram Johnson of California had long served on the Commerce Committee of the Senate—which held hearings on river and harbor bills sent from the House—and he also sat on the conference committee that ironed out differences between House and Senate versions of the 1928 flood control legislation. His seniority put him in the perfect position to horse-trade, particularly after Senator Newlands—who had opposed the creation of any new water projects until Congress had created a permanent inland waterways commission—died in 1917. As Johnson explained in a letter to a friend, "I was very glad to be upon the flood control conference because . . . then I could protect the Sacramento Flood control item, which [Congressman

Charles F.] Curry [of Northern California] so ably succeeded in getting into the bill in the House." Not only did Johnson confront sectional differences within the United States and the West; California itself was split into two commonwealths. Northern California demanded flood control, and Southern California, Boulder Dam; the two projects were linked. Given Southern California's phenomenal population growth during the 1920s, Northern Californians deeply feared losing political and economic power to Los Angeles and its surrounding communities.[72]

The history of Boulder Dam has been well told.[73] It was the capstone of a package of discrete Colorado River water projects linked together more by politics than the dictates of efficiency. During World War I, residents of Southern California realized that an omnibus bill combining the water needs of different parts of the Southwest would have the best chance of winning approval in Congress. Before 1920, flood control and irrigation took precedence, but during the 1920s hydroelectric power and water for Los Angeles assumed greater importance. The Imperial Valley of California contained five hundred thousand immensely fertile acres, but much of that land was lower than the Colorado River, making it flood prone, and the diversion canal that linked the valley and river ran partly through Mexico. The Colorado inundated the valley in 1905, and in 1911 and 1914, the Mexican Revolution and hostility to the American invasion of Veracruz threatened to cut off the valley's water supply. California's governor sent the state militia into the valley, whose residents were prepared to invade Mexico to keep the water flowing. An All-American Canal was first proposed in 1918, but it was not integrated into the Boulder Dam Project until 1921, the year before the Swing-Johnson Bill first surfaced in Congress.[74]

The second part of the Boulder Dam Project grew out of high crop prices during World War I and the anticipated demand for land among returning veterans. The Reclamation Bureau wanted to serve both the urban and rural West, not redirect its focus entirely to rapidly growing cities such as Los Angeles. It began comprehensive studies of the Colorado River in 1914, and it published reports of those investigations in 1918 and 1919. Two million acres of irrigable land adjoined the proposed reservoir sites on the Colorado, and the 1928 Boulder Dam Act authorized an investigation of the largest potential project, the Parker-Gila Project, which covered six hundred thousand acres in southwestern Arizona. In California, eight hundred thousand acres could be served by the All-American Canal, including more than five hundred thousand in the Imperial Valley. The Coachella Valley, near Indio, California, contained another seventy-two thousand acres, and there were seventy-nine thousand more in the Palo Verde Project, near Blythe. The agricultural depression of the 1920s turned this feature of the project into a liability, but it was not abandoned. Many westerners, including Herbert Hoover, believed that eventually the growing American population would require new farmland, and

Southern California's burgeoning cities would provide excellent markets for agricultural commodities. Equally important, securing the political support of Arizona and Nevada required that Boulder Dam provide them with direct benefits, including the promise that their populations would be increased.[75]

The third part of the project first appeared in the mid-1920s. In 1923, William Mulholland, the chief engineer of the Los Angeles Water Bureau, proposed an aqueduct from the Colorado River to Los Angeles to expand the city's water supply. The city surveyed potential routes in 1923 and 1924, and in 1925, Los Angeles voters overwhelmingly approved a bond issue to pay for aqueduct surveys. A bill to create a special district to deliver water to the communities of Southern California—what became the Metropolitan Water District (MWD)—passed the California legislature in 1927. Although the aqueduct began at Parker Dam, downstream from Boulder Dam, the high dam provided the power needed to pump the water to Los Angeles. In 1928, proponents of Boulder Dam thought that revenue from power sales to the MWD would ensure repayment—and get the Boulder Dam legislation through Congress. The MWD solidified support for Boulder Dam within many parts of Southern California.[76]

The alliance between Los Angeles and the Bureau of Reclamation drove and sustained the project. Between 1900 and 1925, the city's population nearly doubled, and the county grew at an even faster rate. In 1928, Herbert Hoover remarked that the city "represents one of the most remarkable human migrations in history."[77] In 1922, the city happily contributed seventy-five thousand dollars to help fund government surveys of the two most likely sites for a high dam on the Colorado, Boulder Canyon and Black Canyon. By the middle of the 1920s, it became clear that Congress would pay for a high dam only if the structure could generate sufficient power to return the money spent on construction to the national treasury within a reasonable number of years. Navigation and flood control benefits would be deducted from the bill, but they were assumed to constitute a small fraction of the project's total cost. Construction would not begin until contracts had been signed for the sale of water and power.[78]

The Boulder Dam Bill, cosponsored by Representative Phil Swing of the Imperial Valley and California senator Hiram Johnson, first appeared in Congress in 1922. It received little attention or debate. Hostility and division among the Colorado River Basin states proved to be the most important obstacle. The interests of six Colorado River states appeared to have been sacrificed to those of one—California. Political conflict within the Colorado River drainage basin closely resembled that within the Mississippi River Basin: downstream interests encountered strong suspicion and resentment among upstream interests, who thought they had been shortchanged by federal water policies.

In April 1926, Hiram Johnson lamented privately that the Boulder Canyon Project was "of such magnitude and there are so many diverse interests,

[that] haste is impossible. . . . Days, and weeks, and even months have been spent by us with the upper-basin States. . . . It has been a tremendous task to endeavor to reconcile . . . the western senators. Few others [outside the West] even understand or care for the measure, and a process of education will have to be conducted with them." According to Johnson, nine of the fourteen senators who represented the Colorado Basin states opposed his bill. Late in 1927, the four governors of the upper-basin states pledged to resist the Swing-Johnson Bill until all seven states had approved the pending Colorado River Compact. In Johnson's mind, the lack of consensus posed a profound question: if the West itself could not agree to build Boulder Dam, how could other parts of the country be persuaded to support it?[79]

The old mercantilist view that one state or region's gain was, inevitably, another's loss remained powerful during the 1920s. To westerners outside the Colorado River Basin, the Boulder Dam legislation favored the development of irrigation and power in one part of the West at the expense of the rest. Therefore, politicians in many western states hoped to attach pet reclamation projects to the Swing-Johnson legislation, creating an omnibus bill to authorize many projects simultaneously. Others favored the McNary-Smith Bill, which spread federal appropriations for irrigation evenly across the West, much as the Reclamation Act of 1902 had attempted to do.[80]

Residents of the Pacific Northwest saw Boulder Dam as a direct threat to federal construction of a high dam in the Columbia Valley, as well as to smaller government irrigation projects in Oregon and Washington. Typical of politicians in that region was Charles McNary of Oregon. A member of the Senate Irrigation and Reclamation Committee, McNary stood for reelection in 1926. If he supported the Swing-Johnson Bill, that would open him to public criticism that his vote had hampered Oregon's economic development. Who could be sure that Congress would approve a dam for the Pacific Northwest? Therefore, McNary opposed the Boulder Canyon Project. In April 1926, Johnson explained in a letter to George Young, editor of the *Los Angeles Examiner:* "In many states which have not advanced as rapidly as ours, there is a feeling which is often the concomitant of inferiority, and of jealousy, of California because of our growth, great prosperity, and tremendous possibilities. There is a disposition among some of these states, and strangely enough, it is more marked in the west than elsewhere, to talk of California's great wealth, and California's desire to appropriate to herself more than she ought."[81]

Supporters of the Boulder Dam Project also had their differences. Initially, many members of the Imperial Irrigation District's board opposed linking flood control on the lower Colorado and the All-American Canal to a high dam, fearing that an omnibus bill would delay or prevent construction of the canal and cost at least twice as much as a smaller dam designed solely for flood control and irrigation. The more ambitious the bill, the more likely it was to promote opposition upstream.[82] Southern Nevada contained little irrigable land, little immediate need for additional electricity, and little prospect of substantial urban or industrial growth. In the age before air-conditioning, Las Vegas was more village than city. The Swing-Johnson Bill ran the risk, therefore, that all power produced at Boulder Dam would be contracted to private companies or municipalities in Southern California. In 1926 and 1927, Senator Key Pittman of Nevada urged that either a share of the power be reserved to his state, no matter how long the Silver State took to use it, or that Nevada be granted part of the revenue it produced.[83] This was a dangerous tactic. If Nevada or other basin states asked for too much, then Congress might refuse to appropriate money for the dam on the grounds that the cost of building it could not be repaid within a reasonable period of time.[84]

A maverick Republican, Hiram Johnson complained that the Coolidge administration—led behind the scenes by Herbert Hoover (whom he despised)—had conspired to prevent his bill from reaching the floor. The House leadership strongly opposed the legislation—as it had opposed the Reclamation Act in 1902—so Johnson faced a parliamentary dilemma. His bill would receive a fairer hearing in the Senate, where the West was much better represented, but House members regarded it as a revenue measure that should originate in that chamber. Therefore, Johnson modified his legislation so that the construction of Boulder Dam would be paid for by a bond issue rather than by a reimbursable appropriation from the general treasury. In that way, it could bypass the powerful House Appropriations Committee, which was dominated by easterners. The Swing-Johnson Bill finally reached the House floor in December 1926, more than four years after it first appeared in Congress.[85]

Boulder Dam was closely linked to the All-American Canal, but at a time of substantial crop surpluses, few legislators—especially those who represented states in the Midwest—favored opening *new* land to irrigation anywhere. Doubts also arose that the Bureau of Reclamation could find a market for the power. As noted in chapter 8, the cost of producing electricity by steam engines declined rapidly in the 1920s. Therefore, hydroelectric power lost some of its allure—especially when it had to be transmitted great distances, as from the Colorado River to Los Angeles. A few engineers claimed that the dam site was unstable, or that the salt content of the water rendered it unfit for domestic use. More claimed that even a high dam would fill with silt in ten or twenty years: for hundreds of miles above Black Canyon and Boulder Canyon, the Colorado River carved its channel through soft sandstone and clay shale, and it carried an enormous quantity of soil in suspension. Other objections included anticipated cost overruns; that the Swing-Johnson Bill was much ado about nothing, because it could not take effect until the Colorado River Compact had been ratified by six if not all seven states within the basin—which seemed very unlikely in 1925 or 1926; that the rights of the states to the Colorado's surplus water should be settled by the U.S. Supreme Court *before* Congress authorized any dam; and, most important, that the project was public power masquerading as flood control and irrigation.[86]

Given strong congressional opposition to Boulder Dam in 1922, 1924, and 1926, how did it finally win approval in 1928? The answer is complicated, but changing public perceptions of the electrical-power industry played a large part. During the 1920s, utility companies replaced the railroads as the "mother of trusts." At the end of April 1928—the same month Congress adopted the flood control bill—Federal Trade Commission hearings revealed that utility trade associations had created a slush fund of more than four hundred thousand dollars to buy, manufacture, and cultivate public opinion against Boulder Dam. Private power companies hired writers to prepare pamphlets opposing public power, lecturers to attack it from the podium, and lobbyists to fight it in Congress and the state legislatures. They even distributed literature to elementary and secondary schools in an effort to turn children against public power. Little wonder that the *Washington Herald* likened the tactics of the power companies to a totalitarian regime: "One reads that in Russia the Bolshevist government has set about deliberately to educate a rising generation in the principles of communism and in hostility to all religion. But even that policy was deliberately adopted by a de facto government. Our American Power Trust has not yet been attested as quite a de facto government. It has made considerable advances in that direction, but has not been accorded recognition." In private correspondence Hiram Johnson declared that the "power trust" was the "biggest thing that has developed since I took an interest in public affairs. . . . Its influence and its power . . . permeate every avenue of our social, economic, and political life. It is this horrible influence that I have to combat in the Boulder Dam fight."[87]

In the spring of 1928, as Congress debated the Mississippi River flood control legislation, Johnson made a strategic decision not to push Boulder Dam at that time. If the Colorado River project was to be a quid pro quo for the Mississippi River legislation, then he needed to move fast. Yet the Senate was preoccupied with the tax bill, and if Congress passed too much public works legislation at one session, Coolidge would be more likely to veto it. In exchange for Johnson removing his bill from the legislative agenda, Senate leaders promised that Boulder Dam would receive top priority when Congress reconvened in December. Johnson made a wise decision. By December, many senators who had opposed the legislation earlier in the year favored it out of fear that a negative vote would brand them as stooges of the vilified power trust. In the middle of December, the Boulder Dam Bill passed the Senate by a vote of 64 to 11 and the House by 166 to 122. Of the seventeen states west of the Mississippi, two-thirds were unanimous in support of Boulder

Dam, and only in Arizona did both United States senators vote against the legislation. The Colorado River project cost $165 million, which included $71.6 million for the dam and reservoir; $38.2 million for the power plant; $38.5 million for the seventy-five-mile-long All-American Canal to the Imperial Valley; and $17.7 million in interest. Of this amount, $25 million was written off as a nonreimbursable flood control benefit.[88]

Without extensive vote trading, Congress would have rejected both the Flood Control Act of 1928 and the Colorado River project. In committee, lawmakers considered including Boulder Dam and the Sacramento River Projects in the Flood Control Act, but given President Coolidge's calls for tax relief, southern politicians feared that such overt logrolling would invite a presidential veto. Speaking in opposition to the flood control bill, Congressman James A. Frear of Wisconsin observed: "Every legislative project from farm relief to Boulder Dam, flood control, and lesser measures involving countless millions have been joined into an omnibus movement to rush through Congress these great measures by widespread legislative trades, while telegrams and letters from political supporters back home deluge the average Member who seeks to do his duty to the Government and to measure up to his legislative responsibility." William Mullendore, one of Herbert Hoover's assistants in the Commerce Department in the early 1920s and a lobbyist for the Southern California Edison Company from 1926 to 1928, informed company officials that "[Phil] Swing is trading with everyone he can reach. He told a Louisiana Congressman that he would not vote, nor would the California delegation vote for Miss. relief unless they were promised flood relief on the Colorado also via Boulder Dam. . . . [T]he threats are dangerous and are undoubtedly resulting in some blocks of votes."[89] In announcing passage of the Colorado River legislation, the *Times-Picayune* of New Orleans observed, "Party lines were obliterated in the final vote on passage. Senators Broussard and Ransdell of Louisiana, Harrison and Stephens of Mississippi and Heflin and Black of Alabama all voted for the bill."[90] No longer were Southern Democrats rigid champions of states' rights, and the flood of 1927 had contributed greatly to that transformation.

THE BATTLE FOR THE NEW WEST:
THE CORPS OF ENGINEERS AND THE BUREAU OF RECLAMATION

Much remained to be done following passage of the Boulder Dam Act.[91] Congress had not established a policy to apportion the cost of multiple-use dams— as it had apportioned the cost of flood control in the 1928 Mississippi River legislation. It was impossible, therefore, to predict in advance what local interests and the states would pay toward the construction of future projects, what costs should be written off to navigation and flood control, how the proceeds from electricity would be used, and whether the Bureau of Reclamation or Corps of Engineers would build those projects. Until 1933, when Congress created the Tennessee Valley Authority, the corps seemed likely to construct and administer the nation's second multiple-use project, in the Tennessee Valley. It had already designed the capstone of that project, Wilson Dam, in 1928. Historian Marc Reisner has traced the rivalry between the Corps of Engineers and the Bureau of Reclamation to the late 1930s and finds its fullest expression in the Pick-Sloan Plan of 1944, but the turf war began in earnest during the 1920s.[92]

The construction work of the Corps of Engineers expanded dramatically during the 1920s and early 1930s. In 1915, 575 river and harbor projects were under way. That number increased to 930 in 1930. As its work increased, so did its influence in Congress. The 1925 River and Harbor Act ordered the Corps of Engineers and Federal Power Commission to estimate the cost of investigating the nation's navigable streams and their tributaries *as entire units*—at least those streams where the generation of hydroelectric power or flood control seemed feasible. This was a dramatic shift from the limited investigations authorized by earlier river and harbor bills. The new surveys laid the foundation for "multiple-purpose" development of those streams, including the reclamation of arid lands.[93]

Congress funded the investigations in 1927. The "308 reports," named after the House document that listed the first streams to be inspected, resulted from Herbert Hoover's comprehensive water policies and from the need to protect power sites on navigable streams from the burgeoning utility industry. As noted earlier, the Flood Control Act of May 15, 1928, extended the 1927 legislation by authorizing a study of whether reservoirs on tributaries of the Mississippi River would substantially reduce flooding in the lower Mississippi. But Congress asked the Corps of Engineers to investigate the impact of these reservoirs on soils, forests, agriculture, and navigation, as well as on flooding. It authorized the corps to spend more than $7.3 million on surveys, and the Flood Control Act of 1928 added an additional $5 million to that amount. To put the figure in perspective, the $12.3 million was more than the Reclamation Bureau had spent on hydrographic surveys during its entire lifetime. By the middle of 1933, more than 150 "308 reports" had been filed by the corps, covering such major rivers as the Columbia, Hudson, Sacramento, Potomac, and James.[94]

The 308 reports opened a new chapter in the turf war between the corps and the Bureau of Reclamation. The war was fought on two major fronts— in the Columbia Valley of Washington State and the Central Valley of California. The Northwest had the second largest concentration of people in the West after California, and the Columbia River carried ten times more water than the Colorado. As within the Colorado Basin, strong rivalries divided the region's agricultural districts. Most of the federal money spent on irrigation in Washington had gone to the Yakima Valley, which competed for markets with central Washington and Spokane, but central Washington contained the largest potential reclamation project, and the Grand Coulee of the Columbia—a trough from one to six miles wide with walls as high as nine hundred feet—offered an excellent reservoir site. The first extensive proposal to dam it came in 1918. Completion of the Great Northern Railroad's line up the Columbia River in 1914, soaring wheat prices during the war, a drought in 1918–19, and the river's vast potential to generate electricity contributed to interest in the project. Two million acres could be readily irrigated in central Washington, and, as on the lower Colorado, cheap Columbia River power promised to subsidize agriculture and industry. Historian Robert Ficken has observed that "Grand Coulee meant nothing less than the industrialization of the Pacific Northwest, the transformation of an entire raw-material-rich region into a manufacturing complex. . . . All sorts of industrial enterprises—sawmills, chemical and fertilizer plants, [and] aluminum manufacturers—would be drawn to the upper Columbia by the availability of cheap and abundant electricity, there to exploit the forested and mineralized wealth of the Cascades."[95]

Nevertheless, neither the Bureau of Reclamation nor the Corps of Engineers showed much interest in central Washington until the late 1920s. Construction of a high dam in Washington State, bureau officials feared, would prevent or postpone the construction of Boulder Dam, and it would be very expensive. A survey conducted by the bureau in 1925 considered five plans to develop farms in the Columbia Basin. It concluded that the cost would run from $200 million to $300 million, two or three times the projected price of Boulder Dam, and between $157 and $229 an acre. Farmers would need $2,500 to $4,500 just to get started. Twenty-five years would be needed to settle the project, and ten or twenty years would elapse before repayment would begin. The most likely crops were alfalfa, potatoes, wheat, sweet clover, and small grains—much of which would be fed to livestock, not people. "The project has been compared to the Panama Canal, and the claim made that it should be developed for reasons of public policy, like the canal undertaking," *Engineering News-Record* editorialized in September 1925. "Everything considered, it is well that the project has been shelved. It should be allowed to sleep for a generation or two."[96]

The corps launched its 308 study of the Columbia River in 1929 without consulting the Bureau of Reclamation, which, in the same year, began surveys of the Grand Coulee dam site. The corps spent 10 percent of the money originally appropriated for the 308 reports on the Columbia, and it identified ten dam sites, including one at Grand Coulee. Initially, the corps refused to share the information it gathered with the Interior Department, and it also refused to cooperate in common endeavors, such as dam-site test borings. On April 6, 1929, R. F. Walter, then chief engineer of the bureau, noted: "I am informally advised by officers of the War Department who have visited this office during the past year, that they expect their [investigatory] operations to continue and to grow into one of the largest governmental activities in the west and middle west, and eventually to cover all streams without regard to their navigability, or need for flood control which is the basis of present justification for this work." A month later, Secretary of the Interior Ray Lyman Wilbur sent the secretary of war an urgent "Memorandum Concerning Duplication of Activities in the War and Interior Departments." It began:

> The last Congress appropriated $5,000,000.00 for the investigation of flood control and related matters to be disbursed by the War Department. With the exceptionally large sums thus provided, the Engineer Corps of the Army has extended its influence into fields hitherto removed from the accepted activities of the military branch of the Government. It is now duplicating work which for many years has been entrusted by Congress to the bureaus of the Department of the Interior [the Geological Survey and Reclamation Bureau]. That the results of this invasion of Interior Department functions do not promise a more economical administration, better performance, or simplified procedure is apparent from knowledge already gained of the activities and plans of the Engineer Corps. . . . On the contrary, it is submitted that the Interior Department's cooperative relationship with state governments and portions of the civilian population is being threatened; records acquired as a result of years of investigations by the Interior Department are being obtained by Army Engineers from Interior field officers without the prior knowledge and consent of the responsible heads of Interior bureaus; large sums of money are being expended on projects which could be more economically executed by the technical staff of the Interior Department; and the success of engineering and economic developments for which the Interior Department is responsible and for which the Government is in the position of a creditor seeking repayment for millions of dollars invested, is being undermined.[97]

Wilbur's fears were well founded. Power, flood control, and irrigation could not be neatly separated, and many politicians, as well as water users, thought the corps had more to offer than the Reclamation Bureau. The corps paid the entire cost of preliminary dam surveys, while the bureau asked water users to finance half the cost up front. Even more important, river and harbor appropriations did not require reimbursement by water users, and the corps was not constrained by the 160-acre limitation in the Reclamation Act of 1902. That made the construction of high dams by the corps attractive to large farmers and land speculators. Only a few days before Wilbur wrote the memo just quoted, Senator Burton K. Wheeler of Montana introduced legislation that would have permitted the Corps of Engineers to construct a multiple-purpose dam "for the regulation of the flow and control of the floods of the Flathead River, Clark Fork, and the Columbia River," a dam that would have stored water for the irrigation of a large tract of government land.[98]

At the end of 1929, a friend of the Reclamation Bureau in Congress, Representative Louis C. Cramton of Michigan, echoed Wilbur's complaint that corps' studies of reclamation were "usurping the powers of the Bureau of Reclamation." The army engineers, Cramton charged, had gone "further than Congress ever dreamed they would." Indeed, the corps threatened the future of federal reclamation. "It has taken several years of intensive effort to bring collections [on government irrigation projects] up to their present satisfactory condition," Cramton remarked, "and the Interior Department can not see them jeopardized without a vigorous protest."[99] If the corps began building multiple-purpose dams, paying for them with river and harbor appropriations, and writing off much of the cost to flood control and navigation, the Bureau of Reclamation could not compete. The West—indeed, the entire nation—would belong to the corps.[100]

Secretary Wilbur's fears ultimately proved premature. Neither navigation improvement nor anticipated demands for electricity justified a series of dams on the Columbia, the corps concluded. The Pacific Northwest already had a power surplus, and Grand Coulee was situated in a scantily populated desert seventy-five miles from the nearest urban market, Spokane, which contained little more than a hundred thousand people. Private power companies could produce electricity much more cheaply from tributaries of the Columbia. The chief engineer of the Montana Power Company predicted that even if the government provided power from Grand Coulee to Seattle and Tacoma free of charge, transmitting it 250 miles would cost more than generating the same amount of power from streams that emptied into Puget Sound. Seattle and Tacoma already had municipal electrical plants and low rates. The Columbia River 308 report went to the corps' Board of Engineers for Rivers and Harbors in July 1931. Six months later, the nation's agricultural surpluses, the enormous anticipated cost of the dam, and the limited local markets for power persuaded the board to recommend against the construction of any dam on the Columbia.[101]

At hearings held at the beginning of 1932, local interests protested the corps' action, even though they disagreed about whether the first dam should be built at Grand Coulee, the Dalles, or near Bonneville, forty miles east of Portland. More important, presidential candidate Franklin D. Roosevelt promised that "the next great hydro-electric development to be undertaken by the Federal Government must be on the Columbia River." Providing work soon took precedence over immediate needs for water or power. Secretary of the Interior Harold Ickes and FDR insisted that the Reclamation Bureau build Grand Coulee Dam, and Congress authorized that project in July 1933. Shortly thereafter, Congress also authorized the corps to construct multiple-purpose dams at Bonneville and at Fort Peck, in Montana. Eventually, World War II justified their construction, but in 1933, few westerners anticipated a need for more water for either power or irrigation.[102]

The construction of Boulder Dam also encouraged residents of California's Central Valley to seek federal construction and funding of a high dam. The Central Valley Project (CVP) was originally conceived as a state project, but the Great Depression prevented California from borrowing money at a low enough interest rate to build it. The federal government could finance the project at 3.5 percent interest, while the state could not sell its bonds at less than 4.5 percent interest. Over the fifty-year life of a loan, one percentage point made an enormous difference. In the Sacramento and San Joaquin Valleys, the drought of 1929 and 1930 prompted local water users to request that the corps investigate a dam on the upper Sacramento River at Kennett (later Shasta), a second reservoir on the upper San Joaquin River at Friant, canals from the Sacramento–San Joaquin Delta into the upper San Joaquin Valley, and an aqueduct to serve water-starved land south of the Kings River. The Corps of Engineers 308 survey of the Sacramento River appeared in early 1931.[103]

The corps tolerated diversions for irrigation in the Sacramento Valley, even though the rapid expansion of rice cultivation during the first decades of the twentieth century all but destroyed waterborne commerce above Sacramento. A high dam on the upper Sacramento would restore water transportation, and the army engineers sought to maintain a navigable depth of six feet between Sacramento and Chico. Such a dam would also protect communities strung along the river—Marysville and Yuba City, as well as Sacramento—from flooding. Finally, since the late 1890s, the corps had had nominal authority to protect water quality. Diversions and drought increased the salinity of water downstream, in the Sacramento–San Joaquin Delta and on the north end of San Francisco Bay. This threatened irrigation in the delta, as well as the domestic water supplies of cities on the north arm of San Francisco Bay.[104]

In 1930, the division engineer for the Sacramento Valley suggested that only the federal government could finance the Central Valley Project, but other corps engineers balked at becoming involved in such a large undertaking. In 1931, Major Lytle Brown, the chief of engineers, recommended against any federal contribution to Friant Dam, and he warned that both Kennett and Friant were "on the border line of economic feasibility." The panel of army engineers who reviewed the 308 report on the Sacramento River agreed. They were willing to support a $4 million federal contribution to a high dam on the Sacramento River in the name of navigation, but they did not support a federally financed project. The agricultural depression would encourage water users to repudiate all debts to the government, particularly if the project proved disappointing—as had so many federal reclamation schemes in the past. The State of California and the beneficiaries ought to fund the CVP, the review board decided.[105]

Public works spending expanded dramatically during Franklin D. Roosevelt's first term, and the Corps of Engineers' opposition to a federally financed and constructed CVP softened, as had its opposition to dams on the

Columbia. In 1933, the corps suggested that the federal government contribute $7.7 million to the construction of Kennett Dam and fund as much as 30 percent of the rest of the state plan from river and harbor appropriations. The 1935 Rivers and Harbors Act contained the first authorization for federal construction of the $170 million Central Valley Project, and that legislation provided for construction by the corps. Secretary of the Interior Harold Ickes complained to Roosevelt that the Reclamation Bureau should have exclusive jurisdiction over the CVP. A month after passage of the rivers and harbors bill Ickes, who also headed the Public Works Administration, turned the first phase of the project, Friant Dam, on the San Joaquin River, into a PWA project and assigned it to the Reclamation Bureau. Nevertheless, Roosevelt left the door open as to which agency would build other features of the CVP, particularly the multiple-purpose dam on the Sacramento River. He argued that the *primary function* of a dam, not what part of the country in which the site was situated or which agency local water users preferred, should determine whether it was built by the corps or Bureau of Reclamation.[106]

Thus, Roosevelt's 1935 decision to assign Friant Dam to the Bureau of Reclamation did not decide which agency would build the other parts of the Central Valley Project. Friant offered drought relief for two hundred thousand acres of productive agricultural land in the San Joaquin Valley that would return to desert without additional water. Kennett Dam was expected to cost seven times more than Friant, but it would provide hydroelectric power, flood control, and navigation improvement as well as irrigation. It would not be easy to determine the dam's primary purpose. And although FDR considered proposed dams on the Kings and Kern Rivers primarily irrigation structures, the chair of the House Flood Control Committee, William Whittington of Mississippi, regarded them mainly as flood control works. Multiple-purpose dams made it possible to shift costs from one use of water to another, but they also made it difficult to determine the primary purpose of those dams. Friant Dam was completed in 1942. Shasta Dam was authorized in July 1938, but it was not completed until 1945, and it did not begin to generate electricity until 1950. Just as Southern California Edison received a large share of the power from Boulder Dam, in 1951 Congress granted the Pacific Gas and Electric Company the right to transmit the power generated by Central Valley Project dams. It also prohibited the Reclamation Bureau from distributing power directly to consumers.[107]

As the debate over which federal agency should build multiple-purpose dams raged in the Central Valley and Washington State, the Corps of Engineers demonstrated that it knew as much or more about rivers and hydraulic engineering as the Bureau of Reclamation. Before the Mississippi flood of 1927, the corps and its friends in Congress had opposed the creation of a waterways laboratory to study the behavior of rivers. Models could never replicate flooding, they argued, particularly on streams that carried a great deal of silt, such as the Missouri and Mississippi. They also feared that civilian control over the lab would threaten their future work and appropriations.[108]

The 1927 flood, however, led to new calls for a lab, which was authorized by the Flood Control Act of 1928. The army opened its hydraulic facility at Vicksburg, Mississippi, in 1930. There, scientists and engineers studied the five variables that influenced the flow of rivers: velocity, channel width, channel depth, slope or gradient, and composition of the bed. By the mid-1930s, more than two hundred people worked at the facility, including engineers, draftspeople, photographers, carpenters, and laborers. During the first few years of operation, the corps constructed sixty-five models. The first represented the Illinois River—a 528-foot replica that mimicked 130 miles of the stream in nature. The most ambitious movable model was constructed in 1935. It replicated the Mississippi River from Helena, Arkansas, to Donaldsonville, Louisiana, reducing the 600 river miles to a representative 1,100 feet. The models demonstrated the effect of cutoffs, revetments, levee seepage, and the operation of various types of navigation dams and locks, and they proved, for example, that cutoffs increased the capacity of meandering rivers to carry floodwater. The lab not only modeled rivers, it also collected more than six hundred samples of bed material from the lower Mississippi and its tributaries.

A replica of Fort Peck dam became the Corps of Engineers' first dam model. By the 1940s the lab had made it possible for the corps to study subjects far removed from its original mission, such as the impact of forest cover on soil erosion. Despite their initial opposition, army engineers quickly recognized the lab's value, even if the models never provided "the key to supposed universal laws governing water movement," in the words of historian Martin Reuss, as some hydraulic engineers had hoped. Reuss argues that the lab at Vicksburg was consistent with "the empirical principles and inductive approach that had guided the Corps of Engineers from the agency's inception." It was also a symbol of the corps' increasing role in federal water policy during the 1920s and 1930s.[109]

Paradoxically, when Boulder Dam was completed in 1935, the future of the Corps of Engineers seemed brighter than that of the Bureau of Reclamation. The corps had completed surveys of many of the nation's rivers and had eclipsed both the Bureau of Reclamation and the U.S. Geological Survey in the study of water. In 1934, Secretary of War George H. Dern urged FDR to support a comprehensive survey of the nation's rivers by the corps, in cooperation with the Public Health Service, to determine the best ways to protect them from pollution. And in 1937, a bill to permit the corps to prepare a comprehensive water plan covering flood control, the development of hydroelectric power, and water and soil conservation, as well as irrigation, made it all the way through Congress; Roosevelt vetoed it. FDR, who was strongly influenced by his powerful secretary of the interior, Harold Ickes, opposed giving the War Department the role of national planning agency for water. In the president's words, the corps lacked the "experience and background," to prepare a comprehensive water plan. Unlike Progressive Era water planners, he thought that "such a process of national planning should start at the bottom . . . in the State and local units." In the West, planning should come from river basin authorities that answered directly to the president, rather than from the War Department, which answered to Congress. "The local and regional basis of planning would be ignored," Roosevelt complained, "and there would be no review of the whole program, prior to its presentation to Congress, from the standpoints of national budgetary considerations and national conservation policies." Privately, however, FDR predicted that the corps would make the survey eventually, given its strong support in Congress. One thing had not changed since 1902: in Congress, the Reclamation Bureau was still seen as an agency that answered to the president through the secretary of the interior, while the corps answered directly to Congress.[110]

Bureaucratic rivalries intensified during the New Deal, as the enormous growth in public works spending reinforced the personal ambitions of strong department chiefs, such as Secretary of the Interior Harold Ickes and Secretary of Agriculture Henry Wallace.[111] Historians often portray the 1930s as a decade that witnessed a massive centralization of power in Washington. Yet even if one ignores how federal programs increased the power of the states, or how Congress protected *local* interests, it is important to recognize that the huge increase in public works spending resulted not just in a proliferation of agencies but in the scattering of appropriations among many competing bureaus. If anything, bureaucratic rivalries deepened during the 1930s, making coordinated water planning, let alone the reorganization of government, all but impossible.[112]

CONCLUSION

Boulder Dam became the quintessential American dam. Two hundred feet taller than the Washington Monument, it contained more concrete than *all* the dams built by the Reclamation Bureau before 1928—and a greater storage capacity. The reservoir trapped more than a year's flow of the Colorado River, enough water to cover the entire state of Connecticut to a depth of ten feet. The dam had the potential to generate twice as much power as Niagara Falls, four times the power generated by the Tennessee Valley Authority dams at Muscle Shoals, and as much electricity each year as had been produced by *all* of California's power plants in 1917. The dam was finished in 1935, the generators began turning on September 11, 1936, and by the end of 1941, Boulder Dam produced more electricity than any other power plant in the world.[113]

Boulder Dam created the illusion of planning and efficiency, an illusion the Reclamation Bureau carefully cultivated and perpetuated. In the 1920s and early 1930s, water projects became larger, and flood control and hydroelectric power became as important as irrigation and transportation. Yet even as Herbert Hoover and Franklin D. Roosevelt began to look at entire river basins, water policy became increasingly fragmented. After Roosevelt became president, water projects were chosen primarily to put men to work, not for reasons of technological efficiency or the greatest good for the greatest number. By putting jobs first, the New Deal water policy represented a step backward toward the old system of treating public works as local relief rather than parts of a comprehensive plan. Many smaller projects undertaken during the depression had little or no value, except as work relief. In 1929 or 1930, for example, Congress appropriated $15 million to improve the channel of the Missouri River—which carried few passengers and virtually no freight.[114]

Boulder Dam became a symbol of technological mastery, but it ushered in an age of policy drift. The high dams that followed it did not lead to a coherent federal water policy, nor did the Bureau of Reclamation adopt a formal power policy. There would be no Division of Power within the Interior Department until 1941, when the requirements of World War II demanded one. Nor did Interior create a policy to ensure that power benefits were shared by the greatest number of beneficiaries. Nor did it determine how to distribute profits after the construction costs of high dams had been repaid. Nor did it establish a formula to decide which part of the cost of each dam would be reimbursable to the government and how long farmers would have to pay. Nor did it find a way to cooperate with the Army Corps of Engineers.

The size of the high dams, and the fact that they were undertaken primarily as work relief, undermined the earlier dreams of the Reclamation Bureau. It was easier for the bureau to deal with large landowners rather than small, and urban utility districts rather than rural irrigation districts. Not surprisingly, the Interior Department excused much of the land served by the new generation of dams from the 160-acre limitation—including the Imperial Valley, and farmland irrigated by the Central Valley Project and Colorado–Big Thompson Project. Although the 1930s have been portrayed as an age that saw a major expansion of federal control over water,[115] they also were an age of deferred decisions. Ultimately, the high dams were better suited to the country's needs to fight World War II and the cold war than they were to creating family farms or public power.

10

Conclusion

Retrospect and Significance

From 1902 to 1935, federal water policies reflected remarkably consistent attitudes toward nature.[1] Part of the larger conservation movement, these policies sought to transform "natural resources" into predictable, manageable, and measurable units—as well as commodities that could be bought, sold, and traded. At all levels of government, water policy exemplified the American will to order and dominate the physical world, an almost primal impulse to "complete" an evolutionary process dictated by God or culture. In 1902, federal reclamation promised to "subdue worthless land," turn the desert wilderness into a garden, and convert the West into a commonwealth of small farms. In the decades immediately following passage of the Reclamation Act, several constraints limited the scale and scope of water projects: the technology of dam building, the western demand that every state and territory profit from federal reclamation, the antagonism within Congress toward "government paternalism," the inability to transmit electricity great distances, and the absence of markets for power. Rarely did the Reclamation Service transport water or power more than ten or twenty miles from a project's main dam. But the 1920s produced vast water projects capable of altering the environment far beyond the rivers themselves, as the growth of Los Angeles demonstrated for the Colorado. The goal of federal reclamation shifted from "taming the land" through discrete local projects to promoting economic growth and stability within a sphere of influence that extended hundreds of miles from the river itself. Hydroelectric power, as the historian Richard White has demonstrated, helped to transform rivers into "organic machines." Nature had defined watersheds fairly clearly, but after the 1930s many of the nation's rivers were as much the creations of people as they were of nature.[2]

Continental imperialism constituted a second important theme—the federal government's attempt to incorporate the American hinterland or outback. The "conquest of arid America" helped integrate the West into the nation, as did the depression and World War II. In many ways, federal reclamation was the last stage of Manifest Destiny—the process of creating an integrated nation that stretched from sea to sea. The rivalry between empire and colony, nation and state, core and periphery, metropolis and hinterland, North and South, and East and West all suggest that the sheer size of the United States encouraged Americans to think spatially, deeply affecting politics at all levels of government. From Bacon's Rebellion to the Sagebrush Rebellion of the 1980s, "westerners" assumed that they were overtaxed, underrepresented, and misunderstood by Washington, and water policy must be understood in that context. One of the most debated issues in natural resource policy was whether economic growth should be promoted through public institutions or private ones. The incorporation of the West was a joint operation, a partnership between government and capitalism.

Finally, federal water policy suggests a third major theme: the difficulty of maintaining centralized control and vision in a political system designed to protect and promote local interests. When the federal government began to subsidize the construction of a "continental" railroad in 1862, it did so without debating what sort of West it was trying to create. Similarly, federal reclamation proceeded without a central plan. Never did Congress, the Interior Department, or the bureau itself create a blueprint for a "new West." From its inception, therefore, the Reclamation Bureau's mission was ambiguous. Regional economic development counted for as much as the creation of small farms; bureau leaders sought to build up towns and cities as well as agriculture. The bureau never reconciled these goals. The Great Depression nominally expanded the power of the central government, but it also expanded opportunities for local water users. American government, therefore, must be understood as the interaction of national and local institutions.

RETROSPECT: THE SIGNIFICANCE OF FEDERAL RECLAMATION

In March 1902, four months before the passage of the Reclamation Act, Congressman George Ray of New York, chair of the House Judiciary Committee and a member of the Arid Lands Committee, wrote the latter committee's minority report in opposition to the legislation. Later he led the floor debate against the measure. From the 1870s through the 1890s, the nation had experienced declining wheat, corn, and cotton prices. The agricultural depression had lifted by 1902, but Ray worried that it might return. Federal reclamation might stall the recovery. The eastern half of the nation contained plenty of arable land, he said, and there was no need to create new farms in the West. Irrigation companies, land speculators, and land grant railroads were the driving force behind federal reclamation, not would-be farmers who thirsted for new land. The crusade to move "landless men" to "manless land" merely dressed self-interest in respectable clothes. No federal reclamation program should be adopted, Ray warned, without new water laws. For example, the federal government needed clear authority over interstate streams so that it could build dams in one state to store water for use in another. Even more important, Ray regarded federal reclamation as another method to tax the many and reward the few. The argument that the irrigation program would cost the nation nothing because the sale of public lands would pay for it was specious. Since proceeds from those sales fed into the general treasury, but would no more after passage of the Reclamation Act, the whole nation would be taxed to pay for a program that benefited one region. To make matters worse, Ray predicted that proceeds from land sales would prove inadequate to fund the new program. Government farmers would refuse to repay the cost of construction, and, ultimately, the West would demand appropriations from the general treasury.

Ray's warnings proved prophetic, but there was no lack of prophetic criticism in the spring of 1902. For example, George Maxwell and Elwood Mead cautioned that a wholesale revision of American land laws should precede or be included in any federal reclamation bill, and the secretary of agriculture predicted that the cost of setting up a farm in the West would be "prohibitive for all except men of considerable means." Why, then, did the legislation pass? Granted that spreading American institutions across the continent had an almost mythic appeal, even in the East. But even more important, in the West federal reclamation was considered an entitlement. Westerners in the U.S. Senate threatened to stall or block future river and harbor bills unless easterners accepted federal reclamation of arid lands. Whether or not the West *needed* government reclamation—given the growth of private irrigation in the 1870s and 1880s—did not matter. Nor was it relevant to ask whether such a program could be administered *efficiently*. After all, the nation's river improvement program was notoriously wasteful and inefficient. The East had its program, and the West demanded one of its own.

In addition, Theodore Roosevelt wanted to strengthen the Republican Party, particularly in states soon expected to enter the union, such as Arizona, New Mexico, and Oklahoma. That could be done only if his party supported a program to develop the West. Roosevelt cherished the family farm, but he cherished the future of the Republican Party even more. Therefore, he not only changed his mind about building a few experimental irrigation projects so that the leaders of federal reclamation could learn from their mistakes, he also refused to push legislation to amend the nation's land laws. Grazing interests and such stalwart western Republicans as Francis E. Warren, Frank Mondell, and Henry M. Teller strongly opposed revision. Roosevelt could ill afford to disappoint them.[3]

Federal reclamation also suffered from arrogance and conceit. Those who drafted the Reclamation Act of 1902 forgot or ignored the lessons of the past. Just as settlers clamored for free land in 1800, they clamored for free water a century later. For more than eighty years, Congress had wisely refused to sell land on credit—in large part because the Land Act of 1800, which gave buyers up to four years to pay, had proved to be a disaster. The Reclamation Act sold irrigation works on credit rather than land, but it gave farmers ten years to repay their debt, rather than four. The result was similar to the experience of a century earlier. Both the 1800 and 1902 laws encouraged speculation and invited farmers to renege on their debt to the government. In the 1820s and 1830s, Congress passed a series of relief acts, just as it would a century later.

The proponents of federal reclamation also forgot or ignored the lesson of the swampland acts of 1849 and 1850, which deeded millions of acres of wetlands to midwestern and southern states to encourage draining and leveeing it. Water covered one-third of Louisiana, for example, and the land beneath it had little value to the federal government. Under this legislation, nearly 65 million acres passed from the public domain to private control—far more acres than the land eventually reclaimed by federal reclamation in the West. But the results were the same. Along the Mississippi River, the swampland acts contributed to the spread of plantation agriculture rather than to the family farm. In California, the San Joaquin Valley land syndicate of Miller and Lux ended up with more than eighty thousand acres of swampland, and a rival company patented thirty-four thousand acres. As the historian Paul Wallace Gates has noted, judging "by the records of the disposal of swamplands in Indiana, Illinois, Louisiana, and California the greater part of the lands went to parties who were already large investors in land which they might or might not be developing."[4] Virtually every large transfer of land in the nation's history resulted in huge monopolies and rampant speculation. The Reclamation Act was no exception.

Even more important was the link between the Homestead Act (1862) and the Reclamation Act. Gates called the Homestead Act part of an "incongruous land system." He meant "incongruous" in two ways. First, giving land away clashed with the policy of selling it—a policy that continued to be followed even after passage of the Homestead Act. Indeed, from 1862 to 1904, the federal government sold four times more land than it gave away. Second, Gates considered American land laws incongruous because Congress piled them one on top of another, and often the statutes acted at cross-purposes. Theoretically, American land laws discouraged monopoly—most restricted the amount of acreage that could be taken—but they did not operate that way in practice. Stockmen, land companies, speculators and others parlayed the Homestead Act, Timber Culture Act (1873), and the Desert Land Act (1877) into princely estates. The Reclamation Act might have broken with the past had it been part of an overall reform of the land laws. But just as the Homestead Act was incomplete by itself—part of a *system* of laws, not an act that stood on its own feet—the Reclamation Act of 1902 promised "free land," but did little to protect that promise.[5]

Paying for federal reclamation through land sales was a devil's bargain. Public land subject to irrigation was the first to sell, and the Reclamation Act gave the secretary of the interior no power to reserve tracts susceptible to irrigation from entry under earlier land laws. Therefore, the law stimulated rather than discouraged land speculation. From 1902 to 1904, the Reclamation Service set aside more than 40 million acres that fell within potential irrigation projects, much of it along the Rio Grande and the Colorado River. However, from 1898 to 1922, more than three times that amount of land was claimed for dry farming on the upper Great Plains—and much of it was irrigable. Land left the public domain so fast that by 1910 few potential irrigation projects that contained any sizable tracts of public land remained anywhere on the Great Plains. In October 1903, Theodore Roosevelt created a Public Lands Commission to revise the land laws, partly in the hope of protecting irrigable acreage for the Reclamation Service. But under heavy pressure from Republican senators in the Rocky Mountains and Great Plains, Roosevelt ultimately turned his back on reforming the land laws, making it even more difficult for the Reclamation Act to accomplish its objectives. In the early 1930s, the federal government irrigated fewer than 3 million acres, but private individuals, water companies, and irrigation districts watered many times that amount from land that had been part of the public domain in the late 1890s.[6]

The Homestead Act taught another lesson ignored by the Reclamation Service. When Congress adopted the principle of "free land," it tacitly recognized that most resources within the public domain had little or no intrinsic value. Conquest and labor, not paper titles, created value. In principle, therefore, the Homestead Act resembled the policy of "free mining," which, beginning with the California gold rush, gave away gold or silver extracted from the public domain to those with the skill and energy to take it. Miners paid nothing for the privilege of extracting precious metals, in part because the central government lacked a bureaucracy large enough to administer law on the frontier, but also because Americans deeply believed that work created wealth: natural resources should belong to those who put them to use. That was all the more true because putting land into cultivation symbolized the advance of civilization and the retreat of wilderness.

The nineteenth-century legacy can be seen in many other parts of the federal reclamation program. In the nineteenth as well as the early twentieth centuries, it was axiomatic that the majority of the first settlers to occupy "virgin land" would not become permanent residents. Shock troops of the frontier, some failed so that others could later succeed. Frederick H. Newell and his lieutenants in the Reclamation Service regarded the agricultural settlement of the West as a Darwinian struggle: pioneering was a process that sorted out the fit and the unfit. In 1923, a prominent official in the Reclamation Service recounted that the region around Billings, Montana, which he claimed "has been one of the most successful sections in the West," had gone through "at least three cycles in the past forty years, the first settlers [most of whom came from cities] at twelve or thirteen years had fully 90% gone, the next cycle about the same, and we now have the third cycle, which looks permanent, they are mostly foreigners, the American seems to be continually on the move." More alarming still, by the end of the 1920s tenants cultivated one-third of all farms within federal irrigation projects. By the 1920s, the only hope of breaking the speculative cycle was for the federal government to purchase all the privately held land within existing and proposed government projects. Every attempt to regulate the price of private land within the projects failed.[7]

Another link to the past was the competition *within* the West for federal aid. In 1902, it seemed inconceivable that the demand for arable land would ever abate.[8] The population of the United States grew by 30 percent in the 1870s, 26 percent in the 1880s, 21 percent in the 1890s, and another 21 percent in the first decade of the twentieth century.[9] The Reclamation Service assumed that this increase would continue and would require a substantial increase in cultivated land. American agriculture had always been characterized by the exchange of poor, exhausted land for virgin soil. It was natural to conclude that eventually all the West's irrigable land would be settled and that its first irrigation projects would fill up quickly, over the span of no more than a few years. The Reclamation Service did not plan for settlement over decades. Therefore, it was forced to saddle the early settlers on many projects with far higher construction costs, and higher maintenance and operation charges, than its original estimates.

In 1902 the Reclamation Service could not anticipate most of the problems it would soon face. In the late 1890s, many who favored federal reclamation simply wanted the federal government to build dams and canals, leaving the states to dole out water. At that time, most westerners conceived of federal reclamation as a program to aid established farmers and to stimulate private enterprise. The federal government would build reservoirs to supplement, extend, and consolidate the water supply of existing systems. Some new land would be reclaimed, but most of it would be within established agricultural districts. This plan had limited appeal in Congress. Therefore, the salesmen of federal reclamation pulled out all the stops in an appeal to the family farm, a return to the land, and a restoration of the ideals of rural America. They broadened the program to include virgin public land. This was a fateful step. Taking it meant that the government would have to build not just reservoirs, but new main canals as well. Setting up new farms proved far more expensive than aiding established farmers.

Congress refused to give the Reclamation Service authority to screen potential settlers, and many of those settlers were poor. Not surprisingly, the first wave demanded that the government construct the lateral canals that led to their land, as well as the main canals. And eventually, they demanded that the Reclamation Service build drainage ditches to prevent the buildup of alkali, and that it maintain and operate the hydraulic systems. By 1910, federal reclamation was a far more comprehensive engineering program than had been conceived a decade earlier, and the per-acre cost of reclamation ran far higher than engineers in the Reclamation Service had anticipated. Farmers and would-be farmers expected the federal government to build much higher quality, longer-lasting irrigation works than private enterprise, but the service had no choice but to cut corners where it could. In 1937, John C. Page, the commissioner of reclamation, admitted, "Construction under the early [1902] law was done as cheaply as possible, expecting that when the investment was retired local funds could rebuild and replace the short-lived structures without hardship. Wooden headgates, culverts, bridges, etc., were installed instead of concrete and steel as is now the practice."[10]

Not only did farmers expect the government to do more than the Reclamation Service anticipated doing in 1902, but the service's method of constructing projects invited cost overruns. Private companies did most of the work under contract. In 1900 or 1901, the proponents of federal reclamation assumed that projects would be built all at once, rather than in stages, and they based cost predictions on the deflationary period of the 1890s. But in the early years of the twentieth century, inflation drove up the cost of construction, and the limited amount of money in the reclamation fund, the need to spread that money as broadly as possible, and the slow pace of settlement quickly convinced the Reclamation Service to scale back its original plans. It decided to build projects in phases, using separate contracts. At a time of rapidly increasing construction costs, that made it impossible to charge farmers who settled on an addition to an original project the same price for construction as those who took up land on the original project. This was one of many ways that the Reclamation Service created classes of settlers and sowed disunity within its projects. Was it equitable for someone who settled land within a project five or ten years after it opened to pay 50 percent more in construction charges—often to farm land that had far less agricultural potential?

Almost from the beginning of its life, the Reclamation Service faced chronic money shortages. The Warren Act of 1911 provided for the sale of surplus government water, stimulating private irrigation projects. And in many ways the Boulder Dam Act simply continued the principle established in 1911: that the Reclamation Bureau should create as large a service area as possible and seek to blend levels of government, as well as public and private institutions. The Reclamation Service encouraged the states to grant land or money to the federal government and also encouraged the formation of irrigation districts that would raise money by bonding the land. Congress left the agency little choice but to seek a hybrid program. The central government had no power to tax the land it reclaimed, and, given their police powers, the states could ensure the repayment of loans to farmers. The cooperative road-building program launched by the U.S. Department of Agriculture in the second decade of the twentieth century served as the immediate inspiration for many of these schemes. But the roots of federal-state cooperation in the construction and administration of public works stretched far back into the nineteenth century. The Chesapeake and Ohio Canal included stock subscriptions from Maryland, Virginia, and the communities of Georgetown, Alexandria, and Washington, as well as the federal government. The Chesapeake and Delaware Canal was also a mixed enterprise, and the federal government bought two hundred thousand dollars in stock in the Dismal Canal Company. River and harbor legislation also set a precedent for cooperation. By the early years of the twentieth century, local communities began contributing to "river improvement" work, following the lead of Dallas, Texas. For example, the Rivers and Harbors Act of 1905 required that city to spend $66,000 on improving the Trinity River before the federal appropriation of $161,300 could be used.[11]

The Reclamation Act of 1902 encouraged states to form new institutions to manage water. Moreover, western politicians assumed that their states would be more likely to receive federal aid if they were represented by engineers who spoke the language of the Reclamation Service and could take the lead in settling water rights disputes, and Nevada, Utah, Idaho, Montana, and South Dakota created state engineering offices in direct response to passage of the Reclamation Act. There was also a considerable interchange of personnel between state engineering offices and the Reclamation Bureau, which helped to link the two levels of government. As always, however, the western states were torn between their desire for federal aid and their desire to maintain local control over water rights. By the middle of the 1920s, California, Colorado, Oregon, North and South Carolina, and Washington had created land settlement boards with the power to acquire state, school, or other undeveloped lands and render the land habitable and productive. California established two irrigation communities—at Durham and Delhi—and Washington State established one near Hanford. Some westerners saw this legislation as a prelude to the states contracting with the Reclamation Bureau to construct irrigation projects administered by land settlement companies or irrigation districts. The states were no less interested in cooperative agricultural schemes than the Reclamation Bureau, but constitutional prohibitions against debt, and the western states' expectation that they were *entitled* to direct federal aid to promote agriculture, limited cooperation.[12]

The Lane-Mondell soldier settlement bill of 1919–20 was the first legislation to push for cooperation along lines popularized by the Reclamation

Bureau during the 1920s. States interested in reclaiming wet or dry land could either donate unimproved acreage to the federal government or assume at least 25 percent of the financial burden of drainage or irrigation. Under this scheme, the Reclamation Bureau would have become purely a construction agency; the states would have assumed the responsibility for screening applicants and administering the completed projects. The bureau came closest to achieving this goal during the 1920s, when it conducted cooperative surveys in several southern states.

Nevertheless, all attempts to centralize power in the name of planning failed. During the 1920s and 1930s, conservationists disagreed over the best method to achieve comprehensive management of water in the West. Some, including Harold Ickes, favored the creation of a Department of Natural Resources to eliminate jurisdictional squabbles between the Department of Interior, Department of Agriculture, and Department of War. Others, like Senator George Norris of Nebraska, favored relatively autonomous river-basin authorities—an option strenuously opposed by the federal bureaucracies. A third group, which included Herbert Hoover, nominally supported river-basin management, but by established state and federal bureaucracies rather than autonomous units of government. Still others hoped that the National Resources Committee, created early in the New Deal, would take the lead in planning, leaving the established agencies to implement its plans. Franklin D. Roosevelt created many water planning committees, including the Water Resources Committee and the Great Plains Drought Committee, but they did little to direct or even coordinate federal water policies. The leaders of established departments of government often dominated such committees—as, for example, Ickes headed the National Resources Committee in 1937—making them just as vulnerable to turf wars as the cabinet departments. The agencies staffed by "independent experts" were ignored, because they had no turf at all.

In 1902, the Reclamation Service's leaders knew little about desert soils, community planning, or the pitfalls of farming in the West. Nor did they anticipate how rapidly the expectations of farmers would change in the early decades of the twentieth century. With the memory of the joblessness and homelessness of the depression of the 1890s fresh, the Reclamation Service saw subsistence as the basic goal of its projects, not maximum profits. Yet only a few years after the federal reclamation program had begun, Senator Henry Hansbrough of North Dakota remarked: "Forty or fifty years ago a settler would take 160 acres of land, and about all he wanted was a comfortable log house, a good coon dog, and a squirrel rifle, and he was willing to stay there five or any number of years before securing title. But . . . times have changed. . . . The man who goes upon the public domain to-day wants a white frame house and a big red barn, four horses and a gang plow. That is the difference."[13]

If American farmers appeared stubbornly independent, they gradually became slaves of market agriculture and the new consumer culture. By the 1930s, family gardens, home-cured meats, and homespun clothes had become far less common than in 1900. Now, the farm table was supplied from all parts of the nation, and rural families yearned for cars, electric lights, radios and other appliances, and movies. The new consumer goods drove up the cost of living for farm families, who faced additional expenses ranging from machinery to the higher taxes required to pay for paved roads, modern school buildings, and year-round schools. The western farmers who watered their land after 1900 could not practice subsistence agriculture even if they wanted to; irrigation required substantial capital just to meet expenses.

As the historian Hal Barron has shown, the process of "modernizing" the countryside was complicated. Farm folk both resisted and embraced new products, fashions, and entertainment. For example, the most popular single item sold by Montgomery Ward's mail-order company was the Singer sewing machine. It symbolized the popularity of factory-made clothing and fashions, even in rural America. But by keeping production at home, rural women economized and maintained traditional "homespun" ways. They picked and chose among available clothing patterns, maintaining the illusion of self-sufficiency. Much the same was true of the automobile. Ford first marketed the Model T to rural customers for business, not pleasure. "Some advertisers," according to Barron, "argued that the Ford automobile—as distinguished from higher priced luxury models more attractive to urban residents—was the ultimate farm machine whose motor could be used to run all sorts of other machinery, such as pumps. Or, it could be justified as cheaper to maintain than horses." And though the automobile often gave rural residents access to large cities, at first farmers used their cars to travel among rural towns rather than to big cities. They shopped at home, reducing their dependence on mail-order businesses. In short, the Model T, like the sewing machine, fit into the existing culture of the countryside. Similarly, when radio first appeared, it was seen as congenial to rural values. Barron observed that "the rural culture instituted on the airwaves paradoxically celebrated old-fashioned virtues of localism and neighborliness even as it rendered the specific communities more marginal culturally. . . . Much of the integration of the northern countryside into the consumer culture of the 1920s, then, fostered a hybrid rural version of that culture rather than a replication of more mainstream patterns." Initially, companies such as Westinghouse and General Electric used the radio mainly to sell radios. In the 1920s, magazines were a much more potent form of advertising.[14]

That said, the forces of capitalism were relentless and inexorable, and they had the strongest impact on those who invested the most in their farms—including irrigation farmers. Just as national magazines advertised appliances such as washing machines, phonographs, radios, and electric stoves, farm journals hawked the latest agricultural implements, including windmills, weeders, threshers, harvesters, grain binders, graders, milking machines, and a wide variety of tractors. As crop prices soared during World War I, profits seemed limitless. Farm families that were frugal and conservative when they shopped for clothing, food, furniture, and other household items threw caution to the wind in working the land. Jonathan Raban has observed:

> When it came to farm machinery, the same people spent like kings. The banks egged them on. The advertising copywriters told the prospective customer that he was not really buying the new tractor but saving by its purchase. It was an investment, that cherished adman's word. Its percentage yield would be incalculably higher than the $5\frac{1}{2}$ per cent needed to service the loan. The extension lecturers drove from schoolhouse to schoolhouse, counseling the homesteaders to mechanize and prosper. Government, industry and finance worked in consort to persuade people that ownership of a Bates Steel Mule or a Lauson Full Jewel was itself a symbol of their thriftiness, and perfectly in keeping with the patched sleeve and turned shirt-collar.[15]

In 1916, the federal government contributed to rural debt when it passed the Federal Farm Loan Act, which permitted farm land banks to offer forty-year loans to farmers at 6 percent interest. Once in debt, of course, it was hard to get out. The farmer who bought a gasoline-powered tractor soon learned that all manner of new machines could be hitched to it: "Once you started to mechanize, you were in for the long haul, coupling expensive gizmo to expensive gizmo, until the train of farm machinery stretched far over the foreseeable horizon."[16]

Put simply, by the 1930s much of the countryside had become tributary to the factory and the city, not the realm of autonomous family farms envisioned by proponents of the Reclamation Act in 1902. One-third of the American population lived on farms in 1900, but only one-fifth did so in 1940. Farmers remained individualistic in spirit, but by the Great Depression debt was a chronic feature of agriculture in all parts of the nation. Luxury became necessity, and the day of the pioneer was gone. Little wonder that it became more and more difficult for the Reclamation Bureau to find men and women with the necessary "grit" to become farmers. Even with the enormous subsidy from hydroelectric power and the sale of water to cities promised by high dams, few potential farmers were willing to gamble their modest life savings, and face years of hard labor and privation, before receiving any return on their investment.[17]

WATER AND AMERICAN GOVERNMENT

Historians have neglected the relationship between natural resources and the nature of American government in the early twentieth century. Intent on demonstrating that the existing "hydraulic empire" cannot be sustained, the two best-known histories of water in the West—Marc Reisner's *Cadillac Desert* and Donald Worster's *Rivers of Empire*—focus on present-day concerns that are undeniably important, including the vast environmental damage created by high dams, the immense amount of money the federal government has wasted on unnecessary water projects, and the injustice of the huge subsidies provided to agribusiness.[18] Westerners, Reisner and Worster predict, will pay for their arrogance and conceit. Reisner considers the American West as a "beachhead." "And if history is any guide," he concludes, "the odds that we can sustain it would have to be regarded as low." The conquest of the West has been an illusion. The deserts will return, as they have in other parts of the world where civilization depended on moving large quantities of water from one place to another.[19]

Both these studies are "declensionist," and in both the decline begins with the Reclamation Act of 1902, which Reisner calls the "first and most durable example of the modern welfare state." Indeed, he insists that water projects became a vital part of American politics. "To a degree that is impossible for most people to fathom," he observes, "water projects are the grease that lubricates the nation's legislative machinery. Congress without water projects would be like an engine without oil; it would simply seize up." After the 1930s, logrolling allowed the Reclamation Bureau and the Army Corps of Engineers to work their combined will on the West. The two agencies competed in an open field, with the full cooperation of Congress—or, at least, their client committees in Congress. Nevertheless, if 1902 represented a turning point, Reisner pays little attention to water politics before the 1930s, or to the many constraints on the Bureau of Reclamation, Corps of Engineers, and other federal agencies, or to what water policies tell us about the American state in the "Progressive Era." At best he provides a sensational, highly oversimplified view of the political process.[20]

Rivers of Empire considers the nature of the American state much more directly than *Cadillac Desert*. It is a passionate, almost lyrical book. The marriage between government and private capital created a "Leviathan," Worster insists, a "big bruiser of a state" that served the rich and powerful rather than the common good. Government at any level represents the imperatives of capitalism, and the Reclamation Act of 1902 "put the federal government irrevocably in charge of almost all future irrigation development in the West." A seamless web of institutions and private corporations subverted popular rule. "The long-term trend in that society [the American West] . . . has been toward more and more concentration of power, allowing less and less real input from the citizenry." It was and is a region "built by state power, state expertise, state technology, and state bureaucracy." Ultimately, the West forfeited a sustainable civilization for maximum short-run profits, and the marriage of government and private capital resulted in great damage to the land

and to American democracy. Worster calls the West a "hydraulic society," linking it to empires of the ancient Middle East—all of which erroneously assumed that they could exterminate the deserts. To Worster, the state is simply an extension of the capitalist system; it has no autonomy, nor do the bureaucracies contained within it possess individual personalities.[21]

Reisner and Worster teach us much about the arrogance of American attempts to manage and control nature, but they also present a distorted view of the past. Both write history from the "top down" and understate the complexity of politics and power. The Reclamation Bureau was much weaker prior to World War II than either Reisner or Worster admits. Far from dictating water policy toward the West, the agency succeeded only where it formed partnerships with state and local governments. Federal reclamation had a greater impact on the West than the scant number of acres it irrigated directly, but until well after World War II, reclamation by mutual water companies, private water companies, irrigation districts, and other groups of water users served far more land than the federal government did. Moreover, westerners supported water projects not because they had been duped or deceived, but because those projects stimulated economic growth in what appeared to be a "capital starved" region. The "High Dam Era" ended in the 1960s and 1970s, when the public became skeptical of the value of water projects.

Samuel P. Hays remains the historian who has said the most about the relationship between natural resources and government in the early decades of the twentieth century. His brilliant and original book *Conservation and the Gospel of Efficiency*—an extension of his earlier *Response to Industrialism*—first appeared in 1959.[22] Hays's thesis has been absorbed into most subsequent histories of modern America, and few historians have questioned his view of conservation or government.

It is hardly surprising that a book as subtle and perceptive as Hays's would enjoy such influence. Hays considered industrial capitalism, and more specifically the rise of the business corporation, as essential to the evolution of the federal government. Big business begat big government. "The history of modern America is, above all, a story of the impact of industrialism on every phase of human life," he said at the beginning of *Response to Industrialism*. As with many other historians who wrote in the 1950s and 1960s, the decline of local and the rise of national institutions dominated his approach. The modern American state, in his view, grew inevitably out of weaknesses in government at the state and local levels. Industrial capitalism eroded local autonomy, but Hays was quick to concede that many American values reinforced localism and democracy rather than nationalism and efficiency. Regionalism also played a part in his story, because the West and South—locked into "a colonial economic pattern as a source of raw materials and markets for northeastern industry"—challenged the concentration of power in Washington. Politicians in both sections "lived under the shadow of a far more highly developed area, which, they felt, deliberately imposed restraints upon the economic growth of the regions." Far removed from the nation's factories, both regions had a much larger percentage of their workers in extractive industries than did the East. And as colonies of the East, both had a hard time generating the surplus capital needed to diversify their economies.[23]

Government was not simply an agent of the new industrial order, and Hays regarded bureaucratization—symbolic of the expansion of executive authority vis-à-vis Congress—as a good thing. An interdependent, modern industrial society could function only with large-scale comprehensive planning from the top down. In the aftermath of the Great Depression and World War II, and in the age of the cold war and the civil rights movement, it made sense to see the central government as more significant than those of states, counties, cities, and towns. Hays wanted to know how government became modern, and the ebb and flow of power toward and away from the center served as one measure of modernization. In addition to new executive bureaus, Theodore Roosevelt created a series of commissions independent of Congress, including the Country Life Commission, the National Conservation Commission, and the Inland Waterways Commission. Therefore, conservation played a large part in "the transformation of a decentralized, nontechnical, loosely organized society, where waste and inefficiency ran rampant, into a highly organized, technical, and centrally planned and directed social organization which could meet a complex world with efficiency and purpose."[24]

Hays did not regard conservation as inherently antibusiness or as a popular revolt against the monopolization of the nation's natural resources by rapidly expanding corporations. He broke with the "Progressive History" that prevailed in the 1930s to 1950s, an interpretation of the American past as a persistent struggle between "the people" and "the interests," the haves and the have nots, the exploited and the exploiters. The conservation movement, the pre-Hays interpretation argued, promoted the greatest good for the greatest number. It was, therefore, a chapter in the evolution of American democracy. Hays, however, shifted the discussion from democracy to bureaucracy by focusing on the "organizational revolution"—the professionalization of science and the consequent centralization of power in Washington.[25] To him, conservation was rational planning, the coordination of a multitude of single-purpose policies and competing resource uses.

Theodore Roosevelt wanted to transform, not just expand, government, and such bureaus as the Reclamation Service and the Forest Service articulated his vision of a unified, planned society. The Inland Waterways Commission, first proposed in 1907, substituted for the multitude of federal agencies interested in water an impartial body independent of Congress and immune to the tug-of-war of sectional interests. Rivers would be developed systematically and consistently, and flood control, irrigation, navigation, and hydroelectric power would be coordinated. The idea of "multiple use"—one resource with many uses—dated to the Progressive Era, even though most historians before Hays saw that idea as the product of the High Dam Era and the 1930s. By 1907, Hays argued, the Reclamation Bureau, Forest Service, and U.S. Geological Survey had accepted the notion that every stream was a unit from source to mouth. The Army Corps of Engineers, however, cast its fate with Congress, which represented local interests and preferred to conduct river and harbor work in a piecemeal fashion. The corps, therefore, was the federal agency most responsible for the failure of comprehensive river-basin planning.

The failure of planning, according to Hays, came as much from local politics as from interagency rivalries at the national level. Federal conservation policies challenged the corruption and localism of nineteenth-century politics as well as the haphazard use of natural resources. Nevertheless, the new duties of government encouraged the growth of pressure groups—such as the National Irrigation Association, the National Irrigation Congress, and the Lakes-to-the-Gulf-Waterways Association—which made the ethics of planning and wise use difficult, if not impossible, to implement. "A multiple-purpose water program collapsed," Hays observed in *Response to Industrialism,* "as each interest group, seeking influence and power in resource management, obtained from Congress a special program for its particular concern, be it flood control, drainage, reclamation or navigation."[26] Localism and democracy competed against efficiency and coordination. Single-purpose water policies won out because "they provided opportunities for grass-roots participation in decision-making. They enabled resource users to feel that they had some degree of control over the policies that affected them." In the end, "centralized and coordinated decisions . . . conflicted with American political institutions which drew their vitality from filling local needs. This conflict between the centralizing tendencies of effective economic organization and the interests presented problems to challenge even the wisest statesman."[27]

Conservation and the Gospel of Efficiency made enormous contributions to our understanding of government, conservation, and politics in the early twentieth century. Prior to its publication, most historians of conservation considered the creation of national forests as the most important element in the conservation program, but Hays recognized that water management had far greater impact on the national economy and American institutions. And if Hays exaggerated the differences in administrative style between new agencies such as the Reclamation Bureau and Forest Service and old ones like the General Land Office and Corps of Engineers, he was one of the first historians to discuss how interagency rivalries undermined national conservation policies. He also recognized that the West itself was deeply divided. For example, neglected parts of the region—those that had failed to secure federal water projects under the 1902 Reclamation Act—tended to favor

Francis G. Newlands's Inland Waterways plan, because it promised to pay for water projects through bond issues rather than the reclamation fund.

Yet despite its usefulness and durability, there are many flaws and holes in Hays's thesis. For example, Hays pays far more attention to "science" than to the moralism that infected the leaders of the conservation movement and pervaded conservation policies. As the historian Gordon B. Dodds pointed out decades ago, science in 1900 depended more on observation than experimentation, and much of what was taken as "scientific truth" was simply common sense or general knowledge. "[The conservationists'] commitment was to a cause, not to scientific evidence, if the evidence contravened the cause," Dodds has written. "[T]he conservationists, as Progressives were wont to do, framed their arguments in moralistic terms by stigmatizing their enemies as militarists, monopolists, traditionalists, and other opprobrious creatures."[28]

Neither "science" nor "efficiency," as we understand those terms today, did much to shape federal reclamation. Indeed, according to A. Hunter Dupree, the Reclamation Bureau was more a "construction company than a scientific organization, research playing a minimum role." Except in designing dams and canals, the bureau's leaders showed little curiosity, let alone vision.[29] Progressive Era conservationists were not so much exemplars of science as forerunners. Most of today's scientific fields resulted from the rise of scholarly foundations and the modern research university—neither of which existed in 1900 or 1910. The new branches of engineering that appeared in the late nineteenth and early twentieth centuries depended on advances in science, but some were rooted in theory and others in experiment. Engineering was just becoming a profession, and it utilized intuition and practical observation more than the laboratory science associated with the twentieth-century university, corporation, or think tank.[30]

Nor does Hays define what he means by "bureaucratization." Scientific expertise and the allegiance to a profession are but two components of bureaucracy. A strong sense of civic virtue and noblesse oblige are just as important. Bureaucratization depends not just on the jobs performed by bureaus, but on how the employees of those bureaus view themselves and their role in government. In Europe, bureaucracy meant not just efficiency, but a class of civil servants trained to see the political and moral consequences of their decisions—a self-conscious "administrative caste" that did not exist in the United States. Many prominent leaders in the Reclamation Bureau left government to take jobs with private companies or the states, and the reverse was also true. The flow of engineers in and out of government, and the blurred line between public and private realms, worked against the creation of a bureaucratic class.

Hays also overstated the differences between the new natural resource agencies tied to the executive branch and the old ones linked to Congress. His interpretation of federal water policy hinged on the multiple-use concept of water planning, which Hays claimed the Bureau of Reclamation embraced and the Corps of Engineers rejected. "The hostility of the Corps of Engineers to the Newlands [Inland Waterways Commission] Bill," he wrote, "sprang from three sources: its interest in navigation alone, its willingness to defer to Congress, and its desire for complete autonomy in administration.... While the Forest Service, the Geological Survey, and the Bureau of Reclamation considered water as a single resource with many possible functions, the Corps limited its concern to navigation."[31] Hays regarded the water commission first proposed by Newlands in 1907 as a *practical* policy alternative. But even though Frederick H. Newell served on the original commission and nominally supported the multiple-use idea, officials in the Reclamation Service never exhibited enthusiasm for the legislation. Indeed, the Reclamation Service, no less than the corps, feared government by commission. Who would dominate an Inland Waterways Commission? Would heavily populated sections of the country win greater appropriations than the arid West, where the Reclamation Service enjoyed dominance? Would the creation of such a commission prompt Congress to abolish the reclamation fund and pay for water projects through bonds? And, most important, was the idea practical? Even in 1928, only a few river basins afforded sites for huge multiple-use dams. In 1907, the technology to build those dams, and the technology to transmit electricity great distances, did not exist. Therefore, engineers who opposed multiple-use did so not because they were wedded to local interests or Congress, but because they considered the idea unworkable.

Hays argued that the Progressive Era did as much as the New Deal to shape the American state, but his approach did not pay sufficient attention to the "trigger events" of the 1890s that led to the Roosevelt conservation policies—such as the impact of the depression on the economy of the American West—or to the continuity in the size of the federal government between the late nineteenth and early twentieth centuries. The political scientist Robert Higgs rejects the argument that the need to modernize, conserve, or economize had much to do with the evolution of the national government. Wars and depressions had a greater impact, he argues, than the ideals of reformers or perceived needs to expand national power. The state grew out of crisis, not from attempts by reformers to regulate the economy, expand social welfare, redistribute income, promote efficiency, or provide comprehensive planning. Ideology served as a mediating force, but only because many reformers used war and depression as an excuse to implement preexisting ideas.[32]

Another weakness in the Hays approach is that he does not look closely enough at the Interior Department's chief rival, the Department of Agriculture. In an excellent recent study, the political scientist Daniel Carpenter compares the evolution of bureaucracy in the Post Office, Department of Agriculture, and Interior Department. Carpenter, like Hays, concludes that the bureaucratic state emerged during the late nineteenth and early twentieth centuries, not during the 1930s or after. In the early decades of the twentieth century, he argues, the USDA passed from being a distributive department that provided farmers with free seeds and information to an autonomous department dedicated to science and planning. At the end of the nineteenth century, the emergence of such agencies within the USDA as the Divisions of Forestry and the Biological Survey transformed the department into "an organizational center (perhaps *the* center) of American environmentalism. No other organization could boast such expertise in mammalogy, ornithology, and forestry, to say nothing of soil expertise, insect research, and dozens of other problems in which a growing swell of nature enthusiasts was interested." In short, the department transformed its mission from pork barrel spending to rational experimentation.[33]

By comparison, the Reclamation Service began its life with a great deal of autonomy and forfeited its ability to engage in either science or comprehensive planning. It squandered broad administrative discretion rather than expanded it. The lack of bureaucratic autonomy could be seen in the too narrow focus on the construction of hydraulic works, the failure to estimate the cost of construction, the failure to properly assess soil quality and drainage, the failure to teach desert agriculture, and the failure to engage in community planning. Above all, the Reclamation Service failed to "develop political affiliations in the West" as the USDA did. In the end, "[o]ne of the prized aims of Francis Newlands, the planning of neo-Jeffersonian communities of small farms, was abandoned by the service's leaders in favor of purely numerical program expansion: more dams, more settlers, more farms."[34]

Carpenter focuses on two paradoxes: How did the Interior Department, which counted "beneficiaries across classes, of both sexes, and in every state," as in its distribution of Civil War pensions, lose its identity as a national institution? How did a department with great formal authority in the nineteenth century become "perhaps the most politically feeble agency in American government before the New Deal," despite the Reclamation Act of 1902?[35] And second, how did the Reclamation Bureau, devoted as many of its supporters were to the rational management of humans and nature, develop such a narrow perspective on natural resource management? In discussing the emergence of the "modern American state," most political scientists and sociologists have focused on political parties, the power of localism in Congress, and clashes between geographical sections. Instead, Carpenter looks at dynamics within the departments themselves, from their administrative structures, to their leaders, to their alliances with pressure groups, to the ways they publicized their activities using newspapers and magazines. The administrative structure of the Interior Department was different from that of the Agriculture Department. "The early troubles of American reclamation," Carpenter writes, "were traceable to the Interior Department's stifling administrative structure, exacerbated by program leadership that emphasized administrative isolation and extreme centralization. Among these failures, three were most critical: (1) the overcommitment of service resources, (2) massive cost overruns, and (3) the systematic neglect of planning for sustainable agriculture." Decisions on federal reclamation had to "gain approval from several (if not five or more) administrative checkpoints in the Secretary's Office."[36] Equally important, "In the western areas into which officials of the Interior Department eagerly charged with abundant funds lay a political vacuum, without any networks that the department might have mobilized into action around the 1902 act. The department attempted to create a clientele basis when it fostered water users' associations, but its success in nurturing these groups was limited."[37]

The most significant structural flaw in the Interior Department was not that it was the "Great Miscellany" but that "[t]he twelve divisions of the Secretary's Office closely scrutinized the [Reclamation] service. All service decisions involving legal issues (even tangentially) required review and approval by the department's assistant attorney general. All operations requiring expenditure required approval by the Finance Division. The Publications Division reviewed at length all of the service's scientific studies requiring publication. Most critically, the divisions conducted these reviews *before* the secretary could weigh in on any decision. The only way for the service's directors to speed up administrative reviews was to lobby the secretary personally, a tactic used ever more frequently after 1905. Because the secretary's schedule was constrained, however, lobbying was an unreliable strategy. On a daily basis, the divisions ruled the Reclamation Service." For example, the Reclamation Bureau and the General Land Office "could communicate to the secretary only through the Lands and Railroads Division."[38]

Carpenter concludes his discussion of federal reclamation with a counterfactual scenario:

Had the [Reclamation] service nursed the reclamation fund through a selective choice of projects, it surely would not have exhausted its funds so quickly, and it might have been able to survive early project failures, in part by highlighting and building on a few early successes. Had the service developed lasting and stable political ties to water users' associations and professional groups, it would have been able to defend itself against congressional and executive-branch critics more effectively after 1907. The most fascinating counterfactual scenario comes when we ask how reclamation would have evolved had the Interior Department looked more like the USDA. Had the service been led by the USDA's Ellwood *[sic]* Mead or a similar official with broad affiliations in Progressive society, and had it retained a corps of officials capable of developing legislative and partisan trust in the service and with broad support outside the department, then political attacks on the service would have been much more costly for politicians to launch. Indeed, the promise of the reclamation program was larger than even these separate counterfactuals will allow. With careful project selection, incremental development, stronger ties to water users' associations, stable and knowledgeable personnel, and diverse network support, the Interior Department would probably have housed in its Reclamation Service the most autonomous bureau in the federal government."[39]

This is a challenging thesis, but it rests on the assumption that properly administered, the federal reclamation program might have succeeded. Given the grandiose expectations of those who supported federal reclamation in 1902, and given the changing nature of agriculture and American society in the early decades of the twentieth century, that assumption is highly questionable. More likely, the agencies within USDA succeeded because they had more limited objectives than the Reclamation Bureau. Carpenter identifies many of the flaws in federal reclamation, particularly the inability of the Reclamation Bureau to build local support for its public works until the "High Dam Era" of the 1930s and after. Yet he neglects or denies the importance of many other forces that constrained the Reclamation Service, particularly the actions of Congress, legal obstacles, and weaknesses in the 1902 law itself. Moreover, the correspondence of leaders of the bureau reveals little impatience with the administrative structure of the Interior Department. Indeed, the Ballinger-Pinchot controversy grew in part from the fact that during the presidency of Theodore Roosevelt the leaders of the Reclamation Service became accustomed to carrying their concerns directly to the secretary, or even to the president. Reclamation Service officials thought that Congress, the courts, and individual secretaries of the interior—not the structure or organization of the department itself—imposed the most important limitations on their authority. Indeed, until the 1930s the most common complaint of secretaries of the interior was that the Reclamation Bureau acted independently of the secretary, considered itself beyond administrative accountability, and "cooked" statistics to improve its image.

Carpenter is one of many perceptive political scientists, sociologists, and anthropologists who have studied the American state in the decades since Hays published *Conservation and the Gospel of Efficiency*. Most have focused on the origins of the modern American welfare state and on centralized state bureaucracies and social welfare programs such as social security and medicare, not on natural-resource programs. A more serious bias involves the use of European nations as a bellwether against which to compare the United States. That is, the urban-industrial state is taken as a given, as a norm toward which all states aspire. Because European states antedated the United States, and assumed social welfare responsibilities before the 1930s, the fundamental question becomes, Why was the United States so slow to mimic European institutions and programs? This study suggests that the sheer size of the United States, its great population "imbalance," and the existence of a huge body of public land did as much to shape American government as welfare functions did. Disposing of the public domain, keeping the nation's largest rivers open to navigation, and instituting federal reclamation all helped set the United States apart from Europe.[40]

This book reinforces the simple truth that studied from the top down or bottom up, government is a series of interlocking institutions and a process of negotiation, not just a set of formal policies. Students of federal conservation have generally argued that the expansion of state and federal control over natural resources resulted in a loss of local control.[41] Yet the untold story of the twentieth century is the proliferation of special districts and their relationship to county, state, and federal institutions of government. These include housing authorities, port authorities, municipal utility districts, flood control agencies, and a multitude of water districts. Special districts tax, float bonds, and provide essential public services. The number of municipalities in the United States increased only modestly from World War II to the end of the 1980s, and the number of counties and townships actually decreased. Special districts more than tripled, however, and many pertained to natural resources, particularly flood control and water districts. Much remains to be done to show the interaction of planning and power at different levels of government, and the intersection of public and private realms of authority.[42] In a recent dissertation on flood control, the sociologist Karen Marie O'Neill suggests that the state's capacity to administer land and water is different from its efforts to manage finance, industry, and social welfare. The state is not just a central bureaucracy, O'Neill points out, but also the interaction of state officials "with the different social groups associated with each activity." The central government can be understood only in relation to the state and local institutions it spawns. In O'Neill's case, the history of levee and flood control districts, and the interaction of federal, state, and local land and water policies, suggests a seamless, unified government far more active than historians have suggested in the past. Historians would do well to follow her lead.[43]

A few words by way of conclusion. This book considers the failure of American government to live up to the ideals that animated the boldest peacetime program undertaken in the twentieth century.[44] As in so many other areas of early-twentieth-century "reform," federal reclamation now seems more conservative and less idealistic than it appeared to historians in the 1940s, 1950s, or 1960s. Obviously, it failed to accomplish its original objectives. It did not restore the family farm; it did not put "surplus men on surplus land"; it did not make the West's population less migratory; it did not reduce land speculation; and it did not create a more virtuous society. It did far more to support the status quo than to reform rural institutions, and far more to aid the large landowner than the small. In the first three decades of this century, conservationists claimed to look at natural resources as interrelated rather than separate. But the files of the Reclamation Bureau show far greater interest in engineering and bare-knuckle politics than in the relationship of water to other natural resources, or science, or the shape of rural society. The refusal of the Reclamation Service to test desert soils before constructing water projects, and its chronic problems with drainage, exemplify its narrow vision and its fear of admitting mistakes or giving Congress an excuse to assign its responsibilities to another agency. It spent far more time protecting its turf than studying the composition of western soils. Day-to-day concerns, not high ideals, animated the leaders of the Reclamation Bureau.

Furthermore, by most standards, the accomplishments of federal reclamation from 1902 to 1935 were modest. Irrigation expanded little outside the seventeen western states, and its growth was inconsistent within the West. The region's irrigated land increased from 7.5 million acres in 1899, to 14 million in 1909, to 18.6 million in 1919, and then barely grew to 18.9 million acres in 1929. California and Colorado, the two leading irrigation states, contained more than 40 percent of that acreage. The annual average expenditure for federal reclamation was $52 million a year from 1933 to 1940, as opposed to an average of less than $9 million from 1902 to 1933, but there was very little increase in the West's irrigated land from 1920 to 1940.[45] Throughout the first half of the twentieth century, irrigation aided ranching more than farming. In 1950, more than 75 percent of the West's 25 million irrigated acres were in pasture. Of the remaining 25 percent, alfalfa raised for hay covered 3.4 million acres; cotton 2.4 million acres; rice 1.8 million acres; and orchards, vineyards, and planted nut trees a scant 1.6 million acres. Put another way, by the middle of the twentieth century, cash receipts from stock sales exceeded those from crops in eight of the seventeen western states. Overall, livestock returned 90 percent of the value of all crops.[46]

From 1900 to 1930, the expansion of private reclamation easily outpaced government reclamation, although separating the two is not always easy. In 1932, projects that had been launched by individuals, partnerships, mutual water companies, irrigation districts, and other groups of farmers still constituted the vast majority of the nation's more than seventy-five thousand irrigation projects. The federal government operated only thirty, which covered less than 10 percent of the irrigated land in the western United States and less than 1 percent of all land cropped in the United States. Expenditures for private reclamation ran many times those spent on federal reclamation, and they increased at a much faster rate than those of the federal government. As late as 1950, the federal government served less than 25 percent of the region's irrigated land.[47] Nevertheless, because many irrigation districts bought water from the federal government, the influence of federal reclamation was great. In 1950, federal reclamation served as many acres of land outside federal projects as within. Long before the Boulder Dam Act, federal reclamation had become an adjunct to private enterprise. It subsidized private as well as public projects.[48]

Any plan as large and ambiguous as federal reclamation, particularly one that benefited the least populated part of the nation, could never live up to expectations. Nevertheless, my story is not solely one of failure and disappointment. Federal reclamation helped shatter the idea of the "great American desert" once and for all. In so doing, it also destroyed the notion that the West would forever remain one large pasture punctuated by scattered mines, or simply a storehouse of raw materials, or a refuge or dumping ground for Native Americans, criminals, scoundrels, and the victims of respiratory diseases. Federal reclamation also provided direct economic benefits to the region. In 1929 alone, the crops produced on government projects returned more than the entire cost of constructing all the dams and canals built since 1902.[49] Finally, federal reclamation contributed to the settlement of Phoenix, Salt Lake City, and Los Angeles, as well as dozens of smaller communities such as Rupert and Twin Falls. Ultimately, the urban West would rely on water from federal projects as much as the rural West.

To assess success or failure, of course, we must assume that the Reclamation Bureau might, under ideal circumstances, have produced a significantly different West and that a wholesale remodeling of society would have been a good thing. It is instructive, therefore, to look beyond western Europe to colonizing, authoritarian regimes whose growth and legitimacy depended upon asserting control over natural resources. The political scientist James C. Scott has examined both urban and rural planned settlement schemes in Russia, Brazil, Tanzania, and Third World countries. He demonstrates that ambitious state-directed settlement schemes rarely work. Unlike political scientists concerned with social welfare programs, Scott argues that the modern authoritarian state is built on natural-resource policies that attempt to achieve "legibility and simplification"—that is, to reduce complicated natural phenomena to statistics that can be compiled and maintained by modern state bureaucracies in an effort to consolidate power and produce an orderly, disciplined society. Such states are obsessed with land and water planning, not just in the name of efficiency but to justify their existence and maintain control over their subjects.

In the first three decades of the twentieth century, the American West represented the antithesis of planned societies in other parts of the world. The United States government attempted to build a modern economy on the foundation of the family farm, which, given its autonomy, clashed with the ideal of increasing state control over natural resources. In Russia, the state abolished the small farm in favor of collectivization at the same time that the United States moved in an opposite direction. Nevertheless, the American experience with planned settlement was not completely different from that of authoritarian regimes. Theodore Roosevelt understood only too well that expanding presidential power depended on enlarging executive management of natural resources—as the creation of national parks and forests suggests. Much of the formal state apparatus created in the early decades of the twentieth century derived from natural-resource management. The United States was also susceptible to what Scott calls "high modernist ideology," or "self-confidence about scientific and technical progress." In the United States as elsewhere, the basic goal of science was to simplify and rationalize nature, not to protect it. No less than in Russia, social reformers in the United States assumed that they could remake society and that only they were qualified to inform and direct that process. Water policy on Indian reservations went far beyond the policies toward non–Native Americans. There we see an American state much closer to the oppressive regimes Scott discusses—a state that used coercive power to implement extensive plans to transform the lives of Indians that did far more harm than good. What Scott says about authoritarian leaders also applies to the many American conservationists: they "regarded themselves as far smarter and farseeing than they really were and, at the same time, regarded their subjects as far more stupid and incompetent that *they* really were."[50]

Nevertheless, the United States was also different, not just because it had a larger "private sphere of activity in which the state and its agencies may not legitimately interfere," thus preventing the state from achieving a monopoly of "economic sovereignty," but also because it provided institutions through which opposition to a planned society could be marshaled. Unlike Russia, where war, revolution, and economic collapse undermined democratic institutions and rendered the populace more receptive to authoritarian designs, American institutions were remarkably stable through time. War and revolution had far less impact on the United States than on European nations. American federalism, often seen as an impediment to planning and the ally of wastefulness, served as a firewall to protect the nation from potentially dangerous schemes doomed to fail. Scott's book reminds us that the flexible, adaptable, and decentralized institutions that federalism provides have great advantages over the alternative—at least as measured by authoritarian regimes. As Scott puts it, "I am . . . making a case against an imperial or hegemonic planning mentality that excludes the necessary role of local knowledge and know-how." No central government completely represents the ideals, values, and aspirations of the people it serves, but the government of the United States has done better than most. Perhaps we should be grateful that the grandest scheme for social planning ever conceived in the United States, federal reclamation, did not, and could not, live up to expectations.[51]

ARCHIVAL ABBREVIATIONS

The following archival records are in the Washington, D.C., area, at either the main National Archives in downtown Washington or in nearby College Park, Maryland. Regular shuttle bus service connects these two government repositories. The only exception is Records Group 115, Records of the Bureau of Reclamation, housed at the Federal Records Center, Denver, Colorado.

RG 8	Records Group 8:	Records of the Bureau of Agricultural Engineering; Office of Experiment Stations, General Correspondence, 1898–1912
RG 16	Records Group 16:	Records of the Department of Agriculture
RG 51	Records Group 51:	Records of the Bureau of Efficiency
RG 48	Records Group 48:	Records of the Office of the Secretary of the Interior
RG 49	Records Group 49:	Records of the General Land Office
RG 57	Records Group 57:	Records of the United States Geological Survey
RG 60	Records Group 60:	Records of the Department of Justice
RG 75	Records Group 75:	Records of the Bureau of Indian Affairs
RG 115	Records Group 115:	Records of the Bureau of Reclamation

NOTES

PREFACE

1. Donald J. Pisani, *To Reclaim a Divided West: Water, Law, and Public Policy, 1848–1902* (Albuquerque: University of New Mexico Press, 1992).
2. Most books that discuss water policy from 1902 to 1935 have done so as part of the larger Progressive Era "conservation movement." These include Samuel P. Hays, *Conservation and the Gospel of Efficiency: The Progressive Conservation Movement, 1890–1920* (Cambridge: Harvard University Press, 1959); Elmo Richardson, *The Politics of Conservation: Crusades and Controversies, 1897–1913* (Berkeley: University of California Press, 1962); and Donald C. Swain, *Federal Conservation Policy, 1921–1933* (Berkeley: University of California Press, 1963). Monographs published in the 1950s and 1960s generally looked at federal water policy in a positive light, but more recent surveys of water in the American West go to the opposite extreme. See, for example, Donald Worster, *Rivers of Empire: Water, Aridity, and the Growth of the American West* (New York: Pantheon Books, 1985), and Marc Reisner, *Cadillac Desert: The American West and Its Disappearing Water* (New York: Viking, 1986). Full-length histories of the Bureau of Reclamation are uncritical—indeed, laudatory. These include William Warne, *The Bureau of Reclamation* (New York: Praeger, 1973), and Michael Robinson, *Water for the West: The Bureau of Reclamation, 1902–1977* (Chicago: American Public Works Association, 1979). However, many scholars, environmental organizations, and public interest groups have produced notable critiques of the bureau. See, for example, Doris Ostrander Dawdy, *Congress in Its Wisdom: The Bureau of Reclamation and the Public Interest* (Boulder, Colo.: Westview Press, 1989), and Richard L. Berkman, *Damming the West: Ralph Nader's Study Group Report on the Bureau of Reclamation* (New York: Grossman Publishers, 1973). Of course, many other authors have produced excellent books and articles that look at state and local water policies. Their work is cited throughout my notes.
3. For the arguments offered in support of irrigating the deserts of the West, see Pisani, *To Reclaim a Divided West*, 273–325.

299

300 NOTES TO PAGES XII-3

4. The quotation from Bryan's speech is as reprinted in Henry Steele Commager, ed., *Documents of American History* (New York: Appleton-Century-Crofts, Inc., 1958), 177.

5. John A. Widtsoe, *Success on Irrigation Projects* (New York: John Wiley and Sons, 1928), 138.

6. Robert Higgs, *Crisis and Leviathan: Critical Episodes in the Growth of American Government* (New York: Oxford University Press, 1987), 77–105. On the impact of the depression, also see David Thelen, "Social Tensions and the Origins of Progressivism," *Journal of American History* 56 (September 1969): 323–41, and his book *The New Citizenship: Origins of Progressivism in Wisconsin, 1885–1900* (Columbia: University of Missouri Press, 1972), as well as David M. Wrobel, *The End of American Exceptionalism: Frontier Anxiety from the Old West to the New Deal* (Lawrence: University Press of Kansas, 1993), 29–41.

7. Pisani, *To Reclaim a Divided West,* 225–72.

8. Ibid., 273–97. By 1896, Warren believed that ceding all or part of the arid lands to the states would not encourage private capital to build dams and canals. Instead, it would permit the federal government to escape its responsibility to develop the American West. In addition, the promoters and executives of land grant railroads opposed cession because they feared that it would be more difficult to shape policies favorable to their interests in the multitude of state legislatures rather than in Congress. They owned millions of acres that they hoped would soar in value if Congress adopted a federal irrigation program.

9. Pisani, *To Reclaim a Divided West,* 275–85.

10. *Engineering News* 70 (November 13, 1913): 987.

CHAPTER 1. SAVING LOST LIVES

1. The epigraph comes from *The Works of Theodore Roosevelt,* vol. 16 (New York: Charles Scribner's Sons, 1926), 133. On the genesis of the Reclamation Act, see Donald J. Pisani, *To Reclaim a Divided West: Water, Law, and Public Policy, 1848–1902* (Albuquerque: University of New Mexico Press, 1992), 298–319.

2. *Forestry and Irrigation* 9 (October 1903): 475–76.

3. F. H. Newell, *Irrigation in the United States* (New York: Thomas Y. Crowell and Co., 1902), 406.

4. F. H. Newell, "The Reclamation of the West," *National Geographic* 15 (January 1904): 15. Borah's remark is from the *Congressional Record,* 61st Cong., 2d sess., Senate, February 17, 1910: 2015.

5. Frederick H. Newell, *Water Resources: Present and Future Uses* (New Haven: Yale University Press, 1920), 192; Ray P. Teele, *Irrigation in the United States* (New York: D. Appleton and Co., 1915), 13.

6. Newell, *Irrigation in the United States,* 53, 300.

7. *Fourteenth Census of the United States, 1910,* vol. 7 (Washington, D.C.: GPO, 1922), 31–32; Dorothy Lampen, *Economic and Social Aspects of Federal Reclamation* (Baltimore: Johns Hopkins University Press, 1930), 57; *New York Times,* October 23, 1902, and May 27 and September 18, 1903.

8. Elwood Mead to Charles F. Manderson, December 16, 1901, RG 8, Box 1.

9. As reprinted in Brookings Institution, Institute for Government Research, *The*

U.S. Reclamation Service: Its History, Activities, and Organization (New York: D. Appleton and Co., 1919), 19.

10. Theodore Roosevelt to Ethan Allen Hitchcock, July 2, 1902, Theodore Roosevelt Papers, Library of Congress, Washington, D.C. In his *Autobiography* (New York: Charles Scribner's Sons, 1925), 388, T. R. noted: "The impatience of the Western people to see immediate results from the Reclamation Act was so great that red tape was disregarded, and the work was pushed forward at a rate previously unknown in government affairs." Yet he and the Interior Department were no less "impatient." According to Newell, T. R. took "a keen personal interest" in the details of reclamation work, including construction contracts and design details, "details which you might imagine would be left to subordinates." F. H. Newell, "The Work of the National Reclamation Service," *Official Proceedings of the Fifteenth National Irrigation Congress* (Sacramento, Calif.: News Publishing Co., 1907), 106.

11. Ethan Allen Hitchcock to Theodore Roosevelt, July 9, 1902, RG 48, Entry 195, Hitchcock Letterbooks. Also see Hitchcock to Charles D. Walcott, June 18, 1902, in the same collection, and Theodore Roosevelt to the Secretary of the Interior, June 17, 1902, Theodore Roosevelt Papers, Library of Congress.

12. *Report of the Secretary of the Interior, 1904* (Washington, D.C.: GPO, 1904), 95–96; *National Geographic* 13 (October 1902): 387, and 14 (April 1903): 165; *Forestry and Irrigation* 9 (April 1903): 179; *Chicago Record-Herald,* March 31, 1903; F. H. Newell to Charles D. Walcott, February 2, 1903, RG 115, General Administrative Records, 1902–1919, Box 100, "(131): Corres. re Administration: Policies and Organization thru 1905." When Newell sent the list of proposed projects to A. P. Davis, the Reclamation Service's chief engineer, the puzzled Davis—who looked at the projects mainly as experiments in engineering—responded: "In regard to the order of importance or precedence of the various projects, I am greatly interested in the list you send. There are doubtless some [political] considerations, as the attitude of the people, etc., that I do not understand so well as you." Davis had hoped to concentrate on fewer and larger projects in more promising locations, such as on the Colorado and Sacramento Rivers. See A. P. Davis to F. H. Newell, November 5, 1902, in "(131): Corres. re Administration: Policies and Organization thru 1905."

13. Brookings Institution, *U.S. Reclamation Service,* 24–25. F. H. Newell described the major works constructed by the Reclamation Service in *Water Resources,* 148–78.

14. *Official Proceedings of the Tenth National Irrigation Congress Held at Colorado Springs, Colorado* (Colorado Springs: Consolidated Publishing Co., 1902), 240; *Cheyenne Daily Leader,* June 30, 1902; "Our National Irrigation Problem," *Harper's Weekly* 48 (July 30, 1904): 1164; F. E. Warren to George W. Perry, March 9, 1904, Warren Letterbook, February 12, 1904, to July 31, 1904, and Warren to F. H. Newell, April 24, 1905, Warren Letterbook, January 29, 1905, to May 5, 1905, both in the Francis E. Warren Collection, American Heritage Center, University of Wyoming, Laramie.

15. For example, Donald C. Swain, in *Federal Conservation Policy, 1921–1933* (Berkeley: University of California Press, 1963), 77, erroneously concluded that the Reclamation Service shunned "all areas but the arid West" and "refused to consider the drainage of Southern swamp lands as within its rightful sphere. It con-

strued reclamation exclusively as the process of reclaiming the desert lands of the western United States."

16. Elwood Mead, "Irrigation in the United States," *Transactions of the American Society of Civil Engineers* 54 (1905): 85.

17. F. H. Newell, "The Undrained Empire of the South," speech delivered March 2, 1911, in Box 6, F. H. Newell Collection, Library of Congress, Washington, D.C.; C. R. Van Hise, *The Conservation of Natural Resources in the United States* (New York: Macmillan, 1914), 199–201.

18. *New York Times*, May 28, 1871, October 29, 1873, and January 5, 1896; *Report of the Commissioner of Agriculture, 1873* (Washington, D.C.: GPO, 1874), 283; "Irrigation in the Eastern States," *Scientific American* 83 (November 3, 1900): 274; "Irrigation for the East," *Irrigation Age* 15 (November 1900): 42–43; E. B. Voorhees, "Irrigation in the East," *Proceedings of the Ninth Annual Session of the National Irrigation Congress, Held at Central Music Hall, Chicago, Ill., November 21, 22, 23, 24, 1900* (St. Louis: Interstate Manufacturer, n.d.), 150–54; Milo B. Williams, "Irrigation in the Humid States," *Official Proceedings of the Nineteenth National Irrigation Congress Held at Chicago, Illinois, December 5–9, 1911* (Chicago: R. R. Donnelley and Sons, 1912), 148–50.

19. J. W. Powell to J. A. Pickler, August 12, 1890, RG 57, Outgoing Correspondence, April 14–Sept. 1, 1890. The assumption that water carried natural fertilizers leached from the soil was a great comfort to western irrigation boosters. As late as 1917, George Wharton James, in *Reclaiming the Arid West: The Story of the United States Reclamation Service* (New York: Dodd and Mead, 1917), 25, confidently proclaimed: "The scientist now tells us—and the cultivation of millions of acres in the arid West has proved its truth—that the very condition of aridity is an assurance of great fertility when water is applied." Virgin soils had stored up nutrients over the ages, nutrients that only irrigation could unleash.

20. Liberty Hyde Bailey, "Shall We Irrigate Orchards in New York?" *Garden and Forest* 8 (June 12, 1895): 236. Also see C. S. Sargent, "The Arid West and Irrigation," *Garden and Forest* 1 (July 25, 1888): 253, and "Irrigation in the United States," *The Nation* 47 (November 15, 1888): 392; "Relative Value of Rain and Irrigation," *Popular Science Monthly* 42 (November 1892): 141; *Report of the Secretary of Agriculture, 1892* (Washington, D.C.: GPO, 1893), 83; "Profits of Irrigation in the Eastern Part of the United States," *Scientific American* 88 (March 21, 1903): 208; "Profits of Irrigation in the East," *Forestry and Irrigation* 9 (April 1903): 165–66; *Official Proceedings of the Eleventh National Irrigation Congress Held at Ogden, Utah, September 15–18, 1903* (Ogden: The Proceedings Publishing Co., 1904), 169.

21. *Official Report of the Fifth National Irrigation Congress Held at Phoenix, Arizona, December 15, 16, and 17, 1896* (Phoenix: The Arizona Republican, 1897), 34–37; *Official Proceedings of the Twelfth National Irrigation Congress Held at El Paso, Texas, Nov. 15–16–17–18, 1904* (Galveston: Clarke and Courts, 1905), 344 (quote). The remarks and papers devoted to humid land reclamation are reprinted on pp. 344–58. Also see *Report of the Secretary of Agriculture, 1901* (Washington, D.C., 1901), 87; *The Citrograph* (Redlands, Calif.), Feb. 4, 1899; "Irrigation in Florida," *Forestry and Irrigation* 8 (July 1902): 340–41 (and see pp. 298–300 in the same issue); and Guy E. Mitchell, "Sociological Aspects of the Irrigation Problem," *Forestry and Irrigation* 9 (January 1903): 32–34.

22. Donald J. Pisani, *From the Family Farm to Agribusiness: The Irrigation Crusade in California and the West, 1850–1931* (Berkeley: University of California Press, 1984), 129–53 and 250–82.

23. John Wesley Powell's famous 1878 report anticipated that one day the submerged lands of the South would be "redeemed from excessive humidity," and he claimed that "their fertility is almost inexhaustible, and the agricultural capacity of the United States will eventually be largely increased by the rescue of these lands from their present valueless condition." In 1878, he was mainly concerned with the arid West, but he hoped to survey the swamplands later. See his *Report on the Lands of the Arid Region of the United States, with a More Detailed Account of the Lands of Utah,* H. Ex. Doc. 73, 45th Cong., 2d sess., serial 1805 (Washington, D.C.: GPO, 1878), viii.

24. "Reclamation Fund Threatened" (editorial), *Forestry and Irrigation* 12 (March 1906): 112–13. Apparently, Hansbrough prepared a second bill that dedicated 90 percent of the receipts from timber sales within the national forests to an irrigation and drainage fund administered by the Department of Agriculture—a direct challenge to the Geological Survey's work in the South and East. See Guy E. Mitchell to George H. Maxwell, March 9, 1906, and Charles Walcott (Director of the USGS) to George H. Maxwell, March 19, 1906, "Maxwell Correspondence," Box 2, in the Charles Walcott Collection, Smithsonian Institution Archives, Washington, D.C.

25. Guy Elliott Mitchell, "Land Reclamation by Drainage," *Forestry and Irrigation* 12 (March 1906): 134–38; *Forestry and Irrigation* 12 (November 1906): 492.

26. *Official Proceedings of the Fifteenth National Irrigation Congress,* 60–61, 267; F. H. Newell to Arthur F. Francis, October 6, 1906, RG 115, General File, 1902–1919, Box 205, "(676–1): Trans-Mississippi Commercial Congresses"; Herbert M. Wilson, "Reclaiming the Swamp Lands of the United States," *National Geographic* 18 (May 1907): 292–301; Robert H. Chapman, "A Drowned Empire," *National Geographic* 19 (March 1908): 190–99; "Reclaiming Our Swamp Lands," *Forestry and Irrigation* 13 (November and December 1907): 562–63, 567; "Shall Uncle Sam Drain the Swamps?" *Forestry and Irrigation* 14 (April 1908): 207–9.

27. Theodore Roosevelt, *State Papers as Governor and President, 1899–1909* (New York: Charles Scribner's Sons, 1926), 445. In a speech before the National Irrigation Congress at Boise in 1906, Vice President Charles Fairbanks also urged that irrigation be extended throughout the nation, warning, "We can see the limit of our arable areas, but we cannot see the limit of our increasing population nor the extent of the demand of millions in foreign countries for American food supplies." *New York Times,* September 4, 1906.

28. *Reclamation Record* 4 (January 1913): 14; Ibid. 5 (May 1914): 171; Ibid. 5 (December 1914): 446; Ibid. 15 (January 1924): 16.

29. C. J. Blanchard, "The Home-Making Work of the Government," *Official Proceedings of the Seventeenth National Irrigation Congress [1909]* (Spokane: Shaw and Borden Co., n.d.), 347–71, esp. 351–52.

30. Blanchard, "The Home-Making Work of the Government," 354, 356–57. For similar panegyrics from a vast literature, see Alexander O. Brodie, "Reclaiming the Arid West," *Cosmopolitan* 37 (October 1904): 715–22; Frank Vrooman, "Uncle Sam's Romance with Science and the Soil," *Arena* 35 (January 1906): 36–46; Ira E. Bennett, "Western Affairs at Washington—Men and Problems," *Pacific*

Monthly 18 (October 1907): 470–83; and Arthur W. Page, "The Real Conquest of the West: The Work of the United States Reclamation Service," *World's Work* 15 (December 1907): 9691–704.

31. *Reclamation Record* 14 (August 1923): 271–72.
32. "Yakima Project Offers Splendid Opportunities to Right People," *New Reclamation Era* 18 (January 1927): 14.
33. Richard Lowitt and Judith Fabry, *Henry A. Wallace's Irrigation Frontier: On the Trail of the Corn-Belt Farmer, 1909* (Norman: University of Oklahoma Press, 1991), 30, 63. For other evidence of hard times on government projects, see pp. 110–11, 126, 141–42, 148–49, and 150–51.
34. *Reclamation Record* 5 (December 1914): 455.
35. "Don't Knock Your Project," *Reclamation Record* 5 (May 1914): 179.
36. *Reclamation Record* 14 (September 1923): 287. Also see the poem of the same name in *Reclamation Record* 6 (September 1915): 393.
37. A notable exception was the honest and revealing letter from a farmer on Washington's Yakima Project, printed in *Reclamation Record* 5 (September 1914): 323–24. The main purpose of boosting, the writer complained, was to drive up land prices, and boosters made it harder for legitimate farmers to succeed:

> It's real pitiable to see a city or town man, or a man from some other profession, buy a ranch at several times what it's worth and begin to improve it. As a rule his money gets away from him in a surprisingly short time, he's disappointed, and a disappointed man usually knocks hard. Some of these fellows paid $400 an acre for raw land. No farmer paid such prices, mind you, but the booster didn't work on farmers. My conviction is that we'll never get anywhere by misrepresenting the facts. It requires a real farmer with sand in his craw to make a success under any of the projects I've seen or in any new country. . . . You realize that most of these projects are far from markets and after a farmer has grown a crop such as potatoes or onions he often can't sell it. . . . The man who knows his business and is willing to hustle 12 or 15 hours a day can't find a better place.

38. Francis G. Newlands, "National Irrigation as a Social Problem," *Pacific Monthly* 16 (September 1906): 296–97 (quote); F. H. Newell, "Reclaiming an Empire," *Pacific Monthly* 18 (October 1907): 478.
39. United States Reclamation Service, typescript Memorandum no. 9, "Rural Settlements," May 21, 1906, in RG 115, "(262-C): Establishment of Townsites & Villages." This memo, written by F. H. Newell, emphasized that it was "the intention of Congress to encourage the concentration of irrigators under Reclamation Projects in numerous small villages. It is believed that this policy is not only the intent of the [Townsite] act, but would be conducive to the prosperity, culture, and happiness of the irrigators under Reclamation Projects, by enabling them to enjoy material and social advantages incident to village residence, combined with the health and freedom of rural life." The 1906 Townsite Act permitted the Reclamation Service to sell surplus power and water to towns and cities on or near its projects. It was hoped that this law would encourage farmers to cluster in villages rather than live on isolated farms.

40. B. E. Stoutmeyer to Supervising Engineer, June 8, 1911, and "Testimony before the House Committee of Arid Lands on March 13, 1912, on HR 10443," in RG 115, "(262-C): Establishment of Townsites & Villages."

41. Frank A. Waugh to F. H. Newell, December 2, 1912, and J. Horace McFarland to Newell, December 3, 1912, McFarland Papers, American Civic Association General Correspondence, Newell file, MG [Manuscript Group] 85, Pennsylvania State Archives. I am grateful to Gail Evans for sharing her research in the ACA papers with me. Some correspondence between the ACA and Reclamation Service can also be found in the townsite files within RG 115, cited in note 44.

42. John Nolen, Frederick Law Olmsted, Frank A. Waugh, Harlan P. Kelsey, and Warren H. Manning to Walter L. Fisher, January 8, 1913, McFarland Papers, ACA General Correspondence, Warren H. Manning file, MG 85, Pennsylvania State Archives.

43. C. J. Blanchard to J. Horace McFarland, January 28, 1913, McFarland Papers, American Civic Association, General Correspondence, C. J. Blanchard file, MG 85, Pennsylvania State Archives.

44. D. W. Ross to the director of the Reclamation Service, January 2, 1908; Walter Fisher to J. Horace McFarland, December 18, 1912; J. Horace McFarland to Walter Fisher, December 23, 1912; A. P. Davis to W. E. Weld, October 16, 1917, all in RG 115, "(262-C): Establishment of Townsites & Villages"; C. J. Blanchard to George H. Maxwell, September 6, 1918, RG 115, Records of the National Reclamation Association, Box 5, "Corres. Sept. 1916–1917"; *Eleventh Annual Report of the Reclamation Service, 1912* (Washington, D.C.: GPO, 1912), 18–22; *Sixteenth Annual Report of the Reclamation Service, 1917* (Washington, D.C.: GPO, 1917), 8–9; Paul Wallace Gates, *History of Public Land Law Development* (Washington, D.C.: GPO, 1968), 660.

45. On the irrigation crusade in the 1890s, see Pisani, *To Reclaim a Divided West,* 273–325.

46. Ibid., 285–94. For Maxwell's career before 1902, see Gordon E. Nelson, *The Lobbyist: The Story of George H. Maxwell, Irrigation Crusader* (Bowie, Md.: Headgate Press, 2001). The best single source on Maxwell's career after 1902 is "George Hebard Maxwell—Conservation Pioneer," an anonymous biography dated 1948 contained within the National Reclamation Association files in RG 115. Also see Andrew Hudanick, Jr., "George Hebard Maxwell: Reclamation's Militant Evangelist," *Journal of the West* 14 (July 1975): 108–21; Laura Lovett, "Land Reclamation as Family Reclamation: The Family Ideal in George Maxwell's Reclamation and Resettlement Campaigns, 1897–1933," *Social Politics* 7 (Spring 2000): 80–100; and Robert Autobee, "Every Child a Garden: George H. Maxwell and the American Homecroft Society," *Prologue* 28 (Fall 1996): 195–206.

47. Seven railroads—the Great Northern, Northern Pacific, Southern Pacific, Santa Fe, Union Pacific, Burlington, and Rock Island—paid fifty thousand dollars a year to support Maxwell's National Irrigation Association, which not only lobbied for federal reclamation but also published several journals. See *Country Gentleman* 69 (April 14, 1904): 348; *Irrigation Age* 19 (April 1904): 168a; and *Irrigation Age* 20 (March 1905): 135–38.

48. The quotations are from "Paper Prepared by Mr. James J. Hill on Irrigation, Read at National Irrigation Congress, Portland, Oregon, August 21, 1905," pp. 3 and 9,

at the James J. Hill Library, St. Paul, Minnesota. Also see James J. Hill to Theodore Roosevelt, March 20, 1908, and Hill to Fisher A. Baker, October 30, 1909, in Personal and Private Correspondence, James J. Hill Collection, Letterbook March 14, 1908–March 17, 1910, James J. Hill Library. In a book published in 1910, Hill called the 1902 law "[t]he single intelligent advance on practical lines made by public authority within the last quarter of a century." See Hill, *Highways of Progress* (New York: Doubleday, Page and Co., 1910), 21. For a recent biography of Hill, see Michael P. Malone, *James J. Hill: Empire Builder of the Northwest* (Norman: University of Oklahoma Press, 1996).

49. Ray Lyman Wilbur, *Conservation in the Department of the Interior* (Washington, D.C.: GPO, 1931), 41.

50. Michael P. Malone and Richard B. Roeder, *Montana: A History of Two Centuries* (Seattle: University of Washington Press, 1976), 183; James J. Hill to Jonathan S. Kennedy, May 16, 1902, and Hill to Paris Gibson, July 29, 1902, Personal and Private Correspondence, James J. Hill Collection, James J. Hill Library. In the *New York Times*, October 21, 1903, Hill pointed out that in 1882 the Great Northern hauled slightly more than a million tons of freight at an average rate of $2.51 per ton per hundred miles; by 1902 it moved more than 16 million tons at 85 cents per ton per hundred miles. Public criticism of the railroads made it imperative to keep rates as low as possible.

51. "Great Irrigation Enterprises," *World's Work* 1 (December 1900): 252–53; *Los Angeles Times*, November 26, 1901; *San Francisco Chronicle*, November 26, 1901; *Montana Daily Record*, September 25, 1903; *Helena Daily Independent*, September 26, 1903; *Proceedings of the Tenth National Irrigation Congress*, 183. George Maxwell to Paris Gibson, December 8, 1900, Paris Gibson File, Box 1; Maxwell to F. H. Newell, March 31, 1900, and F. H. Newell to George H. Maxwell, October 6, 1900, Newell File, Box 2; and Maxwell to R. M. Lewis, August 23, 1900, Box 4, all in George Maxwell Collection, Louisiana State Museum, New Orleans; James J. Hill to F. H. Newell, November 2, 1905, Hill Letterpress Book, November 18, 1902–February 20, 1906, James J. Hill Library.

52. *Salt Lake City Tribune*, April 11, 1902; *Salt Lake City Telegram*, April 10, 1902; *Cheyenne Daily Leader*, April 25, 1902.

53. F. H. Newell to George H. Maxwell, March 19, 1904, Great Northern Papers, President's Subject Files no. 4013, Minnesota Historical Society, St. Paul; George H. Maxwell to T. E. Higgins, Aug. 13, 1903, Box 8, no. 271, Maxwell Collection, Louisiana State Museum, New Orleans; also see George Maxwell to F. G. Newlands, September 21, 1915, Box 52, Folder 555, Newlands Papers, Sterling Library, Yale University.

54. "The Milk River Project," *Forestry and Irrigation* 10 (May 1904): 226–27; Fred Whiteside, "Government Irrigation in Montana," *Official Proceedings of the Nineteenth National Irrigation Congress Held at Chicago, Illinois, December 5–9, 1911* (Chicago: R. R. Donnelley and Sons Co., 1912), 44–49; James J. Hill to C. S. Mellon, January 12, 1903, Personal and Private Correspondence, Letterbook June 1, 1902–June 7, 1905, James J. Hill Library.

55. Louis W. Hill to J. W. Blabon (Fourth Vice President, Great Northern Railroad), August 22, 1904, Great Northern Papers, President's Subject Files no. 4013, Minnesota Historical Society. Also see Hill to A. P. Davis, March 14, 1910; F. L. Whit-

ney to Blabon, April 5, 1904; and Thomas H. Carter to W. M. Wooldridge, December 27, 1906, in the same file, and Thomas Cooper to Howard Elliott, September 29, 1904, Northern Pacific Papers, President's Office Subject Files, 1. C. 1. 4F, file 19-D (George Maxwell Correspondence), Minnesota Historical Society. For later criticism of Newell by railroad leaders, see *New York Times,* June 7, 1913.

56. James J. Hill to George H. Maxwell, March 17, 1905, Personal and Private Correspondence, James J. Hill Collection, Letterbook June 1, 1902–June 7, 1905, James J. Hill Library; *Christian Science Monitor,* March 12, 1913.

57. Thomas Cooper, "Reclaiming the Arid Lands of the Northwest," *Forestry and Irrigation* 11 (May 1905): 226–30; E. T. Perkins to B. Campbell, February 20, 1905, Great Northern Papers, President's Subject Files no. 4013, Minnesota Historical Society. *Minnesota Journal,* January 16, 1910; *St. Paul Pioneer Press,* January 16, 1910; A. P. Davis to L. W. Hill, March 2, 1910, Great Northern Papers, President's Subject Files no. 4013, Minnesota Historical Society; Elwood Mead to John D. Works, December 24, 1912, Mead File, John Works Collection, Bancroft Library, University of California, Berkeley.

58. During the early and mid-1890s, prior to becoming a publicist for federal reclamation, Maxwell worked as a water rights lawyer in California. He supported federal reclamation in part to drive up the price of land he had been given by clients whom he defended in California irrigation-district suits. He also held town lots in Great Falls, Montana, and there were rumors that he owned additional land in Arizona and New Mexico. True or not, the Salt River Project cost more than any other. By 1917, 12 percent of all the money spent on federal reclamation since 1902 had been expended in central Arizona. See George H. Maxwell to Paris Gibson, May 29, 1903, Paris Gibson File, Box 1, and F. H. Newell to Maxwell, Newell File, Box 2, both in the George Maxwell Collection, Louisiana State Museum, and Donald J. Pisani, "George Maxwell, the Railroads, and American Land Policy, 1899–1904," *Pacific Historical Review* 63 (May 1994): 177–202.

59. The Maxwell letter is as reprinted in Karen L. Smith, "The Campaign for Water in Central Arizona, 1890–1903," *Arizona and the West* 23 (Summer 1981): 141.

60. T. R.'s interest in Arizona politics is discussed in the Gifford Pinchot diary, July 2 and 3, 1902, Gifford Pinchot Collection, Library of Congress, Washington, D.C. Also see B. A. Fowler to Maxwell, February 18, 1903, Fowler file, Box 1, and Maxwell to F. H. Newell, February 1, May 25, and May 30, 1903, Box 17, George Maxwell Collection, Louisiana State Museum.

61. On the decision to end financial support to Maxwell, see D. Miller to J. W. Blabon, March 11, 1904; D. Miller to Howard Elliott, June 3, 1904; Louis W. Hill to George H. Maxwell, July 23, 1904; George H. Maxwell to Louis W. Hill, July 26, 1904, all in Great Northern Papers, President's Subject Files no. 4013. Also see Howard Elliot to D. Miller, May 14, 1904; Miller to Elliott, June 3, 1904; Elliott to Miller, June 6, 1904; and George H. Maxwell to Howard Elliott, September 21, 1904, all in Northern Pacific Papers, President's Office Subject Files, 1. C. 1. 4F, file 19-D (George Maxwell Correspondence) Minnesota Historical Society.

62. George H. Maxwell to Thomas R. Bard, July 14, 1904, in "Irrigation, National, I," Box 9-A, Thomas R. Bard Collection, Huntington Library, San Marino, California. Also see *Irrigation Age* 19 (May 1904): 199.

63. The depression of the 1890s had demonstrated the value of urban agriculture. Some cities hired farmers to teach the unemployed about agriculture, including how to raise and market produce. Hazen Pingree, Detroit's mayor, encouraged the unemployed to turn vacant lots into gardens, which permitted a thousand families to survive the brutal winter of 1895–96. No charity was involved, and children and the elderly also tended the gardens. See "Farming on Vacant City Lots," *Garden and Forest* 9 (March 4, 1896): 91–92.

64. George H. Maxwell, "The Cost of Living: Irrigation and Homemaking on the Land," address to the Manufacturer's Club of Philadelphia, December 19, 1904, in RG 115, Records of the National Reclamation Association, entry 57, "Printed Booklets." Many of Maxwell's ideas were also spread by Guy Elliott Mitchell, Maxwell's associate in his National Irrigation Association. See, for example, Mitchell's "Giving Men Homes on Land," *Forestry and Irrigation* 11 (January 1905): 30–34.

65. *Maxwell's Talisman* 6 (March 1906), 1.

66. George H. Maxwell, "Homecroft: The Making of a Word," *Maxwell's Talisman* 6 (April 1906): 5. For a summary of Maxwell's ideas, see his "Homecrofts—The Talisman of Today," parts 1 and 2, *Maxwell's Talisman* 9 (March 1908): 17–19; and 9 (April 1908): 27.

67. George Maxwell, "The Homecrofters Guild: A New Sociological Experiment at Watertown," *Maxwell's Talisman* 6 (July 1906): 10, 15, and "The Arizona Homecroft Village," Ibid. 6 (August 1906): 21–22; *Irrigation Age* 24 (May 1909): 205–6.

68. George Maxwell, "A Postal Savings Bank," *Maxwell's Talisman* 7 (January 1907): 14; "The National Homecroft Bill," Ibid. 7 (February 1907): 45–46; "A Postal Savings Bank," Ibid. 7 (March 1907): 79; "A Trinity of National Service," Ibid. 6 (November 1906): 3–4; "The National Homecroft Bill: Reasons Why Congress Should Make It a Law," Ibid. 6 (November 1906): 5–7; and Maxwell to Gifford Pinchot, October 19, 1907, Box 697, Gifford Pinchot Collection, Library of Congress.

69. George Maxwell to Brush Runabout Works, July 18, 1914, RG 115, Records of the National Reclamation Association, Box 1, "Corres. 1911–July 1914," and Maxwell to the National Reclamation Association, March 29, 1918, in Box 6, "Corres. 1918–1919"; *Duluth Herald,* September 30, 1914; *Indianapolis News,* May 28, 1920; *Michigan City News,* July 17, 1920.

70. George Maxwell to Guy E. Mitchell, June 30, 1915, RG 115, Records of the National Reclamation Association, Box 3, "Corres. 1915–Jan. 1916." Maxwell also warned of "the physical and racial deterioration now going on at such an appalling rate among the masses of our wageworkers" in *Our National Defense: The Patriotism of Peace* (Cambridge, Mass.: The University Press, 1915), 118, 124 (quote), and 127.

71. George H. Maxwell to Roger Babson, February 3, 1920, and Maxwell to Charles K. Holmburg, March 6, 1931, RG 115, National Reclamation Association Files.

72. On Maxwell's mental state, see his letters to Charles Walcott of March 13, 1906, and May 24, 1913, in the Maxwell correspondence within the Charles D. Walcott Collection, Smithsonian Institution Archives, and George H. Maxwell to Walter Parker, February 17, 1935, in RG 115, Records of the American Homecroft Society, "General Records, 1920–1921"; also see Maxwell to Charles K. Holmburg, March 6, 1931, RG 115, National Reclamation Association Files.

73. Norris Hundley, jr., *Water and the West: The Colorado River Compact and the Politics of Water in the West* (Berkeley: University of California Press, 1975), 159–64, 233–34; Maxwell, *Our National Defense*, 154–55; George H. Maxwell to Warren G. Harding, November 25, 1922, in Colorado River Commission records, Box 7, "George H. Maxwell, 1922," Herbert Hoover Papers, Hoover Presidential Library, West Branch, Iowa.

74. William Ellsworth Smythe, *The Conquest of Arid America* (New York: Harper and Bros., 1900; New York: Macmillan, 1905).

75. William Ellsworth Smythe, *Constructive Democracy: The Economics of a Square Deal* (New York: Macmillan, 1905), 62.

76. Ibid., 258.

77. William E. Smythe, "The Unfinished Task," *Official Proceedings of the Thirteenth International Irrigation Congress, 1905* (Portland: Bushong and Co., 1905), 257, and "New Zealand Institutions," *Out West* 16 (February 1902): 202–9.

78. Bolton Hall, *A Little Land and a Living* (New York: The Arcadia Press, 1908). Also see Hall's *Three Acres and Liberty* (New York: Macmillan, 1918).

79. Lawrence B. Lee, "William Ellsworth Smythe and San Diego, 1901–1908," *Journal of San Diego History* 19 (Winter 1973): 10–24, and "The Little Landers of San Ysidro," *Journal of San Diego History* 21 (Spring 1975): 28.

80. In addition to the excellent articles by Lawrence B. Lee cited in the preceding note, see Smythe, "The New Gospel: A Little Land and a Living," *Official Proceedings of the Eighteenth National Irrigation Congress Held at Pueblo, Colorado, Sept. 26–30, 1910* (Pueblo, Colo.: The Franklin Press, 1910), 115–25, and Smythe, "For a Nation of Little Landers," *Proceedings of the Nineteenth National Irrigation Congress,* 176–180. Lee points out that other Little Lander colonies in California, near Glendale and Hayward, fared no better. See Lee, "Little Landers," 44.

81. John Wesley Powell to the Secretary of the Interior, June 11, 1889, in RG 57, Outgoing Correspondence, March 30–July 15, 1889; Frederick Haynes Newell, "Memoirs," Box 1, F. H. Newell Collection, American Heritage Center, University of Wyoming, Laramie; Allen B. McDaniel, "Frederick Haynes Newell," *Transactions of the American Society of Civil Engineers* 98 (1933): 1597–1600.

82. Pisani, *To Reclaim a Divided West,* 304–5.

83. All of the biographical information on Newell is taken from his typescript "Memoirs," in the F. H. Newell Collection, American Heritage Center, University of Wyoming.

84. On the engineering profession, see Raymond H. Merritt, *Engineering in American Society, 1850–1875* (Lexington: University Press of Kentucky, 1969); Edwin T. Layton, *The Revolt of the Engineers* (Cleveland: Press of Case Western Reserve University, 1971); Monte Calvert, *The Professionalization of the American Mechanical Engineer, 1830–1910* (Baltimore: Johns Hopkins University Press, 1967); and Murray I. Mantell, *Ethics and Professionalism in Engineering* (New York: Macmillan, 1964).

85. Layton, *Revolt of the Engineers,* 58–59 (quote), 134–49, 189–90; Samuel Haber, *Efficiency and Uplift: Scientific Management in the Progressive Era, 1890–1920* (Chicago: University of Chicago Press, 1964).

86. As Samuel Haber has pointed out, "efficiency" could mean an effective worker, social harmony, and leadership by the competent as well as the energy ratio or

output of machines, or the cost of producing a product. See *Efficiency and Uplift,* ix–x.

87. Arthur T. Hadley, "The Professional Ideals of the Twentieth Century," *Engineering* 33 (July 1907): 640–42.

88. Frederick H. Newell, "The Engineer in the Public Service," address delivered May 29, 1912, in the Frederick Haynes Newell Collection, Box 6, "Newell 1912," Library of Congress, Washington, D.C.

89. Frederick Haynes Newell, "Awakening of the Engineer," *Engineering News* 74 (September 16, 1915): 568–69. Also see Newell, "The Emphasis on the Human Factor in Industry," Ohio State University College of Engineering *Bulletin,* no. 16 (January 1917), 102–6; "The Engineer's Part in After-the-War Problems," *Scientific Monthly* 8 (March 1919): 239–46; and "Ethics of the Engineering Profession," *Annals of the American Academy of Political and Social Science* 101 (May 1922): 76–85.

90. F. H. Newell, "The Public Lands of the United States," *Scientific American* 78 (March 12, 1898): 163; Newell, "The Annexation of the Arid West," *Independent* 50 (August 11, 1898): 408–10.

91. The quotation is from F. H. Newell's speech "Reclamation of the Arid West," published in *Science* 33 (May 5, 1911): 681–82. For similar sentiments, see these additional works by Newell: "Home-Making through Conservation," a speech delivered to the Sons of the American Revolution on March 15, 1911, in the Newell Collection, Box 6, Library of Congress; "The National Irrigation Situation," in *Proceedings of the Seventeenth National Irrigation Congress,* 52–61; "Reclamation and Home-Making," *Scientific American* 105 (August 12, 1911): 144–45. Such sentiments cannot be taken entirely at face value. They must be considered in light of criticisms of federal reclamation as unsympathetic to the needs of farmers on government projects, which were leveled at the federal reclamation program after 1909. Nevertheless, Newell made similar statements in private or semiprivate meetings with reclamation officials. See, for example, the transcript "Irrigation Managers' Conferences during 1912," in the folder "Irrigation and Reclamation of Arid Lands," Box 10, John D. Works Collection, Bancroft Library, University of California, Berkeley.

92. C. J. Blanchard, "Millions for Moisture: An Account of the Work of the U.S. Reclamation Service," *National Geographic* 18 (April 1907): 230–31, 239, 243; "Home-Making by the Government: An Account of the Eleven Immense Irrigating Projects to be Opened in 1908," *National Geographic* 19 (April 1908): 250; "The Call of the West: Homes Are Being Made for Millions of People in the Arid West," *National Geographic* 20 (May 1909): 404, 434; "Reclaiming the Desert," *Mentor* 6 (October 15, 1918): 11. Also see Blanchard, "The Spirit of the West: The Wonderful Agricultural Development since the Dawn of Irrigation," *National Geographic* 21 (April 1910): 333–60.

93. *Eleventh Annual Report of the Reclamation Service,* 5–6 ("The characteristics . . ."); F. H. Newell, "Federal Land Reclamation: A National Problem," *Engineering News-Record* 91 (November 15, 1923): 803.

94. F. H. Newell, *Irrigation Management,* 3 (quote), 32, 35.

95. *Twelfth Annual Report of the Reclamation Service, 1912–1913* (Washington, D.C.: GPO, 1914), 9.

96. F. H. Newell, "Meeting of Irrigation Men," memorandum (quoting a Blanchard survey) dated September 30, 1912, in Box 6, F. H. Newell Collection, Library of Congress; F. H. Newell to Gifford Pinchot, October 6, 1913, in General Correspondence, 1913, L-N, Box 168, Gifford Pinchot Collection, Library of Congress.

97. F. H. Newell to Oliver C. Haga, January 19, 1915, RG 115, General File, 1902–1919, Box 90, "(110-E): Corres. re Irrigation Laws; Water Codes; Etc"; Newell, "The Conservation and Utilization of Natural Resources: The National Problem of Land Reclamation," *Scientific Monthly* 16 (April 1923): 337–43; "Newell on History of Western Irrigation Development," *Transactions of the American Society of Civil Engineers* 90 (1927): 703.

98. F. H. Newell, "Water," in *Conservation of Our Natural Resources,* ed. Loomis Havemeyer (New York: Macmillan Co., 1931), 154–64, The quotes are from pp. 154 and 163.

99. Newell was not the only Reclamation Service official to claim that federal reclamation had failed largely because of changes in the character and expectations of American farmers. In 1914, C. J. Blanchard candidly admitted that there had been "dark days" for settlers on the Truckee-Carson Project. Many had "failed and given place to others," but that was the story of every new country. "As on every [irrigation] project, the first settlers, as a rule, were men of small means. Many were wholly inexperienced and not a few were quite unfit for the arduous task they had set out to accomplish. Most of those who were unfit are gone, but those who were imbued with courage and who stuck to their land are today where they can look over the long hill and see a smiling landscape beyond." Congress could interfere with this Darwinian process only at the nation's peril. See C. J. Blanchard, "The Truckee-Carson Project," *Reclamation Record* 5 (November 1914), 415–16. Many engineers in the Reclamation Service shared this view. See for example, C. E. Grunsky, "C. E. Grunsky on History of Western Irrigation Development," *Transactions of the American Society of Civil Engineers* 90 (1927): 700; Thomas H. Means, "Thomas H. Means on Reclamation Bureau and Land Settlement" in the same volume, p. 738, and Copley Amory, "Farmers: Inventory and Appraise Character!" *New Reclamation Era* 17 (March 1926): 46–47.

CHAPTER 2. THE PERILS OF PUBLIC WORKS

1. *Forestry and Irrigation* 12 (March 1906): 110.

2. Benjamin Harrison, "Third Annual Message [to Congress]," December 9, 1891, in James D. Richardson, ed., *Messages and Papers of the Presidents, 1787–1897,* vol. 9 (Washington, D.C.: GPO, 1900), 205–6. The U.S. Geological Survey's Irrigation Survey (1888–1890) reserved 30 million acres of irrigable land and 147 reservoir sites: 33 in California, 46 in Colorado, 27 in Montana, 39 in New Mexico, and 2 in Nevada. Most of the irrigable land was restored to the public domain at the end of August 1890, but the reservoir sites remained off limits until February 1897. See Donald J. Pisani, *To Reclaim a Divided West: Water, Law, and Public Policy, 1848–1902* (Albuquerque: University of New Mexico Press, 1992), 163–64.

3. *U.S. Statutes at Large* 26 (1889–1891): 454, and 27 (1891–1893): 110.

4. Charles C. Allen, "National Control of the Pollution of Public Waterways," *American Law Review* 38 (May–June 1904): 321–33.

5. *U.S. Statutes at Large* 30 (1897–1899): 36 (emphasis added).

6. *Cruse* v. *McCauley*, 96 Fed. 369 (1899), 373; *Smith* v. *Denniff*, 24 Mont. 20 (1900), 21; *Benton* v. *Johncox*, 17 Wash. 277 (1897), 289; *Morris* v. *Bean*, 123 Fed. 618 (1903); *Hoge* v. *Eaton*, 135 Fed. 411 (1905); *Anderson* v. *Bassman*, 140 Fed. 10 (1905); *Morgan* v. *Shaw*, 47 Ore. 333 (1906), 337; *LeQuime* v. *Chambers*, 15 Idaho 405 (1908).

7. *Howell* v. *Johnson*, 89 Fed. 556 (1898), 558, 560. The Montana circuit court upheld the same principle in another case pertaining to Sage Creek. See *Morris* v. *Bean*, 123 Fed. 618 (1903), and *Bean* v. *Morris*, 221 U.S. 485 (1911).

8. *United States* v. *Rio Grande Dam and Irrigation Company*, 174 U.S. 690 (1899), 703.

9. For a concise summary of these two views of water rights, see Robert Dunbar, *Forging New Rights in Western Waters* (Lincoln: University of Nebraska Press, 1983), 61–81.

10. After graduating from the University of California in 1879 with a degree in civil engineering, Morris Bien worked for the United States Geological Survey until 1893, when he moved to the General Land Office. In 1902, he returned to the USGS as chief legal officer for the new Reclamation Service. Meanwhile, in 1895 he had graduated from Columbian University Law School (now George Washington University) and in the following year received a Master of Laws degree from National University. *Forestry and Irrigation* 11 (February 1905): 59. Also see Bien's typescript "Autobiography" in the Morris Bien Collection, American Heritage Center, University of Wyoming, Laramie.

11. For Morris Bien's theory of national water rights, see Binger Hermann, Commissioner of the General Land Office (written by Morris Bien) to the Secretary of the Interior, January 13, 1902, RG 49, Division A, Press Copies of Letters Sent Relating to Congressional Bills, vol. 20, December 20, 1901–April 2, 1902; Bien, "Relation of Federal and State Laws to Irrigation," in *Official Proceedings of the Eleventh National Irrigation Congress, Ogden, Utah, September 15–18, 1903* (Ogden: The Proceedings Publishing Co., 1904), 397–402; Bien, "Memorandum Concerning the Origin of the Right of Appropriation of the Waters of the Public Domain," dated February 6, 1904, and "Informal Statement Concerning the Right of Appropriation of Water and Riparian Rights in the Arid Regions," 1906, RG 115, "(762): Legal Discussions—General"; Bien, *Relation of Federal and State Laws to Irrigation*, USGS, Water Supply and Irrigation Paper no. 93 (Washington, D.C.: GPO, 1904).

12. *U.S. Statutes at Large* 14 (1865–1867), 253.

13. Ibid. 16 (1869–1871), 218.

14. Ibid. 19 (1875–1877), 377.

15. Bien, "Informal Statement."

16. For example, see Frederick H. Newell's "To Whom Belong the Unappropriated Rights in the Water?" in vol. B, Box 7, F. H. Newell Collection, Library of Congress; Arnold Kruckman to Ottamar Hamele (Chief Counsel, Bureau of Reclamation), August 8, 1922, RG 115, Central Administrative Files, 1919–1929, Box 35, "(032): General Corres. Re Water Rights; Settlement of; Exchange; Transfer, etc. thru 1929," and F. W. Dent (Acting Commissioner of Reclamation) to L. Ward

Bannister, September 3, 1929, Box 73, "(101.9): General Corres. re State Jurisdiction over Government Projects and Activities"; Ottamar Hamele, "Federal Water Rights in the Colorado River," American Academy of Political and Social Science, *Annals* 135 (January 1928): 143–49, and his testimony before the House Committee on Irrigation and Reclamation re H.R. 2903, *Colorado River Bill,* 68th Cong., 1st sess. (Washington, D.C.: GPO, 1924), 881–900; and Ethelbert Ward (Special Assistant to the U.S. Attorney General), "Memorandum: Federal Irrigation Water Rights," dated January 22, 1930, item no. 588, Wells Hutchins Collection, California Water Resources Archives, University of California, Berkeley.

17. C. S. Kinney predicted in his *Treatise on the Law of Irrigation and Water Rights and the Arid Region Doctrine of the Appropriation of Water* (San Francisco: Bender-Moss Co., 1912), 692, that Congress at any time could pass a law providing for the disposition of water on the public domain that completely bypassed state laws. Also see Samuel C. Wiel, *Water Rights in the Western States* (San Francisco: Bancroft-Whitney Co., 1905), 49–69.

18. John Truesdell to J. F. Richardson (Truckee-Carson Irrigation Project manager), May 29, 1918, Truckee Carson Irrigation District Records, Fallon, Nevada. Also see Truesdell to Richardson, May 15, 1918, and Richardson to Truesdell, May 22, 1918, in the same collection. The *Twenty-third Annual Report of the Bureau of Reclamation, 1923–1924* (Washington, D.C.: GPO, 1924), 32, declared that the Justice Department construed Section 8 of the Reclamation Act as "directory, in the interests of comity, but not mandatory." For a brief statement of the Justice Department's interpretation of federal water rights, see the *Annual Report of the Attorney General of the United States, 1914* (Washington, D.C.: GPO, 1914), 39.

19. Edwin S. Corwin *The Twilight of the Supreme Court: A History of Our Constitutional Theory* (New Haven: Yale University Press, 1934), 11–12.

20. See Teller's speech on water rights in the *Congressional Record,* 60th Cong., 1st sess., Senate, March 31, 1908: 4155–67 (the quotes are on p. 4159). The United States, Teller argued, had long before established the principle of state control over water used for commerce. In *Martin* v. *Waddell's Lessee* (1842), a case involving a claim to land lying under navigable water in New Jersey, Chief Justice Roger Brooke Taney remarked: "For when the Revolution took place, the people of each State became themselves sovereign; and in that character held the absolute right to all their navigable waters and the soils under them for their own common use, subject only to the rights since surrendered by the Constitution to the general government" (*Martin* v. *Waddell's Lessee,* 41 U.S. 367 [1842], 367 [quote]). According to Teller, this case did not enunciate a new principle; it simply confirmed rights granted by colonial charters.

21. Delph E. Carpenter, "Conflict of Jurisdiction Respecting Control of Waters in Western States," *Rocky Mountain Law Review* 2 (April 1930): 162–72. The quotes are from pp. 165 and 170–71. Also see the Carpenter speech to the Conference of Governors, Salt Lake City, August 26–27, 1929, *Congressional Record,* 71st Cong., 1st sess., September 13, 1929: 3576–79.

22. Morris Bien, "Relation of Federal and State Laws to Irrigation," in *Official Proceedings of the Eleventh National Irrigation Congress,* 401.

23. Morris Bien to F. H. Newell, January 5, 1904, RG 115, General File, 1902–1919, Box 90, "(110-E): Corres. re Irrigation Laws; Water Codes, Etc."

24. *Thirteenth Annual Report of the Reclamation Service, 1913–1914* (Washington, D.C.: GPO, 1915), 16.
25. Donald J. Pisani, "Water Law Reform in California, 1900–1913," *Agricultural History* 54 (April 1980): 295–317; Pisani, *From the Family Farm to Agribusiness: The Irrigation Crusade in California and the West, 1850–1931* (Berkeley: University of California Press, 1984), 335–80.
26. On Wyoming's reform effort—which served as a model for some parts of the West—see Dunbar, *Forging New Rights*, 99–112.
27. *Morning Oregonian* (Portland), December 2, 1904. For conditions in Oregon, also see the *Oregonian* of August 5, 17, and 23, September 3 and 10, and October 11, 1904.
28. For summaries of the Bien Code, see Bien's undated 1903 "Memorandum of Principles to Be Incorporated in State Irrigation Laws" as well as subsequent versions of the code in RG 115, General Files, 1902–1919, "(110-E): Legislation: Corres. re Irrigation Laws; Water Codes, Etc."; *Official Proceedings of the Twelfth National Irrigation Congress Held at El Paso, Texas, November 15–16–17–18, 1904* (Galveston: Clarke and Courts, 1905), 169–85.
29. Zera Snow to F. H. Newell, February 24, 1904, and John T. Whistler to F. H. Newell, October 14, 1904, in RG 115, General Files, 1902–1919, "(110-E2): Legislation: Irrigation Laws; Water Codes; Etc. Oregon; thru 1904"; Morris Bien, typescript "Autobiography," pp. 17–18, Morris Bien Collection, American Heritage Center; *Morning Oregonian* (Portland), September 21 and October 10 and 21, 1904; *Seattle Daily Times*, January 20 and 21, and February 2, 1905.
30. *Seattle Daily Times*, January 11, 1905.
31. D. W. Ross to F. H. Newell, January 30, 1905; John T. Whistler to Newell, February 2, 1905; and Whistler to J. B. Lippincott, March 15, 1905, in "(110-E2): Legislation: Irrigation Laws; Water Codes; Etc., Oregon; 1905 on"; T. A. Noble to Newell, February 1, 1905, and D. W. Ross to Newell, February 6, 1905, in "(110-E16): Legislation: Irrigation Law; Water Codes; Etc. Washington thru 1910," all in RG 115, General Files, 1902–1919. Also see *Morning Oregonian* (Portland), September 21 and October 10 and 21, 1904; *Seattle Daily Times*, January 20 and 21 and February 2, 1905.
32. Donald J. Pisani, "State vs. Nation: Federal Reclamation and Water Rights in the Progressive Era," *Pacific Historical Review* 51 (August 1982): 271–72. See also D. W. Ross to Morris Bien, December 29, 1903, and L. G. Carpenter (State Engineer of Colorado) to Bien, October 27, 1904, in RG 115, General File, 1902–1919, Box 90, "(110-E): Corres. re Irrigation Laws; Water Codes, Etc."
33. *Kansas v. Colorado*, 206 U.S. 46 (1907). Also see *Kansas v. Colorado*, 185 U.S. 143 (1902). The legal literature on this case is immense. For a good introduction, see James Earl Sherow, *Watering the Valley: Development along the High Plains Arkansas River, 1870–1950* (Lawrence: University Press of Kansas, 1990). Also see Michael Brodhead, *David J. Brewer: The Life of a Supreme Court Justice, 1837–1910* (Carbondale: Southern Illinois University Press, 1994).
34. *United States v. Rio Grande Dam and Irrigation Company*, 174 U.S. 690 (1899).
35. H. M. Hoyt (Solicitor General) to A. C. Campbell, July 16, 1906, file no. 25749, Box 625, Kansas v. Colorado, RG 60.
36. "Petition of Intervention on Behalf of the United States," October 1903, 10–11,

and H. M. Hoyt (Solicitor General) to A. C. Campbell, July 16, 1906, file no. 25749, Box 625, Kansas v. Colorado, RG 60; Campbell to W. J. Hughes, August 13, 1906, file no. 25749, Box 625, RG 60.

37. A. E. Chandler, "Federal vs. State Control of Waters," in *Transactions of the Commonwealth Club of California* 9 (March 1914): 121.

38. *Kansas v. Colorado,* 27 Sup. Ct. 662 (1907), 663.

39. Ibid., 663, 665.

40. Elwood Mead formally suggested the study based on a precedent set by the American Bar Association, which appointed special committees to promote uniform state laws related to a wide variety of subjects, including divorce and bankruptcy. See Mead, "The Evolution of Irrigation Institutions," in *Official Proceedings of the Fourteenth National Irrigation Congress Held at Boise, Idaho, Sept. 3–8, 1906* (Boise: Statesman Printing Co., 1906), 80, 237, 240.

41. *Proceedings of the Fifteenth National Irrigation Congress* (Sacramento, Calif.: News Publishing Co., n.d.), 257–61. The quote is from p. 260.

42. "An Engineer's Committee to Draft a Federal Water Law," *Engineering News* 70 (November 6, 1913): 934.

43. John H. Lewis, "State and National Water Laws, with Detailed Statement of the Oregon System of Water Titles," *Transactions of the American Society of Civil Engineers* 76 (December 1913): 637–76.

44. See, for example, Newell's paper "Irrigation" in the *Report of the National Conservation Commission, February, 1909,* vol. 2 (Washington, D.C.: GPO, 1909), 66.

45. For a summary of these conflicts, see Newell's "Interstate Difficulties over Water Rights," *Engineering Record* 70 (July 11, 1914): 42.

46. See the undated, unpaginated document "A National Water Law," vol. A, Box 7, Frederick Haynes Newell Collection, Library of Congress, Washington, D.C.

47. Ibid.

48. "American Society of Civil Engineers, Special Committee on a National Water Law, Historical," vol. B, Box 7, Newell Collection, Library of Congress.

49. American Society of Civil Engineers, *Proceedings* 41 (December 1915): 2747–51, and *Proceedings* 42 (February 1916): 68, 97.

50. American Society of Civil Engineers, *Proceedings* 43 (December 1917): 2462. Also see *Proceedings* 42 (August 1916): 414–15.

51. F. H. Newell to Morris Bien, December 16, 1918, RG 115, "(1253): Correspondence re Publicity for Colonization and Settlement of Reclamation Project Lands," and Newell to John W. Alvord, March 9, 1920, Box 5, A. P. Davis Papers, American Heritage Center, University of Wyoming, Laramie.

52. American Society of Civil Engineers, *Proceedings* 46 (February 1920): 153–54; *Proceedings* 46 (May 1920): 471–72.

53. For an overview of many of these conflicts, see Allan J. Soffar, "Differing Views on the Gospel of Efficiency: Conservation Controversies between Agriculture and Interior, 1898–1938" (Ph.D. diss., Texas Tech University, 1974).

54. Pisani, *To Reclaim a Divided West,* 143–63.

55. Richard Hinton to E. S. Willits, Acting Secretary of Agriculture, April 29, 1891, RG 16, Copies of Letters Sent by the Office of Irrigation Inquiry, February 28, 1891 to August 26, 1891. For a brief sketch of Hinton's life, see Harwood P. Hinton, "Richard J. Hinton and the American Southwest," in *Voices from the South-*

west: A Gathering in Honor of Lawrence Clark Powell, ed. Donald C. Dickinson, et al. (Flagstaff, Ariz.: Northland Press, 1976), 82–91.

56. F. E. Warren to Elwood Mead, February 12, March 4, March 16 (quote), March 20, and April 8, 1898, and Warren to James Wilson (Secretary of Agriculture), April 11, 1898, Warren Letterbook, January 7, 1898–April 18, 1898, Warren Collection, American Heritage Center, University of Wyoming, Laramie. In December 1892, Mead had been offered the job of director of a department of irrigation in Agriculture. Fearful that the Republican Party would not win re-election, he had refused. See Mead to Edwin Willits (Assistant Secretary of Agriculture), December 27, 1892, Mead Letterbook, December 10, 1892–October 20, 1893, Elwood Mead Collection, University of Wyoming Archives, Cheyenne. On Mead's life, see James R. Kluger, *Turning on Water with a Shovel: The Career of Elwood Mead* (Albuquerque: University of New Mexico Press, 1992). Kluger discusses Mead's career from 1890 to 1902 on pp. 14–40.

57. F. E. Warren, "Reasons for Creating Division of Irrigation," undated memorandum (probably January 1898), in Warren Letterbook, January 7, 1898–April 18, 1898, Warren Collection.

58. "Irrigation Investigations," undated memorandum signed "Allen" [E. T. Allen?] in Gifford Pinchot Collection, Box 602, Library of Congress. Also see Milton Conover, *The Office of Experiment Stations: Its History, Activities, and Organization* (Baltimore: Johns Hopkins University Press, 1924), 89–93. Mead's most important cooperative project, one that gave him substantial political clout in California, was a 1900 survey of water rights on eight California streams, which permitted his agency to join forces with a powerful conservation league, the California Water and Forest Association, using personnel from the University of California and Stanford. See Pisani, *From the Family Farm to Agribusiness,* 335–43.

59. F. E. Warren to Elwood Mead, May 20, June 1, July 15, and August 20, 1901; Warren Letterbook, May 6–October 26, 1901; Elwood Mead to Frank Adams, May 28, 1901, RG 8, Box 1. The rivalry was not entirely within the Department of Agriculture. In the Interior Department, there was tension between the General Land Office and the U.S. Geological Survey, especially after the appointment of William A. Richards, the former governor of Wyoming, as commissioner of the Land Office in July 1903. Since the Land Office, not the Reclamation Service, interpreted the land laws and processed the applications of prospective settlers on federal water projects, it was destined to have a powerful role in the national irrigation program.

60. Elwood Mead to George Maxwell, December 6 and December 21, 1898, and James Wilson to Francis E. Warren, November 30, 1898, all in Box 12, George Maxwell Collection, Louisiana State Museum, New Orleans.

61. On the Mead-Newell relationship prior to 1902, see Pisani, *To Reclaim A Divided West,* 306–9.

62. Elwood Mead, "Problems of Irrigation Legislation," *Forum* 32 (January 1902): 581; Elwood Mead to Francis E. Warren, February 21, 1902, RG 8, Box 1.

63. F. E. Warren to Elwood Mead, October 4, 1902, Warren Letterbook, July 24, 1902–February 9, 1903; Elwood Mead to Platt Rogers, October 29, 1902, RG 8, Box 1.

64. George H. Maxwell to Thomas R. Bard (U.S. senator from California), Novem-

ber 26, 1902, in Box 9-A, file "Irrigation, National, I," Thomas R. Bard Collection, Huntington Library, San Marino, California.

65. *Denver Republican,* October 10, 1902; *Official Proceedings of the Tenth National Irrigation Congress Held at Colorado Springs, Colorado* (Colorado Springs: Consolidated Publishing Co., 1902), 245–50 (the quote is from p. 247); George H. Maxwell, "Reclamation of the Arid Region," *Forestry and Irrigation* 8 (November 1902): 444–47 (the quote is from p. 445).

66. Mead's letter, "An Open Letter to the Delegates to the National Irrigation Congress at Colorado Springs, October 6–9, 1902," dated October 15, 1902, was published in *Irrigation Age* 18 (November 1902): 13–17.

67. C. B. Boothe to Thomas R. Bard, December 19, 1902, Box 9-A, "Irrigation, National, I," Thomas R. Bard Collection.

68. In 1902 and 1903, the editor of *Irrigation Age,* D. H. Anderson, published a series of editorials attacking George Maxwell. Mead wanted to avoid a public feud with Newell, and doubtless advised Anderson to train his guns on Maxwell, who had no formal position in the Reclamation Service but exercised great influence over its policies. In 1903, Anderson collected many of his editorials in a pamphlet entitled *Influences in the National Irrigation Program* (n.p., n.d.), a copy of which is contained in Reel 13 of the Ballinger Papers, Special Collections, University of Washington, Seattle. Anderson exposed many inconsistencies in Maxwell's thought and actions. Maxwell had called for "home rule" in irrigation, but torpedoed the irrigation district law in California. Originally, he insisted that federal reclamation could not work without sweeping reforms of state water laws, but by 1902 he argued against such reforms. He had once favored leasing public grazing lands to settlers who farmed land adjoining the public commons at nominal rates, but rejected that plan by 1902. Anderson attributed these inconsistencies to Maxwell's ties to the railroads—and to large private landowners in Arizona. He portrayed Newell as honest, but weak and vain— Maxwell's dupe.

69. F. H. Newell to Gifford Pinchot, July 2, 1903, Box 602, Gifford Pinchot Collection.

70. Elwood Mead to Gifford Pinchot, July 2, 1903, Box 602, Gifford Pinchot Collection.

71. A. C. True to Gifford Pinchot, December 10, 1903, Box 602, Gifford Pinchot Collection.

72. See the unpublished "Report of the Committee on Organization of Government Scientific Work to President Roosevelt," July 20, 1903, p. 7, in Box 603, "Government Organization & Adm. PS Government Scientific Work Committee on," Gifford Pinchot Collection.

73. Donald J. Pisani, "Forests and Reclamation, 1891–1911," *Forest and Conservation History* 37 (April 1993): 73–75. In a November 18, 1905, letter to J. B. Lippincott, Newell suggested that imposing a small rental fee on public grazing lands might replenish the then exhausted reclamation fund. Nevertheless, he was well aware that this would clash with Gifford Pinchot's plans to use such fees to expand the work of the forestry office. Newell concluded, "The subject is one which it is probably not wise at present to discuss as coming from the Reclamation Service." The letter is contained in the Newell file, George Pardee Collection, Bancroft Library, University of California, Berkeley.

74. F. H. Newell, *Irrigation in the United States* (New York: Thomas Y. Crowell and Co., 1902), 10, 12; Brookings Institution, Institute for Government Research, *The U.S. Reclamation Service: Its History, Activities, and Organization* (New York: D. Appleton and Co., 1919), 42.

75. Elwood Mead, "Irrigation in the United States," *Transactions of the American Society of Civil Engineers* 54 (1905): 84.

76. As early as 1904, the USDA's Bureau of Soils conducted a few cooperative soil surveys on federal reclamation projects, but funding proved inadequate and most projects were ignored. Not until 1914 did the Agriculture Department began testing project soils systematically. Yet as late as the mid-1920s, the soils on 40 percent of the projects had not been investigated, and some of the remainder had been surveyed only partially. The boards of review appointed by the Reclamation Service to consider the feasibility of irrigation projects never included representatives from the Department of Agriculture or farmers experienced in cultivating desert soil. See *Reclamation Record* 5 (May 1914): 156–57; *Congressional Record*, 58th Cong., 1st sess., House, June 7, 1924: 11235–36.

77. Wallace McMartin, "The Economics of Land Classification for Irrigation," *Journal of Farm Economics* 32 (November 1950): 553–70. Soil scientist John Widtsoe noted that the annual growing season on federal irrigation projects ranged from 335 days on the Yuma Project to 113 days on the Milk River Project. Per-acre returns depended directly on the number of days above freezing. The Milk River Project produced an average annual income of less than fifteen dollars per acre per year, the Salt River Project nearly four times that amount. See Widtsoe, *Success on Irrigation Projects* (New York: J. Wiley and Sons, 1928), 22.

78. California contained little arable public land within a reasonable distance from water, but there were dozens of defunct irrigation districts that had been created during the late 1880s and early 1890s. They covered nearly 2 million acres, and the bondholders and land speculators who had invested in them hoped that the federal government would rescue some districts and purchase at face value the bonds that had been sold to build irrigation works, which by 1902 sold at a deep discount. See Donald J. Pisani, *Water, Land, and Law in the West: The Limits of Public Policy, 1850–1920* (Lawrence: University Press of Kansas, 1996), 104.

79. *Caldwell Tribune* (Caldwell, Idaho), August 14, 1909.

80. H. C. Hansbrough, "A National Irrigation Policy," *Forestry and Irrigation* 8 (March 1902): 103. A. P. Davis outlined the Reclamation Service's policies toward private irrigation companies in his letter to J. B. Lippincott, July 30, 1904, Thomas R. Bard Collection, Box 7-D, file "Irrigation, III," Huntington Library. Also see the *Chicago Record-Herald*, March 31, 1903; *Philadelphia Item*, March 25, 1903; *Boston Transcript*, April 8, 1903; *Cincinnati Christian Leader*, April 14, 1903; *Los Angeles Times*, April 18, 1903.

81. The first Newell quote is from Guy E. Mitchell, "Millions Appropriated for Levees," *Irrigation Age* 15 (October 1900): 7, and the second is from the *Morning Oregonian* (Portland), August 8, 1904. Also see Frederick H. Newell, "Reclamation of Arid Public Lands," *Independent* 54 (May 22, 1902): 1244; Newell, *Irrigation in the United States,* 405; *National Irrigation* 6 (October 1901): 138; Brookings Institution, *The U.S. Reclamation Service,* 18.

82. A. P. Davis to J. B. Lippincott, July 30, 1904, Box 7-D, file "Irrigation, III," Thomas R. Bard Collection.

83. "The Gardens of the West," *National Geographic* 16 (March 1905): 123.

84. See F. H. Newell, "Fallacies of Irrigation Statistics," undated speech in Box 6, Newell Collection. Also see Newell, "Progress of National Reclamation," *Proceedings of the Fourteenth National Irrigation Congress,* 56; *Reclamation of Arid Lands,* S. Rept. 254, 57th Cong., 1st sess., serial 4257 (Washington, D.C., 1902), 3; Morris Bien, typescript "Autobiography" pp. 26–27; and Charles D. Walcott to Francis G. Newlands, February 4, 1911, in Box 2, Charles D. Walcott Collection, Smithsonian Institution Archives.

85. In 1903, British India contained more than 44 million acres of irrigated land, half of them watered from canals built by the British government at an average cost of about $7.50 per acre. Some canals operated at a loss, but collectively they returned a net annual revenue of 6.3 percent on the cost of construction. The problem with comparing these canals to those in the American West was that labor was much cheaper in India, the population more concentrated, and the populace used to a strong centralized government. See "Irrigation, An Informal Discussion," in *Transactions of the American Society of Civil Engineers* 62 (March 1909): 32–33.

86. See the statement of Wyoming State Engineer Clarence T. Johnston in the *Cheyenne Daily Leader,* June 21, 1902; *Congressional Record,* 56th Cong., 2d sess., House, February 19, 1901: 2660; *Reclamation of Arid Lands,* S. Rept. 254, 3; Dorothy Lampen, *Economic and Social Aspects of Federal Reclamation* (Baltimore: Johns Hopkins University Press, 1930), 66–68; Widtsoe, *Success on Irrigation Projects,* 8; *Forestry and Irrigation* 9 (December 1903): 573; *Philadelphia Record,* May 24, 1904; F. H. Newell, "The Reclamation Service," *Popular Science Monthly* 66 (December 1904): 106–16.

87. Ray P. Teele, *Irrigation in the United States* (New York: D. Appleton and Co., 1915), 235. Newell later confirmed Teele's figures. See Newell, "National Efforts at Home Making," *Annual Report of the Smithsonian Institution, 1922* (Washington, D.C.: GPO, 1924), 527.

88. F. H. Newell, "Development of Water Resources," *Forester* 7 (August 1901): 197; *New York Times,* October 4, 1903.

89. *Official Proceedings of the Tenth National Irrigation Congress Held at Colorado Springs, Colorado,* 223; George H. Maxwell to Franklin K. Lane, March 23, 1914, Francis G. Newlands Collection, Box 45, Folder 467, Sterling Library, Yale University.

90. *Third Annual Report of the Reclamation Service, 1903–1904* (Washington, D.C.: GPO, 1905), 53–54. For the location of the reserved lands, see the map facing p. 30 in the *Fourth Annual Report of the Reclamation Service, 1904–1905* (Washington, D.C.: GPO, 1906). Also see *Congressional Record,* 61st Cong., 2d sess., House, June 21, 1910: 8683, and *Addresses and Proceedings of the Second National Conservation Congress* (Washington, D.C.: National Conservation Congress, 1911), 113.

91. The following discussion relies heavily on Ira Clark, *Water in New Mexico: A History of Its Management and Use* (Albuquerque: University of New Mexico Press, 1987), 90–99; Clark, "The Elephant Butte Controversy: A Chapter in the Emer-

gence of Federal Water Law," *Journal of American History* 61 (March 1975): 1006–33; and Douglas R. Littlefield's excellent "Interstate Water Conflicts, Compromises, and Compacts: The Rio Grande, 1880–1938," which the author kindly allowed me to read in manuscript. Since Littlefield's study is not yet widely available, I have not cited page numbers. It is based on his 1987 doctoral dissertation in history at the University of California, Los Angeles, which bears the same title.

92. Clark, *Water in New Mexico,* 92.

93. Paul Wallace Gates, *History of Public Land Law Development* (Washington, D.C.: GPO, 1968; New York: Arno Press, 1979), 461.

94. *United States* v. *Rio Grande Dam and Irrigation Company,* 174 U.S. 690 (1899).

95. Clark, *Water in New Mexico,* 98–99.

96. *Irrigation Age* 21 (June 1906): 241.

97. See Newell's testimony in *Hearings before the Committee on Irrigation of Arid Lands of the House of Representatives, Jan. 28 to Feb. 9, 1901* (Washington, D.C.: GPO, 1901), 8, 88. Also see his untitled speech in *Proceedings of the Eleventh National Irrigation Congress,* 201, and his article "The Reclamation of the West," *National Geographic* 15 (January 1904): 15. In 1909, Newell publicly reiterated that "[t]he speculative element has been largely absent" from federal reclamation projects. See Newell, "The National Irrigation Situation," *Official Proceedings of the Seventeenth National Irrigation Congress [1909]* (Spokane: Shaw and Borden Co., n.d.), 54. Privately, he told a different story. In 1911, for example, he informed the secretary of the interior that the price of privately held land on the government projects was "a condition which seems to prevail throughout a great part of this country and is holding back development. Few intelligent farmers will sell land in Iowa or Illinois and purchase raw land here, which will require years to be subdued, at present prices." See Frederick H. Newell to Walter L. Fisher, September 29, 1911, "Reclamation, Part I," Walter L. Fisher Collection, Library of Congress, Washington, D.C.

98. *Forestry and Irrigation* 11 (October 1905): 443–44.

99. *Report of the Secretary of the Interior, 1905* (Washington, D.C.: GPO, 1906), 80.

100. "The Public-Land Problem and Irrigation," *The Nation* 77 (September 24, 1903): 241–42; *Forestry and Irrigation* 10 (February 1904): 86.

101. Paris Gibson, "The Repeal of Our Objectionable Land Laws," *Forestry and Irrigation* 9 (October 1903): 484–89; *New York Tribune,* June 15, 1903; Guy E. Mitchell, "The New Montana," *Forestry and Irrigation* 10 (August 1904): 365–67. Also see Donald J. Pisani, "George Maxwell, the Railroads, and American Land Policy, 1899–1904," *Pacific Historical Review* 63 (May 1994): 177–202.

102. *U.S. Statutes at Large* 36 (1910): 836; R. A. Ballinger to Thomas H. Carter, July 30, 1909, Entry 4–50, Ballinger Papers, Special Collections, University of Washington, Seattle.

103. Richard Lowitt and Judith Fabry, eds., *Henry A. Wallace's Irrigation Frontier: On the Trail of the Corn Belt Farmer, 1909* (Norman: University of Oklahoma Press, 1991), 129.

104. A. E. Chandler, "The Reclamation of Nevada," *Sunset* 14 (February 1905): 339–48; *Forestry and Irrigation* 10 (February 1904): 58; Katherine Coman, "Some Unsettled Problems of Irrigation," *American Economic Review* 1 (March 1911):

18. Other projects experienced the same problem. For example, see *Pittsburgh Dispatch,* October 21, 1902; *Los Angeles Times,* November 9, 1902; *Denver Republican,* January 24, 1903; *Salt Lake City Herald,* June 24, 1903; *Forestry and Irrigation* 10 (June 1904): 247, and 10 (November 1904): 511–12. Squatters on the Minidoka Project—who moved onto government land years before water became available—have been well described by William Darrell Gertsch in "The Upper Snake River Project: A Historical Study of Reclamation and Regional Development" (Ph.D. diss., University of Washington, 1974), 143–45.

105. William E. Warne, "Land Speculation," *Reclamation Era* 33 (August 1947): 176–80, 186. The *average* value of irrigated land in Washington State increased from fifty dollars an acre in 1890 to two hundred dollars an acre in 1910, but the value of irrigated land within the Yakima Project increased at a much faster rate than in the state as a whole. Robert C. Nesbit and Charles M. Gates, "Agriculture in Eastern Washington, 1890–1910," *Pacific Northwest Quarterly* 37 (October 1946): 289.

106. Charles F. Lambert, "Land Speculation and Irrigation Development in the Sacramento Valley, 1905–1907," 24, oral history transcript dated 1957 at the Bancroft Library, University of California, Berkeley.

107. *Reclamation Record* 2 (July 1910): 62, and 5 (December 1914): 445; William K. Brown to Richard A. Ballinger, May 6, 1910, RG 48, Box 1707, "Reclamation Service: Miscellaneous Charges."

108. Frederick H. Newell to George Pardee, June 5, 1906, Newell file, George Pardee Papers, Bancroft Library. Also see Newell's statement before the House Committee on Irrigation of Arid Lands on January 27, 1912, as reprinted in Warne, "Land Speculation," p. 179, and Newell, "The National Irrigation Situation," *Proceedings of the Seventeenth National Irrigation Congress,* 59. At the end of 1911, Newell informed Secretary of the Interior Walter Fisher that on the Umatilla Project in Oregon only forty-five hundred out of seventeen thousand irrigable acres were producing crops. The unirrigated land was held for as much as two hundred dollars an acre by speculators who had used the Desert Land Act to acquire it. "It is generally recognized that these conditions are not unique," Newell noted, "that there are literally millions of acres throughout the arid West which have been reclaimed at costs of from \$40–\$50 per acre and upwards, but which are not being cropped." Obviously, too much land stimulated speculation as much as too little. See F. H. Newell, "Memorandum for Secretary Fisher," December 7, 1912, RG 48, Box 1707, "Reclamation Service: Miscellaneous Charges."

109. *National Geographic* 13 (October 1902): 386–88; *Forestry and Irrigation* 11 (October 1905): 441–42; *Forestry and Irrigation* 8 (December 1902): 516–17; *Congressional Record,* 57th Cong., 1st sess., House, June 12, 1902: 6676.

110. *Fourth Annual Report of the Reclamation Service, 1904–05* (Washington, D.C., 1906), 31; Daniel E. Willard, "The Planting of Trees on Prairie Lands Where Irrigation Is Impossible," *Proceedings of the Eleventh National Irrigation Congress,* 286; *Forestry and Irrigation* 12 (July 1906): 305–6.

111. F. H. Newell, "Newell on History of Western Irrigation Development," *Transactions of the American Society of Civil Engineers* 90 (1927): 700; A. P. Davis, "Davis on History of Western Irrigation Development," Ibid., 696.

112. H. A. Storrs, "Irrigation Development in North Dakota," *Proceedings of the Twelfth National Irrigation Congress,* 199–201; *Forestry and Irrigation* 11 (April 1905): 181–82; *Forestry and Irrigation* 12 (September 1906): 428; F. H. Newell, "Progress on Pumping Projects," *Forestry and Irrigation* 12 (December 1906): 551–52.

113. *New York Times,* October 4, 1903; F. H. Newell, "The Reclamation of the West," *National Geographic* 15 (January 1904): 20–21. Reclamation Service officials initially hoped that farmers would distribute the water impounded in government dams, but "on a long sandy lateral where considerable care is necessary in order to force water to flow down to the farms at the lower end, the majority of the land owners living near the upper end would not exert themselves or limit their supply in favor of their neighbors living miles away at the far end, who, in turn, complained that they did not receive water at the right time or in sufficient amount and consequently could not make payment." To ensure the repayment of construction charges and to reduce friction among irrigators, the Reclamation Service assumed the additional expense of supervising the operation of even the smallest ditches. The reluctance of farmers to cooperate forced the service to deliver water to individual farms, not just groups of farmers. See Brookings Institution, *The U.S. Reclamation Service,* 63–64.

114. Francis E. Warren to Elwood Mead, May 28, 1903, Francis E. Warren Collection; Elwood Mead to Platt Rogers, October 29, 1902, RG 8, Box 1.

115. Karen L. Smith and Shelly C. Dudley, "The Marriage of Law and Public Policy in the Southwest: Salt River Project, Phoenix, Arizona," *Western Legal History* 2 (Summer-Fall, 1989): 246–51; H. E. Meredith, "Reclamation in the Salt River Valley, 1902–1917," *Journal of the West* 7 (January 1968): 78.

116. *Reclamation Record* 2 (July 1910): 61–62.

CHAPTER 3. CASE STUDIES IN IRRIGATION AND COMMUNITY

1. Richard Lowitt and Judith Fabry, eds., *Henry A. Wallace's Irrigation Frontier: On the Trail of the Corn Belt Farmer, 1909* (Norman: University of Oklahoma Press, 1991), 159.

2. William Darrell Gertsch, "The Upper Snake River Project: A Historical Study of Reclamation and Regional Development, 1890–1930" (Ph.D. diss., University of Washington, 1974), 20–21, 48; Hugh T. Lovin, "Water, Arid Land, and Visions of Advancement on the Snake River Plain," *Idaho Yesterdays* 35 (Spring 1991), 4. For an imaginative, sophisticated history of the relationship between irrigation and the environment in the Snake River Valley, see Mark Fiege, *Irrigated Eden: The Making of an Agricultural Landscape in the American West* (Seattle: University of Washington Press, 1999). Unfortunately, that book did not appear until after this chapter had been written.

3. On the genesis and early history of the Carey Act, see Donald J. Pisani, *To Reclaim a Divided West: Water, Law, and Public Policy, 1848–1902* (Albuquerque: University of New Mexico Press, 1992), 251–65.

4. At the turn of the twentieth century, most of Idaho's irrigated farms were situated along the Snake River forty miles upstream from what would become the Minidoka Project, where primitive ditches flooded two hundred thousand acres of meadowland at American Falls.

5. Mikel H. Williams, *The History of Development and Current Status of the Carey Act in Idaho* (Boise: Idaho Department of Reclamation, 1970), 15–81; Leonard Arrington, *History of Idaho*, vol. 1 (Moscow: University of Idaho Press, 1994), 471; Benjamin Hibbard, *A History of the Public Land Policies* (New York: Macmillan, 1924), 436–37; Hugh T. Lovin, "Footnote to History: 'The Reservoir . . . Would Not Hold Water,'" *Idaho Yesterdays* 24 (Spring 1980): 12.

6. Randall R. Howard, "Irrigation Frauds in Ten States," *Technical World Magazine* 17 (July 1912): 513.

7. Byron Hunter and Samuel B. Nuckols, *An Economic Study of Irrigated Farming in Twin Falls County, Idaho*, United States Department of Agriculture Bulletin no. 1421 (Washington, D.C.: GPO, 1926).

8. Merrill D. Beal and Merle W. Wells, *History of Idaho*, vol. 2 (New York: Lewis Historical Publishing Co., 1959), 138–45; H. J. Kingsbury, *Bucking the Tide* (New York: Ganis and Harris, 1949), 45–55; Louise Morgan Sill, "The Largest Irrigated Tract in the World," *Harper's Weekly* 52 (October 17, 1908): 11–12.

9. Anna E. Hayes Oral History Transcript, August 24, 1970, OH 46, Idaho State Library, Boise; C. S. Walgamott, *Reminiscences of Early Days* (Twin Falls: Idaho Citizen Printing Co., 1926); J. Howard Moon, "The Twin Falls Land and Water Company," in *A Tribute to the Past, a Legacy to the Future*, ed. Donna Scott (Twin Falls: Twin Falls County Business History, 1990), 8.

10. D. W. Ross to State Board of Land Commissioners, October 12, 1900, in Idaho Department of Reclamation Records, AR 20, Carey Act Files, Box 17, file "Twin Falls—South Side," Idaho State Archives, Idaho State Historical Society, Boise; James Stephenson, *Irrigation in Idaho*, USDA Office of Experiment Stations Bulletin 216 (Washington, D.C.: GPO, 1909), 43; Alfred R. Golze, *Reclamation in the United States* (New York: McGraw-Hill Book Co., 1952), 155–56.

11. *New York Times*, March 29, 1903. The Twin Falls Project, dominated by eastern investors who were regarded as more sober and responsible than the typical western entrepreneur, received nationwide attention. For example, see William Allen White, "The Boom in the Northwest," *Saturday Evening Post* 170 (May 21, 1904): 2; E. G. Adams, "America's Greatest Irrigation Enterprise," *Pacific Monthly* 12 (November 1904): 281–87; and Henry F. Cope, "Making Gardens Out of Lava Dust," *World Today* 10 (June 1906): 621–28.

12. Patricia Wright, *Twin Falls Country: A Look at Idaho Architecture* (Boise: Idaho State Historical Society, 1979), 13; Anna E. Hayes Oral History Transcript, pp. 18–19, Idaho State Library; *Idaho Statesman* (Boise), August 2, 1931.

13. *Twin Falls News*, August 17, 1911; *Caldwell Tribune* (Caldwell, Idaho), June 13 and 27 and July 18, 1903; Gertsch, "The Upper Snake River Project," 64–65; Walgamott, *Reminiscences*, 118–19; James D. Schuyler, "New Irrigation Construction on Snake River, Idaho," in *Official Proceedings of the Eleventh National Irrigation Congress, Ogden, Utah, September 15–18, 1903* (Ogden: The Proceedings Publishing Co., 1904), 354–62.

14. *Twin Falls News*, October 28, 1904, and February 3, 1905; *The First Hundred Years: A History of the Twin Falls Area from 1811 to 1911* (Twin Falls: Times-News Publishing Co., n.d.), 38, 42; J. Howard Moon, "The Twin Falls Investment Company," in *Tribute to the Past*, 20.

15. *Twin Falls News*, June 23, 1905.

16. *Twin Falls News,* October 28, 1904; March 3 and 17, August 4 and 11, and December 22, 1905 (quote).
17. *Twin Falls News,* December 29, 1905, January 12 and 19, September 7, 1906. F. R. Gooding, "Development of Idaho under the Carey Act," in *Official Proceedings of the Seventeenth National Irrigation Congress [1909]* (Spokane: Shaw and Borden Co., n.d.), 317.
18. Stephenson, *Irrigation in Idaho,* 45.
19. *Twin Falls News,* April 21 and 28 and December 29, 1905; February 9 and October 19, 1906; May 24, 1907; *Rupert Pioneer-Record,* May 6, 1909. The company's support for an opera house was not purely cultural. It was part of a campaign to make Twin Falls the seat of a new county and provide a meeting hall large enough to host the state conventions of Idaho's political parties.
20. *Twin Falls News,* March 17, 1905; November 23, 1906; February 7 and 14, 1908.
21. *Twin Falls News,* March 24, 1905; January 25, 1907; April 10, 1908.
22. In 1908, Fred A. Voigt, secretary of the Twin Falls Land and Water Company, also served as mayor, and many members of the city council had close ties to the company.
23. Fred Voigt, Twin Falls Land and Water Co., to S. Loave, July 17, 1906, Box 3, Twin Falls Land and Water Company Records, Idaho State Historical Society, Boise. Also see the company's promotional pamphlet, *Idaho, the Land of Opportunity,* dated January 1, 1906, in Box 5. It promised a "perfect climate," the "absolute elimination of water controversies and litigation," and soil that would grow fruits, nuts, and even tobacco.
24. Fred Voigt, Twin Falls Land and Water Co., to W. A. Wotherspoon, March 26, 1907, Box 5, Twin Falls Land and Water Co. Records.
25. *Twin Falls News,* October 28, 1904.
26. *Twin Falls News,* September 13, 1907; September 24 and October 1, 1909; August 25, 1905.
27. Hunter and Nuckols, *Economic Study,* 8, 25.
28. *Twin Falls News,* August 25, 1905, and October 9, 1908. An April 5, 1907, advertisement for the C. E. Evans real estate company urged buyers to "Buy a lot in Terrace Park Place. They will advance $50 per lot in the next Thirty Days." A typical blurb in the editorial column of the February 15, 1907, issue noted: "The advance in the price of farm lands in Rock creek canyon has been phenomenal of late."
29. Fred Voigt, Twin Falls Land and Water Company, to Ernest E. Jewett, May 1, 1905, Box 3, and Secretary to George A. Snow, November 20, 1909, Box 5, Twin Falls Land and Water Company Records.
30. Tax laws often favored one industry over another, particularly in frontier states. In 1904, the assessed value of Idaho's railroads was only 13 percent of real value, while livestock was taxed at 31 percent. Put another way, while the railroads owned nearly 27 percent of the state's property, they paid only 15 percent of the taxes. The tax burden rested heaviest on livestock owners, next heaviest on farmers, and lightest on the railroads. See the *Rupert Record,* December 27, 1906.
31. Fred Voigt, Twin Falls Land and Water Co., to Trowbridge and Niver Co., July 25, 1906, Box 5, Twin Falls Land and Water Co. Records.
32. *Rupert Record,* September 28, 1905, and January 25 and May 10, 1906; *Twin Falls News,* May 4, 1906, and August 3, 1911.

33. *Twin Falls News,* December 7, 1906 (quote); August 23, 1907; July 3, August 28, and September 18, 1908; August 10 and 24, 1911.

34. *Twin Falls News,* July 19 and October 11, 1907; August 7, 1908.

35. *Twin Falls News,* February 15 and 22, and April 26, 1907; August 20 and 27, 1909; March 10, 1910; *The First Hundred Years,* 30, 32-33.

36. *Twin Falls News,* April 26, 1907.

37. *Twin Falls News,* August 10 and 31 (quote), September 7, 14, and 21, 1906; April 26 and May 10, 1907.

38. *Twin Falls News,* April 12, 1907; February 7, 1908; August 6, September 17, and November 5, 1909.

39. *Twin Falls News,* September 25, 1908.

40. *Twin Falls News,* March 15 and 29, and June 28, 1907.

41. *Twin Falls News,* February 9, March 2, and December 28, 1906; April 5 and 12, May 17, July 26, and December 16, 1907; October 2, 1908; March 12, 1909; December 13, 1910; *Rupert Pioneer-Record,* September 24, 1908; March 18 and August 19, 1909.

42. *Rupert Record,* February 1, 1906; *Twin Falls News,* January 4, July 26, December 20 and 27, 1907, and November 2, 1911; F. A. Voigt to S. H. Hays, January 23, 1907, and Hays to Voigt, June 5, 1907, Box 2, Twin Falls Land and Water Company Records.

43. F. H. Buhl to R. W. Faris, October 1, 1906, Box 6, Twin Falls Land and Water Company Records, Idaho State Historical Society; *Twin Falls News,* November 30 and December 7, 14, and 21, 1906; July 5, 19, and 27, 1907; January 3 and 10, and December 18, 1908; May 7, October 1, and December 10, 1909.

44. *Twin Falls News,* December 28, 1906; April 26, September 6 and 27, October 4, and November 22, 1907; March 27 and September 4 and 11, 1908; December 10 and 24, 1909; November 25, 1910; *Caldwell Tribune,* January 26, 1907.

45. S. H. Hays to Trowbridge and Niver Co., May 14, 1906, Box 5, Twin Falls Land and Water Co. Records.

46. *Rupert Pioneer-Record,* October 6, 1909.

47. *[USGS] Irrigation Survey—First Annual Report* (Washington, D.C.: GPO, 1890), 106, 107-8 (quote); *Irrigation Survey—Second Annual Report* (Washington, D.C.: GPO, 1890), 77-92, 192, 197-98.

48. P. M. Fogg, "A History of the Minidoka Project, Idaho, to 1912 Inclusive," typescript dated August 1915, pp. 10-11, 19, in the Idaho State Library, Boise. Fogg was one of the Minidoka Project's early managers, and his detailed history is a particularly valuable source. Also see *First Annual Report of the Reclamation Service from June 17 to December 1, 1902* (Washington, D.C.: GPO, 1903), 171, and *Second Annual Report of the Reclamation Service, 1902-3* (Washington, D.C.: GPO, 1904), 251-79.

49. *Rupert Record,* December 28, 1905.

50. Fogg, "History of the Minidoka Project," 27, 33-34; Lovin, "Water, Arid Land, and Visions of Advancement," 9.

51. May Jones Oral History Transcript, June 12, 1973, OH 183, and Herman A. Johnson Oral History Transcript, December 5, 1972, OH 209, Idaho State Library; Alvin C. Holmes, *Swedish Homesteaders in Idaho on the Minidoka Irrigation Project* (Twin Falls: Ace Printing, Inc., 1976), 82; Mildred D. Curtis, *In Only Ten Years*

(n.p., n.d.; in the collection of the Idaho State Library, Boise), 6, 8; Gerhard Riedesel, ed., *Arid Acres: A History of the Kimama-Minidoka Homesteaders, 1912–1932* (Pullman, Wash.: G. A. Riedesel, 1969), 2.

52. *Rupert Record,* October 12, 1905.

53. *Caldwell Tribune* (Caldwell, Idaho), December 24, 1904.

54. *Rupert Record,* February 1, March 1, and November 15 and 22, 1906, March 7, 1907; Charles Coate, "Federal-Local Relationships on the Boise and Minidoka Projects, 1904–1926," *Idaho Yesterdays* 25 (Summer 1981): 2–9.

55. Fogg, "History of the Minidoka Project," 33–35, 132–33, 136, 140; Stephenson, *Irrigation in Idaho,* 33; *Rupert Pioneer-Record,* April 1 and May 27, 1909.

56. *Rupert Record,* August 22 and September 5, 12, and 26, 1907.

57. The first Newell quote is from his February 14, 1908, letter to A. C. DeMary, U.S. land commissioner in Rupert, as reprinted in the *Rupert Record,* February 27, 1908. The second is as reprinted in Coate, "Federal-Local Relationships," 4. In the February 27 issue of the *Record,* Secretary of the Interior James Garfield claimed that one in five Minidoka entrants had done nothing to improve his claim. Such entrants had not conformed to the requirements of the Reclamation Act and Homestead Act, but they were rarely challenged. Also see the comments of the chief engineer of the Reclamation Service, A. P. Davis, in the *Record* of March 12, 1908.

58. *Rupert Pioneer-Record,* March 10, 1910; Fogg, "History of the Minidoka Project," 139.

59. *Rupert Record,* December 13, 1906. *Rupert Pioneer-Record,* February 25, 1909; February 2, 9, and 15, March 9, and April 6, 1911.

60. *Rupert Record,* March 29, 1906. In his "History of the Minidoka Project," project manager P. M. Fogg observed: "It should be understood that the farm population was composed of people from nearly every walk in life; many had never farmed at all, some had farmed land in other states and under totally different circumstances; many were foreigners attracted by the idea of 'free' land, and possessed but little, if any, capital" (pp. 133–34).

61. *Rupert Record,* September 28, 1905, and August 23 and September 13, 1906; *Rupert Pioneer-Record,* June 4 and September 17, 1908; Fogg, "History of the Minidoka Project," 144.

62. *Rupert Record,* March 8 and January 23 and 30, 1906; *Rupert Pioneer-Record,* April 2 and 9, July 16, and December 11, 1908; February 18 and October 15, 1909; July 20, 1911.

63. Historians have largely ignored the environmental impact of irrigation. Canals required large embankments, so their construction generally left open pits or low areas near the ditch. In Idaho, where the soil was very porous, water seeped through the earthen wall and entered the pits, creating ponds. These were popular with children, who used them for skating in the winter and wading in the summer. But, as one writer has pointed out, the marshes created by irrigation soon "became full of water bugs, snails, algae, moss and minute organisms. The kids' legs got red and inflamed. The ponds were becoming swamps with a disagreeable odor. Cattails and willows began growing everywhere. Muskrats became numerous. Snipes and ducks moved in. Killdeers were running and chirping along the water edge, eating insects. The bordering land was turning white with

alkali. Foxtail grass grew everywhere. The land was being ruined for agriculture."
Rising groundwater also poisoned wells and created quicksand, a menace to domestic animals. See Holmes, *Swedish Homesteaders,* 60.

64. *Rupert Record,* December 27, 1906, and February 14 and November 7, 1907; *Rupert Pioneer-Record,* March 11, June 17 and 24, and July 29, 1909; Fogg, "History
of the Minidoka Project," 45, 50.

65. *Rupert Pioneer-Record,* May 18, 1911.

66. *Rupert Record,* December 21, 1905, and October 24 and November 14, 1907; *Rupert Pioneer-Record,* July 16 and 23, November 26, and December 31, 1908; Fogg,
"History of the Minidoka Project," 150.

67. *Rupert Record,* November 2, 1905; January 4 and 25, 1906; January 28, 1908. *Rupert Pioneer-Record,* June 11, July 23, August 6, November 19, and December 17
and 24, 1908; February 23, 1911.

68. *Rupert Record,* November 2, 1905.

69. *Rupert Record,* August 23, 1906.

70. As early as November 1905, the editor of the *Record* observed that a bridge would
give Rupert access to Albion, Cassia County's capital, thirteen miles away. "Rupert is a leader," he observed, "and in time will have roads leading in from every
point of the compass." *Rupert Record,* November 9, 1905. Apparently, the state
legislature appropriated ten thousand dollars to build the bridge on condition
that Lincoln and Cassia Counties contribute a thousand dollars apiece; that
money was raised by subscription. See *Rupert Pioneer-Record,* June 2, 1910.

71. *Rupert Record,* October 5 and December 7, 14, and 28 (quotes), 1905. Also see
Rupert Record, June 14, 1906. In the late nineteenth and early twentieth centuries,
westerners used the term *opera house* very loosely. Rupert's was thirty by seventy
feet, constructed in two weeks by two men who originally had intended to build
a dance hall. The grand opening was held on October 13, 1905.

72. *Rupert Record,* October 26, 1905; January 18 and August 16 and 30, 1906; December 19, 1907. *Rupert Pioneer-Record,* September 23, 1909; February 17 and
April 14, 1910. At the sale of 412 lots held on April 8, 1910, local buyers predominated, with notable exceptions. M. M. Mackey, Lincoln County assessor, half
owner of a Shoshone land company, and a former resident of Rupert, purchased
the largest number of lots, fifty-seven. Most other speculators lived in Boise.

73. Herman A. Johnson Oral History Transcript p. 8.

74. *Rupert Record,* June 14 and August 2, 1906.

75. *Twin Falls News,* October 6, 1905; *Rupert Record,* October 12, 1905.

76. The most important bills introduced from 1905 to 1910 were H.R. 18530
(French), 58th Cong., 3d sess.; H.R. 5362 (French) and S. 4862 (Dubois), 59th
Cong., 1st sess.; H.R. 20700 (French) and S. 6018 (Borah), 60th Cong., 1st sess.;
S. 8376 (Borah), 60th Cong., 2d sess. Also see *Sale of Lands in Reclamation Town
Sites,* S. Rept. 1524, 59th Cong., 1st sess. (Washington, D.C.: GPO, 1906); *Al-
lowing Certain Settlers to Buy Lots in Heyburn and Rupert, Idaho,* H. Rept. 2471, 59th
Cong., 1st sess. (Washington, D.C.: GPO, 1906); *Rupert Record,* November 16,
December 14, 1905; January 11, February 15, March 15 and 29, April 12, May 31,
June 21, and July 5, 1906; December 12, 1907; March 12, 1908. *Rupert Pioneer-
Record,* March 19, April 9, May 7, 14, and 21, and October 29, 1908; February 4,
1909.

77. *Congressional Record,* 60th Cong., 1st sess., Senate, April 29, 1908: 5424–25.

78. *Rupert Record,* May 2 and June 6, 1907; *Rupert Pioneer-Record,* September 8, 1910.

79. *Rupert Record,* July 16, 1908. The *Idaho Statesman* of September 20, 1909, was equally candid:

> The progress and growth of Rupert has been retarded and held back to a great extent on account of its being a government townsite, in the first place, as no money was available for advertising purposes and to push the town to the front. In the second place, anyone desiring to purchase property was compelled to pay cash in full, as the government gives no terms, except cash with the order. With the publicity and boosting the other towns of Southern Idaho have had in the last two or three years it is no wonder Rupert was over-looked, temporarily at least.

80. The Reclamation Service continued to urge the expenditure of at least part of the receipts from town lot sales on municipal improvements. Congress continued to insist that the proceeds be credited against construction charges. The Minidoka and Belle Fourche Projects produced the largest income from lot sales. A. P. Davis to Secretary of the Interior, November 11, 1912, in RG 115, General Administrative Records, 1902–1919, Box 332, "(1079): General. The President's Economy and Efficiency Commission [1911–1913]"; *Reclamation Record* 5 (April 1914): 134–35.

81. *Rupert Pioneer-Record,* August 26, 1909, and August 25, 1910.

82. *Rupert Record,* April 26, May 3, and June 14 and 21, 1906; January 30, 1908. *Rupert Pioneer-Record,* April 2, 1908; April 22, May 20, June 17, and September 2 and 23, 1909; March 24, May 12 and 19, June 2, and November 10, 1910.

83. *Rupert Record,* September 19, 1907. *Rupert Pioneer-Record,* September 1 and 8 and December 8, 1910; January 5 and 12, 1911.

84. *Rupert Record,* May 2, 1907; *Minidoka County News,* September 25, 1947.

85. Minidoka County Historical Society, *A History of Minidoka County and Its People, 1985* (Dallas: Taylor Publishing Co., 1985), 49–50; *Rupert Record,* October 12, 1905; September 19, 1907; March 12, 1908. *Rupert Pioneer-Record,* August 20 and December 31, 1908; February 18, 1909.

86. *Rupert Pioneer-Record,* March 25, June 10, June 17, and September 23, 1909; November 17 and December 22, 1910.

87. Stephenson, *Irrigation in Idaho,* 58.

88. *Rupert Record,* January 25 and November 1, 1906. *Rupert Pioneer-Record,* March 3 and April 28, 1910; July 13 and September 7 and 14, 1911.

89. *Thirteenth Census of the United States, 1910: Agriculture General Report and Analysis* (Washington, D.C.: GPO, 1914), 845; *Fourteenth Census of the United States, 1920: Irrigation and Drainage* (Washington, D.C.: GPO, 1922), 15; *Fifteenth Census of the United States, 1930: Irrigation of Agricultural Lands* (Washington, D.C.: GPO, 1932), 15; Gertsch, "The Upper Snake River Project," 96; Hugh T. Lovin, "The Carey Act in Idaho, 1895–1925: An Experiment in Free Enterprise Reclamation," *Pacific Northwest Quarterly* 78 (October 1987): 126.

90. Donald J. Pisani, *From the Family Farm to Agribusiness: The Irrigation Crusade in Cali-*

fornia and the West, 1850–1931 (Berkeley: University of California Press, 1984), 129–53, 250–82. In 1921, the Idaho legislature established a Reclamation District Bond Commission, which, in the words of historian Hugh T. Lovin, "obtained independent appraisals of irrigation district bonds and certified the bonds to purchasers on the basis of such ratings; moreover, certification officially informed investors that the 'faith and credit' of the irrigation district stood behind the bonds. For a brief period, this legislation helped to make district bonds more marketable, but investors developed new mistrust because districts took advantage of the law and piled up too much debt." Even more important, the severe agricultural depression of the 1920s sharply reduced the demand for irrigated land. Lovin, "The Carey Act in Idaho," 131. Also see Lovin, "Water, Arid Land," 7.

91. Donald J. Pisani, "Water Law Reform in California, 1900–1913," *Agricultural History* 54 (April 1980): 295–317.

92. Gertsch, "The Upper Snake River Project," 43–44, 82, 84, 91, 93.

93. Hugh T. Lovin, "Free Enterprise and Large-Scale Reclamation on the Twin Falls–North Side Tract, 1907–1930," *Idaho Yesterdays* 29 (Spring 1985): 4, 6. Also see Lovin, "How Not to Run a Carey Act Project: The Twin Falls–Salmon Falls Creek Tract, 1904–1922," *Idaho Yesterdays* 29 (Fall 1986): 11–13, and "A 'New West' Reclamation Tragedy: The Twin Falls Oakley Project in Idaho," *Arizona and the West* 20 (Spring 1978): 5–24.

94. For typical criticisms of the Idaho Land Board, see the *Caldwell Tribune*, November 20 and December 4, 1909, and October 14, 1910.

95. S. Doc. 1097, 62d Cong., 3d sess. (Washington, D.C.: GPO, 1913); Randall R. Howard, "Irrigation Frauds in Ten States," *Technical World Magazine* 17 (July 1912): 504–14; Ray P. Teele, *Land Reclamation Policies in the United States,* USDA Department Bulletin no. 1257 (Washington, D.C.: GPO, 1924), 7; R. E. Shepherd, "The Financing of Irrigation Developments by Private Capital," *Transactions of the American Society of Civil Engineers* 90 (1927): 715; Robert G. Dunbar, *Forging New Rights to Western Waters* (Lincoln: University of Nebraska Press, 1983), 40.

96. *Twin Falls News,* January 26, 1906; Paul Bickel (Twin Falls Investment Company) to Thomas H. Carter (U.S. senator from Montana), November 14, 1904, in Box 6, "Paul S. A. Bickel" file, Twin Falls Land and Water Company Records; F. W. Hunt to Fred Dubois (U.S. senator from Idaho), November 22, 1903, Folder 16, Box 37, Fred Dubois Collection, Special Collections, Idaho State University, Pocatello; Gertsch, "The Upper Snake River Project," 119.

97. *Twin Falls News,* May 17, 1907. Also see the *News* of December 15, 1905, and June 26, 1908, and the *Caldwell Tribune,* January 2, 1904.

98. *Reclamation Project Data* (Washington, D.C.: GPO, 1948), 197; Leonard Arrington, *History of Idaho,* vol. 2 (Moscow: University of Idaho Press, 1994), 28–30. For an excellent case study of how federal reclamation blocked, undermined, and absorbed Carey Act projects, see Hugh T. Lovin, "Idaho's White Elephant: The King Hill Tracts and the United States Reclamation Service," *Pacific Northwest Quarterly* 83 (January 1992), 12–21.

99. *Twin Falls News,* December 29, 1905.

100. *Rupert Record,* December 28, 1905; March 22, 1906; January 10, August 8, and October 31, 1907.

101. *Rupert Pioneer-Record,* March 25 and April 23, 1908.

102. *Idaho State Business Directory, 1910–1911* (Denver: The Gazetteer Publishing Co., 1910), 611; *Polk's Idaho Gazetteer and Business Directory, 1930–31* (Salt Lake City: R. L. Polk and Co., 1930), 778, 805.

103. One historian of reclamation has observed, "By its intensive action, settlement [on the Carey Act projects near Twin Falls] was effected in about 4 years which under ordinary circumstances would have required 20 years or more." See Golze, *Reclamation in the United States,* 159.

104. As quoted in Wright, *Twin Falls Country,* 9.

105. *The Twin Falls Country Southern Idaho* (Twin Falls: Kingsbury Printing Company, 1913), 5.

106. *Fifteenth Census of the United States [Population]: 1930* (Washington, D.C.: Government Printing Office, 1932), vol. 3, 343–48, 553–88; *Fifteenth Census of the United States [Agriculture]: 1930* (Washington, D.C.: GPO, 1932), vol. 2, 113–23, 171–217.

107. William Ellsworth Smythe, *The Conquest of Arid America* (New York: Harper and Bros., 1900; New York: Macmillan, 1905.) On Smythe's career, see Patricia Nelson Limerick, *Desert Passages: Encounters with the American Deserts* (Albuquerque: University of New Mexico Press, 1985), 77–90; Lawrence B. Lee, "William Ellsworth Smythe and the Irrigation Movement: A Reconsideration," *Pacific Historical Review* 41 (August 1972): 287–311; and Martin E. Carlson, "William E. Smythe: Irrigation Crusader," *Journal of the West* 7 (January 1968): 41–47.

108. Robert Dykstra, *The Cattle Towns* (New York: Knopf, 1968), 366. For a sampling of literature on the small town in the American West, see Daniel Boorstin, *The Americans: The National Experience* (New York: Random House, 1965), 90–97, 113–68; Lewis Atherton, *Main Street on the Middle Border* (Chicago: Quadrangle Books, 1966); Don Harrison Doyle, *The Social Order of a Frontier Community: Jacksonville, Illinois, 1825–1870* (Urbana: University of Illinois Press, 1978); Doyle, "Social Theory and New Communities in Nineteenth-Century America," *Western Historical Quarterly* 8 (April 1977): 151–66; Robert V. Hine, *Community on the American Frontier: Separate but Not Alone* (Norman: University of Oklahoma Press, 1980), 127–52; W. Turrentine Jackson, *Treasure Hill: Portrait of a Silver Mining Camp* (Tucson: University of Arizona Press, 1963); and Paula Nelson, *After the West Was Won: Homesteaders and Town-Builders in Western South Dakota, 1900–1917* (Iowa City: University of Iowa Press, 1986), 81–118.

109. John Walton, *Western Times and Water Wars: State, Culture, and Rebellion in California* (Berkeley: University of California Press, 1992), 91–92. Eventually, Twin Falls created many cooperative institutions, including the Twin Falls County Bean Growers' Association and the Twin Falls County Dairymen's Association, both established in the early 1920s. But these institutions resulted more from economic hard times—and the consequent desire to eliminate middlemen—than from the creative spirit of voluntarism and self-rule. See Kingsbury, *Bucking the Tide,* 69–73.

110. Paula Nelson has studied the impact of drought on farm populations in western South Dakota at the beginning of the twentieth century. Three counties lost nearly half their population in the five years following the severe drought of 1910 and 1911. Nelson, *After the West Was Won,* 88, 130. The droughts of the late 1880s and early 1890s and the late 1920s and early 1930s had a similar impact.

111. Dean L. May, *Three Frontiers: Family, Land, and Society in the American West, 1850–1900* (New York: Cambridge University Press, 1994), 105.

CHAPTER 4. AN ADMINISTRATIVE MORASS

1. Donald C. Jackson, "Engineering in the Progressive Era: A New Look at Frederick Haynes Newell and the U.S. Reclamation Service," *Technology and Culture* 34 (July 1993): 554–55; *Irrigation Age* 19 (December 1903): 39.
2. *Irrigation Age* 19 (September 1904): 327.
3. See the Arthur Powell Davis obituary in Box 6, Correspondence, A. P. Davis Collection, American Heritage Center, University of Wyoming, Laramie. For an overview of Davis's life that portrays him as a social reformer, see Gene M. Gressley, "Arthur Powell Davis, Reclamation, and the West," *Agricultural History* 42 (July 1968): 241–57. Also see Norris Hundley, jr., *Water and the West: The Colorado River Compact and the Politics of Water in the American West* (Berkeley: University of California Press, 1975), 5–16.
4. *Irrigation Age* 19 (December 1903): 39.
5. Jackson, "Engineering in the Progressive Era," 574.
6. As quoted in David Billington, Donald C. Jackson, and Martin Melosi, "Federal Dams," pp. 16–17, in manuscript.
7. David G. McCullough, *The Johnstown Flood* (New York: Simon and Schuster, 1987); Donald C. Jackson, *Building the Ultimate Dam: John S. Eastwood and the Control of Water in the West* (Lawrence: University Press of Kansas, 1995), 11–12.
8. Donald C. Jackson, "Considering the Multiple Arch Dam: Theory, Practice, and the Ethics of Safety in a Case of Innovative Hydraulic Engineering," *Natural Resources Journal* 32 (Winter 1992): 77–100.
9. On Elwood Mead's early career, see Donald J. Pisani, *To Reclaim a Divided West: Water, Law, and Public Policy, 1848–1902* (Albuquerque: University of New Mexico Press, 1992), 234–35, 237–40, 296–98, 308–13. On Frederick Newell's career, see Pisani, "Reclamation and Social Engineering in the Progressive Era," *Agricultural History* 57 (January 1983): 46–63.
10. Andrew Denny Rodgers III, "Federal Reclamation's Pioneer Period: A Biographical Study of Its Origins, Organization, and Early Work of Its Engineer Corps," 212–13, typescript manuscript in the United States Bureau of Reclamation Library, Federal Center, Denver.
11. F. H. Newell, "The United States Reclamation Service," *Engineering News* 53 (June 15, 1905): 610–11; Charles D. Walcott to Ethan Allen Hitchcock, June 18, 1902, and A. P. Davis to F. H. Newell, May 20, 1903, in RG 115, Entry 3, General Administrative Records, 1902–1919, Box 101, "(131): Corres. re Administration: Policies and Organization thru 1905," and "Report of Committee on Organization to the Chief Engineer," January 16, 1905, Box 147, "(273 and Subs): Committees and Reports." Also see Brit Storey, *Bureau of Reclamation Historical Organizational Structure* (Denver: Bureau of Reclamation History Program, 1997), 5–7.
12. Brookings Institution, Institute for Government Research, *The U.S. Reclamation Service: Its History, Activities, and Organization* (New York: D. Appleton and Co., 1919), 81, 86–87.
13. Charles Walcott to F. H. Newell, July 12, 1906, RG 115, Entry 3, General Ad-

ministrative Records, 1902–1919, Box 186, "(369): Reclamation Service Office Systems."

14. F. H. Newell, "Bookkeeping: Historical," memo prepared by Newell dated January 26, 1906, and F. H. Newell to N. E. Webster, Jr., January 8, 1909, RG 115, Entry 3, General Administrative Records, 1902–1919, Box 113, "(188): Bookkeeping and Accounting thru 1910."

15. Chief Engineer to H. N. Savage, October 3, 1905; Morris Bien, "Memorandum for the Director," dated June 10, 1907; "Memo to Mr. Luney," dated March 12, 1918; Senior Clerk to the Director, May 27, 1919; and Director to Senior Clerk, June 19, 1919, all in RG 115, Entry 3, General Administrative Records, 1902–1919, Box 232.

16. The best discussion of use of the press by conservation leaders is Stephen Edward Ponder, "News Management in the Progressive Era, 1898–1909: Gifford Pinchot, Theodore Roosevelt, and the Conservation Crusade" (Ph.D. diss., University of Washington, 1985). Also see Gifford Pinchot, *Breaking New Ground* (New York: Harcourt, Brace, 1947), 301; Stephen Fox, *The American Conservation Movement: John Muir and His Legacy* (Madison: University of Wisconsin Press, 1981), 129–30; and Arthur A. Ekirch, Jr., *Man and Nature in America* (New York: Columbia University Press, 1963), 92.

17. William Harper Dean, "The Master Movie Maker," *Technical World Magazine* 22 (January 1915): 730–32; C. J. Blanchard, "Memorandum for Mr. McCoy," June 9, 1914, in RG 115, Entry 3, General Administrative Records, 1902–1919, Box 186, "(369): Reclamation Service Office System."

18. Will R. King to the Secretary of the Interior, September 8, 1917, and A. P. Davis to Mr. Bradley, September 24, 1917, RG 115, Entry 3, General Administrative Records, Box 196, "(525): General Correspondence re the Reclamation Record."

19. State of Colorado, House Joint Memorial no. 5, dated March 8, 1913, in RG 115, General Administrative and Project Records, 1902–1919, Box 240, "(783): Establishment and Extension of Forest Reserves"; Ponder, "News Management in the Progressive Era," 174–75.

20. Thomas R. Bard to Secretary of the Interior, February 19, 1904, in RG 48, Entry 632, Box 1; and Bard to C. B. Boothe, December 28, 1904, in the Thomas R. Bard Collection, Box 9-A, "Irrigation, National, I," Huntington Library, San Marino, California.

21. See, for example, *Hearings before the House Committee on the Irrigation of Arid Lands concerning Western Reclamation Projects*, January 13–February 13, 1905, H. Doc. 381, 58th Cong., 3d sess., serial 4832 (Washington, D.C.: GPO, 1905).

22. *Hearings Conducted by the Senate Committee on the Irrigation and Reclamation of Arid Lands*, S. Rept. 1281, 61st Cong., 3d sess., serial 5846 (Washington, D.C.: GPO, 1911), 11, 26, 32. Many farmers who testified before the committee were far less optimistic than the committee. For a scathing indictment of federal reclamation as of 1909, see the statement of the Buford-Trenton Water Users Association as reprinted on pp. 199–202 in the transcript of the hearings. Also see the complaints of settlers on the Minidoka Project, pp. 584–85; the North Platte Project, pp. 607–8; the Truckee-Carson Project, pp. 683–85; and the Klamath Project, pp. 716–19.

23. Paolo E. Coletta, *The Presidency of William Howard Taft* (Lawrence: University Press of Kansas, 1973), 82–83.

24. R. A. Ballinger to Thomas H. Carter, February 9, 1910, 4–50, Ballinger Papers, Special Collections, University of Washington, Seattle.

25. *Rupert Pioneer-Record* (Rupert, Idaho), February 18 and June 10, 1909; *Twin Falls News* (Twin Falls, Idaho), June 11, 1909. At the end of the year, Carter tried to create a new administrative position to administer federal reclamation in Interior, responsible only to the secretary, leaving the supervision of engineering to Newell. This was the opposite of Henry Hansbrough's reorganization scheme. Undoubtedly, Carter hoped that such an arrangement would force Newell to resign. See the *Rupert Pioneer-Record,* December 9, 1909.

26. Don M. Carr to H. M. Whigham, April 12, 1910, 4–45, Ballinger Papers.

27. "President Taft on Conservation and the Work of the Reclamation Service," *Engineering News* 62 (October 7, 1909): 380–81. Taft summarized his views in an undated memo entitled "President Taft's Views on Reclamation Work," probably prepared for the Ballinger-Pinchot hearings in 1910. It is included in RG 115, Box 90, File "(110-E): Corres. re Irrigation Laws; Water Codes; Etc." Also see William Howard Taft to Richard A. Ballinger, September 13, 1909, Reel 13, Ballinger Papers.

28. *Investigation of the Department of the Interior and the Bureau of Forestry,* 61st Cong., 3d sess., S. Doc. 719, serial 5892 (Washington, D.C.: GPO, 1911), 3687.

29. *Rupert Pioneer-Record,* May 19, 1910.

30. Pinchot, *Breaking New Ground,* 410. Later, after an examination of the land, Ballinger "re-withdrew" more than 420,000 acres of the land Garfield had set aside.

31. See the "Memorandum" prepared by E. T. Perkins dated June 29, 1910, in 12–38, Ballinger Papers.

32. See Perkins's "Memorandum" and the statements on Newell and Davis prepared by Perkins in the spring of 1910 in Entry 10–42, Ballinger Papers.

33. See, for example, *Rupert Pioneer-Record,* June 17 and July 15, 1909.

34. Richard A. Ballinger to Walter E. Clark *(New York Sun),* August 25, 1909, and Ballinger to E. F. Baldwin *(Outlook),* August 25, 1909, Reel 2, Ballinger Papers.

35. Richard Ballinger to Walter E. Clark, August 7, 1909, 4–68, Ballinger Papers; *Investigation of the Department of the Interior and of the Bureau of Forestry,* S. Doc. 719, 3684; James L. Penick, Jr., *Progressive Politics and Conservation: The Ballinger-Pinchot Affair* (Chicago: University of Chicago Press, 1968), 166.

36. F. H. Newell to R. A. Ballinger, July 14, 1910, 4–43, Ballinger Papers. To the end of his tenure as director of the Reclamation Service, December 1914, Newell refused to admit that *any* project was a failure. A. P. Davis, however, acknowledged that the Hondo, Garden City, and Williston Projects, in New Mexico, Kansas, and North Dakota, respectively, should never have been constructed. As for Hondo, Davis observed: "No; it never has filled; it runs out too rapidly; two or three hundred second-feet leak out through the bottom, so that it fills for a little while, but quickly leaks out." The water bled into subterranean caverns through gypsum deposits. See *Hearings before the [House] Committee on Irrigation of Arid Lands* on the appropriation for the Reclamation Service, 63d Cong., 3d sess., December 16–18 and 21, 1914 (Washington, D.C.: GPO, 1915), 97.

37. On February 21, 1912, Newell wrote to Francis G. Newlands, noting that many "unfortunate individuals" on government projects were "entitled to great consideration and sympathy." The problem was that project farmers had to be treated equally. "I am calling this to your attention," Newell wrote, "because of the fact that we must have very rigid laws which do not permit the exercise of sympathy." See Box 27, folder 265, Francis G. Newlands Collection, Sterling Library, Yale University, New Haven.

38. Oscar Lawler to Richard A. Ballinger, July 21 and August 13, 1909, folders 8–48 and 8–49, and Walter E. Clark (Editor, *New York Sun*) to Ballinger, August 1, 1909, 4–68, Ballinger Papers; "Secretary Ballinger and the Reclamation Service," *Engineering News* 63 (January 13, 1910): 46–48.

39. Morris Bien to George Pardee, June 20, 1909, Bien File, George Pardee Collection, Bancroft Library, University of California, Berkeley. Long before Ballinger took office, Newell worried about being fired as director of the Reclamation Service. For example, see his letter to Gifford Pinchot, May 28, 1907, Box 759, Gifford Pinchot Collection, Library of Congress, Washington, D.C.

40. The best single study of this famous battle over the administration of natural resources is Penick, *Progressive Politics and Conservation.*

41. "Memorandum on Opinion of the Attorney-General of May 26, 1909, in the Matter of Cooperation Certificates," in Box 434, "Cooperative Certificates" file, Gifford Pinchot Collection.

42. Penick, *Progressive Politics and Conservation,* 68–72; *Investigation of the Department of the Interior and of the Bureau of Forestry,* S. Doc. 719, 85–88; R. A. Ballinger to F. H. Newell, September 9, 1909, and George Wickersham (U.S. Attorney General) to Ballinger, September 8, 1909, Box 434, "Cooperative Certificates" file, Gifford Pinchot Collection; Ballinger to Oscar Lawler, June 7, 1909, 8–47; Lawler to Ballinger, July 21, 1909; and Ballinger to Lawler, August 6, 1909, all in 8–48, Ballinger Papers.

43. *Investigation of the Department of the Interior and of the Bureau of Forestry,* S. Doc. 719, 3643.

44. *Washington Post,* May 4, 1910; *New York Times,* July 5 and 6, 1910; *Salt Lake City Tribune,* July 15, 1910; Richard A. Ballinger to William H. Taft, June 29, 1910, 12–38; Ballinger to Taft, July 1, 1910, 12–39; and Ballinger to John J. Vertrees, July 1, 1910, 13–43, Ballinger Papers.

45. *Fund for the Reclamation of Arid Lands,* H. Doc. 1262, 61st Cong., 3d sess., serial 6022 (Washington, D.C.: GPO, 1911); *New York Times,* July 3, 1910; Don M. Carr (Ballinger's secretary) to Senator Henry M. Teller (Colorado), July 12, 1910, 13–10, and William L. Marshall to Richard A. Ballinger, July 25, 1910, 9–38, Ballinger Papers. For a brief biography of Marshall, see *Reclamation Record* 5 (December 1914): 462.

46. F. H. Newell to George Pardee (Governor of California), July 6, 1906, Newell file, George Pardee Collection, Bancroft Library, University of California, Berkeley.

47. President Taft had justified such a loan months before the bill appeared in Congress. See Taft, "The Conservation of Our National Resources," *Official Proceedings of the Seventeenth National Irrigation Congress [1909]* (Spokane: Shaw and Borden Co., n.d.), 521.

48. *Congressional Record,* 61st Cong., 2d sess., Senate, February 17, 1910: 2014; *Rupert Pioneer-Record,* March 31 and April 7, 1910.

49. As reprinted in *Rupert Pioneer-Record,* June 30, 1910.

50. *Congressional Record,* 61st Cong., 2d sess., 1910, Senate: 2013–22 (quote p. 2020), and House: 8673–98 (quote p. 8693).

51. *New York Times,* March 3, 1910; *Rupert Pioneer-Record,* March 10, 1910.

52. *Congressional Record,* 61st Cong., 2d sess., House, June 21, 1910: 8685–87.

53. Brookings Institution, *The U.S. Reclamation Service,* 29–30, 59; Dorothy Lampen, *Economic and Social Aspects of Federal Reclamation* (Baltimore: Johns Hopkins University Press, 1930), 58; F. H. Newell to R. A. Ballinger, July 14, 1910, 4–43, Ballinger Papers.

54. *Contracts for Disposition of Waters of Projects under Reclamation Act,* S. Rept. 442, 61st Cong., 2d sess., serial 5583 (Washington, D.C.: GPO, 1910).

55. *Congressional Record,* 61st Cong., 2d sess., Senate, March 25, April 5, April 6, April 14, 1910: 3740–48, 4259–60, 4314–24, and 4662–69. The Burkett quote is from p. 4317. Also see 61st Cong., 3d sess., House, February 17, 1911: 4662–69.

56. I am indebted to Dr. Alan Newell of Historical Research Associates, Inc., in Missoula, Montana, for sharing with me his extensive knowledge of the Warren Act.

57. F. H. Walter, "Land Settlement on the Federal Reclamation Projects," *New Reclamation Era* 18 (January 1927): 6; Carroll H. Wooddy, *The Growth of the Federal Government, 1915–1932* (New York: McGraw-Hill Book Co., 1934), 534.

58. The Curtis Act of February 13, 1911, is contained in *U.S. Statutes at Large* 36 (1911): 902.

59. *Reclamation Record* 3 (May 1912): 85.

60. As quoted in J. Leonard Bates, *The Origins of Teapot Dome: Progressives, Parties, and Petroleum, 1909–1921* (Urbana: University of Illinois Press, 1963), 79–80.

61. The quotes are from Keith W. Olson, *Biography of a Progressive: Franklin K. Lane, 1864–1921* (Westport, Conn.: Greenwood Press, 1979), 107, and the *Annual Report of the Secretary of the Interior, 1919,* vol. 1 (Washington, D.C.: GPO, 1919), 7. For Lane's early reclamation plans, see the *New York Times,* December 24, 1913.

62. *Fallon Standard* (Fallon, Nevada), July 29, 1909, and *Rupert Pioneer-Record,* August 31, 1911; Arthur P. Davis, "Memoirs of the Reclamation Service," November 3, 1915, Box 11, A. P. Davis Collection, American Heritage Center, University of Wyoming, Laramie.

63. Olson, *Biography of a Progressive,* 77; *Reclamation Record* 4 (June 1913): 113; "The Reclamation Service: A Review," *Outlook* 104 (July 12, 1913): 560–62; Franklin K. Lane, "The Nation's Undeveloped Resources," *National Geographic* 25 (February 1914): 209; Lane, "Our Paternal Uncle," *Sunset* 33 (September 1914): 512–18; *New York Times,* February 14, 1915.

64. Anne W. Lane and Louise H. Wall, eds., *The Letters of Franklin K. Lane* (Boston: Houghton-Mifflin Co., 1922), 137, 139–40.

65. "Pioneering without Pain," *Independent* 71 (August 17, 1911): 383.

66. Davis, "Memoirs of the Reclamation Service," Davis Collection.

67. *New York Times,* May 29, 1913; Franklin K. Lane, reorganization order dated December 13, 1913, in RG 115, Entry 3, General Administrative Records, 1902–1919, Box 101, "(131): Corres. re Administration; Policies & Organization, 1906

thru 1913." Also see A. P. Davis, "Memorandum Regarding Organization of the Reclamation Service," April 4, 1916, in Box 11, Davis Collection; Franklin K. Lane to F. H. Newell, December 3, 1914, Box 50, folder 527, Newlands Collection; Brookings Institution, *The U.S. Reclamation Service*, 24, 74; *New York Herald,* January 18, 1915, and *Boston Transcript,* January 18, 1915.

68. Davis, "Memoirs of the Reclamation Service," Davis Collection.

69. F. H. Newell, "Memoirs," 1914 and 1915, Box no. 1, F. H. Newell Collection, American Heritage Center, University of Wyoming, Laramie.

70. Newell, "Memoirs," 1914 and 1915; *New York Times,* December 24, 1913; *Engineering News* 71 (February 12, 1914): 337.

71. *U.S. Statutes at Large* 38 (1914): 686. From the beginning of federal reclamation, some western politicians, led by U.S. senator Thomas Carter of Montana, favored giving Congress, rather than the secretary of the interior, the right to select projects. Congress, Carter argued, would allocate the reclamation fund more judiciously than the secretary. In the competition for projects, Montana would fare better at the hands of Congress, which was likely to divide up the reclamation fund as it distributed river and harbor appropriations. Apparently, the first bill to transfer control to Congress was drafted in 1906. See *Twin Falls News,* February 2, 1906, and *Rupert Record,* February 8, 1906.

72. James R. Kluger, *Turning on Water with a Shovel: The Career of Elwood Mead* (Albuquerque: University of New Mexico Press, 1992), 74–75; *Reclamation Record* 6 (March 1915): 95–96.

73. Elwood Mead to John D. Works, September 7, 1915, Box 4, and Mead to Works, October 29, 1915, Mead file, John D. Works Collection, Bancroft Library, University of California, Berkeley.

74. Elwood Mead to Franklin K. Lane, July 26, 1915, in Mead file, John D. Works Collection.

75. Elwood Mead to John D. Works, October 29, 1915, Mead file, John D. Works Collection.

76. George Maxwell to F. G. Newlands, July 9, 1915, Box 52, folder 551, Newlands Collection.

77. F. H. Newell, "History and Problems of Irrigation Development in the West," *Transactions of the American Society of Civil Engineers* 90 (1927): 705.

78. See *Reclamation Record* 4 (February 1913): 38, and the irrigation census tables prepared by Ray P. Teele in *Official Proceedings of the Nineteenth National Irrigation Congress Held at Chicago, Illinois, December 5–9, 1911* (Chicago: R. R. Donnelley and Sons, 1912), 330–35.

79. Donald J. Pisani, *From the Family Farm to Agribusiness: The Irrigation Crusade in California and the West, 1850–1931* (Berkeley: University of California Press, 1984), 443–48.

80. *Hearings [on extension of the period of payment under reclamation projects] before the [House] Committee on Irrigation of Arid Lands,* 63d Cong., 2d sess., February 28, 1914 (Washington, D.C.: GPO, 1914); *Reclamation Record* 5 (April 1914), 113–14; Donald C. Swain, *Federal Conservation Policy: 1921–1933* (Berkeley: University of California Press, 1963), 76; Brookings Institution, *The U.S. Reclamation Service,* 41; Lampen, *Economic and Social Aspects,* 60.

CHAPTER 5. BOOM, BUST, AND BOOM

1. Harold U. Faulkner, *The Decline of Laissez Faire, 1897–1917* (New York: Rinehart and Co., 1951), 315–16.

2. For an overview of agricultural conditions after World War I, see David B. Danbom, *Born in the Country: A History of Rural America* (Baltimore: Johns Hopkins University Press, 1995), 185–205.

3. *Sixteenth Annual Report of the Reclamation Service, 1916–1917* (Washington, D.C.: GPO, 1917), 16; *Twentieth Annual Report of the Reclamation Service, 1920–1921* (Washington, D.C.: GPO, 1921), 8; F. B. Headley, *The Work in 1918 of the Newlands (Formerly Truckee-Carson) Reclamation Project Experiment Farm,* USDA Circular no. 80 (Washington, D.C.: GPO, 1920), 3; William E. Borah to W. H. Krause, January 1, 1917, and Borah to F. H. Sherwood, January 11, 1917, Box 543, "Irrigation Districts, 1916–1917," William E. Borah Collection, Library of Congress, Washington, D.C.

4. Arthur P. Davis, "Results of National Irrigation," *Reclamation Record* 12 (December 1919): 546–47. Also see Davis, "The Results of National Irrigation," *Literary Digest* 64 (January 17, 1920): 100–03, and Davis's statement before the House Committee on Appropriations' hearings on the Reclamation Service, December 23, 1921, 67th Cong., 2d sess. (Washington, D.C.: GPO, 1922), 608–23.

5. *Congressional Record,* 70th Cong., 2d sess., House, February 22, 1929: 4077–84.

6. William Ellsworth Smythe, et al., "Reconstruction," November 4, 1920, in RG 115, Central Administrative Records, Box 11, "(144): General Corres. re Soldier Settlement Legislation (Federal) through 1929." The same document is in the Albert B. Fall Papers, Box 67 (17), "U.S. Bureau of Reclamation, 4 Nov. 1920–9 Feb. 1923," Huntington Library, San Marino, California. Smythe had preached much the same message during the depression of the 1890s. See Donald J. Pisani, *To Reclaim a Divided West: Water, Law, and Public Policy, 1848–1902* (Albuquerque: University of New Mexico Press, 1992), 235–37, 248–51.

7. Secretary of the Interior Franklin K. Lane estimated that since 1880, more than 10 million acres of improved land had been abandoned in the northeastern states of New York, New Jersey, Pennsylvania, and the five New England states—more than three times the amount of land the government had reclaimed in the West. See Lane, "The Soldier Settlement Policy from the Standpoint of the American Business Man," November 11, 1919, Box 279, "Leg.—Irrigation" file, Thomas Walsh Collection, Library of Congress, Washington, D.C.

8. Smythe, et al., "Reconstruction."

9. *New York Times,* April 26, May 29, and June 8, 1919; *Engineering News-Record* 81 (August 22, 1918): 361–64; *Engineering News-Record* 83 (October 2, 1919): 680; A. P. Davis, "Homes for Returning Veterans," undated memo, Box 9, Arthur P. Davis Papers, American Heritage Center, University of Wyoming, Laramie.

10. *Report of the Department of the Interior for the Fiscal Year Ended June 30, 1920,* vol. 1 (Washington, D.C.: GPO, 1920), 8–9.

11. "New Democracy Seen by Franklin K. Lane," *New York Times,* March 1, 1920 (quote); *Engineering News-Record* 80 (April 18, 1918): 751–52.

12. Franklin K. Lane outlined his plan to provide farms for soldiers returning from

Europe in a long letter to Woodrow Wilson dated May 31, 1918, reprinted in Anne W. Lane and Louise H. Wall, eds., *The Letters of Franklin K. Lane* (Boston: Houghton Mifflin Co., 1922), 284–90. Also see *Report of the Secretary of the Interior, 1918* (Washington, D.C.: GPO, 1919), 4–13; *Report of the Secretary of the Interior, 1919* (Washington, D.C.: GPO, 1920), 25–32; *New York Times,* September 15, 1918, and May 25, 1919.

13. James R. Kluger, *Turning on Water with a Shovel: The Career of Elwood Mead* (Albuquerque: University of New Mexico Press, 1992), 75–81.

14. Franklin K. Lane, "Memorandum for the Director [of the Reclamation Service]," January 9, 1919, RG 115, General File, 1902–1919, Box 92, "(110-F): Corres. re National Legislation (Soldier's Settlement Act), Jan. and Feb. 1919." The Lane quote is as reported in the memo. Also see *Engineering News-Record* 83 (August 7, 1919): 291; *Reclamation Record* 10 (March 1919): 98–99; *New York Times,* May 25, 1919.

15. See Lane's letters to various public officials in RG 48, Central Files, 1907–1936, Box 172, "Reclamation Service, Soldier Settlement, General, Dec. 16, 1918–Feb. 12, 1919." Also see "Proposed draft of bill for cooperation between states and the U.S. to provide employment and homes for soldiers, sailors, and marines, etc.," December 2, 1918, and Elwood Mead's memorandum, "Cooperative Legislation," October 21, 1918, RG 115, General File, 1902–1919, Box 92, "(110-F): Corres. re National Legislation (Soldier's Settlement Act), thru 1918."

16. Kluger, *Turning on Water,* 83.

17. Elwood Mead to A. P. Davis, June 19, 1919, RG 115, General File, 1902–1919, Box 93, "(110-F): Corres. re National Legislation (Soldier and Settlement Act), March 1, 1919 thru [?]."

18. Department of the Interior, "Memorandum for the Press, November 13, 1919," RG 115, Central Administrative Records, Box 111, "(144): General Corres. re Soldier Settlement Legislation (Federal) through 1919"; Thomas J. Walsh (U.S. senator from Montana) to F. B. Connelly, December 12, 1919, Box 279, "Leg.—Irrigation," Walsh Collection; *New York Times,* July 22, 1919.

19. It cost $1.24 million to settle thirty thousand farm families on the western reclamation projects. At that rate, homes for five hundred thousand soldiers and their families would cost more than $2 billion. See *World War Adjusted Compensation,* Congressional report to accompany H.R. 14157, H. Rep. 1020, 66th Cong., 2d sess., serial 7654 (Washington, D.C.: GPO, 1920), 9–10.

20. *Congressional Record,* 66th Cong., 2d sess., Senate, February 6, 1920: 2537, 2538. Franklin K. Lane responded to his critics in the *New York Times,* December 28, 1919.

21. E. W. R. Ewing, "Memorandum for Chief Counsel," July 8, 1919, RG 115, General Administrative Files, 1919–1929, Box 111, "(144): General Corres. re Soldier Settlement Legislation (Federal) through 1929."

22. *National Soldier Settlement Act,* H. Rept. 216, 66th Cong., 1st sess., serial 7592 (Washington, D.C.: GPO, 1919), 15–17; Charles J. McNary to Thomas J. Walsh, March 23, 1922, and P. N. Bernard to Walsh, April 3 and 6, 1922, Box 308, "Leg.—Irrigation," Walsh Collection; C. H. Norcross to A. P. Davis, January 30, 1919, RG 115, General File, 1902–1919, Box 92, "(110-F): Corres. re National Legislation (Soldier Settlement Act), Jan. and Feb. 1919"; George H. Maxwell

to William E. Smythe, April 1, 1920, RG 115, Central Administrative Records, Box 111, "(144): General Corres. re Soldier Settlement Legislation (Federal) through 1929"; F. H. Newell to Franklin K. Lane, November 5, 1919, and A. P. Davis to F. H. Newell, November 12, 1919, RG 48, Central Files, 1907–1936, Box 1712, "Reclamation Bureau Congresses, National Drainage Congress."

23. S. 3477 (Smoot), introduced December 3, 1919; S. 3942 (Fletcher), introduced February 19, 1920; and S. 4372 (Borah), introduced May 12, 1920—all 66th Cong., 2d sess. (1919–20). Also see William Ellsworth Smythe, "Reclamation and Settlement," memo dated February 21, 1920, and A. P. Davis to Elwood Mead, March 23, 1920, in RG 115, Central Administrative Records, Box 111, "(144): General Corres. re Soldier Settlement Legislation (Federal) through 1929."

24. Charles L. McNary to Stephen A. Lowell, May 13, 1921, and McNary to D. W. Davis, July 9, 1921, Box 43, "S. 3254, Reclamation Bill: McNary Bill," Charles McNary Collection, Library of Congress.

25. *Thirteenth Census of the United States, 1910: Agriculture General Report and Analysis* (Washington, D.C.: GPO, 1914), 845; *Fourteenth Census of the United States, 1920: Irrigation and Drainage* (Washington, D.C.: GPO, 1922), 15.

26. "Hearings before the Committee on Ways and Means," September 18, 1919, 66th Cong., 2d sess. (Washington, D.C.: GPO, 1919), 15–16. Also see the hearing held on January 20, 1920, as well as Elwood Mead, "Advance Statement by the Commissioner of Reclamation on Economic Conditions on the Reclamation Projects," February 14–15, 1928, in RG 115, Central Administrative Records, 1919–1929, Box 66, "(101): Matters of Policy, 1926–1929"; Mead to Thomas J. Walsh, February 13, 1929, Box 308, "Leg.—Reclamation" file, Walsh Collection; William C. Gregg, "What's Wrong with Reclamation," *Outlook* 141 (September 30, 1925): 154–56.

27. *Annual Report of the Bureau of Reclamation, 1922–23* (Washington, D.C.: GPO, 1923), 1; "Ten-Year Crop Value One Billion Dollars," *New Reclamation Era* 18 (September 1927): 133; Joseph Kinsey Howard, *Montana: High, Wide, and Handsome* (New Haven: Yale University Press, 1959), 207–8.

28. Elwood Mead, "Present Policy of the United States Bureau of Reclamation Regarding Land Settlement," *Transactions of the American Society of Civil Engineers* 90 (1927), 730–49; Augustus Griffin, "Land Settlement of Irrigation Projects," Ibid., 750–72; Department of the Interior, "Memorandum for the Press," dated December 7, 1923, Box 308, "Leg.—Reclamation" file, Walsh Collection; John A. Widtsoe, *Success on Irrigation Projects* (New York: John Wiley and Sons, 1928), 94.

29. *New York Times*, September 5, 1926.

30. *U.S. Daily,* October 29, 1926, and August 14, 1928.

31. F. H. Walter, "Land Settlement on the Federal Reclamation Projects," *New Reclamation Era* 18 (January 1927), 6; C. L. Stewart, "The Persistent Increase of Tenant Farming," February 9, 1922; "Continued Increase Shown in Tenant Farming," November 22, 1922; "Tenancy on the Irrigated Farms on the Projects of the Bureau of Reclamation, 1920 and 1924"; H. A. Brown, "Memorandum for the Commissioner," August 24, 1925 (quote); and Elwood Mead to E. J. Bell, October 15, 1928, all in RG 115, General Administrative Files, 1919–1929, Box 359, "(507): General Correspondence re Tenancy thru 1929."

32. "Plan for Curbing Reclamation Land Speculation," *New Reclamation Era* 16 (May 1925): 70–72.

33. Walter, "Land Settlement," 7; Kluger, *Turning on Water,* 120–21.

34. "Curbing Land Speculation on the Federal Reclamation Projects," *New Reclamation Era* 19 (October 1928): 151; Richard L. Berkman and W. Kip Viscusi, *Damming the West* (New York: Grossman Publishers, 1973), 140.

35. Paul Wallace Gates, *History of Public Land Law Development* (Washington, D.C.: GPO, 1968; New York: Arno Press, 1979), 29; Carroll H. Wooddy, *The Growth of the Federal Government, 1915–1932* (New York: McGraw-Hill Book Co., 1934), 533; *Reclamation Record* 15 (January 1924), 16; *Twenty-Ninth Report of the Commissioner of Reclamation, 1929–1930* (Washington, D.C.: GPO, 1930), 1; *Report of the Commissioner of Reclamation, 1946* (Washington, D.C.: GPO, 1946), 116.

36. Hubert Work to Wesley Jones, January 23, 1926, Wesley Jones Collection, 74–1, Special Collections, University of Washington, Seattle; *Great Falls Tribune* (Great Falls, Montana), January 27, 1926.

37. Donald J. Pisani, *From the Family Farm to Agribusiness: The Irrigation Crusade in California and the West, 1850–1931* (Berkeley: University of California Press, 1984), 335–43.

38. William Ellsworth Smythe to State Irrigation Convention, October 7, 1904, Smythe File, George Pardee Papers, Bancroft Library, University of California, Berkeley. Also see Smythe to Pardee, July 1, October 24, and December 14, 1904, in the same file.

39. W. E. Smythe, "A Success of Two Centuries," *Out West* 22 (January 1905): 72–76; Smythe, *Constructive Democracy: The Economics of the Square Deal* (New York: Macmillan, 1905), 381–85; "The Reclamation Service," *Forestry and Irrigation* 11 (June 1905): 280; F. G. Newlands to Secretary of the Interior, January 26, 1905, and Charles Walcott (Director, USGS) to Secretary of the Interior, June 3, 1905, in RG 48, 1420–1904, "Miscellaneous Projects: State Irrigation under National Control, F. G. Newlands."

40. B. E. Stoutmeyer, "Irrigation Districts: Their Relation to the Reclamation Service," *Reclamation Record* 5 (October 1914): 362.

41. E. B. Hoffman, "Cooperative Plan," memo dated May 5, 1915, RG 115, General Files, 1902–1919, Box 85, "Legislation—Corres. re Legislation and Laws Affecting the Reclamation Act thru 1915." Also see B. E. Stoutmeyer to Elwood Mead, December 6, 1924, in RG 115, General Administrative Files, 1919–1929, Box 367, "(522): General Corres. re Cooperation by States with the Bureau in Colonizing and Settling Lands thru 1929," and *Reclamation Record* 5 (December 1914): 455–56.

42. A. E. Chandler to F. H. Newell, October 26, 1909, RG 115, General File, 1902–1919, Box 87, "(110-D): Corres. re Legislation; Laws, etc. re formation and operation of Irrigation Districts and corres. re Legislation to provide turning over projects. Thru 1915"; "Co-operative Reclamation," *Engineering News-Record* 93 (September 18, 1924), 450–51. On state mercantilism, see Pisani, *To Reclaim a Divided West,* 169–223.

43. *Congressional Record,* 67th Cong., 2d sess., House, March 7 and 8, 1922: 3572–3589 (the quote is from p. 3573); Alfred R. Golze, *Reclamation in the United States* (New York: McGraw-Hill Book Co., 1952), 100, 104.

44. Donald J. Pisani, "Federalism and the American West, 1900–1950," in *Frontier and Region: Essays in Honor of Martin Ridge,* ed. Robert C. Ritchie and Paul Andrew Hutton (San Marino, Calif.: The Huntington Library Press, 1997), 94–97; Tom Lewis, *Divided Highways: Building the Interstate Highways, Transforming American Life* (New York: Viking, 1997).

45. *Engineering News-Record* 94 (April 23, 1925): 705, and *Engineering News-Record* 94 (June 18, 1925): 1003–4; Hubert Work to Calvin Coolidge, December 11, 1924, Box 308, "Leg.—Reclamation" file, Walsh Collection; Department of the Interior, "Memorandum for the Press," March 6, 1926, Box 75, "Reclamation Bureau" file, Key Pittman Papers, Library of Congress, Washington, D.C.; Hubert Work to F. E. Warren, January 23, 1926, RG 115, General Administrative Files, 1919–1929, Box 356, "(500): General Correspondence re Colonization & Settlement, 1925–1929"; Elwood Mead to F. E. Schmit, March 10, 1925, and J. E. Erickson (Governor of Montana) to Elwood Mead, December 21, 1925, Box 367, "(522): General Corres. re Cooperation by States with the Bureau in Colonizing and Settling Lands thru 1929."

46. Elwood Mead, "Federal Reclamation: What It Should Include," speech of June 25, 1926, Box 75, "Reclamation Bureau" file, Key Pittman Papers; Mead to Walter M. Pierce (Governor of Oregon), March 10, 1926, RG 115, General Administrative Files, 1919–1929, Box 367, "(522): General Corres. re Cooperation by States with the Bureau in Colonizing and Settling Lands, thru 1929"; *San Diego Union,* April 17, 1926; *Great Falls Tribune,* March 14, 1926.

47. *Engineering News-Record* 95 (December 10, 1925): 941–42; *Congressional Record,* 69th Cong., 1st sess., House, January 6, 1926: 1571–73, 1656–70 (the quote is from p. 1573).

48. Mae A. Schnurr, "Establishing a Home on the Land," *New Reclamation Era* 19 (October 1928): 152; Albert Z. Guttenberg, "The Land Utilization Movement of the 1920s," *Agricultural History* 50 (July 1976): 477–90.

49. *Reclamation Record* 15 (January 1924): 4; *New Reclamation Era* 18 (August 1927): 120.

50. "Building a Community House," *New Reclamation Era* 20 (June 1929): 88–89.

51. "Memorandum for the Press," text of an address delivered by Elwood Mead before the Western Society of Civil Engineers, October 26, 1925, in RG 115, Central Administrative Records, 1919–1929, Box 66, "(101): Matters of Policy, 1925."

52. Congress adopted other blanket moratoriums on project debt in 1924, and from 1931 to 1936. Donald C. Swain, *Federal Conservation Policy, 1921–1933* (Berkeley: University of California Press, 1963), 79; Swain, "The Bureau of Reclamation and the New Deal, 1933–1944," *Pacific Northwest Quarterly* 61 (July 1970): 141; *New York Times,* September 28, 1925.

53. Eugene P. Trani, "Hubert Work and the Department of the Interior, 1923–1928," *Pacific Northwest Quarterly* 61 (January 1970): 31–40; "A Statement by Secretary of Interior Work," March 5, 1923, RG 115, Central Administrative Records, 1919–1929, Box 66, "(101): Matters of Policy, etc. thru 1924"; Department of the Interior, "Memorandum for the Press," October 15, 1923, Box 308, "Leg.—Reclamation" file, Thomas Walsh Collection (quote).

54. The Work quotations are from Gregg, "What's Wrong with Reclamation," 154. For additional statements of Work's views of federal reclamation, see Department

of the Interior, "Memorandum for the Press," April 6, 1923, RG 115, Central Administrative Records, 1919–1929, Box 66, "(101): Matters of Policy, etc. thru 1924"; *Federal Reclamation by Irrigation,* S. Doc. 92, 68th Cong., 1st sess., serial 8238 (Washington, D.C.: GPO, 1924), 26; and *To Provide Aided and Directed Settlement on Government Irrigation Projects,* H. Rept. 1628, 68th Cong., 2d sess., serial 8931 (Washington, D.C.: GPO, 1925), 4–5.

55. Department of the Interior, "Memorandum for the Press," December 7, 1923, Box 308, "Leg.—Reclamation" file, Walsh Collection.

56. *New York Times,* June 19 and 27, August 28, and October 15, 1923, and October 17, 1924; *Engineering News-Record* 91 (August 2, 1923): 197; Ibid. 91 (August 23, 1923): 320; Ibid. 91 (August 30, 1923): 361; Ibid. 91 (September 20, 1923): 490; Ibid. 91 (October 18, 1923): 653; Ibid. 92 (January 10, 1924): 89; Ibid. 92 (April 10, 1924): 629; Arthur P. Davis to Joseph Jacobs, July 5, 1923, and Davis to Philip P. Wells, July 9, 1923, in Box 3, "Dismissal Comments" file, A. P. Davis Collection, American Heritage Center, University of Wyoming, Laramie.

57. Department of the Interior, "Memorandum for the Press," September 10 and 20, 1923, Box 308, "Leg.—Reclamation" file, Walsh Collection; *Reclamation Record* 14 (August 1923): 268–69; Ibid. 14 (September 1923): 277–78; and Ibid. 14 (October 1923): 295–96. Also see *Reclamation Record* 15 (March 1924) and 15 (April 1924).

58. The May, June, and July issues of *Reclamation Record* summarized the report of the Fact Finders' Commission. Even before the commission began its deliberations, an independent study of the Bureau of Reclamation conducted by agents from two other departments concluded that it was "organized along unbusinesslike lines and . . . the results achieved were not commensurate with the effort and the money expended." The earlier report suggested a reorganization of the bureau, and at the end of 1923, twelve high-salaried employees were dismissed. *Reclamation Record* 14 (November–December, 1923): 311. For an excellent overview of the commission, see Brian Q. Cannon, "'We Are Now Entering a New Era': Federal Reclamation and the Fact Finding Commission of 1923–1924," *Pacific Historical Review* 66 (May 1997): 185–211. Also see *Federal Reclamation by Irrigation,* S. Doc. 92.

59. See, for example, the reforms suggested in Mead's October 29, 1915, letter to California U.S. senator John D. Works in the John D. Works Collection, Bancroft Library, University of California, Berkeley.

60. *Annual Report of the Bureau of Reclamation, 1923–1924* (Washington, D.C.: GPO, 1924), 8–9; *Engineering News-Record* 92 (April 24, 1924): 726–29; Elwood Mead, "Irrigation Profiteers," *Country Gentleman* 89 (December 20, 1924): 6, 38–39; "To Liquidate Irrigation Debts," *Literary Digest* 81 (May 3, 1924): 16; R. F. Walter, "Land Settlement on the Federal Reclamation Projects," *New Reclamation Era* 18 (January 1927): 4–17; Swain, *Federal Conservation Policy,* 81.

61. *New Reclamation Era* 16 (June 1925): 88; Elwood Mead, "Memorandum for Senator McNary," April 5, 1926, RG 115, General Administrative Files, 1919–1929, Box 366, "(515): Corres. re Plans, etc. for Aided & Directed Settlement."

62. Elwood Mead to William Kent, October 2, 1924, Box 41, William Kent Papers, Sterling Library, Yale University, New Haven, Connecticut; Mead, "Federal Reclamation: What It Should Include," speech dated June 25, 1926, Key Pittman

Papers, Box 75, "Reclamation Bureau" file, Library of Congress; Mead, "The Relation of Land Settlement to Irrigation Development," February 1, 1924, RG 115, General Administrative Files, 1919–1929, Box 366, "(515): Corres. re Plans, etc. for Aided & Directed Settlement through 1925."

63. By 1930, two kinds of repayment contracts were in force on federal reclamation projects: those that specified a fixed sum repayable in forty years, and those that required payment of 5 percent of gross crop income over a period longer than forty years (the term depended on the project). Neither carried any interest. Low crop prices, however, led to moratoria on most of the construction charges during the early 1930s, with no payment of interest on the deferred debt.

64. The reclamation legislation enacted by Congress in December 1924 is summarized and discussed in the *New Reclamation Era* issues of February and April, 1925 (vol. 16). Also see Kluger, *Turning on Water,* 111–13, and Dorothy Lampen, *Economic and Social Aspects of Federal Reclamation* (Baltimore: Johns Hopkins University Press, 1930).

65. *Annual Report of the Bureau of Reclamation, 1923–1924* (Washington, D.C.: GPO, 1924), 4.

66. Elwood Mead to William Kent, September 15, 1924, Box 41, Kent Papers, Sterling Library, Yale University, New Haven.

67. James Kluger, *Turning on Water,* 57–73, 85–101; Paul K. Conkin, "The Vision of Elwood Mead," *Agricultural History* 34 (April 1960): 88–97; Pisani, *From the Family Farm to Agribusiness,* 443–48.

68. Elwood Mead to W. W. Robertson, July 29, 1926, RG 115, Central Administrative Records, 1919–1929, Box 66, "(101): Matters of Policy, 1926–1929."

69. Department of the Interior, "Memorandum for the Press," text of an address before the Western Society of Civil Engineers by Elwood Mead on October 26, 1925, RG 115, Central Administrative Records, 1919–1929, Box 66, "(101): Matters of Policy, 1925."

70. Elwood Mead to John W. Haw, December 22, 1927, in Northern Pacific Papers, President's Office Subject Files, 19-Q, Folder 16, Minnesota Historical Society, St. Paul. Also see Mead, "Economic Problems of Federal Reclamation," speech delivered at the annual meeting of the American Society of Civil Engineers, October 4, 1928, RG 115, Central Administrative Records, 1919–1929, Box 66, "(101): Matters of Policy, 1926–1929," and Mead, "Speculating in Sagebrush," *Country Gentleman* 89 (December 6, 1924): 42.

71. *Engineering News-Record* 94 (January 22, 1925): 153; *New York Times,* June 23, 1925.

72. *Engineering News-Record* 93 (August 21, 1924): 317; *New Reclamation Era* 15 (October 1924): 1; *New York Times,* June 24, 1924.

73. George C. Kreutzer, "The Value of Careful Selection of Settlers," *New Reclamation Era* 17 (February 1926): 28–29; Department of the Interior, "Memorandum for the Press," September 14, 1925, Box 357, "(503.2): General Correspondence re Boards for Selection of Settlers, thru 1929," and Elwood Mead, "Advance Statement by the Commissioner of Reclamation on Economic Conditions on the Reclamation Projects," February 14–15, 1928, Box 66, "(101): Matters of Policy, 1926–1929," RG 115, Central Administrative Records, 1919–1929.

74. *Engineering News-Record* 93 (December 18, 1924): 1011; Ibid. 94 (February 12,

1925): 291; Ibid. 94 (February 19, 1925): 303; Ibid. 94 (March 12, 1925): 452; *To Provide for Aided and Directed Settlement on Government Land in Irrigation Projects,* S. Rept. 955, 68th Cong., 2d sess., serial 8388 (Washington, D.C.: GPO, 1925); Elwood Mead to George C. Kreutzer, November 19, 1924, and Mead to Hubert Work, November 21, 1924, RG 115, General Administrative Files, 1919–1929, Box 366, "(515): Corres. re Plans etc. for Aided & Directed Settlement through 1925."

75. Elwood Mead, "Present Policy of the United States Bureau of Reclamation Regarding Land Settlement," *Transactions of the American Society of Civil Engineers* 90 (1927): 734; *Congressional Record,* 69th Cong., 1st sess., House, January 7, 1926: 1663–70; Elwood Mead to Richard R. Lyman, March 19, 1926, RG 115, General Administrative Files, 1919–1929, Box 366, "(515): Corres re Plans, etc. for Aided & Directed Settlement"; Kluger, *Turning on Water,* 122.

76. *Engineering News-Record* 100 (March 8, 1928): 419–20; *To Provide for Aided and Directed Settlement on Federal Reclamation Projects,* H. Rept. 1039, 70th Cong., 1st sess., serial 8836 (Washington, D.C.: GPO, 1928); Elwood Mead to H. C. Baldridge (Governor of Idaho), November 5, 1928, RG 115, General File: 1919–1945, Box 105, "(140): General Correspondence re National or State Legislation, 1922 thru 1929."

77. John A. Widtsoe, *Success on Irrigation Projects* (New York: John Wiley and Sons, 1928), 92–93; A. P. Davis to *New York World,* March 17, 1920; Davis to Rex Lampman, March 23, 1920; and Davis to Joseph W. Forney, March 26, 1920, RG 115, Central Administrative Records, Box 111, "(144): General Corres. re Soldier Settlement Legislation (Federal) through 1929." Also in RG 115, Central Administrative Records, see J. B. Beadle to E. W. Packard, August 31, 1921, Box 356, "(500): General Correspondence regarding Colonization and Settlement thru 1924"; "Summary of the Economic and Financial Conditions on Belle Fourche and Lower Yellowstone Projects and Part of the Fort Laramie Division of the North Platte Project," undated report in Box 356, "(500): General Correspondence re Colonization & Settlement, 1925–1929."

78. Elwood Mead, "Memorandum for the Secretary," November 18, 1926, Box 66, "(101): Matters of Policy, 1926–1929," and Mead to George Young, January 9, 1929, Box 365, "(515): Corres. re Plans, Etc. for Aided & Directed Settlement, 1928–1929," RG 115, Central Administrative Records, 1919–1929. Another solution was to create a private corporation beyond politics to administer collections and supervise reclamation as a business. See R. E. Shepherd, "The Financing of Irrigation Developments by Private Capital," *Transactions of the American Society of Civil Engineers* 90 (1927): 716–17.

79. *Engineering News-Record* 96 (February 11, 1926): 254; Ibid. 96 (February 18, 1926): 280; Ibid. 96 (June 10, 1926): 960; *New York Times,* July 25, 1926; Lampen, *Economic and Social Aspects,* 59. In a candid letter to Edward F. Adams, October 12, 1925, RG 115, Central Administrative Records, 1919–1929, Box 66, "(101): Matters of Policy, 1925," Mead observed:

On the North Platte project . . . where more than half of the farms are held by speculators and mortgage companies, they have an organized political combination which they believe will enable them to do as they please [e.g., abandon their debt to the government], and their local congressman comes in here and tells me where we will get off if we don't follow instructions. Heretofore they encountered a Secretary who wanted to hold onto his job, and a Commissioner [A. P. Davis?] who was young enough to have a future. Our Secretary [Hubert Work] don't [sic] care, and as for me, I am mainly concerned in saving whatever reputation I made in the past, and we are going through with this thing [getting project farmers to repay construction costs] unless stopped by Congress."

80. Elwood Mead, "Present Policy of the United States Bureau of Reclamation Regarding Land Settlement," *Transactions of the American Society of Civil Engineers* 90 (1927): 731 (quote), 737; Elwood Mead, "Federal Reclamation: What It Should Include," speech dated June 25, 1926, in Box 75, "Reclamation Bureau" file, Key Pittman Collection; Swain, *Federal Conservation Policy,* 84; *Congressional Record,* 58th Cong., 1st sess., House, June 7, 1924: 11215.

81. *New York Times,* August 5, 1926; *Annual Report of the Commissioner of Reclamation, Fiscal Year 1924* (Washington, D.C.: GPO, 1924), 26–27; *Engineering News-Record* 97 (December 9, 1926): 974; Elwood Mead to Charles L. McNary, September 13, 1926, and Mead, "Memorandum for Secretary Work Relative to a Ten-Year Reclamation Program," March 3, 1926, RG 115, Central Administrative Files, 1919–1929, Box 66, "(101): Matters of Policy, 1926–1929." In the same file, see the Interior Department memoranda for the press of March 6 and March 17, 1926. Also see Elwood Mead to Charles B. Stafford, November 8, 1928, in Box 365, "(515): Corrcs. re Plans, Etc. for Aided & directed Settlement, 1928–1929."

82. *New Orleans Times-Picayune,* July 14, 1916; George C. Kreutzer, "Land Settlement an Essential Part of Reclamation," *New Reclamation Era* 19 (August 1928): 114.

83. Elwood Mead, "Community Small Farms," *New Reclamation Era* 20 (July, 1929): 99.

84. Elwood Mead to W. Brookings, January 11, 1922, "U" incoming file, Box 2, Elwood Mead Collection, Bancroft Library, University of California, Berkeley; Hubert Work to Howard Elliott, November 9, 1926, and Elwood Mead, "Plan for the Creation of Organized Rural Communities in the South," speech delivered December 12, 1927, RG 48, Central Classified Files, 1907–1936, Box 1714, "Reclamation Bureau: Southern Reclamation and Rural Development, Nov. 8, 1926–July 9, 1930."

85. *New York Times,* September 13, 14, 15, 17, and 27, 1925, and March 7, 1926; Franklin K. Lane, "Farms for Returned Soldiers: A Quarter of a Billion Acres of Unused Land," *Scientific American* 119 (November 9, 1918): 372–73; Bill G. Reid, "Franklin K. Lane's Idea for Veterans' Colonization, 1918–1921," *Pacific Historical Review* 33 (November 1964): 447–61; Reid, "Agrarian Opposition to Franklin K. Lane's Proposal for Soldier Settlement, 1918–1921," *Agricultural History* 41 (April 1967): 167–79; and Paul Conkin, "The Vision of Elwood Mead," *Agricultural History* 34 (April 1960): 88–97.

86. The other two members were George Soule, a well-known economist and director of the National Association for Economic Research, and Daniel C. Roper, a former commissioner of the Internal Revenue Service long involved in South Carolina agriculture.

87. Department of the Interior, "Memorandum for the Press," November 27, 1926, and Hubert Work to J. B. Aswell, January 6, 1927, RG 48, Central Files, 1907–1936, Box 1714, "Reclamation Bureau: Southern Reclamation and Rural Development, Nov. 8, 1926–July 9, 1930"; *Creation of Organized Rural Communities,* H. Rept. 1217, 70th Cong., 1st sess., serial 8837 (Washington, D.C.: GPO, 1928), 5.

88. "Report of the Secretary of Agriculture," in *Yearbook of Agriculture, 1927* (Washington, D.C., GPO, 1928), 25–28.

89. *Engineering News-Record* 84 (February 19, 1920): 375–77; Wooddy, *Growth of the Federal Government,* 530–31; *Congressional Record,* 69th Cong., 2d sess., House, January 7, 1926: 1666, and February 28, 1927: 5089; *New York Times,* September 5, 1926; *Twenty-Eighth Annual Report of the Commissioner of Reclamation, 1928–1929* (Washington, D.C.: GPO, 1929), 6–7; *Development of Unused Lands,* H. Doc. 262, 66th Cong., 1st sess., serial 7644 (Washington, D.C.: GPO, 1919), 38–41.

90. For representative criticism of federal reclamation, see Garet Garrett, "The Tale of Uncle Sam's Voyage in an Irrigating Ditch," *Saturday Evening Post* 197 (January 17, 1925): 8–9, 119, 120, 125, 126; "Politics in Western Lands," *Independent* 115 (October 10, 1925): 406; French Strother, "The End of Uncle Sam as Santa Claus?" *World's Work* 51 (January 1926): 295–300.

91. B. B. Fleming to Elwood Mead, March 18, 1925, RG 115, Central Administrative Files, 1919–1929, Box 366, "(515): Corres. re Plans, etc. for Aided & Directed Settlement through 1925."

92. Elwood Mead to John W. Haw, December 22, 1927, Northern Pacific Papers, President's Office Subject Files, 19-Q, Folder 16, Minnesota Historical Society; Elwood Mead to J. G. Woodworth (Vice President, Northern Pacific Railway Co.), February 4, 1929, RG 115, General Administrative Files, 1919–1929, Box 365, "(515): Corres. re Plans, Etc. for Aided & Directed Settlement, 1928–1929" (quote); Elwood Mead to Hugh MacRae, October 8, 1929, RG 115, General Administrative Files, 1919–1929, Box 365, "(515): Corres. re Plans, Etc. for Aided & Directed Settlement, 1928–1929."

93. Ray Lyman Wilbur, *The Hoover Policies* (New York: Charles Scribner's Sons, 1937), 276–78; *New Reclamation Era* 19 (November, 1928): 1; *Wall Street Journal,* March 15, 1929; *Engineering News-Record* 103 (September 5, 1929): 355–56; Ibid. 103 (September 12, 1929): 427–29; and Ibid. 103 (November 7, 1929): 714–15. Elwood Mead to Albert Shaw (Editor, *Review of Reviews*), November 22, 1928, RG 115, General Administrative Files, 1919–1929, Box 365, "(515): Corres. re Plans, Etc. for Aided & Directed Settlement, 1928–1929."

94. *Annual Report of the Secretary of the Interior for the Fiscal Year Ended June 30, 1931* (Washington, D.C.: GPO, 1931), 98; *Annual Report of the Secretary of the Interior for the Fiscal Year Ended June 30, 1932* (Washington, D.C.: GPO, 1932), 94, 101; *Annual Report of the Secretary of the Interior for the Fiscal Year Ended June 30, 1933* (Washington, D.C.: GPO, 1933), 8, 20, 34.

95. For the Reclamation Bureau's report, see *Annual Report of the Secretary of the Interior for the Fiscal Year Ended June 30, 1930* (Washington, D.C.: GPO, 1930), 21–22, 80.

96. Wooddy, *Growth of the Federal Government,* 534; *Thirty-Second Annual Report of the Commissioner of Reclamation, 1932–1933* (Washington, D.C.: GPO, 1933), 114; Kluger, *Turning on Water,* 126, 128.

97. *Annual Report of the Secretary of the Interior for the Fiscal Year Ended June 30, 1934* (Washington, D.C.: GPO, 1934), 22–23, 27.

98. Ibid., 24, 41–43.

99. *Annual Report of the Secretary of the Interior for the Fiscal year Ended June 30, 1935* (Washington, D.C.: GPO, 1935), 44–45.

CHAPTER 6. UNEASY ALLIES

1. W. T. Sherman to C. Delano, November 7, 1871, in RG 75, Irrigation Division, General Correspondence, Entry no. 653, Box 52, "Ft. Apache, 1871–1918"; L. W. Cooke to Commissioner of Indian Affairs, October 20, 1893, RG 75, Special Cases, Entry no. 190, "Blackfeet" Box; *Report of the Commissioner of Indian Affairs, 1902* (Washington, D.C.: GPO, 1903), 63–64; *Report of the Commissioner of Indian Affairs, 1909* (Washington, D.C.: GPO, 1910), 10.

2. *Report of the Commissioner of Indian Affairs, 1906* (Washington, D.C.: GPO, 1907), 13–15 (the quote is on p. 13); *Report of the Commissioner of Indian Affairs, 1908* (Washington, D.C.: GPO, 1908), 58. Also see *Report of the Commissioner of Indian Affairs, 1897* (Washington, D.C.: GPO, 1897), 29; *Report of the Commissioner of Indian Affairs, 1911* (Washington, D.C.: GPO, 1912), 14; *Report of the Commissioner of Indian Affairs, 1916* (Washington, D.C.: GPO, 1917), 41, 44.

3. Frederick E. Hoxie, *Parading through History: The Making of the Crow Nation in America, 1805–1935* (New York: Cambridge University Press, 1995), 228, 231, 273–78; *Report of the Commissioner of Indian Affairs, 1891* (Washington, D.C.: GPO, 1892), 51 (quote); *Report of the Commissioner of Indian Affairs, 1896* (Washington, D.C., 1897), 29; *Report of the Commissioner of Indian Affairs, 1897*, 33; *Report of the Secretary of the Interior, 1892* (Washington, D.C.: GPO, 1893), 54; *Report of the Secretary of the Interior, 1896* (Washington, D.C.: GPO, 1896), 46; *Report of the Secretary of the Interior, 1898* (Washington, D.C.: GPO, 1898), 47; *Board of Irrigation, Executive Departments*, S. Doc. 36, 54th Cong., 1st sess., serial 3349 (Washington, D.C.: GPO, 1896), 15–16.

4. W. H. Graves to the Commissioner of Indian Affairs, October 25, 1892; October 14, 1894; August 9, 1895; and March 10, 1898 (quotes), in RG 75, Special Cases, Entry no. 190, "Crow'; *Report of the Commissioner of Indian Affairs, 1898* (Washington, D.C.: GPO, 1898), 49. Reservation agents had good reason to exaggerate Indian enthusiasm and progress. Their jobs depended on demonstrating success, and many expected to profit personally from the irrigation of reservation land.

5. *Report of the Commissioner of Indian Affairs, 1910* (Washington, D.C.: GPO, 1911), 22.

6. *Report of the Secretary of the Interior, 1892* (Washington, D.C.: GPO, 1893), 54; *Report of the Commissioner of Indian Affairs, 1892* (Washington, D.C.: GPO, 1892), 92–93; *Report of the Commissioner of Indian Affairs, 1893* (Washington, D.C.: GPO, 1893), 47–50; *Report of the Commissioner of Indian Affairs, 1894* (Washington, D.C.: GPO, 1894), 24–26; *Report of the Commissioner of Indian Affairs, 1895* (Washington, D.C.: GPO, 1896), 28.

7. R. Douglas Hurt, *Indian Agriculture in America: Prehistory to the Present* (Lawrence: University Press of Kansas, 1987), 118; Hiram Price, "The Government and the Indians," *Forum* 10 (February 1891): 715 (quote).

8. Laurence F. Schmeckebier, *The Office of Indian Affairs: Its History, Activities, and Organization* (Baltimore: Johns Hopkins University Press, 1927), 239.

9. Hurt, *Indian Agriculture,* 170–71.

10. "The American Indian and Irrigation," *Forestry and Irrigation* 9 (May 1903): 236.

11. Leonard A. Carlson, *Indians, Bureaucrats, and Land: The Dawes Act and the Decline of Indian Farming* (Westport, Conn.: Greenwood Press, 1981); Carlson, "Federal Policy and Indian Land: Economic Interests and the Sale of Indian Allotments," *Agricultural History* 57 (January 1983): 33–45.

12. *Report of the Commissioner of Indian Affairs, 1901* (Washington, D.C.: GPO, 1902), 6; *Report of the Commissioner of Indian Affairs, 1903* (Washington, D.C.: GPO, 1904), 2.

13. The quote is from the *Report of the Commissioner of Indian Affairs, 1905* (Washington, D.C.: GPO, 1906), 7. Also see Francis E. Leupp, "Outlines of an Indian Policy," *Outlook* 79 (April 15, 1905): 949–50. Leupp's ideas were developed at length in his books *The Indian and His Problem* (New York: Charles Scribner's Sons, 1910) and *In Red Man's Land* (New York: Fleming H. Revell Co., 1914).

14. Francis Paul Prucha, *The Indians in American Society* (Berkeley: University of California Press, 1985), 6–10.

15. As quoted in Theodore Roosevelt to Charles Walcott, March 28, 1906, RG 115, General Administrative Files, Box 99, "(127): Uintah Indian Reservation—Utah, 1904 thru [?]"

16. Francis E. Leupp, "The Story of Four Strenuous Years," *Outlook* 92 (June 5, 1909): 328–31. The quote is on p. 331.

17. Francis Paul Prucha, *The Great Father,* vol. 2 (Lincoln: University of Nebraska Press, 1984), 864–65, 870.

18. F. H. Newell to George Maxwell, October 1, 1900, Newell File, George Maxwell Collection, Louisiana State Museum, New Orleans.

19. Henry L. Dawes, "Have We Failed with the Indians?" *Atlantic* 84 (August 1899): 283.

20. Donald J. Pisani, *From the Family Farm to Agribusiness: The Irrigation Crusade in California and the West, 1850–1931* (Berkeley: University of California Press, 1984), 314–15. The 1904 law (*U.S. Statutes at Large* 33 [1904]: 224) is reprinted in *Fifth Annual Report of the Reclamation Service, 1906* (Washington, D.C.: GPO, 1907), 21–22.

21. *Estimate of Appropriation for Truckee-Carson Irrigation Project as Related to Paiute Allotments,* H. Doc. 211, 59th Cong., 2d sess., serial 5152 (Washington, D.C.: GPO, 1906); *Report of the Commissioner of Indian Affairs, 1906,* 148–50; *Report of the Commissioner of Indian Affairs, 1909,* 42.

22. Elihu B. Reynolds to the Commissioner of Indian Affairs, March 2, 1900, RG 75, Special Cases, Entry no. 190, "Ft. Hall, 1898–1907."

23. E. A. Keys (Inspector, U.S. Reclamation Service), "Memorandum for the Secretary [of the Interior]," May 21, 1909, RG 48, Central Classified Files, 1907–36, 5–6 Irrigation, Box 1436, "Indian Office, General, Irrigation, June 25, 1907– Aug. 5, 1909," and "Memorandum for Mr. Wells," dated January 10, 1912, in the same box, "Indian Office, General Investigations, Jan. 2, 1912–April 26, 1930"; F. H. Newell to Secretary of the Interior, July 11, 1911, and Walter Fisher

(Secretary of the Interior) to Comptroller of the Treasury, July 13, 1911, Entry 5–1, Box 1189, "Flathead: Irrigation, Cooperation."

24. F. H. Newell to A. P. Davis, November 25, 1905, RG 115, General Administrative Files, 1902–19, Box 226, "(757. D1): Cooperation with Office of Indian Affairs."

25. *Report of the Commissioner of Indian Affairs, 1907* (Washington, D.C.: GPO, 1907), 50–51; *Ninth Annual Report of the Reclamation Service, 1909–1910* (Washington, D.C.: GPO, 1911), 32; *Fifteenth Annual Report of the Reclamation Service, 1915–1916* (Washington, D.C.: GPO, 1916), 547.

26. Donald J. Pisani, "George Maxwell, the Railroads, and American Land Policy, 1899–1904," *Pacific Historical Review* 63 (May 1994): 177–202.

27. *Lone Wolf v. Hitchcock,* 187 U.S. 553 (1903).

28. For a recent survey of this case, see Blue Clark, *Lone Wolf v. Hitchcock: Treaty Rights and Indian Law at the End of the Nineteenth Century* (Lincoln: University of Nebraska Press, 1994), especially pp. 14, 67–76, 82, 97.

29. *U.S.* v. *Winans,* 198 U.S. 371 (1905), 381. This rule had been established in a long series of cases beginning with *Worcester v. Georgia,* 31 U.S. 515 (1832). Neither Winans nor any other case limited the power of Congress to interpret treaties. As the leading student of Indian rights observed in 1942, "The powers of sovereignty have been limited from time to time by special treaties and laws designed to take from the Indian tribes control of matters which, in the judgment of Congress, these tribes could no longer be safely permitted to handle. The statutes of Congress . . . must be examined to determine the limitations of tribal sovereignty." Felix Cohen, *Handbook of Federal Indian Law* (Washington, D.C.: GPO, 1942), 122.

30. *U.S. Statutes at Large* 24 (1887): 388; Ibid. 26 (1891): 745; Ibid. 28 (1894): 118; Ibid. 30 (1899): 924. Also see *U.S. Statutes at Large* 34 (1906): 53; Ibid. 35 (1908): 559; and Ibid. 35 (1909): 782.

31. For excellent summaries of the Winters case, see John Lytle Shurts, *Indian Reserved Water Rights: The Winters Doctrine and Its Social and Legal Context, 1880s–1930s* (Norman: University of Oklahoma Press, 2000); Norris Hundley, jr., "The Dark and Bloody Ground of Indian Water Rights: Confusion Elevated to Principle," *Western Historical Quarterly* 9 (October 1978): 455–82, and "The 'Winters' Decision and Indian Water Rights: A Mystery Reexamined," *Western Historical Quarterly* 13 (January 1982): 17–42. The best general account of Indian water rights in the twentieth century is Daniel McCool, *Command of the Waters: Iron Triangles, Federal Water Development, and Indian Water* (Berkeley: University of California Press, 1987). McCool discusses the Winters case on pp. 36–65.

32. *Winters* v. *United States,* 143 Fed. 740 (1906), 741.

33. "Brief for the United States," in U.S. Supreme Court, *Records and Briefs,* vol. 207 [*Winters* v. *United States,* 1907], Library of Congress Law Library, 5; "Brief of the Appellee in United States Circuit Court of Appeals for the Ninth Circuit," undated, and C. F. Larrabee (Acting Commissioner of Indian Affairs) to the Secretary of Interior, June 9, 1905, in RG 60, file no. 58730, Box 221 [*Winters* v. *United States,* 1907].

34. C. F. Larrabee (Acting Commissioner of Indian Affairs) to Secretary of the Interior, June 9, 1905, RG 60, file no. 58730, Box 221.

35. Carl Rasch to U.S. Attorney General, August 28, 1905, RG 60, file no. 58730, Box 221.

36. Ibid.

37. "Transcript of Record upon Appeal from the United States Circuit Court for the District of Montana," RG 60, file no. 58730, Box 221, 85, 86.

38. "Brief of the Appellee in United States Circuit Court of Appeals for the Ninth Circuit," 13–34, 46, 48, 55–56, 62; C. S. Kinney, *A Treatise on the Law of Irrigation and Water Rights, and the Arid Region Doctrine of Appropriation of Water* (San Francisco: Bender-Moss, 1912), sec. 135, p. 205, and sec. 145, pp. 220–21.

39. Carl Rasch to Attorney General, August 28, 1905, RG 60, file no. 58730, Box 221.

40. *Winters* v. *United States*, 143 Fed. 740 (9th Cir. 1906); *Winters* v. *United States*, 148 Fed. 684 (9th Cir. 1906). As Judge Hawley emphasized in the first appeal, a reservation was just that: something reserved, not something granted. To interpret the treaty in any other way "would be in violation of the true intent and meaning of the terms of the treaty. We must presume that the government and the Indians, in agreeing to the terms of the treaty, acted in utmost good faith to each other." See 143 Fed. 740 (9th Cir. 1906), p. 745.

41. *Winters* v. *United States*, 28 Sup. Ct. 207 (1908), 211.

42. *Winters* v. *United States*, 207 U.S. 564 (1908), 577.

43. Charles E. Corker, "Water Rights and Federalism—The Western Water Rights Settlement Bill of 1957," *California Law Review* 45 (1957): 626.

44. *U.S.* v. *Powers*, 59 Sup. Ct. 344 (1939).

45. Donald J. Pisani, "Irrigation, Water Rights, and the Betrayal of Indian Allotment," *Environmental History Review* 10 (Fall 1986): 157–76.

46. "Memorandum: Conflicting Attitude Dept. Justice on Irrigation Matters," December 8, 1905; Attorney General to the President, December 18, 1905; and Ethan Allen Hitchcock to the President, January 5, 1906, RG 60, file no. 58730, Box 221; "Attitude of the Department of Justice on Irrigation Matters," December 20, 1905, RG 115, General File, 1902–1919, Box 231, "Legal Discussions—General, thru December 31, 1907."

47. W. H. Code to James W. Martin (Superintendent of Irrigation, Indian Irrigation Service), August 16, 1911, RG 75, Irrigation Division, General Correspondence, Entry no. 653, Box 14, "Yakima, June–December 1911."

48. William Reed to Commissioner of Indian Affairs, March 26, 1913, RG 75, Irrigation, General Correspondence, Entry no. 653, "Wm. Reed, 1912–15," and "Water Rights," undated memo (probably 1914 or 1915), Entry no. 653, Box 3.

49. W. H. Code to Secretary of the Interior, January 27, 1909, and Code to Chief Engineer, United States Reclamation Service, RG 115, General Administrative Files, 1902–1919, Box 99, "(127): Uintah Indian Reservation—Utah, 1904 thru [?]"; Code to Secretary of the Interior, March 22, 1909, RG 75, Indian Office, General Correspondence, Entry no. 653, Box 26, "Uintah, 1909," and Code to the Secretary, February 23, 1911, in the same box, "Uintah, 1911–12."

50. *Report of the Commissioner of Indian Affairs, 1913* (Washington, D.C.: GPO, 1914), 12–13; "Memorandum for Commissioner Burke, in re Irrigation of Uintah Lands," October 31, 1921, RG 75, Irrigation Division, General Correspondence, Entry no. 653, Box 27, "Uintah, 1920–21."

51. "Allotments of Dead Indians for Lease," undated circular; advertisement dated September 22, 1915, and *The Uintah Basin and Its Indian Lands* (Nyton, Utah: The Reservation News Print, 1916), RG 75, Irrigation Division, General Correspondence, Entry no. 653, Box 27, "Uintah, 1916."

52. *Irrigable Lands on the Uintah Reservation, Utah*, S. Doc. 414, 66th Cong., 3d sess., serial 7794 (Washington: GPO, 1921), 4.

53. E. B. Merritt to Walter Fisher, January 2, 1913, RG 48, Central Classified File, 1907–1936, Entry 5–1, Box 1387, "Uintah & Ouray Irrigation, 1912–1918"; E. W. Burr, "Memoranda—Proposed Suit to Establish Rights of the Indians to the Yakima River," December 1, 1913, 77–12, Wesley Jones Papers, University of Washington, Special Collections, Seattle.

54. *U.S. Statutes at Large* 34 (1906): 375; *U.S. Statutes at Large* 35 (1908): 558; *Report of the Commissioner of Indian Affairs, 1906*, 83. As the Bureau of Indian Affairs law clerk E. B. Merritt noted in a letter to Commissioner Robert G. Valentine, "I find that the principle laid down in the very favorable decision of the Supreme Court . . . in the Winters case . . . has been practically nullified by various acts of Congress and as the result of such legislation the water rights of Indians are now dependent on beneficial use in a large number of reservations." See Merritt to Valentine, November 17, 1911, RG 48, Central Classified File, 1907–1936, Entry 5–1, Box 1387, "Uintah & Ouray Irrigation, April 9, 1907–April 12, 1912." Similar wording appears in Secretary of the Interior to Robert G. Gamble (Chair, Committee on Indian Affairs, U.S. Senate), no date [probably January 1913], in the same box, "Uintah & Ouray Irrigation, 1912–1918."

55. Robert G. Valentine to Secretary of the Interior, December 1, 1911, RG 48, Central Classified Files, 1907–36, Entry 5–1, Box 1299, "Pima, Irrigation, Nov. 2, 1911–Apr. 19, 1913"; Valentine to Secretary, March 15, 1912, RG 75, Irrigation Division, General Correspondence, Entry 653, Box 14, "Yakima, 1912–13"; *Report of the Commissioner of Indian Affairs, 1913* (Washington, D.C.: GPO, 1914), 19; S. M. Brosius, "Indian Water-Rights for Irrigation," speech to a conference of Friends of the Indian, Mohonk Lake, New York, October 23, 1912, RG 48, Central Classified File, 1907–1936, Entry 5–1, Box 1412, "Yakima, Irrigation, General, October 25, 1912–Mar. 15, 1913." On Winters and the Yakima Reservation, see the long legal brief prepared by E. W. Burr and submitted to the chief counsel of the Reclamation Service in 1913 in E. W. Burr to W. L. Jones, December 24, 1913, 77–12, Wesley Jones Papers, and W. J. Burke, "The Doctrine of the Winters Case and Its Application to the Yakima River," memo dated September 20, 1940, in RG 115, General Correspondence File, 1930–1945, "(032): Correspondence re Settlement; Exchange; Transfer, Etc. of Water Rights, January 1940 thru December 1941."

56. House Joint Resolution 250 (Stephens), *Congressional Record*, 62d Cong., 2d sess., House, February 22, 1912: 2344.

57. Franklin K. Lane, "From the War-Path to the Plow," *National Geographic* 27 (January 1915): 87.

58. Franklin K. Lane to Speaker of the House of Representatives, December 7, 1914, RG 75, Irrigation Division, General Correspondence, Entry 653, Box 28, "Uintah No. 3"; *Irrigation Projects on Shoshone or Wind River Reservation*, H. Doc. 1274, 63d Cong., 3d sess., serial 6888 (Washington, D.C.: GPO, 1914), 3.

59. "A Bill," undated, probably late 1913 or early 1914, in RG 75, Irrigation, General Correspondence, Entry 653, Box 3. Phillip P. Wells, a legal official in the Interior Department, or E. B. Meritt, the Indian Office's law clerk, prepared similar legislation in November or December, 1911. See RG 48, Central Classified File, 1907–1936, Entry 5–1, Box 1387, "Uintah & Ouray Irrigation, April 9, 1907–April 12, 1912."

60. The House paid less attention to Indian water rights in 1914. However, it did consider an amendment to the appropriations bill for the Flathead Irrigation Project that would have reserved sufficient water for all the land "allotted or to be allotted" on the Flathead Reservation in Montana. See the *Congressional Record*, 63d Cong., 2d sess., House, February 19, 1914: 1891.

61. *Congressional Record*, 63d Cong., 2d sess., Senate, June 20, 1914: 10773–10780.

62. Ibid., 11020, 11021 (quote), 11029.

63. Ibid., 10773, 10774.

64. Ibid., 11024, 11027.

65. Ibid., 10598, 10777, 10788, 10795, 11024, 11027–28.

66. Ibid., 11019; "Senator Robinson's Record in the Senate: 1913–1930," Joseph T. Robinson Collection, Series 5, Box 20, folder 16, Special Collections, University of Arkansas, Fayetteville.

67. Joseph T. Robinson to Sam Peel, November 10, 1915, Joseph T. Robinson Collection, Series 7, Box 56, folder 6; Nevin E. Neal, "A Biography of Joseph T. Robinson" (Ph.D. diss., University of Oklahoma, 1958), 125–39; Jerry J. Vervack, "The Making of a Politician: Joe T. Robinson, 1872–1921" (Ph.D. diss., University of Arkansas, 1990), 195–96, 198.

68. Besides Joseph Robinson, the joint committee consisted of Senator Harry Lane of Oregon and Congressmen James H. Stephens of Texas, Charles H. Burke of South Dakota, and Charles D. Carter of Oklahoma.

69. *U.S. Statutes at Large* 38 (1914): 583; *U.S. Statues at Large* 41 (1920): 409. Before 1914, much of the cost of Indian irrigation projects was not reimbursable. In fiscal year 1910, for example, $325,000 was appropriated unconditionally and $551,000 was subject to repayment. See the *Report of the Commissioner of Indian Affairs, 1910* (Washington, D.C.: GPO, 1911), 21. In 1927, Congress increased the twenty-year repayment schedule mandated in 1920 to forty years. In addition to construction costs, the pro rata costs of operating and maintaining dams and canals were included in the liens on individual allotments.

70. Some Indians favored this legislation in the hope that it would increase their annuity money and allow them to purchase livestock as well as farm equipment. For example, see "Petition of Confederated Bands of Ute Indians of the Uintah and Ouray Agency, Utah, August, 1913," RG 75, Irrigation Office, General Correspondence, Entry 653, Box 26, "Uintah, 1913–14–15."

71. As early as 1910, an official in the Interior Department informed the secretary of the interior that if the BIA forced whites who took up Indian land on the Flathead Reservation to pay the full cost of the water they received from Indian irrigation works, then the value of Indian land would fall by 50 percent. At the time, the Department of Interior ruled that whites who purchased Indian allotments *before* the construction of an irrigation system had to pay full construction costs. If the system had already been completed, white farmers were

exempt from such charges. And if construction was under way at the time of entry, the white purchaser was exempt for all charges up to the time of purchase. See Stanley Scearce to Secretary of the Interior, November 15, 1910, RG 48, Central Classified File, 1907–1936, Entry 5–1, Box 1190, "Flathead: Irrigation, Water Rights."

72. Cato Sells to Secretary of the Interior, October 20, 1919, and John F. Truesdell, "Memorandum for the Commissioner," October 18, 1920, RG 75, Irrigation Division, General Correspondence, Entry 653, Box 28, loose correspondence; Samuel J. Flickinger to Commissioner of Indian Affairs, October 14, 1926, RG 75, Central Classified Files, General Service, 1907–39, 341, Box 962, file 50093–1926; Charles Burke to John H. Edwards (Assistant Secretary of the Interior), September 8, 1928, in RG 75, Central Classified Files, General Service, 1907–39, Entry 341, Box 963, file 1973–1927; Charles H. Burke to A. P. Davis (Director, U.S. Reclamation Service), May 4, 1923, and Ethelbert Ward, "Memorandum for Mr. Hamele," May 21, 1923, RG 115, Project Files, 1919–1929, Box 518, "(032): Flathead Reservation; Settlement of Water Rights"; Acting Commissioner of Indian Affairs to Secretary of the Interior, July 13, 1925, RG 48, Central Classified File, 1907–1936, Entry 5–1, Box 1300, "Pima, Irrigation, June 13, 1922–July 16, 1930"; *Report of the Commissioner of Indian Affairs, 1926* (Washington, D.C.: GPO, 1926), 24.

73. Janet McDonnell, *The Dispossession of the American Indian, 1887–1934* (Bloomington: Indiana University Press, 1991), 33; Hurt, *Indian Agriculture,* 164–65; Donald J. Pisani, *Water, Land, and Law in the West: The Limits of Public Policy, 1850–1920* (Lawrence: University Press of Kansas, 1996), 178; *Report of the Commissioner of Indian Affairs, 1919* (Washington, D.C.: GPO, 1920), 38; *Report of the Commissioner of Indian Affairs, 1920* (Washington, D.C.: GPO, 1920), 23.

74. As reprinted in McDonnell, *Dispossession of the American Indian,* 33.

75. *Report of the Commissioner of Indian Affairs, 1922* (Washington, D.C.: GPO, 1922), 14; *Report of the Commissioner of Indian Affairs, 1930* (Washington, D.C.: GPO, 1930), 22. As historian R. Douglas Hurt has pointed out, in 1927 almost 40 percent of all irrigated Indian land in the West was on the Pima Reservation in Arizona and the Uintah Reservation in Utah. See Hurt, *Indian Agriculture,* 171.

76. *Report of the Commissioner of Indian Affairs, 1926* (Washington, D.C.: GPO, 1926), 24–25; *Extension of Time for Payment of Charges Due on Indian Irrigation Projects,* S. Rept. 586, 71st Cong., 2d sess. (Washington, D.C.: GPO, 1930); *Report of the Commissioner of Indian Affairs, 1930* (Washington, D.C.: GPO, 1930), 22; *Report of the Commissioner of Indian Affairs, 1932* (Washington, D.C.: GPO, 1932), 18; "Report of the Commissioner of Indian Affairs," in *Report of the Secretary of the Interior, 1937* (Washington, D.C.: GPO, 1937), 217.

77. McDonnell, *Dispossession of the American Indian,* 122; Superintendent, Blackfeet Agency, to Commissioner of Indian Affairs, March 31, 1923; W. M. Reed to Charles Burke, July 17, 1924; Reed to Secretary of the Interior, October 1 (quote) and 2, 1928, all in RG 75, Central Classified Files, General Service, 1907–39, Entry 341, Box 939, file 38841–1920.

78. Chief Engineer, Indian Irrigation Service, "Memorandum: Laws Pertaining to Irrigation on the Flathead Reservation," January 29, 1914, RG 75, Irrigation Division, General Correspondence, Entry 653, Box 36, "Flathead, 1910–16." Con-

ditions were not much different on the Crow Reservation, whose irrigation system had been constructed and supervised by the Indian Irrigation Service. By the end of 1923, $2.5 million of Crow money had been spent on ditches and canals that irrigated fewer than ten thousand acres of Indian land. See Samuel Blair, Special Inspector, "Crow Indian Reservation Irrigation Systems," June 12, 1924, RG 75, Irrigation Division, General Correspondence, Entry 653, Box 35, "Crow, 1923–24."

79. McDonnell, *Dispossession of the American Indian,* 41; *Report of the Commissioner of Indian Affairs, 1907,* 52; *Report of the Commissioner of Indian Affairs, 1915* (Washington, D.C.: GPO, 1916), 46; *Eighth Annual Report of the Reclamation Service, 1908–1909* (Washington, D.C.: GPO, 1910), 90–96.

80. Lewis Meriam, *The Problem of Indian Administration* (Washington, D.C.: Institute for Government Research, 1928), 491.

81. Ibid., 39, 488, 490–91, 496.

82. Ibid., 510–15, 783 (quote).

83. Porter J. Preston and Charles A. Engle, "Report of Advisors on Irrigation on Indian Reservations," in *Survey of Conditions of the Indians in the United States,* Hearings before a Subcommittee of the Committee on Indian Affairs, U.S. Senate, July 8, 10, 11, 12, and 17, 1929 (Washington, D.C.: GPO, 1930), 2217–18, 2220 (quote).

84. Ibid., 2218.

85. Ibid., 2213. Preston and Engle discuss the *Winters* decision on pp. 2231–32 and 2269–72.

86. *Annual Report of the Secretary of the Interior for the Fiscal Year Ending June 30, 1930* (Washington, D.C.: GPO, 1930), 30–31; Charles Burke to John H. Edwards (Assistant Secretary of the Interior), September 8, 1928, RG 75, Central Classified Files, General Service, 1907–39, Entry 341, Box 963, file "1973–1927."

87. Hurt, *Indian Agriculture,* 172.

88. *Annual Report of the Secretary of the Interior for the Fiscal Year Ended June 30, 1933* (Washington, D.C.: GPO, 1933), 89.

89. *Annual Report of the Secretary of the Interior for the Fiscal Year Ended June 30, 1935* (Washington, D.C.: GPO, 1935), 149–51; "Report of the Commissioner of Indian Affairs," in *Report of the Secretary of the Interior, 1938* (Washington, D.C.: GPO, 1938), 222. In 1948, Indians still cultivated only 25 percent of the land provided with water by the BIA. See Alfred R. Golze, *Reclamation in the United States* (New York: McGraw-Hill Book Co., 1952), 31, table 1–6.

90. Ray Lyman Wilbur, *Conservation in the Department of the Interior* (Washington, D.C.: GPO, 1931), 118.

91. Leonard A. Carlson, *Indians, Bureaucrats, and Land: The Dawes Act and the Decline of Indian Farming* (Westport, Conn.: Greenwood Press, 1981), 116, 120, 130.

92. Indians did not suffer equally from federal irrigation policies. For a case study of a tribe that maintained traditional patterns of life and enjoyed considerable agricultural success in the twentieth century, see Thomas R. Wessel, "Phantom Experiment Station: Government Agriculture on the Zuni Reservation," *Agricultural History* 61 (Fall 1987): 1–12. Also see Wessel, "Agriculture on the Reservations: The Case of the Blackfeet, 1885–1935," *Journal of the West* 18 (1979): 17–24.

93. The Collier phrases are from the annual report of the Commissioner of Indian Affairs for 1940, as published in the *Report of the Secretary of the Interior, 1940* (Washington, D.C.: GPO, 1940), 357.

94. Board of Indian Commissioners, "Brief on Indian Irrigation," 1915, RG 75, Irrigation Division, General Correspondence, Entry 653, Box 3.

95. Douglas Hurt recounts that as early as 1881, the agent at the Pine Ridge Reservation in Dakota Territory observed, "White men well trained in farming have tried to till the soil in this vicinity in Northern Nebraska and have lost all the money invested, and have not produced enough to pay for the seed. I can confidently venture to state that, if the experiment were tried of placing 7,000 white people on this land, with seed, agricultural implements, and one year's subsistence, at the end of that time they would die of starvation, if they had to depend on their crops for their sustenance." Hurt, *Indian Agriculture,* 132.

96. *Report of the Secretary of the Interior, 1882* (Washington, D.C.: GPO, 1882), 9; *Report of the Commissioner of Indian Affairs, 1895,* 26; Hurt, *Indian Agriculture,* 109.

97. Schmeckebier, *Office of Indian Affairs,* 238; McDonnell, *Dispossession of the American Indian,* 26; *Congressional Record,* 63d Cong., 2d sess., Senate, June 17, 1914: 10590 (quote).

98. A few examples speak volumes. At the Oto Agency in Nebraska, Indians used knives, tin cups, and even their hands to dig postholes on the agency farm. At the Ponca Agency in Dakota Territory, Indians harvested wheat with butcher knives. Three times the number of Kiowa, Comanche, and Wichita in Oklahoma wanted to farm than the agency could supply with plows. And all too often, those lucky enough to receive plows found Indian ponies too weak to pull them. Hurt, *Indian Agriculture,* 125, 147.

99. Hurt, *Indian Agriculture,* 110–11, 134, 169; Schmeckebier, *Office of Indian Affairs,* 247. Thomas Wessel has pointed out the irony of the Indian Office's position. Lewis Henry Morgan, one of the leading ethnographers of the late nineteenth century, argued that stock raising was an intermediate stage on the evolutionary ladder—a rung up from savage hunters and a rung down from civilized farmers. As Morgan wrote in 1878: "We have overlooked the fact that the principal Indian tribes have passed by natural development out of the condition of savages into that of barbarians. In relative progress they are now precisely where our own barbarous ancestors were when by the domestication of animals they passed from a similar into a higher condition of barbarism, though still two ethnical periods below civilization." In short, the myth that Indians could not "progress" unless they practiced settled agriculture was questioned even at the time. See Thomas R. Wessel, "Agent of Acculturation: Farming on the Northern Plains Reservations, 1880–1910," *Agricultural History* 60 (Spring 1986): 235.

100. For an overview of the neglected subject of Indian wage labor, see Alice Littlefield and Martha C. Knack, eds., *Native Americans and Wage Labor: Ethnohistorical Perspectives* (Norman: University of Oklahoma Press, 1996).

CHAPTER 7. CASE STUDIES IN WATER AND POWER

1. John Arthur Bower, Jr., "The Hydrogeography of Yakima Indian Nation Resource Use" (Ph.D. diss., University of Washington), 1990, 4–9.

2. Ibid., 32-35, and Richard D. Daugherty, *The Yakima People* (Phoenix: Indian Tribal Series, 1973), 41-46.

3. Bower, "Hydrogeography of Yakima Resource Use," 98.

4. In 1913—at a time when the Yakima Indians had little more than twenty thousand dollars in their treasury—the acting commissioner of Indian Affairs estimated that the reservation's timber supply was worth four times its unallotted land. See F. H. Abbott to Miles Poindexter, February 28, 1913, 76-8, Miles Poindexter Papers, University of Washington Special Collections, Seattle.

5. Bower, "Hydrogeography of Yakima Resource Use," 246; James Black Fitch, "Economic Development in a Minority Enclave: The Case of the Yakima Indian Nation, Washington" (Ph.D. diss., Stanford University, 1974), 79; Lucullus V. McWhorter, *The Crime against the Yakimas* (Yakima: Republic Press, 1913), 37. McWhorter ("Old Wolf"), an adopted member of the Yakima Tribe, regularly participated in tribal councils and represented the Yakima before Congress and the national Indian Rights Association.

6. As quoted in Bower, "Hydrogeography of Yakima Resource Use," 119.

7. Barbara G. Leibhardt, "Law, Environment, and Social Change in the Columbia River Basin: The Yakima Indian Nation as a Case Study, 1840-1933" (Ph.D. diss., History and Jurisprudence and Social Policy Programs, Boalt Hall Law School, University of California, Berkeley, 1990), 131-32, 250-54; Fitch, "Economic Development," 86, 89; Brad Asher, "Beyond the Reservation: Indian / White Relations and the Law in Washington Territory, 1853-1889" (Ph.D. diss., University of Chicago, 1996), 104; Rose M. Boening, "History of Irrigation in the State of Washington," *Washington Historical Quarterly* 9 (October 1918): 260, 272.

8. Asher, "Beyond the Reservation," 88-92.

9. Helen Schuster maintains that those Indians who already farmed generally favored dividing up the reservation, while the "Wild Yakima" and those who used reservation land to graze horses and cattle did not. Nevertheless, those who favored allotment seldom favored the sale of unallotted reservation land. Helen Shuster, "Yakima Indian Traditionalism: A Study in Continuity and Change" (Ph.D. diss., University of Washington, Seattle, 1975), 251, 254. Schuster describes allotment on pp. 249-62.

10. Bower, "Hydrogeography of Yakima Resource Use," 255-76.

11. Barbara G. Leibhardt, "Allotment Policy in an Incongruous Legal System: The Yakima Indian Nation as a Case Study, 1887-1934," *Agricultural History* 65 (Fall 1991): 78-103; Leibhardt, "Law, Environment, and Social Change," 136-57; Fitch, "Economic Development," 91-92.

12. *Report of the Commissioner of Indian Affairs, 1872* (Washington, D.C.: GPO, 1873), 61.

13. On leasing, see Janet McDonnell, *The Dispossession of the American Indian, 1887-1934* (Bloomington: Indiana University Press, 1991), 43-70; D. S. Otis, *The Dawes Act and the Allotment of Indian Lands* (Norman: University of Oklahoma Press, 1973), 98-123; and Frederick E. Hoxie, *A Final Promise: The Campaign to Assimilate the Indians, 1880-1920* (Lincoln: University of Nebraska Press, 1984). The case for leasing Yakima land is well described in Leibhardt, "Law, Environment, and Social Change," 157-62.

14. Fitch, "Economic Development," 96; Leibhardt, "Law, Environment, and Social Change," 161.

NOTES TO PAGES 185-88

15. By 1905 or 1906, the Wapato Development Company—a real estate company that specialized in Indian land—was selling an average of three eighty-acre allotments per week. By 1909, more than five hundred non-Indians had secured ownership of Indian allotments. Shuster, "Yakima Indian Traditionalism," 257.

16. McWhorter, *The Crime Against the Yakimas*, 9.

17. Bower, "Hydrogeography of Yakima Resource Use," 350–53.

18. *Report of the Commissioner of Indian Affairs, 1903* (Washington, D.C.: GPO, 1904), 44. In fiscal year 1903, two-thirds of the money spent by the Bureau of Indian Affairs on irrigation went to the Yakima Reservation in Washington and the Zuni Reservation in New Mexico.

19. Calvin B. Coulter, "The Victory of National Irrigation in the Yakima Valley, 1902–1906," *Pacific Northwest Quarterly* 42 (April 1951): 115–16; Commissioner of Indian Affairs to Secretary of the Interior, March 15, 1912, RG 75, Irrigation Division, General Correspondence, Entry no. 653, Box 14, "Yakima, 1912–13."

20. Emmett K. Vandevere, "History of Irrigation in Washington" (Ph.D. diss., University of Washington, 1948), 165.

21. *Morning Oregonian* (Portland), December 14, 1904; John Fahey, *The Inland Empire: Unfolding Years, 1879–1929* (Seattle: University of Washington Press, 1986), 91–92.

22. "Memorandum Relative to Cases Involving Water Rights of Indians in Montana and Washington," undated, and Ethan A. Hitchcock to Theodore Roosevelt, January 5, 1906, in RG 60, file no. 58730, Box 221 [*Winters v. United States*]; Bower, "Hydrogeography of Yakima Resource Use," 356; McWhorter, *The Crime Against the Yakimas*, 10–11; Click Relander, "The Battleground of National Irrigation," *Pacific Northwest Quarterly* 52 (October 1961): 144–51.

23. The report of the House Indian Committee is reprinted in McWhorter, *The Crime Against the Yakimas*, p. 7. Also see *Report of the Commissioner of Indian Affairs, 1906* (Washington, D.C.: GPO, 1907), 89, and *Fifth Annual Report of the Reclamation Service, 1906* (Washington, D.C.: GPO, 1907), 21–23.

24. The excerpt from Newell's letter to D. C. Henny, November 21, 1905, is as quoted in Bower, "Hydrogeography of Yakima Resource Use," 374.

25. W. H. Code to Secretary of the Interior, November 29, 1905, in RG 75, Irrigation Division, General Correspondence, Entry no. 653, Box 12, "Yakima, 1905–06."

26. The Jones Act, approved on March 6, 1906, is in *U.S. Statutes at Large* 34 (1906): 53. It is reprinted in the *Fifth Annual Report of the Reclamation Service, 1906* (Washington, D.C.: GPO, 1907), 22–23. The principle of using money from the sale of surplus land to pay for the irrigation of Indian land had been established in December 1904 (see *U.S. Statutes at Large* 33 [1904]: 595). However, this law pertained to unallotted land and contemplated irrigation works undertaken by the Indian Irrigation Service rather than the Reclamation Service.

27. Jay Lynch to W. H. Code, February 3, 1906, RG 75, Irrigation Division, General Correspondence, Entry no. 653, Box 12, "Yakima, 1905–06." In western states that recognized both riparian rights and prior appropriation—such as Washington and California—riparian rights took precedence unless the riparian owner tolerated a diversion without protest for a certain number of years. Since Lynch had protested white diversions as early as 1890 or 1891, no white farmer could claim water rights acquired through "adverse possession" Adverse pos-

session was the acquisition of a claim to property, including water, through uncontested use over a stipulated period, which was as short as five years in the western states.

28. W. H. Code to Secretary of the Interior, September 20, 1905, RG 75, Irrigation Division, General Correspondence, Entry no. 653, Box 12, "Yakima, 1905–06."

29. Francis Leupp to Ethan Allen Hitchcock, September 12, 1906, RG 75, Irrigation Division, General Correspondence, Entry no. 653, Box 12, "Yakima, 1905–06." Also see Jay Lynch to A. G. Avery, July 1, 1907, RG 48, Central Classified File, 1907–1936, Entry 5–1, Box 1387, "Yakima, Irrigation, Ahtanum Creek, June 18, 1907–Nov. 9, 1912"; Wesley Jones to Erastus Brainerd, March 5, 1906, Erastus Brainerd Papers, 3–22, University of Washington Special Collections, Seattle.

30. McWhorter, *The Crime Against the Yakimas*, 14.

31. W. H. Code to the Secretary of the Interior, April 27, 1911, RG 48, Central Classified File, 1907–1936, Entry 5–1, Box 1413, "Yakima, Irrigation, Wapato Unit, May 10, 1907–Sept. 9, 1911"; McWhorter, *The Crime Against the Yakimas*, 30.

32. L. V. McWhorter to Miles Poindexter, March 28, 1912, 74–5, Poindexter Papers; Commissioner of Indian Affairs to Poindexter, undated letter concerning grazing rights in folder 78–5, Poindexter Papers; McWhorter, *The Crime Against the Yakimas*, 25, 38, 40–41.

33. Leibhardt, "Law, Environment, and Social Change," 319–82; Bower, "Hydrogeography of Yakima Resource Use," 202–7, 285, 332–34.

34. Bower, "Hydrogeography of Yakima Resource Use," 250–52.

35. W. H. Code to the Secretary of the Interior, April 27, 1911, in RG 75, Irrigation Division, General Correspondence, Entry no. 653, Box 14, "Yakima, Jan.–May, 1911." The Indians recognized that a claim to twenty acres would be just as precarious as their existing claim to eighty. Whites did not welcome the prospect of having Indian neighbors. H. M. Gilbert, a leading speculator in Yakima land, noted in a May 27, 1909, letter to Wesley Jones that it would be far better if the government forced the Indians to sell the full eighty acres and then segregated them in the upper valleys or mountains. What Gilbert neglected to say was that most of that land was unfit for farming. See Gilbert's letter as reprinted in McWhorter, *The Crime Against the Yakimas*, 23–24.

36. As reprinted in Fitch, "Economic Development," 99.

37. See, for example, the many letters from Louis Mann, recording secretary of the Yakima Council, to Washington's U.S. senator Miles Poindexter, covering the years from about 1909 to World War I, in the Poindexter Papers.

38. Commissioner of Indian Affairs to Secretary of the Interior, March 15, 1912, RG 75, Irrigation Division, General Correspondence, Entry no. 653, Box 14, "Yakima, 1912–13."

39. F. H. Newell to Secretary of the Interior, March 29, 1912, and Philip Wess, "Memorandum," March 30, 1912, RG 48, Central Classified File, 1907–1936, Entry 5–1, Box 1412, "Yakima, Irrigation, General."

40. Walter Fisher to Director of the Reclamation Service and Commissioner of Indian Affairs, January 23, 1913, RG 75, Irrigation Division, General Correspondence, Entry no. 653, Box 14, "Yakima, 1912–13." Subsequently, Fisher called for legislation to give the secretary explicit power to allocate the water on In-

dian reservations "as an incident to his administrative power over the Indians and the public lands reserved for them." See McWhorter, *The Crime Against the Yakimas,* 44.

41. Indian Rights Association, *Thirtieth Annual Report, 1912,* 49–54; *Thirty-First Annual Report, 1913,* 52, 72–75; and *Thirty-Second Annual Report, 1914,* 29, in Indian Rights Association Papers, Microfilm Reel 103, Western History Collections, University of Oklahoma, Norman.

42. *Memorial of the Yakima Tribe of Indians,* June 8, 1912, H. Doc. 1304, 62d Cong., 3d sess., serial 6500 (Washington, D.C.: GPO, 1919), 3; McWhorter, *The Crime Against the Yakimas,* 44, 48; S. M. Brosius, Indian Rights Association, "Indian Water-Rights for Irrigation," speech to the Conference of Friends of the Indian, Mohonk Lake, N.Y., October 23, 1912, RG 48, Central Classified File, 1907–1936, Entry 5–1, Box 1412, "Yakima, Irrigation, General, Oct. 25, 1912–Mar. 15, 1913."

43. F. H. Newell to Miles Poindexter, January 17, 1913, 76–13, Poindexter Papers.

44. *Joint Commission on Indian Tuberculosis Sanitarium in New Mexico and Yakima Reservation Project in Washington,* S. Doc. 337, 63d Cong., 2d sess., serial 6572 (Washington, D.C.: GPO, 1914). Also see *Indian Tuberculosis Sanitorium in New Mexico and Yakima Reservation Project in Washington,* H. Doc. 505, 63d Cong., 2d sess., serial 6754 (Washington, D.C.: GPO, 1914).

45. *Report of the Commissioner of Indian Affairs, 1917* (Washington, D.C.: GPO, 1918), 35; *Irrigating the Yakima Indian Reservation,* H. Doc. 1472, 63d Cong., 3d sess., serial 6888 (Washington, D.C.: GPO, 1915); Vandevere, "History of Irrigation in Washington," 176–83; E. C. Finney (Solicitor of the Interior Department) to the Secretary of the Interior, June 7, 1929, RG 48, Central Classified File, 1907–1936, Entry 5–1, Box 1412, "Yakima, Irrigation, Ahtanum Creek, March 5, 1919 to July 31, 1930"; Cato Sells to the Secretary of the Interior, January 22, 1918, in the same records group, Box 1413, "Yakima, Irrigation, Wapato Unit, May 10, 1907–Sept. 9, 1911"; Cato Sells to Chief Saluskin, Kiutus James, and Indians of the Yakima Reservation, February 5, 1916, and Louis Mann to Miles Poindexter, January 13–14, 1916, Box 76, file 12, Poindexter Papers.

46. Fitch, "Economic Development," 100–101, 106, 407–8; Leibhardt, "Law, Environment, and Social Change," 93, 301–3.

47. T. D. Mallery, "Rainfall Records for the Sonoran Desert," *Ecology* 17 (January 1936): 110–21, and (April 1936): 212–15; J. W. Hoover, "The Indian Country of Southern Arizona," *Geographical Review* 19 (January 1929): 40.

48. Edward F. Castetter and Willis H. Bell, *Pima and Papago Indian Agriculture* (Albuquerque: University of New Mexico Press, 1942), 39, 49–51, 56–57, 63–72, 145; Frank Russell, "The Pima Indians," in *Twenty-Sixth Annual Report of the Bureau of American Ethnology to the Secretary of the Smithsonian Institution, 1904–1905* (Washington, D.C.: GPO, 1908), 68, 74.

49. Ross Calvin, ed., *Lieutenant Emory Reports: A Reprint of W. H. Emory's "Notes of a Military Reconnaissance"* (Albuquerque: University of New Mexico Press, 1951), 133, 134–35.

50. Russell, "The Pima Indians," 31–32.

51. Bertha P. Dutton, *American Indians of the Southwest* (Albuquerque: University of New Mexico Press, 1983), 206, 209; Paul H. Ezell, "History of the Pima," in *Handbook of North American Indians: The Southwest,* vol. 10, ed. William C. Sturtevant

(Washington, D.C.: Smithsonian Institution, 1983), 158; Castetter and Bell, *Pima and Papago Indian Agriculture*, 16.

52. Robert A. Hackenberg, "Pima and Papago Ecological Adaptations," in *Handbook of North American Indians*, vol. 10, 161–65.

53. R. Douglas Hurt, *Indian Agriculture in America: Prehistory to the Present* (Lawrence: University Press of Kansas, 1987), 49, 125, 139; Frank Russell, *The Pima Indians* (Tucson: University of Arizona Press, 1975), 66, 90; Ezell, *History of the Pima*, 151, 153; Hackenberg, "Pima and Papago Ecological Adaptations," 163–64, 170. Hurt estimates that Pima canals could irrigate thirteen thousand to sixteen thousand acres at the end of the nineteenth century. See *Indian Agriculture*, 49.

54. Whittemore, "The Pima Indians, Their Manners and Customs," 94–95; "The Pima Reservation, Arizona, 1917," memo dated June 18, 1917, in RG 48, Central Classified File, 1907–1936, Entry 5–1, Box 1299, "Indian Office, Pima Investigations." Not all white observers agreed with this glowing assessment of the Pima. Some acknowledged the erosion of traditional Pima values, and the effects of disease, as the Indians came into closer contact with whites during the last half of the nineteenth century. For example, see F. E. Grossmann, "The Pima Indians of Arizona," in *Annual Report of the Board of Regents of the Smithsonian Institution* (Washington, D.C.: GPO, 1873), 412, and Russell, "The Pima Indians," 32.

55. Edward Spicer, *Cycles of Conquest* (Tucson: University of Arizona Press, 1962), 148–49.

56. A. P. Davis, *Report on the Irrigation Investigation for the Benefit of the Pima and Other Indians on the Gila River Indian Reservation, Arizona* (Washington, D.C.: GPO, 1897); *Irrigation upon the Pima Indian Reservation, Arizona* (Washington, D.C.: GPO, 1900); *Reservoir near San Carlos, Ariz.* (Washington, D.C.: GPO, 1901).

57. The quotations from the Pima agent's letter are as reprinted in J. B. Lippincott, *Storage of Water on Gila River, Arizona* (Washington, D.C.: GPO, 1900), 12.

58. Lippincott, *Storage of Water*, 95; William M. Stewart, "Irrigating Indian Reservations," *Irrigation Age* 15 (April 1901): 222–38. The secretary of the interior recommended construction of the San Carlos dam in 1900. See *Report of the Secretary of the Interior, 1900* (Washington, D.C.: GPO, 1900), 99.

59. The Newell comments are as quoted in Davis, *Report on the Irrigation Investigation*, 3. Also see George H. Maxwell to Harry Brook, April 18, 1903, Harry Brook file, Box 1, George Maxwell Collection, Louisiana State Museum, New Orleans, and F. H. Newell to Maxwell, October 1, 1900, and February 5, 1903, F. H. Newell file, Box 2, Maxwell Collection.

60. As quoted in Karen L. Smith, "The Campaign for Water in Central Arizona, 1890–1903," *Arizona and the West* 23 (Summer 1981): 133.

61. *Report of the Commissioner of Indian Affairs, 1900* (Washington, D.C.: GPO, 1900), 59.

62. James R. Garfield (Secretary of the Interior) to Chief Antonio Azul, December 23, 1907, RG 48, Central Classified File, 1907–1936, Entry 5–1, Box 1299, "Pima Irrigation, April 29, 1907 to October 2, 1911."

63. *Report of the Commissioner of Indian Affairs, 1904* (Washington, D.C.: GPO, 1905), 7–21; *Report of the Commissioner of Indian Affairs, 1905* (Washington, D.C.: GPO, 1906), 75; Elwood Hadley to Commissioner of Indian Affairs, July 17, 1901, RG 75, Special Cases, Case no. 190, "Pima, 1901–1907."

64. Owen Wilson, "Rescuing a People by an Irrigating Ditch: The Making Over of

the Pima Indians," *The World's Work* 22 (September 1911): 14815–17; *Report of the Commissioner of Indian Affairs, 1906,* 87; *Report of the Commissioner of Indian Affairs, 1907* (Washington, D.C.: GPO, 1907), 53–54; George H. Wisner and Louis Hill to F. H. Newell, December 15, 1905, RG 115, General Administrative Files, 1902–19, Box 226, "(757-D1): Cooperation with Office of Indian Affairs"; *U.S. Statutes at Large* 34 (1907): 1022.

65. "Irrigation for the Indians," *Forestry and Irrigation* 10 (August 1904): 378–79.

66. M. K. Sniffen, "The Record of Thirty Years: A Brief Statement of the Indian Rights Association, Its Objects, Methods, and Achievements," p. 14, typescript dated April 15, 1913, in Ray Lyman Wilbur Papers, Box 15, "Indian Affairs, 1913–1921," Herbert Hoover Presidential Library, West Branch, Iowa; *Twenty-Ninth Annual Report [of the Indian Rights Association], 1911,* 45–49, in Indian Rights Association Papers, Microfilm Reel 103.

67. For the Pima point of view, see Chief Antonio Azul and other Pimas to Francis E. Leupp, March 1, 1906; Sacaton Reservation Pimas to James R. Garfield, May 20, 1907; and Hugh Patton and Lewis D. Nelson to the Secretary of Interior, May 1, 1908, all in RG 115, General Administrative Files, 1902–19, Box 226, "(757-D1): Cooperation with Office of Indian Affairs." Also see *Letters and Petition with Reference to Conserving the Rights of the Pima Indians, of Arizona, to the Lands of Their Reservation and the Necessary Water Supply for Irrigation,* 62d Cong., 1st sess., House Committee Print H-3840 (Washington, D.C.: GPO, 1911).

68. The five-acre allotments on the Pima Reservation were the same size as the Indian allotments on the nearby Yuma Reservation, much of which was absorbed into the Reclamation Service's Yuma Project. Five irrigated acres per Indian was insufficient, however, because wheat—the crop that made the Pima independent and self-sufficient—returned only about fifteen dollars an acre per year under the best conditions.

69. S. M. Brosius (Indian Rights Association) to Carl E. Grammer (President, Indian Rights Association), July 10, 1909; Brosius to the Secretary of Interior, July 6, 1911; and Robert G. Valentine (Commissioner of Indian Affairs) to the Secretary of the Interior, December 1, 1911, all in RG 48, Central Classified file 1907–1936, Entry 5–1, Box 1299, "Pima Irrigation, April 29, 1907, to Oct. 2, 1911"; Brosius, "Indian Water-Rights for Irrigation"; F. H. Newell to Cato Sells (Commissioner of Indian Affairs), August 19, 1913, RG 115, General Administrative Files, 1902–19, Box 227, "(757-D1): Cooperation with Office of Indian Affairs—Gila River & Pima Indian Res. 1913 thru [?]"

70. Robert G. Valentine (Commissioner of Indian Affairs) to Secretary of Interior, December 1, 1911, RG 48, Central Classified File 1907–1936, Entry 5–1, Box 1299, "Pima, Irrigation, Nov. 2, 1911–Apr. 19, 1913" (quote). Also see Castetter and Bell, *Pima and Papago Indian Agriculture,* 15–16; Hackenberg, "Pima and Papago Ecological Adaptations," 173; Spicer, *Cycles of Conquest,* 150.

71. *Report of the Commissioner of Indian Affairs, 1925* (Washington, D.C.: GPO, 1925), 20–21; Jack L. August, "Carl Hayden's 'Indian Card': Environmental Politics and the San Carlos Reclamation Project," *Journal of Arizona History* 33 (Winter 1992): 1–20. Also see "Statement by Carl Hayden Relative to Water Rights on the Gila River" and "Memorandum Regarding the Coolidge Dam," both in Box 617, file 6, Carl Hayden Collection, Special Collections, Arizona State University, Tempe.

I am indebted to Professor Richard Lowitt of the University of Oklahoma for sharing with me photocopies of documents in the Hayden Collection.

72. As quoted in "Information Service for Advisory Council on Indian Affairs, July 9, 1924," Ray Lyman Wilbur Papers, Box 15, "Indian Affairs, 1923–1928," Hoover Library.

73. *Report of the Commissioner of Indian Affairs, 1919* (Washington, D.C.: GPO, 1920), 41; "Report of the Commissioner of Indian Affairs [1935]," in *Report of the Secretary of the Interior, 1935* (Washington, D.C.: GPO, 1935), 150.

74. *Thirty-Fourth Annual Report [of the Indian Rights Association], 1916*, 41–42, in Indian Rights Association Papers, Microfilm Reel 103.

75. "The Pima Reservation, Arizona, 1917," memo dated June 18, 1917, in RG 48, Central Classified File, 1907–1936, Entry 5–1, Box 1299, "Indian Office, Pima Investigations."

76. Castetter and Bell, *Pima and Papago Indian Agriculture*, 16.

77. Ales Hrdlicka, "Notes on the Pima of Arizona," *American Anthropologist* 8 (January–March 1906): 40.

CHAPTER 8. WIRING THE NEW WEST

1. Louis C. Hunter and Lynwood Bryant, *A History of Industrial Power in the United States, 1780–1930*, vol. 3 (Cambridge: Massachusetts Institute of Technology Press, 1991), 254–72.

2. Recent studies of the electrification of the West include Jay Brigham, *Empowering the West: Electrical Politics before FDR* (Lawrence: University Press of Kansas, 1998), and James C. Williams, *Energy and the Making of Modern California* (Akron, Ohio: University of Akron Press, 1997).

3. John Wesley Powell, "The Non-Irrigable Lands of the Arid Region," *Century* 39 (April 1890): 921; *Irrigation Age* 6 (January 1894): 2, and Ibid. 6 (February 1894): 47; William Baxter, "The Electric Transmission of Water Power," *Popular Science Monthly* 52 (April 1898): 742.

4. Walter B. Henry, "The Water Giant Waits," *The Nation's Business* 7 (March 1919): 16 (quote), 18; Thomas J. Walsh to Norman Hapgood, February 19, 1916, Box 329, "Legislation: Water Power," Thomas J. Walsh Collection, Library of Congress, Washington, D.C.; Carl D. Thompson, "Hydro-Electric and Superpower," *Public Ownership* 4 (October 1922): 3–13.

5. *Pacific Rural Press* 56 (December 31, 1898): 434 (quote); Hunter and Bryant, *History of Industrial Power*, vol. 3, 256–57; Harley W. Nehf, "The Concentration of Water Powers," *Journal of Political Economy* 24 (October 1916): 785.

6. Carl J. Rohrer, "Electricity in Agriculture—I," *Scientific American Supplement* 80 (October 23, 1915): 264–66; Louis J. Taber, "Electrical Sunshine for Agriculture," address to the 48th convention of the National Electric Light Association in San Francisco, 1925, in RG 115, Central Administrative Records, 1919–1929, Box 281, "(325): General Corres. re Power Use on Farms (Rural Electrification)."

7. "Irrigation by Electricity," *Irrigation Age* 7 (November 1894): 228; Joel Shomaker, "Irrigation and Commercial Expansion," *Irrigation Age* 14 (October 1899): 7–11; A. G. Wishon, "Electrical Development of the San Joaquin Valley," *Out West* 40 (December 1914): 356; Henry J. Pierce, "The Vital Necessity for Water Power

Development," pamphlet dated May 1917 in Box 329, "Legislation, Water Power" file, Thomas J. Walsh Collection.

8. A. H. Horton, "Production of Electric Power by Public-Utility Power Plants in the United States," November 1, 1928, Box 2882, Gifford Pinchot Collection, Library of Congress, Washington, D.C.; Calvert Townley, "Hydro-Electric Development," *Scientific American Supplement* 85 (April 27, 1918): 263; "Developed and Potential Water Power of the United States" (editorial), *Science* 57 (January 12, 1923): 57.

9. The U.S. Supreme Court did not decide that commerce included navigation until 1824, and then reinforced that decision in 1865, when it ruled that the navigable waters were the public property of the nation and thus subject to Congressional authority. See *Gibbons* v. *Ogden*, 22 U.S. 1 (1824) and *Gilman* v. *Philadelphia*, 70 U.S. 715 (1865).

10. Thomas K. McCraw, *TVA and the Power Fight, 1933–1939* (Philadelphia: J. B. Lippincott Co., 1971), 7.

11. On federal power policy in the late nineteenth and early twentieth centuries, see Samuel P. Hays, *Conservation and the Gospel of Efficiency: The Progressive Conservation Movement, 1890–1920* (Cambridge: Harvard University Press, 1959), 73–81, 114–21, 160–65. Also see Jerome Kerwin, *Federal Water-Power Legislation* (New York: Columbia University Press, 1926), and Judson King, *The Conservation Fight: From Theodore Roosevelt to the Tennessee Valley Authority* (Washington, D.C.: Public Affairs Press, 1959). Franklin K. Lane outlined his water power policy in his annual reports. In particular, see the *Report of the Secretary of the Interior, 1913* (Washington, D.C.: GPO, 1913), 23–25; *Report of the Secretary of the Interior, 1914* (Washington, D.C.: GPO, 1914), 16–18; and *Report of the Secretary of the Interior, 1915* (Washington, D.C.: GPO, 1915), 18–21.

12. *Congressional Record,* 64th Cong., 1st sess., Senate, March 8, 1916: 3731–32, 3736, 3743, 3755 (quote).

13. *New York Times,* September 22, 1918.

14. *Congressional Record,* 64th Cong., 1st sess., Senate, March 8, 1916: 3750.

15. *New York Times,* July 14, 1916; January 19, 1917; August 30 and September 3, 1918; Henry Solon Graves, "Memorandum for the Secretary [of Agriculture]," December 2, 1916, RG 16, Drawer 301, Incoming Correspondence, 1916, "Water Power"; Thomas J. Walsh to Joseph N. Teal, June 23, 1915, Box 217, "Water Power" file, Thomas J. Walsh Collection.

16. The Borah quotations are from Roy Robbins, *Our Landed Heritage: The Public Domain, 1776–1970* (Lincoln: University of Nebraska Press, 1976), 372–73. Also see William E. Borah to Karl Paine, April 21, 1916; Borah to Edgar Piper, February 23, 1916; and Borah to J. Walter Johnson, January 29, 1916, all in Box 541, "Water Power Development, 1915–1916," and Borah to W. S. Hunt, February 12, 1918, Box 546, "Leasing System, 1917–1918," William E. Borah Collection, Library of Congress, Washington, D.C.

17. *Congressional Record,* 64th Cong., 1st sess., House, January 5, 1916: 554–55. Also see Taylor's statement in the *Record,* 63d Cong., 2d sess., House, August 13, 1914: 13680–81. For summaries of Western arguments on water power legislation, see Hays, *Conservation and the Gospel of Efficiency,* 241–60, and Robbins, *Our Landed Heritage,* 389–97.

18. William Kent to the Secretary of Agriculture, May 11, 1914, RG 16, Drawer 361, Incoming Correspondence, 1914, "Water Power Control on Public Lands, 1914"; William Kent to Woodrow Wilson, June 27, 1914, Box 19, Corres. June 25–30, 1914, William Kent Collection, Sterling Library, Yale University; *New York Times,* January 7, 1915; *Congressional Record,* 63d Cong., 1st sess., House, August 11, 1914: 13630–31, 13671, and August 22, 1914: 14151, both from 64th Cong., 1st sess., January 8, 1916: 733–34, 736.

19. Robert H. Fuller to Walter L. Fisher, April 26 and June 21, 1911, Box 20, "Conservation of Water Power, Part I," Walter Fisher Collection, Library of Congress, Washington, D.C.; C. R. Van Hise, *Conservation of Natural Resources in the United States* (New York: Macmillan, 1914), 157; Milton Conover, *The Federal Power Commission: Its History, Activities, and Organization* (Baltimore: Johns Hopkins University Press, 1923), 13–14; Charles W. Baker, "The Necessity for State or Federal Regulation of Water Power Development," *Annals of the American Academy of Political and Social Science* 33 (May 1909): 592–93.

20. Frederick H. Newell, *Water Resources: Present and Future Uses* (New Haven: Yale University Press, 1920), 28–29.

21. Newton D. Baker, Franklin K. Lane, and David F. Houston to T. W. Sims, February 15 and 27, 1918, and George P. Hampton to Woodrow Wilson, August 19, 1918, RG 16, Drawer 275, Incoming Correspondence, 1918, "Water Power" and O. C. Merrill, Memorandum on Water Power Legislation, October 31, 1917, Drawer 41, Incoming Correspondence, 1917, "Water Power."

22. D. F. Houston to Woodrow Wilson, November 30, 1917, RG 16, Drawer 41, Incoming Correspondence, 1917, "Water Power" (quote). Also see Newton D. Baker (Secretary of War) to Franklin K. Lane, and David F. Houston to T. W. Sims, both February 15, 1918, in Drawer 275, Incoming Correspondence, 1918, "Water Power" and O. C. Merrill, Memorandum Concerning Federal Power Commission, September 10, 1920, Box 519, Gifford Pinchot Collection.

23. *New York Times,* February 3 and 16, 1919, and November 6, 1921; Judson C. Welliver, "Superpower: The Next Industrial Revolution," *American Review of Reviews* 66 (September 1922): 285–96. By the middle of the 1920s, Gifford Pinchot was predicting, "The time is almost here when electric utility companies will be interconnected all the way from Chicago to the Gulf, and from the Atlantic Coast to the Great Plains. . . . Leaders of the electric industry do not hesitate to forecast interconnection in the near future over all the United States." See Pinchot's introduction in *Annals of the American Academy of Political and Social Science* 118 (March 1925): ix–x.

24. *New York Times,* August 20, 24, and 30, and September 3 and 17, 1918; George Otis Smith (Director, U.S. Geological Survey) to Truman C. Bigham, March 11, 1927, RG 57, Office of the Director: General Classified Files, Box 316, file "613." Some conservationists favored Oregon senator Harry Lane's proposal that the federal government construct a unified, coordinated national hydroelectric system. Once completed, the power plants would be sold to the states, which would have fifty years to repay the cost at 2 percent interest. This, the senator thought, would prevent the award of franchises to a few people "with a provision that at the expiration of 50 years their grandchildren may perhaps be granted the right to recover . . . , if they can . . . that which already belongs to them!" See Lane's

comments in the *Congressional Record*, 64th Cong., 1st sess., Senate, March 8, 1916: 3740–41.

25. Thomas J. Walsh to Seattle Commercial Club, November 22, 1915, Box 217, "Water Power" file, Department of the Interior, "Memorandum for the Press," December 21, 1916 and Henry J. Pierce, "The Vital Necessity for Water Power Development," May, 1917, Box 329, "Legislation: Water Power" file, Thomas J. Walsh Collection; George Otis Smith (Director, U.S. Geological Survey) to Nathan A. Cole, April 29, 1919, RG 57, Office of the Director: General Classified Files, Box 316, file "613."

26. Franklin K. Lane to Woodrow Wilson, January 8, 1917, in Arthur Link, ed., *The Papers of Woodrow Wilson,* vol. 40 (Princeton: Princeton University Press, 1982), 424; *New York Times,* March 3 and April 9, 1918, and February 27, 1919; Conover, *The Federal Power Commission,* 60–62.

27. On the 1920 act, see Hays, *Conservation and the Gospel of Efficiency,* 81, 239–40; O. C. Merrill, Memorandum Concerning Federal Power Commission, September 10, 1920, Box 519, Gifford Pinchot Collection; Merrill, "Benefits Accruing to Municipalities through the Federal Water Power Act," *American City* 23 (November 1920): 476–78; William E. Borah to W. W. Deal, May 11, 1920, and Borah to Cornelius F. Bruns, May 26, 1920, Box 550, "Water Power Bill, 1919–1920," William E. Borah Collection; Gifford Pinchot to Thomas J. Walsh, January 5, 1920, Box 330, "Leg. Water Power" file, Thomas J. Walsh Collection.

28. Federal Water Power Act of 1920, *U.S. Statutes at Large* 41 (1919–21): 1063–77; section 27 is on p. 1077. Also see "Federal Water-Power Bill Passes Both Houses," *Engineering News-Record* 84 (June 3, 1920): 1127–28.

29. *New York Times,* January 17 (quote), and May 29, 1920; O. C. Merrill, "Memorandum Concerning Federal Power Commission, September 10, 1920," Box 519, and Federal Power Commission, "Memorandum for the Press: First Report of the Federal Power Commission," December 10, 1921, in Box 761, Gifford Pinchot Collection; A. H. Horton, "Water-Power Resources of the United States," May 21, 1920, RG 57, Power Resources Division, Box 273, "Production of Electric Energy, 1–63, 1919–1924."

30. Federal Power Commission, "Memorandum for the Press, July 8, 1921," "Memorandum for the Press: First Report of the Federal Power Commission," December 10, 1921, and O. C. Merrill, "The Administration of the Federal Water Power Act," address delivered at Princeton University, April 16, 1929, Box 761, Gifford Pinchot Collection; *U.S. Daily,* April 18, 1929.

31. Swain, *Federal Conservation Policy,* 113; Conover, *The Federal Power Commission,* 63–66, 75.

32. O. C. Merrill, "Memorandum on Organization and Work of Federal Power Commission up to Close of Business on March 3, 1921," RG 16, Drawer 72, Incoming Correspondence, 1921, "Water Power"; Federal Power Commission, "Memorandum for the Press, July 8, 1921, Box 761, Gifford Pinchot Collection; Ruth Finney, "The Power Fight Goes On," *The Nation* 131 (December 24, 1930): 697.

33. *Engineering News-Record* 89 (August 3, 1922): 171; Ibid. 89 (October 5, 1922): 581; Ibid. 89 (November 30, 1922): 950; Ibid. 89 (December 7, 1922): 985; Ibid. 91 (November 22, 1923): 862; Ibid. 92 (April 10, 1924): 618; Ibid. 99 (November 24, 1927): 822, 851, 854; and Ibid. 105 (November 6, 1930): 715.

34. O. C. Merrill, Memorandum for the Federal Power Commission, April 7, 1921, RG 16, Drawer 72, Incoming Correspondence, 1921, "Water Power."
35. O. C. Merrill, "The Administration of the Federal Water Power Act," address delivered at Princeton University, April 16, 1929; William Leuchtenburg, *Flood Control Politics: The Connecticut River Valley Problem, 1927–1950* (Cambridge: Harvard University Press, 1953), 6.
36. William Kent to W. C. Boyden, October 28, 1924, Box 41, 1924 (quote) and press release by Philip P. Wells, November 1, 1922, Box 77, "Conservation—Water Power," William Kent Collection; O. C. Merrill, "Memo for the Secretary of Agriculture, January 12, 1924, RG 16, Drawer 516, Incoming Correspondence, 1924, "Water Power"; *Engineering News-Record* 104 (April 10, 1930): 629; Ibid. 104 (June 26, 1930): 1069; Ibid. 105 (December 25, 1930): 993–94; Frank Smith, *The Politics of Conservation* (New York: Pantheon Books, 1966), 171.
37. Binger Hermann (by Morris Bien) to Secretary of the Interior, February 8, 1902, RG 49, Division A, "Press Copies of Letters Sent Relating to Congressional Bills, v. 20, December 20, 1901–Apr. 2, 1902"; H. A. Storrs, "Electrical Transmission of Power for Pumping," *Official Proceedings of the Eleventh National Irrigation Congress Held at Ogden, Utah, September 15–18, 1903* (Ogden: The Proceedings Publishing Co., 1904), 397; George Wharton James, *Reclaiming the Arid West: The Story of the United States Reclamation Service* (New York: Dodd, Mead and Co., 1917), 84. The Secretary of the Interior first acknowledged that proceeds from water power could be used to subsidize other uses of water in the *Report of the Secretary of the Interior, 1911* (Washington, D.C.: GPO, 1912), 15. Also see the *Congressional Record*, 62d Cong., 2d sess., House, August 22, 1912: 11568 and 11571, and 62d Cong., 3d sess., Senate, February 13, 1913: 3057, and *Power of Federal Government over Development and Use of Water Power*, S. Doc. 246, 64th Cong., 1st sess., serial 6951 (Washington, D.C.: GPO, 1916), 17.
38. *U.S. Statutes at Large* 34 (1906): 116; Elwood Mead to Hubert Work, December 17, 1925, RG 115, General Files: 1919–1945, Box 106, "(140.1): General Corres. re Legislation Governing Power Development"; W. B. Hoyt, "Memorandum Concerning Water Policies of the Department of the Interior with Special Emphasis on Priorities of Use," dated September 1944, RG 115, General Correspondence File, 1930–1945, Box 681.
39. J. C. Stevens, "Stream Regulation with Reference to Irrigation and Power," *Transactions of the American Society of Civil Engineers* 90 (1927): 958–93.
40. F. H. Newell, "Electrical Features of the U.S. Reclamation Service," *Proceedings of the American Institute of Electrical Engineers* 33 (October 1914): 1583–98; F. H. Newell to Chief Electrical Engineer, March 17, 1913, and "Memorandum for Mr. Seideman," August 5, 1914, RG 115, General File, 1902–1919, Box 116, "(190-D): Repayments—Sale of Power"; E. C. Finney, "Hydroelectric Power Development on Public Lands in Relation to Irrigation," *Reclamation Record* 5 (October 1914): 364–66.
41. *Forestry and Irrigation* 12 (December 1906): 573; *Tucson Daily Star*, April 18, 1903.
42. The Territorial Insane Asylum, the Indian School, the Phoenix Street Railway, and the Consolidated Copper Company escaped the PG&E monopoly by stringing their own transmission lines to the point of generation. Most residents of Phoenix, of course, did not have that option.

43. Louis C. Hill to F. H. Newell, May 22, 1907, RG 115, General File, 1902–1919, Box 116, "(190-D): Repayments—Sale of Power"; E. C. Finney to Acting Secretary of the Interior, October 12, 1909, and Walter L. Fisher (Secretary of the Interior) to the Attorney General, December 20, 1912, RG 48, Central Files, 1907–1936, Box 1644, "Reclamation Service, Salt River Project, Arizona, Contracts, Pacific Gas and Electric Company."

44. Charles E. Arnold to H. H. Schwartz, January 13, 1910, Walter L. Fisher to the Attorney General, December 20, 1912, F. H. Newell to Walter Fisher, April 9, 1913, and "Memorandum for the Secretary," April 12, 1913, in RG 48, Central Files, 1907–1936, Box 1644, "Reclamation Service, Salt River Project, Arizona, Contracts, Pacific Gas and Electric Company"; Joseph H. Kibbey to L. C. Hill, March 31, 1913, and Kibbey to F. H. Newell, April 23, 1913, RG 115, General File, 1902–1919, Box 101, "(131): Corres. re Administration, Policies and Organization, 1914–1916."

45. *Reclamation Record* 5 (May 1914): 175–76; James, *Reclaiming the Arid West,* 65–85; L. N. McClellen, "Power Development on Government Projects," (March 1929), RG 115, Central Administrative Records, 1919–1929, Box 280, "(320): General Corres. re Power Development thru 1929."

46. *Rupert Record* (Rupert, Idaho), April 19, 1906, and March 12, 1908.

47. O. H. Ensign, "Electric Power for Irrigation," *Engineering News* 66 (July 6, 1911): 4–9; F. H. Newell, "Notes on Irrigation Managers' Conference During 1912," pp. 31–32, in Box 10, "Irrigation and Reclamation of Arid Lands, John D. Works Collection, Bancroft Library, University of California, Berkeley; L. N. McClellen, "Power Development on Government Projects," March 1929, and Elwood Mead to George W. Norris, December 27, 1929, RG 115, Central Administrative Records, 1919–1929, Box 280, "(320): General Corres. re Power Development thru 1929."

48. The Minidoka Project was the second-largest power producer among federal reclamation projects, but in 1915, its electrical sales returned only 10 percent of those on the Salt River Project. See the power charts for individual reclamation projects in RG 115, General File, 1902–1919, Box 116, "(190-D): Repayments—Sale of Power." Occasionally, the Reclamation Bureau carried power directly to businesses—including a sugar beet factory near Burley, Idaho—if the user was willing to pay for the transmission lines. See F. H. Newell to First Assistant Secretary Adams, April 12, 1912, and Acting Director and Chief Counsel to the Secretary of the Interior, September 7, 1917, RG 48, Central Files, 1907–1936, Box 1617, "Minidoka: Lease of Power, Burley, Idaho." Also see R. F. Walter to the Commissioner, September 26, 1927, RG 115, Central Administrative Files, 1919–1929, Box 280, "(320): General Corres. re Power Development thru 1929."

49. Department of the Interior, "Memorandum for the Press," May 26, 1926, RG 115, Central Administrative Files, 1919–1929, Box 280, "(320): General Corres. re Power Development thru 1929." Also see "Minidoka Project Homes Enjoy Electrical Aids," *New Reclamation Era* 17 (July 1926): 119.

50. *Reclamation Record* 4 (July 1913): 137–38; "Commercial Power on the Minidoka Project, 1924," *New Reclamation Era* 16 (April 1925): 57; R. S. Moy, "Rural Homes on the Minidoka Project," *New Reclamation Era* 17 (April 1926): 65; "Possible Power Production in the Western States," undated memo in RG 115, Gen-

eral File, 1902–1919, Box 116, "(190-D): Repayments—Sale of Power"; James, *Reclaiming the Arid West,* 153–57; F. H. Newell and Daniel W. Murphy, *Principles of Irrigation Engineering* (New York: McGraw-Hill Book Co., 1913), 128; Newell, *Water Resources,* 261; William Darrell Gertsch, "The Upper Snake River Project, 1890–1930: A Historical Study of Reclamation and Regional Development" (Ph.D. diss., University of Washington, 1974), 134–35.

51. As early as 1916, A. P. Davis recognized that some of the larger dams under consideration by the Bureau of Reclamation on the Sacramento, Columbia, and Snake Rivers would have the potential to generate enormous amounts of electricity, but most were far removed from major centers of population. See Davis, "Power Possibilities of Federal Irrigation Projects," *Engineering News* 75 (May 11, 1916): 875.

52. *Reclamation Record* 14 (January 1923): 4; E. C. Finney to M. P. Kinkaid, July 15, 1922 and Albert B. Fall to Calvin Coolidge, September 18, 1922, in RG 115, General File: 1919–1945, Box 106, "(140.1): General Corres. re Legislation Governing Power Development." Courtland L. Smith, in *The Salt River Project: A Case Study in Cultural Adaptation to an Urbanizing Community* (Tucson: University of Arizona Press, 1972), 48, notes that as of 1968, landowners and water users paid only 9 percent of the total annual budget of the Salt River Project Water Users Association; revenue from power sales took care of the rest.

53. For examples of the Reclamation Bureau's faith in the ability of electricity to transform farm life, see *Reclamation Record* 14 (October 1923): 293; Ibid., 15 (January 1924): 4; and Ibid. 19 (November 1928): 167–68.

54. F. W. Dent to R. F. Walter, September 9, 1927, RG 115, Central Administrative Files, 1919–1929, Box 280, "(320): General Corres. re Power Development thru 1929." Also see Hubert Work to Calvin Coolidge, December 11, 1924, Box 308, "Leg.—Reclamation" file, Thomas J. Walsh Collection.

55. *Annual Report of the Secretary of the Interior for the Fiscal Year Ended June 30, 1932* (Washington, D.C.: GPO, 1932), 99–100; Carroll H. Wooddy, *The Growth of the Federal Government, 1915–1932* (New York: McGraw-Hill Book Co., 1934), 539; Department of the Interior, "Memorandum for the Press," May 26, 1926, RG 115, Central Administrative Files, 1919–1929, Box 280, "(320): General Corres. re Power Development thru 1929"; *U.S. Daily,* June 11, 1928. Knowing that revenue from power sales could be greatly increased, Commissioner of Reclamation Elwood Mead wanted to build new power plants on the projects *purely* to generate revenue. "The question arises," he observed in 1929, "should not the power revenue be kept entirely apart from the irrigation revenue, and after the works are paid for the power revenues be used to assist in the construction of new works?" Despite the Boulder Dam legislation, which clearly anticipated that proceeds from the sale of hydroelectric power would subsidize irrigation in Southern California, Congress refused to accept his recommendation as a general principle that would apply to future reclamation power projects. See Elwood Mead, "Memorandum on Reclamation," November 23, 1929, RG 115, Central Administrative Records, 1919–1929, Box 66, "(101): Matters of Policy, 1926–1929."

56. Samuel Insull pioneered the use of holding companies in 1912. By the 1920s, his Chicago-based utility empire was the biggest in the nation, and Insull became one of the nation's best-known businessmen—as notable in the twenties as J. P.

Morgan had been at the beginning of the century. By 1925, Insull was delivering electricity to customers in thirty-nine states, but in the early months of 1932 his pyramid of 95 holding companies and 255 operating companies began to crumble, and he fled to France. Extradited to Chicago in 1934, he was tried three times on a variety of charges, including fraud and embezzlement. Each time he was acquitted. See Forrest McDonald, *Insull* (Chicago: University of Chicago Press, 1962).

57. For a small sampling of the vast literature on the Tennessee Valley Authority, see David E. Lilienthal, *TVA: Democracy on the March* (New York: Harper, 1953); Arthur E. Morgan, *The Making of TVA* (Buffalo, N.Y.: Prometheus Books, 1974); Thomas K. McCraw, *Morgan vs. Lilienthal: The Feud within the TVA* (Chicago: Loyola University Press, 1970); Steven M. Neuse, *David E. Lilienthal: The Journey of An American Liberal* (Knoxville: University of Tennessee Press, 1996); Roy Talbert, *FDR's Utopian: Arthur Morgan of the TVA* (Jackson: University Press of Mississippi, 1987); Walter L. Creese, *TVA's Public Planning: The Vision, the Reality* (Knoxville: University of Tennessee Press, 1990); and Marguerite Owen, *The Tennessee Valley Authority* (New York: Praeger, 1973). For brief introductions to the river basin authority in the West, see Donald J. Pisani, "Federal Water Policy and the Rural West," in *The Rural West since World War II*, ed. R. Douglas Hurt (Lawrence: University Press of Kansas, 1998), 120–27, and Pisani, "Beyond the Hundredth Meridian: Nationalizing the History of Water in the United States," *Environmental History* 5 (October 2000): 472–74.

58. Paul K. Conkin, "Intellectual and Political Roots," in *TVA: Fifty Years of Grass-Roots Bureaucracy*, ed. Erwin C. Hargrove and Paul K. Conkin (Urbana: University of Illinois Press, 1983), 4, 12–13; W. B. West, "America's Greatest Dam," *Scientific American* 121 (May 7, 1921): 364–65; Harry Burgess, "The Muscle Shoals Section of the Tennessee River," U.S. Army Corps of Engineers, *Professional Memoirs* 8 (January–February 1916): 61–62.

59. Conkin, "Intellectual and Political Roots," 5, 79; Burgess, "The Muscle Shoals Section of the Tennessee River," 66, 70; W. C. Weeks and S. C. Godfrey, "Notes on the Construction of the Wilson Dam," *Military Engineer* 13 (March–April 1921): 112.

60. *Sioux City Journal*, July 2, 1917; *Portland Oregonian*, July 9, 1917.

61. *Engineering News-Record* 80 (March 7, 1918): 478; King, *The Conservation Fight*, 62–63, 71, 79.

62. W. B. West, "America's Greatest Dam," *Scientific American* 124 (May 7, 1921): 364–65.

63. Conkin, "Intellectual and Political Roots," 5–6.

64. In 1922, the *Engineering News-Record* reported that nation's entire demand for ammonium nitrate was only 20 percent of the capacity of the Muscle Shoals plants. Using the cyanamide process, the American Cyanamid Company could extract nitrogen from the atmosphere at its Niagara Falls plant much more cheaply than could be done at Muscle Shoals. See *Engineering News-Record* 88 (April 20, 1922): 669.

65. *Engineering News-Record* 84 (January 8, 1920): 106; *Military Engineer* 15 (July–August 1923): 339.

66. *Engineering News-Record* 88 (March 2, 1922): 345; King, *The Conservation Fight*, 98–122.

67. See Ford's statement in *Engineering News-Record* 91 (October 18, 1923): 652.

68. McCraw, *TVA and the Power Fight,* 18–25; Conkin, "Intellectual and Political Roots," 15; King, *The Conservation Fight,* 98–122.

69. King, *The Conservation Fight,* 143–44, 177–78, 245.

70. *Engineering News-Record* 88 (June 8, 1922): 973.

71. *Congressional Record,* 67th Cong., 2d sess., Senate, March 10, 1922: 3659–60 and May 11, 1922, 6709. On Muscle Shoals, see Preston J. Hubbard, *Origins of TVA: The Muscle Shoals Controversy, 1920–1932* (Nashville: Vanderbilt University Press, 1961); Richard Lowitt, *George W. Norris: The Persistence of a Progressive, 1913–1933* (Urbana: University of Illinois Press, 1971), 197–216, 244–71; and Frank Smith, *The Politics of Conservation* (New York: Pantheon Books, 1966), 101–2, 178–203.

72. Lowitt, *George W. Norris,* 197–216, 244–71; Hubbard, *Origins of the TVA,* 217–89; Richard Colignon, *Power Plays: Critical Events in the Institutionalization of the Tennessee Valley Authority* (Albany: State University of New York Press, 1997), 49–50, 78.

73. *Engineering News-Record* 100 (June 14, 1928): 919; Ibid. 101 (December 6, 1928): 857.

74. *Engineering News-Record* 110 (April 20, 1933): 508; Ibid. 110 (May 11, 1933): 579–83, 600–601; Ibid. 110 (May 25, 1933): 696–97.

75. Hubbard, *Origins of the TVA,* 124, 193, 217, 223–24, 270; Judson King, "The Next Phase of the Power Fight," *New Republic* 65 (December 10, 1930): 91–93.

76. George Woodruff to Herbert Hoover, February 15, 1930, RG 48, Office of the Secretary: Central Classified File, 1907–1936, Box 1579, "Reclamation Bureau, Colorado River Administrative, January 2–July 9, 1930"; Thomas Walsh to Hiram Johnson, January 20, 1930, and Ray Lyman Wilbur to Hiram Johnson, February 3, 1930 (and attached memo of E. C. Finney dated January 6, 1930), in Hiram Johnson Collection, Bancroft Library, University of California, Berkeley; *New York Times,* January 29, 1930. Also see the editorial "The People's Power," *The Nation* 130 (April 2, 1930): 385–86.

77. O. C. Merrill (Executive Secretary, Federal Power Commission) to the President, June 29, 1922, Box 47 (10), "Colorado River Project, 21 September 1921–9 February 1923," Albert B. Fall Collection, Huntington Library, San Marino, California; John B. Miller (President, Southern California Edison Company), statement dated December 7, 1921, RG 48, Office of the Secretary: Central Classified File, 1907–1936, Box 1583, "Reclamation Service, Colorado River Storage, General, October 13, 1914–February 28, 1922"; O. C. Merrill, "Power Development on the Colorado River," speech delivered on April 11, 1922, and Merrill to the Secretary of Agriculture, November 23, 1923, in RG 16, Drawer 388, Incoming Correspondence, 1923, "Water Power: Boulder Canyon" and "Memorandum for Federal Power Commission," dated October 19, 1925, in Drawer 105, Incoming Correspondence, 1925, "Water Power: Boulder Canyon"; William Mullendore, "Projected Construction of a Dam and Other Works in the Colorado River," William Mullendore Collection, Box 9, "Colorado River Commission / Hoover Dam, Boulder Dam: Comments On," Herbert Hoover Presidential Library, West Branch, Iowa.

78. For the full story of these famous negotiations, see Norris Hundley, jr., *Water and the West: The Colorado River Compact and the Politics of Water in the American West*

(Berkeley: University of California Press, 1975). Also see Key Pittman to Federal Water Power Commission, October 13, 1925, in Colorado River Commission Records, Box 8, "Senator Key Pittman, 1925," Herbert Hoover Collection; L. Ward Bannister to Herbert Hoover, October 8, 1927, Colorado River Commission Records, Box 29, "Bannister, L. Ward 1927–28," Hoover Library; A. P. Davis to Albert Fall, March 18, 1922, Fall to Davis July 7 and 17, 1922, and Fall to Warren G. Harding, September 24, 1921, April 5 and July 7, 1922, in Box 47 (10), "Colorado River Project, 21 September 1921–9 February 1923," Albert B. Fall Collection; John W. Kemp (President, Public Power League of California) to A. B. Fall, March 23, 1922, RG 48, Office of the Secretary: Central Classified Files, 1907–1936, Box 1584, "Reclamation Service, Colorado River Storage, General, March 4, 1922-May 26, 1924."

79. The quote from Hoover's 1928 speech is as reprinted in King, *The Conservation Fight,* 182–83. The quotes from his 1931 veto message are as reprinted in Edwin Vennard, *Government in the Power Business* (New York: McGraw-Hill Book Co., 1968), 92.

80. Richard Coke Lower, *A Bloc of One: The Political Career of Hiram W. Johnson* (Stanford: Stanford University Press, 1993), 233; Hiram Johnson to C. C. Young, February 2, 1927, Hiram Johnson Collection; William Starr Myers, ed., *The State Papers and Other Public Writings of Herbert Hoover,* vol. 2 (New York: Doubleday, Doran and Co., 1934), 481; "Abstract of Secretary Hoover's Statement on the Colorado River before the House Committee on Irrigation and Reclamation, March 3, 1926," in Colorado River Commission Records, Box 8, "Publicity, General, 1920–26," Hoover Library. Also see William C. Mullendore, "Memorandum for Mr. Ballard," February 27, 1926, William Mullendore Collection, Box 12.

81. Key Pittman to George Malone, June 6, 1929, RG 48, Office of the Secretary: Central Classified Files, 1907–1936, Box 1588-A, "Boulder Canyon Project, General Regulations; Leases and Contracts for Hoover Dam Power" (quote); Hiram Johnson to Hubert Work, January 21, 1928, and "Boulder Dam Project—Questions and Answers," Department of the Interior press release dated October 1, 1930, in Johnson Collection, Part 6, Carton 1, "Boulder Dam Project" file. George W. Malone, "Boulder Dam Legislation," memo dated December 14, 1928, in "Boulder Dam" folder, Tasker L. Oddie Correspondence, 1928, Tasker Oddie Collection, Nevada Historical Society, Reno.

82. Paul L. Kleinsorge, *The Boulder Canyon Project: Historical and Economic Aspects* (Stanford: Stanford University Press, 1941), 274–75, 294–97; Robert Gottlieb and Margaret FitzSimmons, *Thirst for Growth: Water Agencies as Hidden Government in California* (Tucson: University of Arizona Press, 1991), 8; E. F. Scattergood (Chief Electrical Engineer, Los Angeles Bureau of Power and Light) to Herbert Hoover, July 28, 1922, and Scattergood to Clarence Stetson (Executive Secretary, Colorado River Commission), September 28, 1922 (quote), in Box 19, Colorado River Commission Records; "Los Angeles Bureau of Power and Light," and Charles C. Stetson to Thomas C. Yager, August 8, 1922, Box 11, "Boulder Canyon, 1921–22," Hoover Collection. Also see Albert B. Fall to Warren G. Harding, September 24, 1921, Box 47 (10), "Colorado River Project, 21 Sept. 1921–9 Feb. 1923," Albert B. Fall Collection.

83. For an excellent discussion of water and annexation, see Norris Hundley, jr., *The*

Great Thirst: Californians and Water: A History, rev. ed. (Berkeley: University of California Press, 2001), 123–71, 215–20, 223–34. Also see Kazuto Oshio, "Urban Water Diplomacy: A Policy History of the Metropolitan Water Supply in Twentieth Century Southern California" (Ph.D. diss., University of California, Santa Barbara, 1992); *History and First Annual Report [of the Metropolitan Water District of Southern California] for the Period Ending June 30, 1938* (Los Angeles: Haynes Corporation, 1939), 26–51; and Vincent Ostrom *Water and Politics: A Study of Water Policies and Administration in the Development of Los Angeles* (Los Angeles: Haynes Foundation, 1953), 145–47, 168–97.

84. "Memorandum for the Secretary [of the Interior]," October 12, 1929, RG 48, Office of the Secretary, Central Classified Files, 1907–1936, Box 1588-A, "Boulder Canyon Project, General Regulations: Leases and Contracts for Hoover Dam Power"; *San Bernardino Sun,* December 15, 1929; Beverley Bowen Moeller, *Phil Swing and Boulder Dam* (Berkeley: University of California Press, 1971), 31.

85. *Annual Report of the Secretary of the Interior for the Fiscal Year Ended June 30, 1932,* 14–15; *Twenty-Ninth Annual Report of the Commissioner of Reclamation, 1929–1930* (Washington, D.C.: GPO, 1930), 3; *Los Angeles Examiner,* October 22, 1929.

86. Van Hise, *Conservation of Natural Resources,* 131–32; Conover, *The Federal Power Commission,* 2. Hunter and Bryant, *History of Industrial Power,* vol. 3, 355–57; H. W. Buck, "The Status of Water Power Development," *Scientific American Supplement* 82 (September 9, 1916): 166–67.

87. O. C. Merrill, "The Administration of the Federal Water Power Act," address delivered at Princeton University, April 16, 1929; Ellis L. Armstrong, ed., *History of Public Works in the United States, 1776–1976* (Chicago: American Public Works Association, 1976), 386.

88. *Annual Report of the Secretary of the Interior, Fiscal Year Ended June 30, 1946* (Washington, D.C.: GPO, 1946), 15; Hunter and Bryant, *History of Industrial Power,* vol. 3, 353, 360, 364; Thomas H. Gammack, "Hydroelectric Myths," *World's Work* 58 (May 1929): 120; William H. Easton, "When the Water Power Works for Us," *Independent* 86 (April 10, 1916): 57–58; Calvert Townley, "Hydro-Electric Development," *Scientific American Supplement* 85 (April 27, 1918): 262–63; A. H. Horton, "Total Developed Power in Horsepower in the United States," January 16, 1920, and Memorandum dated January 12, 1927, in RG 57, Power Resources Division, Box 273, "Production of Electric Energy, 1–63, 1919–1924," and Department of the Interior, "Memorandum for the Press," September 19, 1927, Power Resources Division, in "C" (Coal) file, no. D-272, "Correspondence, Reports & Records File, 1920–1946: Fuels, B-W."

89. McCraw, *TVA and the Power Fight,* 2; Harding, *Water in California,* 129, 132. The quotation from Roosevelt's September 1932 speech is as reprinted in Armstrong, *History of Public Works,* 349.

90. Brigham, *Empowering the West,* 26.

91. Ostrom, *Water and Politics,* 181, 207–8, 217.

92. William C. Mullendore to R. H. Ballard (General Manager, Southern California Edison Co.), February 2, 1926, in Box 12, "Colorado River Commission / Hoover Dam Southern California Edison Co. Correspondence & Memoranda 1926 January–March" file, William Mullendore Collection. In the early 1920s, Mullendore was an aide to Herbert Hoover in the Commerce Department. When

he left Washington in the middle of the decade, he became Southern California Edison's chief lobbyist in Washington and played an active role in opposing the construction of Boulder Dam. The position of private power companies toward Boulder Dam and other government dams can be traced in his remarkably revealing papers at the Hoover Library.

CHAPTER 9. GATEWAY TO THE HYDRAULIC AGE

1. Stephen Skowronek, *Building a New American State: The Expansion of National Administrative Capacities, 1877-1920* (New York: Cambridge University Press, 1982), 20; Leonard D. White, *Trends in Public Administration* (New York: McGraw-Hill Book Co., 1933), 330.
2. Herbert D. Brown (Chief, U.S. Bureau of Efficiency), "Economy through Consolidation and Readjustments of Administrative Departments," December 6, 1932, in RG 51, 1.02, Box 20, "Departmental Reorganization, 1931-Dec. 15, 1932."
3. The Budget and Accounting Act of 1921 transferred the responsibility for preparing the federal budget from committees of Congress to the president. It created a budget bureau within the Treasury Department, under a director appointed by the president, and a General Accounting Office to conduct independent audits of governmental expenses.
4. *Reorganization of the Executive Departments,* H. Rept. 937, 68th Cong., 1st sess., serial 8229 (Washington, D.C.: GPO, 1924), 25-28.
5. In England, interdepartmental committees promoted communication and cooperation among different agencies and departments, but that arrangement did not work in the United States. "Ministers expect the members of Her Majesty's civil service to come up with sensible and agreed solutions, even if an agency must yield a point," the political scientist Herbert Emmerich has remarked. "In the American scene it is considered a species of disloyalty if a departmental representative makes important concessions to a rival agency. Loyalties in the United States government accrue to the highly specialized program components, not to the government as a whole." In the United States, specialization contributed to inefficiency as well as efficiency. As agencies became professionalized in the early years of the twentieth century, they became more resistant to control by those outside the profession or professions they represented. Below the rank of bureau chief, moreover, the new civil service system made career bureaucrats less accountable than they had been under the old patronage system. See Herbert Emmerich, *Federal Organization and Administrative Management* (University: University of Alabama Press, 1971), 18-19.
6. David F. Houston, *Eight Years with Wilson's Cabinet, 1913-1920,* vol. 1 (Garden City, N.Y.: Doubleday, Page and Co., 1926), 125-26 (quote); David F. Houston to Woodrow Wilson, November 30, 1917, in Arthur S. Link, ed., *The Papers of Woodrow Wilson,* vol. 45 (Princeton: Princeton University Press, 1984), 168-69.
7. Robert W. Harrison, *Alluvial Empire: A Study of State and Local Efforts toward Land Development in the Alluvial Valley of the Lower Mississippi River* (Little Rock, Ark.: Pioneer Press, 1961), 217.
8. A. Hunter Dupree, *Science in the Federal Government: A History of Policies and Activities to 1940* (Cambridge: Harvard University Press, 1957), 184-214.

9. Gordon B. Dodds, *Hiram Martin Chittenden: His Public Career* (Lexington: University Press of Kentucky, 1973), 160–61.
10. On average, each West Point class contributed ten or fifteen officers to the Corps of Engineers. The number increased during World War I, but not fast enough to meet wartime needs. See *Engineering News* 76 (September 14, 1916): 530.
11. Martin Reuss, "Andrew A. Humphreys and the Development of Hydraulic Engineering: Politics and Technology in the Army Corps of Engineers," in *The Engineer in America*, ed. Terry S. Reynolds (Chicago: University of Chicago Press, 1991), 112–13.
12. H.R. 7855 (Breckinridge), 48th Cong., 2d sess., introduced January 5, 1885, *Congressional Record*, p. 448.
13. H.R. 9628 (King), 49th Cong., 1st sess., introduced June 21, 1886, *Congressional Record*, p. 5974. Also see W. F. Smith, "A New Executive Department," *Forum* 3 (May 1887): 296–304.
14. Smith, "A New Executive Department," 304.
15. New York Board of Trade and Transportation, *Should a National Department of Public Works Be Created?* pamphlet dated January 8, 1908, in Theodore Burton Papers, Series 2, Container 35, Folder 5, Theodore Burton Papers, Case Western Reserve University, Cleveland; *Waterway Journal* 21 (April 14, 1908): 9; Samuel P. Hays, *Conservation and the Gospel of Efficiency: The Progressive Conservation Movement, 1890–1920* (Cambridge: Harvard University Press, 1959), 94–95.
16. *Engineering News* 63 (May 12, 1910): 563.
17. George H. Maxwell, *Our National Defense: The Patriotism of Peace* (Cambridge, Mass.: The University Press, 1915), 49, 304, 305, 306. Maxwell discusses the Corps of Engineers on pp. 301–16.
18. "Engineers Urge Policies for Public Works," *Engineering News-Record* 81 (December 19, 1918): 1145–46; "A Federal Department of Public Works," *Engineering News-Record* 82 (February 20, 1919): 359.
19. *Bulletin of the Associated General Contractors of America* 11 (January 1920): 43–44; *Constructor* 10 (January 1923): 73.
20. *Engineering News-Record* 82 (May 1, 1919): 855–60.
21. *New York Times*, March 14 and 22, and November 27, 1920; *Engineering News-Record* 83 (July 3, 1919): 41–42; Ibid. 84 (February 19, 1920): 394–95; Ibid. 85 (October 28, 1920): 834–35; Ibid. 85 (December 2, 1920): 1107–8.
22. National Public Works Department Association, *A Department of Public Works* (n.p., n.d.), pamphlet in folder "Debate over Creation of Public Works Agency, 1920–1928," in box titled "Civil Works Reorganization, 1870–1929, III-1," U.S. Army Corps of Engineers, Office of History, Fort Belvoir, Maryland; Isham Randolph, "National Public Works Department versus Corps of Engineers," *Engineering News-Record* 83 (September 18, 1919): 561–62; *Hearings on Reorganization of Executive Departments Jan. 7–31, 1924* (Washington, D.C.: GPO, 1924), 72–73.
23. This became a standard argument used by the corps during the 1920s. For example, see the testimony of Secretary of War John W. Weeks in *Hearings on Reorganization of the Executive Departments, Jan. 7–31, 1924*, parts 1–3, 68th Cong., 1st sess. (Washington, D.C.: GPO, 1924), 116–17, and *Engineering News-Record* 92 (January 17, 1924): 128.
24. John J. Lenney, *Caste System in the American Army: A Study of the Corps of Engineers*

and Their West Point System (New York: Greenberg, 1949), 58–75; *Washington Post,*
July 25, 1920; *Engineering News-Record* 84 (January 22, 1920): 162–63; *Engineering News-Record* 85 (December 30, 1920): 1273–76.

25. Neither Harding nor his secretary of the interior, Hubert Work, favored establishing a Department of Public Works. They wanted to divide Interior into two major branches, one devoted to public works and the other to the public domain, each under an assistant secretary. See *Hearings on Reorganization of Executive Departments,* appendix B.

26. *Report of the Joint Committee on Reorganization Created under the Joint Resolution Adopted December 17, 1920* (Washington, D.C.: GPO, 1924), 20–21; *Engineering News-Record* 92 (June 12, 1924): 1034.

27. On the Interior Department scandals, see Burl Noggle, *Teapot Dome: Oil and Politics in the 1920s* (Baton Rouge: Louisiana State University Press, 1962).

28. Carroll H. Wooddy, *The Growth of the Federal Government, 1915–1932* (New York: McGraw-Hill Book Co., 1934), 503, 504 (quote), 510, 540; *Reorganization of the Executive Departments: Report of the Joint Committee on Reorganization,* H. Doc. 356, 68th Cong., 1st sess., serial 8274 (Washington, D.C.: GPO, 1924); W. F. Willoughby, *The Reorganization of the Administrative Branch of the National Government* (Baltimore: Johns Hopkins University Press, 1923), 205–24; *New York Times,* January 18, November 13, and December 2 and 11, 1924, and May 17, 1931.

29. *Engineering News-Record* 98 (January 20, 1927): 130, 154–55; Ibid. 99 (October 27, 1927): 687–90; Ibid. 100 (April 12, 1928): 605. The Great Depression revived the campaign for reorganization. Those who favored public works projects as an antidote to unemployment were just as interested in restructuring government as those who called for economy and retrenchment. In the fall of 1932, Hoover again proposed transferring the civilian work of the corps to a public works division in Interior. See *Congressional Record,* 72d Cong., 2d sess., House, January 19, 1933: 2113 and 4137–40.

30. Washington's remarks are as reprinted in John Seelye, *Beautiful Machine: Rivers and the Republican Plan, 1755–1825* (New York: Oxford University Press, 1991), 59–60. Hoover's comment is from his article "The Improvement of Our Mid-West Waterways," *Annals of the American Academy of Political and Social Science* 135 (January 1928): 24. For a view of the meaning of rivers to Americans in the eighteenth and nineteenth centuries, see Donald J. Pisani, "Beyond the Hundredth Meridian: Nationalizing the History of Water in the United States," *Environmental History* 5 (October 2000): 466–73.

31. Biographies of Hoover include Joan Hoff-Wilson, *Herbert Hoover, Forgotten Progressive* (Boston: Little-Brown, 1975); David Burner, *Herbert Hoover: A Public Life* (New York: Knopf, 1979); and George H. Nash, *The Life of Herbert Hoover* (New York: W. W. Norton, 1983).

32. On Herbert Hoover and conservation, see Kendrick A. Clements, *Hoover, Conservation, and Consumerism: Engineering the Good Life* (Lawrence: University Press of Kansas, 2000).

33. The Hoover quote is from Ray Lyman Wilbur, *The Hoover Policies* (New York: Charles Scribner's Sons, 1937), 261–62. Hoover discussed his plans for water development in *The Memoirs of Herbert Hoover,* vol. 2, *The Cabinet and the Presidency, 1920–1933* (New York: Macmillan, 1952), 112–31 and 226–36. Also see Wilbur,

The Hoover Policies, pp. 254–87; Wilbur F. Decker, "The Mississippi System of Waterways," *Review of Reviews* 74 (December 1926): 605–6; Norman F. Titus, "The Mississippi Waterway," *Annals of the American Academy of Political and Social Science* 142 (March 1929): 283–90; Franklin Snow, "Waterways as Highways," *North American Review* 227 (May 8, 1929): 592–98; "A River-Minded President on the Rampaging Ohio," *Literary Digest* 103 (November 9, 1929): 8–9; and Uthai Vincent Wilcox, "Progress of America's Inland Waterways," *Current History* 34 (April 1931): 68–72. For a guide to Hoover's speeches and articles on water, see Kathleen Tracey, ed., *Herbert Hoover—A Bibliography: His Writings and Addresses* (Stanford, Calif.: Hoover Institution Press, 1977).

34. "The Great Lakes and the Gulf of Mexico Meet," *Literary Digest* 116 (July 8, 1933): 9.

35. Hoover, "Our Mid-West Waterways," 15–24 (the quote is from p. 17).

36. *New York Times,* June 15, 1928.

37. "Waterway Policy Plea," *Traffic World* 38 (August 28, 1926): 482 (quote); "Hoover Favors Inland Waterway Development," *Engineering News-Record* 96 (March 11, 1926): 421, 424.

38. "Waterway Policy Plea," 483; Hoover, *Memoirs,* vol. 2, 114; *New York Times,* March 10, 1926, and August 28, 1927. For a map of Hoover's proposed waterway improvements, see his article "Why Inland Waterways Should Be Developed," *Review of Reviews* 74 (December 1926): 598.

39. Hoover, "Our Mid-West Waterways," 23.

40. *Los Angeles Times,* June 12, 1927; *New York Times,* July 21, 1927.

41. *New York Times,* October 24 and 27 (quote), and December 4, 1929.

42. "Wanted—A Waterways Plan," *Independent* 116 (April 3, 1926): 378; Clarence E. Cason, "Waterways for Farm Relief," *Independent* 120 (April 21, 1928): 374–76.

43. *New York Times,* December 8, 1926.

44. *New York Times,* May 18, 1930, January 4, 1931, April 16, 1932.

45. "The Great Lakes and the Gulf of Mexico Meet," *Literary Digest* 116 (July 8, 1933): 9; Charles H. Ambler, *A History of Transportation in the Ohio Valley* (Glendale, Calif.: Arthur Clark Co., 1932); R. E. Banta, *The Ohio* (New York: Rinehart and Co., 1949); and Leland R. Johnson, *The Ohio River Division: U.S. Army Corps of Engineers* (Cincinnati: U.S. Army Corps of Engineers, 1992). The volume of freight shipped on the Ohio tripled during the 1920s, as coal, steel, and other bulky commodities moved from Pittsburgh and Cincinnati west by water rather than east by rail. The Ohio project included an elaborate system of forty-nine movable dams and locks, the first authorized in 1879 and most of the rest in 1910. These dams created a series of slack-water pools but had no influence on flooding and produced no hydroelectric power. The project cost over $100 million—more than Boulder Dam.

46. Wilbur, *The Hoover Policies,* 269; Ray Lyman Wilbur, "The Water Cure," *World's Work* 60 (February 1931): 24–28.

47. Hoover, *Memoirs,* vol. 2, 117, 124, 227, 230–31, 234. Also see Norris Hundley, jr., *Water and the West: The Colorado River Compact and the Politics of Water in the American West* (Berkeley: University of California Press, 1975), 5–16. As an example of Hoover's refusal to share credit for major water projects, A. P. Davis, whom historian Norris Hundley, jr., identifies as the father of the Boulder Dam project, is entirely ignored in Hoover's story. "I had visited the site [of Boulder Dam] be-

fore the war," Hoover remembered, "and soon after I became Secretary of Commerce I designated it as one of the first of the great multiple-purpose water conservation works to be undertaken" (Hoover, *Memoirs,* vol. 2, 115).

48. William G. Hoyt and Walter B. Langbein, *Floods* (Princeton: Princeton University Press, 1955), 50–53.

49. Glenn R. Conrad and Carl A. Brasseaux, *Crevasse! The 1927 Flood in Acadiana* (Lafayette: University of Southwestern Louisiana, Center for Louisiana Studies, 1994), 10–11. For a history of Mississippi floods, see J. P. Kemper, *Rebellious River* (Boston: Bruce Humphries, Inc., 1949).

50. John M. Barry, *Rising Tide: The Great Mississippi Flood of 1927 and How It Changed America* (New York: Simon and Schuster, 1997), 15, 175, 179, 189.

51. Harrison, *Alluvial Empire,* 58–60.

52. Karen Marie O'Neill, "State Building and the Campaign for U.S. Flood Control, 1824–1936" (Ph.D. diss., University of California, Los Angeles, 1998), 124–25, 131, 136 (quote).

53. Pete Daniel, *deep'n as it come: The 1927 Mississippi River Flood* (New York: Oxford University Press, 1977), 9–10, 147, 154; Arthur D. Frank, *The Development of the Federal Program of Flood Control on the Mississippi River* (New York: Columbia University Press, 1930), 192, 199; Bruce Alan Lohof, "Hoover and the Mississippi Valley Flood of 1927: A Case Study of the Political Thought of Herbert Hoover" (Ph.D. diss., Syracuse University, 1968), 85–86, 121–22; *United States Daily,* July 2, 1927; *Los Angeles Times,* June 12, 1927; *New York Times,* July 8, 1927.

54. *Congressional Record,* 70th Cong., 1st sess., House, April 17, 1928: 6651.

55. William E. Leuchtenburg, *Flood Control Politics: The Connecticut River Problem, 1927–1950* (Cambridge: Harvard University Press, 1953), 28–29.

56. Calvin Coolidge, Message to Congress, December 6, 1927, *Congressional Record,* 70th Cong., 1st sess., Senate, December 6, 1927: 103–9. The quote is on p. 107.

57. *Congressional Record,* 70th Cong., 1st sess., House, April 17, 1928: 6668.

58. *Los Angeles Times,* June 12, 1927 (quote); Hoover, "Our Mid-West Waterways," 16. On November 7, 1927, the House Flood Control Committee began more than two months of hearings that included three hundred witnesses. Those testifying in favor of a federally funded flood control program included the United States Chamber of Commerce, American Federation of Labor, American Bankers' Association, and many engineering organizations. *Congressional Record,* 70th Cong., 1st sess., House, April 17, 1928: 6645. Also see "Paying for Flood Control," *Engineering News-Record* 99 (December 29, 1927): 1029.

59. "President Coolidge and the Mississippi Valley Overflow," *Manufacturers' Record* 91 (May 12, 1927): 54.

60. Frank, *The Federal Program of Flood Control,* 16–30.

61. John E. Ferrell, "From Single- to Multi-Purpose Planning: The Role of the Army Engineer in River Development Policy, 1824–1930," draft ms. dated February 1976, Office of the Chief of Engineers, Army Corps of Engineers, Washington, D.C.

62. The 1917 flood control bill is reprinted in *Congressional Record,* 70th Cong., 1st sess., House, April 17, 1928: 6663. Also see pp. 6644–45; Ferrell, "From Single- to Multi-Purpose Planning," 186–88; Frank, *The Federal Program of Flood Control,* 151–52; Lohof, "Hoover and the Mississippi Valley Flood," 51–52; and Martin

Reuss and Paul Walker, *Financing Water Resources Development: A Brief History* (Fort Belvoir, Va.: U.S. Army Corps of Engineers, 1983), 28.

63. *Congressional Record,* 64th Cong., 2d sess., Senate, February 26, 1917: 4290–99, 4775–76. The Thomas Walsh quote is from p. 4296.

64. Donald J. Pisani, *To Reclaim a Divided West: Water, Law, and Public Policy, 1848–1902* (Albuquerque: University of New Mexico Press, 1992), 274, 319; *Congressional Record,* 57th Cong., 2d sess., Senate, March 1, 1902: 2279.

65. *Chicago Record-Herald,* August 14, 1909; *Official Proceedings of the Eighteenth International Irrigation Congress, 1910* (Pueblo, Colo.: The Franklin Press, 1910), resolution nos. 3 and 4; *Proceedings of the Twenty-First International Irrigation Congress [1914]* (Ottawa: Government Printing Bureau, 1915), 33.

66. Paul Wallace Gates, *History of Public Land Law Development* (Washington, D.C.: GPO, 1968; New York: Arno Press, 1979), 670–71.

67. *New Orleans Times-Picayune,* March 24 and 29, April 4 and 28, and May 3, 1928; *Washington Star,* March 28, 1928.

68. Reservoirs were popular in parts of the lower Mississippi, not just upstream. For example, the Atchafalaya River contained between 750,000 and a million acres of private land that the Corps of Engineers wanted to use as a floodway to relieve pressure on the main stem of the Mississippi. Some of it was rich in oil and minerals, so valuable property would be sacrificed to protect other property. At from two to five dollars an acre and more, the cost of condemning this land was a substantial part of the cost of flood control. Moreover, land removed from the tax rolls reduced the revenue available to levee boards and doubled or tripled the tax burden of land within districts outside the floodway. See Edwin S. Broussard to Walter J. Burke, March 6, 1928, 132–16, Reel 80, Edwin Broussard Collection, Special Collections, University of Southwestern Louisiana, Lafayette.

69. *New Orleans Times-Picayune,* March 25, and April 14 and 19, 1928; *Congressional Record,* 70th Cong., 1st sess., House, April 19, 1928: 6776 (quote) and 6779, and April 23, 1928: 7007 and 7013; W. W. DeBerard, "Mississippi River Flood Control," *Engineering News-Record* 100 (January 12, 1928): 63.

70. For Coolidge's message to Congress, see note 56; the quote is on p. 107 of that document. Also see *Congressional Record,* 70th Cong., 1st sess., House, April 17, 1928: 6661–62. For the April 1928 debate over the flood control bill, see pp. 6640–6938 and 6999–7031.

71. *New Orleans Times-Picayune,* April 11, 1928; *Congressional Record,* 70th Cong., 1st sess, House, April 17, 1928: 6643, 6658.

72. Hiram Johnson to Charles K. McClatchy, May 12, 1928, Hiram Johnson Collection, Bancroft Library, University of California, Berkeley (quote), and Johnson to "My dear Boys," May 12, 1928, in Robert E. Burke, ed., *The Diary Letters of Hiram Johnson, 1917–1945,* vol. 4 (New York: Garland Publishing Company, Inc., 1983). Letters in this set are unpaginated but arranged chronologically.

73. For example, see Norris Hundley, jr., *The Great Thirst: Californians and Water: A History,* rev. ed. (Berkeley: University of California Press, 2001), 205–34; Hundley, *Water and the West;* Paul L. Kleinsorge, *The Boulder Canyon Project: Historical and Economic Aspects* (Stanford: Stanford University Press, 1941); and Beverley Bowen Moeller, *Phil Swing and Boulder Dam* (Berkeley: University of California Press, 1971).

74. Hundley, *Water and the West,* 30.

75. "Boulder Canyon Project–Questions and Answers," October 1, 1930, in Ray Lyman Wilbur Papers, Box 10, "Hoover Dam: 1930, August–December," Herbert Hoover Presidential Library, West Branch, Iowa. In 1926, Hoover noted that "it will take ten years after [the completion of a dam] to bring any very substantial area into high productivity. In these twenty years the population of the United States will have increased by 30,000,000 people and we will need this production by that time." See "Abstract of Secretary Hoover's Statement on the Colorado River Before the House Committee on Irrigation and Reclamation, March 3, 1926," in Colorado River Commission Records, Box 8, "Publicity, General, 1920–26," Hoover Library.

76. Metropolitan Water District of Southern California, *History and First Annual Report for the Period Ending June 30, 1938* (Los Angeles: Haynes Corporation, 1939), 29–31. The best general history of the MWD is Kazuto Oshio, "Urban Water Diplomacy: A Policy History of the Metropolitan Water Supply in Twentieth-Century Southern California" (Ph.D. diss., University of California, Santa Barbara, 1992).

77. *Eberle Economic Service* 6 (December 9, 1929): 289–91; *Congressional Record,* 69th Cong., 1st sess., Senate, April 24, 1926: 8148; *New York Times,* August 18, 1928.

78. Moeller, *Phil Swing and Boulder Dam.*

79. Hiram Johnson to Chester H. Rowell, April 14, 1926; Johnson to George Young, April 26, 1926; and Johnson to George Norris, May 11, 1926, Outgoing Correspondence, Part 3, Hiram Johnson Collection.

80. Phil D. Swing to George Young, October 16, 1926, in Colorado River Commission Papers, Box 9, "George C. Young, 1925–27," Hoover Library.

81. *Portland Oregonian,* March 22, 1922; Hiram Johnson to George Young, January 21, February 9, and April 26, 1926, Outgoing Correspondence, Hiram Johnson Collection.

82. Moeller, *Phil Swing and Boulder Dam,* 26–27, 34–35.

83. Arizona was the first to ask for a royalty from power sales at Boulder Dam. See Malcolm B. Parsons, "Origins of the Colorado River Controversy in Arizona Politics, 1922–1923," *Arizona and the West* 4 (Spring 1962): 40–41.

84. Betty Glad, *Key Pittman: The Tragedy of a Senate Insider* (New York: Columbia University Press, 1986), 140; Key Pittman to Ed Clark, February 24, 1926, Pittman to Hiram Johnson, April 27, 1926, Pittman to J. G. Scrugham, April 28, 1926, transcript of Pittman speech at the Colorado River Conference held at Denver, Colorado, August 22 to September 2, 1927, and "Resolution Offered by Senator Key Pittman on Behalf of the Nevada Commission to the Conference of Governors and the Commissioners of the Colorado Basin States in Session at Denver, Colorado, August 29, 1927," all in Box 129, "Boulder Dam, 1919–1926," Key Pittman Collection, Library of Congress. Also see Hiram Johnson to George Young, April 26, 1926, Outgoing Correspondence, Part 3, Hiram Johnson Collection; and L. Ward Bannister to Herbert Hoover, October 8, 1927, in Colorado River Commission Papers, Box 29, "Bannister, L. Ward 1927–28," Hoover Library. Pittman claimed that the states had two claims to power from the dam, one based on their collective ownership of the river's surplus water and the other on the location of the walls of the dam in Nevada and Arizona. Arizona, like Nevada, had little *immediate* use for water or power from the Col-

orado River, but politicians in that state agreed with Pittman, though some argued that the primary justification for the two states receiving a share of the power proceeds was that a government power plant would not be subject to state taxation.

85. *New York Times,* February 28 and December 23, 1926; Hiram Johnson to C. K. McClatchy, December 9, 1925; Johnson to George Young, March 19, April 26, May 22 and 24, 1926; Johnson to George W. Norris, May 11, 1926; Johnson to W. A. Johnstone, May 21, 1926, all in Outgoing Correspondence, Hiram Johnson Collection, Bancroft Library. Also see the unpaginated letters to "My dear Boys" of January 8 and February 2, 1927, in Burke, *The Diary Letters of Hiram Johnson,* vol. 4, as well as the letters to Archibald M. Johnson dated March 20, 1926, and February 11, 1927.

86. Moeller, *Phil Swing and Boulder Dam,* 108.

87. *Washington Herald,* May 4, 1928; Hiram Johnson to C. K. McClatchy, June 1, 1928, Outgoing Correspondence, Hiram Johnson Collection. Also see the *Washington Times,* May 17, 1928, and Richard Coke Lower, *A Bloc of One: The Political Career of Hiram W. Johnson* (Stanford: Stanford University Press, 1993), 235. The FTC investigation forced the power companies to change their anti–Boulder Dam strategy from attacking public power to defending states' rights. Now they focused on the high cost of the project, the uncertainty of repayment, and possible defects in engineering.

88. William C. Mullendore, "2nd Series—No. 1," March 22, 1928, "No. 6," March 30, 1928, "No. 16," April 13, 1928, and "No. 21," April 24, 1928, Box 11, "Colorado River Commission / Hoover Dam Diary of Mullendore, 1927–28," Mullendore Papers, Hoover Library; *Washington Post,* December 15, 1928; *New York Times,* December 15 and 19, 1928.

89. *Congressional Record,* 70th Cong., 1st sess., House, April 17, 1928: 6656; *New York Times,* October 13, 1927; *Washington Times,* November 24, 1928; William C. Mullendore, "2nd Series—No. 1," March 22, 1928, in the William Mullendore Papers, Box 11, "Colorado River Commission / Hoover Dam Diary of Mullendore, 1927–28," Hoover Library. Also see Harry J. Brown to Mullendore, September 26, 1927, Box 9, "Colorado River Commission / Hoover Dam Correspondence, 1927." For other reports of vote trading, see "There's Another Flood Coming," *Collier's* 80 (July 2, 1927): 34, and the *New Orleans Times-Picayune,* April 12, 1928. The *Collier's* piece observed that "all parts of the country are maturing vast schemes for raids upon the public treasury" and that "[t]he Mississippi flood may turn out to have swept away more than the levees" (p. 34).

90. *New Orleans Times-Picayune,* December 15, 1928.

91. William Mullendore predicted that the legislation would prove unworkable. "There will be years of debate on it yet," he reported to Southern California Edison officials. Even if the dam were constructed, political divisions within the West would undermine its usefulness. "The shame of the situation is that we will have another Muscle Shoals [e.g., white elephant], only many times bigger and more complicated." See William C. Mullendore, "No. 12" and "No. 14," December 8 and 12, 1928, Box 11, "Colorado River Commission / Hoover Dam Diary of Mullendore, 1927–28," Mullendore Papers, Hoover Library; *Arizona v. California,* 283 U.S. 439 (1931); Hundley, *Water and the West,* 288–90.

92. Marc Reisner, *Cadillac Desert: The American West and Its Disappearing Water* (New York: Viking Press, 1986), 183–94.

93. Not until 1939 did Congress authorize the Reclamation Bureau to expand its studies of rivers to include hydroelectric power, navigation, flood control, and municipal needs.

94. *U.S. Statutes at Large* 45 (1927–1929): 538. The corps also required local water users to pay half the cost of surveys, but only if Congress approved the construction of a project.

95. Robert E. Ficken, *Rufus Woods, the Columbia River, and the Building of Modern Washington* (Pullman: Washington State University Press, 1995), 49, 60, 65, 96 (quote); Paul C. Pitzer, *Grand Coulee: Harnessing a Dream* (Pullman: Washington State University Press, 1994), 14, 17.

96. *Engineering News-Record* 95 (September 24, 1925): 495. Also see Ibid. 86 (April 28, 1921): 733, and Ibid. 94 (March 5, 1925): 400.

97. The Walter and Wilbur statements are from letters cited in "Facts Respecting Attempts at Cooperation between the Bureau of Reclamation and the Corps of Engineers," memorandum dated October 17, 1944, in RG 48, Records of the Office of the Secretary of the Interior, Program Staff Central Files, 1947–1953, Box 53. Also see the letter from Elwood Mead, Commissioner of Reclamation, to Louis C. Cramton, June 26, 1930, reprinted in *Congressional Record*, 71st Cong., 2d sess., House, June 27, 1930: 11924–25.

98. For the Wheeler bill, see *Congressional Record*, 71st Cong., 1st sess., Senate, April 30, 1929: 664. The bill was referred to the Committee on Irrigation and Reclamation and died there.

99. For the debate over the conflict between the Corps of Engineers and Department of Interior, see *Congressional Record*, 70th Cong., 2d sess., House, February 18, 1929: 3692–93; 71st Cong., 2d sess., House, December 11, 1929: 492–93 (quote), and June 27, 1930: 11922–25.

100. *Estimate of Cost of Examinations, etc., of Streams Where Power Development Appears Feasible*, H. Doc. 308, 69th Cong., 1st sess., serial 8579 (Washington, D.C.: GPO, 1926); *Report of the Chief of Engineers, U.S. Army, 1933*, vol. 1 (Washington: GPO, 1933), 1231–35.

101. John R. Jameson, "Bonneville and Grand Coulee: The Politics of Multipurpose Development on the Columbia," unpublished manuscript, U.S. Army Corps of Engineers, Office of History, Alexandria, Va.; Richard F. Sullivan, "Wanted: A New Authority by a Dam-Site," *New Outlook* 164 (July 1934): 48–52; *Engineering News-Record* 109 (July 14, 1932): 52. The eighteen-hundred-page Columbia River 308 report was published as *Columbia River and Minor Tributaries*, H. Doc. 103, 73d Cong., 1st sess., serial 9756 (Washington: GPO, 1933).

102. *Engineering News-Record* 111 (August 3, 1933): 145; Ibid. 111 (October 5, 1933): 420; Ibid. 111 (November 9, 1933): 557; and Ibid. 112 (April 5, 1934): 441. Franklin D. Roosevelt's view of developing the nation's rivers differed little from Hoover's—or from that of Progressive Era conservationists. As early as August 1920, in a speech at Spokane, FDR said: "I look for the day, and that at no distant time, when every gallon of water in our streams will be used for practical purposes, instead of allowing it to run to waste." As quoted in Jameson, "Bonneville and Grand Coulee," 24.

103. On the origins of the Central Valley Project, see Donald J. Pisani, *From the Family Farm to Agribusiness: The Irrigation Crusade in California and the West, 1850–1931* (Berkeley: University of California Press, 1984), 381–439.

104. Alan Paterson, "Rivers and Tides: The Story of Water Policy Management in California's Sacramento–San Joaquin Delta" (Ph.D. diss., University of California, Davis, 1978); W. Turrentine Jackson and Alan M. Paterson, *The Sacramento–San Joaquin Delta: The Evolution and Implementation of Water Policy* (Davis: University of California Water Resources Center, 1977). For an excellent discussion of corps activities in the Sacramento Valley before the 1930s, see Robert Kelley, *Battling the Inland Sea: American Political Culture, Public Policy, and the Sacramento Valley, 1850–1986* (Berkeley: University of California Press, 1989).

105. *Central Valley Project Documents* (Washington, D.C.: GPO, 1956), 263–73, 390.

106. The Rivers and Harbors Act of 1937 gave the Reclamation Bureau the authority to build the Central Valley Project with the proviso that the money appropriated in 1935 to build Friant Dam would not be reimbursable under the Reclamation Act of 1902—thus making the Reclamation Bureau more attractive to residents of the San Joaquin Valley.

107. *Central Valley Project Documents,* 558–59, 561, 565, 567–69; Edgar B. Nixon, ed., *Franklin D. Roosevelt and Conservation, 1911–1945,* vol. 2 (Hyde Park, N.Y.: Franklin D. Roosevelt Library, 1957), 583–84, 586–87; James C. Williams, *Energy and the Making of Modern California* (Akron, Ohio: University of Akron Press, 1997), 266.

108. Martin Reuss, "The Art of Scientific Precision: River Research in the United States Army Corps of Engineers to 1945," *Technology and Culture* 40 (April 1999): 292–323; *Engineering News-Record* 89 (July 13, 1922): 82; Ibid. 100 (April 19, 1928): 641; Ibid. 102 (February 7, 1929): 249; Ibid. 104 (May 1, 1930): 741–42.

109. Martin Reuss, "The Art of Scientific Precision," 321, 323. Also see Herbert D. Vogel, "The U.S. Waterways Experiment Station," *Military Engineer* 23 (March–April 1931): 152–53; Vogel, "Research at Waterways Experiment Station," Ibid. 24 (July–August 1932): 331–35; Vogel, "Experiments with River Models," Ibid. 25 (January–February 1933): 26–28; Vogel, "Organization and Operation of the Waterways Experiment Station," Ibid. 26 (March–April 1934): 121–22; Martin Reuss, *Designing the Bayous: The Control of Water in the Atchafalaya Basin, 1800–1995* (Alexandria, Va.: U.S. Army Corps of Engineers, 1998), 151, 176; *Engineering News-Record* 106 (June 11, 1931): 979; Ibid. 107 (July 16, 1931): 84; and Ibid. 111 (July 6, 1933): 14–17. About the same time the corps opened its Vicksburg facility, the Reclamation Bureau established a hydraulic laboratory in Denver. But it was far smaller than the corps' research center, and its early work focused entirely on Boulder Dam; the Bureau of Reclamation exhibited little interest in studying rivers as a whole.

110. Nixon, *Roosevelt and Conservation,* vol. 2, 102–3, 107, 244, 343–44, 522–23. The Roosevelt quotations are from p. 102. The Bureau of Reclamation also faced threats from its other old rival, the Department of Agriculture, which Congress in 1937 authorized to build water projects on the Great Plains. Harold Ickes complained that the 1937 legislation granted the USDA even broader powers than the Reclamation Act of 1902 had conferred on the Department of the Interior. See Ibid., 375.

111. For a brief introduction to the bureaucratic rivalries over natural resource policy during the 1930s, see Donald J. Pisani, "The Many Faces of Conservation: Natural Resources and the American State, 1900–1940," in *Taking Stock: American Government in the Twentieth Century,* ed. Morton Keller and R. Shep Melnick (New York: Woodrow Wilson Center and Cambridge University Press, 1999), 141–48.

112. By 1960, the budget of the Corps of Engineers was four or five times larger than that of the Bureau of Reclamation. In the 1980s, the corps had thirty-nine thousand employees and the Bureau of Reclamation seventy-three hundred. The federal "water agency" with the second-largest staff was not the Reclamation Bureau but the Tennessee Valley Authority. The fragmentation that retarded planning earlier in the century had become even more pronounced. Thirty-five federal agencies in ten cabinet departments participated in water policy formulation, along with five river basin commissions. These agencies included the Environmental Protection Agency, the Fish and Wildlife Service, the Soil Conservation Service, the Rural Electrification Authority, and the Public Health Service, as well as the Bureau of Reclamation, Forest Service, Corps of Engineers, Federal Power Commission, U.S. Geological Survey, and National Park Service. In addition, twenty-seven congressional committees—fourteen in the House and thirteen in the Senate—had some say over water management, along with countless subcommittees. See Peter Rogers, *America's Water: Federal Roles and Responsibilities* (Cambridge: MIT Press, 1993), 12, 16, 99.

113. Department of the Interior Press Release, October 14, 1941, in RG 115, General Administrative Files, 1930–1945, Box 335, "(320): Colorado River, General Corres. Re Power Development."

114. Hoover, *Memoirs,* vol. 2, 234; *New York Times,* October 10, 1931; *Engineering News-Record* 110 (April 6, 1933): 448.

115. Richard Lowitt, *The New Deal and the West* (Norman: University of Oklahoma Press, 1993), 81–99, 138–71, 189–202.

CHAPTER 10. CONCLUSION

1. Critics did not challenge federal reclamation on environmental grounds until the 1960s and 1970s, save for aesthetic conservationists, who opposed the construction of dams within national parks, which included the headwaters of many of the West's largest streams. The legislation that created Glacier National Park (1910), Rocky Mountain National Park (1915), Lassen National Park (1916), and Grand Canyon National Park (1919) permitted the secretary of the interior to use any part of those parks for the development and maintenance of government water projects. In 1921, however, Congress decided that thereafter no dam or canal could be built within a national park or monument without its approval. See W. B. Hoyt, "Memorandum Concerning Water Policies of the Department of the Interior with Special Emphasis on Priorities of Use," September 1944, RG 115, General Correspondence File, 1930–1945, Box 681.

2. Richard White, The Organic Machine: The Remaking of the Columbia River (New York: Hill and Wang, 1995).

3. Donald J. Pisani, *To Reclaim a Divided West: Water, Law, and Public Policy, 1848–1902* (Albuquerque: University of New Mexico Press, 1992), 314–19.
4. Paul Wallace Gates, *History of Public Land Law Development* (Washington, D.C.: GPO, 1968; New York: Arno Press, 1979), 181 (quote), 321–32; Karen Marie O'Neill, "State Building and the Campaign for U.S. Flood Control, 1824–1936" (Ph.D. diss., University of California, Los Angeles, 1998), 152.
5. Paul Wallace Gates, "The Homestead Law in an Incongruous Land System," *American Historical Review* 41 (July 1936): 652–81. For Gates's most important articles on land, see his collection of articles, *The Jeffersonian Dream: Studies in the History of American Land Policy and Development,* edited with a perceptive introduction by Allan G. Bogue and Margaret Beattie Bogue (Albuquerque: University of New Mexico Press, 1996). The figures on land disposal are from Richard B. Morris, *Encyclopedia of American History* (New York: Harper and Row, 1961), 464–65.
6. Donald J. Pisani, "George Maxwell, the Railroads, and American Land Policy, 1899–1904," *Pacific Historical Review* 63 (May 1994): 177–202.
7. I. D. O'Donnell to Thomas J. Walsh, December 15, 1923, Box 308, "Leg.–Irrigation" file, Thomas J. Walsh Collection, Library of Congress, Washington, D.C.; Gates, *History of Public Land Law Development,* 681.
8. Even during the 1920s—as the demand for desert farms fell with crop prices— officials in the Reclamation Bureau assumed that the nation's population increase alone would demand 240 million acres of new farmland by 1950. "If the entire twenty to thirty millions of remaining irrigable acres in the United States were reclaimed," the *Reclamation Era* editorialized in 1925, "the normal increase in farm population, requiring annually 100,000 farms, would settle such an area in half a dozen years, if the settlement were thus concentrated." The editorial pointed out that as much land was abandoned annually as was reclaimed by irrigation and drainage projects, and that poor land was constantly exchanged for better land. In short, agriculture in the United States now involved intensive use of the best lands and the abandonment of marginal farmland. See "The Development of Our Unused and Idle Land," *New Reclamation Era* 16 (May 1925): 68.
9. Morris, *Encyclopedia of American History,* 468. The nation's population growth tailed off to 15 percent from 1910 to 1920 and 16 percent from 1920 to 1930.
10. John C. Page to James Roosevelt, Secretary to President Franklin D. Roosevelt, December 31, 1937, quoted in Edgar B. Nixon, ed., *Franklin D. Roosevelt and Conservation, 1911–1945,* vol. 2 (Hyde Park, N.Y.: Franklin D. Roosevelt Library, 1957), 163.
11. Martin Reuss and Paul Walker, *Financing Water Resources Development: A Brief History* (Fort Belvoir, Va.: U.S. Army Corps of Engineers, 1983).
12. B. Henderson, "State Policies in Agricultural Settlement," *Journal of Land and Public Utility Economics* 2 (July 1926): 284–96.
13. As quoted in E. Louise Peffer, *The Closing of the Public Domain: Disposal and Reservation Policies, 1900–1950* (Stanford: Stanford University Press, 1951), 49–50.
14. Hal S. Barron, *Mixed Harvest: The Second Great Transformation in the Rural North, 1870–1930* (Chapel Hill: University of North Carolina Press, 1997), 172, 198, 240, 241.
15. Jonathan Raban, *Bad Land: An American Romance* (New York: Pantheon Books, 1996), 178–79.

16. Ibid., 183.

17. In addition to Barron's *Mixed Harvest,* on the transformation of rural America in the late nineteenth and early twentieth centuries see David B. Danbom, *The Resisted Revolution: Urban America and the Industrialization of Agriculture, 1900–1930* (Ames: Iowa State University Press, 1979); Danbom, *Born in the Country: A History of Rural America* (Baltimore: Johns Hopkins University Press, 1995); and William L. Bowers, *The Country Life Movement in America, 1900–1920* (Port Washington, N.Y.: Kennikat Press, 1974).

18. Marc Reisner, *Cadillac Desert: The American West and Its Disappearing Water* (New York: Viking Press, 1986); Donald Worster, *Rivers of Empire: Water, Aridity, and the Growth of the American West* (New York: Pantheon Books, 1985).

19. Reisner, *Cadillac Desert,* 3.

20. Ibid., 111, 319, 503–4.

21. Worster, *Rivers of Empire,* 13, 51, 64, 131, 279. Also see Worster, *An Unsettled Country: Changing Landscapes of the American West* (Albuquerque: University of New Mexico Press, 1994), 37, 40, 43.

22. Samuel P. Hays, *Conservation and the Gospel of Efficiency: The Progressive Conservation Movement, 1890–1920* (Cambridge: Harvard University Press, 1959); Hays, *The Response to Industrialism, 1885–1914* (Chicago: University of Chicago Press, 1957).

23. Hays, *Response to Industrialism,* 1, 116, 128–29, 136–37, 190.

24. Hays, *Conservation and the Gospel of Efficiency,* 249, 265.

25. For a brief introduction to modernization theory, see Martin J. Sklar, *The United States as a Developing Country: Studies in U.S. History in the Progressive Era and the 1920s* (New York: Cambridge University Press, 1992), 45–55.

26. Hays, *Response to Industrialism,* 158.

27. Ibid., 275.

28. Donald J. Pisani, "The Many Faces of Conservation: Natural Resources and the American State, 1900–1940," in *Taking Stock: American Government in the Twentieth Century,* ed. Morton Keller and R. Shep Melnick (New York: Woodrow Wilson Center and Cambridge University Press, 1999), 134–37; Gordon B. Dodds, *Hiram Martin Chittenden: His Public Career* (Lexington: University Press of Kentucky, 1973), 183 (quote).

29. A. Hunter Dupree, *Science in the Federal Government: A History of Policies and Activities to 1940* (Cambridge: Harvard University Press, 1957), 248.

30. Edwin Layton, "Mirror-Image Twins: The Communities of Science and Technology in Nineteenth-Century America," in *The Engineer in America,* ed. Terry S. Reynolds (Chicago: University of Chicago Press, 1991), 229–47.

31. Hays, *Conservation and the Gospel of Efficiency,* 208–9.

32. Higgs also suggests that while politics may have changed dramatically during the Progressive Era, the size of the federal government changed very little. The federal budget did not increase substantially during the first three decades of the twentieth century. As a percentage of the gross national product, federal spending rose from 6 or 7 percent in the early twentieth century to more than 21 percent during World War I. It remained higher after the war than it had been before, but as a percentage of gross national product it was only slightly higher than from 1900 to 1916. During the New Deal, however, the share increased to 14 to 15 percent, and it soared to nearly 50 percent during World War II. Spend-

386   NOTES TO PAGES 289-92

ing returned to an average of 20 percent during the cold war years of the 1950s and 1960s. Nevertheless, generalizing on the basis of total spending can be misleading. For example, the 1920s clearly laid the foundation for the large public works projects of the 1930s and after. And in a decade known for fiscal conservatism, the nation spent four or five times more on public works during the 1920s than it did before World War I. Even considering the postwar inflation, the increase in spending was real. Robert Higgs, *Crisis and Leviathan: Critical Episodes in the Growth of American Government* (New York: Oxford University Press, 1987). Higgs discusses the general arguments used to explain the growth of the modern American state on pp. 6-34 and 150.

Other useful works include Stephen Skowronek, *Building a New American State: The Expansion of National Administrative Capacities, 1877-1920* (New York: Cambridge University Press, 1982), and Richard Franklin Bensel, *Yankee Leviathan: The Origins of Central State Authority in America, 1859-1877* (New York: Cambridge University Press, 1990).

33. Daniel Carpenter, *The Forging of Bureaucratic Autonomy: Reputations, Networks, and Policy Innovation in Executive Agencies, 1862-1928* (Princeton: Princeton University Press, 2001), 208.

34. Ibid., 327.

35. Ibid., 3.

36. Ibid., 52-53.

37. Ibid., 338, 331.

38. Ibid., 56, 333.

39. Ibid., 352.

40. For a small sampling of this literature, see Theodore J. Lowi and Edward J. Harpham, "Political Theory and Public Policy: Marx, Weber, and a Republican Theory of the State," in *Contemporary Empirical Political Theory*, ed. Kristen Renwick Monroe (Berkeley: University of California Press, 1997); Ann Shola Orloff, "The Political Origins of America's Belated Welfare State," in *The Politics of Social Policy in the United States*, ed. Margaret Weir, Ann Shola Orloff, and Theda Skocpol (Princeton: Princeton University Press, 1988), 37-80; Theda Skocpol, "Bringing the State Back In: Strategies of Analysis in Current Research," in *Bringing the State Back In*, ed. Peter B. Evans, Dietrich Rueschemeyer, and Theda Skocpol (New York: Cambridge University Press, 1985), 3-37; Skocpol, *Protecting Soldiers and Mothers: The Political Origins of Social Policy in the United States* (Cambridge: Harvard University Press, 1992); and Theda Skocpol and John Ikenberry, "The Political Formation of the American Welfare State in Historical and Comparative Perspective," *Comparative Social Research* 6 (1983): 87-148.

41. For a provocative and intriguing recent example of this thesis, see Karl Jacoby, *Crimes against Nature: Squatters, Poachers, Thieves, and the Hidden History of American Conservation* (Berkeley: University of California Press, 2001). Whether sponsored by the federal government or the states, Jacoby suggests, conservation undermined the ability of local interests to use or manage the natural resources that fell under federal or state control. Yet there were many varieties of conservation, and the leaders of conservation were far more divided than historians have recognized. Jacoby's thesis makes more sense applied to park and forest

policies than to water, grazing, or mining. There are winners and losers in any program undertaken by government. Those most able to mold federal and state water policies were those best able to organize and apply political pressure in their state legislatures as well as Congress, and those who benefited from federal water policies were different from the intended beneficiaries in 1902. It makes more sense to look at which local interests "win" and which "lose" than to speak of a general loss of authority.

42. For an introduction to local districts and local government in the United States, see John C. Bollens, *Special District Governments in the United States* (Berkeley: University of California Press, 1957) and Nancy Burns, *The Formation of American Local Governments: Private Values in Public Institutions* (New York: Oxford University Press, 1994).

43. O'Neill, "State Building and the Campaign for U.S. Flood Control," 513. I am deeply indebted to Professor O'Neill for her reading of an early version of my manuscript and for making many useful suggestions, particularly regarding the nature of American government.

44. Of course, grand reforms rarely live up to expectations. For example, see Steven M. Gillon, *"That's Not What We Meant to Do": Reform and Its Unintended Consequences in Twentieth-Century America* (New York: W. W. Norton and Co., 2000).

45. *Thirteenth Census of the United States, 1910: Agriculture General Report and Analysis* (Washington, D.C.: GPO, 1914), 845; *Fourteenth Census of the United States, 1920: Irrigation and Drainage* (Washington, D.C.: GPO, 1922), 15; *Fifteenth Census of the United States, 1930: Irrigation of Agricultural Lands* (Washington: GPO, 1932), 15; *U.S. Census of Agriculture, 1950*, vol. 3, *Irrigation of Agricultural Lands* (Washington: GPO, 1952), 8–9; Clayton R. Koppes, "Public Water, Private Land: Origins of the Acreage Limitation Controversy, 1933–1953," *Pacific Historical Review* 47 (November 1978): 609.

46. Alfred R. Golze, *Reclamation in the United States* (New York: McGraw-Hill Book Co., 1952), 47; *Irrigation of Agricultural Lands*, 10.

47. Carroll H. Wooddy, *The Growth of the Federal Government, 1915–1932* (New York: McGraw-Hill Book Co., 1934), 538; Golze, *Reclamation in the United States*, 277.

48. *Fifteenth Census of the United States, 1930: Irrigation of Agricultural Lands*, 54; Golze, *Reclamation in the United States*, 13–14; Mont Saunderson, *Western Land and Water Use* (Norman: University of Oklahoma Press, 1950), 164.

49. *Annual Report of the Secretary of the Interior for the Fiscal Year Ended June 30, 1930* (Washington, D.C.: GPO, 1930), 19.

50. James C. Scott, *Seeing Like a State: How Certain Schemes to Improve the Human Condition Have Failed* (New Haven: Yale University Press, 1998), 4, 343.

51. Ibid., 6.

INDEX

Alabama Power Company, 225, 226
All-American Canal, 257, 259, 260
American Civic Association, 12–13
American Society of Civil Engineers, 42–44, 148
Anderson, D. H., 317n68
Army Corps of Engineers: competition with Geological Survey of, 237–38; criticism by Maxwell of, 239; failure of river-basin planning and, 286; proposals to reorganize, 241, 242; rivalry with Reclamation Service of, 263–70; "308 reports" study of, 263–64; Tennessee River work of, 222, 226; waterways laboratory, 268
Associated General Contractors of America, 240

Bailey, Liberty Hyde, 5–6
Ballinger, Richard, 58, 104–6, 107–10, 114–15
Bard, Thomas R., 104
Barron, Hal, 281
Baruch, Bernard, 210
Belle Fourche Project, 50
Bien, Morris, 41, 312n10; criticism of Ballinger by, 108–9; on federal water rights, 35–36, 37–38; on hydroelectric power, 214; model water code of, 38, 39–40
Black, Hugo, 225
Blackfeet Reservation, 172, 173
Blanchard, C. J., 9, 26–27, 102, 103, 311n99

Boise-Payette Project, 78, *fig. 17*
Borah, William E., 2, 104, 111, 128, 170, 208
Boulder Dam, 221; opposition to, 20, 258–59; private and public enterprise on, 232–33; as symbol, 202, 232–33, 270–71; three parts of, 257–58
Boulder Dam Act, 229, 230–31, 257, 261–62
Boyd, Nathan, 54
Brewer, David Josiah, 34, 41
Brown, Major Lytle, 267
Bryan, William Jennings, xii
Buford-Trenton Project, 61
Bureau of Indian Affairs: accommodation with Reclamation Service of, 154, 160; Indian water rights and, 166–68, 169, 171–72, 176; irrigation projects of, 154, 155–57, 160, 183
Burkett, Elmer, 113–14

California Water and Forest Association, 132
Carey Act of 1894, xiv, 66–67, 89–91
Carpenter, Daniel, 288–91
Carpenter, Delph E., 36, 37
Carter, Thomas, xv, 105, 112, 333n25, 336n71
Central Valley Project, 267–68
Civilian Conservation Corps, 179
Clay, Alexander S., 112
Code, W. H., 167, 187, 188
Collier, John, 177
Colorado River Project, 139. *See also* All-American Canal; Boulder Dam

Text: 10/12 Baskerville
Display: Baskerville
Cartographer: Madge L. Kelley
Indexer: Andrew Christenson
Compositor: Integrated Composition Systems
Printer: Sheridan Books, Inc.